PEARSON BACCALAUREATE

WORLD HISTORY

Causes and Effects of 20TH Century Wars

2nd Edition

KEELY ROGERS • JO THOMAS

Supporting every learner across the IB continuum

Published by Pearson Education Limited, 80 Strand, London, WC2R 0RL.

www.pearsonglobalschools.com

Text © Pearson Education Limited 2015
Edited by Jill Morris
Proofread by Jill Morris, Sarah Nisbet, and Sarah Wright
Designed by Astwood Design
Typeset by Phoenix Photosetting, Chatham, Kent
Original illustrations © Pearson Education 2015
Illustrated by Tech-Set Ltd and Phoenix Photosetting
Cover design by Pearson Education Limited

The rights of Joanna Thomas and Keely Rogers to be identified as authors of this work have been asserted by them in accordance with the Copyright, Designs and Patents Act 1988.

First published 2015

20 19 18 17
IMP 10 9 8 7 6 5 4 3 2

British Library Cataloguing in Publication Data
A catalogue record for this book is available from the British Library

ISBN 978 1 447 98415 3
eBook only ISBN 978 1 447 98416 0

Printed in Slovakia by Neografia

Acknowledgements
The authors and publisher would like to thank Tom Buchanan for his invaluable help with and feedback on this title, and Malcolm Price for his expert help in the structuring and writing of the Theory of Knowledge section in this book.

We would like to thank the following for their kind permission to reproduce their photographs:

(Key: b-bottom; c-centre; l-left; r-right; t-top)

Alamy Images: akg-images 62, Homer Sykes 324t; **Bridgeman Art Library Ltd:** Germany's children starve! 1924 (charcoal on paper), Kollwitz, Kathe Schmidt (1867-1945) / Deutsches Historisches Museum, Berlin, Germany / copyright DHM 73t, Italian cartoon depicting the German Kaiser as 'The Glutton' trying to eat the world (colour litho), Italian School, (20th century) / Private Collection / Peter Newark Military Pictures / Bridgeman Images 25, US Ambassador Patrick Jay Hurley, Zhou Enlai and Mao Zedong, Whittlesey Hall, Yan'an, China, 1945 (b / w photo), German Photographer, (20th century) / SZ Photo 272; **Brooklyn Public Library:** Brooklyn Collection 151; **Corbis:** 19, 22, 59b, 64t, 64b, 80, 194, 207, 256, 258, 348, Archives Barrat-Bartoll 291, 299, Bettmann 16l, 16r, 31, 37, 56, 60b, 132, 155, 172, 192, 296b, Christel Gerstenberg 127, Horacio Villalobos 311, Hulton-Deutsch Collection 60t, 73b, 76, 101, 109, 169, Hulton-Deutsch Collection 60t, 73b, 76, 101, 109, 169, Hulton-Deutsch Collection 60t, 73b, 76, 101, 109, 169, Hupton-Deutsch Collection 21t, 175, Jacques Pavlovsky 335t, Maurice Zalewski 284, Michael S. Yamashita 147, Patrick Robert / Sygma 6, Peter Turnley 332, 335b, 352, Philadelphia Museum of Art 231, Swim Ink 2, LLC 190l, The Art Archive 243; **courtesy www.psywarrior.com:** Ed Rouse 347; **FotoLibra:** Jackie Fox 88; **Getty Images:** 124, Alinari Archives 10, Buyenlarge 210, Central Press 140, David Levenson 312, Davis 289, Education Images 44, Fred Ramage 187, H. S. Wong 148, Horace Abrahams / Stringer 198, Hulton Archive 2, 308, Imagno 131, Keystone 286t, Keystone-France 214r, Lawrence Thornton 146, Max Alpert 7, Mondadori 273, Paul Popper / Popperfoto 214l, PhotoQuest 111, Popperfoto 160, 164, Print Collector 252, Rolls Press / Popperfoto 220, Sovfoto 4, Stringer 340, Three Lions 286b, ullstein Bild 288, UniversalImagesGroup 117t; **Illustrated London News Picture Library:** Ingram Publishing / Alamy 221; **Louis Raemakers Foundation:** 49; **Magnum Photos Ltd:** Robert Capa copyright International Centre of Photography 232cl; **Mary Evans Picture Library:** 23, 67, 173, Epic / AGIP 246, J. Bedmar / Iberfoto 238, Library of Congress 51, M.C.Esteban / Iberfoto 236, ONSLOW AUCTIONS LIMITED 48b, Robert Hunt Collection 59t, WEIMAR ARCHIVE 135; **N&S Syndication and Licensing:** Michael Cummings, Daily Express, 29 Sep 1961 118; **National Archives and Records Administration (NARA):** 77, 179; **PhotoDisc:** Photodisc 3; **Press Association Images:** PA Archive 322; **Punch Cartoon Library:** 26b, 36, 54, 71, 103, 115, 117b; **Randall Bytwerk:** 110; **Rex Features:** John W Jockel 353; **Ronald Grant Archive:** 245, CASBAH 296t; **Solo Syndication / Associated Newspapers Ltd:** Daily Mail 18 / 02 / 1942 197, Daily Mail, 16 / 09 / 1946 278; **Telegraph Media Group:** 326, 330, 351; **The Herb Block Foundation:** A 1933 Herblock cartoon 136; **TopFoto:** 1999 Topham Picturepoint 319, 2002 / AP 226b, 2002 / PA 318, 2004 267, 2004 Roger-Viollet 349, 152, 167t, 226t, AP 328, copyright 2003 Topham Picturepoint 26t, Print Collector / HIP 255, The Granger Collection 139t, 156, 190r, ullsteinbild 106, 304; **United Nations Archives at Geneva:** 98

Cover image: *Front:* **Imperial War Museum**

Inside front cover: **Shutterstock.com**, Dmitry Lobanov

All other images © Pearson Education

We are grateful to the following for permission to reproduce copyright material:

Tables
Table on page 305 from *The search for Modern China*, W.W. Norton & Company Inc (JD Spence 1999) p.507. Copyright © 1990 by Jonathan Spence. Used by permission of W.W.Norton & Company, Inc

Text
Extract on page 29 from *The Origins of the First World War*, Routledge (Joll,J) p.280; Extract on page 31 from *How Wars Begin*, New ed. (Taylor, A.J.P 1980), John Wiley & Sons Ltd; Article on page 35 from *BBC History magazine*, February 2014, 26 (Ferguson,N), BBC Magazines with permission; Extract on page 36 from *The War that Ended Peace: How Europe abandoned peace for the First World War*, Profile Books (MacMillan,M), Profile Books Ltd with permission and Random House Inc; Extract on page 37 from *Germany's Aims in the First World War*, W. W. Norton & Company (Fischer,F). Copyright © 1961 by Droste Berlad und Druckerei GmbH, Dusseldorf. English translation copyright © 1967 by W.E.Norton & Company, Inc; Extracts on page 38, page 108 from *The Origins of the First World War (Lancaster Pamphlets)* 3 edition, Routledge (Henig, R); Extract on page 38 from *The First World War*, Pimlico (Keegan,J 1999) p.51, reprinted by permission of The Random House Group Limited.; Extract on page 40 from *Origins of the First World War: Revised 3rd Edition (Seminar Studies In History)*, 3 ed. Routledge (Martel G) p.85; Extract on page 40 from *The Origins of the First World War (Lancaster Pamphlets)* 3 ed, Routledge (Henig, R) p.44; Extract on page 40 from *Aspects of European History 1789-1980 (University Paperbacks)* Rev Ed edition, Routledge (Lee SJ) p102; Extract on page 41 from *The War that Ended Peace: How Europe abandoned peace for the First World War*, Profile Books (MacMillan, M) p.xxi, Profile Books Ltd with permission and Random House Inc; Extract on page 57 from *The First World War*, Random House Group (Keegan, J 1999). Reprinted by permission of The Random House Group Limited.; Extract on page 60 from *The Great War: 1914-1918 (Modern Wars In Perspective)*, 2 edition, Routledge (Beckett, I) p.239; Article on page 61 from *The Oxford History of Modern War*, New Updated Ed, OUP Oxford (John Bourne in Townsend C (ed.) p133; Extract on page 66 from Siegfried Sassoon, 'The General' 1917, Barbara Levy Literary Agency with permission; Extract on page 67 from *Great Britain and the War of 1914-1918* Methuen (Woodward,L 1967); Extract on page 67 from *The First World War*, Random House Ltd (Keegan J 1999). Reprinted by permission of The Random House Group Limited; Article on page 68 from *BBC History Magazine*, March 2005 p16, BBC Magazines; Article on page 68 from Stabbed at the Front, *History Today*, 58 (Watson A), http://www.historytoday.com/alexander-watson/stabbed-front, History Today Ltd with permission; Extract on page 71 from *The Monopoly of Violence: Why Europeans Hate Going to War*, Faber and Faber (Sheenan, J 2008) P.84; Extract on page 72 from *The Monopoly of Violence: Why Europeans Hate Going to War*, Faber and Faber (Sheenan, J 2008) P.86; Extract on page 72 from *The War of the World: History's Age of Hatred*, Penguin (Ferguson N) p91, copyright © 2006 by Niall Ferguson. Used by permission of Penguin Press, an imprint of Penguin Publishing Group, a division of Penguin Random House LLC; Extract on page 74 from *The First World War (Questions and Analysis in History)*, Routledge (Cawood I, McKinnon-Bell D); Extract on page 88 from *The Harold Nicolson Diaries: 1907-1964: 1907-1963 (Diary,1919)*, New Ed, W&N (Nicolson H) p.23, Orion Publishing Group Ltd; Extract on page 91 from *The Twentieth-Century World and Beyond: An International History since 1900* 6 ed, OUP USA (Keylor, WR) p.88; Extract on page 100 from *The Globalizing of America 1913–1945*, Cambridge University Press (Iriye A) p.68; Extract on page 102 from *Versailles and After, 1919–1933*, Routledge (Henig, R 1995) p.35; Extract on page 102 from *The Twenty Years' Truce* Longmans (Rayner, RM 1943), Pearson Oxford; Extract on page 102 from *The Origins of the Second World War* New Ed, Penguin Books (Taylor AJP) p.86, 430 words from THE ORIGINS OF THE SECOND WORLD WAR by A.J.P. Taylor (Hamish Hamilton 1961, Penguin Books 1964, 1987, 1991) Copyright © A J P Talory, 1961, 1963; Extracts on page 105, page 110 from *Twentieth-Century Europe: Unity and Division*, 1st Ed.,Bloomsbury Academic (Bell,P.M.H.), © Bloomsbury Publishing Plc; Extract on page 110 from *The Monopoly of Violence: Why Europeans Hate Going to War*, 1st Ed., Faber & Faber (Sheehan,J); Extract on page 112 from *The Road to War*, 2nd ed, Vintage (Overy, R) pp.411–412, From THE ROAD TO WAR by Richard Overy & Andrew Wheatcroft Published by Vintage Reprinted by permission of The Random House Group Limited; Extract on page 118 from *The Origins of the Second World War in Europe (Origins Of Modern Wars)*, 1 ed. Longman (Bell PMH) pp.63–64, with permission from Taylor & Francis Group; Extract on page 127 from *Mein Kampf*, Houghton Mifflin (Hitler, A), From Mein Kampf by Adolf Hitler, translated by Ralph Manheim. Published by Hutchinson and reproduced by permission of The Random House Group Ltd and translated by Ralph Manheim. Copyright © 1943, renewed 1971 by Houghton Mifflin Harcourt Publishing Company. Reprinted by permission of Houghton Mifflin Harcourt Publishing Company. All rights reserved; Extract on page 129 from *Questions in History - Hitler and the Road to War*, Collins Educational (Townley,T). Reprinted by permission of HarperCollins Publishers Ltd; Extract on page 137 from *The Storm of War. A new History of the Second World War*, Allen Lane (Roberts, A) p.10, 129 words from The Storm of War: A New History of the Second World War by Andrew Roberts. (Penguin Press 2009). Copyright © Andrew Roberts, 2009.; Extract on page 137 from *Hitler's War Aims: Ideology, the Nazi State, and the Course of Expansion: Ideology, the Nazi State and the Course of Expansion*, New Ed edition, W. W. Norton & Company, Inc (Rich, N) p.4. Copyright © 1973 by W.W. Norton & Company, Inc. Used by permission of W.W. Norton &Company, Inc.; Extract on page 138 from *Hitler in History (Tauber Institute)*, Brandeis University Press (Jackel, E), © University Press of New England, Lebanon, NH. Reprinted with permission; Extract on page 156 from *Pacific War, 1931-1945: A Critical Perspective on Japan's Role in World War II*, 1st Paperback Ed edition (Pantheon Asia Library) Presidio Press (Lenaga S) p.85, Excerpt(s) from PACIFIC WAR: WWII AND JAPANESE by Saburo Ienaga, translation; copyright © 1978 by Random House, Inc. Used by permission of Pantheon Books, an imprint of; the Knopf Doubleday Publishing Group, a division of Penguin Random House LLC. All rights; reserved; Quote on page 159 from The diplomat John Paton Davies describing the relationship between the USA, Japan and China Two Hundred Years of American Foreign Policy: American and East Asia by John Paton Davies, ESSAY January 1977 Issue Foreign Affairs, with permission; Extract on page 161 from *The Triumph of the Dark: European International History 1933-1939 (Oxford History of Modern Europe)*, OUP (Steiner,Z 2013) pg1065; Extract on page 162 from *The Making of Modern Japan.*, 2nd Revised ed, Houghton Mifflin (Pyle,KB) p.204, The making of modern Japan by Pyle, Kenneth B. Reproduced with permission of Houghton Mifflin College Division in the format Republish in a book via Copyright Clearance Center; Extract on page 162 from *The Road to War*, 2nd ed, Vintage (Overy, R) pp.405-406, published by Vintage. Reprinted by permission of The Random House Group Limited, copyright ©1989, 1999 by Richard Overy & Andrew Wheatcroft and used by permission of Viking Books, an imprint of Penguin Publishing Group, a division of Penguin Random House LLC.; Extracts on page 163 from *Japan's Imperial Conspiracy*, 1st Edition ed, William Heinemann Ltd (Bergamini, D) Nov. 1971, reprinted by permission of Peters Fraser Dunlop (www.petersfraserdunlop.com) on behalf of David Bergamini; Extract on page 168 from *The Oxford History of Modern War*, New Updated Ed, OUP Oxford (John Bourne in Townsend C (ed.)p140; Extracts on page 168 from a speech delivered by Winston Churchill to the House of Commons, 18 June 1940 (Curtis Brown), Copyright © The Estate of Winston S. Churchill; Extract on page 172 from *Europe at War 1939-1945: No Simple Victory*, Reprints ed., Pan (Davies,N), Copyright © Norman Davies, 2007. Pan Macmillan Publishers with permission; Extract on page 177 from *Aspects of European History 1789-1980*, Rev Ed ed (University Paperbacks) Routledge (Lee SJ) p187; Extract on page 178 from *Why the Allies Won*, New Ed ed, Pimlico (Overy,R) p.399, from WHY THE ALLIES WON by Richard Overy Published by Jonathan Cape. Reprinted by permission of The Random House Group Limited and used by permission of W.W. Norton & Company, Inc.; Extract on page 178 from *Why the Allies Won*, Pimlico (Overy,R 2006) p.398, From WHY THE ALLIES WON by Richard Overy Published by Jonathan Cape Reprinted by permission of The Random House Group Limited. and used by permission of W.W. Norton & Company, Inc.; Extract on page 180 from *The Second World War*, 1997, New Ed ed. Pimlico (Keegan, J) p 229, from The Second World War by John Keegan, published by Hutchinson. Reproduced by permission of The Random House Group Ltd. and copyright ©1989 by John Keegan. Used by permission of Viking Books, an imprint of Penguin Publishing Group, a division of Penguin Random House LLC.; Extract on page 182 from *The War of the World: History's Age of Hatred*, Penguin (Ferguson, N) p 574. From THE WAR OF THE WORLD: TWENTIETH-CENTURY CONFLICT AND THE

Random House LLC.; Extract on page 186 from *The Second World War, 1997*, New Ed, Pimlico (Keegan, J) p 95. From The Second World War by John Keegan, published by Hutchinson. Reproduced by permission of The Random House Group Ltd. and copyright © 1989, 1999 by Richard Overy & Andrew Wheatcroft. Used by permission of Viking Books, an imprint of Penguin Publishing Group, a division of Penguin Random House LLC.; Extract on page 188 from *Why the Allies Won*, New Ed., Pimlico (Overy,R) p.162, From WHY THE ALLIES WON by Richard Overy and Published by Jonathan Cape and reprinted by permission of The Random House Group Limited. and used by permission of W.W. Norton & Company, Inc.; Extract on page 189 from *Postwar: A History of Europe Since 1945*, Vintage (Judt, T 2010) p.14, by Tony Judt and Published by William Heinemann. Reprinted by permission of The Random House Group Limited and Copyright © Tony Judt 2005, used by permission of The Wylie Agency (UK) Limited; Extract on page 191 from *The War of the World: History's Age of Hatred*, Penguin (Ferguson N) p.xxxiv .From THE WAR OF THE WORLD: TWENTIETH-CENTURY CONFLICT AND THE DESCENT OF THE WEST by Niall Ferguson, copyright © 2006 by Niall Ferguson. Used by permission of Penguin Press, an imprint of Penguin Publishing Group, a division of Penguin Random House LLC.; Extract on page 192 from *The War of the World: History's Age of Hatred*, Penguin (Ferguson N) p.xxxiv, From THE WAR OF THE WORLD: TWENTIETH-CENTURY CONFLICT AND THE DESCENT OF THE WEST by Niall Ferguson, copyright © 2006 by Niall Ferguson. Used by permission of Penguin Press, an imprint of Penguin Publishing Group, a division of Penguin Random House LLC.; Extract on page 200 from *Postwar: A History of Europe Since 1945*, Vintage (Judt, T 2010) p.14, From POSTWAR by Tony Judt and Published by William Heinemann and Reprinted by permission of The Random House Group Limited. and 4 extracts from POSTWAR by Tony Judt. and Copyright © Tony Judt 2005, used by permission of The Wylie Agency (UK) Limited; Extract on page 202 from *The Triumph of the Dark: European International History 1933-1939 (Oxford History of Modern Europe)*, OUP (Steiner,Z 2013) p.1066; Extract on page 202 from *Why the Allies Won*, New Ed ed, Pimlico (Overy,R) p.3, from WHY THE ALLIES WON by Richard Overy and Published by Jonathan Cape and reprinted by permission of The Random House Group Limited used by permission of W.W. Norton & Company, Inc.; Extract on page 203 from *Postwar: A History of Europe Since 1945*, Vintage (Judt, T 2010) p.14, from POSTWAR by Tony Judt and Published by William Heinemann and reprinted by permission of The Random House Group Limited. Copyright © Tony Judt 2005, used by permission of The Wylie Agency (UK) Limited; Extract on page 205 from George Marshall's speech Harvard University on 5 June 1947, Central Intelligence Agency; Extract on page 206 from *Japan: a Concise History*, 4th Revised ed., Rowman & Littlefield Publishers (Meyer, MW), Japan : A Concise History by Meyer, Milton W. Reproduced with permission of Rowman & Littlefield Publishers in the format Republish in a book via Copyright Clearance Center; Extract on page 206 from *The Making of Modern Japan*, 2nd Revised ed.Houghton Mifflin (Pyle,K) p225, The making of modern Japan by Pyle, Kenneth B. Reproduced with permission of Houghton Mifflin College Division in the format Republish in a book via Copyright Clearance Center; Extract on page 212 from *The Origins of the Second World War* New Ed., Penguin Books (Taylor AJP) p.336, 430 words from THE ORIGINS OF THE SECOND WORLD WAR by A.J.P. Taylor (Hamish Hamilton 1961, Penguin Books 1964, 1987, 1991) Copyright © A J P Talory, 1961, 1963; Extract on page 213 from *The Morbid Age. Britain between the wars*, Allen Lane (Overy R) p.70, 102 words from The Morbid Age: Britain and the Crisis of Civilisation, 1919 - 1939 by Richard Overy. (Penguin Press 2009). Copyright © Richard Overy, 2009; Extract on page 226 from *The Bombing War: Europe, 1939-1945*, Allen Lane (Overy, R) pp.609,610, 175 words from THE BOMBING WAR: EUROPE 1939-1945 by Richard Overy. (Penguin Books 2014). Copyright © Richard Overy, 2014; Extract on page 217 from *Modern Europe 1870-1945 (Longman Advanced History)* 1 ed., Longman (Culpin,C Henig,R) p.143, Pearson Education Limited; Extract on page 217 from *Twentieth-Century Europe: Unity and Division*, 1st Edition ed Bloomsbury Academic (Bell,P.M.H.) p.84, © Bloomsbury Publishing Plc; Extract on page 217 from *Modern Europe 1870-1945 (Longman Advanced History)* 1 ed., Longman (Culpin,C Henig,R) p.339, Pearson Education Ltd; Extract on page 218 from *Postwar: A History of Europe Since 1945*, Vintage (Judt, T 2010) p.40, From POSTWAR by Tony Judt and Published by William Heinemann and reprinted by permission of The Random House Group Limited and used by permission of The Wylie Agency (UK) Limited; Extract on page 218 from *Modern Europe 1870-1945 (Longman Advanced History)* 1 edition, Longman (Culpin,C Henig,R) p.142, Pearson Education Limited; Extract on page 218 from *International History of the Twentieth Century and Beyond*, 3 edition, Routledge (Best A et al) p.149; Extract on page 218 from *Twentieth-Century Europe: Unity and Division*, 1st ed. Bloomsbury Academic (Bell,P.M.H.) p.85, © Bloomsbury Publishing Plc; Extracts on page 221, page 230, page 245 from *The Battle for Spain: The Spanish Civil War 1936–1939*, New Ed., W&N (Beevor, A), Orion Publishing Group Ltd; Extract on page 222 from *The Spanish Civil War: Reaction, Revolution and Revenge*, Reprint. Ed., Harper Perennial (Preston,P) p.17, , Reprinted by permission of HarperCollins Publishers Ltd; Extract on page 230 from *The Spanish Civil War 1936-1939 (Essential Histories)* Osprey Publishing (Lannon F) p.7, Osprey Publishing with permission; Extract on page 243 from *The Spanish Civil War, 1971*, HarperCollins Publishers Ltd (Mitchell, D), Reprinted by permission of HarperCollins Publishers Ltd; Extract on page 260 from *Restless Empire: China and the World Since 1750*, the Bodley Head (Westad, OA 2012) pp.163,164, published by The Bodley Head Reprinted by permission of The Random House Group Limited, Odd Westad, copyright © 2012. Reprinted by permission of Basic Books, a member of The Perseus Books Group; Extract on page 268 from *Mao: The Unknown Story* New Ed edition, Vintage (Halliday J, Chang J) p.203, ISBN-13: 978-0099507376, Published by Jonathan Cape. Reprinted by permission of The Random House Group Limited, copyright © 2005 by Globalflair Ltd. Used by permission of Alfred A. Knopf, an imprint of the Knopf and Doubleday Publishing Group, a division of Penguin Random House LLC. All rights reserved; Extract on page 271 from *Modernization and Revolution In China: From the Opium Wars to the Olympics*, 4 ed., Routledge (June Grasso, Jay Corrin and Michael Kort) p.114, copyright 2009. From Modernization and Revolution In China: From the Opium Wars to the Olympics by June Grasso, Jay Corrin and Michael Kort. Reproduced by permission of Taylor and Francis Group, LLC, a division of Informa plc; Extracts on page 271, page 279 from *China in Disintegration: The Republican Era in Chinese History, 1912-1949 (Transformation of Modern China Series)*, The Free Press (Sheridan,J 1977) p.264.Reprinted with the permission of Free Press, a Division of Simon & Schuster, Inc., from CHINA IN DISINTEGRATION: THE REPUBLICAN ERA IN CHINESE HISTORY, 1912-1949 by James Sheridan. Copyright © 1975 by The Free Press, a Division of Macmillan Publishing Co.Inc. All rights reserved; Extract on page 273 from *China in Disintegration: The Republican Era in Chinese History, 1912-1949 (Transformation of Modern China Series)*, The Free Press (Sheridan,J 1977) p.269. Reprinted with the permission of Free Press, a Division of Simon & Schuster, Inc., from CHINA IN DISINTEGRATION: THE REPUBLICAN ERA IN CHINESE HISTORY, 1912-1949 by James Sheridan. Copyright © 1975 by The Free Press, a Division of Macmillan Publishing Co.Inc. All rights reserved; Extract on page 278 from *The Rise of Modern China*, 3rd Revised edition edition, Oxford University Press Inc (Hsu,I 1983) p.639; Extract on page 278 from *Rebellions and Revolutions: China from the 1880s to 2000 (Short Oxford History of the Modern World)*, 2 edition, OUP Oxford (Gray,J); Extract on page 279 from *Restless Empire: China and the World Since 1750*, the Bodley Head (Westad, OA 2012) p.291, published by The Bodley Head and reprinted by permission of The Random House Group Limited, Odd Westad, copyright © 2012. Reprinted by permission of Basic Books, a member of The Perseus Books Group.; Extract on page 279 from *Mao: The Unknown Story* New Ed edition, Vintage (Halliday J, Chang J) pp.329,331, published by Jonathan Cape and reprinted by permission of The Random House Group Limited, copyright © 2005 by Globalflair Ltd.. Used by permission of Alfred A. Knopf, an imprint of the Knopf and Doubleday Publishing Group, a division of Penguin Random House LLC. All rights reserved; Extract on page 301 from *Algeria,1830-2000: A Short History (Cornell Classics in Philosophy)*, Cornell University Press (Stora,B) p.29; Extract on page 294 from *France and Decolonisation (The Making of the Twentieth Century)*, Palgrave Macmillan (Betts,R), reproduced with permission of Palgrave Macmillan; Extract on page 294 from *The Oxford History of Modern War*, New Updated Ed., OUP Oxford (Townsend C (ed.) p191; Extract on page 295 from *Algeria,1830-2000: A Short History (Cornell Classics in Philosophy)*, Cornell University Press (Stora,B) p.50; Extract on page 300 from *Africa. A Modern History*, New ed., Atlantic Books (Arnold,G) Atlantic Books with permission; Extract on page 302 from *Introduction to Global Military History*, 2 ed., Routledge (Black J) p169; Extract on page 343 from *The Gulf War 1991 (Essential Histories)*, 1st Ed, Osprey Publishing (Finlan A), Osprey Publishing with permission; Extract 15.189 from *The Sleepwalkers* Allen Lane. Pearson (Clark C 2012) pp. 560-561, 161 words from THE SLEEPWALKERS: HOW BRITAIN WENT TO WAR IN 1914 by Christopher Clark (Allen Lane 2012, Penguin Books 2013) Copyright © Christopher Clark, 2012; Extract 15.190 from *The Idea of History*, OUP (Collingwood RG 1946); Extract on page 305 from Guerrilla Warfare and its Role during the "Heroic Years" of the Algerian War by Hanafi S, http://www.asfar.org.uk/guerrilla-warfare-and-its-role-during-the-heroic-years-of-the-algerian-war/, Asfar, © Asfar 2015; Extract on page 306 from *The struggle in the Chingkang Mountains*, Foreign Languages Press (Zedong, M 1968) B0018V6S7O; Extract on page 306 from *Algeria,1830-2000: A Short History (Cornell Classics in Philosophy)*, Cornell University Press (Stora,B) p.63, ISBN-13: 978-0801489167; Extract on page 311 from *The Land that Lost its Heroes*, Bloomsbury (Burns, J) p.128,129, © Bloomsbury Publishing Plc; Extract on page 311 from *One of Us*, New Edition ed., Pan (Young,H), Copyright © Hugo Young, 2013.Pan Macmillan Publishers with permission; Extract on page 311 from *One of Us*, New Ed., Pan (Young,H), Copyright © Hugo Young, 2013. Pan Macmillan Publishers with permission; Extract on page 313 from *Thatcher (Reputations)*, Bloomsbury Academic (Green E. H. H.) p156, © Bloomsbury Publishing Plc; Extract on page 315 from *The Battle for the Falklands*, Main Market Ed. edition Pan Books (Hastings, M Jenkins, S) p.77, Copyright © Max Hastings and Simon Jenkins, 2010. Pan Macmillan Publishers with permission and reprinted by permission of Peters Fraser & Dunlop (www.petersfraserdunlop.com) on behalf of Max Hastings and Simon Jenkins; Extract on page 317 from *Thatcher's Britain: The Politics and Social Upheaval of the 1980s*, Simon and Schuster (Vinen,R) p.150, Simon and Schuster, with permission and copyright © Richard Vinen, 2009, used by permission of The Wylie Agency; Extract on page 323 from *The Land that Lost its Heroes*, Bloomsbury (Burns, J) p. 394-395, © Bloomsbury Publishing Plc; Extract on page 326 from *Reagan and Thatcher. The Difficult Relationship*, Norton. New York. USA (Aldous, R) p.109,110, From REAGAN AND THATCHER:THE DIFFICULT RELATIONSHIP by Richard Aldous. © 2012 by Richard Aldous. Used by permission of W.W.Norton & Company,Inc. Extract on page 327 from *Reagan and Thatcher. The Difficult Relationship*, Norton. New York. USA (Aldous, R) p.101, From REAGAN AND THATCHER:THE DIFFICULT RELATIONSHIP by Richard Aldous. © 2012 by Richard Aldous. Used by permission of W.W.Norton & Company,Inc.; Extract on page 328 from *Falklands Aftermath: Picking Up The Pieces*, First Ed., Leo Cooper. London. UK Pen & Sword Books Ltd (Major General Edward Fursdon) p.83, Pen and Sword Books (previously Leo Cooper) with permission; Extract on page 330 from Margaret Thatcher House of Commons Statement Hansard HC [25/729-41], 15/06/1982, Open Parliament Licence © Parliamentary Copyright; Extract 16.195a from *Mao: The Unknown Story* New Ed edition, Vintage (Halliday J, Chang J) p.254, From MAO: THE UNKNOWN STORY by Jung Chang & Jon Halliday and Published by Jonathan Cape and reprinted by permission of The Random House Group Limited. Used by permission of Alfred A. Knopf, an imprint of the Knopf and Doubleday Publishing Group, a division of Penguin Random House LLC. All rights reserved; Extract on page 338 from *International History of the Twentieth Century and Beyond*, 3 edition, Routledge (Best A et al) p.544; Extracts on page 338, page 349 from *Why Nations Go to War*, 9th Revised ed., Wadsworth Publishing Co Inc (Stoessinger, JG), republished with permission of Cengage Learning, Inc, permission conveyed through Copyright Clearance Center, Inc.; Extract on page 339 from *The Gulf Conflict: 1990-1991: Diplomacy and War in the New World Order*, New Ed., Faber and Faber (Freedman L, Karsh E); Extract on page 339 from *The Generals' War: The Inside Story of the Conflict in the Gulf*, Back Bay Books (Atlantic Books) (Gordon and Trainor) p.29; Extract on page 345 from *The Generals' War: The Inside Story of the Conflict in the Gulf*, Back Bay Books (Atlantic Books) (Gordon and Trainor) p.29; Extract on page 348 from *Into the Desert; reflections on the Gulf War*, Oxford University Press (Engel) p.135; Extract on page 348 from *A History of Iraq*, 3rd edition, Cambridge University Press (Tripp C 2007) p.251; Extract on page 350 from *Introduction to Global Military History*, 2 edition, Routledge (Black J) p254; Extract on page 354 from *Illusions of Triumph: Arab View of the Gulf War*, HarperCollins (Heikal, M 1993), Reprinted by permission of HarperCollins Publishers Ltd © Mohamed Heikal 1993; Extract on page 353 from *Thatcher's Britain: The Politics and Social Upheaval of the 1980s*, Pocket Books, Simon and Schuster. London. UK (Vinen, R) p.221, Simon and Schuster with permission and extract from THATCHER'S BRITAIN by Richard Vinen. Copyright © Richard Vinen, 2009, used by permission of The Wylie Agency (UK) Limited; Extract on page 357 from *The Pacific War [Taiheiyo Senso] 1931-45*, Iwanami Shoten, Japan Translation Random House. USA 1978 (Lenaga S) p.133, translation copyright © 1978 by Random House, Inc. Used by permission of Pantheon Books, an imprint of the Knopf Doubleday Publishing Group, a division of Penguin Random House LLC. All rights reserved; Extract on page 357 from *The Triumph of the Dark: European International History 1933-1939 (Oxford History of Modern Europe)*, OUP (Steiner, Z 2013) p.1065; Extract on page 359 from *Germany's Aims in the First World War*, W. W. Norton & Company (Fischer,F) p.88,copyright © 1961 by Droste Berlad und Druckerei GmbH, Dusseldorf. English translation copyright © 1967 by W.E.Norton & Company, Inc

Every effort has been made to trace the copyright holders and we apologise in advance for any unintentional omissions. We would be pleased to insert the appropriate acknowledgement in any subsequent edition of this publication.

The assessment objectives have been reproduced from IBO documents. Our thanks go to the International Baccalaureate for permission to reproduce its intellectual copyright.

This material has been developed independently by the publisher and the content is in no way connected with or endorsed by the International Baccalaureate (IB).

There are links to relevant websites in this book. In order to ensure that the links are up to date and that the links work we have made the links available on our website at www.pearsonhotlinks.com. Search for this title or ISBN 9781447984153.

Contents

Introduction

How will this book help you in your IB examination?

This book is designed to be your guide to success in your International Baccalaureate examination in History. It covers a range of suggested examples from Causes and Effects of 20th-century Wars, Topic 11, and emphasizes the key themes that the IB has identified within the Wars topic that you will need to answer essay questions on in Paper 2. In addition, although it is specifically for Paper 2, the book also helps you to develop and practise the source-based skills you need to answer questions on Paper 1.

Each chapter covers a regional or cross-regional conflict. We have also included:

- analysis of the key causes, events, and results of each war
- discussion of major themes and issues relating to each war
- a summary of, or reference to, up-to-date historiography
- discussion on how to answer essay questions
- essay planning techniques
- timelines to help you put events into context
- comparisons and contrasts between wars
- comparisons and contrasts of key themes
- review and research activities to help you develop your understanding of the key issues and concepts
- some practise of the source analysis skills you will need for Paper 1.

In the separate review chapters, we have highlighted activities and guidance on how to compare and contrast conflicts. We have also used examples from different regions for these sections to encourage the study of cross-regional exemplars.

The regular use of command terms, inquiry-based research tasks, source-based activities, and links to Theory of Knowledge and reflection will not only prepare you fully for the Paper 2 essay questions; it will also help to prepare you for the requirements of your Paper 1 examination and your Internal Assessment.

Notes on the second edition

Key concepts

Throughout the book we focus on and develop the six key concepts that have particular prominence in the Diploma History course: change, continuity, causation, consequence, significance, and perspectives. These concepts have always been key components of the History course; however, they are now specifically highlighted in this new guide.

New content

The new course Topic 11: Causes and Effects of 20th-century Wars has some content continuity with the last curriculum guide's Topic 1. A difference is that there is no material for detailed study and the two questions that you will be asked on this topic in the exam will be 'open' and can be addressed using any relevant case study. There is, however, more emphasis on a thematic and conceptual approach to this topic and the requirement to consider comparative and cross-regional case studies. In this second edition we have approached the case studies thematically and regionally. We have also included new chapters to address the comparisons and contrasts between cross-regional case studies. Each case study is developed in terms of its causes, the practices of war, and their impact on the outcome, culminating in the effects of war.

Approaches to learning

'Approaches to teaching and learning' (ATL) reflects the IB learner profile attributes and is designed to enhance your learning and assist preparation for IAs and examinations. ATL runs throughout the IB Middle Years Programme (MYP) and Diploma Programme (DP), and encourages you to think of common skills that are necessary in all subjects. The variety of skills covered will equip you to continue to be actively engaged in learning after you leave your school or college.

There are five categories of ATL skills: thinking skills, communication skills, social skills, self-management skills, and research skills. These skills encompass the key values that underpin an IB education.

ATL skills are addressed in the activity boxes throughout the book. ATL activities can also be found in the e-book that accompanies this book.

International mindedness

The Causes and Effects of 20th-century Wars topic is 'international' in its study of a range of cross-regional case studies and their impact on international relations in the 21st century. In addition, the emphasis in this course is to consider different perspectives and to analyse events in different regions, which will further your understanding of how key events are viewed around the world. As we go through the book we will further highlight the interconnected nature of 20th-century conflict and the events of today.

How this book works

You will see a number of coloured boxes interspersed throughout each chapter. Each of these boxes provides different information and stimulus, as follows.

Interesting fact boxes

These boxes contain information that will deepen and widen your knowledge, but which does not fit within the main body of the text.

The Spanish flu

Spanish flu was a flu pandemic that hit the world in 1918, causing millions of deaths. It first appeared in the United States, but spread to nearly every part of the world.

Essay questions

The essay questions that are at the start of each chapter offer topic-specific questions for you to think about while working through the chapter. At the end of the chapter there will be additional Paper 2-style questions. Some of these will ask you to compare the case study you have just covered with another case study from an earlier chapter.

As you read this chapter, consider the following essay questions:

- Examine why one peace treaty failed to establish a lasting peace.
- Assess the economic and social consequences of one war.

Key terms

Important terms or concepts are highlighted in bold in the main body of the text and explained in the glossary.

International mindedness

Where there is an activity that promotes international mindedness by looking at comparisons of regional case studies, focusing on different perspectives or by getting students to link an event with issues of today, an IM box will be shown.

What examples can you see of nationalism today causing tension between different groups of people?

Challenge yourself

These boxes contain open questions that encourage you to think about the topic in more depth, or to make detailed connections with other topics. They are designed to be challenging and to make you think.

CHALLENGE YOURSELF

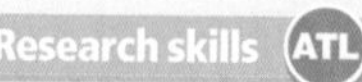

Enquire into how Hitler and other leading Nazis developed the party after the failure of the Munich Beer Hall Putsch. What were the SA and SS? How did the Nazis use modern propaganda and media techniques in the late 1920s?

Hints for success

These boxes can be found alongside questions, exercises, and worked examples and provide insight into how to answer a question in order to achieve the highest marks in an examination. They also identify common pitfalls when answering such questions, and suggest approaches that examiners like to see.

When you are asked to look for an answer in a source, underline the relevant points and then focus on the information that you need to answer the question. Do not list everything – only what is relevant.

Weblinks

Relevant websites are recommended in weblinks boxes at the end of each chapter. They can also be found in the Further Reading section at the end of the book.

To access websites relevant to this chapter, go to www.pearsonhotlinks.com, search for the book title or ISBN, and click on 'chapter 1'.

Theory of Knowledge

There are also Theory of Knowledge (ToK) boxes throughout the book – see page ix for more information about these.

eBook

In the eBook you will find the following:

- additional worksheets containing student activities
- an interactive glossary
- practice examination quizzes (testing knowledge and essay-planning skills)
- revision quizzes
- biographies of key figures covered in the book
- links to relevant websites
- enlargeable photos of useful resources, such as maps and source cartoons.

For more details about your eBook, see pages x–xi.

IB History assessment objectives

This book covers the four IB assessment objectives that are relevant to both the core externally examined papers and to the internally assessed paper. So, although this book is essentially designed as a textbook to accompany the Paper 2: Causes and Effects of 20th-century Wars Topic 11, it addresses *all* of the assessment objectives required for the History syllabus. In other words, as you work through this book, you will be learning and practising the skills that are necessary for each of the core papers. Nevertheless, the main focus will be the assessment objectives assessed in Paper 2.

Specifically, these assessment objectives are:

Assessment Objective 1: Knowledge and understanding

- demonstrate detailed, relevant, and accurate historical knowledge
- demonstrate understanding of historical concepts and context
- demonstrate understanding of historical sources (IA and Paper 1).

Assessment Objective 2: Application and analysis

- formulate clear and coherent arguments
- use relevant historical knowledge to effectively support analysis
- analyse different perspectives on historical issues, events and developments
- analyse and interpret a variety of sources (IA and Paper 1).

Assessment Objective 3: Synthesis and evaluation

- integrate evidence and analysis to produce a coherent response
- evaluate different perspectives on historical issues and events, and integrate this evaluation effectively into a response
- evaluate sources as historical evidence, recognizing their value and limitations (IA and Paper 1)
- synthesize information from a selection of relevant sources (IA and Paper 1).

Assessment Objective 4: Use and application of appropriate skills

- structure and develop focused essays which respond effectively to the demands of the question
- reflect on the methods used by, and challenges facing, the historian (IA)
- formulate an appropriate, focused question to guide an historical enquiry (IA)
- demonstrate evidence of research skills, organization, referencing, and selection of appropriate sources (IA).

Mark schemes

For the externally assessed components – Paper 1, Paper 2, and Paper 3 – there are two different assessment methods used:

- mark bands
- detailed specific mark schemes for each examination paper.

For the internally assessed/moderated IA there are set assessment criteria. You should refer to the Paper 2 mark bands when you attempt the practice essay questions in each chapter. We will also offer some question-specific material for the essay questions set in the book. These will give indicative content for the set question.

Causes and effects of 20th-century wars: key themes

As you read and work through this book, you will be covering the major themes for this History topic. At the end of the book, we will review these themes by considering how to answer possible thematic essay questions. Where and when appropriate, usually after examining two case studies from different regions, there is a chapter that focuses on comparative themes and questions.

Cross-regional case studies

World War One and World War Two are considered to be 'cross-regional' wars, and can be used as cross-regional case studies (for example, World War One in Europe compared with World War Two in Asia). However, you cannot use the *same* war to give cross-regional examples in a response, such as World War Two in Europe with World War Two in Asia. We have identified the specific region for each of the other case studies to encourage the study of cross-regional examples where possible. The examination may require students to consider examples from two different regions.

Different types of warfare

The different types of war – interstate, civil, guerrilla, total mobilization of human and economic resources, and limited mobilization of resources – are explained in Chapter 1 and then discussed further in each relevant case study. This book has two examples of each of the different types of war from different regions to give you enough material for essay questions.

Causes of war

The origins and causes of each war in the book are divided into long-term and short-term causes. In addition, the economic, ideological, political, territorial, and other causes are discussed where relevant.

Practices of war and their impact on the outcome

For each war, the characteristics of the fighting are discussed. Depending on the war, this discussion could include an analysis of the tactics and weaponry used in the fighting on land, on sea, and/or in the air. Where relevant, there will also be discussion of the impact of technological developments on the course and the outcome of the war. The economic and social impact of wars is also considered. Where appropriate, the influence and/or involvement of foreign powers is covered as well.

The effects of war

The results of the wars are analysed at the end of each chapter. There is an examination of the successes and failures of peacemaking and a consideration of wars where there is no concluding peace agreement or treaty. Territorial, political, economic, and social impacts are discussed and, where appropriate, changes in the role and status of women.

Theory of Knowledge

History is a Group 3 subject in the IB Diploma. It is an 'area of knowledge' that considers individuals and societies. In the subject of IB History, many different ways of obtaining knowledge are used.

When working through this book you should reflect on the methods used not only by professional historians but also by yourself, as a student of history, to gain knowledge. The methods used by historians are important to highlight, as it will be necessary to compare and contrast these with the other 'areas of knowledge', such as the Group 4 Sciences (Physics, Chemistry, and Biology). You should think about the role of individuals in history, the difference between bias and selection, and the role played by the historian. You will reflect in detail on these types of question in the final section of your Internal Assessment.

Theory of Knowledge boxes

There are ToK boxes throughout the book. These boxes will enable you to consider ToK issues as they arise, and in context. Often they will just contain a question to stimulate your thoughts and discussion.

How do political leaders attempt to maintain their 'credibility'? Which is more important for this – using reason, ethics, or emotion when addressing the public?

This book also includes a chapter on Theory of Knowledge, which has been updated for the latest ToK curriculum with the help of ToK expert Malcolm Price. In it, you will be encouraged to reflect on the methods used by historians by thinking about questions such as:

- What is the role of the historian?
- What methods do historians use to gain knowledge?
- Who decides which events are historically significant?

These types of questions require you to reflect on and engage with how historians work and will help you with the reflection section of the Internal Assessment.

How to use your enhanced eBook

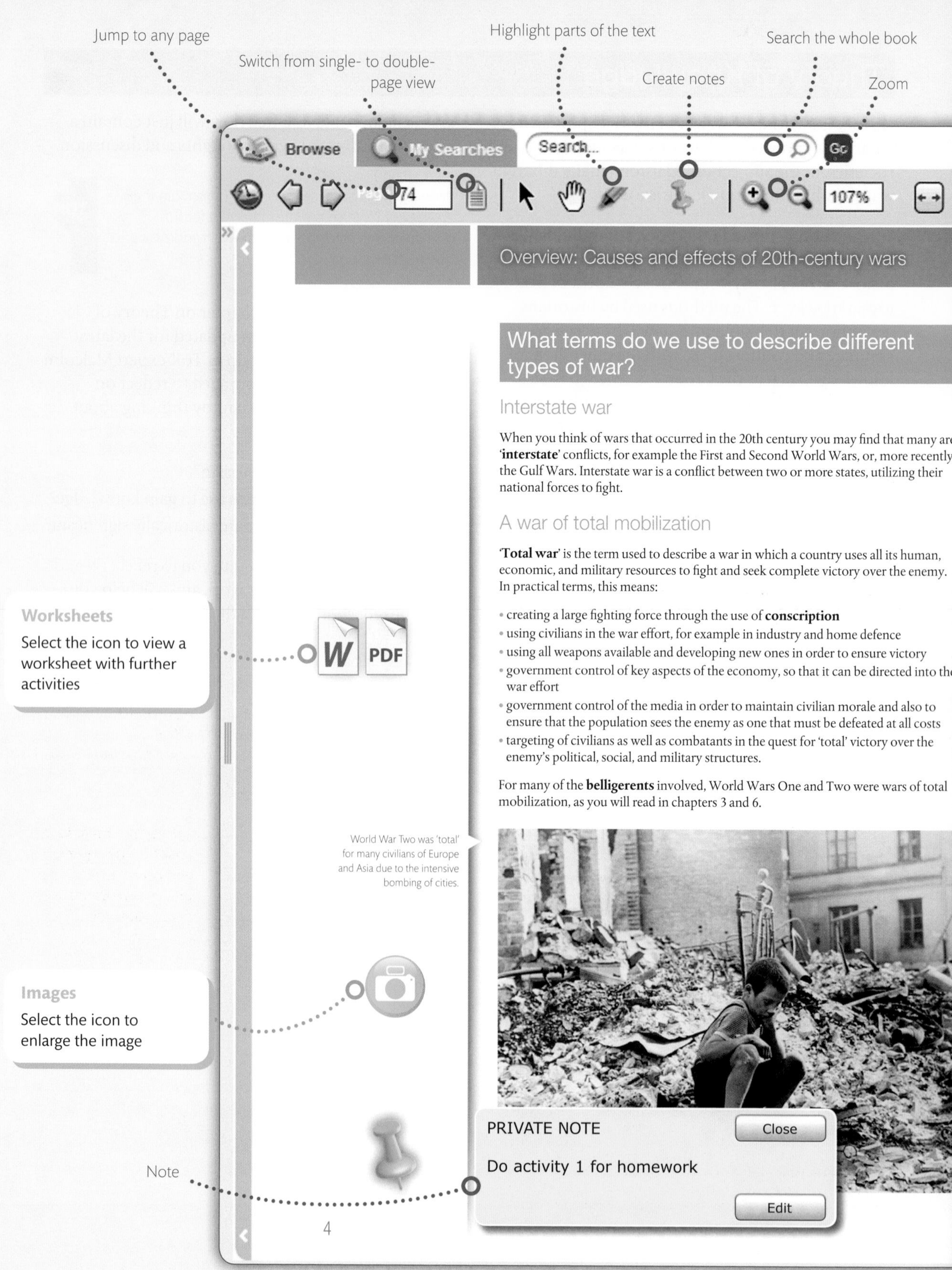

Jump to any page
Switch from single- to double-page view
Highlight parts of the text
Create notes
Search the whole book
Zoom
Browse
My Searches
Search...
Go
74
107%
Overview: Causes and effects of 20th-century wars
What terms do we use to describe different types of war?
Interstate war
When you think of wars that occurred in the 20th century you may find that many are 'interstate' conflicts, for example the First and Second World Wars, or, more recently, the Gulf Wars. Interstate war is a conflict between two or more states, utilizing their national forces to fight.
A war of total mobilization
'Total war' is the term used to describe a war in which a country uses all its human, economic, and military resources to fight and seek complete victory over the enemy. In practical terms, this means:
• creating a large fighting force through the use of conscription
• using civilians in the war effort, for example in industry and home defence
• using all weapons available and developing new ones in order to ensure victory
• government control of key aspects of the economy, so that it can be directed into the war effort
• government control of the media in order to maintain civilian morale and also to ensure that the population sees the enemy as one that must be defeated at all costs
• targeting of civilians as well as combatants in the quest for 'total' victory over the enemy's political, social, and military structures.
For many of the belligerents involved, World Wars One and Two were wars of total mobilization, as you will read in chapters 3 and 6.
World War Two was 'total' for many civilians of Europe and Asia due to the intensive bombing of cities.
Worksheets
Select the icon to view a worksheet with further activities
W
PDF
Images
Select the icon to enlarge the image
PRIVATE NOTE
Close
Do activity 1 for homework
Edit
Note
4

 This is an approximation of what your eBook will look like and not an exact reproduction

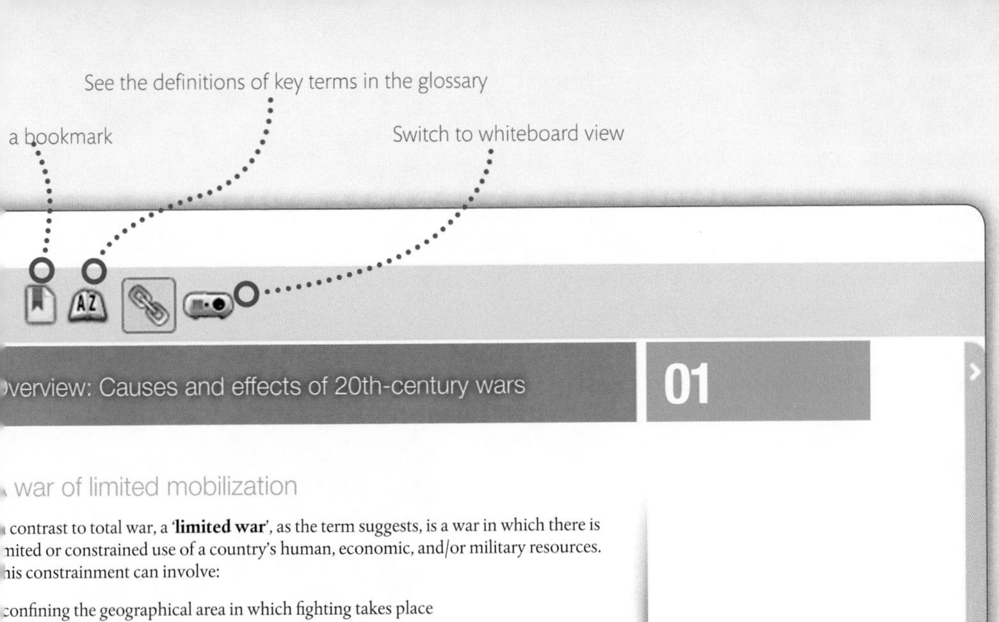

war of limited mobilization

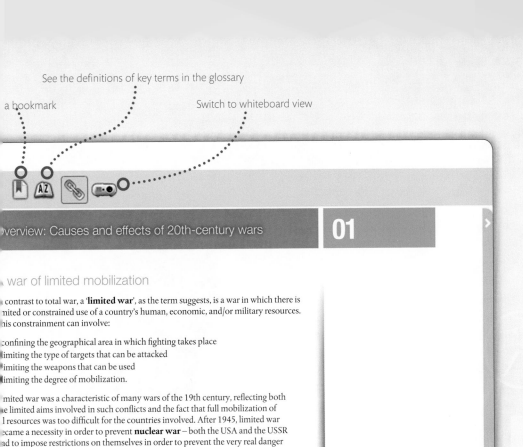

contrast to total war, a '**limited war**', as the term suggests, is a war in which there is nited or constrained use of a country's human, economic, and/or military resources. his constrainment can involve:

- confining the geographical area in which fighting takes place
- limiting the type of targets that can be attacked
- imiting the weapons that can be used
- limiting the degree of mobilization.

mited war was a characteristic of many wars of the 19th century, reflecting both e limited aims involved in such conflicts and the fact that full mobilization of l resources was too difficult for the countries involved. After 1945, limited war ecame a necessity in order to prevent **nuclear war** – both the USA and the USSR ad to impose restrictions on themselves in order to prevent the very real danger f a Superpower confrontation involving nuclear weapons. Thus both the Korean Var (1950–1953) and the Vietnam War (1963–1975) can be classed as 'limited' wars ecause they did not involve the USA using all of its military and economic resources hough, of course, for the Koreans and the Vietnamese these wars were total). xamples of limited war considered in this book are the Falklands War (1982) and the ulf War (1990–1991).

Activity 1 ATL Thinking skills

Find examples of wars before the 20th century. Which ones would you class as wars of limited mobilization, and why? Can you find any examples of wars of total mobilization before the 20th century? Again, explain why you would consider them to be total wars.

ivil wars

ivil wars are conflicts fought between two factions or regions of the same country, e warring sides clashing over ethnic, religious, political, territorial, or **ideological** sues. An example of a civil war is the Spanish Civil War (1936–1939), fought between **epublicans** and **Nationalists**. Generally speaking, during a civil war the combatants m to take control of the political and legal institutions of the state, although the iolence is longer lasting than in a ***coup d'état***. Usually, civil war combatants can be lentified as either **incumbents** or **insurgents**. Often there is foreign involvement or tervention in civil wars, and, depending on its role and impact, this could be viewed s broadening a civil war into an international conflict.

uerrilla warfare

uerrilla warfare (from the Spanish word for 'little war') was a key feature of 20th-entury conflicts. It is described as 'unconventional warfare' because, rather than ying to attack an enemy head-on with conventional tactics, small groups of fighters se tactics such as ambush and small-unit raids against a larger and less mobile formal rmy. The forces of Chinese Communist leader **Mao Zedong**, for example, used uerrilla tactics in the Chinese Civil War from the late 1920s through to 1949. This ype of warfare became common after 1945 for several reasons:

- Many conflicts after 1945 involved peoples of Asia and Africa trying to free themselves from the **colonial** rule of powerful European countries. With only limited military resources, the insurgents used guerrilla tactics as a way of attempting to achieve their goals. The use of guerrilla tactics has been promoted by the fact

5

Biographies

Select the icon to open biographies of key figures mentioned in the text

Quiz

Select the icon to take an interactive quiz to test your knowledge or practise answering exam essay questions

01 Overview: Causes and effects of 20th-century wars

US soldiers wearing gas masks walk through plumes of smoke during World War One.

> *I see it only as a century of massacres and wars.*
>
> **René Dumont.**

> *without doubt the most murderous century of which we have record by the scale, frequency and length of the warfare which filled it.*
>
> **From Eric Hobsbawm, *The Age of Extremes: The Short Twentieth Century* 1914–1991 (Michael Joseph, 1994), p.13.**

At the end of the 19th century, many people were convinced that war could no longer be used as a 'tool of **diplomacy**', yet war would become the dominant theme of the 20th century. There were two 'world' wars, each of which killed millions of people; World War Two (1939–1945) alone cost the lives of more than 50 million people. However, terrible as these wars were in terms of death toll, they were only two of many other conflicts that took place during the 20th century. In between the world wars and after 1945, there were numerous wars both between nations and within nations, in which casualties were often high.

The changing nature of warfare in the 20th century not only dramatically increased the number of casualties, but also blurred the distinctions between combatant and non-combatant. At the beginning of the century, there were eight times as many military casualties in war as there were civilian casualties. By the 1990s, the situation had reversed.

The technological development of weapons has also brought the threat of the total destruction of humanity. Nuclear weapons have raised the destructive potential of any war; their use in 1945 and the clear dangers they posed to the future of humankind also affected the way that wars were fought in the second half of the century.

Why is the study of war important?

As you can see from the map on page 9, and as we have suggested above, wars played a pivotal role in the 20th century. World War One swept away empires and the 'old order' and set the stage for new social and political developments in Europe. World War Two led to the emergence of the USA and USSR as **superpowers** and also to the decline of European powers such as Britain and France. These effects in turn led to the Cold War and the collapse of European empires: developments that dominated world politics after 1945 and shaped the world in which we live today.

A nuclear bomb detonating. Nuclear weapons are the ultimate tools of total war.

What terms do we use to describe different types of war?

Interstate war

When you think of wars that occurred in the 20th century you may find that many are 'interstate' conflicts, for example World Wars One and Two, or, more recently, the Gulf Wars. Interstate war is a conflict between two or more states, in which they utilize their national forces to fight.

A war of total mobilization

'**Total war**' is the term used to describe a war in which a country uses all its human, economic, and military resources to fight and seek complete victory over the enemy. In practical terms, this means:

- creating a large fighting force through the use of **conscription**
- using civilians in the war effort, for example in industry and home defence
- using all weapons available and developing new ones in order to ensure victory
- government control of key aspects of the economy, so that it can be directed into the war effort
- government control of the media in order to maintain civilian morale and also to ensure that the population sees the enemy as one that must be defeated at all costs
- targeting of civilians as well as combatants in the quest for 'total' victory over the enemy's political, social, and military structures.

For many of the **belligerents** involved, World Wars One and Two were wars of **total mobilization**, as you will read in chapters 3 and 6.

World War Two was 'total' for many civilians of Europe and Asia due to the intensive bombing of cities.

A war of limited mobilization

In contrast to total war, a **'limited war'**, as the term suggests, is a war in which there is limited or constrained use of a country's human, economic, and/or military resources. This constrainment can involve:

- confining the geographical area in which fighting takes place
- limiting the type of targets that can be attacked
- limiting the weapons that can be used
- limiting the degree of mobilization.

Limited war was a characteristic of many wars of the 19th century, reflecting both the limited aims involved in such conflicts and the fact that full mobilization of all resources was too difficult for the countries involved. After 1945, limited war became a necessity in order to prevent nuclear war – both the USA and the USSR had to impose restrictions on themselves in order to prevent the very real danger of a superpower confrontation involving nuclear weapons. Thus both the Korean War (1950–1953) and the Vietnam War (1963–1975) can be classed as 'limited' wars because they did not involve the USA using all of its military and economic resources (though, of course, for the Koreans and the Vietnamese these wars were total). Examples of limited war considered in this book are the Falklands War (1982) and the Gulf War (1990–1991).

Activity 1

1. Find examples of wars before the 20th century. Which ones would you class as wars of **limited mobilization**, and why? Can you find any examples of wars of total mobilization before the 20th century? Again, explain why you would consider them to be total wars.

Civil wars

Civil wars are conflicts fought between two factions or regions of the same country, with the warring sides clashing over ethnic, religious, political, territorial, or **ideological** issues. An example of a civil war is the Spanish Civil War (1936–1939), fought between Republicans and Nationalists. Generally speaking, during a civil war the combatants aim to take control of the political and legal institutions of the state, although the violence is longer lasting than in a ***coup d'état***. Usually, civil war combatants can be identified as either **incumbents** or **insurgents**. Often there is foreign involvement or intervention in civil wars, and, depending on its role and impact, this could be viewed as broadening a civil war into an international conflict.

Guerrilla warfare

Guerrilla warfare (from the Spanish word for 'little war') was a key feature of 20th-century conflicts. It is described as 'unconventional warfare' because, rather than trying to attack an enemy head-on with conventional tactics, small groups of fighters use tactics such as ambush and small-unit raids against a larger and less mobile formal army. The forces of Chinese Communist leader Mao Zedong, for example, used guerrilla tactics in the Chinese Civil War from the late 1920s through to 1949. This type of warfare became common after 1945 for several reasons:

- Many conflicts after 1945 involved peoples of Asia and Africa trying to free themselves from the **colonial** rule of powerful European countries. With only limited military resources, the insurgents used guerrilla tactics as a way of attempting to achieve their goals. The use of guerrilla tactics has been promoted by the fact that many post-1945 conflicts have been fought in areas where the terrain has aided guerrilla fighting, e.g. jungles in Vietnam, bush in Rhodesia, and mountains in Afghanistan. In these conflicts the guerrilla fighters have often also had the support of the local population and good knowledge of the terrain. In contrast, combatants of the European countries often faced local hostility and mobility problems in places that lacked a developed **infrastructure**.

- The development of the **Cold War** after 1945 also encouraged guerrilla warfare; in a situation where all conflicts were seen in the context of a struggle against either **Communism** or **Capitalism**, unpopular governments were often supported by one or other of the superpowers, meaning that the local opposition often had no choice but to resort to guerrilla warfare. In fact, given that the dangers of direct confrontation in the Cold War were too great, the USSR and USA often fought war 'by **proxy**', sponsoring local insurgencies rather than fighting themselves.
- The spread of **Marxism** has also had an influence. The belief that the masses must rise up against established Capitalist governments clearly supports the idea of guerrilla warfare, and indeed many successful guerrilla movements have been Marxist in orientation.
- In the post-Cold War world, guerrilla warfare has become increasingly central, as has been seen in **al-Qaeda**'s war against the West, because **democratic** political systems are particularly vulnerable to guerrilla tactics.
- Technological developments have enabled insurgents to become more formidable warriors than was possible at the beginning of the 20th century, and to take advantage of the global distribution of weapons such as shoulder-launched missiles and powerful **small arms**.
- The international coverage of the mass media now provides the kind of publicity that guerrilla fighters need in order to win support for their cause.

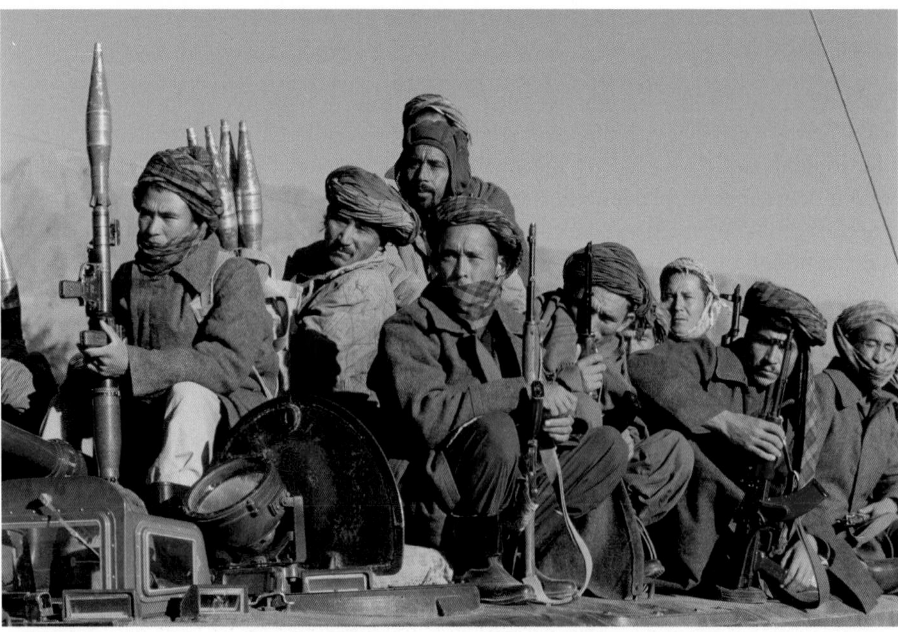

Mujahideen fighters in Afghanistan. In their war against the Soviet Union the Mujahideen used the techniques of guerrilla warfare.

Key terms

When studying wars, historians not only use labels such as 'civil' or 'limited', but they also divide both the causes and the effects of wars into different categories. Most wars will be caused by, and result in, a combination of the factors listed below.

Economic causes

This term refers to conflict over economic resources. For instance, a war could be fought over a country's need to secure foreign markets or raw materials. An example is the Gulf War of 1990–1991, in which the Iraqi leader, Saddam Hussein, looking to solve Iraq's drastic economic problems, invaded neighbouring Kuwait in an attempt to capture its oil reserves.

Economic effects

War can have a dramatic impact on the economic situation of a country, resulting in effects such as **inflation** or food **rationing**. The economic consequences of World War One for Germany, for example, were so severe that they contributed to the internal collapse of Germany in 1918.

Territorial causes

This term refers to conflict over the possession or control of land. For example, a war could be fought between states over control of a particular territory. A war could also be fought within a state between different groups seeking to gain control of land; sometimes it involves disputes over border territories. Often, territorial conflicts relate to economic causes, as a disputed territory may include natural resources such as rivers or farmland. However, territorial causes can also relate to ethnic and religious factors.

Territorial effects

The territorial effects of war can mean changes to the borders of states, the loss of land, and even a dramatic movement or shift in the boundaries of a country. Territorial changes as a result of war can have a significant impact on a country, for example in terms of its national identify and economic wealth (both mineral and farmland), lead to demographic, ethnic, and religious changes, and create refugee problems.

A key impact of 20th-century wars has been to displace people and create refugees.

Social causes

Wars are often caused by tensions between different social groups or classes in a country or region. Such tensions were a key element in the Spanish Civil War.

Social effects

The structures, customs, and traditions of a society are frequently changed by war. For example, World War One brought about huge transformations in European society, including a shift in the status of women and the beginning of the collapse of the traditional ruling classes.

Political causes

A political cause refers to wars that begin through a clash between different political factions, such as occurred in the Spanish Civil War.

Political effects

Wars can change the structure of a government or nation and result in a complete reconfiguration of how a country is run. For example, a key political result of World War One was the break-up of empires and the creation of new states.

Ideological causes

A fundamental clash of ideas between different groups about how government and society should be run is another leading cause of conflict. For example, at the root of the political clashes that caused the Spanish Civil War in 1936–1939 were clear differences in ideology. Many saw the war as a clash between **Fascism** and Communism.

Ideological effects

War can also affect the ideological position of a country or of groups within a country. For example, World War One provided some of the conditions in which the Communist revolution in Russia took place in 1917.

Consider the following technological developments of the 19th and 20th centuries. How has each one affected the conduct of war? Can you give examples of wars in which these developments have had an impact?

- the industrial and technological revolutions (which saw the rise of mass production and technological advances in manufacturing)
- the development of the railways
- the growth of the mass media
- the invention of the aeroplane
- the development of nuclear weapons
- globalization
- satellite technology
- the internet
- smart phones.

Activity 2

1. Look at the conflicts on the map on page 9. Using the information above, decide into which category – interstate, civil, or guerrilla – each war would fit. (You may find that wars can fit into more than category.)
2. Which wars have involved:
   a) total mobilization
   b) limited mobilization
3. What other wars do you know of that are not shown on the map? What wars do you know about that are still being fought today?
4. Wars can be given many other labels. How would you explain the following definitions of wars?
   - revolutionary war
   - territorial war
   - colonial war
   - ideological war
   - defensive war
   - religious war
   - **neo-colonial** war.

The impact of war on societies can be dramatic and permanently transform the social, economic, and political systems and structures of a country. Sometimes a war can create the conditions for social, economic, and political modernization.

1. Can war ever be seen as a 'positive' force within and between societies?
2. Discuss this in pairs and attempt to find examples of when and where war has brought about 'social change and political modernization'.

TOK

The statistics on casualties for these wars vary in different historical sources. Why might this be the case? What does this suggest about the use of statistics for the historian?

1. **World War One** (1914–1918)
2. **World War Two** (1939–1945)
3. **Mexican Revolution** (1910–1920)
4. **Nicaraguan Revolution** (1976–1979)
5. **Falklands/Malvinas War** (1982)
6. **Spanish Civil War** (1936–1939)
7. **Algerian War** (1954–1962)
8. **Nigerian Civil War** (1966–1970)
9. **Arab-Israeli Conflict** (1960–present)
10. **Iran–Iraq War** (1980–1988)
11. **First Gulf War** (1990–1991)
12. **Indo-Pakistan Wars** (1947–1949, 1965, 1971)
13. **First and Second Vietnam Wars** (1946–1954, 1964–1975)
14. **Chinese Civil War** (1928–1937, 1946–1949)
15. **Korean War** (1950–1953)
16. **North Yemen Civil War** (1962–1970)
17. **Chaco War** (1932–1935)
18. **Contra War** (1981–1990)
19. **The Balkan Wars** (1990s)
20. **Russian Civil War** (1917–1922)
21. **Irish War of Independence** (1919–1921)
22. **Russo-Japanese War** (1904–1905)

A century of conflict. This map shows only some of the wars fought in the 20th century.

02

Cross-regional war: World War One – Causes

Key concepts: Causation and perspective

As you read this chapter, consider the following essay question:

- Examine the long-term and short-term causes of one 20th-century war.

One of the most brutal and destructive wars in human history began in Europe in August 1914. It would last until November 1918. By the end of 1918, 60 declarations of war had been made between countries. Contemporaries and historians have argued ever since 1918 over what caused this catastrophe. This chapter looks at the long-term, short-term and immediate events that led the Great Powers of Europe, their empires, and their allies into armed conflict.

Timeline of the causes of World War One: 1871–1914		
1871		End of Franco-Prussian War/German Empire proclaimed
1873		The Three Emperors' League
1879		Dual Alliance
1881		The Three Emperors' Alliance
1882		Triple Alliance
1887		Reinsurance Treaty (Germany, Russia)
1888		Wilhelm II becomes German Emperor
1890		Bismarck resigns
		Reinsurance Treaty lapses
1892–1894		Franco-Russian Alliance
1897		Austro-Russian Agreement
1898		Fashoda Incident
		German Naval Law
1900		Second German Naval Law
1902		Anglo-Japanese Alliance
1904		Russo-Japanese War
		Entente Cordiale (Britain, France)
1905		First Moroccan Crisis
1906		Algeciras Conference
1907		Anglo-Russian Entente
		Triple Entente (Russia, France, and Britain)
1908		Annexation of Bosnia by Austria-Hungary
1911		Second Moroccan Crisis
1912		First Balkan War
1913		Second Balkan War
1914	**28 June**	Archduke Franz Ferdinand assassinated
	5 July	German 'blank cheque' to Austria-Hungary
	23 July	Austro-Hungarian ultimatum to Serbia
	30 July	Russia orders mobilization
	1 Aug	Germany declares war on Russia
	3 Aug	Germany invades Belgium and declares war on France
	4 Aug	Britain declares war on Germany

The Archduke Franz Ferdinand of Habsburg during a hunting trip (before his assassination led to the start of World War One in 1914).

TOK

When analysing the causes of a key event in history, the historian must decide 'when' the causes began – a starting date. However, if historians have to determine this themselves, how can they reach a decision?

If one historian focuses on events in the short term, will that necessarily lead to a different view of what was an important cause when compared to a historian whose focus is on events and issues in the longer term?

Discuss in small groups how this problem in historians' methodology might impact on their conclusions.

In this chapter, we begin looking at the causes of World War One with an earlier conflict that destabilized the balance of power in Europe before the start of the 20th century. This conflict was the Franco-Prussian War (1870–1871), which created a unified Germany.

The Franco-Prussian War (1870–1871)

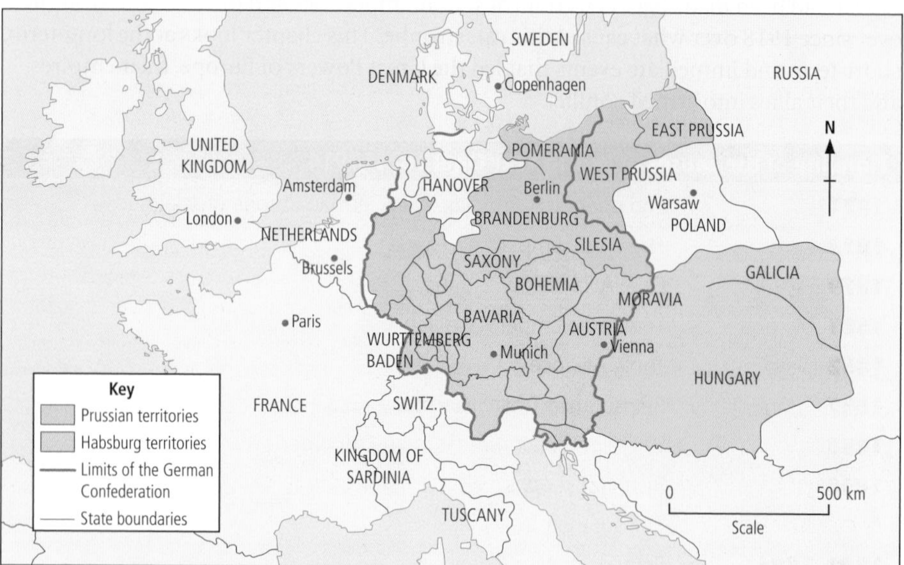

This map depicts Europe during 1815 and shows the 39 states of the German Confederation.

After the Napoleonic Wars, which ended in 1815, there were 39 separate Germanic states in Europe. The two largest were Austria and Prussia. The Prussians, under the leadership of their Chancellor, Otto von Bismarck, fought three wars with the objective both of consolidating these smaller states into a new German state and of asserting themselves as the dominant Germanic state instead of Austria. The Prussians defeated Denmark in 1864, Austria in 1866, and finally France in 1871.

The final war in 1870–1871 saw the well-equipped Prussian army not only defeating, but also humiliating, France. In early September 1870, at Sedan, one French army was forced to surrender its 80,000 men. The core of the French army, some 150,000 men, was encircled for 2 months at Metz and surrendered in October. The war continued for another three months. Paris, which had been under siege since mid-September, finally fell in January 1871. Cut off from the rest of France, Paris had suffered horrendously, and there were some clear signs of the effectiveness of modern technology in supporting warfare, for example, in Prussia's use of railways to deliver men and material to the battlefield. Prussia won the military battles and crippled Paris in an economic **blockade**.

The terms for peace were severe. France lost the territory of Alsace-Lorraine, had to pay an **indemnity** of 5,000 million marks, and suffered Prussian occupation of parts of France until this sum had been paid. There was also a Prussian victory march through Paris. In January 1871, the king of Prussia was proclaimed the German emperor in the Hall of Mirrors in the Palace of Versailles. German unification (without Austria) was complete.

In France, political and **socio-economic** problems followed the humiliation of defeat. There was a desire for revenge in France that manifested itself in the political ***revanche*** movement.

> *From tomorrow, France will have only one thought: to reconstitute its forces, gather its energy, feed its sacred anger, raise its generation ... form an army of the whole people, work relentlessly to study the processes and talents of our enemies, to become again the great France, the France of 1792, the France of the idea and the sword ... Then suddenly one day it will rise ... regain Lorraine, recapture Alsace.*
>
> **French poet Victor Hugo, 1871.**

Internationally, the war had far-reaching consequences. Germany was a new power in Europe, and France's position had been undermined. This situation shifted the balance of power in continental Europe. Germany now had the potential to be dominant. The Prussian wars of unification also offered important military lessons for the rest of Europe – the emphasis in modern warfare had to be on rapid **mobilization** and fast **deployment**. Modern armies had to be well trained and well equipped, and to a certain extent educated and probably conscripted. The general staff of an army (the personnel distributing the orders of the top leadership down to the field officers) had to be competent, and able to plan and coordinate the use of railways in deploying millions of men and their equipment. Another lesson that seemed to come from the unification wars was that modern warfare would rely on movement and be relatively short in duration.

Activity 1

Review questions

1. What was the impact of the Franco-Prussian War on France?
2. Why would the other European powers have been worried about the unification of Germany?

What were the key characteristics of the Great European Powers, c.1900?

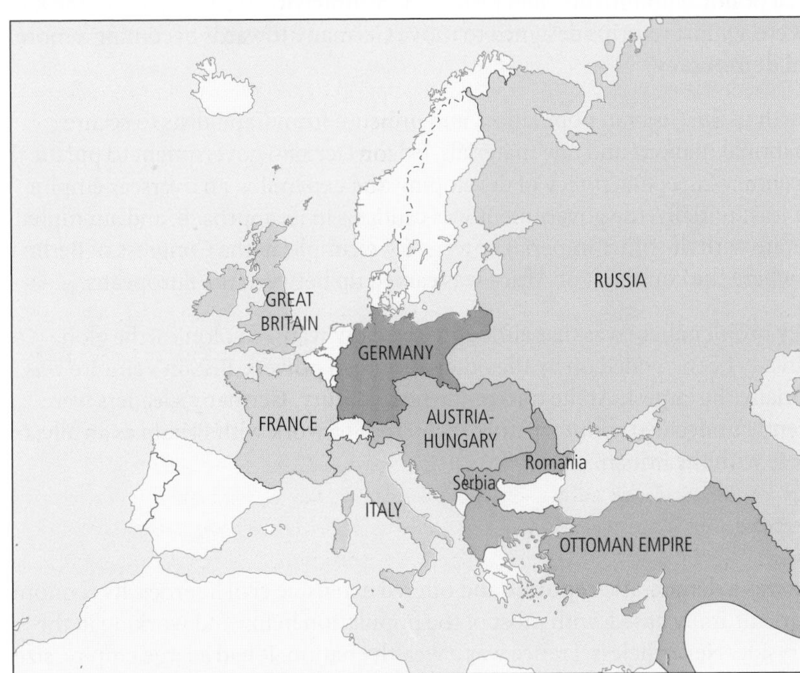

The Great Powers, c.1900.

Before reviewing the key developments in Europe that led up to World War One, it is important that you have a clear idea of the characteristics of the Great Powers of Europe by 1900.

Activity 2 — ATL Communication and social skills

Group activity

Using the information below on each of the European countries, complete the following table. This can be done as a group activity; each group researches a country and feeds back its information to the rest of the class.

	Austria-Hungary	Britain	France	Germany	Russia	Turkey
Economic strength						
Foreign policy						
Key aims/fears						
Key strengths/weaknesses						
Political system						
Socio-economic problems						

Germany

Germany was a **constitutional monarchy**; its system was **authoritarian**, with power held by the **Kaiser** and the Chancellor. The power of the German parliament, the Reichstag, was limited. In the 30 years following the Franco-Prussian War, Germany became the strongest industrial power in Europe. By 1900 it had overtaken Britain in industrial output. However, although its economy was strong and effective, Germany had acute social problems. Rapid **industrialization** had produced a large working class in the expanding cities, and a growing middle class. There were socio-economic tensions between these two groups and also between these groups and the authoritarian government. The great Prussian landowning classes, the Junkers, retained political dominance, and promoted **militarism** and allegiance to the Kaiser; they were against reforms designed to move Germany towards becoming a more **liberal democracy**.

A growth in the German population, and pressure from Capitalists to secure international markets and raw materials, led the German government to pursue the 19th-century European policy of developing and expanding an overseas empire. Yet, at least initially, the government was cautious in its approach, and attempted to cooperate with the other imperial powers, for example, at the Congress of Berlin in 1884, where the continent of Africa was carved up between the Europeans.

The key problem here was that although Germany wanted colonies, the globe had already been divided up by the other European powers. Britain's empire was territorially the largest. At the turn of the new century, Germany's leaders were apparently undecided about whether to attempt to work with Britain as an ally, or to compete with the British.

France

France was a democratic **republic** and offered extensive civil liberties. Its economy was agriculturally based, with most of the population living and working in the countryside. Nevertheless, France was a wealthy nation. It had a large empire, sizeable gold reserves, and had made much overseas investment, particularly in Russia. Politically, the nation was broadly divided between the 'pacifist' left wing and the *revanchist* right wing. France was plagued by short-lived governments, which swung between the left to the right. This instability had a serious impact on foreign policy, as the right wing wanted to pursue **imperialist** ambitions and the reclamation of Alsace-Lorraine, whereas the left were against this. France looked for an alliance with Russia to help 'contain' Germany.

Britain

Britain was a well-established **parliamentary democracy** (though universal **suffrage** was not achieved until after World War One) with a **monarchy** that retained limited powers. It had been the first European power to undergo an industrial revolution, and it had built a vast overseas empire and established itself as the most powerful international trader of the 19th century. Britain had indeed been the number one economic power of the 1800s, but by 1900 it was to a certain extent in decline, both in terms of its international dominance of trade and in its position as the primary economic power. Not only had the USA overtaken Britain in industrial production, but by 1900 Germany had too. Britain had similar socio-economic problems to Germany, with much working-class discontent.

The long-standing political system, however, combined a degree of flexibility with coercion and therefore appeared better able to cope than Germany's autocratic fledgling democratic monarchy. The British government had learnt to be alert to public opinion and the power of the popular press.

The changing balance of power in Europe led to a corresponding change in the shape of British foreign policy. In the later 19th century, Britain had followed a policy of 'splendid isolation', not wanting to be drawn into conflicts between other nations, as this could impact negatively on its international trade. By 1900, with competition from the USA and Germany, Britain was starting to review this policy and to look for allies. Britain's major military power was its navy, but in this strength lay Britain's weakness. Britain depended on the navy not only to defend itself against attack, but also to defend its sea-based trade and its vast empire. Resources were overstretched. It was paramount that the navy was invulnerable. Britain's traditional enemies and rivals had been the French and the Russians, and it remained particularly suspicious of Russia regarding its relationship to the overland Asian trade routes to India (see the Interesting Facts box on page 20). Britain's interests lay in maintaining its dominance of the seas, preserving the balance of power in Europe, and defending the Indian trade routes.

Austria-Hungary

Austria-Hungary was a 'dual monarchy': an emperor presided over the Austro-Hungarian Empire, with Austria and Hungary each having their own parliaments. The system was heavily bureaucratic and inefficient.

There had been slow economic growth in this land-based empire. The key problem for the dual monarchy was the national rivalries within its European empire (see the figures on page 16). The 19th century had unleashed powerful **nationalist** forces and ambitions across Europe, leading to demands for national liberation from states within the Austro-Hungarian Empire. The empire lacked military strength, which had been highlighted in the brief war with Prussia in 1866. A key concern for the Habsburgs was the demise of the Ottoman Empire on their border. This process had strengthened the nationalist cause of many **Slavic** peoples, who now strived for

The Habsburgs

The Habsburgs were the rulers of Austria-Hungary, the dual monarchy set up in 1867; the territories under Austrian and Hungarian control were known as the Habsburg Empire.

independence from the Ottomans, and ultimately wanted to unite with their 'brothers' within the borders of the Habsburg Empire. The Austro-Hungarian regime, therefore, pursued a foreign policy of containment in the Balkans, and, as the Ottoman decline left a vacuum of power, Austria-Hungary intended to fill it.

Austria-Hungary was a multi-national European empire in an age of nationalism. In general, the empire lacked cohesion economically, politically, and socially. Its greatest concern was the hostility and aggression of Serbia. The anxiety was accentuated by the support given to the Serb nationalists by Russia, who saw itself as the great defender of the '**Slav** people'.

Franz Josef, Emperor of Austria and King of Hungary.

Tsar Nicholas II of Russia.

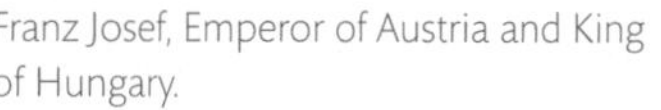

Nationalities of the Habsburg Empire, 1910.

Nationalities of the Habsburg Empire, 1910		
Austria	**Hungary**	**Bosnia-Herzegovina**
Germans 35.6%	Magyars 48%	Croats 21%
Czechs (incl. Slovaks) 23%	Germans 9.8%	Serbs 42%
Poles 17.8%	Slovaks 9.4%	Muslims 34%
Ruthenians 12.6%	Romanians 14.1%	
Serbo-Croats 2.6%	Ruthenians 2.3%	
Romanians 1%	Croats 8.8%	
	Serbs 5.3%	

Russia

Russia was an autocratic 'divine monarchy', the Tsar being perceived by many as having been appointed by God. The state was again heavily bureaucratic and ineffective. There had been rapid industrialization at the end of the 19th century, yet the majority of people in Russia remained peasants, working the land with intensive labour processes long outdated in the modernized European states.

By 1900, discontent towards the regime was growing among the middle classes and among the new urban workers. This mood exploded into revolution in 1905, following defeats in Russia's war with Japan. Although this revolution did not achieve regime change, it led to a very limited degree of democracy being introduced. Working conditions, however, were not improved.

After its defeat in the Crimean War (1853–1856) and then in the Russo-Japanese War (1904–1905), Russia was no longer viewed as a great military power. Russia's strength in 1900, and throughout the 20th century, was its huge resources of people. But again, this strength was also a weakness, as the Russian people were increasingly unhappy with their regime. Russia wanted to encourage Slav nationalism in the Balkans to establish its own influence in the region; however, it also wanted to prop up the ailing Ottoman Empire to prevent any expansion of Austria-Hungary.

Turkey

Turkey was the 'sick man of Europe'. The Ottoman Empire was in decline, and the power of its ruler – the Sultan – had been terminally undermined in most areas. The regime was corrupt and ineffective. Revolts by some national and Islamic groups within the empire could not be contained. Its weakness was exploited by the other European powers for commercial interest, and by 1900 foreign debt and political discontent meant the empire was near collapse. There were divisions between Turks, Slavs, and other Europeans in the Turkish Empire, including between Christians and Muslims. European interference led to widespread Muslim resentment. The Sultan was overthrown in 1909 by the 'Young Turks', a group whose aim was to modernize Turkey economically and politically.

The Ottoman Empire

The Turkish Empire came to be called the 'Ottoman' Empire after a 14th-century leader called Osman I. The Ottoman Empire was an Islamic empire led by a sultan (the Arabic word for 'ruler'). The empire consisted of 29 provinces, and other states under the nominal authority of the **sultanate**.

The Eastern question

The 'question' of what to do about the decaying Ottoman Empire preoccupied the other European powers. As its decline would lead to a power vacuum in the territories it formerly ruled over, there was the potential for a conflict between the powers for the spoils. Most European powers agreed the best solution for the time being was to prop up the Turkish regime and try to persuade it to modernize. The Russians, on the other hand, preferred to promote self-government for the Balkan states, but Austria-Hungary was deeply opposed to this idea.

Summary of key characteristics of the major powers, c.1910	
Austria-Hungary	Dual monarchy / nationalities problems
France	Democratic republic / slow economic growth / empire
Germany	Authoritarian state / military power / industrial power
Great Britain	Parliamentary monarchy / trade / industry / maritime power / empire
Russia	Autocratic tsardom / some industrialization / foreign debt
Turkey	Sultanate / decline of empire

Long-term causes of World War One

As we have seen, the creation of a new state in Europe – particularly one with the economic, military, and imperial potential of Germany – created a certain amount of nervousness among other European countries. France, of course, was particularly hostile in its attitude towards Germany after the humiliation of the war in 1870 and the loss of Alsace-Lorraine. Nevertheless, Germany under its first ruler, Kaiser Wilhelm I, and its Chancellor, Bismarck, did not pursue an aggressive foreign policy.

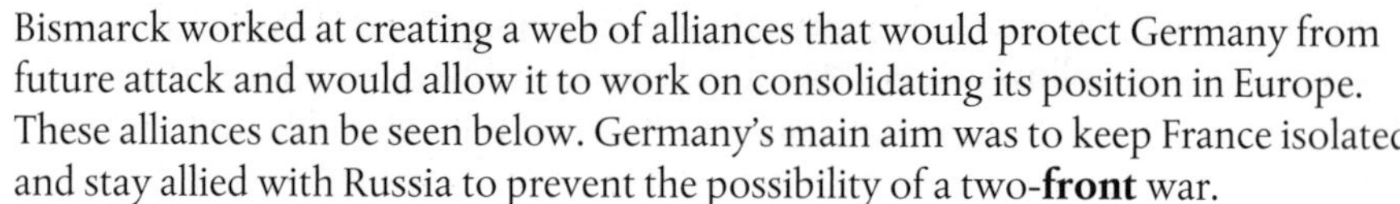

Two-front wars

Military commanders usually want to avoid a two-front war, as it means dividing their forces to meet an enemy in two different places. In the case of World War One, this would have meant the German army sending men, ammunition, supplies, and communications to both the Western and Eastern fronts, thus limiting their capacity to fight on either (see later information on the **Schlieffen Plan**).

Bismarck worked at creating a web of alliances that would protect Germany from future attack and would allow it to work on consolidating its position in Europe. These alliances can be seen below. Germany's main aim was to keep France isolated and stay allied with Russia to prevent the possibility of a two-**front** war.

Bismarck's web of alliances

The *Dreikaiserbund* or Three Emperors' League (1873)

The *Dreikaiserbund* joined Germany, Russia, and Austria-Hungary into an alliance. Its terms were very vague, but it served Bismarck's purpose of keeping France isolated.

The Dual Alliance (1879)

Austria-Hungary and Russia came into conflict over events in the Balkans and the *Dreikaiserbund* collapsed. In its place, Bismarck made a separate treaty with the Austrians. This alliance was part of Bismarck's system to limit the possibility of war between the European powers and was primarily defensive. Germany and Austria-Hungary agreed to assist one another if Russia attacked them. Each country also agreed to remain neutral if the other was attacked by another European country.

The Three Emperors' Alliance (1881)

Russia, feeling isolated in Europe, turned back to Germany, and Bismarck drew up a revised version of the *Drieskaiserbund*. Again, this offered Bismarck security. The terms of the alliance included an agreement that if either Russia, Germany, or Austria were at war with another power, the others would remain neutral. The alliance also tried to resolve Austro-Russian disputes in the Balkans.

Wilhelm II

Wilhelm was the son of Prince Frederick Wilhelm of Prussia and Victoria (who was the daughter of Queen Victoria of Britain). He was a keen advocate of all things military. He loved wearing, and having himself photographed in, his numerous uniforms, and he surrounded himself with the elite of German military society. Wilhelm acted very much as an autocratic monarch and also had a volatile and unpredictable personality. He was a strong opponent of **socialism** and vigorously believed in *Weltpolitik* – increasing the global strength of Germany through building up the German navy and colonial expansion.

The Triple Alliance (1882)

This alliance was between Germany, Austria-Hungary, and Italy. If any of the signatories were attacked by two or more powers, the others promised to provide assistance.

The Reinsurance Treaty (1887)

The Three Emperors' Alliance fell to pieces due to problems in the Balkans in 1885. Thus, this separate treaty with Russia was drawn up in order to avoid any risk of a war on two fronts. Bismarck had to make new arrangements to ensure that Germany stayed friendly with Russia.

The New Course and Weltpolitik

In 1888, the young and ambitious Wilhelm II came to the throne in Germany, and Bismarck was replaced as Chancellor by Leo von Caprivi in 1890. Kaiser Wilhelm II and Caprivi took German foreign policy on a 'new course' that would overturn Bismarck's carefully nurtured system of alliances. The Reinsurance Treaty with Russia was allowed to lapse that year, creating the conditions for the Franco-Russian Alliance of 1894. Militarily, the alliance promised mutual assistance if either was attacked by Germany. It also agreed immediate mobilization in response to deployment of forces by any member of the **Triple Alliance**. There was also a political clause, which agreed mutual support in imperial disputes; the focus of this clause was essentially anti-British. Bismarck's system was destroyed. France was free of its isolation, and Germany now could face a war on two fronts.

Undeterred, however, German policy makers from the mid-1890s began to look beyond Europe and to follow a policy that they hoped would make Germany a colonial power, with an overseas empire and navy. Such a policy would also have the benefit of diverting the German population away from the social and political problems at home. This policy, known as ***Weltpolitik***, was supported by various patriotic groups, such as the **Pan-German League**, within Germany and was bound to have an impact on Germany's relations with other countries.

Kaiser Wilhelm II of Germany.

Activity 3

Source analysis

> *I hope Europe will gradually come to realize the fundamental principle of my policy: leadership in the peaceful sense – a sort of Napoleonic supremacy … I am of the opinion that it is already a success that I, having come to govern at so early an age, stand at the head of German armed might yet have left my sword in its scabbard and have given up Bismarck's policy of externally causing disruption to replace it with a peaceful foreign situation such as we have not known for many years.*
>
> **Kaiser Wilhelm II to Botho Graf zu Eulenburg, July 1892. Eulenburg was a close friend of the Kaiser and served as his Minister of the Interior until 1882.**

1. According to the Kaiser, what did he hope to achieve in foreign policy?

Imperialism

One of the main causes of tension between the European powers in 1880–1905 was colonial rivalry. Over the course of the 19th century, the Europeans had increased their domination of countries in Africa and the Far East and competed to build vast empires. This effort was initially driven by economic motives (cheap raw materials, new markets, and low-cost labour forces). Over the course of the century, however, territorial acquisition increasingly occurred due to a mixture of the social Darwinian belief that the spread of Western civilization was 'God's work' and also nationalistic competition with the other European powers (and to a certain extent the USA).

Social Darwinism

Social Darwinism was the application of some of Charles Darwin's theories of evolution to human societies. Herbert Spencer, an English philosopher, produced a very simplified version of Darwin's ideas that focused on the theory of 'survival of the fittest'. He suggested that countries were destined to evolve like species; through conflict the 'fittest' would triumph and the weakest die out. Peace was not an option – war *was* evolution. This theory gained influence in the latter half of the 19th century across European societies.

Germany's desire to make its influence felt outside Europe was to bring it into conflict with the more established colonial powers, particularly Britain. An example of this effect occurred in 1896, when the German Kaiser caused great offence in Britain over his response to the so-called Jameson Raid of December 1895. The Jameson Raid was a failed attempt by Britain to incite a rising against the Boer Republic of the Transvaal in southern Africa. It was led by a Dr Jameson, who was an administrator in the British South Africa Company, but resulted in the resignation of Cecil Rhodes, the governor of Cape Colony, when it became clear that he was also involved in the planning of this 'illegal' operation. Germany sent a telegram to the Boer leader, Stephanus Johannes Paulus Kruger, on 3 January 1896 congratulating him on his success in resisting the attack:

> *I would like to express my sincere congratulations that you and your peoples have succeeded, without having to invoke the help of friendly powers, in restoring peace with your own resources in face of armed bands which have broken into your country as disturbers of the peace and have been able to preserve the independence of your country against attacks from outside.*

This telegram caused great offence in Britain. The coverage of the affair by the British press led to outrage among the British public.

Activity 4

Research and thinking skills

Research questions

1. By 1914, which European powers had the biggest overseas empires?
2. Where did Germany have colonial possessions?
3. Compare the size of Germany's colonial possessions to those of the other European powers.
4. Why were imperial rivalries a potential cause of tension between the European powers in 1900?

Activity 5

Thinking and social skills

Discussion question

1. Why do you think that the Kruger telegram caused so much fury in Britain?

The emergence of the alliance system

Germany's policy of *Weltpolitik* brought it into conflict with Britain in other ways as well. In 1897, Admiral von Tirpitz was appointed as Secretary of State for the Navy. He shared the Kaiser's belief that Germany should mount a naval challenge to Britain, and within a year he had pushed a naval law through the Reichstag that provided for the building of 17 ships over the next 7 years. This bill was followed by a second naval law in 1900.

Britain quickly responded to this threat to its naval supremacy. It was clear to many that the position of 'splendid isolation' was no longer appropriate or useful. Britain had clashed with France in Sudan over the territory around Fashoda and was a rival with Russia over China in the Far East. Now, with Germany challenging Britain, it seemed the right time to seek security through alliances. Thus, in 1902, Britain made an alliance with Japan, which gave the British an ally in the Far East and allowed the Royal Navy to bring back warships from this area. This alliance was followed by an **entente** with France. Although this entente was not a formal alliance, it settled the rivalry between the two nations over colonial issues, and set a completely new direction for Anglo-French relations.

In 1907, Britain and Russia reached agreement over their relationship with Persia, Tibet, and Afghanistan, again reducing British concern over security in India and the Far East. France had already secured Russia as an ally following Germany's failure to renew the Reinsurance Treaty of 1887. Now Russia, France, and Britain joined together in the **Triple Entente**. German naval expansion had thus forced Britain into seeking an agreement with its former colonial rivals, leaving Germany concerned that it was becoming 'encircled'. Europe was now divided into two alliance systems – the Triple Entente and the Triple Alliance.

The 'Great Game'

The intense rivalry between Britain and Russia between 1813 and 1907 for control over Central Asia has been called the 'Great Game'. Afghanistan was the key focus in the 19th century. The British were determined to protect their land routes to the 'jewel' in their imperial crown – India. Afghanistan, so the British feared, would be the launching ground for a Russian invasion of India. To prevent this, the British attempted to impose a **puppet regime** on Afghanistan in 1838, but this did not last long, and the British were forced to retreat from Kabul in 1852. The British then embarked on another war in Afghanistan in 1878 in retaliation for the Afghans' refusal to accept a British diplomatic mission to Kabul, after they had received one from Moscow. The British were again forced to pull out of Kabul in 1881. There was nearly war between Russia and Britain when the Russians seized Merv in 1882 and fought Afghan forces over Panjdeh. To avert war between the two European powers, Britain accepted Russian control of these territories.

The naval race

A British Dreadnought-class battleship.

The other effect of Germany's maritime challenge to Britain was that it started a naval **arms race.** In 1906, Britain had launched a super-battleship, HMS *Dreadnought*. The battleship's name literally meant that this ship 'feared nothing', as its speed, range, and firepower were far superior to those of any other existing battleship. The irony of the creation of this battleship was that it potentially nullified Britain's historical naval advantage over the other Great Powers. The dreadnought class made all the older battleships obsolete; this meant that in battleship terms Britain had taken the race back to zero and its traditional numerical advantage was lost. A competitor now could construct similar battleships and catch up with Britain. This situation triggered a 'naval scare' in the winter of 1908–1909, as fears grew concerning Germany's rapidly expanding fleet. The British government responded by ordering the construction of eight battleships in 1909.

The naval race also caused a complete change of mood within the British population itself, as newspapers and popular fiction now portrayed Germany (rather than France or Russia) as the new enemy threatening Britain. As historian Norman Lowe observes, Britain's willingness to go to war in 1914 owed a lot to the tensions generated by the naval race.

Tirpitz's Risk Theory

Admiral Alfred von Tirpitz felt that if Germany could build enough ships to make it a threat to Britain, then Britain would decide that it had to avoid conflict with Germany. In fact, he believed that Britain would be inclined to seek accommodation with Germany and thus Germany would be able to pursue *Weltpolitik* without British interference. However, as you can see, the plan pushed Britain into making alliances and also into increasing and modernizing its own navy, while turning government and public opinion against Germany.

Activity 6

ATL Thinking and social skills

European economic and military strength, 1900

	France	Germany	Austria-Hungary	Britain	Russia	Italy
Annual value of foreign trade (£)	460,408,000	545,205,000	151,599,000	877,448,917	141,799,000	132,970,000
Battleships – first class	13	14	0	38	13	9
Battleships – second class	10	0	6	11	10	5
Iron and steel production (tons p.a.)	3,250,000	13,790,000	2,580,000	13,860,000	5,015,000	5,000,000
Merchant fleet (net tonnage)	1,037,720	1,941,645	313,689	9,304,108	633,820	945,000
Personnel in regular army	589,541	589,266	397,316	280,000	860,000	261,728
Population	38,641,333	56,367,176	45,015,000	41,605,323	132,960,000	32,450,000

Study the statistics for the different countries carefully, then in pairs discuss the following questions.

1. Which categories do you think are the most important for indicating the strength of a country in war?
2. Overall, which alliance system seems to be the strongest?
3. To what extent would you agree that Germany's position in 1900 was less secure than it had been in 1890?

The situation in the Balkans

The Balkans was a very unstable area that also contributed to the tensions that existed in Europe before 1914. As you have already read in the introductory section to this chapter, three different empires had interests here – Turkey, Austria-Hungary, and Russia.

Turkey

Turkey had once ruled over the whole of the Balkans. However, the Serbs, Greeks, and Bulgars had already revolted and set up their own independent nation states and now Turkey was struggling to hold on to its remaining Balkan territories.

Austria-Hungary

The Austrians were losing their grip on their multi-ethnic empire by 1900. Of the various ethnic groups in Austria-Hungary, the most forceful in their demands for independence were the southern Slavs – the Serbs, Croats, and Slovenes – who were beginning to look to Serbia for support. They wanted to break away and form a South Slav kingdom with their neighbour, Serbia. Serbia was thus seen as a threat by Austria-Hungary.

Russia

Russia also had ambitions in the Balkans. First, the Russians sympathized with their fellow Slavs; indeed, Russia saw itself as the champion of the Slav people. Second, the Balkans was strategically important to Russia. The Straits of Constantinople had to be kept open to Russian ships *en route* from the Mediterranean to the Black Sea. With ports in the north of Russia's vast empire iced over for 6 months of the year, continued access to warm-water ports was vital. The fact that Turkey's power was so weak and could in fact collapse at any moment led the powers to talk of the 'Eastern question': what would happen in the Balkans if and when this situation arose? Clearly, both Austria-Hungary and Russia hoped to benefit from Turkey's declining power.

King Peter of Serbia.

Growing tension in the Balkans after 1900

In June 1903, the pro-Austrian King Alexander of Serbia was murdered and replaced by the Russophile King Peter, who was determined to reduce Austro-Hungarian influence. This appointment caused great anxiety in Austria-Hungary, which already feared the influence of a strong Serbia on their multi-ethnic empire. A **tariff** war began in 1905–1906, and the Serbs turned to France for arms and finance. Tension increased when the uncompromising Baron von Aehrenthal became Austria's Foreign Minister. He believed that an aggressive foreign policy would demonstrate that Austria was still a power to be reckoned with and would stamp out Serbian aspirations.

Short-term causes: the crisis years (1905–1913)

Between the years 1905 and 1913, there were several crises, which, though they did not lead to war, nevertheless increased tension between the two alliance **blocs** in Europe and also created greater instability in the Balkans.

The Moroccan Crisis (1905)

Germany was worried by the new relationship between Britain and France and set out to expose the weakness of this new friendship and break up the entente by attacking

France in Morocco. As part of the entente agreement, Britain had supported a French takeover of Morocco in return for France recognizing Britain's position in Egypt. (Morocco had been one of the few remaining areas of Africa not controlled by a European power.) The Germans thus announced that they would assist the Sultan of Morocco to maintain his independence and demanded an international conference to discuss the situation.

An atmosphere of crisis and the threat of war was cultivated by the Germans throughout 1905, until the French gave in and agreed to a conference at Algeciras, Spain, in 1906. Much to the surprise of Germany, the British decided to back the French and their demands for influence in Morocco. The Germans had little support at the conference and after several weeks had to admit defeat. Their only gain was a guarantee of their commercial interests.

The results of the first Moroccan Crisis were a disaster for Germany:

- Germany had not gained notable concessions in North Africa, which was a failure for *Weltpolitik* and a blow for German pride.
- Germany had not undermined the Entente Cordiale, but had strengthened it. Military talks between France and Britain were initiated in January 1906. British foreign policy was now directed at supporting French interests.
- Several states had considered war as a possible outcome of the crisis, thus signalling an end to the relatively long period of peaceful relations in Europe.
- Germany was now seen as the key threat to British interests.

Activity 7

ATL Thinking skills

Source analysis

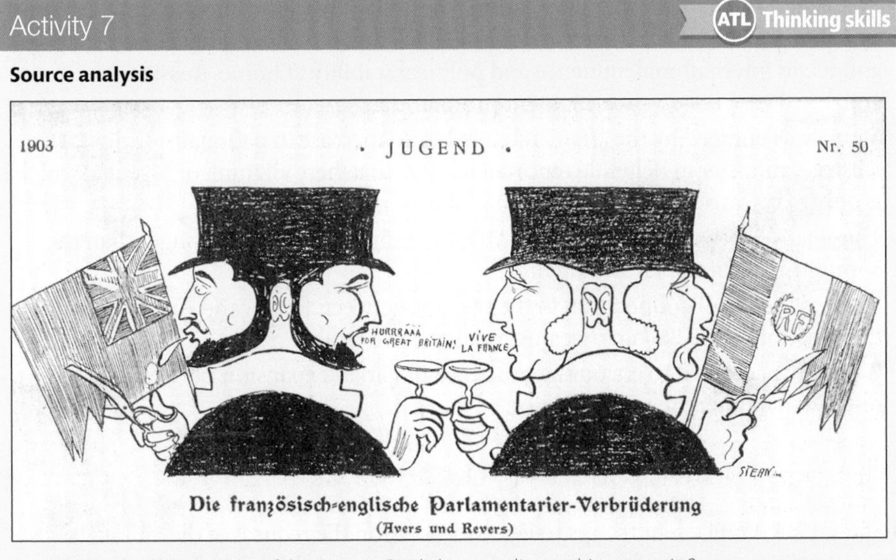

A pre-World War One German cartoon. The caption reads: 'The Franco-English Parliamentarian Alliance (Face and About-face)'.

1. What is the German view of the Entente Cordiale, according to this cartoonist?

In this question, you need to make sure that you structure your answer clearly. You are looking for two points so make it clear to the examiner that you have done this, for example 'The first point that the cartoon is making ... It is also saying that ...' Make sure that you give details from the cartoon to support your answer.

The Bosnian Crisis (1908)

Following the first Moroccan Crisis, the Anglo-Russian Entente of 1907 was signed, thus confirming to many Germans the idea of a conspiracy to encircle and contain them. This fear of encirclement forced Germany into a much closer relationship with its Triple Alliance partner, Austria-Hungary, a shift that was to have an impact in both the Bosnian Crisis of 1908 and the later Balkan Crisis of 1914.

In 1908, an internal crisis in the Ottoman Empire caused by the Young Turk Revolution again raised the issue of the Eastern question, and Austria-Hungary

Entente Cordiale

The Entente Cordiale marked the end of almost a thousand years of periodic conflict between Britain and France. It was a clear demonstration of the re-alignment between the old European powers in response to the perceived threat from the new European power, Germany. The most important of the three documents that made up the Entente Cordiale was an agreement over Egypt and Morocco. The British allowed French influence over Morocco, while the French recognized British influence in Egypt. There was also a guarantee of free passage through the Suez Canal. The other documents recognized British and French rights in West and Central Africa, and in Thailand, Madagascar, and the New Hebrides.

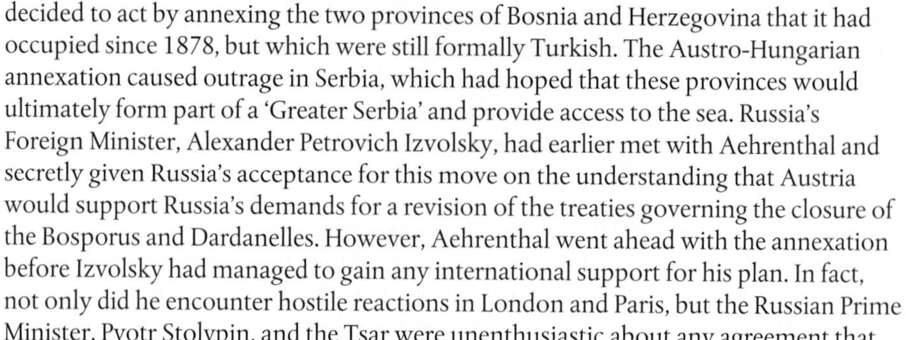

decided to act by annexing the two provinces of Bosnia and Herzegovina that it had occupied since 1878, but which were still formally Turkish. The Austro-Hungarian annexation caused outrage in Serbia, which had hoped that these provinces would ultimately form part of a 'Greater Serbia' and provide access to the sea. Russia's Foreign Minister, Alexander Petrovich Izvolsky, had earlier met with Aehrenthal and secretly given Russia's acceptance for this move on the understanding that Austria would support Russia's demands for a revision of the treaties governing the closure of the Bosporus and Dardanelles. However, Aehrenthal went ahead with the annexation before Izvolsky had managed to gain any international support for his plan. In fact, not only did he encounter hostile reactions in London and Paris, but the Russian Prime Minister, Pyotr Stolypin, and the Tsar were unenthusiastic about any agreement that would give Austria control over fellow Slavs.

Relations between Austria-Hungary and Russia became very strained and there was talk of war. It was at this point, in January 1909, that Germany decided to stand 'shoulder to shoulder' with its ally. Germany reassured Austria-Hungary that it would mobilize in support if Austria-Hungary went to war with Serbia. By contrast, Russia had little support from Britain or France. The Russians – weakened by the 1904–1905 war with Japan – had no alternative but to capitulate to the German 'ultimatum' and recognize the Austro-Hungarian annexation of Bosnia. Given the overwhelming military potential of Austria-Hungary and Germany, Serbia backed down.

The results of the crisis were important factors in raising tension in the region and between the alliance blocs:

- Russia had suffered another international humiliation, following on from its defeat by Japan. It was unlikely that Russia could back down from another crisis situation and retain international influence and political stability at home. Russia now embarked on a massive rearmament programme.
- Serbia was enraged by the affair, and it led to an increase in nationalist feeling. The Austrian minister in Belgrade reported in 1909 that 'here all think of revenge, which is only to be carried out with the help of the Russians'.
- The alliance between Germany and Austria-Hungary appeared stronger than the commitments of the Triple Entente.
- It ended the era of cooperation in the Balkans between Russia and Austria-Hungary; the situation in the Balkans became much more unstable.
- Germany had opted to encourage Austro-Hungarian expansion rather than acting to restrain their approach to the region.

The Second Moroccan (Agadir) Crisis (1911)

In May 1911, France sent troops to Fez, Morocco, on the request of the Sultan, to suppress a revolt that had broken out. The Germans saw this as the beginning of a French takeover of Morocco and sent a German gunboat, the *Panther*, to Agadir, a small port on Morocco's Atlantic coast, hoping to pressurize the French into giving them some compensation for such an action.

The Germans, in demanding the whole of the French Congo, were too ambitious. This assertiveness was popular with public opinion in Germany, but such 'gunboat diplomacy', as it was called by the British, implied the threat of war. Britain, worried that the Germans might acquire Agadir as a naval base that would threaten its naval routes to Gibraltar, made its position clear. David Lloyd George (Britain's Chancellor of the Exchequer) gave a speech – called the Mansion House Speech – to warn Germany off. He said that Britain would not stand by and watch while 'her interests were affected'. This speech turned the Franco-German crisis into an Anglo-German confrontation. In November the crisis was finally resolved when Germany accepted far less compensation – two strips of territory in the French Congo.

The results of this crisis, again, increased tension between the European powers:

- German public opinion was hostile to the settlement and critical of their government's handling of the crisis, which was another failure for the policy of *Weltpolitik*.
- The entente between Britain and France was again strengthened. Naval negotiations between the two began in 1912, and Britain had made a commitment to defend France by 1913.
- There was increased tension and hostility between Germany and Britain.

Thus, although imperial rivalries in themselves did not necessarily mean war given that there had also been many agreements on colonial issues in the years before the war), incidents such as those in Morocco helped to increase mutual suspicion and hostility.

Activity 8

ATL Thinking skills

Source analysis

Source A

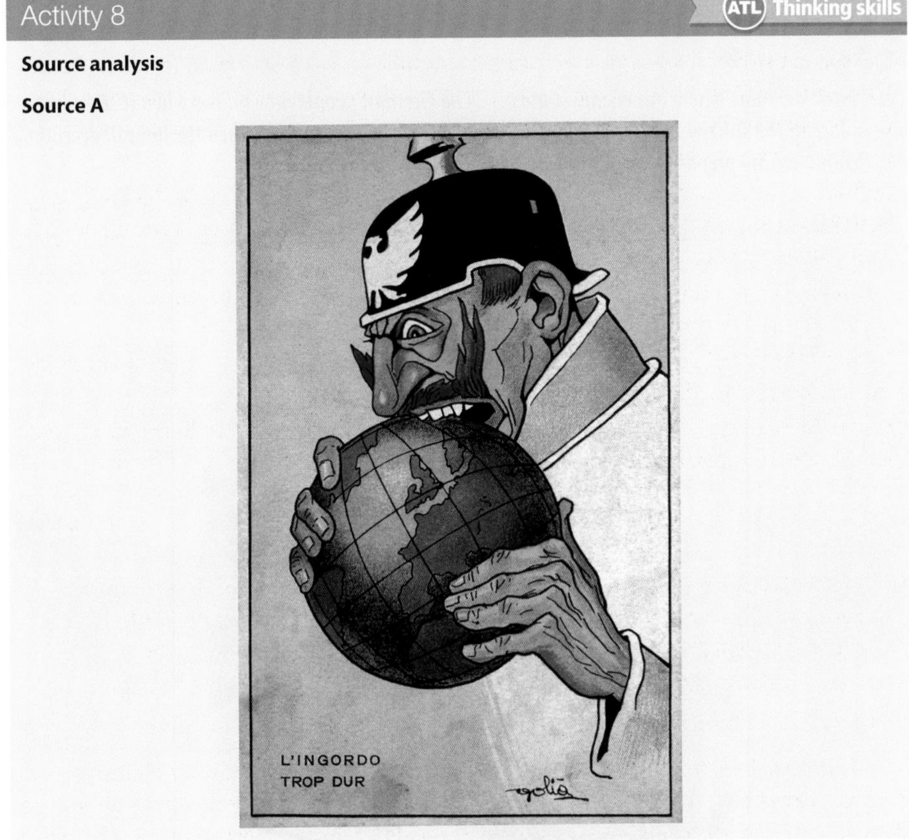

An Italian postcard from the early 1900s shows the Kaiser attempting to eat the world. The caption roughly translates as: 'The glutton finds this too hard.'

Source B

A German cartoon, 'The mailed fist of Agadir', c.1912.

Source C

On 9 November 1905 a leading member of the Reichstag was applauded when he declared:

> *Now we know where our enemy stands … The German people now knows when it seeks its place in the sun, when it seeks the place allotted to it by destiny … When the hour of decision comes we are prepared for sacrifices, both of blood and of treasure.*

Source D

Cartoon in *Punch* magazine, 2 August 1911.

1. What are the messages of Sources A, B, and C regarding the aims and methods of Germany in its quest for colonies?
2. What similarities are there between the messages of Sources B and C?
3. Write a caption for Source D.

Activity 9

ATL Thinking skills

Review questions

1. Why had Germany interfered in Morocco in 1905 and 1911?
2. For what reasons did Germany strengthen its alliance with Austria-Hungary?
3. Why were the results of the Moroccan crises disappointing for Germany?
4. To what extent was German policy 'miscalculated'?
5. Explain why the Balkans situation was more dangerous as a result of the **annexation** of Bosnia-Herzegovina.

The First Balkan War (1912)

In 1912, encouraged by the Russians, the Balkan states of Serbia, Greece, and Montenegro formed a Balkan alliance. Their key objective was to force Turkey from the Balkans by taking Macedonia and dividing it up between themselves. Turkey was already weakened by a war with Italy over Tripolitania the year before and was almost completely driven out of the Balkans in seven weeks. Austria was horrified; it could not accept a strengthened Serbia. Austrian generals called for war. There was a danger, however, that Russia would support its ally, Serbia, and that events could spiral into a wider European war.

Sir Edward Grey, the British Foreign Secretary, was anxious to stop the war spreading, and called a peace conference in London. As a result of this conference, the former Turkish lands were divided up between the Balkan states. Yet Austria-Hungary succeeded in containing Serbia by persuading the conference to agree to the creation of Albania, which was placed between Serbia and the Adriatic Sea. This agreement caused more resentment between Serbia and Austria-Hungary.

The Second Balkan War (1913)

Due to the disagreement over the spoils of the First Balkan War, *another* war broke out in the Balkans in July 1913. Bulgaria now went to war against Serbia and Greece, over territory Serbia had occupied. The Bulgarians felt that there were too many Bulgarians living in areas given to Serbia and Greece, namely Macedonia and Salonika.

The Austro-Hungarian Foreign Minister, Count Leopold Berchtold, did not approach this situation with the same caution that he had displayed towards the First Balkan War. He asked for German assistance, as he believed that the Russians would come in to support the Serbs this time. The German government, however, urged Austrian restraint.

The Serbs, Greeks, and, ultimately, Turkey (which had joined in the fight in an attempt to redress some of its losses from the previous year's fighting) defeated Bulgaria. At the Treaty of Bucharest signed in August 1913, Bulgaria lost nearly all the lands it had won in the first war to Greece and Serbia. The war also had far-reaching consequences for Europe. Although a general war between the European powers had again been prevented, the essential causes of tension were exacerbated:

- Serbia was again successful. This fact encouraged the already strong nationalist feeling within Serbia.
- Serbia had doubled in size as a result of the two Balkan wars.
- Serbia had proved itself militarily, and had an army of 200,000 men.
- Serbia's victories were diplomatic successes for Russia, and encouraged Russia to stand by its ally.

- Austria-Hungary was now convinced that it needed to crush Serbia.
- By association, the outcome of the two wars was a diplomatic defeat for Germany, which now drew ever closer to Austria-Hungary.

Activity 10

ATL Thinking skills

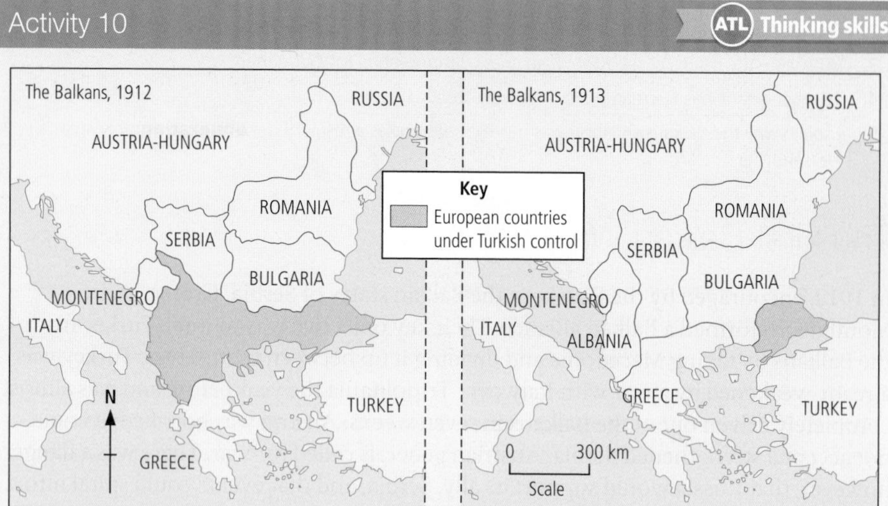

The Balkans 1912–1913.

1. Explain the position of each of the following states following the Second Balkan War:
   - Austria-Hungary
   - Serbia
   - Bulgaria
   - Turkey
2. For what reasons had the Balkan wars of 1912 and 1913 not escalated into a general European war?

The international situation by 1913

The crises of 1905–1913 had seen a marked deterioration in international relations. There was increasing division between the two alliance systems and an increase in the general armaments race, alongside the naval race that already existed between Germany and Britain. Nationalist fervor was rising in European countries. Each crisis had passed without a major European war, but every subsequent crisis exacerbated the tension and made a future conflict more likely. War was by no means inevitable at this stage, though. Clearly, if there was to be another crisis, careful handling of the situation by the Great Powers would be vital.

Other developments 1900–1913

Alongside the international crises, other developments were occurring in European countries. These developments were fed and encouraged by the actual events that you have already read about.

The will to make war

What examples can you see of nationalism causing tension between different groups of people today?

Literature, the press, and educational materials did much to prepare the public of Europe for war by portraying it as something that would be short and heroic. Nationalism had also become a more aggressive force in many of the major states, and this trend was encouraged by the popular press, which exaggerated international incidents to inflame public opinion, and by right-wing pressure groups such as the Pan-German League and Action Française. As James Joll writes:

> *the reactions of ordinary people in the crisis of 1914 were the result of the history they had learnt at school, the stories about the national past which they had been told as children and an instinctive sense of loyalty and solidarity with their neighbours and workmates. In each country, children were taught the duties of patriotism and the glory of past national achievements ... In each country children were being taught to take pride in their historical tradition and to respect what were regarded as characteristic national virtues ... [The] reactions in 1914 ... and the patriotic language with which the war was greeted reflected the sentiments of a national tradition absorbed over many years.*

James Joll, *The Origins of the First World War* (Longman, 1992), p.221.

Activity 11

ATL Research and communication skills

1. Divide the class into the following groups. Each group should research the promotion of war in World War One in their area of popular culture, and attempt to find material from at least two countries in the opposing alliance blocs.
   - the press
   - art and music
   - literature
   - education

Groups could then share their research findings in brief class presentations. Each group should provide the rest of the class with a handout summarizing their research.

The arms race and militarism

The naval arms race was actually part of a more general arms race. Between 1870 and 1914, military spending by the European powers increased by 300 per cent. The increase in the European population made it possible to have large **standing armies**, and conscription was introduced in all continental countries after 1871. In addition, there was a massive increase in armaments. Although there were some attempts to stop the arms build-up – for instance, at conferences at The Hague in 1899 and 1907 – no limits on arms production were agreed upon, although some agreements were made on restricting war practices.

Activity 12

ATL Thinking skills

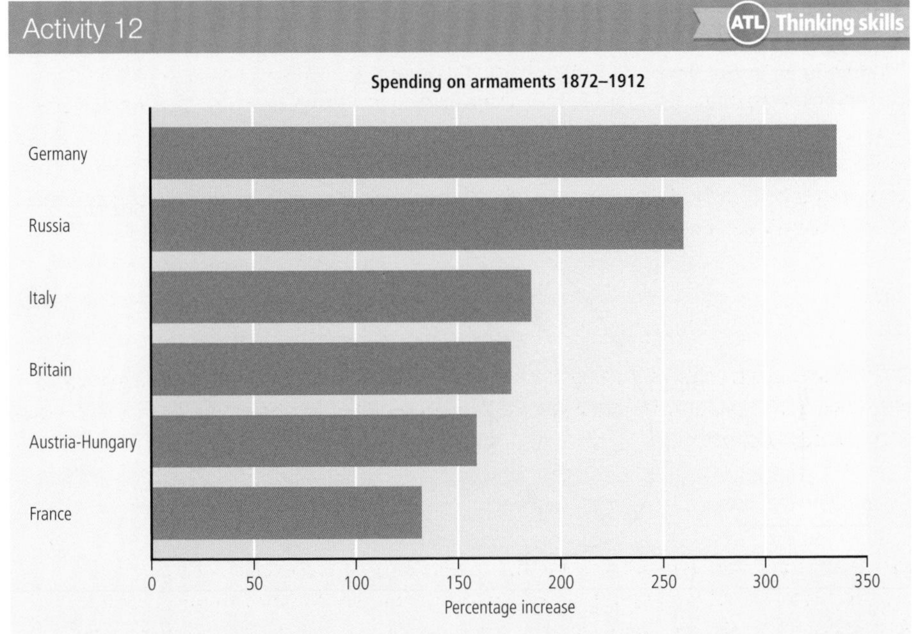

Spending on armaments 1872–1912.

1. How could the growth in military spending and armaments have added to the tension between the powers of Europe between 1900 and 1914?

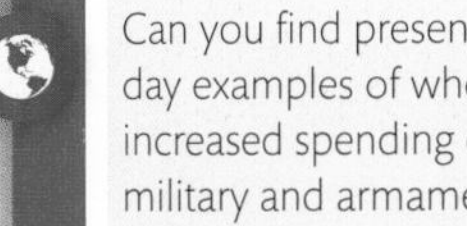

Can you find present-day examples of where increased spending on military and armaments is causing regional tension?

War plans

Every European power made detailed plans regarding what to do should war break out. One of the most important effects of the alliance systems was that they reduced the flexibility of the Great Powers' response to crises, and this issue can be seen most clearly in the German war plan. This plan was drawn up by German Field Marshal **Count Alfred von Schlieffen** and was intended to deal with the implications of the Triple Entente and the difficulty of fighting a two-front war. Knowing that it would take Russia 6 weeks to mobilize, Schlieffen worked out a plan that would involve crushing France first. He calculated that Germany could invade France through Belgium, Holland, and Luxembourg (thus bypassing the French defences along the German–French border), and then move down to encircle Paris. With Paris captured, troops could be moved swiftly to meet the Russian troops along the Eastern Front.

In 1911, Schlieffen's successor, Helmuth von Moltke, modified the plan by reducing the amount of neutral territory that Germany would pass through and by changing the deployment of troops (see map below). However, the plan still remained inflexible, and contained miscalculations regarding the impact of marching though Belgium, the amount of time Russia would take to mobilize, and Britain's effectiveness in coming to the aid of France.

All other countries had war plans as well:

- France's Plan 17 involved a high-speed mobilization of the majority of its forces and a swift attack to capture Alsace and Lorraine before crossing the Rhine into Germany.
- Russia had a plan to attack Austria-Hungary and Germany.
- Austria-Hungary had two plans – Plan R and Plan B. The plans differed in the amount of troops allocated to fighting Russia and Serbia.

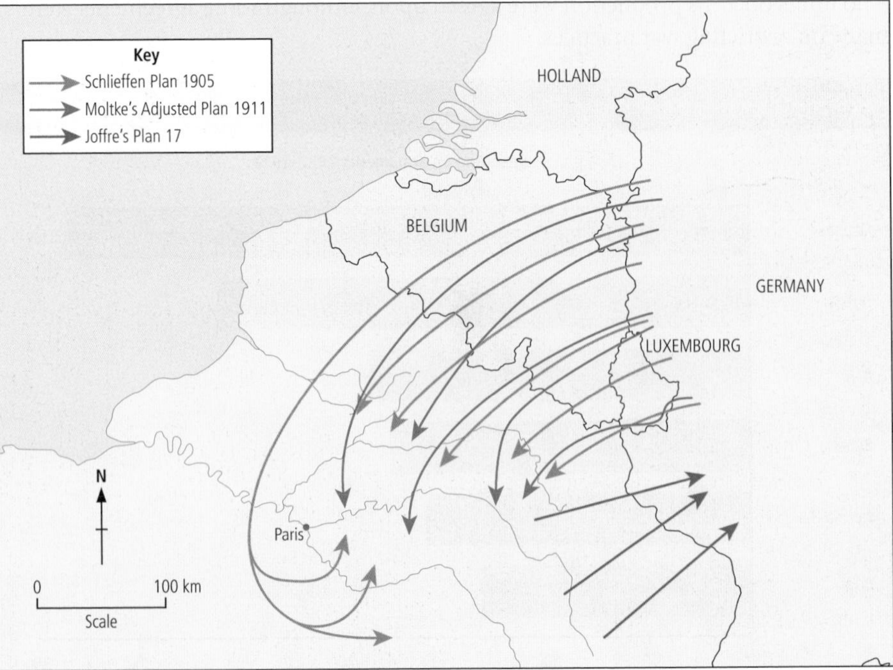

Pre-World War One war plans.

Activity 13

Source analysis

All the great powers had vast conscript armies. These armies of course were not maintained in peace time. They were brought together by mobilisation … All mobilisation plans depended on the railways. At that time the automobile was hardly used, and railways demand timetables.

All the mobilisation plans had been timed to the minute, months or even years before and they would not be changed … [A change] in one direction would ruin them in every other direction. Any attempt for instance by the Austrians to mobilise against Serbia would mean that they could not then mobilise as well against Russia because two lots of trains would be running against each other … Any alteration in the mobilisation plan meant not a delay for 24 hours but for at least six months before the next lot of timetables were ready.

From A.J.P. Taylor, *How Wars Begin* (Hamish Hamilton, 1979), p.117.

1. What point is A.J.P. Taylor making about the war plans?
2. What impact would such war plans have on any European war? Do you think that they made war more or less likely?

Activity 14

1. Historians generally consider that the forces of imperialism, militarism, the alliance systems, and nationalism helped to increase the tensions that led to World War One. Go back over the events of this chapter and pull out examples relating to each one of these issues. Do you agree that they are all equally important in raising tension? Is one more important than the others? Once you have read the next section on the July Crisis, come back to this exercise and add any extra relevant points.

The impact of the July Crisis (1914)

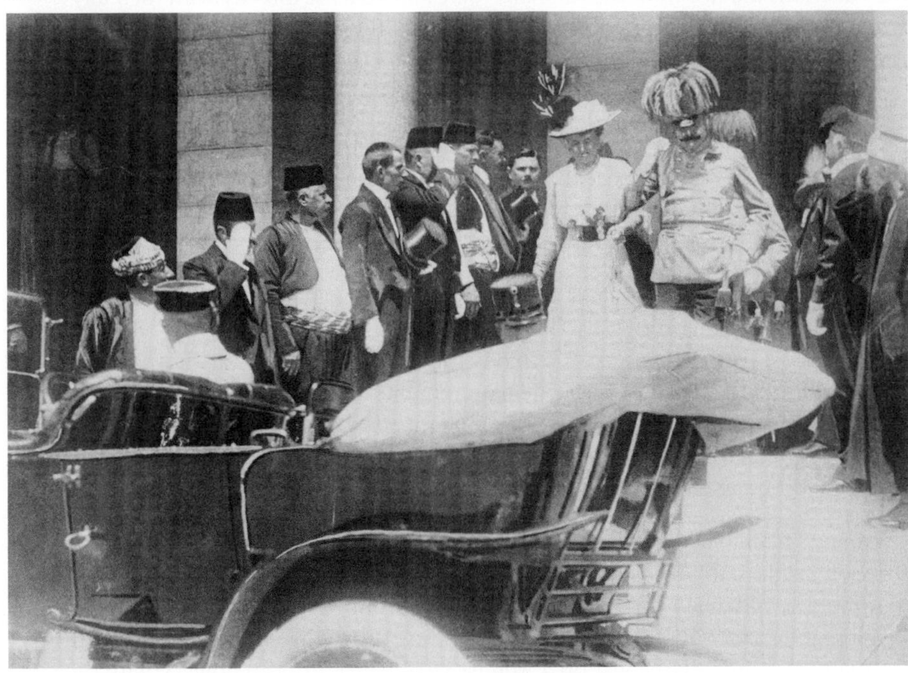

Archduke Franz Ferdinand and his wife, Sophie, on their visit to Sarajevo.

The first few months of 1914 were a relatively calm period between the European states. There was even optimism that should another conflict erupt in the Balkans this would, for a third time in as many years, be contained locally. The event that broke the calm was the shooting dead of the heir to the Austro-Hungarian throne and his wife on 28 June 1914. Archduke Franz Ferdinand was with his wife on an official visit to Sarajevo, the capital of Bosnia, when a 19-year-old terrorist shot them both at point-blank range. The assassin's name was Gavrilo Princip. He had been working with a small group of terrorists, armed by the Serbian Black Hand movement. Their aim in the assassination is not entirely clear, but their objective was the unification of all Slavs from the Austro-Hungarian Empire into a Greater Serbia. The archduke was evidently symbolic of the Austro-Hungarian regime. It was unclear to what degree the Serbian government was involved with the group – the head of the Black Hand was a colonel in the Serbian general staff.

The Austrian government saw its chance to crush Serbia, but initially hesitated. An attack on Serbia would bring in the Russians, so the Austrians needed assurances from their ally, Germany, that they would be supported. On 5 July 1914, the Kaiser and his Chancellor, Theobald von Bethmann-Hollweg, issued Austria a 'blank cheque': the German guarantee of unconditional support. Thus, the Germans were not exercising their power to restrain Austria-Hungary, as they had the previous year.

Had the Austro-Hungarian response and its bombardment of Sarajavo been immediate, it might have averted the escalation of events that followed. Despite the blank cheque, however, the response to the crisis took nearly a whole month to manifest itself. Berchtold wanted an **ultimatum** sent to the Serb government, but he also intended that the demands of the ultimatum be so severe that the Serb sovereign government could never agree to them. The drawing up of the ultimatum took until mid-July, and this delay meant the Austro-Hungarians could no longer present their response as a shock reaction to the assassination; rather, they would appear far more calculating.

Then there was a further delay. The French president was in Russia until 23 July and the Austrians did not want the Russians to be able to liaise directly with their ally France concerning the demands. So finally, on 23 July, the ultimatum was sent, and a response from Serbia was required within 48 hours.

The Russians were shocked when they reviewed the terms on 24 July. Yet the Serb response was conciliatory, and most European powers thought that this might end the crisis – which was not to be the case. Although the Kaiser suggested that the Serb response removed the 'cause for war', the Austro-Hungarians claimed it was too late to change their minds – they declared war on Serbia and bombarded Belgrade on 28 July.

The Russians, determined to take a firm stance this time in the Balkans, ordered general mobilization on 30 July. Thus, the Third Balkan War had begun – Serbia and Russia against Austria-Hungary. Germany then declared war on Russia and began mobilization on 1 August. Due to the requirements of the Schlieffen Plan, Germany sent an ultimatum to France demanding guarantees of French neutrality. When the French responded by declaring that they would follow their 'own interests', Germany declared war on France on 3 August.

Germany's plan to take out France swiftly meant that its forces were to march through Belgium to avoid France's heavily fortified border defences. Britain, choosing to uphold an old treaty agreement with Belgium from 1839, threatened to defend Belgium if Germany did not respect its neutrality. When there was no response from Germany, Britain declared war on 4 August 1914. The European powers, with their vast empires, were at war – the Great War had begun.

Activity 15

Source analysis

The Kaiser's 'blank cheque' to Austria

The following is a report of a famous conversation between Wilhelm II and the Austrian ambassador in Berlin, Count Szogyeny, in which the Kaiser seemed to promise his support for Austria-Hungary under any conditions.

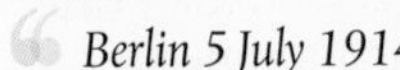

> *Berlin 5 July 1914*
>
> *tel. 237 Strictly Confidential*
>
> *... the Kaiser authorized me to inform our gracious majesty that we might in this case, as in all others, rely upon Germany's full support ... he did not doubt in the least that Herr von Bethmann Hollweg would agree with him. Especially as far as our action against Serbia was concerned. But it was his [Kaiser Wilhelm's] opinion that this action must not be delayed. Russia's attitude will no doubt be hostile, but to this he has for years been prepared, and should a war between Austria-Hungary and Russia be unavoidable, we might be convinced that Germany, our old faithful ally, would stand at our side. Russia at the present time was in no way prepared for war, and would think twice before it appealed to arms ... if we had really recognized the necessity of warlike action against Serbia, he [Kaiser Wilhelm] would regret it if we did not make use of the present moment, which is all in our favour...*
>
> **From Imanuel Geiss (ed.), *July 1914: The Outbreak of the First World War – Selected Documents* (W.W. Norton, 1967), p.77.**

1. With reference to origin, purpose, and content, assess the values and limitations of this source for historians studying the causes of World War One.

Activity 16

1. Create your own timeline of events leading to the outbreak of World War One. You should divide the timeline into long-term and short-term causes.

Alternatively, list all the factors (people, events, underlying forces) that you think contributed to the outbreak of war and try to create a flow diagram or a mind map to show how these factors are linked and how they led to the outbreak of a general war in 1914.

To view a timeline that goes into detail on the events leading up to the outbreak of the war, visit pearsonhotlinks.com, enter the book title or ISBN, and click on weblink 2.1.

On the IB website you can find a copy of the IB Learner Profile, which outlines the key attributes promoted by the IB. IB learners should attempt to live the IB Learner Profile. Consider the approach and decisions made by the European governments and statesmen and attempt to identify when they were acting like IB learners, and when they were not. Try to give specific examples: for example, which of the leaders and statesmen were 'knowledgeable' in their decision-making?

In pairs, reflect on the ways in which the process of crisis management, and the final descent into a general European war, might have been different if the leaders of the Great Powers had been IB learners.

During the July Crisis, what was the contribution of each of the European powers to the outbreak of war?

Germany

The Kaiser had encouraged the Austro-Hungarians to seize the opportunity to attack Serbia in the 5 July blank cheque. However, Germany may have been predicting another Balkans war, not the spread of war generally across Europe. Even as late as 18 July 1914, many in Germany's government believed that a united front of Germany and Austria-Hungary, together with a swift response, would keep the Russians from involving themselves. The Kaiser went off on a cruise, and on his return declared that the Serb response to the Austro-Hungarian ultimatum removed the rationale for a war.

Nevertheless, Germany was risking drawing the powers into a general war. What was the motive?

- It had to support its ally, Austria-Hungary.
- It had to prevent itself and Austria-Hungary being crushed by the entente powers.
- Russia's military modernizations were increasing the country's potential for mobilization, and this could undermine the Schlieffen Plan.
- German generals, such as von Moltke, believed that it was a favourable time for Germany to go to war with its enemies.
- War would provide a good distraction and a unifying effect, which would help to overcome rising domestic problems in Germany.
- War could improve the popularity of the Kaiser.

Once the Russians ordered mobilization, the Schlieffen Plan prescribed that Germany would have to draw in the French.

> *… it seems very unlikely that the Russians positively desired a major war. Mobilization for them meant preparation for a possible war. The Germans, however, interpreted mobilization as the virtual equivalent to a declaration of war, and Germany's Schlieffen Plan meant that the German army would have to attack and defeat France before moving eastwards to combat Russian forces.*
>
> **From Robert Pearce and John Lowe, *Rivalry and Accord: International Relations, 1870–1914* (Hodder & Stoughton, 2001), p.105.**

Thus Germany's responsibility for the beginning of war was:

- urging Austria-Hungary on with the 'blank cheque'
- declaring war on Russia on 1 August
- violating Belgian neutrality
- invading France
- bringing Britain into the conflict.

Austria-Hungary

It is clear that Austria-Hungary was determined to respond to the Sarajevo incident, and saw it as an opportunity 'to eliminate Serbia as a political factor in the Balkans'.

The contribution of Austria-Hungary to the outbreak of war was that it:

- exaggerated the potential threat of Serbia and was determined to make war
- delayed responding to the assassination, which contributed to the development of the July Crisis
- declared war on Serbia on 28 July, only five days after the delivery of the ultimatum (which in any case had a time limit of only 48 hours)
- refused to halt its military actions even though negotiations with Russia were scheduled for 30 July.

Russia

The Russian foreign minister saw in the ultimatum to Serbia a 'European war'. Sergei Sazonov was determined to take a firm stand, as he believed that the Germans had seen weakness in Russia's previous responses to Balkan crises. Although the Tsar was in favour of partial mobilization, his generals ordered general mobilization on 30 July.

The contribution of Russia to the beginning of the war was that it:

- did not try to restrain Serb nationalism, even though it was likely to lead to instability in the Balkans
- supported Serbia, which deepened the conflict and possibly caused Serbia to reject the ultimatum
- mobilized, thus triggering a general European war.

France

France's government was hesitant about getting involved in a war, and, after the ignominious defeat of 1871, it did not want to provoke a general war. France's ally Russia mobilized without consulting the French, and then the Germans declared war on France on 3 August. France had not decided to go to war: it was swept into it.

The responsibility of France for the start of the war was that it gave Russia assurances of support before the July Crisis.

Britain

The violation of the neutrality of Belgium led to some popular demands for war with Germany, and gave the British government grounds, based on the treaty of 1839, to declare war. It was also a popular reason with the British public. However, regardless of Belgium, the British were unlikely to stand by and let Germany defeat France and thus dominate the continent and the channel ports. The responsibility of Britain for the start of the war was that it should have made its position – that it would stand 'shoulder to shoulder' with the French – clearer during the July Crisis, as this might have deterred the Germans from pursuing the Schlieffen Plan. Yet Grey himself did not have a mandate to make his position clear, due to the mixed opinions of the cabinet.

John Lowe also makes the following point:

> *… the most serious charge against Britain, however, is that her naval talks with Russia in 1914 convinced the German chancellor that the ring of encirclement around her was now complete. Grey's false denial of these secret talks also destroyed his credibility as a mediator in German eyes in the July crisis.*
>
> **From Robert Pearce and John Lowe, *Rivalry and Accord: International Relations 1870–1914* (Hodder & Stoughton, 2001), p.105.**

Niall Ferguson argues that it would have been better for Britain to invade Europe later in the conflict and that it suffered from inadequate war planning before 1914:

> *The right way for Britain to proceed was not to rush into a land war but rather to exploit its massive advantages at sea and in financial terms. Even if Germany had defeated France and Russia, it would have had a pretty massive challenge on its hands trying to run the new German-dominated Europe, and would have remained significantly weaker than the British empire in naval and financial terms. Given the resources that Britain had available in 1914, a better strategy would have been to wait and deal with the German challenge later when Britain could respond on its own terms, taking advantage of its much greater naval and financial capacity … The problem with British policy in 1914 is that it was neither one thing nor another. It was not a credible continental commitment, which would have required conscription and a much larger land army. Nor was it a clearly thought-through maritime strategy to deal with the possibility of a German victory over France and Russia.*
>
> **Niall Ferguson, BBC *History* magazine, February 2014, p.26.**

Historiography: Causes of World War One

> *The current consensus on why World War One broke out is 'that there is no consensus'.*
>
> **Margaret MacMillan, *The War that Ended Peace* (Profile, 2014).**

Activity 17

ATL Thinking skills

Source analysis

THE TRIUMPH OF "CULTURE."

'The Triumph of Culture', a cartoon from the satirical British magazine *Punch*.

1. What is the message of this cartoon, which was published on 26 August 1914, following Germany's invasion of Belgium?

Central Powers

The Central Powers were the countries that fought against the entente powers, namely Germany, Austria-Hungary, Turkey, and Bulgaria. They were called the Central Powers due to their geographical position in Central Europe.

Responsibility for causing World War One was placed on the Central Powers by the Versailles settlement in 1919. In the **war guilt clause** of the Treaty of Versailles with Germany (Article 231), Germany had to accept responsibility as one of the aggressors. (This is discussed in more detail in chapter 4.) While the Treaty of Versailles was being drawn up by the victorious powers, the German foreign office was already preparing documents from its archives in an attempt to prove that *all* belligerent states were to blame. To this end, between 1922 and 1927, the Germans produced 40 volumes of documents backing up this claim.

Other governments felt the need to respond by producing their own volumes of archives. Britain published 11 volumes between 1926 and 1938, France its own version of events in 1936, Austria produced 8 volumes in 1930, and the Soviet Union brought out justificatory publications in 1931 and 1934. Germany's argument gained international sympathy in the 1920s and 1930s. There was a growing sentiment that the war had been caused by the failure of international relations rather than the specific actions of one country. Lloyd George, writing in his memoirs in the 1930s, explained that 'the nations slithered over the brink into the boiling cauldron of war'.

S.B. Fay and H.E. Barnes were two American historians who, to some extent, supported the **revisionist** arguments put forward by Germany regarding the causes of World War One. Barnes argued in his 1927 book, *The Genesis of the War*, that Serbia, France, and Russia were directly responsible for causing the war, that Austro-Hungarian responsibility was far less, and that least responsible were Germany and Britain. He supported this view by arguing that the Franco-Russian alliance became offensive from 1912, and their joint plans intended to manipulate any crisis in the Balkans to provoke a European war. Both countries decided that Serbia would be central to their war plans and early in 1914 officers in the Serbian general staff plotted the assassination of Franz Ferdinand. The Russian and French motives for starting a European war were to attain their key objectives: the seizure of the Dardanelles Straits and the return of Alsace-Lorraine, which could only be realized through war.

An Italian historian, Luigi Albertini, wrote a thorough and coherent response to the revisionist argument in the 1940s. Albertini's argument focused on the responsibility of Austria-Hungary and Germany in the immediate term: Austria for the ultimatum to Serbia, and Germany for its 'naivety' in demanding a localized war. Overall, Germany was in his view fundamentally to blame, as it was clear that Britain could not have remained neutral in a war raging on the continent.

Fritz Fischer

In 1961, historian Fritz Fischer published *Germany's Aims in the First World War*; this was later translated into English. Fischer's argument focused responsibility back on Germany. He discovered a document called the 'September Programme' written by the German Chancellor, Bethmann-Hollweg. This memorandum, which was dated 9 September 1914 (after war had started), set out Germany's aims for domination of Europe (see the next chapter for more discussion of this aspiration). Fischer claimed that the document proved that the ruling elite had always had expansionist aims and that a war would allow them to fulfil these. War would also consolidate their power at home and deal with the threat of socialism. Fischer went on to argue in another book that the War Council of 1912 proved that Germany planned to launch a continental war in 1914. At this War Council, von Moltke had commented that 'in my opinion war is inevitable and the sooner the better'.

German Chancellor Bethmann-Hollweg.

Fischer's argument is persuasive, as he links longer-term policies from 1897 to short-term and immediate actions taken in the July Crisis. He concludes that:

> *As Germany willed and coveted the Austro-Serbian war and, in her confidence in her military superiority, deliberately faced the risk of a conflict with Russia and France, her leaders must bear a substantial share of the historical responsibility for the outbreak of a general war in 1914.*
>
> **Fritz Fischer, *Germany's Aims in the First World War* (W.W. Norton, 1967), p.88.**

Fischer's arguments have been criticized in the following ways:

- Fischer argues 'backwards' from the German 'September war aims'. There is limited evidence to prove Germany had specific expansionist aims prior to September 1914.
- The December War Council is also limited evidence; its importance is debatable as the imperial Chancellor was not present.
- Fischer considers the domestic crisis in Germany as central to why war was triggered in 1914. However, Bethmann-Hollweg dismissed war as a solution to the rise of socialism.
- It could be argued that German policy lacked coherency in the decade before 1914.
- Fischer focuses too much on Germany; this priority leads to an emphasis on German actions and he neglects the role played by other powers.

After Fischer

Since Fischer's theses on German guilt, historians have continued to debate the degree of German responsibility. Conservative German historians such as Gerhard Ritter rejected Fischer's view in the 1960s, although Imanuel Geiss defended Fischer by publishing a book of German documents that undermined the arguments of the revisionists of the 1920s. However, the majority of historians around the world now agree that Germany played a pivotal role in the events that led to war, through its policy of *Weltpolitik* and its role in the July Crisis, though this was not necessarily as part of any set 'plan', as Fischer had argued.

> *It has been widely asserted that German policy held the key to the situation in the summer of 1914 and that it was the German desire to profit diplomatically and militarily from the crisis which widened the crisis from an Eastern European one to a continental and world war.*
>
> **Ruth Henig, *The Origins of the First World War* (Routledge, 1993), p.42.**

Other historians have stressed different issues in explaining the outbreak of war, however.

John Keegan

Military historian John Keegan focuses on the events of the July Crisis. He suggests that although there were long-term and short-term tensions in Europe, war was in fact not inevitable; war was unlikely due to the interdependence and cooperation necessary for the European economy, plus royal, intellectual, and religious links between the nations.

The key to Keegan's theory is the lack of communication during the July Crisis. He highlights the fact that the Kaiser had 50 people advising him – mostly independent and jealous of one another: 'The Kaiser … in the crisis of 1914 … found that he did not understand the machinery he was supposed to control, panicked and let a piece of paper determine events' (*The First World War* [Bodley Head, 2014], p.51). Keegan suggests that had Austria-Hungary acted immediately, the war might have been limited to a local affair. It was Austria-Hungary's reluctance to act alone, and its alliance with Germany, that led to the escalation.

No country used the communications available at the time, such as radio. Information was arriving fitfully, and was always 'incomplete'. The crisis that followed the expiration of the ultimatum to Serbia was not one that the European powers had expected and the key problem was that each nation failed to communicate its aims during the crisis:

- Austria-Hungary had wanted to punish Serbia, but lacked the courage to act alone. It did not want a general European war.
- Germany had wanted a diplomatic success that would leave its Austro-Hungarian ally stronger in European eyes. It did not want a general European war.
- Russia did not want a general European war, but had not calculated that support for Serbia would edge the danger of war closer.
- France had not mobilized, but was increasingly worried that Germany would mobilize against it.
- Britain only awoke to the real danger of the crisis on Saturday 25 July, and still hoped on Thursday 30 July that Russia would tolerate the punishment of Serbia. It would not, however, leave France in danger.

None of the European powers had communicated their objectives clearly in the July Crisis. Therefore, for Keegan, it was the events of 31 July that were the turning point. The news of Russia's general mobilization and the German ultimatum to Russia and France made the issue one of peace or war. The Great Powers could step back from the brink, but a withdrawal would not be compatible with the status of each as a Great Power. The Serbs, a cause of the crisis in the first place, had been forgotten.

James Joll

Joll attempts to link impersonal forces – factors beyond the specific control or influence of an individual leader, regime, or government – to personal or human forces. He suggests an atmosphere of extreme tension was created by impersonal forces in the long and short terms, while personal decisions made in the July Crisis led to war. Joll explains the outbreak of war in terms of the decisions taken by the political leaders in 1914, but argues that these decisions were shaped by the impersonal factors, which meant that the leaders had only limited options open to them in the final days of the crisis.

Personal forces	vs	Impersonal forces
expansionist aims		Capitalism
war plans		international anarchy
calculated decisions		alliances

Marxist historians have focused on the roles of Capitalism and imperialism as the key causes of World War One, but a limitation with focusing on impersonal factors is that they do not seem to explain why the war broke out when it did. Joll's argument links the impersonal factors to the personal decision-making that took place during the July Crisis and, thus, apparently, overcomes this problem.

Niall Ferguson

In *The Pity of War* (1998) Niall Ferguson suggests that Germany was moving away from a militaristic outlook prior to World War One, and highlights the increasing influence of the Social Democrat Party there. The German Social Democrat Party was founded as a socialist party, with a radical agenda for Germany. By 1912 it had gained the most votes in the Reichstag and its influence increasingly alarmed the Kaiser's regime. Ferguson sees Britain as heavily implicated in the causes of war by its involvement in 1914, which Ferguson argues was unnecessary. Ferguson does not see war as inevitable in 1914, despite the forces of militarism, imperialism, and secret diplomacy. He argues that these long-term factors and their impact in increasing tension in Europe have been stressed too much by historians. When war came it was in fact a surprise to most people, and Ferguson argues that it could have been avoided.

Activity 18

1. Draw up a grid summarizing the views of the key historians that you have read about in this chapter. Also include the views of the historians in the sources activity below.

Activity 19

Source analysis

Study the sources below. As you read, decide what factor each historian is stressing as the key cause for war.

Source A

The First World War was not inevitable. Although it is essential to understand the underlying factors that formed the background to the July Crisis, it is equally essential to see how the immediate circumstances of the crisis fit into this background in a particular, and perhaps unique, way. Europe was not a powder keg waiting to explode; one crisis did not lead necessarily to another in an escalating series of confrontations that made war more and more difficult to avoid. Europe had successfully weathered a number of storms in the recent past; the alliances were not rigidly fixed; the war plans were always being revised and need not necessarily have come into play. It is difficult to imagine a crisis in the Far East, in North Africa or in the Mediterranean that would have unleashed the series of events that arose from the assassination in Sarajevo. The First World War was, in the final analysis, fought for the future of the near east; whoever won this struggle would, it was believed, be in a position to dominate all of Europe. Germany and her ally made the bid for control; Russia and her allies resolved to stop them.

From Gordon Martel, *The Origins of the First World War* (Longman, 1987), p.76.

Source B

[For Germany] … war seemed to offer … a solution to both domestic and foreign antagonisms. And if that war could be made appealing to all sections of the population – as a war against Tsarist Russia most certainly would be, even to ardent socialists – then so much the better. There can be no doubt that German leaders were prepared for war in 1914 and exploited the crisis of June–July 1914 to bring it about … Just as the Germans sought to increase their power, so Britain and France sought to contain it, by military means if necessary. In this sense it could be argued that both powers fought to try to restore the balance of power to Europe.

Countries went to war because they believed that they could achieve more through war than by diplomatic negotiation and that if they stood aside their status as great powers would be gravely affected …

From Ruth Henig, *The Origins of the First World War* (Routledge, 1993), p.54.

Source C

It used to be held that the system of alliances was in itself sufficient explanation for the outbreak of war, that the very existence of two camps made war inevitable sooner or later. But this approach has, for two reasons, an over-simple appreciation of the individual alliances. In the first place, the primary purpose of the alliances was defensive … Second, the way that war actually broke out bore little relation to treaty obligations …

There were, however, two ways in which the alliances did affect international relations and contribute to the growth of tension in Europe in the decade before 1914. First, they provided the links across which crises could spread from peripheral areas like North Africa and the Balkans to the major powers themselves. Normally, the dangers were seen and the connections cut; hence the Moroccan crises of 1906 and 1911 were allowed to fizzle out. But, as the sequence of events after Sarajevo showed only too clearly, the means existed whereby a local conflict could be transformed into a continental war. Second, the alliances had a direct bearing on the arms race and the development of military schedules.

From Stephen J. Lee, *Aspects of European History 1789–1980* (Taylor & Francis, 1988), pp.152–153.

Source D

We must remember, as the decision-makers did, what had happened before that last crisis of 1914 and what they had learned from the Moroccan crises, the Bosnian one, or the events of the First Balkan Wars. Europe's very success in surviving those earlier crises paradoxically led to a dangerous complacency in the summer of 1914 that, yet again, solutions would be found at the last moment and the peace would be maintained. And if we want to point fingers from the twenty-first century we can accuse those who took Europe into war of two things. First, a failure of imagination in not seeing how destructive such a conflict would be and second, their lack of courage to stand up to those who said there was no choice left but to go to war. There are always choices.

Margaret MacMillan, *The War that Ended Peace* (Profile, 2014), p.605.

Source E

The outbreak of World War One in 1914 is not an Agatha Christie drama at the end of which we will discover the culprit standing over a corpse in the conservatory with a smoking pistol. There is no smoking gun in this story; or rather, there is one in the hands of every major character. Viewed in this light, the outbreak of war was a tragedy, not a crime. Acknowledging this does not mean that we should minimise the belligerence and imperialist paranoia of the Austrian and German policy-makers that rightly absorbed the attention of Fritz Fischer and his historiographical allies. But the Germans were not the only ones to succumb to paranoia. The crisis that brought war in 1914 was the fruit of a shared political culture. But it was also multipolar and genuinely interactive – that's what makes it the most complex event of modern times and that is why the debate over the origins of the First World War continues, one century after Gavrilo Princip fired those two fatal shots on Franz Joseph Street.

Christopher Clarke, *The Sleepwalkers* (Penguin, 2013), p.561.

1. Read Sources A, B, C, D, and E. Briefly summarize the points made in each source. Compare and contrast these arguments with those of the historians discussed on pages 36–39.

TOK

Consider the methodologies used by historians in attempting to find 'historical truth' (see chapter 16 for a review of historians' methodologies). Why do historians reach different conclusions on what caused World War One? What are the strengths and limitations of the historians' methodologies?

How do I write a history essay?

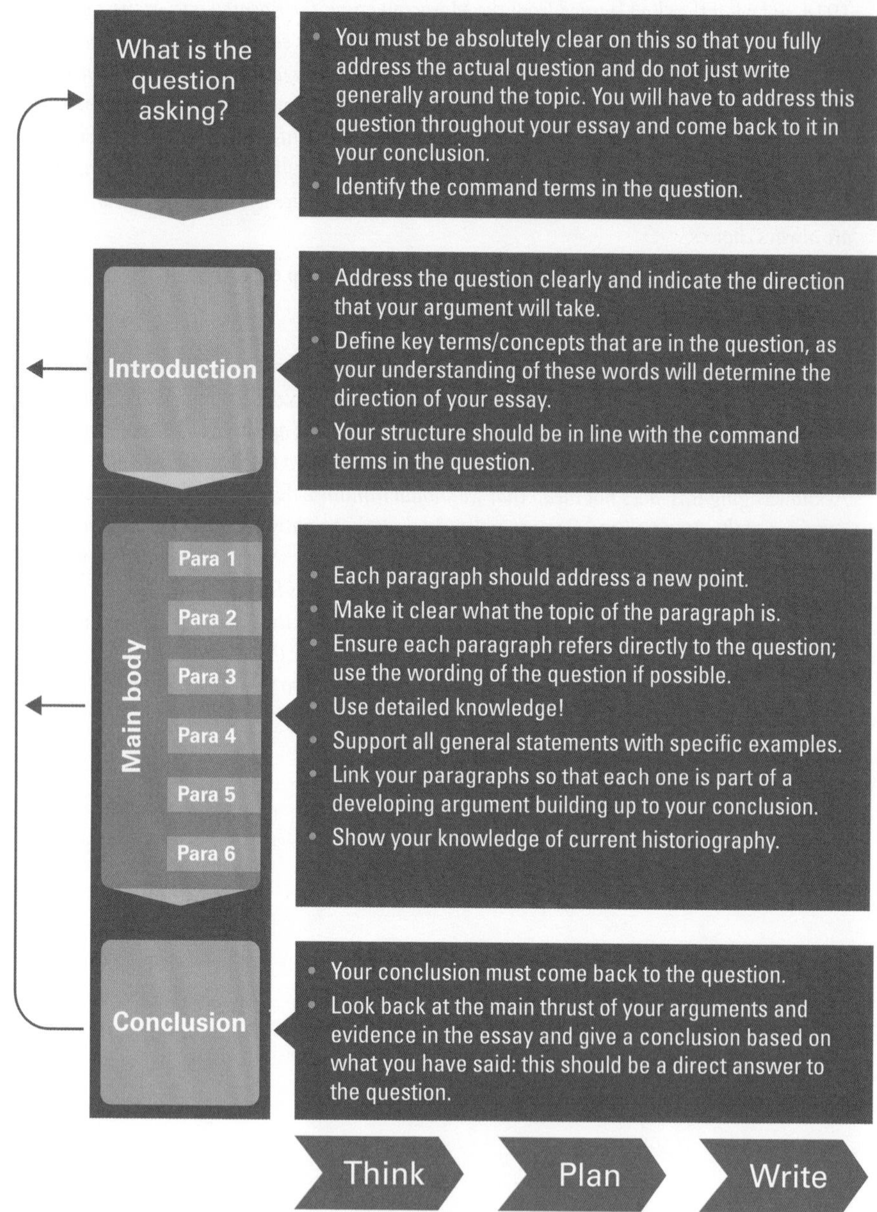

What is the question asking?
You must be absolutely clear on this so that you fully address the actual question and do not just write generally around the topic. You will have to address this question throughout your essay and come back to it in your conclusion.
Identify the command terms in the question.
Introduction
Address the question clearly and indicate the direction that your argument will take.
Define key terms/concepts that are in the question, as your understanding of these words will determine the direction of your essay.
Your structure should be in line with the command terms in the question.
Main body
Para 1
Para 2
Para 3
Para 4
Para 5
Para 6
Each paragraph should address a new point.
Make it clear what the topic of the paragraph is.
Ensure each paragraph refers directly to the question; use the wording of the question if possible.
Use detailed knowledge!
Support all general statements with specific examples.
Link your paragraphs so that each one is part of a developing argument building up to your conclusion.
Show your knowledge of current historiography.
Conclusion
Your conclusion must come back to the question.
Look back at the main thrust of your arguments and evidence in the essay and give a conclusion based on what you have said: this should be a direct answer to the question.
Think
Plan
Write

Activity 20

ATL Thinking skills

Essay planning

Consider the following essay question:

> ***'Long-term causes were more important than short-term causes in explaining the outbreak of one 20th-century war.' To what extent do you agree with this statement?***

Below is an essay frame to help you structure your answer. As you are writing your answer, keep referring to the 'How do I write a history essay?' diagram. Check that you have covered all the pointers in the blue boxes.

Introduction: State that the case study you will use is World War One. Set the question into context, for example: that war broke out in 1914 following the July Crisis, but that tensions in Europe had been increasing in the years before this. Also show that you understand this debate about the origins of World War One

– that historians are divided as to how important the long-term causes were. Mention historians specifically – Keegan for instance argues that the long-term factors which were causing tension in Europe did not make war inevitable and that it was the July Crisis that caused the war to happen.

Indicate the key causes that you will be looking at in your essay and also set out your main argument: that is, whether you think long- or short-term causes were more important.

Part 1: Always deal directly with the statement that you are given, so look at long-term causes first. You cannot deal with ***all*** long-term factors, so choose two that you want to explain. Make sure that when you are dealing with a cause that you assess its ***importance in causing the war***.

Part 2: Here you need to address the second half of the quotation. Examine the impact of the crises in the years before 1914 and the July Crisis of 1914. Again, make sure you assess their importance in causing the war – do not just describe them!

Conclusion: Make sure that you come back to the actual question. Based on the weight of evidence on each side of the argument, conclude whether long- or short-term causes were more important in causing the war.

Now plan out the following essay questions in pairs. Use the essay plan on page 42 as a guide.

1. ***Discuss the importance of territorial factors in causing one 20th-century war.***
2. ***Examine the impact of ideology in causing one 20th-century war.***

You have read the views of several different historians on the causes of World War One. Try to include some of these views in your essay. Only use historians, however, where they are useful for backing up your arguments.

To access websites relevant to this chapter, go to www.pearsonhotlinks.com, search for the book title or ISBN, and click on 'chapter 2'.

03

Cross-regional war: World War One – Practices

A scene from the Western Front.

Key concepts: Significance and consequence

As you read this chapter, consider the following essay questions:

- To what extent did one 20th-century war see the full mobilization of human and economic resources?
- Discuss the relative importance of a) war on the land, b) war at sea, and c) war in the air in determining the outcome of one 20th-century war.
- Examine the impact of technological developments on the course and outcome of one 20th-century war.

Breakdown of events of World War One, 1914–1918

	General	Western Front	Eastern Front	War at Sea	War in the Air	Africa and Asia
1914	Assassination of Archduke Franz Ferdinand Outbreak of general war Japan enters the war on the Allied side Turkey enters the war on the Central Powers' side	Schlieffen Plan – German invasion of Belgium First Battle of the Marne First Battle of Ypres Christmas 'truce'	Austrian invasion of Serbia Russian invasion of Germany Battles of Tannenberg and Masurian Lakes Austrian invasion of Russia	British blockade Battles of Heligoland, Falkland Islands, and Coronel	Bombardment of British towns by Zeppelins	Conquest of German Togoland and possessions in the Pacific
1915	Italy joins the war on side of Allies Bulgaria joins the war on the side of the Central Powers	Battle of Neuve Chapelle Second Battle of Ypres (gas used) Battle of Loos Battles on the Isonzo between Italy and Austria	Defeat of Serbia Gallipoli campaign Defeat of Russia in Galicia	U-boat warfare *Lusitania* sunk	Zeppelin raids on Britain	Conquest of German South-West Africa
1916	Portugal and Romania join the war on the side of the Allies	Battle of Verdun Battle of the Somme	End of Gallipoli campaign Brusilov's breakthrough	Battle of Jutland	Machine guns are by now standard fittings on fighter planes	Arab revolt in Turkey Surrender of German Cameroon
1917	USA and Greece join war on side of Allies	Nivelle offensive French mutinies Battles of Vimy Ridge and Arras Third Battle of Ypres (Passchendaele) Battle of Cambrai Italians driven back at Caporetto	Russian Revolution – Tsar abdicates Russian armistice	Unrestricted U-boat warfare British convoy system established	Air superiority shifts from the Germans to the Allies	British capture of Baghdad Allenby's campaign
1918	US troops arrive in Europe Abdication of Kaiser	Ludendorff Offensive Allied counter-offensive Armistice signed	Treaty of Brest-Litovsk Surrender of Bulgaria, Turkey, and Austria	Naval mutiny in Germany	British attack on Zeebrugge	Surrender of Turkey

War fever gripped the populations of Europe in August 1914. Many felt the war to be just and necessary and all felt that the war would be short and that soldiers would be home by Christmas. Unfortunately, the quick and glorious victories that were expected did not take place. The war was to last for four long years, during which time the fighting took place on several fronts. The most important of these is known as the Western Front, and this stretched 320 kilometres from the English Channel to the Swiss Alps. Fighting also took place on Germany's Eastern Front, involving both Austria-Hungary and Russia, and both sides continued to hope that they would be able to break through on one of the other **diversionary** fronts that existed in the Balkans, Italy, and the Middle East.

Overview of the war: the Western Front

Following the declarations of war in July and August 1914, governments made their opening moves: Austria-Hungary opened fire on Serbia, Russia mobilized its troops, Britain prepared the British Expeditionary Force (the BEF), and Germany put its Schlieffen Plan into action.

The failure of the Schlieffen Plan

Map showing the failure of the Schlieffen Plan, 1914.

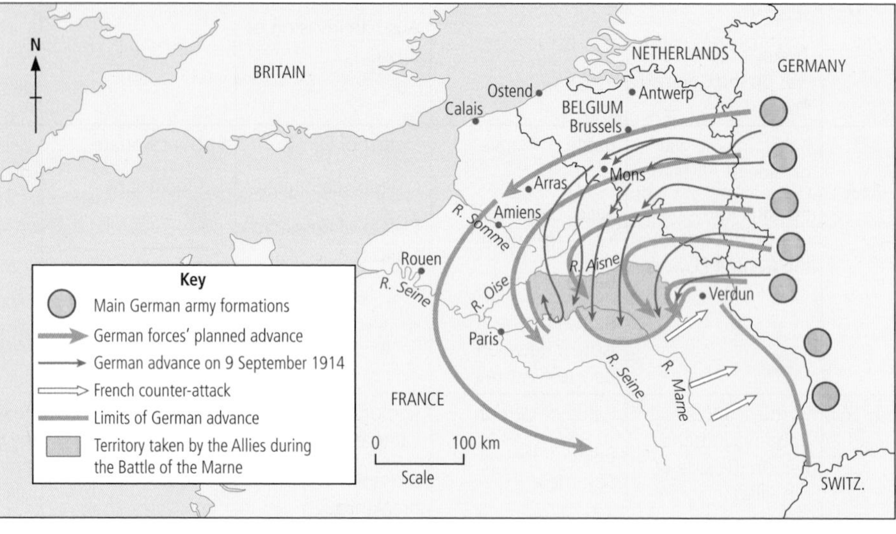

The wars of German unification had convinced strategists at the beginning of the 20th century that future wars would be short, and that rapid mobilization and a strong opening attack would be the key elements necessary for victory. Von Schlieffen's war plan for Germany followed these assumptions. To deal with Germany's nightmare scenario of a two-front war, he decided to use the bulk of German forces to win a speedy victory over France, after which they could be transferred to the east to deal with the Tsar's armies. Specifically, his plan required the German armies to sweep through into northern France via neutral Belgium and then advance to the west of Paris, finally swinging back eastwards to defeat the main French forces, which would still be defending the German border. German troops would then be free to move to the Eastern Front to confront the Russian army, which, given the size of the army and the country, would only just have mobilized.

There were several key reasons for the failure of the Schlieffen Plan:

- Belgian resistance was unexpectedly strong and it took the Germans more than two weeks to capture Brussels, the Belgian capital.

- The attack on Belgium also brought Britain, who was a guarantor of Belgian neutrality through the 1839 Treaty of London, into the war.
- The German delay in getting through Belgium gave the British time to organize themselves and left the Channel ports free, enabling the BEF to land.
- The German forces marching to Paris were weakened by the deployment of some of their troops to the east (where Russia had mobilized faster than expected), and by the difficulties of maintaining supplies. Thus instead of approaching Paris from the west, the Germans swept down too early, making for Paris from the east of the city.
- In Paris, **reservists** were sent to meet the Germans via taxis in the famous 'taxis of the Marne' – thousands of men were transported to the battle via requisitioned Paris taxicabs. The Germans, slowed down by exhaustion and a lack of food and ammunition, were halted by British and French troops at the Battle of the Marne on 9 September.

The 'miracle of the Marne' marked the failure of the Schlieffen Plan and ensured that there would be no short war. Indeed, the Battle of the Marne was followed by a 'race to the sea', as each side tried to outflank the other army in order to get behind them and cut them off. This race eventually resulted in the building of a continuous series of trenches stretching from the Alps to the Channel coast, and it was these trenches that determined the type of warfare that was to exist for the whole of the war along the Western Front. The failures of both the British and the Germans to break through at Ypres in November 1914, and then the failure of the French to break through at Artois and Champagne in December, meant that a **stalemate** situation was in place by the end of 1914.

German war aims

German war aims in 1914 were very comprehensive. In his memorandum of 9 September, Bethmann-Hollweg promised 'security for the German Reich in west and east for all imaginable time', and this was to be done through a combination of territorial expansion and economic control. In Africa, for instance, French, Belgian, and Portuguese colonies would be incorporated into an economic region in Central Africa: *Mittelafrika*. In Europe, Germany would have indirect control over much of Europe through a customs union, which would include Austria-Hungary, Belgium, Denmark, France, the Netherlands, and Poland. Parts of Belgium, France, and Luxembourg would be directly annexed and Russia would have to provide some level of self-determination to nationalities such as the Poles. (Poland had been part of Russia since the 18th century.) Britain's economic supremacy would be weakened by Germany's naval command of key international routes, as well as by Germany's economic domination of Africa and Europe. Such comprehensive aims increased the determination of both sides to fight for total victory, and they made a compromise peace difficult to achieve.

CHALLENGE YOURSELF

Research skills 

Belgium remained under German occupation for the whole of the war. Research the impact that this had on civilians living under occupation. What forms of resistance took place? What was the role of Edith Cavell, a British nurse living in Brussels, in trying to help Allied soldiers escape from occupied Belgium, and what was the international impact of her execution by the Germans?

The rape of Belgium

Belgium not only slowed down the German advance, but the actions of the Germans against the Belgian population provided the basis for much of the anti-German Allied propaganda. When Belgium put up resistance to the German advance, the army took revenge on civilians. Its actions in the Belgium city of Leuven (Louvain), where the medieval library, along with many other buildings, was burnt, 250 people shot, and many others sent on trains back to Germany, shocked the world. In total, the German army executed between 5,500 and 6,500 French and Belgian civilians between August and November 1914, and 1,500,000 Belgians fled the country. In its propaganda, both Britain and America now used images of dead or tortured Belgium woman and children (many exaggerated); the message now focused on the atrocities perpetrated by the Germans and the 'moral' obligation that Britain had to stop Germany and to avenge the 'rape of Belgium'.

1915: stalemate

In 1915, the stalemate continued on the Western Front. Several attempts were made to break this situation, but they all failed: the British tried at Neuve Chapelle and Loos, the French lost thousands of men in an unsuccessful offensive in Champagne, and the Germans were driven back from Ypres in April. It was at this second battle of Ypres that poison gas was first used by the Germans, and although it was initially effective in clearing the British trenches, the gas also prevented the Germans from making any progress, and the attack was halted.

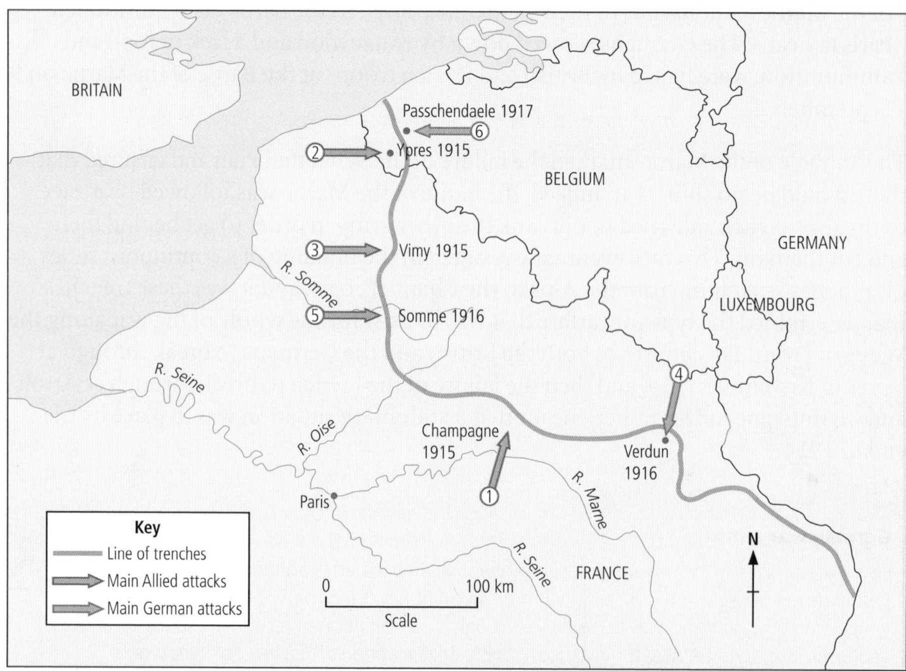

Trench line of the Western Front, with key battles, 1915–1917.

Activity 1

ATL Thinking skills

Source analysis

1. What is the message of this British propaganda poster?

1916: Verdun and the Somme

The two key battles of 1916 were those at Verdun and the Somme – both failed to achieve their aims and both were horrific in terms of loss of life.

Verdun

In February 1916, the Germans launched a massive attack against the important French fortress town of Verdun. The German Commander Erich von Falkenhayn set out his plans:

> *Just behind the French lines on the Western Front there are objectives which the French command must defend to the last man. If it so defends them the French army will be exhausted by its bloody losses in the inevitable combat, regardless of whether or not we win the objectives immediately. If, on the other hand, it lets them go, the damage to French morale will be enormous … The essential question is not to take Verdun … but to pin down the French, pull them towards the battlefield, and since they will have to defend it shoulder to shoulder, we shall bleed them white by virtue of our superiority in guns.*

Attacks were followed by counter-attacks. General Philippe Pétain, the commander in charge of the French troops, held out, but at a huge cost of 315,000 men. He voiced French determination in the phrase '*Ils ne passeront pas*' ('They shall not pass') and by April French counter-attacks had caused huge losses for the Germans – 280,000 men. Falkenhayn was sacked in August 1916, but his policy at Verdun ran on for another four months. The casualties eventually numbered more than 800,000. Overall, the battle broke all previous records for killing and destruction.

Activity 2 — ATL Thinking skills

Review questions

1. What were Falkenhayn's objectives in attacking Verdun?
2. What does this reveal about the way in which war was now being fought on the Western Front?

Activity 3 — ATL Thinking skills

Source analysis

"Father, we must have a higher pile to see Verdun."

'We must have a higher pile to see Verdun', by Dutch cartoonist Louis Raemakers.

1. What point is Raemakers making in this cartoon?

TOK

Casualties are an inevitable element of waging a war. However, the Battle of the Somme has been seen as resulting in unacceptably high casualty figures.

Can high casualty rates in war be justified? What *is* a high casualty figure? Did the sheer number of men in the mass armies of World War One mean that high casualties were unavoidable?

The Battle of the Somme

The Battle of the Somme was a series of attacks led mainly by the British under General Douglas Haig. They began on 1 July 1916 and lasted through to the following November. The aim of these attacks was to take the pressure off the French at Verdun and ensure that the Germans were fully committed so that they could not send reinforcements to the Eastern Front against Russia. The first attack was preceded by the most intensive preliminary artillery bombardment ever made. The aim of this demonstration of firepower was to destroy the forward defences. It failed, however, and as a result the first attack by British soldiers ended in heavy casualties. A second major attack was made in September. This used tanks for the first time, but again, there was no breakthrough and by the end of this battle the Allies had made only limited advances, varying between a few hundred metres and 4 kilometres, along a 50-kilometre front. Losses on both sides were appalling: British killed or wounded totalled 418,000, German casualties were 650,000, and French 194,000.

1917: the USA joins the war

In February 1917, the Germans withdrew behind the heavily fortified **Hindenburg Line** in north-eastern France, which could be more easily defended. During the rest of the year, the French and the British continued offensive actions, without any major breakthroughs, in the Battle of Arras (9–15 April), the Battle of the Aisne in the French Nivelle Offensive (16–20 April), and in the Third Battle of Ypres at Passchendaele (July–November). Failure in the Nivelle Offensive proved intolerable to many soldiers and the French government was faced with mutiny, resulting in the courts martial of 300–400 ringleaders. Only the Battle of Cambrai (20 November–3 December) indicated that there could be an end to the stalemate, when British and Australian forces using tanks broke through German lines and achieved an advance of 8 kilometres. Yet the tank was still mechanically unreliable, and many broke down under the stresses of the advance. The British advance slowed and the Germans were able to counter-attack successfully, forcing the British out of many of the areas they had captured.

Yet the Allies had cause for optimism when the USA entered the war in 1917. America had suffered as a result of the German policy of unrestricted submarine warfare in the Atlantic from February 1917, which had involved attacks on American ships and the consequent loss of American lives. When the Zimmerman telegram was intercepted (see Interesting Facts box on page 51) it was the final straw, and America declared war on Germany on 4 April. Nevertheless, it took time for US troops to arrive in Europe, and at the end of 1917 the situation on the Western Front still looked bleak; the French army was recovering from the mutinies, and, following the success of the **Bolshevik** revolution in Russia, an **armistice** was signed between the Bolsheviks and the Germans. This event led to Russian troops being withdrawn from the Eastern Front, which meant that the Germans could focus their attention on fighting in Western Europe.

The Treaty of Brest-Litovsk

When Lenin took over Russia in October 1917, he was determined to end the war with Germany. However, the 'robber peace' that Russia was forced to sign was extremely harsh. Russia lost Poland, Estonia, Latvia and Lithuania, Ukraine, Georgia, and Finland. These losses included a third of Russia's farming land, a third of its population, two-thirds of its coal mines, and half of its industry. In addition, Russia had to pay an indemnity of 5 billion gold rubles.

US neutrality, unrestricted submarine warfare, and the Zimmerman telegram

At the beginning of the war, the USA had maintained a policy of neutrality, and President Woodrow Wilson had even attempted to negotiate a peace, arguing for a 'peace without victory' in Europe. **Isolationism** – keeping America out of Europe's affairs – was also strongly supported by public opinion in the USA. Neutrality, however, was very difficult when the USA was trading with the combatants, particularly the Allies. Germany's response was to use submarines to attack American ships without warning, a situation that led to the sinking of the ocean liner *Lusitania* in 1915. Germany suspended its **U-boat** attacks, but resumed them in January 1917 (see page 62). Germany knew that this action might draw the USA into the war on the side of the Allies. Thus, in January 1917, Arthur Zimmerman, foreign secretary of Germany, wrote a telegram to the German ambassador of Mexico, Heinrich von Eckhardt, instructing him to approach the Mexican government with a proposal for a military alliance; it offered US territory in return for Mexico joining the German cause. The Zimmerman telegram was intercepted and decoded by the British. Its publication in the US media caused public outrage that helped swing popular opinion in favour of entering the war.

Activity 4 — ATL Thinking skills

Source analysis

An American poster uses the image of the sinking *Lusitania* to encourage young men to enlist in the US Navy.

1. What does this poster tell you about American attitudes to the sinking of the *Lusitania* and about America's position of neutrality?

1918: victory for the Allies

With Germany on the verge of starvation as a result of the success of an Allied blockade, and under the threat of US troops arriving to join the Allies, the German Commander Erich Ludendorff decided to risk everything on a quick victory in his 'Peace Offensive' (*Friedensturm*). Ludendorff's initial attacks were very successful; following the usual preliminary artillery bombardment came attacks of smaller bands of specially trained and lightly equipped 'storm troops' rather than the usual waves of **infantry**. Attacking along the entire frontline, the Germans broke the Allied lines in many places. In March 1918, 35 German divisions on the Somme made gains of about 65 kilometres against the British. In April, a breakthrough was made in Flanders,

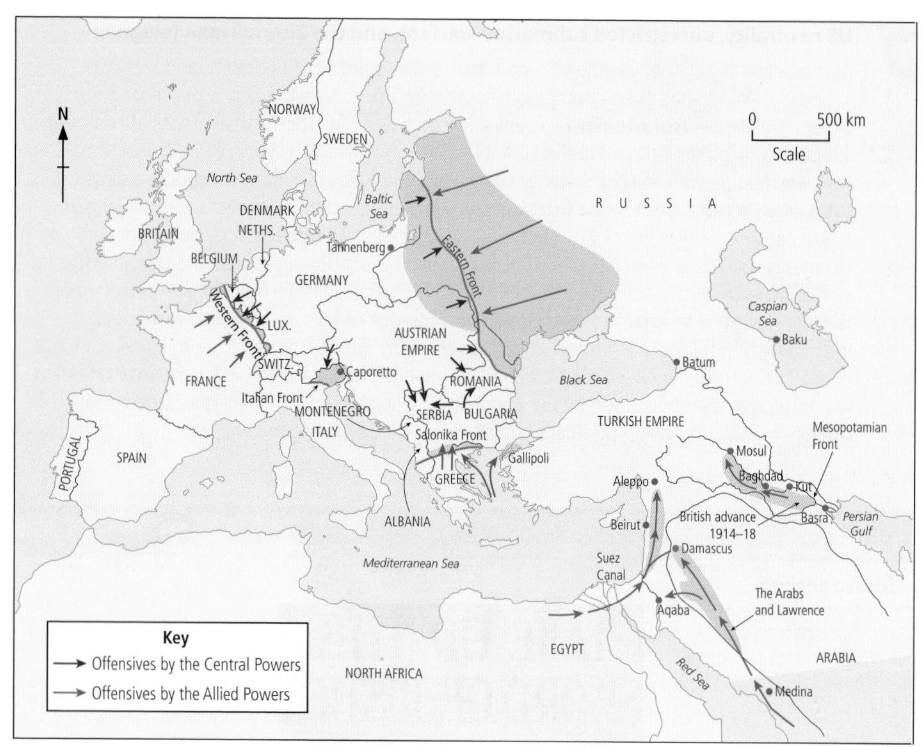

Map showing the different fronts on which fighting took place.

which threatened Allied control of the Channel ports, and in May German troops once again reached the River Marne. They were only 80 kilometres from Paris.

Yet the Germans had overstretched themselves and they had no reserves to call on to replace the 800,000 casualties that they had sustained in the offensive. They made no further progress between May and August. Meanwhile, the Allied forces, now under the coordinated control of General Ferdinand Foch, and using planes and tanks, massed their growing forces around the salient that the German forces had created in their advance. The last German offensive in July met stiff opposition and was unable to make any progress. Instead, the French counter-attack made a breakthrough, forcing Ludendorff's units back to safer ground.

On 8 August – what Ludendorff called 'The Black Day of the German Army' – the Allies achieved the furthest advance since the beginning of the war in 1914. By late September, they had reached the Hindenburg Line. By October, the Germans, now suffering from low morale, hunger, and indiscipline, were in full retreat. Germany was facing other problems – the impact of the blockade and the surrender of its allies. Back in September, Ludendorff had lost his nerve and urged the Kaiser to 'request an armistice without any hesitation'; only a 'quick end' could save the army from destruction. Thus on 11 November 1918, the Armistice came into effect, ending the fighting between the Allies and Germany.

Activity 5

ATL Thinking skills

Review questions

1. Why did a stalemate develop, and continue, on the Western Front?
2. Why did the Americans enter the war?
3. What factors contributed to the Germans agreeing to an armistice in November 1918?

The Armistice

The Armistice was agreed at 5.00am on 11 November, to come into effect at 11.00am Paris time – the eleventh hour of the eleventh day of the eleventh month. The terms contained the following major points:

- termination of military hostilities within six hours after signature
- immediate removal of all German troops from France, Belgium, Luxembourg and Alsace-Lorraine
- removal of all German troops from territory on both sides of the Rhine, with ensuing occupation by Allied troops
- removal of all German troops from the Eastern Front, leaving German territory as it was on 1 August 1914
- renouncement of the Treaty of Brest-Litovsk with Russia and of the Treaty of Bucharest with Romania
- internment of the German fleet and surrender of other weapons.

The agreement was signed by the German delegation in Foch's railway siding in the forest of Compiègne (which Hitler subsequently used for the signing of the armistice that the French made with the Germans in 1940).

The Eastern Front 1914

The aim of the Schlieffen Plan had been for Germany to avoid fighting a war on two fronts. Yet not only did Germany fail to defeat France quickly, but the Russians mobilized their army much faster than Germany had predicted. On 17 August 1914, the Russians moved into East Prussia, forcing the Germans to divert troops from the Western Front. Although the Russians were initially successful against the Austrians, by occupying the province of Galicia and helping to cause the failure of the Schlieffen Plan, they were defeated by the Germans both at Tannenberg in August and the Masurian Lakes in September. (Here was a pattern to be repeated several times – the Russians could defeat the Austrians but not the Germans, and the Germans had to keep coming to the aid of the Austrians.) These defeats boosted German self-confidence, forced Russia out of Germany, and also resulted in the loss for Russia of huge amounts of equipment and ammunition. Russia's position worsened considerably when Turkey entered the war on the side of the Germany, as Turkey could cut Russia's main supply route through the Dardanelles.

1915

This year again saw the Russians defeated by the Germans, who captured Warsaw in August. A combined Austro-German offensive in the Carpathians in May also meant the loss of most of Russia's 1914 gains by late June. By the end of the year, the Russians had withdrawn some 450 kilometres with losses of a million dead and a further million taken prisoner. A Russian general reported to the Tsar, 'A third of the men have no rifles. These poor devils have to wait patiently until their comrades fall so they can pick up their weapons. The army is drowning in its own blood.' The Russians had to establish a new defensive line that extended from Riga on the Baltic Sea to Romania in the Balkans – a line that was soon to become 'six hundred miles of mud and horror'. Russia was also starting to suffer from the effects of the Turkish blockade of the Dardanelles (see page 55).

Activity 6

ATL Thinking skills

Source analysis

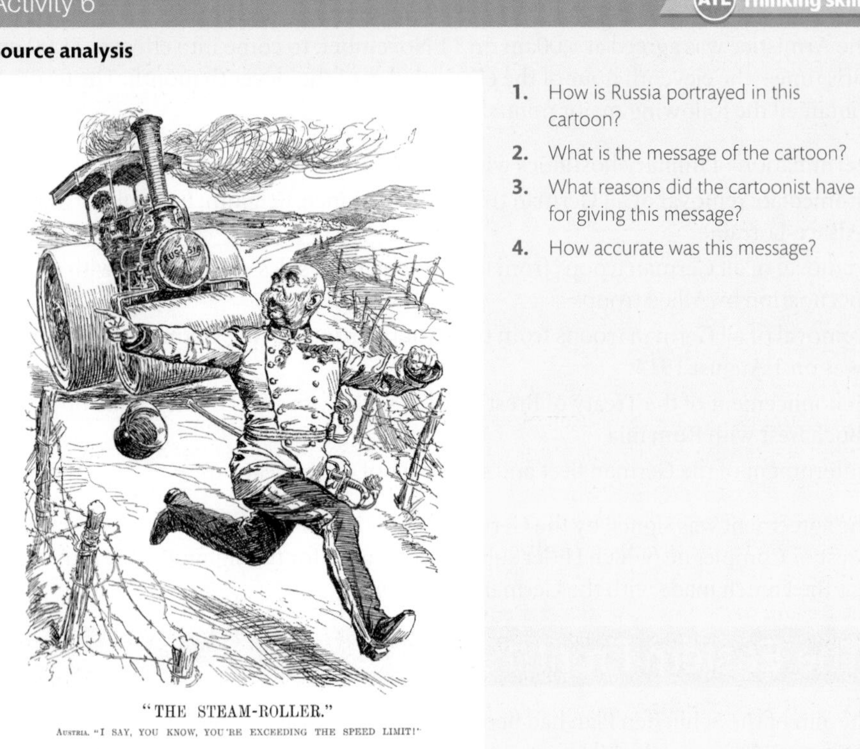

"THE STEAM-ROLLER."
AUSTRIA. "I SAY, YOU KNOW, YOU'RE EXCEEDING THE SPEED LIMIT!"

A British cartoon published in September 1914, which reads: "'The Steam-roller.' Austria – 'I say, you know, you're exceeding the speed limit!'"

1. How is Russia portrayed in this cartoon?
2. What is the message of the cartoon?
3. What reasons did the cartoonist have for giving this message?
4. How accurate was this message?

When analysing any source, the date is a crucial piece of information that needs to be taken into consideration. Look at the sequence of events on the Eastern Front and the date of the cartoon to help you with Question 3.

1916–1917

The following year, 1916, saw the greatest Russian success of the war. Due to a determined effort on the home front, the Russian army had better equipment than it had possessed in 1916, and on 4 June General Aleksei Brusilov, under pressure from France and Britain to divert German resources away from Verdun, launched a massive offensive over a wide front against the Austrians. Initially, this offensive was very successful, advancing 160 kilometres. By early August, however, with the Germans again coming to the support of the Austro-Hungarian army, the Brusilov Offensive came to a halt. It had cost the Russians a million lives.

The offensive had a devastating effect on both the Austro-Hungarian and the Russian empires. In Austria-Hungary the number of casualties – 340,000, with 400,000 more men taken prisoner – caused morale to reach rock bottom. In Russia, the effect of a further million casualties combined with growing hardships at home created yet more opposition to the ruling Romanov dynasty. The mounting pressure exploded in February 1917, when the **Tsar** was forced to abdicate. Although the new **Provisional Government** decided to maintain the war effort, the continued defeats of the Russian army and the ongoing economic crisis on the home front helped increase support for the Bolshevik Party, who were successful in overthrowing the Provisional Government in October of the same year.

The new Bolshevik government then removed Russia from the war in December, ending Germany's need to fight a war on two fronts. The majority of German forces could now be used against the West.

The Balkan Front

Austria-Hungary failed to occupy Serbia in 1914, yet Bulgaria's entry on the side of the Central Powers allowed a successful joint Austro-German–Bulgarian offensive in October 1915. In August 1916, encouraged by the Russian successes, Romania joined the Allies, but was quickly overrun by the forces of Germany, Austria-Hungary, Turkey, and Bulgaria. Allied attempts to relieve Romania by invading through Greece on the Salonika Front failed. It was not until 1918 that the Allies made advances against Bulgaria, leading to its surrender in September 1918.

The Italian Front

Italy joined the war in 1915 on the side of the Allies, having been promised by Britain and France (in the Treaty of London) possession of Austria's Italian-speaking provinces, as well as territory along the eastern shore of the Adriatic Sea. Italy's entry into the war opened up a front between Italy and Austria-Hungary along the River Isonzo. However, fighting in the mountainous terrain was difficult and the Italians made little headway against the Austrians. In October 1917, a major Austro-Hungarian offensive – the Battle of Caporetto – was launched with German support. The Italians were forced to retreat more than 110 kilometres and the Central Powers' advance was halted only by the arrival of British and French reinforcements. Despite these failures, the Italian Front placed a heavy burden on Austria-Hungary, which in 1916 had to deploy half of its forces against the Italians.

Turkey and the Middle Eastern Fronts

Turkey joined Germany and Austria-Hungary in the war on 31 October 1914, mainly with the intention of halting Russian expansion around the Black Sea. The Allies attacked the Turkish Empire in three separate campaigns.

The Gallipoli campaign planned for British warships to sweep through the Dardanelles, attacking Constantinople and driving Turkey out of the war. This success would then open up a sea route to the Russian Front, so that the Allies could get supplies to Russia.

It would also allow the Allies to march through the Balkans and attack Austria-Hungary, thus opening up a new front. The plan was an attractive alternative to the stalemate on the Western Front, seeming to offer the possibility of a quick and unexpected success. Lord Herbert Kitchener, the British Secretary of State for War, believed that it would be the plan that would win the war.

The first stage of the campaign, a naval bombardment of the Turkish forts protecting the narrow straits, was a failure. With British and French ships damaged by a combination of mines and shell fire from the forts, the Allied commanders decided that the risks were too great. They opted instead to launch a land invasion to capture the peninsula. Thus an Allied army, which included a large number of Australians and New Zealanders (Anzacs), landed on the Gallipoli peninsula on 25 April 1915. In the ensuing months, the campaign suffered from shortages, delays, lack of coordinated command, and tactical errors. It was finally abandoned in November, having achieved none of its goals and having cost the Allies 250,000 men, dead, wounded, or captured.

The second campaign against the Turks involved an operation to win control of oil supplies through an expedition to oil-rich Mesopotamia. The Turks, led and supported by German officers, resisted fiercely at first, but by the end of the war British forces were in control of Basra, Baghdad, and Mosul.

TOK

Religion was used as a propaganda tool to motivate and console the different societies fighting in the Great War. Christians on both sides - Entente powers and Central Powers - were reassured that 'God was on their side'. Turkish troops would be told that Allah was supporting the Islamic armies. How could people reconcile their religious beliefs with the death and destruction they saw all around them? Would the impact of war strengthen or undermine religious faith? Discuss your responses with a partner.

Guerrilla warfare in East Africa

The British experienced the impact of guerrilla warfare when Colonel Paul Emil von Lettow-Vorbeck launched a series of successful guerrilla-style attacks against the British in East Africa, including raids against British railways and forts in Kenya and Rhodesia.

With no more than 14,000 troops at his disposal, he tied down as many as 10 to 20 times that number of Allied troops. He officially surrendered to the British in November 1918, having never been defeated.

The third campaign involved British, Anzac, and Indian troops driving the Turks back through Palestine towards Turkey itself. The British were aided in this campaign by guerrilla warfare carried out by the Arabs, who had been promised independence from Turkey after the war. T.E. Lawrence, a British intelligence officer, became a military adviser to the Arabs. Known as 'Lawrence of Arabia', he led a guerrilla force in attacks on Turkish railways and supply lines. Under the leadership of General Edmund Allenby, the British and Empire forces defeated the Turks at Megiddo in September 1918, and the Turks finally surrendered on 3 November.

War in the colonial territories

Most of the major powers fighting in the war had colonies, and so fighting also took place in other parts of the world. Britain's control of the seas, however, meant that attacks on overseas territories and colonies were all Allied attacks. Most colonies were manned by relatively small garrisons and their capture was not difficult, though it was not until 1917 that all German forces in Africa were overcome.

Britain, France, and Germany also involved the people living in their colonies in the fighting; soldiers from India (1.5 million volunteers), Canada, Australia, New Zealand, and South Africa contributed to the British war effort, for example. The French recruited some 600,000 combat troops and a further 200,000 labourers from North and West Africa. Many of these soldiers ended up facing not only the appalling conditions of the Western Front, but also racism from the European troops.

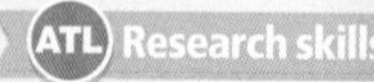

Indian troops from 57th Wilde's Rifles in action, October 1914.

In Asia, meanwhile, Japan joined the war on the side of the Allies and took the opportunity to attack and occupy Germany's islands in the Central Pacific and take over the heavily fortified German fortress at Kiaochow. A New Zealand force took over Samoa and an Australian battalion took New Guinea. By the end of the year, Germany had lost its Asiatic colonies, which Britain promised to their respective conquerors.

CHALLENGE YOURSELF

ATL Research skills

Research the role of one of the colonial countries that contributed troops to the Allied war effort. This activity could include looking at the number of troops sent, casualties, impact on the home life of the country, and impact on the colony's status and relationship with either Britain or France.

How was World War One fought?

War on land – the Western Front

Although fighting took place on several fronts throughout the four years of the war, the Western Front nevertheless remained the most important for several reasons:

- Because of its size and the length of time it remained an operational theatre of war. It was a continuous battlefield stretching for 320 kilometres from the North Sea to the French–Swiss border in the south. Across this line, the Allies and the Germans attacked each other continuously for four years without significantly breaking the position of the line.
- Because it played a key role in the outcome of the Great War. Many of the other conflicts in the war were 'diversionary fronts', which were created to break the deadlock on the Western Front.

- The fighting on the Western Front was to have a significant impact on ideas about and attitudes towards war.

Why did trench warfare lead to a stalemate?

The feature of the Western Front that most affected the way the war was fought was the development of trench warfare. After the 'race to the sea', the conflict settled into static 'positional' warfare. The war of movement was over. In order to hold their positions, and keep out of the line of machine-gun and artillery fire, soldiers had to dig down into defensive positions, thus trenches were dug along the entire length of the front. As it became clear that these hastily dug ditches were to become permanent, they evolved into complex defensive systems on both sides, with the area between opposing trenches known as 'no man's land'.

Trench warfare was deadlier for attackers than defenders; attackers suffered twice as many casualties during an assault on the enemy trench line. A major attack would begin with an artillery barrage, followed by the attacking troops going 'over the top' – climbing out of their trenches and attempting to reach and capture the enemy trenches on the other side of no man's land. Soldiers had to walk or run into the direct firing line of the defenders, while mines and thick rolls of barbed wire slowed down their progress and further increased their chances of being hit by enemy machine-gun fire.

The nature of this type of warfare is described by John Keegan in his account of the Battle of the Somme:

> *Descriptions of zero hour on 1 July abound, of the long lines of young men, burdened by the sixty pounds of equipment judged necessary to sustain them in a long struggle inside the German trenches, plodding off almost shoulder to shoulder; of their good cheer and certainty of success, of individual displays of bravado, as in the battalions which kicked a football ahead of the ranks; of bright sunshine breaking through the thin morning mist; of the illusion of an empty battlefield, denuded of opponents by the weight of bombardment and the explosion of twenty-one chambers, laboriously driven under the German front lines, as the attack began. Descriptions of what happened later abound also; of the discovery of the uncut wire, of the appearance of the German defenders, manning the parapet at the moment the British creeping barrage passed beyond, to fire frenziedly into the approaching ranks, of the opening of gaps in the attacking waves, of massacre in the wire entanglements, of the advance checked, halted and eventually stopped literally dead.*
>
> **From John Keegan, *The First World War* (Random House, 1999), p.317.**

Because of the difficulties of attacking and taking the enemy's trenches, the Western Front became one of stalemate, with little change in the position of the front over the whole four years. Increasingly, the aim of battles became not so much to win territory held by the enemy, but to destroy or wear down the opposing army; it was a **war of attrition** intended to break the morale of the enemy and reduce their numbers.

Clearly the military education and mindset of the generals were inadequate to meet the demands of this new type of warfare in 1914. Similarly, the soldiers themselves were ill-prepared in their training at the start of the war to deal with the horror in which they found themselves.

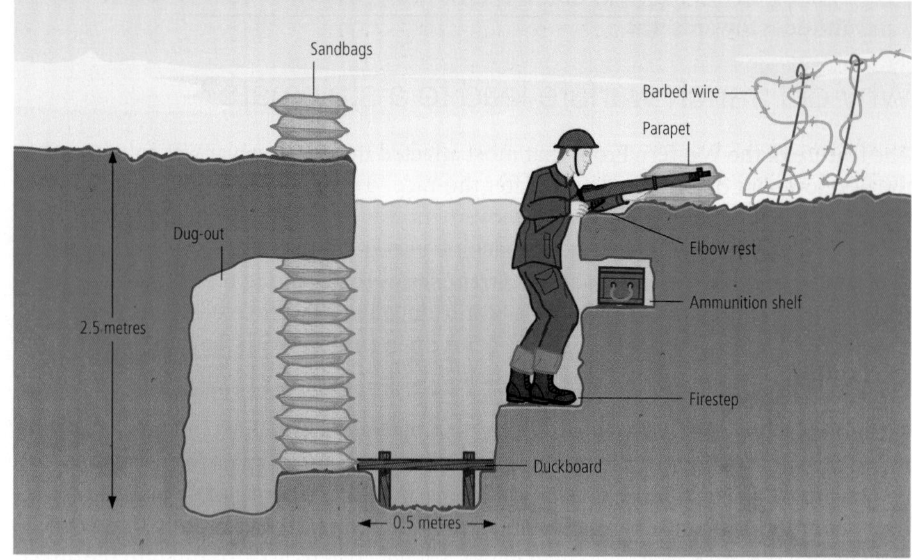

Cross-section of a typical World War One trench system.

CHALLENGE YOURSELF

Find out more about:

- the Christmas truce
- shell-shock
- trench foot
- the work of miners tunnelling beneath the trenches
- communication systems used in the trenches
- **conscientious objectors**
- those who were shot for 'cowardice'

Conditions on the Western Front

Soldiers on the Western Front experienced appalling day-to-day living conditions. Sanitation was poor and soldiers had to deal with the effects of limited washing and toilet facilities, as well as being surrounded by rotting corpses. Rats swarmed everywhere and soldiers became covered with lice. When it rained, the trenches could fill with water, which could lead to a soldier getting 'trench foot' after standing for hours with wet feet; this was an extremely painful skin condition that could lead to amputation if left untreated. When soldiers were not involved in an attack, life at the front could also be monotonous, and days were spent repairing trenches, writing letters, resting, and keeping guard. Soldiers did not spend all their time in the trenches. The trench systems stretched far back on both sides and they would also spend time in the support trenches or behind the lines.

How did new technologies impact the fighting on the Western Front?

Both sides in the war utilized a wide range of weapons in order to try to break the deadlock. The infantry charge explained above remained the key battle tactic used throughout the war, and most weapons were applied or developed with the aim of making this strategy more effective.

Machine guns and grenades

The main weapon of the British soldier was a .303in, bolt-action Lee-Enfield rifle with a magazine that held 10 rounds of ammunition; a bayonet could be attached to the end of the rifle for use in hand-to-hand fighting. Each side had similar types of rifle. The machine gun, however, was far more lethal against mass targets. Whereas an infantryman could fire 25 rounds a minute with a bolt-action rifle, he could fire 600 rounds a minute with a machine gun. The effects were devastating on attackers, as a German machine-gunner here recounts:

> *... the [British] officers walked in front. I noticed one of them walking calmly carrying a walking stick. When we started firing we just had to load and re-load. They went down in their hundreds. You didn't have to aim, we just fired into them.*

Soldiers also used hand grenades, essentially small hand-thrown bombs. The British, for example, used the pineapple-shaped Mills bomb, while the Germans used stick-shaped grenades nicknamed 'potato-mashers'.

Another weapon innovation of World War One was the submachine gun, a lightweight hand-held automatic weapon that fired pistol-calibre ammunition. (By using low-power ammunition, the soldier could control the recoil better than if he was using high-power rifle ammunition.) The submachine gun was known as a 'trench sweeper', a weapon that could deliver heavy firepower at close-quarters during a trench assault.

German soldiers carrying Model 24 stick grenades.

Heavy artillery

Although machine guns killed many thousands of people during World War One, nevertheless it was artillery that was the real killer: it was responsible for 70 per cent of all casualties. With the war being so static, the huge guns could take up permanent positions in strategically good locations, from where they could launch massive numbers of high-explosive shells. Commanders saw artillery as the key to overcoming the defences of the enemy and thus every major attack was preceded by a prolonged artillery barrage.

British artillery position on the Western Front.

Yet the reality was that the artillery was not accurate or effective enough to destroy enemy trench systems completely – unless a shell fell directly into a trench, the occupants were relatively well protected behind their earthen walls. In the Battle of the Somme, for example, the British fired more than 1.5 million shells in 5 days, but these failed to cut the barbed wire or destroy the German trenches. Even if the infantry made a breakthrough, the artillery was not mobile enough to be brought forward to protect the attackers. Another problem with the barrage was that it gave the enemy warning of the attack to come; when the barrage stopped that was the signal for the attack. The effect of the artillery on soldiers was nevertheless grim: brain damage, bleeding ears, shell-shock (a disorder which affected soldiers' mental health). It also churned up the land into a sea of mud and craters, which made attacking across no man's land even more difficult.

British soldiers man a Vickers machine gun while wearing gas masks.

Artillery tactics and **fire-control** technologies evolved over the course of the war to become more versatile, with the use of techniques such as the 'creeping barrage' (a steadily advancing wall of fire) and 'artillery ambush' (a sudden storm of shells against a specific target). It also became possible to locate and attack enemy artillery more effectively; thus British guns could remain silent until the actual attack and then blanket the German guns with fire, bringing back the element of surprise.

Chemical warfare

The first poison gas attack was made at Ypres by the Germans in April 1915. Carried on the wind, the chlorine gas caused panic amongst the Allied soldiers and disabled 6.5 kilometres of trenches. More lethal gases were soon developed: phosgene gas, which was 18 times stronger than the chlorine gas, and the most feared of all, mustard gas, which burned, blinded, or slowly killed the victims over several weeks. However, although gas was a useful weapon for causing panic among troops, it did not actually play any key role in breaking the stalemate. Its big disadvantage was that it was dependent on the wind for distribution and so it could blow back towards the side that was using it; this happened to the British at the Battle of Loos in 1915. In addition, gas masks were quickly developed by scientists, making gas as a weapon much less effective.

Tanks

Use of tanks was another attempt to break the stalemate. Developed by the British and the French, 49 of them were first used at the Battle of the Somme. The tank was able to advance ahead of the infantry, crushing barbed wire fences and attacking the enemy at the same time with machine-gun and cannon fire. Inside the tank, the crew was protected from small-arms fire by the outer metal armour. Even so, the tank was not yet able to break the stalemate. It was slow and unreliable and many tanks broke down before they reached the German trenches. Also, their armour plating was not strong enough to resist artillery, and the use of tanks at the Somme did not have any major effect other than causing initial panic amongst the Germans. The conditions for the tank operators were also appalling. The heat generated inside the tank was tremendous and fumes from the engine and guns nearly choked the men inside.

Larger numbers of tanks were used in the Battle of Cambrai in 1917, but here initial successes were not sustained and breakthroughs were quickly reversed.

> *As a result of the tank's limitations, there was little real agreement within the British Expeditionary Force on whether mechanical warfare truly offered a substitute for manpower. In that sense, tanks during the war remained what GHQ concluded in August 1918, a 'mechanical contrivance' with potential usefulness only as an adjunct to combined infantry and artillery assault.*
>
> **Ian Beckett, *The Great War 1914–1918* (Pearson, 2001), p.239.**

Official photo of a British tank going into action during the Battle of the Somme.

What impact did the technological advances of World War One have on the outcome of the fighting?

As suggested above, none of the technological developments in weaponry or the variations in tactics were ultimately decisive during the fighting on the Western Front. Nevertheless, the developments that did take place during the course of war – in artillery, tanks, combat aircraft, and aerial reconnaissance (see page 64 for more discussion of the air war) – did allow for a change of tactics by the final campaigns of 1918 and played a role in the final success of the Allied advance in 1918.

> *In 1914 the British soldier went to war dressed like a gamekeeper in a soft cap, armed only with rifle and bayonet. In 1918 he went into battle dressed like an industrial worker in a steel helmet, protected by a respirator against poison gas, armed with automatic weapons and mortars, supported by tanks and ground-attack aircraft, and preceded by a creeping artillery barrage of crushing intensity. Firepower replaced manpower as the instrument of victory. This represented a revolution in the conduct of war.*
>
> **John Bourne in Charles Townshend (ed.), *The Oxford History of Modern War* (Oxford University Press, 2005), pp.133–134.**

War at sea

What was the importance of naval warfare in World War One?

From the beginning of the war, it was clear that control of the seas was crucial to both sides. Britain needed to be able to transport men (including from places as far afield as Australia and Canada) and supplies to the battlefields of Europe and the Middle East. As an island, Britain's need for food and industrial supplies from other countries, particularly from the USA, was key to the country's survival. Thus Britain was also cautious in its use of its navies; it could not risk losing many ships to mines and submarines or in surface battles. As Winston Churchill (who served as First Lord of the Admiralty for part of the war) said, it would have been possible for Admiral Jellicoe, the commander of the British fleet, to lose the war in an afternoon.

Germany did not need naval routes to supply and help its allies. However, Germany also needed food and other supplies from overseas. Thus control of trade routes was vital to both sides, both for their own needs and to stop supplies reaching the enemy.

Britain was particularly successful in pursuing the latter objective. Royal Navy vessels went into action against German units stationed abroad, and destroyed one of the main German squadrons at the Battle of the Falkland Islands in 1914. The Allies also started blockading German ports; British naval vessels enforced the right of search on neutral shipping to ensure that Germany and its allies were not getting supplies via other countries.

Mines and submarines

With their surviving warships vulnerable to the might of the Royal Navy, the Germans turned instead to submarine attacks and tried to enforce their own blockade of Britain using U-boats (*Unterseebooten* – meaning 'underwater boats') to sink merchant ships.

TOK

The *Lusitania*, sunk by German U-boats on 7 May 1915, was a luxury liner built to convey its passengers between Britain and the United States. The Germans claimed they had evidence that the liner was transporting munitions as well as civilian passengers across the Atlantic. US President Woodrow Wilson had resisted public demand, particularly in Britain, to respond to the attack with a declaration of war. This choice was seen by some as 'cowardice', and a shell that failed to explode was nicknamed a 'Wilson' in the British trenches.

At the time it was widely believed that the German claim about the ship was false, and was an attempt to justify the effects of unrestricted submarine warfare. In 2006, however, a dive team from Ireland claimed that they had found munitions on board the sunken vessel. These included 15,000 rounds of rifle ammunition in the bow of the ship. These rounds were the same calibre as those used by the British in their rifles and machine guns on the Western Front.

Discuss as a class the implications of this new evidence. What does it suggest about our understanding of the past? Do we have more 'truth' about the past today than was possible at the time of the war?

Submarines, and also the use of sea mines, changed the conduct of naval warfare. Previously, naval actions had been carried out on the surface, often at close range. The development, however, of the torpedo and submarine made the large battleships vulnerable and almost defenceless, and the submarine campaign caused serious losses of Allied ships and cargoes. Yet it was also politically dangerous warfare. Some of the ships sunk belonged to neutral countries. The sinking of the *Lusitania* by torpedo attack and the loss of 1,000 lives, including 128 Americans, led to strong protests from the USA. Although the Germans scaled down their U-boat campaign in September 1915 in an attempt to keep America out of the war, the failure at Jutland (see below) to harm significantly the British Grand Fleet led to a decision to renew the campaign of unrestricted submarine warfare in February 1917. The Germans hoped that the underwater blockade would starve Britain and France into surrender before the USA could have any impact on the war. They were very nearly successful. In February 1917, Britain lost 464,000 tons of shipping. In April it lost 834,000 tons. Britain was soon down to only six weeks' worth of supplies of corn.

Why was Britain able to survive the U-boat blockade?

The success rate of the U-boats was due to the fact that they were attacking unarmed merchant ships that were travelling alone or in small groups without any protection. Lloyd George supported the idea of a convoy system in which large numbers of merchant ships would sail together with a naval escort. Neither the Admiralty nor the shipping companies were enthusiastic about this idea, but they eventually agreed. It was the turning point. By October 1917, a total of 99 homeward-bound convoys had reached harbour safely and only 10 vessels had been lost. The last quarter of 1917 saw 235 ships lost compared to 413 ships in the second quarter of the year.

German poster from 1917: 'The U-boats are out!'

The convoy system did not eliminate the threat of the U-boats completely, but other factors now also came into play to help defeat the U-boat threat:

- As losses went down due to the convoy system, the total tonnage of Allied shipping increased due to the vast increases in output from American shipyards; thus the U-boat campaign was unable to achieve a reduction in the overall volume of Allied shipping.
- Weapons technology progressed so that surface vessels could locate and attack U-boats even when they were submerged. The hydrophone passive listening device enabled ships to 'listen' for U-boat engine noises, and depth charges were developed to attack submarines. By 1918, sonar had been developed and the French were also using echo ranging: both were technologies that allowed U-boat detection. In 1918, the Germans lost 69 U-boats and, at this stage in the war, they were unable to replace them.
- Improved submarine nets were designed and deployed across the entrances to the English Channel, which forced the U-boats to go north around the top of Britain, thus seriously reducing their operational time in the war zone.

The Battle of Jutland

Despite the expectations of a major confrontation between the main German and British fleets and the new dreadnoughts, such a clash did not occur until 1916 – mainly because both sides realized that they had too much to lose if they waged a head-on battle. Instead, the war at sea was dominated by submarines and mines, as explained above. Nevertheless, there was one major challenge to British supremacy of the sea at the Battle of Jutland (31 May–1 June 1916).

The battle began when German Admiral Reinhard Scheer tried to lure part of the British fleet out from its base so that an attack could be made by numerically superior German forces. However, due to the fact that the British could decipher German radio signals, more British ships came out than anticipated, and so Scheer had to fight an engagement involving some 250 ships in total. After several hours of exchanging artillery fire, the Germans decided to sail back to port. Although the Germans could claim victory, having lost 11 ships to Britain's 14, the major result of this encounter was that the Germans had not destroyed the British fleet – Britain was left in control of the surface waters. The German High Seas Fleet stayed in Kiel for the rest of the war, and instead the Germans switched their focus to the submarine warfare outlined above. 'As one journalist famously remarked, the High Seas Fleet had succeeded only in assaulting its gaoler before returning to gaol' (Ian Beckett, *The Great War 1914–1918* [Pearson, 2001], p.184).

The fact that Britain's navy enjoyed supremacy for the course of the war was central in allowing it to move 8.5 million troops across the British Empire, as well as troops and supplies from Britain across the Channel to France. Imports continued to reach Britain, and the Allies were able to establish and maintain the devastating blockade on Germany. Ultimately, they were also able to sustain the convoy system and transport American men and equipment to Europe for the final battles.

Activity 7

1. To what extent can it be argued that German attempts to destroy British naval supremacy were a complete failure?

Activity 8

Source analysis

> *The new policy [of unrestricted submarine warfare] has swept every restriction aside. All vessels, irrespective of cargo and flag, have been sent to the bottom, without help and without mercy. Even hospital and relief ships, though provided with the Germans' safe conduct, were sunk with the same reckless lack of compassion and principle …*
>
> *German submarine warfare is no longer directed against belligerents but against the whole world. All nations are involved in Germany's action. The challenge is to all mankind. Wanton, wholesale destruction has been effected against women and children while they have been engaged in pursuits which even in the darkest periods of modern history have been regarded as innocent and legitimate …*
>
> *There is one choice I cannot make. I will not choose the path of submission, and suffer the most sacred rights of the nation and of the people to be ignored and violated.*
>
> *With a profound sense of the solemn and even tragic character of the step I am taking, and of the grave responsibilities involved, but in unhesitating obedience to my constitutional duty, I advise Congress to declare that the recent course of the German government is nothing less than war against the United States, and the United States accept the status of a belligerent which has been thrust upon it, and will take immediate steps to put the country into a thorough state of defence, and to exert all the power and resource in bringing Germany to terms, and in ending the war …*
>
> **Speech by President Woodrow Wilson to the joint houses of Congress, 2 April 1917.**

1. What is the overall message of this speech with regard to German actions in carrying out unrestricted submarine warfare?

2 a) What is the value of this speech to a historian studying the reasons for US entry into the war?

b) What are the limitations of the speech?

War in the air

One of the major technological leaps in the Great War was the use of aircraft as military weapons. As the war progressed, the importance of aircraft became increasingly evident.

Airships, bombs, and civilian targets

In the early stages of the war, it was the airship that had the most important role in the air. Certainly, military leaders saw them as more useful than aeroplanes because they were more reliable, could carry heavy loads, and had a much greater range. The British used airships mainly for escorting ships and for spotting U-boats (they could then warn the escort ships by radio). The Germans, however, with their more advanced airship called the Zeppelin, soon realized the potential of the airship for carrying out bombing on civilian and industrial targets in Britain. At the start of the war, the Germans had a force of 30 Zeppelins, and although potentially an easy target – they contained 57,000 cubic metres of highly flammable hydrogen – they were initially reasonably safe because of the height at which they flew. Raids on London, the Midlands, and the east coast killed several hundred civilians. As British defences improved, however, Zeppelins became too vulnerable and were replaced with bomber aircraft, the most famous of which was the Gotha. This bomber caused nearly 3,000 casualties in raids against London and south-east England. The British responded with the development of their own bomber fleet as part of the Royal Flying Corps (RFC). The British aircraft also made bombing raids into enemy territory in the last year of the war. By February 1918, there were the first 'round-the-clock' raids, with British DH-4 planes attacking the town of Trier by day and Handley Page aircraft attacking at night. In March, there were raids on Mannheim, Mainz, and Stuttgart during the day. Clearly the idea of attacking civilians from the air had already become a feature of 20th-century war by 1918.

Zeppelin airships were used in air raids against British towns and cities.

The 'Red Baron' – German fighter ace Baron Manfred von Richthofen.

Aircraft: reconnaissance, dog-fights, and ground attack

Aircraft were a relatively recent invention, and thus very primitive and unreliable at the start of the war. Yet they soon came to fulfil important functions over the battlefields. First, their speed and mobility meant that they could be used for detailed reconnaissance work over enemy trenches. Pilots were able to report on troop concentrations, artillery positions, and enemy movements, in addition to directing the fire of their own artillery on to specific targets. Photographs of trench systems and artillery targets were taken from the air, and by 1918 photographic images could be taken from as high as 4,500 metres. Messages could even be dropped from the aircraft. With the development of the aerial wireless, communication was also possible between aircraft and the ground.

The airmen in these reconnaissance planes soon began to experiment with improvised weapons to bring down rival reconnaissance flights. This innovation led to the emergence of aerial 'dog-fights'. At first, pilots tried to attack each other with pistols and rifles, but by 1915 machine guns were fitted and synchronized so that they could shoot through the propeller of the airplane without striking the blades.

Dog-fights became a common sight over the trenches. Aircraft also became increasingly important for attacking enemy ground troops. For example, in 1918 ground-attack aircraft played their part in the Allied victory by dropping 1,563 bombs and firing 122,150 rounds of machine-gun ammunition in support of land offensives.

The growing awareness of the importance of air power meant that the aircraft evolved rapidly during the course of the war. The numbers of aircraft also grew; by 1918, there were more than 8,000 aircraft in operation on all sides. Control of the skies over the battlefield had become essential to victory. Politicians and commanders in all countries realized the potential importance of airpower, including the idea that bombing civilians could play a key role in undermining the enemy's morale. The end of World War One was still determined by what happened on the ground, but in both strategy and tactics, there were signs of what would come in the next war of 1939 to 1945.

Activity 9

ATL Thinking and communication skills

Review activity

Using what you have read in this chapter, copy and fill out the grids below and then answer the questions that follow.

	Western Front (land)	Eastern Front (land)	War in the air	War at sea
Key strategies/ tactics used				
Impact of tactics (consider casualties, land gained, strategic gains)				
Overall impact on outcome of the war				

1. Looking at the battles on both the Western and the Eastern Fronts, what differences can you see in how the war was fought and how it developed along these two fronts? (Refer to the map on page 52 and notice the amount of territory that changed hands on the Western and Eastern Fronts. Also compare casualty figures between the two fronts.)
2. Why do think that there were these differences?
3. What impact would the changing front line in the east have had on the civilian populations of these areas?
4. What impact overall did the war at sea have on the outcome of World War One?
5. What was the impact of the war in the air?
6. Overall, which theatre of war was most important for the outcome of the war?

The war in the air

The idea of honourable combat between fighter 'aces' caught people's imaginations during the war, and all countries had their own heroes. While the soldiers in the trenches remained anonymous, the names of the fighter aces became well known – Major 'Micky' Mannock in Britain, René Fonck in France, and, perhaps the most famous of all, Baron von Richthofen, or the 'Red Baron', from Germany, who headed his 'flying circus' squadron and shot down 80 planes. Governments soon realized the propaganda potential of glamorous war heroes and encouraged dramatic accounts of air combat, which were much better for morale than stories of the horrors of the trenches. However, the development of mass air actions with much greater numbers of aeroplanes led to the end of this 'romantic' individual action.

Strategy and tactics

A strategy is the overall plan of action. It involves looking at the 'bigger picture' and seeing how all the different battles and engagements are linked together. Strategy is different from tactics. Tactics are the actual ways in which a strategy is carried out: that is, how a particular battle is conducted.

Activity 10 — ATL Thinking and communication skills

Complete this grid about the technological developments of World War One in the air, on land, and at sea. Then answer the questions below.

TECHNOLOGICAL DEVELOPMENTS			
	Technological developments	Impact on tactics	Impact on outcome of the war
War on land			
War at sea			
War in the air			

1. How important were technological developments in deciding the outcome of the war?
2. What do you consider to be the most important of the technological developments made?
3. How did these technological developments change the nature of warfare?

World War One controversy

The General

'Good morning, good morning,' the General said,
When we met him last week on our way to the Line.
Now the soldiers he smiled at are most of 'em dead,
And we're cursing his staff for incompetent swine.
'He's a cheery old card,' grunted Harry to Jack,
As they slogged up to Arras with rifle and pack.

But he did for them both by his plan of attack.

Siegfried Sassoon, 'The General', 1917.

One of the key debates for historians is the extent to which the World War One generals were responsible for throwing away the lives of men in futile attacks.

Certainly generals in all countries were unprepared for the nature of the fighting that was to take place. The French, for example, in 1914 believed in *'elan vital'*, which translates as 'the will to win'. This offensive military strategy resulted in French General Foch ordering an attack at the Battle of the Marne when the situation called for a retreat.

Why, he was later asked, did he advance at the Marne when he was technically beaten. 'Why? I don't know. Because of my men, because I had a will. And then – God was there.

Barbara Tuchman, *The Guns of August* (Ballentine, 1962), p.32.

The failure to replace the red trousers of the French army at the beginning of the war also contributed to the horrendous consequences of the French 'Plan 17' as the army attacked through Alsace and Lorraine. As Barbara Tuchman writes:

With the cry of 'En avant!', with waving sword, with all the ardour on which the French Army prided itself, officers led their companies to the attack – against an enemy who dug in and used his field-guns. Field grey merging into the fog and shadows had beaten the too-visible pantaloon rouge; steady, solid, methodical training had beaten élan.

Barbara Tuchman, *The Guns of August* (Ballentine, 1962), p.243.

However, while generals could be excused for misunderstanding the nature of this new type of war in 1914, can it be argued that they failed to learn and adapt after 1914 and instead continued with tactics designed to lead to maximum losses of life with no significant gain?

General Haig has come under particular scrutiny. In 1967, L. Woodward wrote:

> *Haig … failed to comprehend that the policy of 'attrition' or in plain English, 'killing Germans' until the German army was worn down and exhausted, was not only wasteful and, intellectually, a confession of impotence; it was extremely dangerous. The Germans might counter Haig's plan by allowing him to wear down his own army in a series of unsuccessful attacks against a skilful defense. Fortunately the enemy generals were of much the same 'textbook' type as Haig …*

L. Woodward, *Great Britain and the War 1914–18* (Methuen, 1967), p.141.

Cartoon of Douglas Haig, 1919.

This critical view of Haig was also put forward by Alan Clark in 1961 in a book called *The Donkeys*, and more recently by John Laffin, whose book *Butchers and Bunglers* presents the view that Haig was 'criminally negligent'.

Critics of Haig put forward the following criticisms:

- that he was not concerned enough with the degree of casualties and human suffering that was taking place
- he was a poor communicator and did not delegate effectively
- he stayed back from the front line and was out of touch with what was going on in his relatively luxurious HQ
- he did not adapt quickly enough to the new methods of warfare and did not change tactics to use the new technology efficiently enough – continuing with the slaughter and tactics of attrition.

These accusations regarding Haig have also been applied to the other British generals.

However, it is generally accepted now that many of these accusations are unfounded. The majority of British generals, for example, did visit the front lines every day; in fact during the war more than 200 were killed, wounded, or captured. They were also dealing with an unprecedented situation in which it would have been difficult for anyone to act effectively:

> *… holding commands of a size far beyond their experience, with inadequate communications and in a war whose nature took both sides by surprise …*

M. Howard, Review of *The Donkeys* in *The Listener*, 3 August 1961.

John Keegan also stresses the difficulties that the generals faced at this stage due to the development of war technology:

> *While battle-altering resources – reliable armoured, cross-country vehicles, portable two-way radio – lay beyond their grasp … the generals were trapped within the iron fetters of a technology all too adequate for mass destruction of life but quite inadequate to restore to them the flexibilities of control that would have kept destruction of life within bearable limits.*

John Keegan, *The First World War* (Random House, 1999), p.342.

Given this new situation, the generals, including Haig, adapted amazingly well to the new situation. By 1918 the British army was a highly effective fighting force and the final campaign shows that Haig was prepared to adopt all the latest technology and tactics to secure victory.

> *He presided over an army that emerged as a technologically advanced and enormously effective force that won the greatest series of victories in British military history, against a background of changes in warfare so great they amounted to a revolution in military affairs.*
>
> **Gary Sheffield and John Bourne, 'Dropping the Donkey Epithet', BBC *History* magazine, March 2005, p.16**

What were the reasons for Germany's defeat in World War One?

Looking back over this chapter, we can see several reasons for Germany's eventual defeat. These can be grouped into Germany's weaknesses and mistakes and the Allies' successes and strengths.

Germany's weaknesses/failures

Germany made several ambitious gambles that didn't pay off. It gambled on a quick victory with the Schlieffen Plan. Once that gamble had failed, there was no hope of a rapid conclusion to the war. The plan, with its march through Belgium, also resulted in Britain entering the war. The war that resulted, on two fronts, was the one that Germany had always dreaded and tried to avoid. Another gamble – that of Verdun, with its emphasis on wearing down the strength of France and Britain – also failed. The German high-risk strategy of unrestricted U-boat warfare not only failed, but also helped to bring the USA into the war, which was vital to boosting Allied resources in 1918. By August 1918, US troops were arriving at a rate of 300,000 a month.

Germany also suffered due to weak allies. As you have read, Germany constantly had to help out the Austrians. With the defeat of Bulgaria and then the Serbs in September 1918, followed by the defeat of Austria by Italy and then the surrender of Turkey in October, it was only a matter of time before Germany had to surrender.

The failure of the Ludendorff Offensive was critical to overall German defeat. As historian Alexander Watson writes:

> *Their [Ludendorff's and Hindenburg's] desperate desire for peace derived not from any domestic considerations nor even the weakness of Germany's allies; it was due principally to the parlous state of their army. The war had been above all a contest of endurance and, during the course of 1918, the accumulated strain and the hopelessness of its situation had broken the army's will to continue fighting'*
>
> **Alexander Watson, 'Stabbed at the Front', *History Today*, 2008, p.22.**

The Germans were ultimately unable to sustain their losses after the failure of the 1918 offensive. An epidemic of Spanish flu in 1918 made the situation much worse, and morale was very low in the German army. When Ludendorff asked for an armistice in October 1918, he said it was because:

> *No reliance can be put on the troops any longer. Since August 8, it has gone rapidly down hill. Continually units have proved themselves so unreliable that they have hurriedly had to be withdrawn from the front ... the High Command and the German Army are finished.*

On top of military factors, the dire economic situation in Germany by 1918 played an important role in Germany's defeat. Supplies were not reaching the German army and the German population was ready for revolution. This crisis was due partly to the Allied blockade, which prevented imports reaching Germany, and also because the German government proved less efficient at organizing the country for war than the Allied countries. Germany spent 83 per cent of total public expenditure on military items, but just 2 per cent on the civilian sector. The figures in Britain were 62 per cent and 16 per cent respectively. Over the course of the conflict, there was a shift in resources away from the production of civilian goods in Germany. German agriculture was particularly hard hit by the war; production fell by 70 per cent in some areas. The economic situation, combined with the continual failures of the troops, meant that Germany was in a state of internal collapse by the end of 1918.

Even Russia's withdrawal from the war and the harsh terms of the Treaty of Brest-Litovsk did not help Germany. The lengthy deliberations over the treaty seriously disrupted planning for the German spring offensive that was to begin on 21 March 1918. The 1 million men who were needed in the west were still in the east to enforce the treaty and to occupy Ukraine. The chaos in Russia and the impact of the civil war on agriculture also meant that Germany was unable to get badly needed resources from Russia to help deal with shortages at home.

Allied strengths/successes

Ultimately, the Allies had greater numbers of men and resources, and so the longer the war went on the harder it was for the Germans to win. Germany could have beaten France on a one-to-one basis, just as Russia could have beaten Austria-Hungary, but all countries working together and helping each other out meant that the war would become one of **attrition**. This situation, in the long term, benefited the Allies (particularly once the USA had joined the war).

Maintaining control of the sea was decisive for the Allies. The blockade on Germany helped to cause dreadful food shortages, while Britain was still able to import food supplies both from its colonies and from the USA with the help of the convoy system. The British and French were also particularly successful in mobilizing their economies.

In the Allied counter-offensive of 1918, the Allies benefited from a greater coordination of effort and what Beckett calls a 'distinctly "modern" style of warfare' that took advantage of all the technological and tactical developments that had taken place during the war: the use of tanks, artillery, aircraft, and infantry in relatively close cooperation. The contribution of the USA to Allied victory in 1918 was also critical. US troops started arriving in France in June 1918. The 2 million soldiers eventually deployed brought a huge advantage to the Allied side in that they lacked the 'war weariness' of European soldiers already on the Western Front. America's massive economic resources were another key factor in the push for Allied victory. The USA made a substantial difference to the Allied fight, contributing money, weaponry, and warships. Altogether America lent more than $7.7 billion to the Allies during the war. As Akira Iriye puts it in *The Globalising of America 1913–1945* (Cambridge University Press, 1993), 'American participation spelled the defeat of German ambitions' (page 43).

TOK

Before you go on to read about World War One and total mobilization, it is important to consider whether or not there can be effective 'rules' when fighting a war. There had been attempts to limit warfare, and to draw up some rules of engagement, prior to the Great War, at The Hague in 1898 (see chapter 1).

- What rules of engagement *should* there be in war? Should chemical and biological warfare be forbidden? Should civilian targets be outlawed?
- What rules of engagement *have* to be tolerated in warfare?
- How far do ethics matter in wars? Are morality and warfare mutually exclusive ideas?

Discuss these ideas as a class.

World War One as a war of total mobilization

To what extent did World War One see the full mobilization of military, human, and economic resources?

World War One is considered to be the first total war for several reasons:

- Both sides fought the war not for limited aims but for total victory.

- Governments used all weaponry that they had at their disposal in order to win the war. They also developed new technologies and weaponry as the war progressed.
- It involved all people of the major countries – not only soldiers, but also civilians. Civilians were deliberately targeted during the military conflict and they suffered from the economic warfare carried out by both sides. Women also played a major role in the war effort at home.
- In order to fight the kind of battles waged in World War One, and to weld the state into a united, efficient war-making machine, nations developed new ways of controlling the economy and their own populations. In the process of trying to do this, the countries of Europe experienced major changes in government as well as in established social and economic practices.

These points are discussed in more detail below.

World War One as a war of total mobilization.

Activity 11

ATL Self-management skills

Review activity

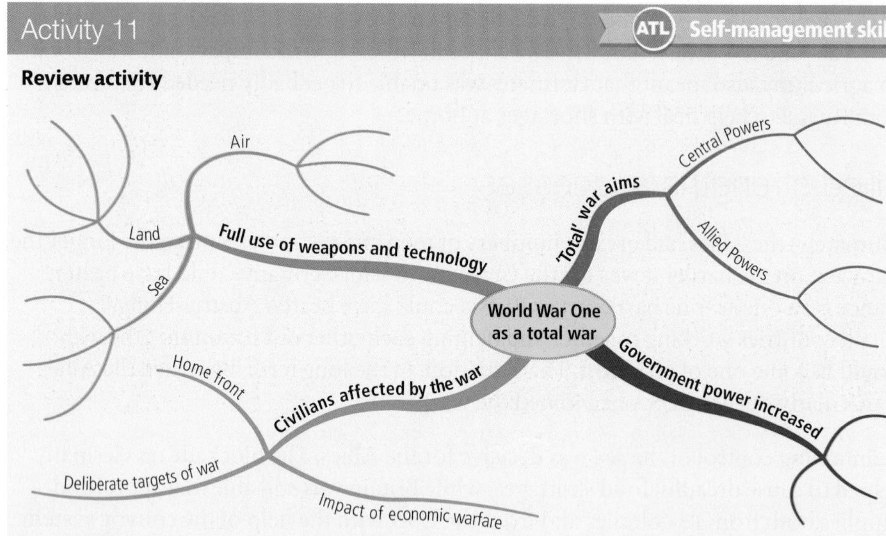

This mind map highlights the key elements of World War One as a war of total mobilization.

1. Copy it out. As you read through the evidence below, add details to your diagram to make it a useful revision tool on World War One as a total war. Also, add links between the different sections where you see an overlap.

The aims of the belligerents

The *aims* of the powers involved in the fighting were 'total' and made any negotiated peace very difficult to achieve. Germany's aims in the September Memorandum have already been discussed on page 47. However, all the Great Powers developed ambitious war aims that they were reluctant to give up. France was determined to regain Alsace-Lorraine and both France and Britain had committed themselves to crushing 'Prussian militarism'. **Propaganda** on both sides reinforced nationalist sentiment, justifying the war and demonizing the enemy. Governments would have had to do a serious turn around in terms of public opinion if they were to seek a compromise.

In 1917, there were several calls for peace, coming from such divergent sources as the Pope, Lenin (the new Bolshevik leader of Russia), and Lord Lansdowne, a British **Conservative**, former viceroy of India, and foreign secretary. Pope Benedict XV called for a return to the territorial status quo of 1914 and a renunciation of all financial demands. Lenin also called for a peace without annexations or financial demands. Lord Lansdowne made the point that the war was costing more in terms of human and economic resources than could ever be regained, even by victory. Yet both sides continued to believe that they *could* win and both sides believed that only total victory could justify the sacrifices that had been made in this war.

Activity 12

ATL Thinking skills

Source analysis

UKRAINE
A GERMAN "PEACE."
(FOR THE INSTRUCTION OF OUR PACIFISTS.)

'A German "peace"'; cartoon from *Punch* magazine, 12 June 1918.

1. What is the message of this British cartoon?

The use of weaponry

As you have read, both sides used the full arsenal of weapons at their disposal and also developed new technologies for land, sea, and air warfare to try to break the deadlock and achieve total victory. This pursuit involved, in the case of gas, breaking international agreements; the Hague Convention of 1899 had prohibited the use of poisons as weapons.

The role of civilians

> *Among the many illusions destroyed in 1914 was the assumption that in the events of European war, a clear distinction between soldiers and civilians could be maintained.*
>
> **James Sheehan, *The Monopoly of Violence* (Faber & Faber, 2008), p. 84.**

The impact of the fighting on civilians

As you have read earlier in this chapter (see p. 47 on Belgium), civilians were affected from the start of the war. This was partly due to the new technologies available to both sides, which allowed civilians to become targets. Paris was shelled from a distance of 126 kilometres by the massive German gun known as 'Long Max', while first the Zeppelins, and later planes, made raids on Britain. British planes also inflicted severe damage on German factories and towns in the last year of the war.

On the Eastern Front, civilians were actually caught up in the battles. Because there was relatively little movement on the Western Front, civilians, after the initial battles, were able to keep away from the actual fighting and casualties only resulted from inaccurate artillery fire. By contrast, the great advances and retreats that took place on the Eastern Front meant that civilians were very much caught up in the violence.

However, it was not just new technology that led to civilian casualties. As Sheehan writes, 'As millions of men, most of them without combat experience moved into enemy territory, the potential for error, over reaction, and panic was great' (p. 86). You have already read about what happened in Belgium, but deliberate attacks on civilians took place elsewhere, particularly on the Eastern Front. In Serbia, thousands of civilians were slaughtered by Austro-Hungarian troops, while Jews – viewed with suspicion by the Russian military – were actively attacked by advancing Russians. Other minorities also suffered: Germans, Roma, Hungarians, and Turks were all deported from Russia's western provinces during the war. Ethnic violence also took place in the Balkans. As Niall Ferguson writes in *The War of the World*:

> *There [the Eastern Front] the death throes of the old Central and East European empires had dissolved the old boundaries between combatant and civilian. This kind of war proved much easier to start than to stop.*
>
> **From Niall Ferguson, *The War of the World* (Penguin, 2006), p.140.**

The lives of civilians in all countries were also affected by the huge losses of soldiers; all families and villages across Europe faced the consequences of the 'lost generation'. The enormous casualties in the early campaigns also led to the introduction of military conscription, in 1915 for France and 1916 for Britain.

Genocide

World War One also witnessed the century's first **genocide**. Turkish propaganda at the time presented the Armenians as saboteurs and a pro-Russian '**fifth column**'. Hundreds of thousands of Armenians died from starvation and thirst when the Ottoman Turks deported them en masse from eastern Anatolia to the Syrian desert, and elsewhere, in 1915–1916.

There is disagreement over the number of Armenians killed. Armenians say 1.5 million, while the republic of Turkey estimates the total to be 300,000. According to the International Association of Genocide scholars, the total was 'more than a million'.

The impact of economic warfare on civilians

Both sides realized the advantages of cutting off supplies to their enemies. They tried to disrupt each other's trade routes, and prevent vital foods and raw materials getting through, by laying minefields at sea or attacking merchant ships with submarines or warships. The British blockade had a devastating effect on Germany, causing desperate food shortages and contributing to Germany's defeat in 1918. The average daily calorie input for a civilian adult dropped from around 1,500 in 1915 to below 1,000 in the winter of 1916–1917. Germany's use of submarine warfare also subjected British civilians to shortages, and Russia suffered as a result of the blockade of the Dardanelles. Rationing was introduced in many countries.

CHALLENGE YOURSELF

ATL Research skills

Artists in World War One

Käthe Kollwitz is one of the many artists who recorded different aspects of the war in their artwork. She was German, and she became an ardent **socialist** and **pacifist** after the war, following the loss of her son in the conflict. In her artwork, she portrayed stark images of the suffering caused by conflict.

Research the lives and work of artists from both sides of the conflict. Find artwork that reveals different aspects of the war.

'The Children are Starving' by Käthe Kollwitz.

Women as part of the war effort

The war saw the rapid growth of industry in all countries as governments tried to keep up with the production demands of total war. In Britain, France and Germany, these demands also meant women joining the workforce as more and more men left to fight in the war. However, in all countries there was resistance to employing women, and it was not until 1915 that serious recruitment of women into industries began. Even then, there was little enthusiasm from employers and trade unions for women entering the workforce, and in Britain there had to be negotiations to reach agreements on women entering 'men's jobs' – in munitions and engineering, for example – that such arrangements were only to be temporary and that the women would not be trained up as 'fully skilled tradesmen'. Women were supposed to receive equal wages to men for doing similar jobs, but rarely did; their wages remained low, though higher than pay for traditional women's work. This situation was despite the fact that the work in munitions in particular was extremely dangerous, with risks of TNT (an explosive) poisoning and accidental explosions. By 1917, one in four war workers was female, leading French General Joseph Joffre to claim that 'if the women in the war factories stopped for 20 minutes, we should lose the war'. Indeed, women were able to prove, as Kate Adie writes, that

Women working in a munitions factory.

> *they could weld, deliver the post, saw off a leg, drive a tram, entertain troops to the sound of shellfire, read the lesson in church and play decent football in front of twenty thousand people – all previously thought utterly, completely and absolutely beyond the a woman …*
>
> **Kate Adie, *Fighting on the Home Front* (Hodder, 2013) p.1.**

CHALLENGE YOURSELF

Research skills 

Research further the work that women did in World War One. How did their work differ from country to country?

The growth of government power

Other changes on the home fronts came with increased centralization of power in the hands of the governments of Britain, France, and Germany. Citizens found themselves being subjected to much greater control from their governments as countries tried to ensure that maximum use was made of human and economic resources. In Britain, the government passed the Defence of the Realm Act (DORA) in 1914, which gave the government wide-ranging powers to police many aspects of people's daily lives, such as restricting the hours of pub opening, preventing the use of binoculars, and limiting the lighting of bonfires. In France, a 'state of siege' was proclaimed by President Raymond Poincaré, who placed eight departments of government under the control of the commander-in-chief, Joffre, and subject to military law. This number was later increased to 33 departments. In Germany, executive power was given to the deputy commanding generals of Germany's 24 military districts. The Tsar in Russia, meanwhile, used the pro-war atmosphere in 1914 as an opportunity to reassert **autocratic** powers and rule without the Duma (Russian parliament).

Government control was exercised in several key areas.

Controlling human resources

To control human resources more effectively, conscription was introduced in most countries. In the UK it was introduced in 1916. This decision was taken not just because of the need for more men, but also because British industry could not afford to lose its skilled workers. So many miners had joined up, for example, that a large number had to be sent back in order to maintain the essential supplies of coal. The controlled direction of human resources was necessary to ensure that both industry and the armed forces were provided for; it has been estimated that it took three civilian workers to keep a soldier fighting in World War One. The government also took the lead in negotiating – with the trade unions – the way for women to work in the munitions factories.

Controlling production

To increase the efficiency of production, governments started to exercise more control over industry. In the UK, this involved nationalizing key industries such as coal mining and shipping, and also regulating wages and prices to ensure that inflation did not get out of hand. In Germany, industrialist Walter Rathenau also tried to bring industry under the control of the War Boards to oversee production, but he was never as successful at achieving this as the British government, and faced frustrating interference from the German military.

In Britain, involvement in the workplace by the government extended to intervention in areas such as provision of canteens and childcare, and the setting up of various committees, such as the Health of Munitions Workers Committee.

> *By 1918, the Ministry of Munitions owned more than 250 factories, administering a further 20,000 and the government employed 5 million workers. A huge experiment in 'state capitalism' was under way, and the significance of this was not lost on workers, employers, unions and Labour politicians. The change in attitude is aptly illustrated by Lloyd George's famous promise of 'habitations for the heroes who have won the war' the day after the armistice, and the subsequent establishment of the Ministry of Health.*
>
> **Ian Cawood and David McKinnon-Bell, *The First World War* (Routledge, 2001), p.66.**

Controlling morale

In order to motivate the home fronts and keep up morale, governments also spent a great deal of time and energy on wartime propaganda. At first, propaganda was used to emphasize the defensive nature of the war; each side produced propaganda to show that it was simply defending its soil and national pride. Later, propaganda became more important to justify the length of the war and to counter opposition to its continuation. Propaganda portrayed the enemy as an inhuman force that must be defeated at all costs. The British government also created a Ministry of Information, making propaganda a key element of its war policy.

Controlling the economy

In order to pay for the war, Britain increased direct taxation. It also abandoned its 19th-century policy of **free trade** by adopting tariffs on certain types of imported goods. All countries borrowed immense sums to pay for the war. The Russians, French, and Italians borrowed heavily from the British and the Americans; the British also borrowed massive amounts from the USA. The governments of all combatants borrowed from their own people through 'war loans', which would be paid with interest after the war.

In Russia, borrowing led to rapid inflation as the amount of money in circulation increased. This contributed to the disastrous economic situation in Russia leading to revolution in 1917. In Germany, money for the war was raised almost entirely through loans and government **savings bonds**, which the government intended to repay when victory came. Only 6 per cent was raised by taxation as against 20 per cent in Britain. Germany planned to pay for the war through the imposition of severe treaties on its vanquished enemies and did not plan for defeat. When defeat came, however, Germany was bankrupt and thousands of Germans lost their savings.

Activity 13

Essay planning

Examine the role of technological developments in determining the outcome of one 20th-century war.

Introduction: Explain which case study you will use, in this case World War One, and put the question into context here. Explain that the war lasted for 4 years and that it only ended when the Germans asked for an armistice in 1918. You need to identify the key points that you will be covering in your essay. New technologies played a role – but what other factors are you going to consider? Also set out your main argument; do you agree that new technologies allowed the Allies to win, or was it other factors?

Part One: Start with the factor that is given in the title: that is new technologies. Describe the new technologies that were having an impact on the Western Front – tanks, aircraft, creeping barrage. These were crucial to the final Allied attacks. Explain how they were effectively being used by 1918.

Part Two: You need to give an alternative argument or 'balance' to your essay. There are several other factors that you could consider which explain the outcome of the war:

- the failure of the Ludendorff Offensive
- the impact of the naval blockade on Germany and the resulting economic and political situation within Germany
- the entry of the US into the war
- the fact that Britain could import food from other countries and so was not facing the same economic situation as Germany.

Conclusion: State your overall argument based on what you have discussed in the main body of your essay.

Now try planning these essays.

- ***To what extent did one 20th-century war see the full mobilization of human and economic resources?***
- ***Discuss the relative importance of war on the land and at sea in determining the outcome of one 20th-century war.***

Constructing good paragraphs in your essay

As indicated by the essay planning guideline on page 42, each of your paragraphs should follow a certain structure. Make sure that you have a clear opening 'signpost' sentence that links to the question and sets out the point that the paragraph will be making. Include precise evidence to support your point and have a final sentence that links back to the question and restates the relevance of the paragraph.

To access websites relevant to this chapter, go to www.pearsonhotlinks.com, search for the book title or ISBN, and click on 'chapter 3'.

04

Cross-regional war: World War One – Effects

Ruins of St. Martin's Church and Cloth Hall in Ypres on the Western Front.

Key concepts: Change and continuity

As you read this chapter, consider the following essay questions:

- Examine the reasons for the failure of one peace treaty in the 20th century.
- Discuss the economic and social consequences of one 20th-century war.

When the delegates of the 'victorious' powers met at Versailles near Paris in 1919 to attempt to create a peace settlement, they faced a Europe that was very different from that of 1914, and one that was in a state of turmoil and chaos. The old empires of Germany, Russia, and Austria-Hungary had disappeared, and various successor states were struggling to replace them. A Communist revolution had taken place in Russia and there appeared to be a real threat of revolution spreading across Europe. In addition, there had been terrible destruction, and the population of Europe now faced the problems of starvation, displacement, and a lethal flu epidemic.

Against this difficult background, the leaders of France, Britain, the USA, and Italy attempted to create a peace settlement. The fact that the settlement was to break down within 20 years has led many historians to view it as a disaster that contributed to the outbreak of World War Two. More recently, however, historians have argued that the peacemakers did not fully comprehend the scale of the problems in 1919, therefore it is not surprising that they failed to create a lasting peace.

The impact of the war on Europe – the situation in 1919

The human cost of the war

The Tyne Cot cemetery at Passchendaele in Belgium.

How did different countries attempt to come to terms with the loss of so many lives? Research the discussions that took place in one country regarding how to remember the dead, the nature of war memorials, and the setting up of the Commonwealth War Graves Commission.

The death toll for the armed forces in World War One was appalling. Around 9 million soldiers were killed, which was about 15 per cent of all combatants. In addition, millions more were permanently disabled by the war; of British war veterans, for example, 41,000 lost a limb in the fighting. In Britain, it became common to talk of a 'lost generation'. This was also a particularly appropriate phrase for the situation in France, where 20 per cent of those between the ages of 20 and 40 in 1914 were killed.

The Spanish flu

Spanish flu was a flu pandemic that hit the world in 1918, causing millions of deaths. It first appeared in the United States, but spread to nearly every part of the world. It is estimated that anywhere from 20 to 100 million people died worldwide, at least more than double the number killed in World War One. It was called the Spanish flu primarily because the pandemic received such great press attention when it moved from France to Spain in November 1918. Spain was not involved in the war and had not imposed wartime censorship.

Although civilians were not killed on the scale that they would be in World War Two, populations had nevertheless become targets of war. In addition to the civilians killed directly in the war, millions more died from famine and disease in the aftermath, and at least a further 20 million died worldwide in the Spanish flu **pandemic** in the winter of 1918–1919.

Economic consequences

The economic impact of the war on Europe was devastating. The war cost Britain alone more than £34 billion. All powers had financed the war by borrowing money. By 1918, the USA had lent $2,000 million to Britain and France; U-boats had also sunk 40 per cent of British merchant shipping. Throughout the 1920s, Britain and France spent between a third and a half of their total public expenditure on debt charges and repayments. Britain never regained its pre-war international financial predominance, and lost several overseas markets.

The physical effects of the war also had an impact on the economic situation of Europe. Wherever fighting had taken place, land and industry had been destroyed. France suffered particularly badly, with farm land (2 million hectares), factories, and railway lines along the Western Front totally ruined. Belgium, Poland, Italy, and Serbia were also badly affected. Roads and railway lines needed to be reconstructed, hospitals and houses had to be rebuilt, and **arable** land made productive again by the removal of unexploded shells. Consequently, there was a dramatic decline in manufacturing output. Combined with the loss of trade and foreign investments, it is clear that Europe faced an acute economic crisis in 1919.

Political consequences

The victorious governments of Britain and France did not suffer any major political changes as a result of the war. However, there were huge changes in Central Europe, where the map was completely redrawn. Before 1914, Central Europe had been dominated by multinational, monarchical regimes. By the end of the war, these regimes had all collapsed. As Niall Ferguson writes, 'the war led to a triumph of republicanism undreamt of even in the 1790s' (*The Pity of War* [Penguin, 2006], p.435).

Germany

Even before the war ended on 11 November 1918, revolution had broken out in Germany against the old regime. Sailors in northern Germany mutinied and took over the town of Kiel. This action triggered further revolts, with socialists leading uprisings of workers and soldiers in other German ports and cities. In Bavaria, an independent socialist republic was declared. On 9 November 1918, the Kaiser abdicated his throne and fled to Holland. The following day, the socialist leader Friedrich Ebert became the new leader of the Republic of Germany.

Russia

As discussed in the previous chapter, Russia experienced two revolutions in 1917. The first overthrew the Tsarist regime and replaced it briefly with a Provisional Government that planned to hold free elections. This government, however, was overthrown in the second revolution of 1917, in which the Communist Bolsheviks seized power and sought to establish a dictatorship. In turn, this, and the peace of Brest-Litovsk that took Russia out of the war, helped to cause a civil war that lasted until the end of 1920.

The Habsburg Empire

With the defeat of Austria-Hungary, the Habsburg Empire disintegrated and the monarchy collapsed. The last emperor, Karl I, was forced to abdicate in November 1918 and a republic was declared. Austria and Hungary split into two separate states and the various other nationalities in the empire declared themselves independent.

Turkey

The collapse of the sultanate finally came in 1922, and it was replaced by the rule of Mustapha Kemal, who established an authoritarian regime.

The collapse of these empires left a huge area of Central and Eastern Europe in turmoil. In addition, the success of the Bolsheviks in Russia encouraged growth of socialist politics in post-war Europe. Many of the ruling classes were afraid that revolution would spread across the continent, particularly given the weak economic state of its countries.

Impact of the war outside of Europe – the situation in 1919

America

In stark comparison to the economic situation in Europe, the USA emerged from the war as the world's leading economy. Throughout the war, American industry and trade had prospered, as US food, raw materials, and munitions were sent to Europe to help with the war effort. In addition, the USA had taken over European overseas markets during the war, and many American industries had become more successful than their European competitors. The USA had, for example, replaced Germany as the world's leading producer of fertilizers, dyes, and chemical products. The war also led to US advances in technology – the USA was now world leader in areas such as mechanization and the development of plastics.

President Woodrow Wilson hoped that America would now play a larger role in international affairs and worked hard at the Versailles Peace Conference to create an alternative world order in which international problems would be solved through collective security (see chapter 5). However, the majority of Americans had never wanted to be involved in World War One, and once it ended they were keen to return to concerns nearer to home: the Spanish flu epidemic, the fear of Communism (exacerbated by a series of industrial strikes), and racial tension, which exploded into riots in 25 cities across the USA. There was also a concern that America might be dragged into other European disputes.

Japan and China

Japan also did well economically out of the war. As in the case of America, new markets and new demands for Japanese goods brought economic growth and prosperity, with exports nearly tripling during the war years. World War One also presented Japan with opportunities for territorial expansion; under the guise of the Anglo-Japanese alliance, it was able to seize German holdings in Shandong province and German-held islands in the Pacific, and to present the Chinese with a list of 21 demands that aimed for political and economic domination of China. At the end of the war, Japan hoped to be able to hold on to these gains.

China, which had finally entered the war on the Allied side in 1917, was also entitled to send delegates to the Versailles Peace Conference. Their hopes were entirely opposed to those of the Japanese: they wanted to resume political and economic control over Shandong and to be released from the Japanese demands.

Problems facing the peacemakers in 1919

The Versailles Peace Conference was dominated by the political leaders of three of the five victorious powers: David Lloyd George (prime minister of the UK), Georges Clemenceau (prime minister of France), and Woodrow Wilson (president of the USA). Japan was only interested in what was decided about the Pacific and played little part. Vittorio Orlando, prime minister of Italy, played only a minor role in discussions, and in fact walked out of the conference when he failed to get the territorial gains that Italy had hoped for.

The first problem faced by the peacemakers at Versailles was the political and social instability in Europe, which called for them to act speedily to reach a peace settlement. One Allied observer noted that 'there was a veritable race between peace and anarchy'. Other political issues, however, combined to make a satisfactory treaty difficult to achieve:

- the different aims of the peacemakers
- the nature of the Armistice settlement and the mood of the German population
- the popular sentiment in the Allied countries.

The aims of the peacemakers

In a speech to Congress on 8 January 1918, Woodrow Wilson stated US war aims in his Fourteen Points, which can be summarized as follows:

1. Abolition of secret diplomacy
2. Free navigation at sea for all nations in war and peace
3. Free trade between countries
4. **Disarmament** by all countries
5. Colonies to have a say in their own future
6. German troops to leave Russia
7. Restoration of independence for Belgium
8. France to regain Alsace and Lorraine
9. Frontier between Austria and Italy to be adjusted along the lines of nationality
10. **Self-determination** for the peoples of Austria-Hungary
11. Serbia to have access to the sea
12. Self-determination for the people in the Turkish Empire and permanent opening of the Dardanelles
13. Poland to become an independent state with access to the sea
14. A **League of Nations** to be set up in order to preserve the peace.

The 'Big Three': Georges Clemenceau (prime minister of France), David Lloyd George (prime minister of the UK), and Woodrow Wilson (president of the USA).

Activity 1

Discuss the following questions in pairs:

1. Look at Wilson's points. What would you consider to be his overall aims for the post-war world?
2. Which of these points would you consider as:
   - easily achievable
   - difficult to achieve in Europe
3. Are there issues not covered by Wilson's Fourteen Points that other countries might want to see addressed? Give reasons for your decisions.

As you can see from his points above, Wilson was an **idealist** whose aim was to build a better and more peaceful world. Although he believed that Germany should be punished, he hoped that these points would allow for a new political and international world order. Self-determination – giving the different ethnic groups within the old empires of Europe the chance to set up their own countries – would, in Wilson's mind, end the frustrations that had contributed to the outbreak of World War One. In addition, open diplomacy, world disarmament, economic integration, and a League of Nations would stop secret alliances, and force countries to work together to prevent a tragedy such as World War One happening again.

Wilson also believed that the USA should take the lead in this new world order. In 1916, he had proclaimed that the object of the war should be 'to make the world safe for democracy' – unlike the ostensibly more selfish aims of the Allied powers, the USA would take the lead in promoting the ideas of democracy and self-determination.

Wilson's idealist views were not shared by Clemenceau and Lloyd George. Clemenceau (who commented that even God had only needed ten points) wanted a harsh settlement to ensure that Germany could not threaten France again. The way to achieve this would be to combine heavy economic and territorial **sanctions** with disarmament policies. **Reparations** for France were necessary not only to pay for the terrible losses inflicted upon their country, but also to keep Germany weak. Clemenceau was also keen to retain wartime links with Britain and America, and was ready to make concessions in order to achieve this aim.

Lloyd George was in favour of a less severe settlement. He wanted Germany to lose its navy and colonies so that it could not threaten the British Empire. Yet he also wanted Germany to be able to recover quickly, so that it could start trading again with Britain and be a bulwark against the spread of Communism from the new Bolshevik Russia. He was also aware that 'injustice and arrogance displayed in the hour of triumph will never be forgotten or forgiven'. He was under pressure from public opinion at home, however, to make Germany accountable for the death and suffering that had taken place.

The aims of Japan and Italy were to maximize their wartime gains. The Italian prime minister, Vittorio Orlando, wanted the Allies to keep the promises they made in the Treaty of London and also demanded the port of Fiume in the Adriatic. Japan, which had already seized the German islands in the Pacific, wanted recognition of these gains. Japan also wanted the inclusion of a racial equality clause in the Covenant of the League of Nations in the hope that this would protect Japanese immigrants in America.

The Covenant of the League of Nations

The first 26 articles of the Treaty of Versailles, and of the other treaties concluded with Germany's allies, formed the Covenant of the League of Nations. The League of Nations was an organization with the broad aim of keeping international peace and preventing a war happening again. Germany, however, along with Russia, was not allowed to join.

The racial equality clause

Japan had wanted a racial equality clause to be included within the Covenant of the League of Nations, to gain recognition that all races should be treated equally. This was because the Japanese faced discrimination in the West, particularly in America, as many Japanese had emigrated there. The clause was opposed by Australia because Prime Minister William Hughes feared it might prevent him from being able to limit Japanese immigration into Australia. Japan suggested a compromise in which the word 'racial' was dropped. This modification still did not meet with unanimous support. Wilson insisted that such a point of principle had to have unanimous, rather than majority, support. Thus no such commitment was included in the League's founding document, though Japan still joined the League and was a permanent member of its Council.

Activity 2

1. How might the demands of France, Britain, Italy, and Japan have gone against the spirit of Wilson's Fourteen Points?

The Armistice settlement and the mood of the German population

When the German government sued for an end to fighting, it did so in the belief that the Armistice would be based on Wilson's Fourteen Points. These offered an alternative to having to face the 'total' defeat that the nature of this war had indicated would happen. In reality, the Armistice terms were very tough, and were designed not only to remove Germany's ability to continue fighting, but also to serve as the basis for a more permanent weakening of Germany. The terms of the Armistice ordered Germany to evacuate all occupied territory, including Alsace-Lorraine, and to withdraw beyond a 10-kilometre-wide neutral zone to the east of the Rhine. Allied troops would occupy the west bank of the Rhine. The Germans also lost all their submarines and much of their surface fleet and air force.

When German soldiers returned home after the new government had signed the Armistice, they were initially greeted as heroes. The German population was not fully aware of the reality, and Germany's defeat came as a shock. The German army had occupied parts of France and Belgium and had defeated Russia. Ordinary Germans had been told that their army was on the verge of victory. Yet its defeat did not seem to have been caused by any overwhelming Allied military victory, and certainly not by an invasion of Germany.

Several days after the Armistice had been signed, Field Marshal Paul von Hindenburg, the most respected German commander, made the following comment: 'In spite of the superiority of the enemy in men and materials, we could have brought the struggle to a favourable conclusion if there had been proper cooperation between the politicians and the army. The German army was stabbed in the back.'

Although the German army was in disarray by November 1918, the idea that Germany had been 'stabbed in the back' soon took hold. The months before the Armistice was signed had seen Germany facing mutinies and strikes, and attempts by some groups to set up a socialist government. Therefore the blame for defeat was put on 'internal' enemies – Jews, socialists, Communists. Hitler would later refer to those who had agreed to an armistice in November 1918 as the 'November Criminals'.

Thus, at the start of the Versailles Peace Conference, the German population believed that they had not been truly defeated; even their leaders still believed that Germany would play a part in the peace conference and that the final treaty, based on Wilson's principles, would not be too harsh. There was, therefore, a huge difference between the expectations of the Germans and the expectations of the Allies, who believed that Germany would accept the terms of the treaty as the defeated nation.

The popular mood in Britain, France, Italy, and the USA

Lloyd George, Clemenceau, and Orlando also faced pressure from the popular mood in their own countries, where the feeling was that revenge had to be taken on the Germans for the trauma of the last four years. Encouraged by the popular press, the people of Britain and France in particular looked to the peacemakers at Versailles to 'hang the Kaiser' and 'squeeze the German lemon until the pips squeak'. The French, having borne the brunt of the fighting, would be satisfied with nothing less than a punitive peace.

The press closely reported all the details of the Versailles conference and helped put pressure on the delegates to create a settlement that would satisfy popular demands. Clemenceau and Lloyd George also knew that their political success depended on keeping their electorates happy, which meant obtaining a harsh settlement. Similarly, Orlando was under pressure from opinion at home to get a settlement that gave Italy the territorial and economic gains it desired, and which would at last make Italy into a great power.

In America, however, the electorate had lost interest in the Versailles settlement and Wilson's aims for Europe. Mid-term elections held on 5 November 1918 saw Americans reject Wilson's appeal to voters to support him in his work in Europe. There were sweeping gains for his Republican opponents, who had been very critical of his foreign policy and his Fourteen Points. When he sailed for Europe in December 1918, Wilson left behind a Republican-dominated **House of Representatives** and **Senate** and a hostile Foreign Relations Committee. He thus could not be sure that any agreements reached at Versailles would be honoured by his own government.

Activity 3

Communication and social skills

Group activity

Before you read what the peacemakers decided at Versailles, consider in more detail the issues they faced. Divide the class into four groups. Groups 1, 2, and 3 should take on the roles of France, Britain, and America. Group 4 is Germany. Groups 1–3 need to look at the issues presented below and decide their standpoint on each one (based on the views of their country as presented on pages 80–81). Each group will then have to make a presentation to the rest of the class based on their decisions.

Germany was not allowed to have any representative at the Versailles conference. In this role-play, however, Group 4 will be given the opportunity to respond to the presentations of the other groups. The German delegation should therefore also consider the bullet points below.

Points that your delegates need to address:

- Look at the map below showing disputed territory around Germany. What decisions will you make concerning each of these areas?
- Germany's armed forces. Will you limit them? If so, how?
- Germany's colonies. Should Germany lose them? If so, why? What should happen to them?

- Should Germany pay **reparations**? What damages, losses, or penalties are these reparations expected to cover?
- Will you make Germany guilty of starting the war? If so, why?
- What other restrictions, if any, would you place on Germany?

At the start of your country's presentation, you need to give a brief speech giving an overview of your country's views regarding the war and any peace settlement, the impact the war has had on your country, and your views on Germany's responsibility.

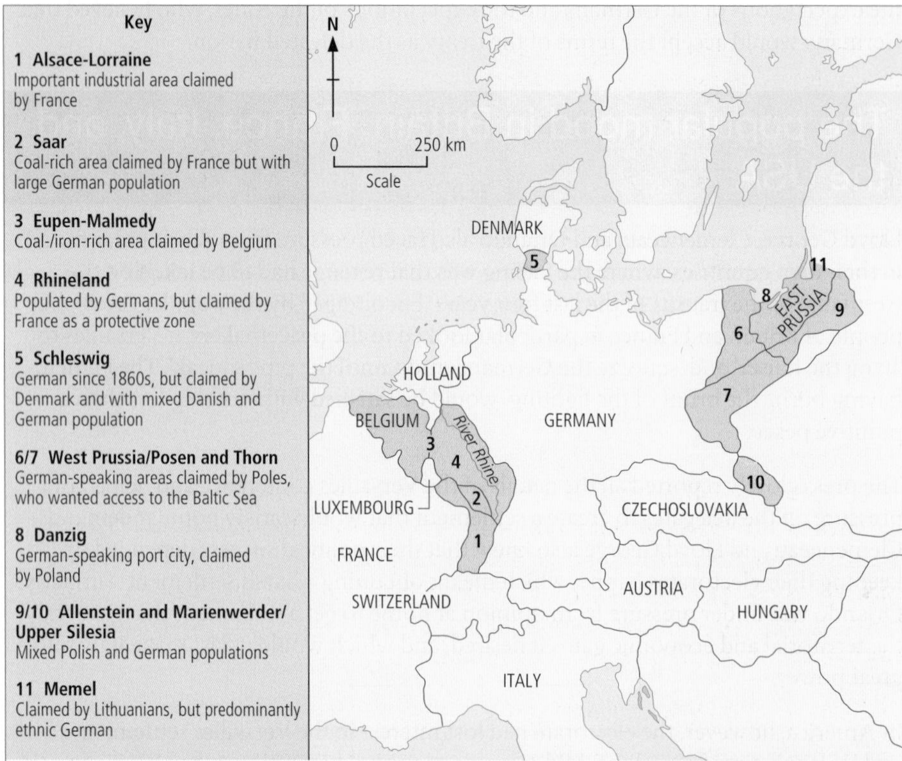

Disputed territories at issue in the Treaty of Versailles.

The terms of the Treaty of Versailles

After six hectic weeks of negotiations, deals, and compromises, the German government was presented with the terms of the peace treaty. None of the powers on the losing side had been allowed any representation during the discussions. For this reason, it became known as the **diktat**. The signing ceremony took place in the Hall of the Mirrors at Versailles, where the Germans had proclaimed the German Empire 50 years earlier following the Franco-Prussian War. The 440 clauses of the peace treaty covered the following areas.

War guilt

The infamous Clause 231, or what later became known as the 'war guilt clause', lay at the heart of the treaty:

> *The Allied and Associated Governments affirm and Germany accepts the responsibility of Germany and her allies for causing all the loss and damage to which the Allied and Associated Governments and their nationals have been subjected as a consequence of the war imposed upon them by the aggression of Germany and her allies.*
>
> **Article 231, Treaty of Versailles, 1919.**

This clause allowed moral justification for the other terms of the treaty that were imposed upon Germany.

Disarmament

It was generally accepted that the pre-1914 arms race in Europe had contributed to the outbreak of war. Thus the treaty addressed disarmament directly. Yet while Germany was obliged to disarm to the lowest point compatible with internal security, there was only a general reference to the idea of full international disarmament. Specifically, Germany was forbidden to have submarines, an air force, armoured cars, or tanks. It was allowed to keep 6 battleships and an army of 100,000 men to provide internal security. (The German navy sank its own fleet at Scapa Flow in Scotland in protest.) In addition, the west bank of the Rhine was **demilitarized** (that is, stripped of German troops), and an Allied army of occupation was to be stationed in the area for 15 years. The French had actually wanted the Rhineland taken away from Germany altogether, but this was not acceptable to Britain and the USA. Finally, a compromise was reached. France agreed that Germany could keep the (demilitarized) Rhineland and in return America and Britain gave a guarantee that if France were ever attacked by Germany in the future, they would immediately come to its assistance.

Territorial changes

Wilson's Fourteen Points proposed respect for the principle of self-determination, and the collapse of large empires gave an opportunity to create states based on the different nationalities. This ambition was to prove very difficult to achieve and, unavoidably, some nationals were left in countries where they constituted minorities, such as Germans who lived in newly formed Czechoslovakia. The situation was made even more complex by the territorial demands of the different powers and of the economic arrangements related to the payment of reparations.

The following points were agreed upon:

- Alsace-Lorraine, which had been seized from France after the Franco-Prussian War in 1871, was returned to France.
- The Saarland was put under the administration of the League of Nations for 15 years, after which a **plebiscite** was to allow the inhabitants to decide whether they wanted to be annexed to Germany or France. In the meantime, the coal extracted there was to go to France.
- Eupen, Moresnet, and Malmedy were to become parts of Belgium after a plebiscite in 1920.
- Germany as a country was split in two. Parts of Upper Silesia, Poznan, and West Prussia formed part of the new Poland, creating a 'Polish Corridor' between Germany and East Prussia and giving Poland access to the sea. The German port of Danzig became a free city under the **mandate** of the League of Nations.
- North Schleswig was given to Denmark after a plebiscite (South Schleswig remained German).
- All territory received by Germany from Russia under the Treaty of Brest-Litovsk was to be returned. Estonia, Latvia, and Lithuania were made independent states in line with the principle of self-determination.
- The port of Memel was to be given to Lithuania in 1922.
- Union (***Anschluss***) between Germany and Austria was forbidden.
- Germany's African colonies were taken away because, the Allies argued, Germany had shown itself unfit to govern subject races. Those in Asia (including Shandong) were given to Japan, Australia, and New Zealand and those in Africa to Britain,

Recreating Poland

Poland had ceased to exist as a country at the end of the 18th century, when it had been partitioned between Russia, Prussia, and Austria. The Polish people, however, had always maintained a strong national identity and Polish independence was proclaimed at the cessation of fighting in 1918 and supported by Point 13 of Wilson's Fourteen Points. The Polish frontiers in the west were fixed by the peacemakers in the Treaty of Versailles. Yet the borders in the east were decided after the Poles fought a victorious battle with the Bolsheviks and forced the Russians back from Warsaw. The resulting Treaty of Riga in 1921 fixed the border in the east on what became known as the Curzon Line.

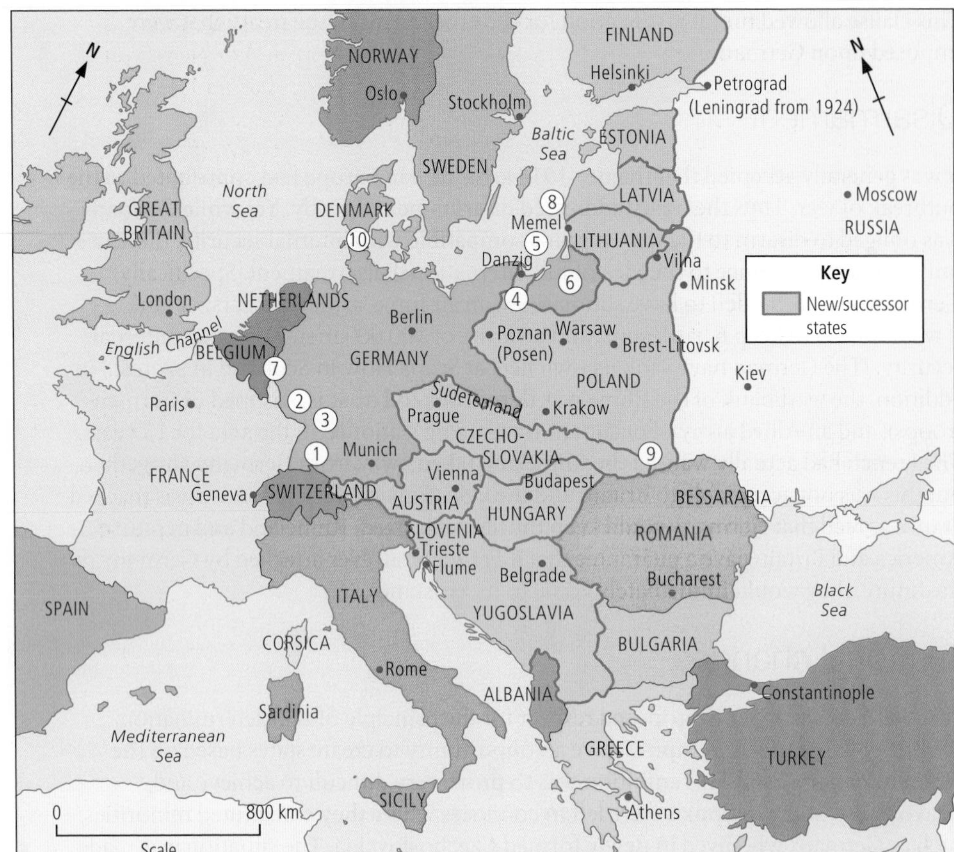

① **Alsace and Lorraine** ▶ *handed back to France*
② **Rhineland** ▶ *demilitarized zone*
③ **Saar** ▶ *under League of Nations for 15 years*
④ **Polish Corridor** ▶ *gave Poland an outlet to the sea*
⑤ **Danzig** ▶ *free city under League of Nations*
⑥ **East Prussia** ▶ *separated from the rest of Germany*
⑦ **Eupen-Malmedy** ▶ *to Belgium*
⑧ **Memel** ▶ *to Lithuania*
⑨ **Upper Silesia** ▶ *to Poland*
⑩ **Northern Schleswig** ▶ *to Denmark*

Territorial changes resulting from the Versailles Treaty.

France, Belgium, and South Africa. All were to become 'mandates', which meant that the new countries came under the supervision of the League of Nations.

Mandates

Germany's colonies were handed over to the League of Nations. Yet Article 22 of the Covenant of the League of Nations reflected a change in attitude towards colonies, requiring all nations to help underdeveloped countries whose peoples were 'not yet able to stand up for themselves'. The mandate system thus meant that nations who were given Germany's colonies had to ensure that they looked after the people in their care; they would also be answerable to the League of Nations for their actions. 'A' mandate countries – including Palestine, Iraq, and Transjordan (given to Britain), and Syria and the Lebanon (given to France) – were to become independent in the near future. Colonies that were considered to be less developed and therefore not ready for immediate independence were 'B' mandates. These included the Cameroons, Togoland, and Tanganyika, and were also given to Britain and France. Belgium also received a 'B' mandate – Ruanda-Urundi. 'C' mandate areas were considered to be in need of the greatest development and were handed over to the powers that had originally conquered them in the war. Thus the North Pacific Islands went to Japan, New Guinea to Australia, South-West Africa to the Union of South Africa, and Western Samoa to New Zealand.

Reparations

Germany's 'war guilt' provided justification for the Allied demands for reparations. The Allies wanted to make Germany pay for the material damage done to them during the war. They also proposed to charge Germany for the future costs of pensions to war widows and war wounded. There was much argument between the delegates at the conference on the whole issue of reparations. Although France has traditionally been blamed for pushing for a high reparations sum, and thus stopping a practical reparations deal, in fact more recent accounts of the negotiations at Versailles blame Britain for making the most extreme demands and preventing a settlement. In the end it was the Inter-Allied Reparations Commission that, in 1921, came up with the reparations sum of £6,600 million.

Punishment of war criminals

The Treaty of Versailles also called for the extradition and trial of the Kaiser and other 'war criminals'. However, the Dutch government refused to hand over the Kaiser, and the Allied leaders found it difficult to identify and find the lesser war criminals. Eventually, a few German military commanders and submarine captains were tried by a German military court at Leipzig and received fines or short terms of imprisonment. These were light sentences, but what is important about the whole process is that the concept of 'crimes against humanity' was given legal sanction for the first time.

Activity 4

1. Consider the positions of the American, British, and French delegations before the Versailles Peace Conference. With which aspects of the treaty would each country be
   a) satisfied
   b) dissatisfied?
2. Which clauses were likely to be most problematic to enforce?
3. Which aspects of the treaty were most likely to
   a) anger Germany
   b) damage Germany?
4. What would be the most likely response of
   a) Japan
   b) China to the treaty?

What was the contemporary response to the Treaty of Versailles?

Read through the sources below and then address the questions in the following activity.

Activity 5

Source analysis

Source A

> *… the future life of Europe was not their concern: its means of livelihood was not their anxiety. Their preoccupations, good and bad alike, related to frontiers and nationalities, to the balance of power, to imperial aggrandisements, to the future enfeeblement of a strong and dangerous enemy, to revenge, and to the shifting by the victors of their unbearable financial burdens onto the shoulders of the defeated.*

From John Maynard Keynes, *The Economic Consequences of the Peace* (Harcourt Brace, 1920), p.56. Keynes was a British economist who worked at the Treasury during World War One and was a chief representative at negotiations prior to the Treaty of Versailles, although he resigned from the British delegation.

Source B

Now that we see [the terms] as a whole, we realise that they are much too stiff. The real crime is the reparations and indemnity chapter, which is immoral and senseless … There is not a single person among the younger people here who is not unhappy and disappointed with the terms. The only people who approve are the old fire-eaters … If I were the Germans, I shouldn't sign it for a moment.

From Harold Nicolson, diary, 1919. Nicolson was a junior member of the British Foreign Office and was attending the Versailles conference.

Source C

The last time I had the opportunity of addressing the House upon this Treaty its main outlines had been settled. I ventured then to call it a 'stern but just Treaty'. I adhere to that description. The terms are in many respects, terrible terms to impose upon a country. Terrible were the deeds that it requites. Terrible were the consequences that were inflicted upon the world. Still more terrible would have been the consequences had they succeeded. What do these terms mean to Germany?

Take the territorial terms. In so far as territories have been taken away from Germany, it is a restoration. Alsace-Lorraine was forcibly taken from the land to which its population were deeply attached. Is it an injustice to restore them to their country? Schleswig-Holstein, the meanest of the Hohenzollern frauds; robbing a small, poor, helpless country, and then retaining that land against the wishes of the population for 50 to 60 years. I am glad the opportunity has come for restoring Schleswig-Holstein. Poland, torn to bits to feed the carnivorous greed of Russian, Austrian and Prussian autocracy. This Treaty has re-knit the torn flag of Poland.

Speech by Lloyd George to the House of Commons, 1919.

Source D

Today in the Hall of Mirrors of Versailles the disgraceful Treaty is being signed. Do not forget it! The German people will with unceasing labour press forward to reconquer the place among nations to which it is entitled. Then will come the vengeance for the same of 1919.

German newspaper, *Deutsche Zeitung*, 1919.

Source E

German cartoon entitled 'Clemenceau the Vampire' from the conservative German newspaper *Kladderadatsch*, July 1919.

1. What are Lloyd George's justifications for the treaty in Source C?
2. What are the main criticisms of the treaty in Sources A and B?
3. Compare and contrast the views expressed about the Treaty of Versailles in Sources A and C.
4. What were Germany's assessments of the treaty (Sources D and E)?
5. With reference to its origin, purpose, and content, assess the value of Source C for historians studying the Treaty of Versailles.

Criticisms of the Treaty of Versailles

As you can see from the sources above, there was already strong criticism of the Treaty of Versailles at the time that it was signed, not just from the Germans but also from among the Allies. These criticisms became stronger in the 1920s, forcefully expressed by contemporary observers like Harold Nicolson and Norman H. Davies, and economist J.M. Keynes. Many historians today also support these criticisms, which are summarized below.

The issue of war guilt

The 'war guilt' clause was particularly hated by the Germans, who felt that all countries should bear responsibility for the outbreak of war in 1914. It was especially harsh to put the whole guilt for the war on the new republic, which was already struggling for survival against the forces of the extreme right. This clause later helped Hitler to gain support, as he was able to play on the resentment and anger felt by the German population towards the war guilt clause, and also towards the fact that it was a *diktat*.

Disarmament clauses

These were hard for the Germans to accept. An army of 100,000 was small for a country of Germany's size. Germany was also very proud of its army. Germany's anger grew when, despite Wilson's call for disarmament in his Fourteen Points, efforts by the other European powers to disarm came to nothing in the 1920s and 1930s.

Reparations and loss of key resources

Keynes (see Source A on page 87) led the criticisms of the treaty in the area of reparations. In *The Economic Consequences of the Peace*, he argued that 'the treaty ignores the economic solidarity of Europe and by aiming at the destruction of the economic life of Germany it threatens the health and prosperity of the Allies themselves'. Not only could Germany not pay the huge reparations bill, but by taking away Germany's coal and iron resources, it also meant that Germany's economy would be unable to recover. Keynes argued that the real problem of the settlement lay not in issues of boundaries 'but rather in questions of food, coal and commerce'. The fact that Germany was to face **hyper-inflation** in the early 1920s seems to provide evidence for his predictions.

Territorial changes to satisfy the issue of self-determination

On this issue, Germany believed that it was treated unfairly. Thus while the Danes were given the chance of a plebiscite in northern Schleswig, the Germans in the Sudetenland and Austria were not given any such choice. Many German-speaking peoples were now ruled by non-Germans. Historian W.H. Dawson claimed in 1933, in his book *Germany under the Treaty*, that Germany's borders 'are literally bleeding. From them oozes out the life-blood, physical, spiritual and material of large populations' (cited in Stephen Lee, *European Dictatorships 1918–1945* [Routledge, 2008], p.13).

Removal of colonies

Wilson's reason for taking away regions like South-West Africa and Ruanda-Urundi from German administration was to remove them from the harsh nature of German rule. Yet this action was clearly hypocritical. States that received German colonies – South Africa and Belgium, for example – could not themselves claim to be model colonial rulers.

The German Problem

The 'German problem' refers to the concern of other European powers regarding the huge potential that Germany had to dominate Europe. Given its geographical position and its economic and military potential, it was in a position to upset the balance of power and threaten other countries.

League of Nations

The failure of the peacemakers to invite Germany to join the League of Nations not only insulted Germany and added to its sense of grievance, but made it less likely that the League could be effective in promoting international cooperation.

Activity 6

1. Read again through the terms of the Treaty of Brest-Litovsk in the information box on page 50. Does this treaty change your views in any way concerning the harshness of the Versailles treaty?

Alternative views of the Treaty of Versailles

Many historians take a different view of the Treaty of Versailles and its impact on the events of Europe after 1920. In fact, it is now argued that the treaty was in fact 'relatively lenient' (Niall Ferguson) and that, given the huge problems facing the peacemakers, it would have been difficult for them to have achieved a more satisfactory settlement. The key arguments of historians such as Sally Marks, Anthony Lentin, Alan Sharp, and Ruth Henig can be summarized as follows.

Compared to the treaties that Germany had imposed on Russia and Romania earlier in 1918, the Treaty of Versailles was quite moderate. Germany's war aims were far reaching and, as shown in the Treaty of Brest-Litovsk, indicate that Germany would have sought huge areas of land from the Allies if it had won. Thus, the Allies can be seen to have exercised considerable restraint. The treaty deprived Germany of about 13.5 per cent of its territory (much of this consisted of Alsace-Lorraine, which was returned to France), about 13 per cent of its economic productivity, and just over 10 per cent of its population. In addition, it can be argued that France deserved to be compensated for the destruction of so much of its land and industry. German land had not been invaded and its farmland and industries therefore remained intact.

The treaty in fact left Germany in a relatively strong position in the centre of Europe. Germany remained a dominant power in a weakened Europe. Not only was it physically undamaged, but it had gained strategic advantages. Russia remained weak and isolated at this time, and Central Europe was fragmented. The peacemakers had created several new states in accordance with the principle of self-determination (see pages 91–92), and this was to create a power vacuum that would favour the expansion of Germany in the future. Anthony Lentin has pointed out the problem here of creating a treaty that failed to weaken Germany, but at the same time left it 'scourged, humiliated and resentful'.

The huge reparations bill was not responsible for the economic crisis that Germany faced in the early 1920s. In fact, the issue of banknotes by the German government was a major factor in causing hyper-inflation. In addition, many economic historians have argued that Germany could have paid the 7.2 per cent of its national income that the reparations schedule required in the years 1925–1929, if it had reformed its financial system or raised its taxation to British levels. However, it chose not to pay the reparations as a way of protesting against the peace settlement.

Thus it can be argued that the treaty was reasonable and not in itself responsible for the chaos of post-war Germany. Why then is the view that the treaty was vindictive and unjust so prevalent, and why is it so often cited as a key factor in the cause of World War Two?

The first issue is that while the treaty was not in itself exceptionally unfair, the Germans thought it was, and they directed all their efforts into persuading others of their case. German propaganda on this issue was very successful, and Britain and France were forced into several revisions of the treaty, while Germany evaded paying reparations or carrying out the disarmament clauses.

The second issue is that the USA and Britain lacked the will to enforce the terms of the treaty. The coalition that put the treaty together at Versailles soon collapsed. The USA refused to ratify the treaty, and Britain, content with colonial gains and with strategic and maritime security from Germany, now wished to distance itself from many of the treaty's territorial provisions. Liberal opinion in the USA and Britain was influenced not only by German propaganda, but also by Keynes's arguments for allowing Germany to recover economically.

France was the only country that still feared for its security and that wanted to enforce Versailles in full. This fact explains why France invaded the Ruhr in 1923 in order to secure reparation payments. It received no support for such actions, however, from the USA and Great Britain, who accused France of 'bullying' Germany. As the American historian William R. Keylor writes,

> *it must in fairness be recorded that the Treaty of Versailles proved to be a failure less because of the inherent defects it contained than because it was never put into full effect.*
>
> ***The Twentieth Century World and Beyond* (Oxford University Press, 2006), p.88.**

The one feature of the Versailles settlement that guaranteed peace and the security of France was the occupation of the Rhineland. Yet the treaty stipulated that the troops should only be there for 15 years. In fact, the last Allied soldiers left in 1930, 5 years earlier than agreed, and just as Germany was recovering its strength.

The settlement of Eastern and South-Eastern Europe

Four separate peace treaties were signed: with Austria (the Treaty of St Germain), Hungary (Treaty of Trianon), Bulgaria (Treaty of Neuilly), and Turkey (Treaty of Sèvres, revised by the Treaty of Lausanne). Following the format of the Treaty of Versailles, all four countries were to disarm, to pay reparations, and to lose territory.

The Treaty of St Germain (1919)

By the time the delegates met at Versailles, the peoples of Austria-Hungary had already broken away from the empire and were setting up their own states in accordance with the principle of self-determination. The conference had no choice but to agree to this situation and suggest minor changes. Austria was separated from Hungary and reduced to a small landlocked state consisting of only 25 per cent of its pre-war area and 20 per cent of its pre-war population. It became a republic of 7 million people, which many nicknamed 'the tadpole state' due to its shape and size.

Other conditions of the Treaty of St Germain were:

- Austria lost Bohemia and Moravia – wealthy industrial provinces – to the new state of Czechoslovakia.
- Austria lost Dalmatia, Bosnia, and Herzegovina to a new state peopled by Serbs, Croats, and Slovenes – a state that, from 1929, became known as Yugoslavia.
- Poland gained Galicia.
- Italy received the South Tyrol, Trentino, and Istria.

In addition, *Anschluss* (union with Germany) was forbidden and Austrian armed forces were reduced to 30,000 men. Austria had to pay reparations to the Allies, and by 1922 it was virtually bankrupt and the League of Nations took over its financial affairs.

The Treaty of Trianon (1920)

Hungary had to recognize the independence of the new states of Czechoslovakia, Poland, Yugoslavia, and Austria. In this treaty it lost 75 per cent of its pre-war territory and 66 per cent of its pre-war population. In addition:

- Slovakia and Ruthenia were given to Czechoslovakia.
- Croatia and Slovenia were given to Yugoslavia.
- Transylvania and the Banat of Temesvar were given to Romania.

Furthermore, the Hungarian army was limited to 35,000 men and Hungary had to pay reparations.

Hungary complained bitterly that the newly formed Hungarian nation was much smaller than the Kingdom of Hungary that had been part of the Austro-Hungarian Empire, and that more than 3 million Magyars had been put under foreign rule.

The Treaty of Neuilly (1919)

In the Treaty of Neuilly, Bulgaria lost territory to Greece and Yugoslavia. Significantly, it lost its Aegean coastline and therefore access to the Mediterranean. However, it was the only defeated nation to receive territory, from Turkey.

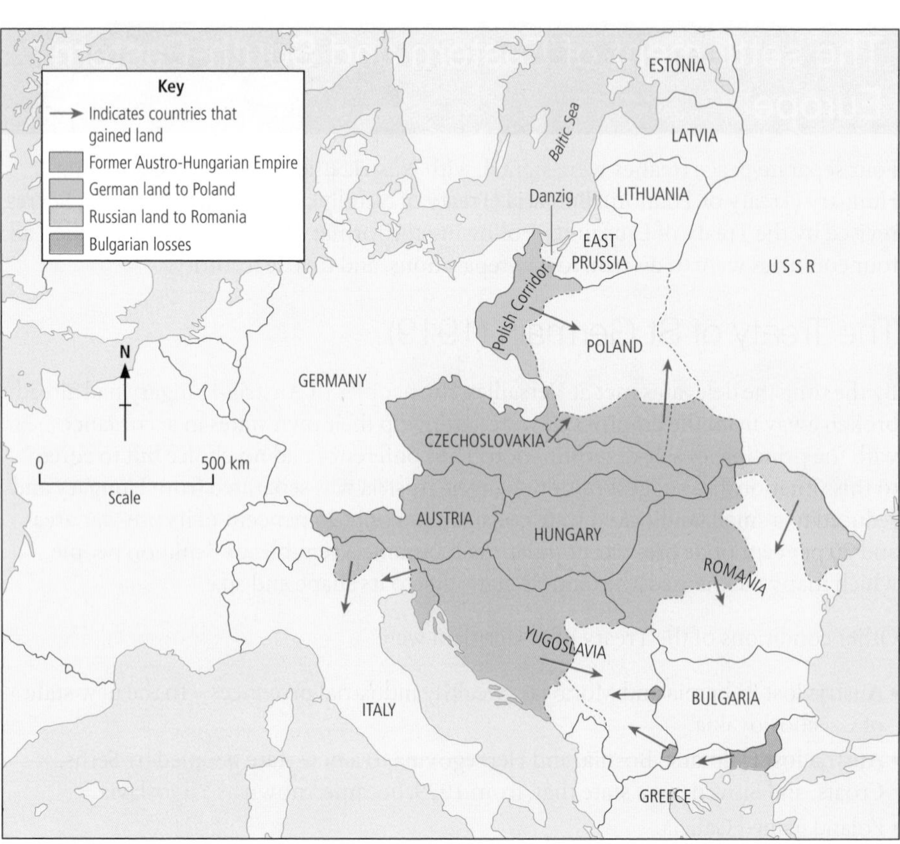

The break-up of the Austro-Hungarian Empire. East Prussia at this time was part of Germany.

The Treaty of Sèvres (1920)

The disintegration of the Ottoman Empire had been long expected and both Britain and France hoped to make some gains in the region. In the Treaty of Sèvres:

- Syria went to France as a mandate.
- Palestine, Iraq, Transjordan, and Cyprus went to Great Britain.
- Eastern Thrace went to Greece.
- Rhodes and the Dodecanese Islands went to Italy.
- Smyrna was occupied by the Greeks for five years and then a plebiscite was due to be held.
- The Straits (exit from the Black Sea) were to become a demilitarized zone administered by the League of Nations: Britain, France, and Italy were to keep troops in Turkey.

The treaty was accepted by Sultan Muhammad VI. Yet there was fierce resentment to the terms. The nationalist leader Mustapha Kemal led a National Assembly at Ankara to pledge the unification of Muslim Turks and the rejection of Sèvres. Greece, ambitious for more land, attempted to take advantage of this internal disorder and declared war, but Kemal smashed the Greek advance, captured and burned Smyrna, and finally ejected all Greek soldiers and civilians from Asia. Kemal advanced on the Straits and for a while it looked as though he intended to attack the British soldiers at the town of Chanak. A compromise was agreed upon, however, which resulted in the Treaty of Sèvres being revised at Lausanne in Switzerland.

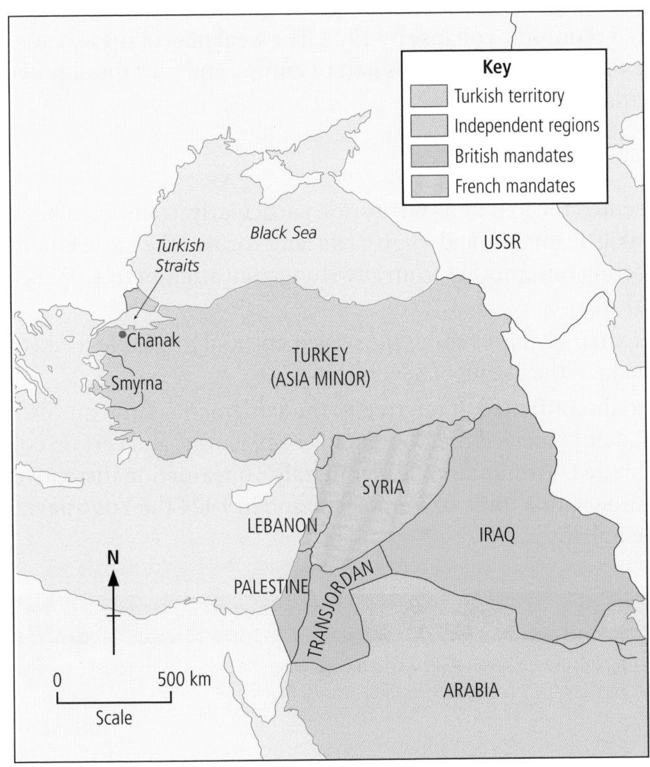

The Treaty of Sèvres and the Turkish Empire.

The Treaty of Lausanne (1923)

The provisions of the Treaty of Lausanne ran as follows:

- Turkey regained Eastern Thrace, Smyrna, some territory along the Syrian border, and several Aegean islands.
- Turkish sovereignty over the Straits was recognized, but the area remained demilitarized.
- Foreign troops were withdrawn from Turkish territory.
- Turkey no longer had to pay reparations or have its army reduced.

Self-determination outside Europe

Applying the principle of self-determination also proved problematic outside Europe. France and Britain were not interested in allowing this principle to operate in their colonies. Ho Chi Minh, a Vietnamese revolutionary, arrived at Versailles with a petition seeking support for the Vietnamese nationalist cause, but he was ignored. Claims from the Indian nationalist press that India's 'deeds and sacrifices justified its claim to an equality within the British Empire' were also unacceptable. Wilson also ignored a memorandum from the black American leader W.E.B. Dubois, which suggested that Africa be reconstructed 'in accordance with the wishes of the Negro race'.

What were the criticisms of the peace settlements in Eastern and South-Eastern Europe?

It was very difficult to apply the principle of self-determination consistently and fairly. Because Czechoslovakia needed a mountainous, defensible border and because the new state lacked certain minerals and industry, it was given the ex-Austrian Sudetenland, which contained around 3.5 million German speakers. The new Czechoslovakia set up on racial lines therefore contained five main racial groups: Czechs, Poles, Magyars, Ruthenians, and German speakers. Racial problems were also rife in the new Yugoslavia, which had at least a dozen nationalities within its borders. Thus the historian Alan Sharp writes that 'the 1919 minorities were probably more discontented than those of 1914' (*Modern History Review*, November 1991, page 30).

As well as ethnic strife, the new states were weak politically and economically. Both Hungary and Austria suffered economic collapse by 1922. The weakness of these new states was later to create a power vacuum in this part of Europe and thus the area became an easy target for German domination.

The treaties caused much bitterness:

- Hungary resented the loss of its territories, particularly Transylvania. Czechoslovakia, Romania, and Yugoslavia later formed the Little Entente, with the aim of protecting one another from any Hungarian attempt to regain control over their territories.
- Turkey was extremely bitter about the settlement, and this led to a takeover by Kemal and the revision of the Treaty of Sèvres.
- Italy was also discontented. It referred to the settlement as 'the mutilated peace' because it had not received the Dalmatian coast, Fiume, and certain colonies. In 1919, Gabriele D'Annunzio, a leader in Italy's ultra-nationalist movement, occupied Fiume with a force of supporters, and in 1924 the Yugoslavians gave Fiume to the Italians.

Activity 7

ATL Thinking skills

1. What do you think the historian Alan Sharp means when he says that the peace settlement was a disappointment 'as much because of its virtues as its faults'?

What was the impact of the war and the peace treaties by the early 1920s?

Political issues

Although Western Europe was still familiar on the map in 1920, this was not the case in Eastern Europe, where no fewer than nine new or revived states came into existence: Finland, Estonia, Latvia, Lithuania, Poland, Czechoslovakia, Austria, Hungary, and Yugoslavia. Meanwhile, Russia's government was now a Bolshevik dictatorship that was encouraging revolution abroad. The frontiers of new states thus became the frontiers of the Europe from which Russia was excluded. Russia was not invited to the Versailles conference and was not a member of the League of Nations until 1934.

The Little Entente

This was a defensive alliance between Czechoslovakia, Yugoslavia, and Romania. France supported the alliance by signing treaties with each member country. A key aim of the Little Entente was to prevent any kind of revision of the Versailles treaty by Germany or Hungary.

The new Europe remained divided not only between the 'victors' and the 'defeated', but also between those who wanted to maintain the peace settlement and those who wanted to see it revised. Not only Germany, but also Hungary and Italy, were active in pursuing their aims of getting the treaties changed. Despite Wilson's hopes to the contrary, international 'blocs' developed, such as that formed by the Little Entente. The peacemakers had hoped for and encouraged democracy in the new states. Yet the people in Central Europe only had experience with autocracy, and governments were undermined by the rivalry between the different ethnic groups and by the economic problems that they faced.

Although Britain and France still had their empires and continued their same colonial policies, the war saw the start of the decline of these powers on the world stage. The role of America in the war had made it clear that Britain and France were going to find it hard to act on their own to deal with international disputes; the focus of power in the world had shifted away from Europe. Furthermore, the war encouraged movements for independence in French and British colonies in Asia and Africa.

Economic issues

As we have seen, the war caused severe economic disruption in Europe. Germany suffered particularly badly, but all countries of Europe faced rising prices. The middle classes of Europe were hit especially hard by inflation, which destroyed the wealth of many **bourgeois** families. In Germany, for example, the total collapse of the currency meant that the savings of middle-class families were made completely worthless.

In Eastern and South-Eastern Europe, the new fragmentation of the area hindered economic recovery. There was now serious disruption in what had been a free trade area of some 50 million inhabitants. From 1919, each country tried to build up its economy, which meant fierce competition and high tariffs. Attempts at economic cooperation foundered and any success was wrecked by the **Great Depression**. As noted, only America and Japan benefited economically from the war, and they went on to experience economic prosperity until the **Wall Street Crash** in 1929.

Social changes

The war also swept away the traditional structures in society. Across Europe, the **landed aristocracy**, which had been so prominent before 1914, lost much of its power and influence. In Russia, the revolution rid the country of its aristocracy completely. In the lands of the Austro-Hungarian Empire, estates were broken up; many governments, such as that of Yugoslavia, undertook land reform and distributed land out to the peasants. In Prussia, the landowners (*Junkers*) kept their lands but lost much of their influence with the decline of the military and the collapse of the monarchy.

Other groups of people benefited from the war. Trade unions were considerably strengthened by the role that they played in negotiating with the governments during the war to improve pay and conditions for the valuable war workers. In both Britain and France, standards of health and welfare also rose during the war, thus improving the lives of the poorest citizens. Measures were introduced to improve the health of children. In Britain, social legislation continued after the war with the Housing Act of 1918, which subsidized the building of houses, and the Unemployment Insurance Acts of 1920 and 1921, which increased benefits for unemployed workers and their families.

How were women affected by the war?

After the war, women gained rights they had previously been denied. Such changes were reflected in a growing female confidence and changes in fashion and behaviour. In Britain and America the so-called flappers wore plain, short dresses, had short hair, smoked cigarettes, and drank cocktails. This kind of behaviour would have been considered unacceptable before the war. In Britain, some professions also opened up to women after the war; they could now train to become architects and lawyers, and were allowed to serve on a jury.

The end of the war also saw women getting the vote in a number of countries: Russia in 1917, Austria and Britain in 1918, Czechoslovakia, Germany, the Netherlands, Poland, and Sweden in 1919, and America and Belgium in 1920. The role that women played in the war effort was a contributory factor to this shift in some countries, though it was not the only factor. In Britain, for instance, the pre-war work of the suffrage movements in raising awareness of women's rights issues was also important. Yet the new employment opportunities that women had experienced during the war did not continue afterwards, with most women giving up their work and returning to their more traditional roles in the home.

Activity 8

Source analysis

> *Unceremoniously, women were tipped out of their wartime jobs to make way for the returning men: their work had always been 'for the duration'. If life were to be returned to 'normal', the women would have to return to the home. Protest was brushed aside – those women who tried to keep their jobs were even met with cries of 'parasites', 'blacklegs' and 'limpets'.*
>
> *In too many households there was no bread winner coming back from the battlefield. Nor, for a generation of women, was there the traditional prospect of marriage and security. Was it some consolation that they knew they had shouldered responsibility and demonstrated skills as never before? That they had proved they could keep the country going, feed the voracious war machine and show courage in the face of danger? Only to a point. They could do it – but it wasn't enough to shift the traditional shape of society – and for so many it was scant consolation in the face of bereavement and insecurity.*
>
> **Kate Adie, *Fighting on the Home Front* (Hodder, 2013), p.301.**

1. According to Kate Adie, what problems did women in Britain face after World War One?

Activity 9

1. Divide into groups. Each group should research a different country in which women received the vote after the war. It should consider:
   - the effect of the war in bringing about this change
   - what other factors contributed to this
   - whether the lives of women in each country changed in any other respect.

   Each group should then feed back its findings to the rest of the groups so that as a class you gain specific examples from a range of countries. This will be important for writing essays on the impact of war on women (see below and also chapter 10).
2. How did the war affect art and culture in the 1920s? Research the artistic movements of Dada and Constructivism. What do these show about the changed attitudes of artists following the horrors of the war?

Activity 10

Essay planning

In pairs plan the following questions.

- ***Evaluate the strengths and weaknesses of one peace treaty in the 20th century.***
- ***With reference to one 20th-century peace treaty, to what extent did the terms meet the aims of the peacemakers?***
- ***Discuss the social and economic effects of one 20th-century war.***
- ***With reference to one 20th-century war, examine the effects of the war on the role and status of women.***
- ***'Peace settlements rarely create a stable peace.' With reference to one 20th-century war, to what extent do you agree with this statement?***

It is very easy with the third essay question in Activity 10 to be too vague or general in your answer. The problem with social, political, and economic effects is that it is not possible to make sweeping generalizations; they varied from country to country and not all were caused solely by the war. You therefore need to ensure that you give very specific examples from a range of countries (European and non-European) to support your arguments.

Note that question 4 takes one social issue only – the impact on women. For this question, you need to refer back to the previous section on the work that women did during the war and combine this with the information in this chapter (along with the research you have done) on the impact that the war had on the position of women in society and the workplace, along with new political rights. Again, you will need specific examples from different countries to support your arguments.

To access websites relevant to this chapter, go to www.pearsonhotlinks.com, search for the book title or ISBN, and click on 'chapter 4'.

05 Cross-regional war: World War Two – Causes I: The failure of collective security

A meeting of the League of Nations Council, Geneva, 1938.

Key concepts: Consequence

As you read this chapter, consider the following essay questions:

- Examine the reasons why collective security failed to keep the peace in the first half of the 20th century.
- To what extent was the League of Nations 'doomed to fail'?
- Discuss how economic crisis led to international tension in the 20th century.

The causes of World War Two are complex, so we have divided the key themes into separate sections. You have already studied the results of World War One and these can be considered as a long-term factor in causing World War Two. In this chapter we will look at another long-term factor – the failure of collective security in preventing the outbreak of another war. We will also consider the impact of the global economic crisis of the 1930s: the Great Depression. In the next section we will look more specifically at Hitler's policies and the policy of appeasement as a cause of war in Europe. In the last section we will consider the actions of the Japanese government and the response of the international community, particularly the USA, which led to the outbreak of war in the Pacific.

Timeline of events 1919–1933	
1919	Treaty of Versailles
	Treaty of St Germain
1920	Establishment of the League of Nations
1922	Treaty of Rapallo between Germany and the USSR
1923	French occupation of the Ruhr
1924	Introduction of the Dawes Plan
1925	Locarno Treaties
1926	Germany admitted to League of Nations
1928	Kellogg-Briand Pact signed
1929	Introduction of the Young Plan
	Wall Street Crash
1932	Lausanne Conference on reparation payments
1933	Hitler appointed Chancellor of Germany

Activity 1

ATL Thinking and self-management skills

Some historians suggest that the settlement at the end of World War One was problematic, and some go further and argue that its terms sowed the seeds for future conflict.

1. Review the criticisms of the Versailles settlement. Identify the states that were:
   a) defeated and unhappy with the settlement
   b) victors and unhappy with the settlement
2. Discuss in pairs the following issues with the settlement that might have challenged post-war stability:
   a) economic issues
   b) territorial issues
   c) political issues
   d) social issues

The failure of 'collective security'

As we have seen, one of Wilson's Fourteen Points led to the creation of the League of Nations, an organization that sought to prevent another war breaking out between states. Akira Iriye writes:

> *It [the League of Nations Covenant] proposed an alternative to the conventional international order, which, Wilson was convinced, had been sustained by force. This had created a dangerous arms race and imperialistic activities abroad. Now military power and expansionism were to be replaced by a rule of law in which 'world public opinion' rather than alliances and armaments would be the key to international order.*
>
> **Akira Iriye, *The Globalizing of America 1913–1945* (CUP, 1993), p.68.**

In the 1920s and 1930s, the League faced many challenges. Although it was successful in some areas, the overall failure of European states to work collectively through the League in dealing with various international crises was a major cause of World War Two.

Collective security and the League of Nations

The principle of **collective security** was the idea that peace could be preserved by countries acting together – collectively – to prevent one country attacking another. Collective security was to be made practically possible by the machinery of the League of Nations. When there was a dispute between countries they would refer the issue(s) to the League's Assembly. If that body could not find a resolution, the Council could then apply 'collective security'. This meant that it could first impose moral pressure and then, if this did not work, the Council could impose economic sanctions to force the country that was deemed to be in the wrong to comply with its decisions.

Activity 2

1. Visit pearsonhotlinks.com, enter the book title or ISBN, and click on weblink 5.1 to watch a video about the League of Nations. Discuss the ideas and motives of Woodrow Wilson in attempting to set up a League of Nations.

The Covenant of the League of Nations

The League met for the first time in Geneva in December 1920. Its key objective was to keep the peace and avoid future conflict by advising on and settling international disputes. It also aimed to promote disarmament, supervise the mandated territories, and promote international goodwill and cooperation through its various organizations dedicated to social and economic development. The initial membership of the League was 32 Allied states and 12 neutral states; however, by 1926, all ex-enemy states had joined. The USSR was not admitted until 1934, and the USA never joined.

There were 26 articles in the League's Covenant (including amendments made in December 1924), which prescribed when and how the League was to operate.

- Articles 1–7 were concerned with the membership and organization of the League, its Assembly, Council, and Secretariat.
- Articles 8–17 were concerned with the prevention of war.
- Articles 18–21 concerned with treaty obligations and the League's expectations of its member states.
- Article 22 concerned the mandated territories.

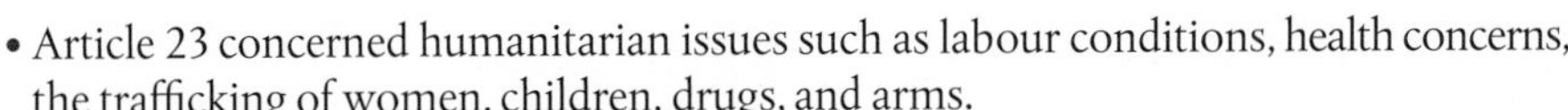

- Article 23 concerned humanitarian issues such as labour conditions, health concerns, the trafficking of women, children, drugs, and arms.
- Article 24 concerned the commissions.
- Article 25 promoted the **Red Cross**.
- Article 26 set down how amendments to the Covenant were made.

Dealing with international disputes

It was set down in the Covenant that member states should refer disputes to one of the following:

- the Permanent Court of International Justice
- **arbitration** (having a neutral person or group of people listening to and judging a dispute)
- an investigation or inquiry by the Council.

The League of Nations in session, 1920.

If member states failed to refer their disputes to the League, or failed to follow its recommendations, the League could then impose economic sanctions, the main tool for the League against aggressors. In the aftermath of World War One, in which the economic blockade of Germany had been effective, this economic weapon appeared to have the potential to be effective in forcing compliance with the League's decisions.

In theory, the League could call for military action as a last resort against an aggressor. Yet the League did not have its own armed forces, and in reality member states did not want to put their sovereign forces under international control. In addition, the Covenant was rather ambiguous as to when and how such armed forces should be used. France had wanted an armed force, or League Army, but Britain had resisted this option. Thus the League lacked military teeth.

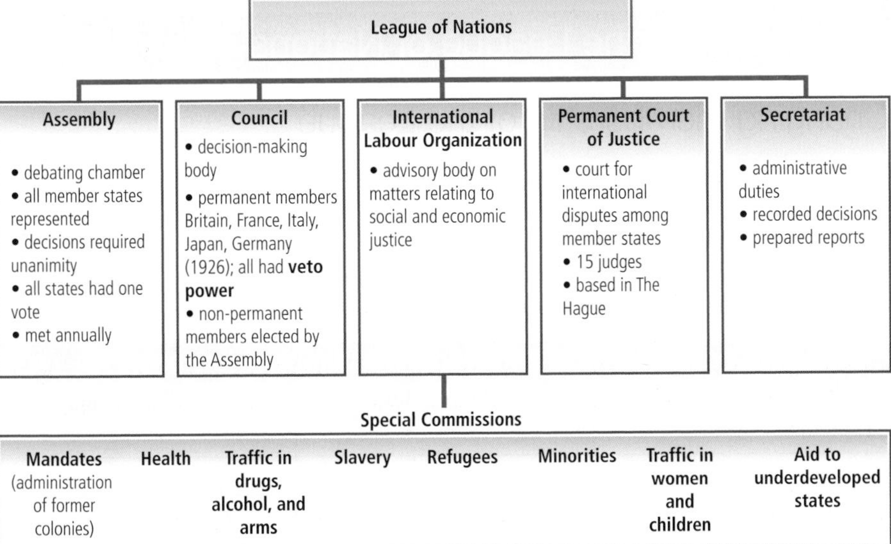
League of Nations
Assembly
• debating chamber
• all member states represented
• decisions required unanimity
• all states had one vote
• met annually
Council
• decision-making body
• permanent members Britain, France, Italy, Japan, Germany (1926); all had veto power
• non-permanent members elected by the Assembly
International Labour Organization
• advisory body on matters relating to social and economic justice
Permanent Court of Justice
• court for international disputes among member states
• 15 judges
• based in The Hague
Secretariat
• administrative duties
• recorded decisions
• prepared reports
Special Commissions
Mandates (administration of former colonies)
Health
Traffic in drugs, alcohol, and arms
Slavery
Refugees
Minorities
Traffic in women and children
Aid to underdeveloped states

The structure of the League of Nations.

Activity 3

ATL Thinking skills

Look up the League of Nations Covenant on the internet. As you read through the document, consider:

1. What aspects of the Covenant made the League of Nations an organization likely to fulfil its aims of collective security?
2. What aspects of the Covenant weakened the League's ability to deliver collective security?

Activity 4

Source A

[the League] depended on the goodwill of the nations to work, though it was the absence of goodwill that made it necessary.

Hugh Brogan, *The Penguin History of the USA* (Penguin, 2001), p.480.

Source B

... successive British governments took care to confine any specific political or military commitments they might make to western Europe, although under article 10 of the League Covenant they had undertaken to 'preserve ... against external aggression the territorial integrity and existing political independence of all members of the League'.

Ruth Henig, *Versailles and After, 1919–1933* (Routledge, 1995), p.35.

Source C

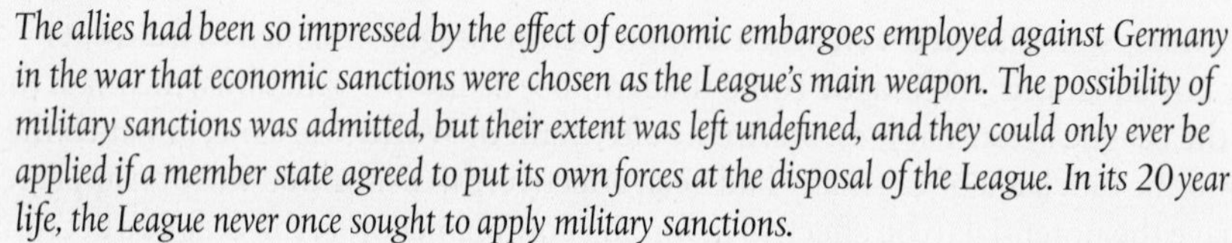

The allies had been so impressed by the effect of economic embargoes employed against Germany in the war that economic sanctions were chosen as the League's main weapon. The possibility of military sanctions was admitted, but their extent was left undefined, and they could only ever be applied if a member state agreed to put its own forces at the disposal of the League. In its 20 year life, the League never once sought to apply military sanctions.

T. Morris and D. Murphy, *Europe 1870–1991* (Collins, 2004), p.336.

Source D

Rival states can be frightened into friendship only by the shadow of some greater danger.

Comment by the British historian A.J.P. Taylor.

1. What potential problems or weaknesses of the League are identified in sources A–D?

Problems for the League of Nations in the 1920s

Changing membership of the League

The changing membership of the League reflected the shifting priorities of its leading members, as the more liberal governments of the 1920s became increasingly polarized following the Wall Street Crash and the ensuing Great Depression. As right-wing governments within the League became more aggressive, so the perceived threat from the USSR shifted to the **Axis powers**.

ACCESSIONS TO AND WITHDRAWALS FROM THE LEAGUE OF NATIONS, 1920-1939

Country	Date of entry	Date of departure
Austria	Dec 1920	Dec 1939*
Ethiopia	Sept 1923	
Ireland	Sept 1923	
Germany	Sept 1926	Oct 1933
Japan	Original member	March 1933
Italy	Original member	Dec 1937
Spain	Original member	May 1939
USSR	Sept 1934	Dec 1939*

*The Council resolved on 14 December 1939 that Austria and the USSR were no longer members.

Absence of major powers

The absence of major powers from the League of Nations had a decisive impact on its working and influence; indeed, this is possibly the key reason why the League ultimately failed to prevent another world war.

The most important absent major power was the USA. The League had been the idea of the Americans and had been championed by President Woodrow Wilson. The US Congress, however, was too concerned that membership would drag the Americans into more disputes and conflicts in Europe, hence the country withdrew into isolationism. The USA had played a pivotal role in bringing World War One to an end, but it did not want to play such a central role in the controversial Versailles settlement.

The absence of the USA seriously weakened the potential of the League to use 'collective security' against aggression, for several reasons. First, the world's most powerful economy would have given the League's economic sanctions real weight, but US absence undermined this one essential weapon. Second, without the USA, the make-up of the permanent members (except for Japan) was distinctly European and lacked the appearance of a genuinely 'worldwide' organization. Third, it highlighted that the new organization might be sidelined in favour of old-style agreements and treaties, as this was clearly how the USA was going to secure its future relationships. Finally, these factors meant that the League was primarily led by European powers that were arguably in decline.

Activity 5

Source A

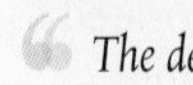

The defeat suffered by Wilsonism in the United States strikes at the very existence of the League of Nations. America's place will remain empty at Geneva, and the two countries that dominate, France and Great Britain, are divided on almost every one of the topics to be discussed.

Marcel Cachin, a French politician, speaking in 1920 about the USA's decision not to join the League of Nations.

Source B

British cartoon 'The Gap in the Bridge', first published in *Punch*, December 1919.

1. According to Source A, what are the most significant problems for the League of Nations caused by the absence of the USA?
2. What are the views of the cartoonist in Source B concerning the USA's absence from the League of Nations?

Absence of the USSR

The USSR was excluded from the League of Nations. The newly established Bolshevik government was regarded as a 'pariah state'; indeed, Western powers had invaded Russia during the Russian Civil War (1918–1921), and had joined the 'White' counter-revolutionary forces. As the Bolsheviks consolidated their position in the Soviet Union after winning the civil war, the old powers of Europe looked on with great concern. Afraid that the 'revolution of the **proletariat**' would spread, they felt that it was expedient to isolate the Soviets rather than to embrace them in a new organization designed to prevent conflict.

Yet the exclusion of Russia further weakened the standing of the League, as it could be perceived by the USSR as a 'club for capitalists' – an organization to protect and promote their interests and empires at the expense of the exploited masses. Indeed, Lenin viewed the League as 'a robbers' den to safeguard the unjust spoils of Versailles'.

Absence of Germany

Germany was initially excluded from the League. This exclusion again undermined the ideals of the League and, perhaps more importantly, suggested that the League was something of a 'victors' club' – the four permanent members of the Council were the victorious Allies. In addition, the exclusion tended to ignore the important fact that Germany remained a strong power at the conclusion of World War One. The assumptions that there had been a clear victory over Germany and that there was now scope for a reordering of European politics were flawed. Germany had been militarily defeated in the west, but not in the east. Its expansionist politics had not evaporated, nor had its economic power. It would therefore seem, particularly with hindsight, vital that Germany was included in the League so that it could work towards its aim of revising the Treaty of Versailles within the confines of the League's machinery. Indeed, following the wave of optimism and positive thinking that ensued after the Locarno treaty, Germany was admitted into the League in September 1926.

Weakness of Central European states

The Austro-Hungarian Empire had collapsed following World War One and had been replaced by a number of smaller states based on the principle of nationality. However, as we saw in the previous chapter, many of these states struggled politically and economically to achieve stability. This meant that instead of another large European state there were now several much smaller states that would require more support from the League, particularly in terms of economic development and territorial security. These states could not offer the League much tangible support in return.

Activity 6

1. To what extent was the League of Nations 'doomed to fail' due to the limitations of its Covenant and structure?
2. Examine why the failure of the USA to join the League may be viewed as critically important.
3. How might countries/regions around the world have perceived the role of the League of Nations differently?

Activity 7

1. Research the work of the commissions shown in the diagram on page 101. How effective was the League of Nations in dealing with the humanitarian issues identified by the commissions?

How successful was the League of Nations in the 1920s?

Peacekeeping 1920–1925

Throughout the 1920s, the League dealt with various disputes arising mainly from the territorial changes of the Versailles settlement. The League had both successes and failures in its handling of these disputes.

Aaland Islands, 1920: These islands were populated mainly by Swedes, but, following the collapse of the Russian Empire, Finland had claimed sovereignty over them. The conflict was taken to the League and Sweden accepted the League's decision to give the islands to Finland.

Vilna, 1920–1923: Both Poland and Lithuania wanted control of the town of Vilna. It had once been the capital of Lithuania, but its people were Polish. The League was unable to prevent the Poles from seizing and retaining Vilna by force. Finally, the Conference of Ambassadors awarded Vilna to Poland.

Upper Silesia, 1921: Both Germany and newly formed Poland wanted control of the important industrial area of Upper Silesia. The League decided to split the area between the two.

Corfu, 1923: Three Italian army officers were shot while working on a boundary dispute between Greece and Albania. Mussolini blamed Greece and ordered compensation. When the Greeks did not pay, Italian soldiers occupied Corfu. Greece appealed to the League, but the Italian government ignored the Council's ruling and left only when compensation had been paid.

Mosul, 1924: The area of Mosul was claimed by both Turkey and Iraq. The League considered the problem and awarded the area to Iraq, a decision that was accepted.

Bulgaria, 1925: Following a Greek invasion of Bulgaria, the League ordered both armies to stop fighting. An investigation by the League blamed Greece for starting the dispute and ordered it to pay damages. Greece accepted the blame and was ordered to pay compensation.

P.M.H. Bell argues that even though the League did not solve all disputes successfully:

> *What was important was that the League had settled down as a valuable forum for the conduct of international affairs. Germany was admitted in 1926, and at once became a permanent member of the Council; so the League was no longer a 'League of victors'. By 1928 every European state was a member (except the USSR). Nearly every foreign minister made a point of attending its sessions. The League was still young, but there seemed a good chance that Europe had found a workable successor to the pre-1914 states system.*
>
> **P.M.H. Bell, *Twentieth-Century Europe* (Bloomsbury, 2006), p.97.**

Activity 8

ATL Thinking skills

1. Which of the disputes outlined above can be regarded as successes for the League and which disputes can be regarded as failures?
2. Are there any common factors that help to explain the successes and failures?
3. What lessons could be drawn for the 1930s from the challenges that had faced the League in the 1920s?

Conference of Ambassadors

The Conference of Ambassadors was set up in January 1920 in Paris to ensure that the peace treaties were implemented. It consisted of the British, Italian, and Japanese ambassadors.

Attempts to strengthen the League

Two attempts were made, in 1923 and 1924, to strengthen the machinery of the League of Nations. These were both initiated by France. The first was the Draft Treaty of Mutual Assistance, which would have required all members of the League to come to the assistance of a victim of aggression. Next, the Geneva Protocol of 1924 would have made arbitration compulsory in all disputes. Both initiatives were rejected by Britain, its dominions, and the Scandinavian powers, who believed that members would not be willing or able to carry out the huge commitment that would result from such a role.

The League thus remained divided between those states that wanted a strong League to enforce the existing territorial agreements and those that wanted to be more selective in dealing with aggression. This division also arose because of the difference in vulnerability of the various states. While France felt highly exposed, others were not so worried and were not prepared to take on what they saw as extra commitments. These differences were to be highlighted further by the Ruhr Crisis, which would deeply undermine the principle of collective security.

Activity 9

ATL Thinking and social skills

1. Discuss in pairs the extent to which France was made vulnerable by the USA's failure to ratify Versailles and join the League of Nations.

The Ruhr Crisis (1923)

A German cartoon from 1923. France is represented by the figure of the woman, and the German text says 'Hands off the Ruhr!'

For France, future security lay in upholding the terms of the Treaty of Versailles. However, France had begun to feel that this security was being undermined within a year of its signing. The USA did not ratify the treaty and signed a separate peace with Germany. In Germany, the political situation seemed unlikely to produce a government keen to comply with its terms. Indeed, reparation payments, crucial for rebuilding the French economy, quickly became a problem. The Germans protested that they could not afford the payments. In October 1921, the Wiesbaden Accords were drawn up, in which France agreed to assist Germany with their reparations by taking a proportion in raw materials and industrial produce rather than cash. The following year, however, even these payments had fallen into arrears.

The French inclination to use force rather than diplomacy to resolve the issue was enhanced by the appointment of the strongly nationalistic Raymond Poincaré as prime minister in January 1922. The issue was brought to a head and became a crisis when Germany asked for reparation payments to be suspended for four years. The French had had enough. They believed that this suspension could jeopardize the enforcement of the treaty as a whole. The French and the Belgians, with the support of Italy, moved troops into the Ruhr Valley in January 1923 to take in kind what they thought they were owed. The German government of Chancellor Wilhelm Cuno protested that this action went against the terms of the Versailles treaty, and in addition instructed German workers to strike. The German government continued to pay the now-striking workers, but found it had to print more paper money to cover the bill.

The floundering German economy now collapsed, and as the government continued to print money, inflation turned into hyperinflation. The French retaliated to this 'passive resistance' by encouraging the unemployed in France and Belgium to work in the Ruhr industries. The descent into economic chaos, indicated by the statistics below, coupled with growing political separatist movements in Germany, led to the replacement of Cuno with Gustav Stresemann in August 1923.

THE IMPACT OF THE RUHR CRISIS ON THE GERMAN ECONOMY	
Value of £ sterling to German mark	
Jan 1914	£1 = 20 marks
Jan 1922	£1 = 760 marks
Nov 1922	£1 = 50,000 marks
Nov 1923	£1 = 16,000,000,000 marks
Coal production in Ruhr	
1922	90 million tonnes
Feb 1923	2.5 million tonnes
Operating iron-smelting furnaces	
1922	70
March 1923	3

Stresemann called for an end to the 'passive resistance' in the Ruhr, and in 1924 the crisis was ended by the Dawes Plan. The plan was named after a commission chaired by US economist Charles Dawes. He produced a report on German reparations in April 1924, which decided the following:

- reparations were to be guaranteed by two mortgages, one on German railways and the second on German industries (supplemented by taxation on the German population)
- a US 'reparations agent' would reside in Germany to supervise repayments
- repayments were to be reduced.

Although reparations were to be reduced, France nevertheless accepted the plan because it brought the Americans back into the picture, involving them in the collection of reparations. In fact, this became known as 'the golden age of reparations' (until 1929), as the Allies received more than they had done before. The Germans were unhappy, however, as there was no fixed date for the completion of repayments. Britain and France were also concerned about the link between German payments and their own payments of war debts to the USA, which they had not wanted.

The Dawes Plan devised a new system of reparation payments. Stresemann promised to comply with this, and French troops were withdrawn from the Ruhr by August 1925. Yet the crisis had thrown up serious problems with the integrity of the League of Nations. Instead of going to the League, France had taken matters into its own hands and attempted to seize payments by force. Indeed, attempts by Britain and Sweden to take the crisis to the League were blocked by the French. This action by a permanent member undermined the League's credibility, as it appeared that the powers would take independent action when it suited them.

Although the hostility of Britain (and the USA) to the invasion of the Ruhr could be seen as a clear condemnation of unilateral action, the overall impact of the invasion was bad for both the League and for international relations. Despite France's economic gains (it had been guaranteed 21 per cent of the Ruhr's production until December 1923, and then this rose to 27 per cent), the results of its actions dramatically increased the tension between France and Germany, making future cooperation all the more problematic. Politically, France had alarmed its former allies, and heightened the sense of patriotism within Germany. In France, Poincaré came under heavy criticism from both left- and right-wing groups. The left argued that this act of aggression had been committed only to benefit capitalist groups in France, and the right were frustrated by Poincaré's withdrawal from the Ruhr, seeing it as a missed opportunity to exert some real control over Germany's economy. There was even unofficial support from certain elements for the promotion of an independent Rhineland.

The Rapallo Treaty

In April 1922, the Germans and Russians signed the Rapallo Treaty. Through this treaty, Germany and Russia entered into diplomatic relations and pledged their future cooperation. Germany fully recognized the Soviet government and both powers denounced reparations. In addition, the Rapallo Treaty provided for close economic cooperation. Arguably a more important consequence of this treaty was that military cooperation would now take place, allowing Germany to rearm and train secretly in Russia. Knowledge of the Rapallo Treaty also made Britain more determined to win over Germany rather than alienate the nation further, lest Germany became even friendlier with Russia.

Activity 10

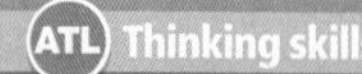

1. What were the reasons for the French occupation of the Ruhr, and how were their aims realized by this occupation?
2. What were the perspectives of other countries in this crisis?
3. How did France's actions undermine the concept of collective security?

Activity 11

> *The invasion of the Ruhr in 1923 had the most serious consequences. Within Germany, it weakened the position of the middle classes in society and diminished their support for the Weimar government. Extremist parties on the right and the left were given a boost, because of the alarm at the prospect of complete economic collapse and social disorder. Many historians argue that the invasion of the Ruhr paved the way for Hitler's subsequent rise to power. Both the British government and the British public were alienated by French policies … The French franc … came under pressure and the French government learned … direct action carried a high political cost … It has been suggested that France's failure to take military action to stop Hitler's remilitarization of the Rhineland in 1936 stemmed largely from the unhappy experience in the Ruhr in 1923.*
>
> **Ruth Henig, *Origins of the First World War* (Routledge, 1993), p.38.**

1. According to Ruth Henig, what was the impact of the Ruhr Invasion on a) Germany and b) France?

The Locarno Era

Following the disastrous Ruhr adventure, the political situation in Europe was improved by the Dawes Plan and the Locarno Pact of 1925, the Kellogg–Briand Pact of August 1928, and the Young Plan of 1929. However, it should be noted that these agreements took place outside the League of Nations.

The Locarno Conference and the 'Locarno spirit' (1925)

Although French forces left the Ruhr, there were allied troops in other Rhineland cities, as dictated by the terms of Versailles. Stresemann wanted to rid Germany of these 'occupying forces', and he was also keen to quell any movement in support of an independent Rhineland. At a conference in Locarno in Switzerland in February 1925, Stresemann proposed a voluntary guarantee from Germany of its western borders. Significantly for the French and Belgians, this meant that Germany was resolved to give up its claims over Alsace-Lorraine, Malmedy, and Eupen. In return, Germany had some reassurance that France would not invade again, and it removed any potential for an independent Rhineland. A series of treaties were signed. The major treaty guaranteed the boundaries between France, Belgium, and Germany. Also present at Locarno were representatives of Italy, Czechoslovakia, and Poland. Germany signed treaties with Poland and Czechoslovakia, agreeing to change the eastern borders with these countries by arbitration only. It was also agreed that Germany should be admitted into the League of Nations.

The Locarno Conference, 1925.

For many in post-war Europe, the Locarno agreement gave hope for future security. It suggested that former enemies could work together to resolve disputes, and to uphold the Versailles settlement. The new mood became known as the 'Locarno spirit'. When Locarno was followed up with a series of agreements involving the USA, this 'spirit' seemed to be embracing even isolationist nations.

The Locarno Pact seemed to bode well for the future of collective security. However, although this agreement appeared to herald a new era of cooperation between the Western European powers (Britain had been in favour of the agreement, as it expunged French excuses for occupation), what the agreement did not guarantee were Germany's eastern borders. Italy, present at Locarno, had not managed to get similar agreements from Germany on its southern border. The treaties France had with Poland and Czechoslovakia were little comfort to these respective countries, as it would be strategically difficult to offer tangible support following Locarno. In addition, France had not changed its view of Germany. Rather, it had just changed its strategy for containing Germany. Instead of confronting the Germans with force, France was now attempting to bring Germany into international agreements that involved the guarantees of other powers. In addition, Locarno had undermined both the Treaty of Versailles and the League of Nations. Security for France had been sought outside the League, and only a component of the Versailles treaty had been guaranteed.

The Young Plan (1929)

The Young Plan attempted to redress some of the problems that remained with the Dawes Plan. The plan:

- further reduced the total sum to be repaid by Germany
- set a date for completion of repayments – 1988
- continued US involvement in reparation payments.

As part of the deal, Britain and France agreed to end their occupation of the Rhineland five years ahead of schedule.

As Keynes had noted in 1926, the foundations for both the Dawes and then the Young Plan, and thus both German and European recovery, was foreign money. Two thirds of investment in Germany during the 1920s came from America. Keynes wrote in 1926 that the reparation arrangements were 'in the hands of the American capitalist'.

Activity 12

ATL Thinking skills

What potential problems with the Dawes and Young plans were highlighted by Keynes?

Activity 13

ATL Thinking skills

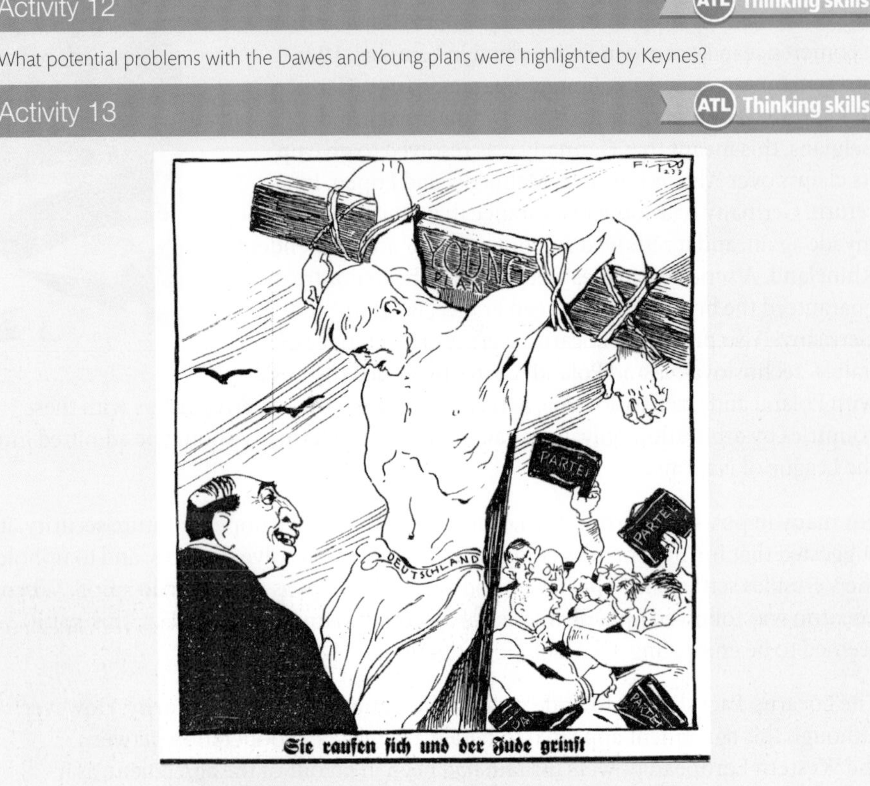

German cartoon, c.1930, from *Der Stürmer*, a very **anti-Semitic** newspaper published by Julius Streicher as part of Nazi propaganda. The cross bears the words 'Young Plan', while German political parties can be seen fighting with each other in the background. The caption translates: 'They fight and the Jew grins.'

1. What message does this German cartoon give about the Young Plan?

Enquire into which countries face debilitating debt repayments today. How are these countries and economies supported? Is 'developing world' debt a 'developing problem'?

The Kellogg–Briand Pact (August 1928)

The Kellogg–Briand Pact was initiated by American Secretary of State William Kellogg and the French Foreign Minister Aristide Briand. The pact renounced 'war as an instrument of national policy' and 62 of 64 invited states signed the agreement (Brazil and Argentina declined).

> *By declaring that Clausewitz's famous definition of war was illegal and guaranteeing that international disputes would be settled peacefully, this treaty … seemed to provide the legal foundation for a new international order.*
>
> **James Sheehan, *The Monopoly of Violence: Why Europeans Hate Going to War* (Faber & Faber, 2008), p.106.**

Contemporary views of the pact were often positive; it was seen as an important declaration by governments that they would pursue their objectives through peaceful means. The pact has been viewed as the high point of 'Locarno spirit' era. Unfortunately, this perspective would prove to be naive, as the encouraging elements of Europe's recovery were very fragile.

It could be argued that there was no major conflict in the 1920s because the main revisionist power – Germany – was still recovering from World War One. In addition, the 1920s were in the main a period of relative economic boom and prosperity, which decreased international tensions and encouraged cooperation. As P.M.H. Bell writes, 'Europe had survived, but was still on the sick list.'

Activity 14

ATL Thinking and social skills

Review questions

In small groups or pairs answer the following questions:

1. What had led to the mood of optimism in the 1920s?
2. Could the 'Locarno spirit' have survived? Why did it not last?
3. Why was there an improvement in relations between Britain, France, and Germany in 1924–1929? In what ways was the international situation more stable in 1929 than it had been in 1923?
4. What had the League of Nations achieved by 1929?

Why did collective security fail in the 1930s?

Although the concept of collective security had some degree of success in the 1920s, the League's failure to resolve key international crises in the 1930s meant that it had completely collapsed by 1939.

The Depression

The unemployed line up at a soup kitchen in the USA.

The worldwide economic depression that followed the Wall Street Crash of October 1929 had far-reaching effects. The USA had become *the* globally dominant economic power, and this meant that the world's economy was ominously linked to its fortunes. The impact of the crisis on the economic, social, and, ultimately, political landscape of the world ushered in a return to a world dominated by national self-interest and the dominance of military forces. The USA's national income fell by almost 50 per cent between 1929 and 1932, and its government struggled to cope with unemployment and popular discontent.

Poverty and despair have often fostered the rise of extremist groups, and the fragile liberal governments of the 1920s found resurgent nationalist and aggressive political groups very difficult to restrict. The delicate European stability that had been nurtured by the resources of American Capitalism was particularly vulnerable to a major economic collapse in the USA. This was equally true of the recently democratic and liberal Japan.

Governments were blamed for the crisis. In France, a moderate government was replaced by a radical left-wing one in the May 1932 election. In Britain, iron and steel production fell by 50 per cent, and political support shifted to right-wing parties. The

The Weimar government

The Weimar government had been established at the end of World War One with the defeat of the German Empire. It replaced the imperial government with a constitution that was seen as one of the most modern in Europe. Universal suffrage was introduced and a lower house of parliament was to be elected every 4 years by a voting system of proportional representation. The president was to be elected every 7 years and a guarantee of basic human rights was included in the constitution.

British Labour government broke up in the financial crisis of 1931 and was almost wiped out by the 1931 election, which led to the formation of a 'National Government' under the Conservatives.

Germany had borrowed £9,000 million between 1924 and 1929. When the money stopped, its economy collapsed; German unemployment stood at 1.4 million in 1928 and rose to over 6 million in 1932. The Weimar government and liberal democracy lost credibility and ended when Franz von Papen assumed the role of virtual dictator in May 1932.

In Japan, in 1931, 50 per cent of factories closed, and silk prices fell by two-thirds. There ensued a radical shift to the right, linked to military factions. By 1932, following a series of assassinations, the era of liberal politics in Japan was over.

In Belgium and Poland, the impact of the Depression led to new government initiatives that looked to improve the countries' defences against a potentially expansionist Germany.

The Depression heightened fears of the USSR's capacity for fostering the spread of Communist revolution into the impoverished working-class streets of European cities. Soviet propaganda claimed that the Depression demonstrated the inherent failings of Capitalism, and its inevitable replacement with the Communist system. Britain and France were also alarmed at the escalating nationalist and independence movements in their respective empires, and the corresponding costs of controlling these. With a pressurized domestic situation, it was particularly difficult to manage the growing forces of **expansionism** in both Europe and Asia. The democratic governments were thus increasingly forced to review their strategies for dealing with international tension. The League's key weapon of economic sanctions was now a weapon most countries would not want deployed as they attempted to protect their own trading interests. The USA pulled away further into isolationism. The British established **protectionism** for trade within their empire in the Ottawa Agreements (1932). Although France and Italy took longer to be affected, as they were not as heavily dependent on international trade, they too had a downturn in their economies.

The responses to the Depression by the democratic states seemed to lead back to an old-style diplomacy – alliances and agreements outside the League. The strategy of appeasing countries in response to aggression became more realistic. Economic sanctions were not palatable and to take on aggressors by force was not, at least in the early 1930s when the Depression was tightening its grip, a viable option.

Activity 15

ATL Thinking and social skills

Source Analysis

The depression that followed the Wall Street Crash was the worst in the history of the industrial world. It struck at a time when confidence in the long-term survival of the social order and world peace was already in the balance. Communism preached the imminent collapse of capitalism; 1929 heralded that collapse. As the crisis deepened governments struggled to protect the established order and prevent social revolution ... The international economic order broke down; 'beggar my neighbour' policies replaced co-operation. Britain and Germany came close to the point of national bankruptcy in 1931. American politicians thought their Republic was closer to revolution in 1932 than at any time in its history ... Economic nationalism became the order of the day; economic considerations openly trespassed into foreign policy, so that economic rivalry was expressed in terms of sharper political conflict. It was no mere chance that economic recovery at the end of the 1930s was fuelled by high levels of rearmament. The 'have-not' nations were determined to improve their economic share of the cake by force.

Richard Overy, *The Road to War*, 2nd ed. (2009), pp.411–412.

1. In pairs, identify the international impact of the Great Depression as suggested by Richard Overy.

The Manchurian dispute

Japan was the only independent Asian power with its own empire – an empire that had expanded in 1920 when Japan took over the Mariana and Caroline Islands as mandates.

Japan was also Asia's greatest industrial and trading power, and so was badly affected by world depression. Some sections of Japanese society believed that the key to Japan's future economic survival was to expand its empire. However, Asia was already dominated by the European colonial powers: Britain, France, and the Netherlands.

These countries would not tolerate any threat to their interests in the region. In addition, the USA was attempting to increase its influence in the Pacific, and would be concerned with any 'aggressive' expansionism there.

In September 1931, the Japanese army in Manchuria, the Kwantung Army (responsible for protecting Japanese interests in the area), claimed that a bomb explosion near the town of Mukden was evidence of growing disorder and used it as an excuse to conquer the province. In reality, the Kwantung Army had planted the bomb, evidence of its desire to expand its influence in the territory. In this incident, one key member of the League had attacked another member – China. China appealed to the League for assistance against an aggressor. Here was exactly the type of incident that 'collective security' was designed to contain. The League of Nations took the following actions:

- It condemned Japan's actions and ordered the withdrawal of Japanese troops. The Japanese government agreed, but their army refused. This outcome exposed the lack of control the Japanese civilian government had over its military.
- It appointed a commission under Lord Lytton to investigate the crisis. The commission took more than a year to report, by which time the invasion and the occupation were complete. The commission found Japan guilty of forcibly seizing part of China's territory.
- It accepted the Lytton Report and instructed all of its members not to recognize the new Japanese state called Manchukuo. It invited Japan to hand Manchuria back to China.

In response, the Japanese said that they were leaving the League. They claimed that the condemnation of their actions in China was hypocrisy by powers such as Britain, which had a long legacy of using force to achieve its objectives in China. They may have had a point, but the new ideas embodied by the League represented a shift in international tolerance of this kind of empire-building.

CHALLENGE YOURSELF

Research skills 

Get into groups of four. Each student should research the impact of the Great Depression on **one** country in a specific region:

- the Americas
- Europe
- Africa and the Middle East
- Asia and Oceania.

Each student should select a different region to ensure the group can feed back on the impact of the economic crises on all four regions. Individuals should then feed back to the group; each group can then share its research with the class. Discuss as a class the extent to which the crises were 'global'. What factors made certain countries more vulnerable to the crash that began in the USA in October 1929?

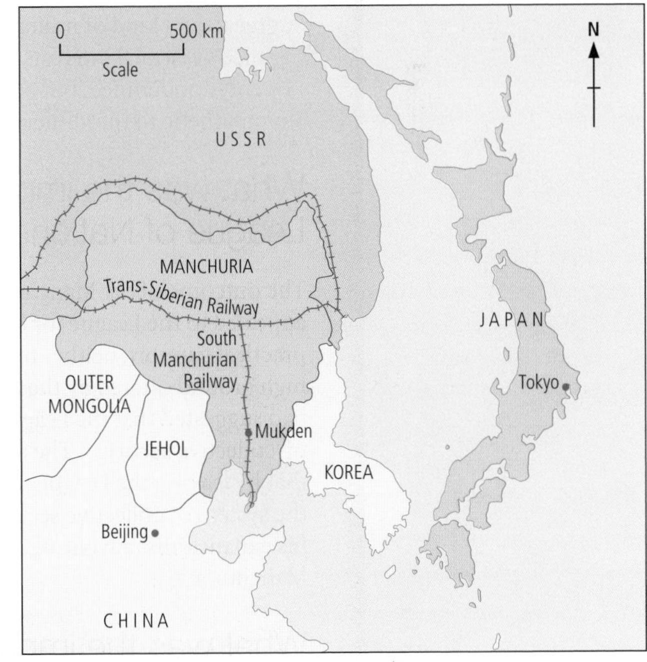

Japanese-controlled Manchuria, 1932.

Activity 16

ATL Thinking skills

Review questions

1. Explain Japan's motivation for attacking Manchuria.
2. What actions did the League of Nations take? What were the problems with these actions?

TOK

In Manchuria today [there is] a collision between twentieth century international machinery and a nineteenth century point of view ... [I] hope that the League's commission will be satisfied with no superficial approach to existing difficulties.

From a speech by the Honourable Vincent Massey, 14 January 1931, to the Empire Club of Canada, published in *The Empire Club of Canada Speeches* 1932.

- What does Vincent Massey mean by 'a nineteenth century point of view'? How was the 'twentieth century' view different? How far is our twenty-first-century view on empire-building different?

Why did the League fail to resolve the Manchurian Crisis?

There are several factors that contributed to the League's failure to resolve the crisis:

- The impact of the Great Depression caused the member states to be too preoccupied with their own troubled domestic situations. It also made them unwilling to apply economic sanctions. In any case, Japan's main trading links were with the USA, which was not a member of the League.
- Imposing any kind of military solution was problematic, as Manchuria was geographically remote, and only Britain and the USA had the naval resources to confront Japan; again the USA was unwilling to do this. Britain was unwilling to act alone and also did not want to risk a naval conflict in the region – it might well have been outnumbered by the Japanese (following the Washington Conference – see pages 119 and 152) and risk threatening colonial interests.
- France and Italy were too occupied with events in Europe and were not prepared to agree to any kind of military or naval action against Japan. Again, as with Britain, France's colonial interests in the region made for a confused response. Japan was openly condemned, but privately the government sent a note suggesting that it was sympathetic to the 'difficulties' Japan was experiencing.

What was the impact of the Manchurian Crisis on the League of Nations?

The outcome of the Manchurian Crisis was a dire failure for the League. China had appealed to the League for help in the face of an aggressor, but had received no practical support, neither militarily nor in terms of economic sanctions. The moral high ground offered by the Lytton Report's verdict was little comfort. The whole affair had suggested that the League lacked the will to follow through with its philosophy of 'collective security'. The aggressor had 'got away with it'. Richard Overy points out that by leaving the League of Nations, Japan had 'effectively removed the Far East from the system of collective security'. In Europe, meanwhile, Mussolini began planning his expansionist adventure into Abyssinia, encouraged by what had happened in Manchuria.

What was the impact of the Manchurian Crisis on the growth of Japanese militarism?

Traditionally, historians have seen the events in Manchuria as the starting point for the dominance of militarism within the Japanese government, which led ultimately to the Pacific War. Some historians, however, view the Manchurian Crisis as less significant to future events in Asia. In *The Manchurian Crisis and Japanese Society, 1931–33* (Routledge, 2002), Sandra Wilson argues that the crisis had a more limited impact on Japanese thinking than has been suggested. Wilson argues that most Japanese regarded the end of fighting in Manchuria in 1933 as a return to normality rather than the beginning of the militarization of Japanese society. Many people in Japanese society even believed that Japan would continue working cooperatively and diplomatically with Britain and the USA. She contends that the post-World War Two idea of a 15-year war beginning in the Pacific in 1931 has affected *our* perception of the Manchurian incident.

Activity 17

ATL Thinking skills

Source A

In 1933 Japan left the League and effectively removed the Far East from the system of collective security. In 1934, in violation of international agreements to preserve an 'Open Door' policy in China, the Japanese government announced the Amau Doctrine, a warning to other powers to regard China as Japan's sphere of influence and to abandon trade with the Chinese and the provision of technical aid to them. There is no doubt that Japanese leaders, spurred on at home by the military, were encouraged to go further after 1932 than they might otherwise have done because of the weak response from the major powers.

R.J. Overy, *Origins of the Second World War*, 2nd ed. (Vintage, 2009), pp.12–14.

Source B

THE ULTIMATUM.

JAPAN. "IF YOU GO ON SAYING I'M NAUGHTY, I SHALL LEAVE THE CLASS."

A cartoon titled 'The Ultimatum', published in the British magazine *Punch*. The caption reads: 'Japan. "If you go on saying I'm naughty, I shall leave the class."'

1. What are the key points made about the League's response in Source A?
2. What is the cartoonist's message in Source B?
3. In pairs, discuss how far political cartoons reflect the public opinion of the time. Can cartoons 'shape' public opinion?

The Abyssinian Crisis (1935)

In 1932, the Italian dictator Benito Mussolini began detailed planning for the annexation of Abyssinia (present-day Ethiopia and Eritrea). At this point, Eritrea was already an Italian colony, and had been since the 1890s.This move was not only an element of his long-term ambition of securing a north African empire, but also a tactic to distract his people from the impact of the Depression.

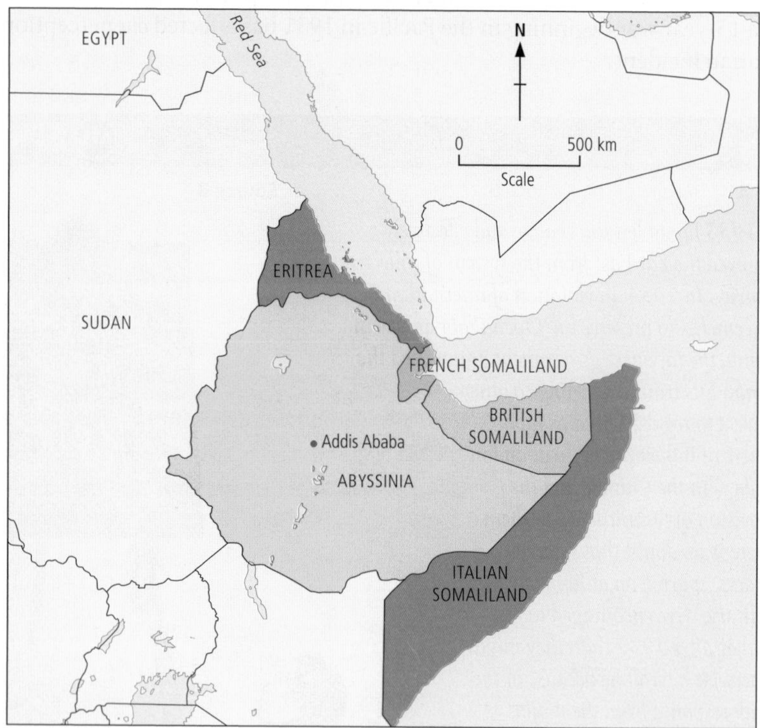

Abyssinia, 1934.

The conquest of Abyssinia would link together two Italian African territories – Eritrea and Italian Somaliland – and provide land for Italians to settle. At the Wal-Wal oasis, 80 kilometres inside the Abyssinian border with Italian Somaliland, Italian and Abyssinian forces clashed in December 1934. A full-scale invasion, however, did not begin until the following October, when Mussolini's forces were ready. He believed that the League would not respond, as Britain and France would not strongly object – Mussolini had been made aware by the French Foreign Minister Pierre Laval that he would be given a free hand in Abyssinia, and the British had wanted to reach an agreement in which Mussolini would have control over the territory without formally annexing it. Neither the French nor the British wanted to lose Italy as an ally against Nazi Germany. The Italians had already prevented Hitler from attempting *Anschluss* in 1934.

It was the brutality and ferocity of the Italian assault on Abyssinia, which began on 3 October 1935, that compromised Britain and France. When the 100,000-strong Italian army invaded, the Abyssinian Emperor, Haile Selassie, appealed to the League.

The League's response came on 18 October. Italy's invasion was condemned and the League decided to employ an escalating programme of sanctions. Britain and France worked for a settlement outside the League in an attempt to avoid a breakdown in relations with Italy. France was hopeful of gaining Italian support for an anti-German alignment that might help to contain Nazi aggression. Britain was faced with possible Japanese aggression in the Far East and also had to consider the dangers of having Italy as an enemy, when Italy occupied an important strategic position in the Mediterranean Sea, a major sea route for Britain through to its imperial possessions.

In December, the British Foreign Minister Samuel Hoare and the French Foreign Minister Laval rekindled a plan that had already been considered by the League in September. The plan, called the Hoare–Laval Pact, was to allow Italian control of around two-thirds of Abyssinia. Mussolini could have accepted this idea, but it was never to be put on the table, as it was leaked to the French press. The pro-League British public was outraged and Hoare was forced to resign. The plan was shelved. Despite this strong public support, the League's sanctions were so diluted that they had little impact on the Italian war effort. No **embargo** was put on oil exports to Italy, and Britain refused to close the Suez Canal to Italian shipping. Mussolini was able to escalate his efforts until May 1936, when the Italians were in control of Abyssinia.

Abyssinian Emperor Haile Selassie.

Activity 18

ATL Research skills

1. Visit pearsonhotlinks.com, enter the book title or ISBN, and click on weblink 5.2 to read Selassie's impassioned speech. Identify the key points he makes to the League on why member states must act to defend Abyssinia.

The British public (generally) supported action by the League, and public opinion was more important at this time, as a general election was pending in November. In France, the **left-wing** element also supported the League, whilst the **right-wing** was more sympathetic to Italy's cause.

Activity 19

ATL Thinking and communication skills

1. What do you think were the different perspectives on the Abyssinian invasion? Consider the permanent members of the League, then consider the smaller nation members, and finally the views of non-members, such as the USA. You may want to work in groups, each group taking a different country. You could take it in turns to be 'hot seated' – where a student or teacher takes on the role of representing a country or person – to present to the rest of the class the perspective and recommendations of your country to the League.

Activity 20

ATL Thinking skills

ABYSSINIAN DISPUTE
THE AWFUL WARNING.
FRANCE AND ENGLAND (together ?).
"WE DON'T WANT YOU TO FIGHT,
BUT, BY JINGO, IF YOU DO,
WE SHALL PROBABLY ISSUE A JOINT MEMORANDUM
SUGGESTING A MILD DISAPPROVAL OF YOU."

A cartoon from the British satirical magazine *Punch*, 1935.

1. What is the message of this cartoon?
2. What evidence can be used to support the cartoonist's viewpoint of the handling of the crisis?

What were the effects of the Abyssinian Crisis on the League of Nations?

For the League, the Abyssinian Crisis was a disaster. A permanent member had again successfully ignored the League and had been victorious through violence and war. The League had proved itself ineffective in using 'collective security' to maintain peace. The crisis had revealed (as had already been seen in Manchuria) that the leading League powers were not prepared to stand up to other major members if their interests were not directly threatened. It was too dangerous to invoke a conflict with a power that – while upholding the idea of collective security – might adversely affect their own power and international position.

Italy, now isolated from its former allies, moved closer to Nazi Germany. The alliance between the British, French, and Italians had collapsed. The League's ultimate weakness was exposed for Hitler to exploit, which he readily did with the militarization of the Rhineland in March 1936.

Many historians have viewed the Abyssinian Crisis as the 'final nail in the coffin' for the League of Nations. Thereafter, the League was simply symbolic of an ideal that had arisen out of the tragedy of World War One – an anomaly amidst old-style militaristic alliances and modern expansionist ideologies. The League of Nations could no longer exert any authority. Collective security had failed.

> *The immediate effects of victory were exhilarating. Mussolini had succeeded where the old Italy had failed. He had defeated not only the Abyssinians but the League of Nations. He abandoned his former cautious approach to foreign affairs and looked for new worlds to conquer.*
>
> **P.M.H. Bell, *Origins of the Second World War* (Longman, 1986), pp.63–64.**

The failure of disarmament

There were attempts to reduce weapons in the 1920s, though these were done outside the League of Nations rather than through it.

Activity 21

ATL Thinking skills

Source A

This cartoon from 10 May 1933 references the 1933 film *King Kong*. The caption on the board reads: 'Professor Geneva will introduce King Kong, The greatest monster in captivity.' The word 'Armaments' is written across King Kong's chest, and 'Peace' on the lady's dress below.

Source B

Article 8.1.

The members of the League recognize that the maintenance of peace requires the reduction of national armaments to the lowest point consistent with national safety and the enforcement by common action of international obligations …

4. *After these plans shall have been adopted by the several governments, the limits therein fixed shall not be exceeded without the concurrence of the several governments.*

5. *The members of the League agree that the manufacture by private enterprise of munitions and implements of war is open to grave objections. The Council shall advise how the evils attendant upon such manufacture can be prevented …*

6. *The members of the League undertake to interchange full and frank information as to the scale of their armaments, their military, naval and air programmes and the conditions of such of their industries as are adaptable to warlike purposes.*

1. In Source A, what point is the cartoonist making regarding the failure of disarmament?
2. Read Source B. What were the key aims of the League of Nations with regard to disarmament?

The Washington Conference (1921–1922)

After World War One, Great Britain, the USA, and Japan in particular continued to build up their navies. The cost of this military growth and the concern that the USA had regarding Japan's growing strength led America to call for the first post-war disarmament conference, held in Washington DC in 1921–1922. The Five-Power Treaty that was a result of this conference set naval tonnage to 525,000 tons for Britain and America, 300,000 for Japan, and 175,000 for France and Italy (a ratio of 5:5:3 for America, Britain, and Japan). The agreement would involve nations destroying battleships until their quota was reached. In addition, no new battleships were to be built for 10 years.

The Washington Conference also addressed other issues in the Far East. America and Canada wished to see Britain distance itself from the 1902 Alliance with Japan, and this was replaced with a Four-Power Treaty involving the USA, Japan, Britain, and France. It guaranteed the rights of all signatories to their possessions in Asia, and they also agreed to come to each other's defence in the case of an attack. A Nine-Power Treaty affirmed the territorial integrity of China and endorsed the concept of an 'open door' through which all nations could trade with China on an equal basis.

The conference was successful in limiting naval armament and was seen as an example of how moves could be made towards disarmament in other areas as well. All countries gained something from the agreements. The fact that so few powers were involved helped make this disarmament conference a success. Nevertheless, the conference highlighted the growing isolation of France, which now had to accept the humiliating position of being on the same level as Italy. It also did not include Germany or Russia in the discussions and agreements.

The London Naval Conference (1930)

The London Naval Conference revised the agreement made at Washington. With the Great Depression now taking hold in Europe, the major powers were still keen to limit their defence spending. The 5:5:3 ratio for the USA, the UK, and Japan was changed to 10:10:7. France and Italy refused to take part in this agreement, though they did agree to continue the ban on building capital ships for five years. Agreements were also reached on the size and numbers of cruisers, destroyers, and submarines, and rules were made to control submarine warfare.

The London Naval Treaty (1936)

In 1935–1936, the major powers met to renegotiate the London treaty of 1930. Yet the international situation had now changed dramatically. Japan no longer wished to limit its naval tonnage and be inferior to the USA and Britain, and so walked out of the conference. The Italians also left. Although Britain, America, and France signed a treaty on cruiser tonnage, all disarmament agreements became meaningless given the rearmament programmes of Germany and Japan.

The Geneva Disarmament Conference (1932–1934)

Between 1926 and 1932, preparations were made for a disarmament conference organized by the League of Nations. When the conference finally convened, 60 nations were represented, including the USA and the USSR. However, even at the preparatory stage, there were disagreements over what types of armament limitations should be discussed and how any resulting agreements should be enforced. By the time that the actual conference took place, in Geneva in 1932, delegates were faced not only with resolving these issues, but they were also faced with a German threat – if League members failed to bring about substantial disarmament, Germany would demand the right to rearm. By this time, Hitler's Nazi Party was the largest party in Germany. Hitler's demands were forceful and they made France even more determined to resist pressure for it to disarm. Germany demanded 'equality of status', but this aspiration clashed with French security. If Germany was equal, France would not be secure; if France was secure, Germany could not be equal.

In October 1933, Hitler (now Chancellor of Germany) dramatically led the German delegation out of the conference, which finally ended in 1934 having failed to secure any of its goals.

Why did the League fail to achieve disarmament?

Supporters of the League of Nations were perhaps most disappointed with its failure to carry through its promises on disarmament. However, there were many factors that made its task in this area almost impossible.

- The economic instability of the 1930s, following the Great Depression, caused, as we have already seen, nations to concentrate on their own problems first rather than work for collective security. Competition for markets grew and with it the dangers of conflict over them. In this position, nations were unlikely to feel that they could reduce their armed forces; indeed, some countries used rearmament as a way of providing employment and thus helping their economies out of the Depression.
- The political instability of Europe, with the new Communist regime in Russia, the fragility of new states in Central Europe, and a discontented Germany, made many states reluctant to limit their arms. France in particular, neighbouring a potentially powerful Germany and lacking any real commitment of support from Great Britain and America, was unwilling to do anything that would increase its vulnerability. Similarly, Czechoslovakia and Poland were looking for increased security given their proximity to both Germany and Russia.
- Japan's invasion of Manchuria undermined the idea of collective security and meant that nations with interests in the Asia–Pacific region were unlikely to welcome disarmament suggestions.

Activity 22

ATL Self-management skills

1. You have read about many conferences/agreements that took place in the post-World War One era. To help remember the key points, look back over the chapter and summarize these conferences and agreements in a grid such as the one below.

	Participants	Terms/agreements	Significance for international situation
Washington Conference 1921–1922			
Geneva Protocol 1921			
Rapallo Treaty 1923			
The Dawes Plan 1924			
The Locarno Conference 1925			
Kellogg–Briand Pact 1928			
The Young Plan 1929			

To access websites relevant to this chapter, go to www.pearsonhotlinks.com, search for the book title or ISBN, and click on 'chapter 5'.

Activity 23

ATL Communication skills

Essay planning

Consider the following essay question:

> ***Examine the reasons for the failure of collective security to keep the peace between 1920 and 1935.***

Introduction: You need to identify and explain key terms/concepts in the actual question. Here you need to explain the concept of 'collective security' and that the League of Nations had been established to facilitate this policy. You also need to show the examiner that you understand the relevance of the dates in the question. How did the situation regarding collective security change between these two dates? What is the relevance of 1935? Don't forget to set out your argument to show the direction that the essay will take.

Section 1: The main instrument for collective security was the League of Nations. In explaining why collective security failed, you need to outline the weaknesses of the League of Nations that were to undermine its ability to perform its task of keeping the peace.

Section 2: Collective security was undermined not just by the machinery of the League, but also by the continued willingness of countries to work outside the League to achieve peace: France in the Ruhr, the various agreements made in the 1920s, and so on.

Section 3: The impact of the Great Depression needs to be examined here, as this had a big effect on the desire/ability of nations to work collectively for peace.

Section 4: Here, analyse the specific events in the 1930s – such as Manchuria, Abyssinia, and disarmament conferences – that showed the inability of the nations in the League to work together.

Opening sentences

As indicated by the essay planning chart on page 42, the opening sentence of each paragraph in your essay is important for indicating the direction of your argument. Each 'topic sentence' should relate back to the question and set out the point that will be argued in that paragraph. A good topic sentence will also lead you into an analytical rather than a narrative approach.

Which of the following opening sentences to the essay above suggest an analytical approach linking to the question? Which suggest a more narrative approach or do not link to the question?

- There were several key events between 1920 and 1935 that created tension in Europe.
- The structure of the League meant that it would be difficult to follow through with the idea of collective security.
- The concept of collective security was damaged by France's unilateral actions in the Ruhr in1923.
- The League of Nations was set up in 1919 with the aim of keeping peace.
- The Locarno conference took place in 1925.
- The Great Depression was triggered by the Wall Street Crash in America in 1929.
- The Manchurian Crisis undermined the credibility of the League and its will to follow through with its philosophy of collective security.
- In 1935, Mussolini invaded Abyssinia.
- The reaction of the League and of key powers such as Britain and France to the Abyssinian Crisis proved conclusively that collective security had failed.
- The League of Nations consisted of an Assembly, Council and Secretariat.
- Collective security was undermined by the impact of the Great Depression.

Now consider the following essay question:

> ***'The League of Nations was inherently weak and therefore could not maintain peace.' To what extent do you agree with this statement?***

Introduction: Begin by identifying the inherent problems with the League's structure, mandate, and membership that made it weak and likely to fail. As this is a 'to what extent' question, you will need to present a counter-argument. State this clearly in your introduction – for example, explain that the League was not inherently flawed, but failed due to the impact of the Great Depression and the self interested actions of key member states and expansionist states.

Section 1: Always start with the argument presented in the question itself and give arguments to support this view, such as:

- weaknesses in structure, mandate, and membership
- failures to keep the peace in the 1920s.

Section 2: Now address an alternative view – that the League had the potential to succeed. Look at:

- strengths in structure, mandate and membership
- evidence of success in peacekeeping in the 1920s
- evidence of support for and strengthening of the League in the 1920s
- the international impact of the Great Depression
- the self-interested actions of key member states and the actions of expansionist states.

Conclusion: Based on the weight of evidence in the main body of the essay, refer back to the question directly.

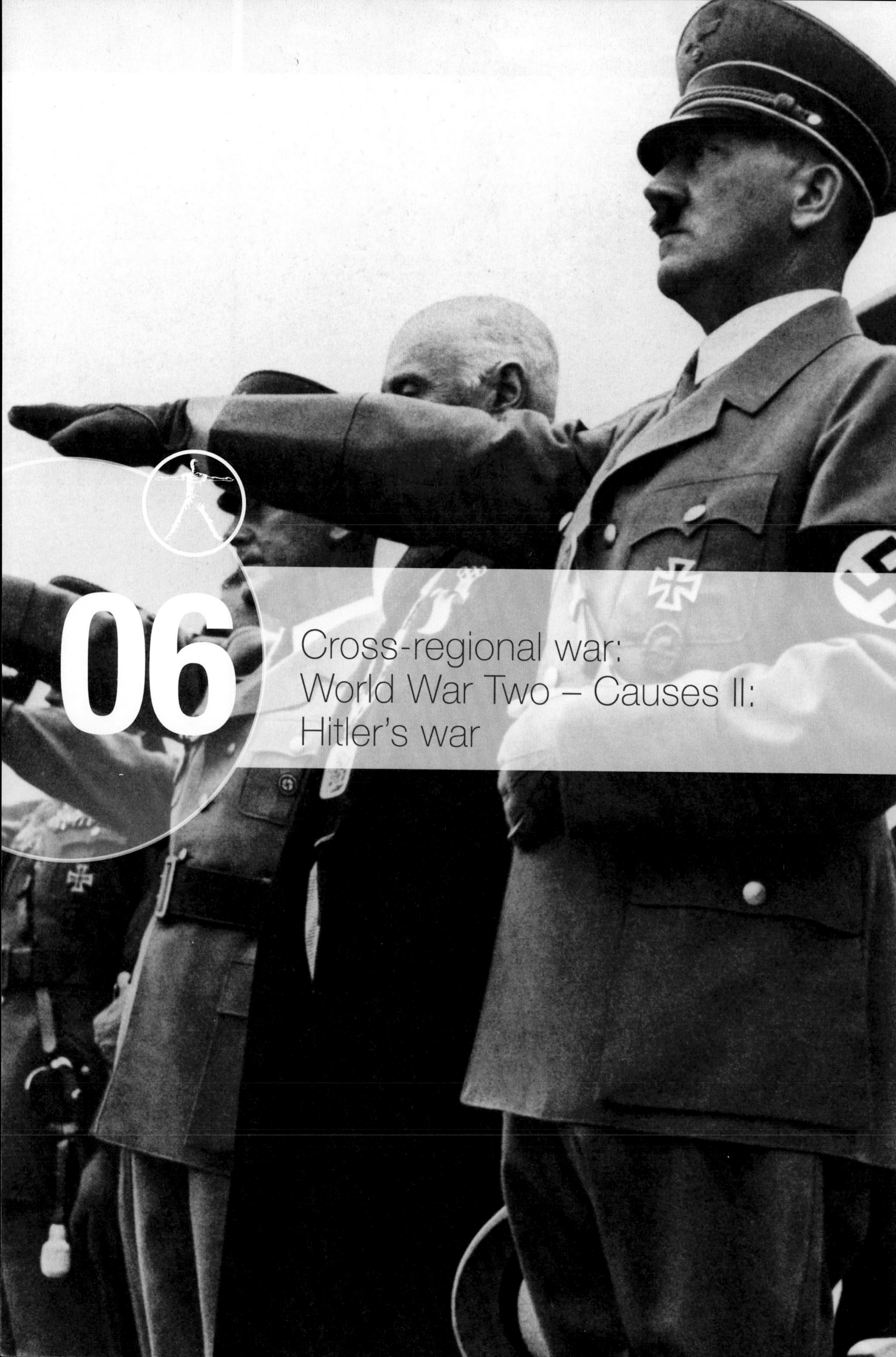

06

Cross-regional war: World War Two – Causes II: Hitler's war

Key concepts: Causation, consequence, and perspective

Adolf Hitler and his staff salute the teams during the opening ceremonies of the XI Olympic Games on 1 August, 1936 in Berlin.

As you read this chapter, consider the following essay questions:

- To what extent did ideology lead to the outbreak of war in the 20th century?
- Examine the role of economic factors as a cause of one 20th-century war.
- Discuss the short-term causes of one war in the 20th century.

As you have read, there were problems with peacekeeping in the 1920s, and there were aggressive and expansionist states that were threatening peace (Japan in Manchuria and Italy in Abyssinia) in the 1930s. Yet according to some historians, and according to Britain's wartime leader, Winston Churchill, World War Two was primarily caused by the ambitions and policies of Adolf Hitler – the conflict was 'Hitler's War'.

Timeline to the outbreak of war, 1933–1939

1933	Jan	Hitler becomes Chancellor of Germany
	Feb	Hitler introduces programme of rearmament
	Oct	Hitler leaves Disarmament Conference/announces intention to withdraw Germany from League of Nations
1934	Jan	Germany signs Non-Aggression Pact with Poland
1935	Jan	Plebiscite in Saar; Germans there vote for return of territory to Germany
	Mar	Conscription reintroduced in Germany. Stresa agreements between Britain, France, and Italy
	June	Anglo-German Naval Treaty
	Oct	Italian invasion of Abyssinia
1936	Mar	Germany remilitarizes the Rhineland
	July	Hitler sends military support to Franco's Nationalists in Spain
	Aug	Hitler's four-year plan drafted for war
	Nov	Anti-Comintern Pact with Japan; Rome–Berlin Axis signed
1937	May	Neville Chamberlain becomes prime minister in Britain
	July	Sino-Japanese War begins
	Nov	Hossbach Memorandum; war plans meeting
1938	Mar	*Anschluss* declared after German troops march into Austria
	Sept	Munich Crisis; Sudetenland Crisis
1939	Mar	Germany occupies rest of Czechoslovakia; Lithuania gives up port of Memel to Germany; Anglo-French guarantee of Poland
	Apr	Introduction of conscription in Britain
	May	Pact of Steel signed between Germany and Italy
	Aug	Anglo-French military mission to Moscow; Nazi–Soviet pact signed between Germany and the USSR; Anglo-Polish treaty signed
	Sept	Germany invades Poland; Britain and France declare war on Germany

In his account of the causes of World War Two, *The Second World War: Volume One, The Gathering Storm*, Churchill asserted that Hitler had a master plan for the domination of Europe, outlined in his book ***Mein Kampf*** ('My Struggle'; 1925–1926). Churchill went on to suggest that the 'granite pillars' of Hitler's plan had been to reunite Germans in a Great German Empire and to conquer Eastern Europe by force. War was inevitable in attaining these goals, and Hitler pursued these ambitions by creating a militarized nation. In Churchill's analysis, the turning point was 1935, when Germany began large-scale rearmament. From this point on, war was the only way to stop Hitler.

As you read through this chapter, consider whether or not you agree with Churchill's perspective on events leading to war in Europe.

Hitler's foreign policy aims 1919–1933

Hitler had fought in World War One and the war left its mark on the young Austrian. He had been temporarily blinded in a gas attack, and it was while he was recovering in hospital that he heard of Germany's surrender. It was then, Hitler has stated, that he decided to 'go into politics'.

With the defeat of Russia on the Eastern Front, and the terms of the Treaty of Brest-Litovsk in 1917, Germany had almost realized the domination of Eastern Europe (Poland and Lithuania became German territories). These gains, however, were lost when Germany was defeated on the Western Front. If you look back to the terms of the Treaty of Versailles in chapter 4, the perceived severity of the treaty meant that Germans, even democratic ones, wanted to reverse the settlement. Most could not accept the severe losses, particularly of territory to Poland. In addition, German commitment to making reparation payments was limited. Nevertheless, as both the Russian and Austro-Hungarian Empires had fallen, Germany was left in a potentially dominant position in continental Europe, even after the peace settlements.

Nazi foreign policy was shaped by this historical context, but Adolf Hitler also had ambitions that went beyond redressing the outcome of World War One. In 1919, Hitler became the 55th member of a new political party led by Anton Drexler – the Deutsche Arbeiterpartei (DAP; German Workers' Party), later renamed the Nationalsozialistische Deutsche Arbeiterpartei (NSDAP; National Socialist German Workers' Party – 'Nazi' for short) in 1920. By 1921, Hitler had become party leader. The **Nazi** Party set down a 25-point programme, which included key objectives such as the union of all Germans, an end to the Treaty of Versailles, a strong state, the creation of a national army, and the exclusion of Jews from German society. The programme is clear evidence that Hitler had long-term objectives that would cause tension and, potentially, conflict in Europe.

In November 1923, Hitler and his Nazis attempted to seize power in a *coup d'état* in Munich known as the Munich Beer Hall Putsch (see the Interesting Fact box below). The attempt failed, and Hitler was sent to prison. It was while serving his sentence in

Munich Beer Hall Putsch

The French invasion of the Ruhr had led to an intensified feeling of nationalism in Germany. A right-wing plot was drawn up late in 1923 by the Bavarian state commissioner, the local Reichswehr commander, the chief of the provincial police, and Hitler's NSDAP to overthrow the Republic. On 8 November, Hitler burst into a political meeting in a Munich beer hall and, supported by units of his ***Sturmabteilung*** (SA) guard, declared that a **putsch** (the German word for coup) was taking place. However, as they were outnumbered on the streets the following day, Hitler attempted to get the local *Reichswehr* to join him. As they marched to the barracks, their path was blocked and 16 Nazis were killed. The rest ran away. After the attempted putsch, General Ludendorff – a supporter of Hitler – and Hitler himself stood trial. Ludendorff was released, but Hitler was sentenced to 5 years in prison. He served only one.

prison that Hitler wrote *Mein Kampf*. The book was a combination of autobiography and political philosophy – it covered racist and authoritarian theories and ideas for the direction of Nazi foreign policy. In this book, Hitler asserted the need for German racial purity and the absolute absolute necessity of acquiring 'living space' – known as ***Lebensraum*** – for the German population.

> *Only an adequate large space on this earth assures a nation of freedom of existence ... We must hold unflinchingly to our aim ... to secure for the German people the land and soil to which they are entitled.*
>
> **From Adolf Hitler, *Mein Kampf*, 1925.**

The historian Andreas Hillgruber suggested that the plans set down in *Mein Kampf* could be viewed as Hitler's *Stufenplan*, or 'stage-by-stage plan'. The first stage would be the termination of the Treaty of Versailles and the formation of an alliance with Britain and Italy. The second stage would be a war against France and her Eastern European allies. The last stage would be a war with the USSR. Hitler, however, did not use the term *Stufenplan* in his book. Indeed, *Mein Kampf*'s value as evidence of war planning by Hitler has been debated by historians. Statements like the quotation above were taken by many people as evidence of Hitler's clear intention for world domination. A.J.P. Taylor, by contrast, sees *Mein Kampf* as rather more irrelevant and just a work of wishful thinking by a then-failed revolutionary.

The Nazi Party did not do well in the German elections in 1928; Hitler retreated to Munich to dictate another book, *Zweites Buch*, known as the 'Secret Book' of 1928. This book provides historians with further evidence of Hitler's longer-term ambitions and his more consistent foreign policy objectives. In the book, Hitler develops many of the foreign policy ideas he discussed in *Mein Kampf*, although he suggests that in the 1930s a final struggle would take place for world **hegemony** between the USA and the combined forces of a 'Greater Germany' and the British Empire. Hitler also wrote here about his admiration for Mussolini, and his anger towards the German Chancellor Gustav Stresemann, whose foreign policy ambition was to return Germany to its pre-1914 borders. Hitler saw this goal as far too limited. He restated his principal aim of attaining vast territories of *Lebensraum*, to be taken from the USSR. The overthrow of Versailles was just the preamble to this objective.

Hitler's rise to power

As we saw in chapter 5, there was a period of optimism in international relations in the 1920s. From Locarno in 1925 to the Kellogg–Briand Pact in 1928 and the commencement of the World Disarmament Conference in 1932, there had been a sense of international cooperation and accord, which was manifest in the new League of Nations organization. Indeed, Germany had signed or been involved with all these agreements. Yet the stability was fragile, and the weaknesses of the League in maintaining peace by collective security had been tested and found wanting before Hitler came to power in Germany. The Great Depression undermined both the League's ability to resist aggressor states, and the willingness of member states to work together.

The impact of the global economic crisis was particularly dramatic in **Weimar** Germany (see chapter 5). The mass unemployment and despair that followed assisted Hitler's rise to power. Indeed, the Nazi Party's success at the polls directly correlated with the degree of unemployment in Germany (see graph on page 128). In the end, Hitler was able to come to power legally; a group of conservative politicians, including the president, General von Hindenburg, concluded that Hitler would be useful to have on their side. They believed that they would be able to control him. Thus, Hitler

CHALLENGE YOURSELF

Research skills 

Enquire into how Hitler and other leading Nazis developed the party after the failure of the Munich Beer Hall Putsch. What were the SA and SS? How did the Nazis use modern propaganda and media techniques in the late 1920s?

A Nazi election poster from the 1930s. The text translates 'Break free now! Vote Hitler.'

became Chancellor of Germany, democratically, in January 1933. He was now able to pursue his long-term ambitions.

Activity 1

ATL Thinking skills

This graph shows German unemployment figures between 1920 and 1932, and the Nazi vote share in the same years.

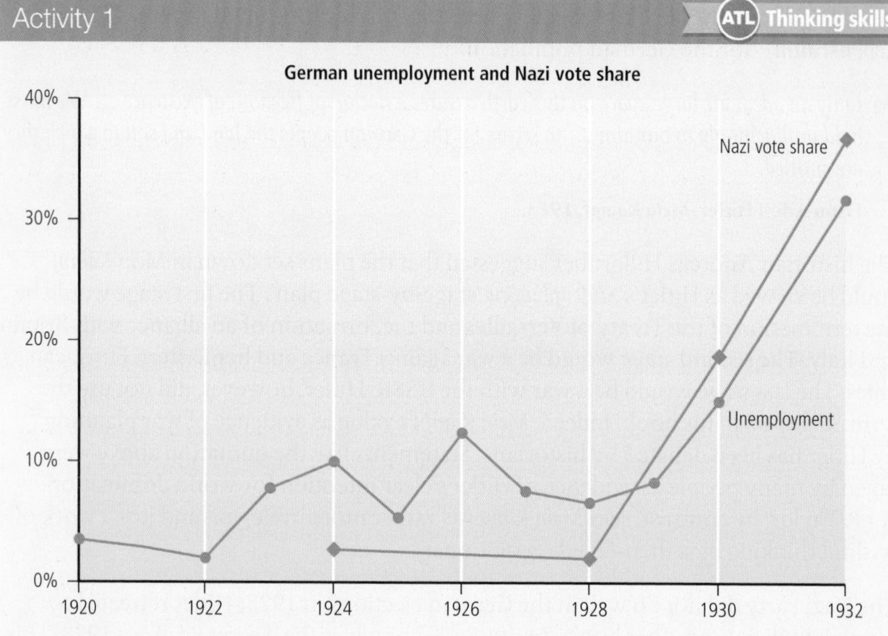

1. In pairs, look at the graph above. What does it suggest about the relationship between economic crisis, unemployment, and the popularity of the Nazi Party in Germany?

It could be argued that Hitler had to pursue certain aggressive foreign policy objectives, as such aims had brought him to power. His attack on the Treaty of Versailles and those who had signed it meant that many Germans believed he and the Nazis would restore Germany's international prestige through crushing the treaty. In addition, Hitler had been brought to power with the assistance of other right-wing parties in the Weimar Republic; much of this support was gained because of the Nazis' stated foreign policy ambitions.

Between 1933 and 1934, Hitler consolidated his control in Germany. He gained the tacit cooperation of the army and the industrialists, who both believed Hitler would bring in a massive programme of rearmament. The Nazi regime was **totalitarian**, and the rights of its citizens were subordinate to the state. Ultimately, this meant that the Nazis could gear domestic policy to meet the needs of their expansionist foreign policy. Military conscription and rearmament, meanwhile, could relieve mass unemployment.

Activity 2

ATL Thinking skills

1. From what you have read so far, what evidence is there that Hitler had a long-term plan that would lead to a general European war?
2. To what extent should the following have been aware of the potential danger of Hitler:
   a) German moderates
   b) foreign governments
3. How far do you agree that the Nazis' popularity was due to the economic crisis in Germany?

Hitler and the short-term causes of World War Two (1933–1938)

As we have seen, there is evidence in the longer term that Hitler had a consistent ambition to control 'race and space' – the Nazis wanted racial purity and *Lebensraum*. These themes are consistent in his speeches, writing, and policy statements throughout the 1920s, and then, once he was in power, appear to be the direction in which Hitler steered Germany through the 1930s. It would seem that neither of these objectives could be obtained *without* war.

Revising the Treaty of Versailles

Between 1933 and 1935, Hitler set about revising the Treaty of Versailles, a process that led to tension in Europe and placed pressure on the League of Nations. Hitler began by attacking reparations. Although repayment of reparations had been suspended before Hitler came to power, in 1933 he announced that the Nazis would not resume payments. The declaration was good propaganda, but was not a major cause of international friction, as most powers had already accepted this. What did increase tension was Hitler's intention to rearm Germany. As we have seen, Hitler manipulated the reluctance of France towards embracing general disarmament to justify Germany's withdrawal from the Disarmament Conference in 1933. German military spending in the year 1934–1935 increased fivefold when compared to that of 1933–1934. Historian Ted Townley writes in *Hitler and the Road to War*, 'For whatever final purpose, Hitler worked at this time to create a German economy that would provide total industrial backing for the German military' (Collins, 1998, p.9).

GERMAN MILITARY EXPENDITURE

Fiscal period	Million marks
1933–1934	750
1934–1935	4,093
1935–1936	5,492
1936–1937	10,271
1937–1938	10,963
1938–1939	17,247

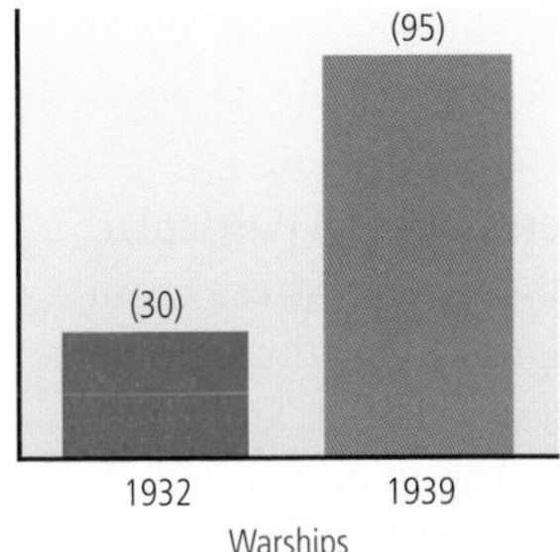

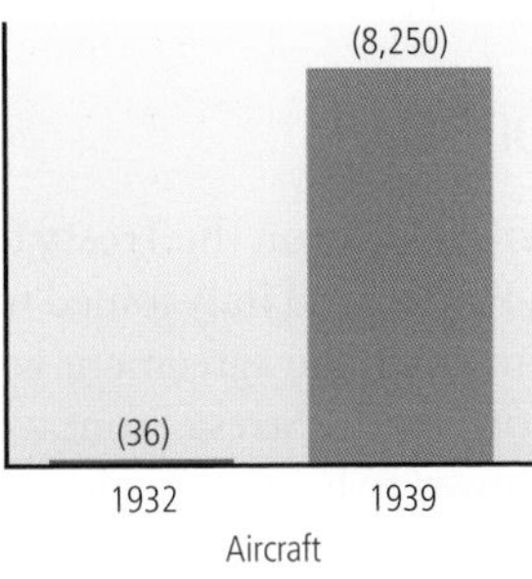

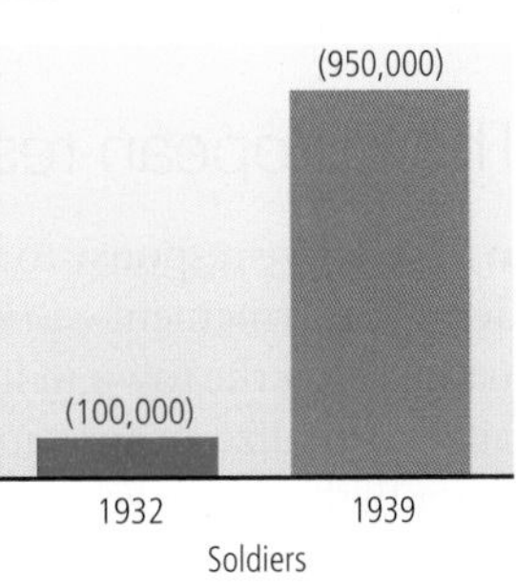

German armed forces in 1932 and 1939.

Hitler again showed his contempt for the Versailles settlement when he withdrew Germany from the League of Nations in 1933. Leaving the League, plus open rearmament, had put Germany on a new path. The Weimar Republic had attempted to work with the international community and the League to rehabilitate Germany. Hitler's new course, by contrast, alarmed the other powers, who were still suffering the effects of the **Depression** and therefore had limited means to respond.

Germany's rearmament can be seen as the fundamental first step in facilitating Hitler's expansionist foreign policy. Hitler's next step was to sign the 10-year 'Non-Aggression Pact' with Poland in January 1934. Although Germany resented Poland on account of the 'Polish corridor' separating Germany from East Prussia, Hitler had gone ahead with this agreement to secure his eastern border. Some historians, for example William Shirer in *The Rise and Fall of the Third Reich*, regard this agreement as evidence of Hitler's plan to dominate Europe.

The terms of the pact not only secured Germany's eastern border with Poland. They also undermined the French alliance system in Eastern Europe – the Little Entente – as it directly countered the Franco-Polish Alliance of 1925. To some extent, it also gave the impression to the international community that Hitler's intentions were ultimately peaceful.

TOK

Consider the extent to which you are personally interested in politics.

- Are you interested in the politics of your own nation, or are you more interested in the politics of other nations?
- What political issues do think are important or engaging?
- Do you agree with the policies of mainstream political parties or do you hold more independent or radical views?

In pairs, discuss why politics is important and why young people often feel remote from current political parties. What are the topics that are most important to you, and what knowledge issues are there in attempting to find answers to political problems?

Hitler's attention then turned to Austria. One of Hitler's stated objectives was to unify Austria with Germany, a policy outlined at some length in *Mein Kampf*. However, unification was forbidden by the Treaty of Versailles, and any attempt to achieve this might lead to confrontation with the European powers. Yet there were pro-Nazi groups in Austria, and in 1934 they murdered the Austrian Chancellor Engelbert Dollfuss and attempted to seize power in a coup. Initially, Hitler saw the coup as an opportunity to obtain his goal of *Anschluss*, but was deterred when the Austrian government crushed the coup and Mussolini sent troops to the border to warn Germany off.

Some historians have focused on this episode as evidence of Hitler's 'improvisation' in foreign policy, and argue that it suggests he did not have a long-term plan. Others, however, argue that Hitler was not yet ready to pursue his expansionist ambitions. He was still developing the Nazi state within Germany.

Hitler was able to use the pro-German Saar plebiscite in 1935 as very positive propaganda. The Treaty of Versailles had set down that there would be self-determination in the Saar by a public vote or plebiscite. The plebiscite was held in 1935, and the result was overwhelming: 9–1 in favour of reuniting with Germany. With the Saar plebiscite acting as a boost to his 'popular mandate', Hitler announced he would introduce compulsory military service in Germany. This step, again, was a violation of the Treaty of Versailles. At the same time he announced the increase of his armaments programme. Hitler now declared the existence of an army of more than 500,000 men, and admitted the existence of an air force. The other powers were deeply concerned, but continued to hope that a revision of Versailles would satisfy the more moderate elements of German society.

The European response

In a collective response to Hitler's attacks on the Treaty of Versailles – in particular German rearmament – Britain, France, and Italy joined together in the 'Stresa Front' (named after the town in Italy in which the agreement was signed). The three powers failed to finalize an agreement on *how* the Stresa Front would stop Hitler, and within a month the Stresa Front was shown to be meaningless when Britain and Germany signed a naval agreement. The Anglo-German Naval Agreement of 1935 allowed for a much larger German navy than was permitted by the Treaty of Versailles, and thus indicated British acceptance of German rearmament. The British had not consulted the French in signing the agreement and were pursuing self-interest, as the agreement was an attempt by Britain to limit German naval expansion. It was another passive victory for Hitler, as Britain had in effect condoned or at least accepted German naval rearmament. It also revealed that Hitler's aggression was successfully intimidating the other European powers.

Hitler was then able to manipulate the new international situation that resulted from the Italian invasion of Abyssinia in October 1935. Abyssinia was a member of the League of Nations, and the invasion led to the breakdown of relations between Italy, Britain, and France. Italy ultimately left the League and, with its humiliation at the hands of a key member state, the League was left impotent. Hitler's expansionist plans, with a rearmed Germany, could enter their next phase.

Activity 3

ATL Thinking skills

1. Which of Hitler's aims, as set down in *Mein Kampf*, had he achieved by 1935?
2. Based on Hitler's stated long-term ambitions, what would his next objectives be?
3. How far do you agree that Germany was the *only* country causing tension in Europe in the first half of the 1930s?

Activity 4

Discuss the question below in pairs and agree a draft response:

1. Based on the evidence in this chapter and the previous chapter, to what extent do you agree that events in the 1920s and early 1930s made a general war in Europe likely?

German remilitarization of the Rhineland

Up until 1936, Hitler had been rather cautious. He had capitalized on the international understanding that his aims were to redress the 'wrongs' meted out to Germany at Versailles. Yet there had also been clear indications that his objectives were more extreme. In 1936 Hitler turned his attention to Germany's western border. Versailles had made the Rhineland a demilitarized zone to help secure the border between Germany and France. France deemed this provision to be a key element in its security, and thus any attempt to remilitarize the area was potentially highly provocative. By this point, Hitler's army had grown, he had the backing of the more extreme nationalists in Germany, and he had the advantage of the divisions between the European 'defenders' of the settlement. Hitler bided his time until it was clear that Italy was going to be victorious in Abyssinia.

Hitler's forces celebrate the reoccupation of the Rhineland, 1936.

Nevertheless, some of Hitler's senior generals were concerned that France would take military action to defend the demilitarized zone; these included his commander-in-chief, Werner von Blomberg. Hitler assured them that he would pull out at the first sign of a French military response. The Germans sent 10,000 troops and 23,000 armed police into the Rhineland in March 1936. There was no response from the French or the British.

In France, there was division over how to react, and no support from the British, who generally were against resistance. Some contemporaries, such as Winston Churchill, argued that this had been a crucial point at which Hitler could and should have been stopped. Not only was the German force relatively small, but stopping Germany at this point would have undermined Hitler's position both politically and militarily. Nevertheless, you will read later in this chapter that the reality of the situation for Britain and France was complicated. Hitler remilitarized the Rhineland and moved on to his next objective, having achieved great popularity at home for this bold move.

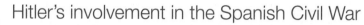

The Anti-Comintern Pact

The Communist International (Comintern) was an international organization set up in the Soviet Union in 1919 with the aim of spreading world revolution. In November 1936, Germany and Japan signed the Anti-Comintern Pact, which was later joined by Mussolini. This pact was directed against the Comintern in general, and the Soviet Union in particular. In case of an attack by the Soviet Union against Germany or Japan, the two countries agreed to consult on what measures to take 'to safeguard their common interests'. They also agreed that neither of them would make any political treaties with the Soviet Union, and Germany also agreed to recognize Manchukuo. When Italy joined the pact, the alliance of what would become known as the Axis powers was now formed.

Hitler's involvement in the Spanish Civil War

Hitler had entered the Rhineland while Mussolini's actions in Africa were occupying international attention. When the League criticized Italian action in Abyssinia, however, Italy and Germany grew closer together. With the outbreak of a civil war in Spain in 1936 (see chapter 11), both Germany and Italy sent support to Franco's forces. Germany's involvement in the Spanish Civil War was more limited than Italy's; for example, there were never more than 10,000 Germans fighting in Spain, whereas Italy had seven times that number. Hitler's motives for getting involved were not simply to benefit from another right-wing government in power in Europe, but also to test out Germany's new and improved armed forces. The nature of the German involvement in Spain is further evidence to support the argument that Hitler was preparing his forces for the realities of war in Europe. Infamously, at Guernica in northern Spain on 26 April 1937, the bombers of Hitler's Condor Legion tested out the effectiveness of civilian aerial bombing. It was an ominous indication of what was to come.

Rome–Berlin Axis and the Anti-Comintern Pact

A treaty of friendship between Germany and Italy was concluded in October 1936, and in November Mussolini first suggested the idea of a Rome–Berlin Axis around which the other European countries would revolve. Hitler broadened his alliance base when Germany signed the Anti-Comintern Pact with Japan in November 1936. In 1937 Italy joined the pact. The Nazi Foreign Minister, Joachim von Ribbentrop, believed Japan could be used as a force to counter Britain and Russia in Asia. The intention was that, by using Japan to apply pressure in Asia, Hitler would meet less resistance to his expansionist aims in Europe.

The Hossbach Memorandum

In August 1936 Hitler launched a 'Four-Year Plan' designed to prepare the German economy for war by 1940. Then, on 5 November 1937, he called a meeting in the Reich Chancellery in Berlin. This meeting was to result in the now infamous 'Hossbach Memorandum'. Present at the meeting were the key military men of Hitler's Germany. According to the minute-taker, Colonel Friedrich Hossbach, Hitler opened the meeting by suggesting that the subject for discussion was of the utmost importance, indeed too important for a wider discussion in the Reichstag. Hitler, Hossbach wrote, then went on to add that in the event of his death, the points he made at the meeting regarding Germany's long-term policy should be regarded as his 'last will and testament'. Hitler proceeded by stating that the key aim of German policy was to secure and preserve the racial community and to enlarge it. He then addressed the questions of when and how. Hitler suggested that after the period 1943–1945, the international situation would not be favourable to German ambitions;

The destroyed city of Guernica. Hitler's Condor Legion bombed the city in April 1937.

the re-equipping and organization of the armed forces was nearly complete, and any delay could result in 'their obsolescence'. The meeting considered scenarios in which France would be less of a threat – for example, in the case of domestic problems or a war with another nation – and the necessity of Germany seizing the initiative to take territory (for instance, Czechoslovakia and Austria). The second part of the conference focused on 'concrete questions of armament'.

This meeting has been seen by some historians as evidence of Hitler planning a general war, while others have questioned its importance. Many historians have agreed with the conclusions of Anthony P. Adamthwaite:

> *... there is no reason why the memorandum should not be accepted as a guide to Hitler's ideas on foreign policy.*
>
> *The Hossbach Memorandum confirms the continuity of Hitler's thinking: the primacy of force in world politics, conquest of living space in the east, anti-Bolshevism, hostility to France. Hitler's warlike intentions were now explicit.*
>
> **Anthony Adamthwaite, *The Making of the Second World War* (Routledge, 1989), p.71.**

Activity 5

Research and thinking skills

1 **a)** What key aims did Hitler set down for German foreign policy during the Hossbach meeting?
   b) Hitler did not seem interested in retaining the minutes of this meeting (none were taken). Is this significant?

2. Compare and contrast the nature and importance of the Hossbach meeting in November 1937 to the German War Council meeting in December 1912 (see chapter 2).

3. Read through a copy of the Hossbach Memorandum at The Avalon Project, which can be found online (see the Further Reading section at the back of this book). Would you identify any other points that suggest Hitler was planning for a general war?

4. The Hossbach Memorandum was used at the Nuremberg War Trials (a series of Allied war trials in 1945–1946) as evidence of Nazi Germany's planning for war. However, the historian A.J.P. Taylor has questioned its importance. Taylor points out that the memorandum is a copy of a copy, and even the original had been written from memory days after the conference. He suggests that historians have misunderstood what the meeting was really about. It was not, in his view, a war-planning meeting at all. Its true purpose was an internal political device to get rid of Hitler's minister for economics, Hjalmar Schacht, who was opposed to the cost of proposed rearmament.

   In pairs, evaluate the value and limitations of the Hossbach document as evidence for historians looking at the causes of World War Two.

Anschluss

In March 1938, Hitler sent troops into Austria. Where he had been resisted in 1934, 4 years later he encountered no military resistance. Italy was now an ally, and Britain, under the leadership of Neville Chamberlain, argued that the Versailles treaty had been wrong to enforce a separation of Germany and Austria. Hitler had seized his opportunity when the Austrian Chancellor Kurt von Schuschnigg had called for a referendum over the issue of *Anschluss*. Hitler's excuse for sending in troops was to ensure the vote was conducted peacefully. With his forces in place, the vote was overwhelmingly in favour – 99.75 per cent. Hitler was now strengthened not only by the Austrian armed forces, but also by the country's rich deposits of gold and iron ore. Tension in Europe increased as Hitler prepared his next move.

Activity 6

1. Read the source below. The historian Denis Mack Smith highlights the change in Mussolini's alignment with the western democracies in the 1920s to Nazi Germany in the 1930s. In pairs, identify the key points Denis Mack Smith makes in this extract.

> *In May 1939 a treaty was at last signed. Mussolini, the great phrase-maker who had coined the word 'axis', called it the 'pact of steel' after prudently discarding his first choice, 'the pact of blood.' His final decision to sign was taken in a moment of pique after foreign journalists reported strong feelings against Germany among the Italian people. He described these reports as lies and perhaps had been deceived by the artificial demonstrations in favour of Germany that he himself had organized. At his insistence, the alliance was drawn up not just for defence: since war against the democracies was unavoidable, it had for preference to be offensive so the optimum moment and occasion could be carefully selected. Whatever he later pretended, Mussolini signed in full knowledge that the Germans saw their next move as an invasion of Poland …*
>
> **Denis Mack Smith, *Mussolini* (Paladin, 1985), p.269.**

2. Examine the role of Mussolini's Italy and the shift in Italian foreign policy and alliances in the 1930s as a causal factor in the outbreak of war in Europe in 1939.

The takeover of Czechoslovakia

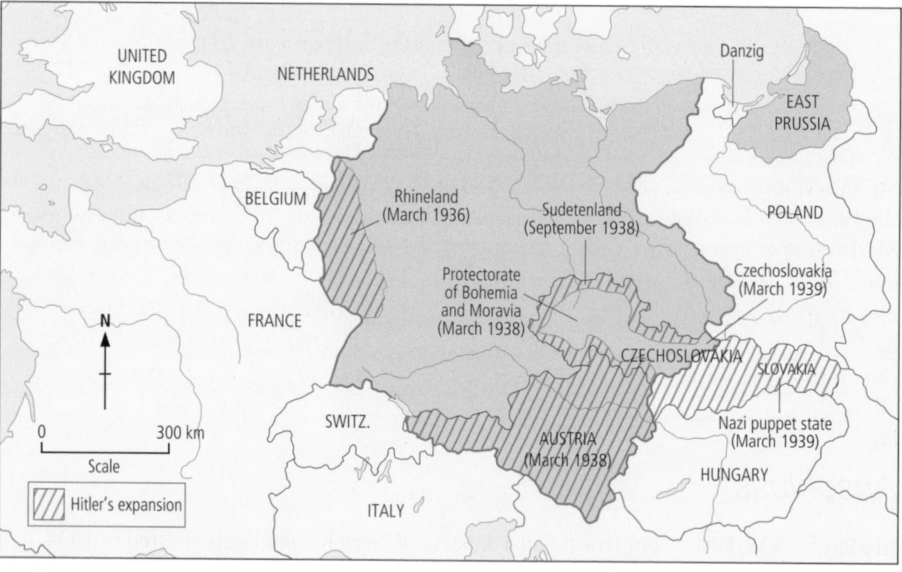

Map of Europe showing Hitler's gains up to August 1939.

Hitler's actions had clearly threatened peace in Europe. In pursuit of his long-term aims, it is apparent that he was methodically revising the terms of the Treaty of Versailles, so his next action was to regain the Sudetenland. The Czechoslovakian leader, Edvard Beneš, was fully aware of the imminent threat to his country, and appealed for help from Britain and France. France, bound by a treaty obligation, agreed to defend Czechoslovakia if it were invaded by Germany, although it was reluctant to do so. Britain then agreed to support the French. In May 1938, Hitler increased the tension by declaring that he would fight for the Sudetenland if he had to.

The Sudetenland

The Sudentenland was territory ceded to Czechoslovakia at the end of World War One. Its 3 million inhabitants were mainly ethnic Germans and the territory consisted of the border territories of Bohemia, Moravia, and Silesia.

This was a bold threat from Hitler, as the Czechs had a modernized army, with state-of-the-art armaments. They also had guarantees of support from Britain, France, and the USSR. However, central to their defences was the Sudetenland, a heavily fortified

region containing key industries and railways. Hitler had initiated a crisis throughout Europe – there was a genuine fear that a war was coming.

On 15 September 1938, Chamberlain attempted to resolve the crisis by meeting with Hitler. At his initial meeting, it seemed as though Hitler wanted a compromise too – he moderated his demands, asking for only parts of the Sudetenland, and only those if a plebiscite showed that the people wanted to be part of Germany. However, at a second meeting on 22 September Hitler increased his demands; he now wanted *all* the Sudetenland. Britain responded by mobilizing its navy. War seemed imminent. A final meeting was held on 29 September. Britain, France, and Italy decided to agree to Hitler's 'ultimatum' and give Germany the Sudetenland. This was known as the Munich Agreement. The three powers did not consult with Beneš and the Czechs, nor with the Soviets. Hitler had again achieved his objective by threatening force.

Although Chamberlain declared that the agreement meant 'peace in our time', he had at the same stroke authorized a massive increase in arms spending. Hitler's policies had led to a renewed arms race in Europe. On 15 March 1939, Germany marched in and occupied the rest of Czechoslovakia. The Munich Agreement was shattered. Hitler had taken over a sovereign territory, and the pursuit of his foreign policy objectives meant that war in Europe was inevitable.

'One People, One Nation, One Leader!' A poster of Hitler, 1938.

Hitler, Poland, and the Nazi–Soviet Pact

Hitler's actions put Europe on the brink of war. He was the aggressor; Britain and France had sought only peace. It was clear that Poland would be Hitler's next target. Britain and France had failed to respond to the occupation of Czechoslovakia, but now warned Germany that an attack on Poland would mean war. The policy of **appeasement** they had pursued throughout the 1930s was at an end. Britain and France attempted to back this threat up with an agreement with the USSR. During the summer of 1939, however, Stalin was also meeting with the German Foreign Minister, von Ribbentrop. On 24 August 1939, Germany pulled off one of the most controversial agreements in modern history – the Nazi–Soviet Pact. Essentially, the two ideological enemies agreed not to attack one another, and secretly they agreed to divide Poland between them. Although Hitler had signed an agreement with the country he intended to invade, this was a short-term strategic triumph, as it would allow Germany to invade Poland without the risk of a two-front war, and gain a launch pad for the later goal of conquering the USSR.

CHALLENGE YOURSELF

Research skills (ATL)

Research different newspaper reports on the Munich Agreement from the time. How was this crisis viewed?

Why did Germany sign an agreement with the USSR?	Why did the USSR sign an agreement with Germany?
• Hitler wanted to avoid a war on two fronts. • He did not believe that Britain and France would intervene to defend Poland once he had a pact with Stalin. • The economic aid which the USSR would give Germany as a part of the pact would negate the impact of any Anglo-French blockade. • Hitler still intended to invade the USSR at a later date – this agreement gave him time to deal with the West first.	• The pact meant that the USSR would not have to get involved in a war in the West. This was important as it faced a threat in the East from Japan, and the Soviet army had been weakened through Stalin's purges (see the Interesting Fact box on page 136). • It gave Stalin time to prepare for war, and there was always the hope that Germany and the West would weaken each other in the war and the USSR would be left as the strongest nation. • As part of the deal, Stalin got half of Poland and the opportunity to take over Finland and the Baltic States. • Germany was still the USSR's major trading partner.

Activity 7

ATL Thinking skills

Source analysis

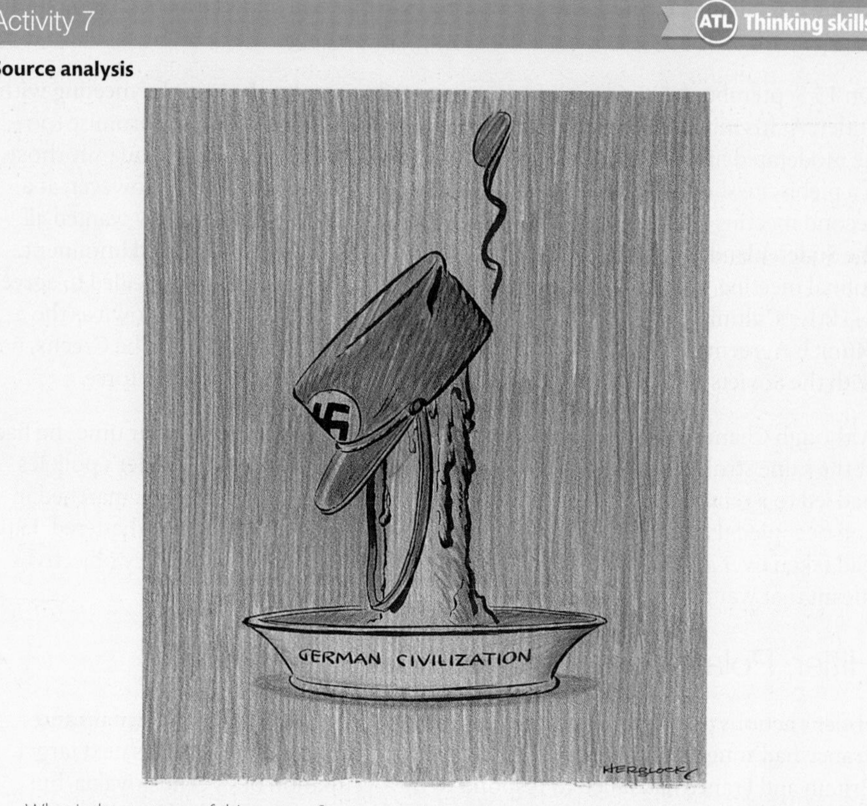

A cartoon by Herblock from 1933. Beneath his original drawing of the cartoon Herblock wrote: 'Light! More light! – Goethe's last words.'

1. What is the message of this cartoon?

Stalin's purges

In 1934, Stalin launched what became known as the 'purges'. Over a 4-year period Stalin arrested, tortured, killed, or sent to the gulag hundreds of party officials and military officers. They were accused of working with Trotsky and/or capitalist states against the USSR. They were often forced to endure highly publicized 'show trials', where they were made to confess to invented crimes. Stalin's aim was to eliminate possible threats to his leadership and to terrorize the masses into obedience. The purges were largely successful in achieving these aims.

The invasion of Poland

The most immediate cause of World War Two was the conflict over the independence of Poland. If you refer back to chapter 4, you will see how the Allied powers had created an independent Polish state that was given a land 'corridor' to the sea through territory that was formerly German. The important German port of Danzig was to be a 'free city', under League of Nations supervision, which meant the Poles could use it. Both sides knew that this solution would be a cause of future tension, and the Germans never accepted it. Soon after Hitler came to power, the National Socialists won a majority in the city's government.

Yet Poland was not only threatened by a resurgent Germany; the Soviets had also laid claim to the newly independent Polish territory. Poland had been given more territory in the east than it had before the peace settlements. In 1920, the Red Army (Soviet army) had invaded in an attempt to crush this new state and consolidate their control in Eastern Europe. The Poles had rallied and managed to defeat the Red Army in the battle for Warsaw. This victory was key to the Poles' new sense of national identity, and it was important in strengthening their determination not to make concessions to either the Soviets or the Germans in 1939. In November 1938, Hitler had told his armed forces to prepare a plan for the forced seizure of Danzig, and by the beginning of 1939 Hitler was demanding the city's return. The Poles decided that they would have to meet German demands with force.

On 3 March 1939, Chamberlain announced that Britain and France would guarantee the independence of Poland. The British now saw the issue as being a case of German ambition to dominate Europe versus the Poles' determination to defend themselves. One month after the British guarantee was made, Hitler ordered preparations for the invasion of Poland. For the Poles, cooperating with the Soviets to deter the Germans seemed abhorrent. Fighting was seen as the only option, and by July 1939 the country was confident and prepared for engagement.

Once Hitler had secured his deal with Stalin on 24 August, he could unleash his attack on Poland. Germany ignored the Anglo-French threat and invaded Poland on 1 September 1939. The reason given for the invasion was that Germany had been acting in 'self-defence' after having been invaded by the Poles. However, in reality, an inmate of a concentration camp had been dressed in a Polish army uniform, taken to a radio transmitting station outside the frontier town of Gleiwitz, and then shot.

> *Operation Himmler as this farcically transparent pantomime was codenamed thus encompassed the very first death of the Second World War. Considering the horrific ways in which fifty million people were to die over the next six years, the hapless prisoner was one of the lucky ones.*
>
> **Andrew Roberts, *The Storm of War: A New History of the Second World War* (Allen Lane, 2009), p.10.**

This time Britain and France kept their word and declared war on Germany. Hitler had started a general war in Europe. It may not have been against the countries he had planned to fight, nor at the time he had expected, but it was Hitler's war.

Activity 8

The role of ideology in Hitler's foreign policy

Read the sources below and answer the questions.

Source A

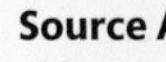

> *The assumption that the past and future of human civilization depended exclusively on the Aryans, that therefore they alone among the peoples of the earth deserved to live and prosper – this was the basis on which rested the entire superstructure of Hitler's ideological program, his concept of the role of party and state, his plans for the future of the German people. Race, far from being a mere propagandistic slogan, was the very rock on which the Nazi church was built. Hitler never appears to have had any doubts about the literal truth of his racial theories, nor did his more fanatic followers.*
>
> **Norman Rich, *Hitler's War Aims* (Norton 1992), p.4.**

Source B

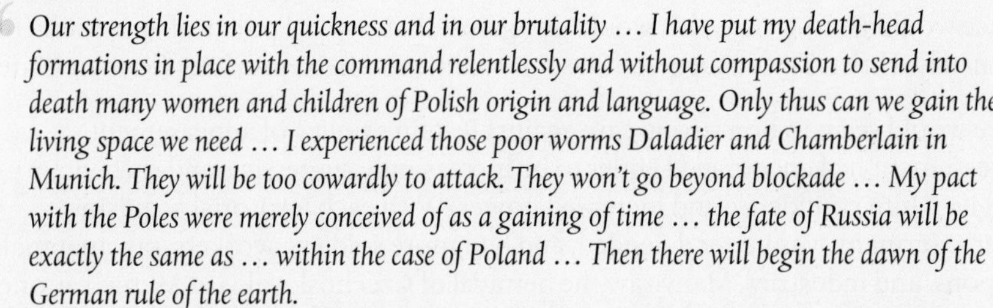

> *Our strength lies in our quickness and in our brutality ... I have put my death-head formations in place with the command relentlessly and without compassion to send into death many women and children of Polish origin and language. Only thus can we gain the living space we need ... I experienced those poor worms Daladier and Chamberlain in Munich. They will be too cowardly to attack. They won't go beyond blockade ... My pact with the Poles were merely conceived of as a gaining of time ... the fate of Russia will be exactly the same as ... within the case of Poland ... Then there will begin the dawn of the German rule of the earth.*
>
> **Speech given by Adolf Hitler to party leaders in Obersalzburg, Germany, on 22 August 1939.**

Source C

> *Hitler's ultimate goal was the establishment of a greater Germany than had ever existed before in history. The way to this greater Germany was a war of conquest fought mainly at the expense of Soviet Russia. It was in the east of the European continent that the German nation was to gain living space [Lebensraum] for generations to come.*
>
> **Eberhard Jackel, *Hitler in History* (Brandeis University Press 1985), p.24.**

1. With reference to Sources A, B, and C, discuss how important ideology was to Hitler's foreign policy.
2. With reference to its origin, purpose, and content, assess the value and limitations of Source B for historians studying Hitler's foreign policy.

Appearement as a cause of World War Two

As you read the next section, consider the following question:

- How important was the policy of appeasement as a cause of World War Two?

Appeasement was the policy followed primarily by Britain in the 1930s in attempting to settle international disputes by satisfying grievances through compromise and negotiation. It has been argued that by pursuing such a policy Britain and France encouraged Hitler's aggression. In consistently and continuously giving in to Hitler's demands, the Western democracies also further alienated the USSR and led Stalin to believe that the policy was designed to allow for German expansion in the East and to promote a conflict between the Nazis and the Soviet communists. In addition, appeasement also meant that Hitler gambled on that policy continuing in the case of Poland, and thus brought about a general European war when Britain and France changed their stance in 1939. Indeed, A.J.P. Taylor, in his 1961 book *The Origins of the Second World War*, disagreed with the view that World War Two was Hitler's war; he suggests that it was at least as much due to the failures of the European statesmen.

Taylor and others have argued that although there is evidence of expansionist aims in Hitler's speeches and writing in the 1920s, this does not mean that he had a 'blueprint' plan of what he would do once in power in the 1930s. They argue that Hitler was not 'acting' to shape, but rather 'reacting' to, the actions of other European leaders. (Taylor dismisses the importance of *Mein Kampf*, suggesting it was written to pass the time in prison rather than as a coherent plan for a future regime.)

Taylor goes on to argue that Hitler's successful dismantling of the Treaty of Versailles was the fault of the other European leaders who failed to contain Germany. It was too late to stop Germany over Poland, and Hitler was not convinced that Britain and France would go to war, as this would go against their typical policy of appeasement. Ultimately, Hitler, Taylor suggests, was not so different from previous German leaders.

There would seem to be a strong case against Britain's policy of appeasement. Appeasement had encouraged Hitler to be increasingly aggressive, and each victory had given him confidence and increased power. With each territorial acquisition, Hitler's Germany was better defended, and had more soldiers, workers, raw materials, weapons, and industries. Many saw the betrayal of Czechoslovakia at Munich as one of the most dishonourable acts Britain had ever committed. Furthermore, this act was all for nothing, as Britain had not rearmed sufficiently to take on Germany in 1939. Appeasement had also led to the USSR signing an agreement with Hitler, thus unleashing World War Two. The Nazi–Soviet Pact meant that Hitler did not have to fear a two-front war and could continue to provoke the West over his claims to Polish territory. Indeed, Hitler's continued expansion would now only mean war to the west, as he had secured his eastern border.

Activity 9

ATL Thinking skills

Source analysis

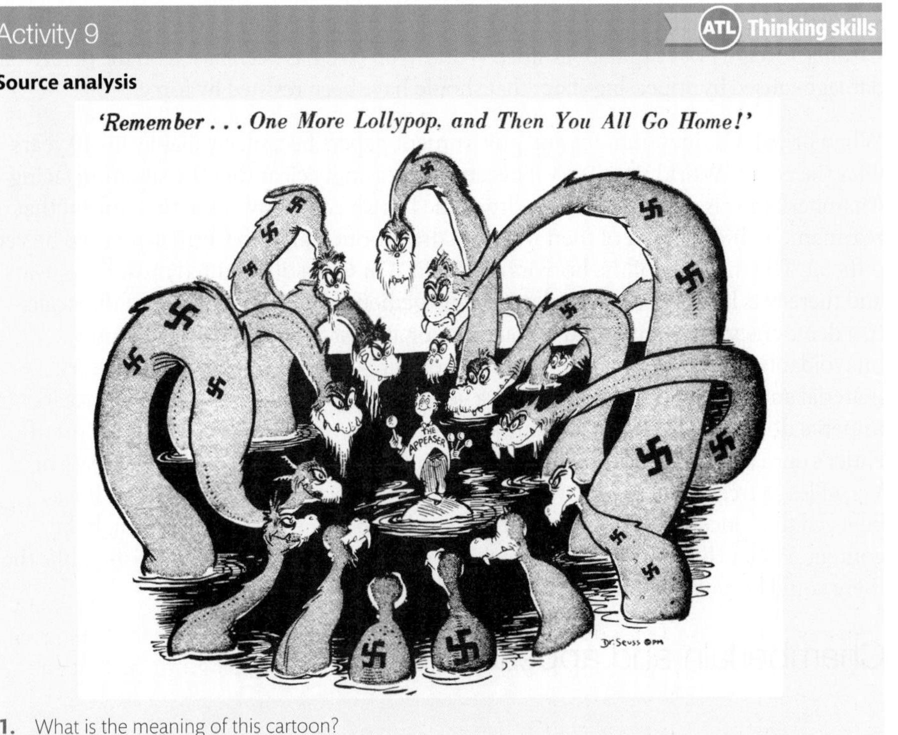

'Remember . . . One More Lollypop, and Then You All Go Home!'
THE APPEASER
Dr. Seuss

A cartoon from August 1941 by the children's author Theodor Seuss Geisel (also known by the pen name Dr. Seuss).

1. What is the meaning of this cartoon?
2. Discuss how the treatment of Stalin and the USSR during the Munich crisis may have led to Soviet negotiations with Nazi Germany and the Nazi–Soviet Pact.

Activity 10

ATL Self-management skills

Appeasement as a cause of war.

Appeasement as a cause of war

- Alienated the USSR – meant no 'anti-fascist alliance'
- Rewarded and encouraged aggression
- Inconsistent as changed policy in 1939 – unpredictable
- Gave Hitler the opportunity to rearm and then expand
- Policy meant Germany became too strong to challenge
- Dishonourable – sacrifice of Czechoslovakia
- Britain did not use the extra time to rearm
- Each time Hitler appeased it strengthened his position domestically and weakened his opposition
- Policy led to Nazi Soviet pact and this unleashed the Second World War

1. After reading the rest of this chapter, create a similar diagram, mind map or infographic to show:
   a) why Hitler's foreign policy can be seen as a cause of war
   b) why appeasement can be seen as a legitimate policy in the 1930s.

Can appeasement as a policy in the 1930s be justified?

Appeasement was viewed by many in the 1940s, and is seen by many today, as a cowardly policy that facilitated the aggression of expansionist states. Much of the justification for hardline foreign policy initiatives since World War Two has been based on the perceived damage caused by appeasing states that should have been resisted by force.

When British Cabinet minutes and government papers became available 30–40 years after the end of World War Two, it became increasingly clear that the situation facing Chamberlain was complex. The reality of the British economy at the time meant that rearmament and the cost of then waging a drawn-out war with Germany would be very difficult. The memory of the horrors of World War One still haunted most Europeans, and there was little popular support for engagement in another conflict of this scale. In a democracy, the people had to *want* war, or at least feel that war was literally unavoidable. This was also true of Britain's empire – in order to get the necessary material and human resources to fight a general war, Britain needed to convince its imperial domains of the 'just' and inescapable nature of war with Germany. Most of Hitler's demands, at least initially, were seen in the context of 'revising the Treaty of Versailles', a treaty that many British people saw as being too harsh anyway. It was believed that once the unfairness of the treaty had been redressed, Hitler might be content. When Hitler broke the Munich Agreement, this showed the British public that there could be *no* negotiated peace with the regime in Germany.

Chamberlain and appeasement

The British Prime Minister, Neville Chamberlain, waves the peace of paper containing the Anglo-German agreement of 1938, assuring the British public that it represented 'peace for our time'.

> *We have a clear conscience. We have done all that any country could do to establish peace, but a situation in which no word given by Germany's ruler could be trusted, and no people or country could feel themselves safe, had become intolerable … For it is evil things we shall be fighting against: brute force, bad faith, injustice, oppression, and persecution. And against them I am certain that right will prevail.*

From Neville Chamberlain's speech to the British nation announcing war with Germany, 3 September 1939.

Chamberlain's policy was grounded in the idea that Germany had three key issues that needed to be resolved – territorial grievances, economic problems, and absence of raw materials. His solutions were to give territorial concessions, economic credits, and colonial concessions. Appeasement would then lead to the strengthening of the more moderate groups in Germany, and a move away from the pursuit of the policy of autarky. Britain would then benefit by being able to reduce arms spending, plus international markets would improve and manufacturers could sell to Germany. Chamberlain summed up his policy to his cabinet on 31 October 1938: 'Our foreign policy is one of appeasement. We must aim at establishing relations with the Dictator powers which will lead to a settlement in Europe.'

Autarky

Autarky means being self-sufficient. This was a key objective of both Hitler and Mussolini – both wanted economic autarky so that they could survive economically without any external assistance or trade. Ultimately, this would enable them to have a degree of military autarky, so that their states could defend themselves without help from another country.

Chamberlain himself did not believe in peace at *any* price, and it has been argued that appeasement was buying time for Britain to rearm. After World War One, Britain had reduced its fighting forces, and was thus militarily unable to oppose Hitler in the mid-1930s. In 1936, the British government launched a Four-Year Plan for rearmament. Between 1934 and 1939 the defence budget increased fourfold. Between 1938 and 1939 it doubled. During the crisis over Czechoslovakia, the British government ordered the digging of air raid shelters and distributed gas masks. Richard Overy argues that appeasement was pragmatic until 1939/1940, when Britain's rearmament was at a stage that the nation could resist, if not defeat, Hitler.

Of course, the French also followed a policy of appeasement, although it can be argued that this was because they had little choice. The French could not act independently, and so they took their lead from Britain. However, their situation was also complex, as the case study of the remilitarization of the Rhineland suggests. Why, given the strategic importance of the Rhineland to the French and their concern that it be remilitarized, had they not challenged the Germans when they sent in troops in 1936? The French government believed that the German army might have forcibly resisted any French counterforce, and they might have received support from the population as they had done in the Ruhr in 1923. The French military were not ready for this kind of campaign; the focus of military planning from 1929 to 1934 had been the Maginot Line chain of border defences, and so the military could not give the government clear advice. In addition, the government in control was weak due to internal divisions, and some suggested that a military response would actually strengthen support for the Nazi regime.

Perhaps the key to understanding the policy of appeasement in the interwar years is the fact that throughout the West there was genuine fear of Communism. Hitler was seen by many, including leading politicians, as the 'lesser of two evils'. Indeed, it was hoped that Hitler's Germany would provide a strong bulwark against the spread of Communism across Europe. In this case, the fear of one extreme ideology fostered another.

Activity 11

ATL Communication skills

1. Organize a class debate on the motion 'The policy of appeasement was the right policy for Britain in the 1930s.'

For the motion: Look at the arguments mentioned above. Also consider the following: Richard Overy argues that Chamberlain's policy was the right one for Britain at the time, and to a certain extent the policy paid off in that Britain forced Germany into a war sooner than it wanted and at a time when Britain stood a chance of ***not*** losing. Overy contends that Hitler's economic and military planning would have led to Germany being a military 'superpower' by the mid-1940s if they had continued without challenge.

Against the motion: Churchill in the 1940s argued that World War Two was an 'unnecessary war', as it could have been prevented by opposing Hitler before he rearmed.

To what extent has the policy of appeasement had a negative impact on international relations since the 1930s?

TOK

How far do historians 'revise' their views of leaders and their actions with the benefit of hindsight? What are the knowledge issues involved in drawing conclusions about an historical leader? When we analyse current leaders, do we do this differently? Are there similar knowledge issues?

Reviewing the causes of war

As we have seen, each of the major European powers in some way made a contribution towards the outbreak of World War Two. Below are some of the most important issues to consider when thinking about their responsibility.

Britain

- Signed the Anglo-German Naval Agreement, undermined the Stresa Front
- did not attempt to use the League of Nations in response to the series of crises in the late 1930s – the League then became obsolete, and with it the possibility of 'collective security'
- failed to encourage a firmer stance from France over the Rhineland
- failed to support the Czechs at Munich
- failed to work harder for an agreement with the USSR
- committed itself to supporting Poland after it had pursued a policy of appeasement; so, it could be argued, Hitler did not believe that Britain would go to war over Poland
- the Polish guarantee made war inevitable.

France

- Committed itself to supporting states in Central Europe in the Little Entente, but did not follow up with military preparations to support them
- like Britain, did not attempt to use the League of Nations in response to the series of crises in the late 1930s – thus undermining the principle of 'collective security'
- failed to support the Czechs in 1938
- followed a defensive strategy focused on the Maginot Line
- did not work hard enough for an agreement with the USSR.

USSR

- Stalin had purged his armies in the 1930s and was militarily weakened; it was in the Soviet interest to work for a delay in a war with Germany
- Stalin believed that the Western powers' policy of appeasement was predominantly anti-Communist
- as the USSR was not invited to the Munich Conference, and attempts to find an agreement in 1939 by Britain and France appeared half-hearted, Stalin saw that his interests were best served by an agreement with Germany
- the Nazi–Soviet Pact unleashed World War Two by allowing Hitler to invade Poland
- the secret clauses in the agreement were cynical and expansionist; Stalin would recoup territories lost after World War One.

Italy

- Dealt a fatal blow to the possibility of collective security when it invaded Abyssinia and undermined the League of Nations; Italy then moved away from the Stresa Front towards Germany
- Italy encouraged the political polarization of Europe by intervening in the Spanish Civil War
- joined alliances with Hitler and with Japan.

Activity 12

Consider the following essay question:

To what extent was ideology the key cause of one 20th-century war?

Introduction: State which case study you will use: that is, the causes of World War Two in Europe. Set up the debate, explaining the two sides of the argument. You should also state what your key argument will be in the essay.

Paragraph 1: Always address the issue given in the title first. Here you need to set out aims of Hitler's/Nazi ideology. Consider the evidence of long-term planning before Hitler comes to power and then link this to the actions that Hitler takes after 1933 in pursuit of his ideology. Bring in the views of historians mentioned in this chapter to support your views.

Paragraph 2: Now consider the role of Communism, or rather the fear of Communism, as a causal factor in the policy of appeasement. Look at the role of appeasement in encouraging Hitler into actions that he might not have considered otherwise. Also, reflect on whether he was brought into a war for which he had not planned. Again, refer specifically to historians here in support of these arguments.

Paragraph 3: A counter-argument could be that the war was a continuation of German foreign policy ambitions rather than a war caused specifically by Nazi ideology. There was in fact a great deal of continuity between World War One and World War Two. This is a major argument of Fritz Fischer, who suggested that there was continuity in the aims of German policy-makers in 1914 and Nazi leaders in the 1930s. This continuity was founded on the powerful industrial and landowning classes, which remained in authoritative positions. They had played a vital role in bringing Hitler to power in 1933. Both **Wilhelmine** and Nazi Germany wanted to establish control over Eastern Europe to provide economic benefits.

When comparing and contrasting the objectives of German foreign policy prior to both world wars, there are some vivid similarities: Wilhelmine Germany was pursuing an expansionist foreign policy before 1914 and attained this goal, temporarily, in Europe in the Treaty of Brest-Litovsk. The domination of Central and Eastern Europe, and the creation of an overseas empire, were objectives for both Kaiser Wilhelm and Hitler.

Conclusion: This should reflect the weighting that you have given the different sides of the argument in the body of your essay.

Now try this essay question:

To what extent were long-term factors more important than short-term factors in causing one 20th-century war?

This question could be argued using Marshal Foch's statement on the Versailles settlement:

'This is not a peace. It is an armistice for 20 years.'

Points that you could develop for this essay include:

- German dissatisfaction with the Treaty of Versailles
- the 'German problem' (see Interesting Facts box on p.90)
- Italian dissatisfaction with the treaty
- how Britain's dissatisfaction with the treaty affected British policy towards Germany in the 1920s and 1930s
- the USA's retreat into isolationism and its impact on the League of Nations
- weakness of Eastern European states after the break-up of the Russian and Austro-Hungarian empires.

Make sure that for each point you refer directly to the question and consider how it contributed to the outbreak of World War Two.

You will then need to set up the counter-argument by considering the short-term factors:

- economic crises/impact of the Great Depression
- Hitler's Germany and Nazi ideology

Here is a third essay question to consider:

Discuss the causes of one 20th-century war.

For this question, you can start with the thesis that World War Two was caused by Nazi ideology. However, you also need to consider a range of other factors:

- fear of Communism
- economic factors/effects of the Great Depression
- weakness of the League of Nations
- the impact of the Versailles settlement and political instability in the 1920s and 1930s.

Again, make sure you link each point to how it contributed to war in 1939.

You will also have to answer questions that compare the causes of wars. Try planning the following:

Compare and contrast the long-term causes of two 20th-century wars.

For this question, review chapters 2 and 3. Consider the ambitions of Kaiser Wilhelm's Germany and compare and contrast these aims with those of Hitler's Germany. Refer to the first essay plan above on Fischer's ideas on this topic.

Contrasts could include collective responsibility/similar ideologies in World War One and conflicting ideologies in World War Two.

Activity 13

Historiography

1. This chapter has covered different perspectives on the reasons why war broke out in Europe in 1939. Review the key arguments presented in this chapter, and research the views of other historians. Attempt to find the views of historians writing at different times, in different languages, and in different regions. Complete a grid like the one below. Add historians from this chapter and historians that you have researched. Share your grids in small groups or to the class. Draw out the grid separately if there is not enough room here.

CONTEMPORARY AND HISTORIANS' VIEWPOINTS	
Contemporary / historian	**Summary of key ideas / evidence**
Winston Churchill	
A.J.P. Taylor	
Richard Overy	

When revising for an exam, plan out as many essay questions as possible on each topic. Have a copy of the curriculum guide in front of you. What key concepts and themes might the examiner ask you to consider? This strategy means that you will have considered all the different 'angles' on a topic before sitting the exam.

It is good to show knowledge of historical debate in your essay and to bring in direct reference to historians. However, these techniques alone will not get you a high grade! Avoid making your essay just a discussion about historians' views and avoid using historians' comments randomly. Historians' views or quotes should be used to support the evidence and viewpoints that you present as part of the overall argument of your essay.

To access websites relevant to this chapter, go to www.pearsonhotlinks.com, search for the book title or ISBN, and click on 'chapter 6'.

07

Cross-regional war: World War Two – Causes III: The war in the Pacific

Key concepts: Causes and consequences

As you read this chapter, consider the following essay question:

- To what extent was militarism the main cause of one 20th-century war?

A view of the USS *Shaw* exploding at the US Naval Base, Pearl Harbor, Hawaii after the Japanese bombing.

On 7 December 1941, Japan attacked an American naval base, Pearl Harbor, in Hawaii. In response, the USA declared war on Japan:

> *Yesterday, December 7th 1941 – a date that will live in infamy – the United States of America was attacked by naval and air forces of the Empire of Japan. The United States was at peace with that nation … No matter how long it may take us to overcome this premeditated invasion, the American people in their righteous might will win through to absolute victory.*
>
> **President Roosevelt's address to the nation, 8 December 1941.**

Japan's responsibility for war in the Pacific: the historical debate

The wars in Europe and Asia became a global war when the USA declared war on Japan and, following this, Hitler declared war on the USA. In the previous chapter, we discussed Hitler's responsibility for causing the war in Europe. We will now consider Japan's role in causing the war in the Pacific.

The flag of Imperial Japan.

Some historians, such as David Bergamini (*Japan's Imperial Conspiracy*, 1971), have argued that Japan had planned a war from the early 1930s and that the emperor had been very much involved. Indeed, Bergamini argues that although Japan appeared willing to negotiate for peace, this was cynically part of its plan to keep the enemy off-guard. Many historians, therefore, suggest Japan planned the war and that it was a clear aggressor whose aim was to conquer Asia.

Other historians, however, suggest that Japan was pursuing a more traditional European-style imperialist policy in Asia, while others emphasize the 'co-prosperity sphere' and Japan's attempts to achieve their aims through diplomacy. This latter view suggests that Japan's actions led to war, not because it had planned for conflict, but as a result of taking too many risks. Initially, gambles paid off, so Japan continued to take them. There is a clear similarity here to the view that Hitler was a gambler who just could not stop. In this view, Japan had attempted to avoid a war with both Britain and the USA, but when negotiations broke down Japan 'stumbled' into war.

The counter-argument to Japanese responsibility can be seen in the Japanese declaration of war, which stated that the USA was to blame for the war in the Pacific. Some historians support a line of argument that suggests that Japan's aim was to 'liberate' Asia from Western domination. Others compare Japan's actions to creating a sphere of influence not dissimilar to the USA's dominance of South America. Both argue that Japan had been continually provoked and mistreated by the West, and in particular the USA. Thus, Japan ultimately fought a *defensive* war that was triggered by American embargoes. Japan had to act when it did or it would be too late.

Unlike Hitler's Germany, the lack of a clear Japanese leader or leadership perhaps makes it more difficult for historians and students to decide on whether or not Japan had intended to cause the Pacific War. Although the head of state was Emperor Hirohito, he was not held responsible by the Allies in 1945 for causing the war. We will discuss his role at the end of this chapter.

A photo taken after the Japanese bombing of Shanghai, 1937.

Timeline of events prior to the Pacific War, 1853-1941		
1853		Commodore Perry first visits Japan
1902		Anglo-Japanese Alliance
1904		Russo-Japanese War breaks out
1915		The 'Twenty-One Demands' made on China
1919		Versailles treaty confirms some of Japan's war gains
1921		Japan participates in the Washington Conference
1926		Hirohito becomes Emperor
1931		Kwantung Army invades Manchuria
1932		Proclamation of 'independent' Japanese puppet state of Manchukuo in Manchuria
		Japanese and Chinese troops skirmish near Shanghai
1933		Tangku Truce establishes ceasefire line in north China. Japan withdraws from the League of Nations
1934		Japan abrogates the Washington Naval Treaty
1936		Japan rejects the principle of nine-power consultation on China issues
		Japanese government decides on fundamental objectives: maintenance of Japan's position on the Asian continent; resistance to Soviet ambitions; expansion into the South Seas
		Japan signs Anti-Comintern Pact with Germany
1937	**June**	Konoe Fumimaro becomes prime minister
	July	Marco Polo Bridge incident near Beijing
		Beijing conquered by Japan
	Aug	Japan captures Shanghai
		Japanese drive Chinese nationalist troops from north China
1937	**Sept**	Konoe calls for 'spiritual mobilization' for a long war against China
	Dec	Japanese conquest of Nanjing results in perhaps 200,000 dead (the 'Rape of Nanjing')
1939	**June**	Japanese army blockades the British concession in Tientsin
		USA notifies Japan that it will cancel the 1911 Treaty of Commerce and Navigation

1940	**Mar**	Japan sets up a puppet government in Nanjing
		Japan demands that Britain and France stop providing aid to China
	Sept	Tripartite German–Italian–Japanese Axis alliance signed in Berlin
		Japan occupies Indochina
		USA embargoes export of scrap iron
1941	**Mar**	Japan signs non-aggression treaty with Soviet Union
	June	Hitler attacks the Soviet Union
	July	Japan occupies southern Indochina
		USA freezes Japanese assets
	Aug	USA embargo on oil and gasoline to Japan
	Dec	Japan attacks Pearl Harbor and the south-western Asia/Pacific region

As with Germany in Europe in the 1930s, Japanese aggression has been seen by many historians as the main cause of war in the Pacific. To analyse this line of argument, we need to look at the development and actions of Japanese foreign policy in the longer term.

Japan and the long-term causes of World War Two in the Pacific

Background: Japanese relations with the West

From the mid-17th century Japan had been isolated from the outside world, a deliberate policy of Japan's rulers – the Shoguns – in response to the threat to their civilization posed by Christianity. The only exception was Dutch traders, but their activities were also severely restricted. For 200 years, the Japanese remained separate. Politically, economically, and socially, Japan functioned as a **feudal** state until the arrival of an American, Commodore Matthew Perry, in 1853. He aimed to negotiate with the Japanese to open up to American requests for trade and refuelling stops.

Due to their isolationist mindset, the Japanese were duly awed by the impressive might of Perry's American gunboats. The government tried to buy time, and Perry agreed to return in one year – with more gunboats. Japan responded realistically. They could not take on the technologically advanced West, and attempting to do so would be suicide. Their much bigger neighbour, China, had attempted to resist Britain in the Opium Wars (1839–1842 and 1856–1860) and had suffered a series of humiliating and unequal treaties. The Treaty of Kanagawa (1854), therefore, gave the USA what it had wanted, but more significantly it 'opened up' Japan to the outside world.

The ruling Shoguns could not recover from their inability to resist American force, and in 1867 power was officially handed back to the Japanese emperor. From 1868 he became known as the Meiji or 'enlightened' emperor, and his government set about modernizing Japan. In the ensuing period of reform, Japan became a limited democracy and stripped away its feudal system, including the rights of the ancient samurai classes. Japan rapidly industrialized and sent its young off to be educated abroad. A key reform was of its military, which was a priority for the new government. A new, modernized army was developed with the introduction of conscription in 1872 and the adoption of German military principles and methods. The Japanese followed the British in their construction of a new navy.

Sino-Japanese War (1894–1895)

With a newly modernized army modelled on the Prussian military and a new navy modelled on the British Royal Navy, Japan went to war with China in 1894. The Chinese were defeated and forced to sign the Treaty of Shimonoseki in 1895. China had to recognize that Korea was an independent kingdom and ceded Taiwan, the Pescadores, and the Liaotung Peninsula. However, the Russians, with the support of France and Germany, advised the Japanese to withdraw from Liaotung, as the Russians wanted the ice-free harbour of Port Arthur. The main results of this war were the emergence of Japan as the key Asian power, the further collapse of China under the influence of the West, and the frustration of Japan at having to relinquish territory to a Western power.

Japan proved the effectiveness of its modernization programme in victory over China in 1894–1895. The results of this victory had far-reaching consequences. Japan became the first non-European nation to be considered by the West as a world power. It was also now an empire that dominated Korea. Imperial growth fostered the idea that an expansionist foreign policy could be successful if it was supported by a strong military. Only generals and admirals could be ministers for the army and navy from 1900, and this meant that the government had a military influence from the beginning of the 20th century.

Japan's second victory was over Russia, which competed with Japanese interests in Manchuria. By the late 1890s, it was clear to Japan that Russia also intended to take over Korea. The Japanese needed a European ally to counter the Russian threat to their own foreign policy ambitions. As the British were at this time coming out of their own isolation, they were willing to consider an alliance with Japan, as this would suit their own policy of containing Russia. Britain also had already been heavily involved in the development of the Japanese navy. In January 1902, the Anglo-Japanese Alliance was signed – it agreed that if either power was attacked by two other states, the other signatory would come to their ally's assistance; if only one power attacked a signatory, the other would remain neutral.

The alliance gave Japan a much stronger position in its rivalry with Russia. Russia was unimpressed with Japan's recent victory in China and with her new alliance; in February 1904 both Russian and Japanese forces entered Korea. Admiral Togo Heichachiro destroyed the Russian fleet in the Tsushima Strait on 27 May 1905, and only 6,000 of 18,000 Russian sailors survived, while just 116 Japanese sailors were killed. The Russians were also convincingly defeated on the land, and they surrendered in March 1905.

The results of the war were far-reaching, as they encouraged Japanese nationalism and expansionism and triggered a revolution in Russia. The Russians were forced by the Treaty of Portsmouth to recognize Japan's 'paramount' political, military, and economic interests in Korea. The indemnity demanded by the Japanese was withheld by the Russians, who simply refused to pay the Japanese for the cost of the war, even though this was a usual component of a peace treaty. The Japanese had no way of enforcing payment from the Russians. In 1910, Japan made further gains by formally annexing Korea. In its actions, Japan had inspired the respect of the West, and the admiration of other Asian nations.

Activity 1

ATL Thinking skills

Source analysis

'The Giant of Brass', a cartoon in the *Brooklyn Eagle* on 2 May 1904. The caption reads 'Not so terrible as it looked'; the boots say 'Army defeats' and 'Navy defeats'.

1. What is the message of this cartoon?

Activity 2

ATL Thinking skills

Review question

1. What characteristics did the new state of Japan show by 1905?

Japan and World War One

During the early 20th century, we can see a consistency in Japan's attempts to expand its influence and make territorial gains in the region, and this ambition would increasingly bring Japan into conflict with the Western powers. World War One gave Japan new opportunities to expand. Japan saw the potential benefit of joining the war on the Allied side, and demanded German colonial possessions in China. This condition, the Japanese argued, was necessary to keep the peace in Asia. When the Germans ignored their demands, Japan declared war on them. In addition, while the Europeans were caught up in total war in Europe, Japan seized the initiative by making further gains in China. The government issued China with 'Twenty-One Demands' in January 1915. These demands would have given Japan the most influential political and economic position in China. International reaction to the demands was hostile. The USA was the most critical, and warned Japan that it would not tolerate any agreement that threatened US interests in the area. US–Japanese relations turned very sour.

After the USA joined the war in 1917, the Americans were determined that the Japanese would not gain more influence in China. The Japanese agreed to the Lansing–Ishii Agreement, which meant the gains they had made up to 1917 were recognized by the Americans, and assurances were given that no further expansion would be pursued at this time. The Chinese felt betrayed by America, which had been overtly sympathetic to their plight.

Japan again saw an opportunity to expand when the Bolsheviks seized power in Russia in October 1917. The Bolsheviks sued for a separate peace with Germany. Their former allies then launched a foreign invading force to support White forces (counter-revolutionary troops) in the ensuing civil war. It was agreed with the USA that Japan would send 7,500 troops to assist the White forces (which included the USA, Britain, and France) in Siberia. However, Japan instead sent 70,000 men. The Bolshevik forces defeated the White generals, but although the USA, France, and Britain withdrew their men in 1920, the Japanese stayed on. Nevertheless, they too were ultimately defeated, and had to withdraw in 1922. The Siberian expedition had failed and was seen as a humiliation at home.

Japan and Versailles: a 'mutilated victory'

During the Versailles meetings, Japan, a victorious power, aimed to increase its gains, and demanded an annexation of the German Pacific territories and the inclusion of a racial equality clause in the Charter of the League of Nations (see chapter 5). The USA, however, was sympathetic to the Chinese delegates' requests for the reversal of gains made by Japan during World War One. Nevertheless, the German concessions on Shandong remained in Japanese hands, which infuriated the Chinese and led to the demonstrations that became known as the May Fourth Movement.

Even though Japan felt that it had not gained what it deserved from Versailles, it did maintain its position in Shandong Province and gained some of Germany's former colonies in the Pacific. Japan had also benefited economically from World War One: the lack of foreign trade resulted in Japan becoming more self-sufficient, and without the competition of the other powers in the region its economy boomed.

Yet Japan's influence over China was still causing concern to both the USA and Britain. In 1921, the Americans initiated the Washington Conference, primarily to discuss tensions in China. As well as the USA, Britain, China, and Japan, there were representatives from France, the Netherlands, Belgium, Italy, and Portugal present. As we have seen, three key agreements were signed: the Four-Power Treaty ended the alliance between Britain and Japan, and the Five-Power Naval Treaty set the following ratios between each power's capital ship tonnage – 5:5–3:1–6:71–6:71 (USA–Britain–Japan–France–Italy). The final agreement was the Nine-Power Treaty, in which the signatories agreed to respect China's sovereignty. Both the Four-Power and the Five-Power agreements actually supported Japanese expansion in the region, the first by giving Japan security from Western attack, and the second by limiting US expansion – Japan could not afford to expand any more than the treaty allowed for, while the US could have expanded, but was prevented from doing so.

Delegates at the Washington Conference, 1921.

The tension between the USA and Japan was eased a little by the Washington agreements. In the 1920s, relations were relatively cordial, but this was due to the more 'peaceful' outlook of the liberal government in Japan, a situation that was to be short lived.

The liberal 1920s: a peaceful Japan?

World War One had made Japan the industrial centre of the East. However, the profits from the war were not invested well, and much was spent on funding various Chinese warlords who did not pay back their debts. Japan's foreign debt therefore remained high. The crisis that hit the banking system led to the printing of extra money, which then led to a steep rise in the cost of living. In 1918, there were riots over rice availability in many cities. The riches from war production had stayed in the hands of the wealthy.

In the 1920s, Japan openly embraced Western culture; architecture, music, fashion, and sport all reflected an enthusiasm for Western style. Hirohito became emperor in 1926. His title was *Showa* ('Bright Peace'), and there was some degree of stability, with the government of Prime Minister Hara lasting from 1918 to 1921. This government introduced social and economic reforms, and the military was contained mainly due to a strong feeling of anti-militarism in the early 1920s. The army was also divided over foreign policy, but the military showed its continued power when it sent more troops to Siberia after the USA pulled out. Japan's government seemed to show its 'peaceful' intentions when Hara ensured that Japanese forces withdrew by 1922. Indeed, Hara's government led Japan into the League of Nations, and its membership of the Council meant that it was accepted as a leading power. But the regime fell into economic difficulties as the wartime boom ended in 1920. Fear of an increasingly strong left-wing movement grew when the Japanese Communist Party (JCP) was founded in 1920. The Communists attempted to exert control over the trade unions, and in response the government clamped down on all 'Communist suspects'.

Despite the power of the left, the undercurrent of right-wing nationalism remained, and surfaced in November 1921, when Hara was assassinated by a right-wing extremist. Korekiyo Takahashi took over. He failed to redress the economic crisis and resigned in June 1922. After Korekiyo, until 1924, Japan was led by three ineffective governments. Kato Tomosaburo's government (1924–1926) was built on constitutional principles, and Kato extended the **franchise** to all men over 25. Kato's attempts to cut costs meant that he came into conflict with the army, as he took 2,000 officers off active duty. But Kato was not tolerant towards the left wing in Japan either. The Peace Preservation Law of 1925 meant that anyone opposed to the government could be imprisoned. Kato pursued a conciliatory policy with China and did not attempt to take advantage of the internal chaos there, a policy with which the army did not agree.

Kato died in 1926 and was replaced by Wakatsuki Reijiro. He too had supported Foreign Minister Shidehara with his policy of cooperative relations with China. His attempts to address another economic crisis failed, and he was forced to resign a year later. Wakatsuki was replaced by General Tanaka Giichi, and, under pressure from the army, a new and more aggressive policy towards China was adopted. The Chinese nationalists under Jiang Jieshi (Chiang Kai-shek) had been quite successful in their campaign to unify China by defeating the warlords. This worried the Japanese, as this success was a threat to their interests in Manchuria. The Kwantung Army attempted to interfere in Chinese politics by assassinating their former Chinese ally in the area. They had acted without permission from the government. Tanaka attempted to get the general staff to punish the offending members of the Kwantung Army, but they refused. It was clear that the army could ignore the government. Liberal parliamentary democracy was in decline, and the military was on the rise.

Osachi Hamaguchi became the new prime minister in 1929, but soon his administration was caught up in the global economic disaster of the Great Depression.

The demand for silk collapsed – this was Japan's key export. Millions became unemployed. The prime minister attempted to cut spending by limiting naval expansion, and cutting military salaries by 10 per cent. The military severely criticized the government, and in November 1930 another right-winger shot Hamaguchi, who died from his injuries in April 1931. Hamaguchi's death heralded Japan's descent into the 'dark valley' of the 1930s.

Activity 3

ATL Thinking skills

Review question

1. What impact did the following have on political developments in Japan?
   - economic problems
   - fear of Communism
   - political issues
   - strength of the Japanese army.

Japan and the short-term causes of the Pacific War: 'the dark valley'

As we have discussed in this chapter, Japan had a history of strong nationalism, which had reaped rewards during the Meiji period. The more liberal era of the 1920s was short lived because the army reasserted itself in the 1930s. As the military gained more and more influence, so Japan became increasingly aggressive. The growing power of the military led Japan down the road to war. Indeed, the attack on Manchuria in 1931 resulted from a plot devised by the Kwantung Army, not the Japanese government. Such unilateral action by the military alarmed the West, particularly the USA. Within Japan itself, the move was popular. The creation of Manchukuo had not been part of government policy, but it was accepted after the military success there. The army did not stop in Manchuria, but went on to Jehol (located to the north of the Great Wall, west of Manchuria and east of Mongolia). Although the Western response to Japan's attack on Manchuria was cautious, relations between Japan and the Western democracies deteriorated in the 1930s for the following main reasons:

- The West was alarmed by the Japanese bombing of Shanghai in 1932.
- In 1933, Japan left the League of Nations after the Council accepted the Lytton Report.
- In 1934, Japan, unhappy at having to have an inferior navy to that of the USA, pulled out of the Washington Naval Treaty and refused to attend another conference.

Sino-Japanese War: no retreat

In May 1933, Japan signed a truce with Chinese nationalists, which led to relative peace until 1937. The military, however, were pressuring for expansion in northern China, and in 1936 a failed attempt at a coup in Tokyo led indirectly to an increase in the power of the military. The attempted coup suggested that the government was not in control of its military and that maybe the military needed more involvement in internal security.

The trigger for the war between Japan and China in 1937 was a clash between Japanese and Chinese forces at the Marco Polo Bridge in Beijing. The Japanese government referred to the fighting as the 'China Incident', and many in the government suggested negotiating. Yet nationalism was running too high on both sides, and the fighting spread.

The war in China was to lead directly to the Pacific War. The Japanese had entered the war with no clear plan of how to end it, and a war on this scale required vast quantities of men and resources. It would be in the quest to acquire raw materials that the conflict with the USA was to intensify.

With the tension increasing in Europe, Britain and France did not want to become enmeshed in a conflict in Asia in 1937. America was also unwilling to get involved. Indeed, the USA only verbally condemned Japan's aggression, and even when – at the end of 1937 – Japanese forces sank the American warship USS *Panay* during their attack on Nanjing, the Americans accepted a Japanese apology and compensation. (So too did the British when HMS *Ladybird* was attacked.) Nevertheless, the USA began to take a harder line in 1938, and in December started to give aid to China. In July 1939, the Americans cancelled the Commerce and Navigation Treaty with Japan.

From 1937, the war with China led to a complete takeover of the Japanese government by the military powers. Prince Konoe Fumimaro, prime minister from June 1937 to January 1939, had announced in November 1938 that Japan was aiming to create a 'New Order' in East Asia – 'cooperation' between China, Manchukuo, and Japan. This idea developed into the Greater East Asia Co-Prosperity Sphere, which was based on the 'one state leading a group of states' model created by the Americans in Latin America. W.G. Beasley suggests that at a Japanese conference of ministers and military leaders in July 1940 it was agreed that Japan should 'establish herself' in Indochina, Thailand, Burma, Malaya, and the Dutch East Indies. (As with the meeting recorded by Hossbach [see the previous chapter], historians argue as to whether this meeting provides evidence of Japanese war planning.)

The Marco Polo incident

On the night of 7/8 July 1937, Chinese soldiers, for reasons that remain unclear, fired at Japanese infantry soldiers on manoeuvres near the Marco Polo Bridge, west of Beijing. This incident was used by the Japanese as an excuse to broaden their attack on mainland China, and within a few days they had ordered air, land, and naval units into action against the Chinese. Their aim was to capture Beijing. Some historians view this incident in 1937 as the beginning of the Sino-Japanese War.

Activity 4

ATL Research skills

Japanese soldiers prepare civilians for execution during the 'Rape of Nanjing'.

Japanese forces captured Shanghai in November 1937. They then moved up the Yangtze River and laid siege to Nanjing, the Chinese nationalists' capital. The Japanese finally took Nanjing in December, and then perpetrated what has become known as the 'Rape of Nanjing' or the 'Nanjing Massacre'.

1. In pairs or small groups, research what happened in Nanjing in December 1937.

Activity 5

ATL Thinking skills

Review questions

1. To what extent was Japan pursuing nationalist and imperialist goals?
2. How far was militarism the driving force in Japan's foreign policy by 1937?

Activity 6

ATL Thinking skills

Source analysis

Source A

> *The army had prepared carefully for war against the Soviet Union, but had done no planning worthy of the name for a general war with China. Army leaders could not conceive of the Chinese putting up a good fight ... How could China be brought to its knees? That was the major problem. Unable to get a negotiated settlement on favourable terms or win a final military success, Japanese leaders sought victory by expanding the conflict.*

From Saburo Ienaga, *The Pacific War* (Iwanami Shoten, 1968), p.85 of English translation.

Source B

A cartoon from 1931 that satirizes the Japanese seizure of Manchuria.

1. What is the message of this cartoon?

Activity 7

ATL Thinking skills

In August 1907, officers of the Japanese navy drew up an operation plan that would become a cornerstone of defence planning. It was a plan to destroy the American fleet in the Pacific. Japan's military planning from the beginning of the 20th century focused on being able to confront the Russians on the land, and the Americans at sea.

1. In pairs, discuss why Japan may have identified these factors as key to its military planning.

Expansion of the war into South-East Asia

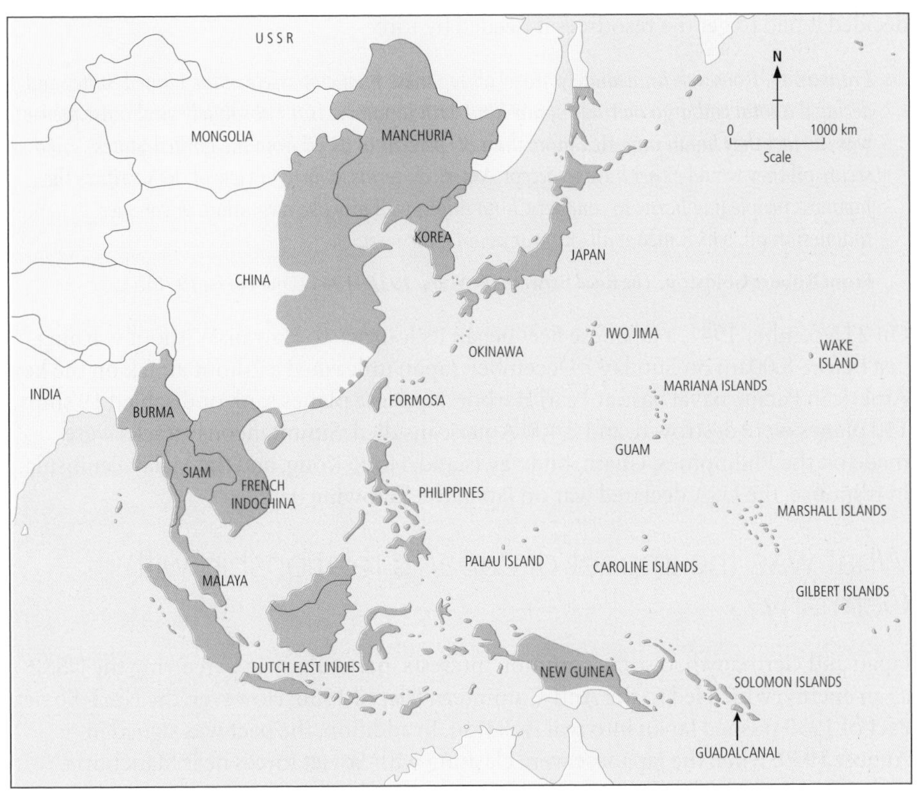

The furthest extent of Japan's Empire in 1942.

The USA responded to Japanese actions in China by cancelling the 1911 Treaty of Commerce and Navigation with Japan. This did not deter the Japanese, and in March 1941 Japan set up a puppet government in Nanjing. In June 1940, with Britain undermined by Hitler's swift victory over France, the Japanese forced the closure of the Burma Road, which was an important supply route for the Chinese. The Americans stepped up their attempts to stop Japan's war in China in September 1940, by banning the export of scrap iron to Japan. This measure had a severe impact on an already fragile economy. Economic growth in Japan in 1930 was 0.5 per cent and unemployment by 1934 was 6.8 per cent. Japan had to import the food and raw materials – such as oil and steel – it needed to sustain its occupation of Chinese territories. It was heavily dependent on its trade with the USA for these goods.

In September, the Japanese signed the Tripartite Pact (see Interesting Facts box). In November, the Americans gave the Chinese nationalist leader, Jiang Jieshi, a massive loan to encourage and strengthen China's ability to resist Japan. Within Japan, the Imperial Rule Assistance Association replaced political parties in 1940, and in October 1941 Prime Minister Konoe was replaced by General Hideki Tojo.

Japan's military was now divided over which specific territory should be targeted next – the USSR or the colonial territories of the Western powers in South-East Asia. After Nazi Germany invaded Russia in June 1941, Japan made its decision and attacked south, occupying southern Indochina. The USA, Britain, and the Netherlands responded by imposing a total trade embargo. Here was a crisis for Japan – there was the danger that the country would run out of oil, and this would mean it could not continue to fight in China.

At this point the Japanese appeared willing to negotiate, but the American demand

The Tripartite Pact

Also called the Three-Power Pact and the Axis Pact, this was signed by Germany, Italy, and Japan in Berlin on 27 September 1940. The pact followed on from the Anti-Comintern Pact, and was intended to re-establish good relations between Japan and Germany following the Nazi–Soviet Pact of August 1939. The signatories agreed to establish a 'new order' and to promote mutual prosperity for the next 10 years. They recognized each other's spheres of influence and agreed to come to the assistance of one another if attacked.

for Japan to withdraw from China was unacceptable to them. When the USA froze Japanese assets in July and then placed an embargo on oil in August 1941, Japan decided it had to get the resources it needed by force.

> *Franklin D. Roosevelt immediately 'froze' all Japanese financial assets in the United States and declared a total embargo on trade of any kind with Japan … [Of] absolutely vital consequence was the fact that Japan imported more than 80 percent of its oil from the United States … To secure oil they would either have to accept American terms, which, in view of the sacrifices the Japanese people had borne to conquer China might well provoke revolution, or conquer Indonesian oil, which meant all-out war against the west.*
>
> **From Robert Goldston, *The Road Between the Wars, 1918–1941* (Dial Press, 1978).**

On 2 December 1941, a Japanese fleet began its journey to Hawaii. Without warning, just before 8.00am on Sunday 7 December, Japan unleashed a 2-hour attack on the key American Pacific naval base at Pearl Harbor. Japanese planes sank or disabled 19 ships, 150 planes were destroyed, and 2,400 Americans died. Simultaneous attacks were made on the Philippines, Guam, Midway Island, Hong Kong, and the Malay Peninsula. In response, the USA declared war on Japan the following day.

What was the impact of Japan's relationship with Germany?

Japan and Germany had some common interests, particularly in perceiving the USSR as an enemy, which led to the Anti-Comintern Pact of 1936. However, the Nazi–Soviet Pact of 1939 pushed Japan into real isolation. In addition, the pact was signed in August 1939, when the Japanese were clashing with Soviet forces near Manchuria.

Motivated by the staggering success of the German campaign in Europe, the Japanese signed the Tripartite Pact in September 1940 with Germany and Italy, which was primarily designed to deter the USA from becoming more involved in the wars in Europe and Asia. Japan's policies were linked to the successes of their ally, Germany; Hitler's successes in Europe encouraged a broader expansionist policy in Japan.

On 11 December 1941, three days after the Japanese attack on Pearl Harbor, Hitler declared war on the USA. In conversation the following month, Hitler gave his view that America was 'a decayed country … That's why, in spite of everything, I like an Englishman a thousand times better than an American … Everything about the behaviour of American society reveals that it's half Judaized, and the other half negrified. How can one expect a state like that to hold together … a country where everything is built on the dollar?'

What was the impact of Japan's relationship with the USSR?

Japan's relationship with Russia/the USSR had been tense, apart from the period 1907–1917 when they were both in alliances with Britain. After the Russian Revolution and the creation of the USSR, Japan was threatened not only territorially by the Russians, but also ideologically. Some historians have suggested that Japan considered the USSR as its only real enemy, and military planning in 1937 focused on this threat. During the initial stage of the Sino-Japanese War, the Soviets were the predominant suppliers of aid to China, and there was fighting between Japanese and Soviet troops on the Manchurian border in 1939. Tens of thousands of troops were deployed in these campaigns even though war was not officially declared. The Japanese defeat at Khalkhin Gol in 1939 helps to explain Japanese reluctance to attack the USSR.

Japan's isolation ended with the increase in hostility between Germany and the USSR in early 1941. The Soviets were now focused on the threat posed by Hitler, and Japan willingly signed a Neutrality Pact with the USSR in early 1941. With the launch of Operation Barbarossa (the German attack on the Soviet Union) in June 1941, the Russian threat to Japan ended. Japan attacked south instead of joining in the assault on the USSR, and it was not until the last week of the war, in August 1945, that the Soviets declared war on Japan.

To what extent was the USA responsible for the war in the Pacific?

> *Japan was the actor, China acted upon. And the US was the self-appointed referee who judged by subjective rules and called fouls without penalties, until just before end of the contest. This provoked the actor into a suicidal attempt to kill the referee.*
>
> **The diplomat John Paton Davies describing the relationship between the USA, Japan, and China.**

At the beginning of this chapter, we briefly explored the historical relationship between the USA and Japan, starting with the 'opening up' of Japan to trade and foreign influence in the middle of the 19th century. Relations between the two nations had at times been strained, but were also often cordial, with the Japanese embracing American culture and trading relations. The Americans were suspicious of Japan's alliance with Britain, however, and did not want an Asian competitor to their interests in the region. Following World War One, the USA set out to contain Japan, first by limiting Japanese gains at Versailles and second by ending Japan's relationship with Britain.

Japan was very offended when the National Origins Act was passed by the American Congress in May 1924. The act set quotas on immigration to the USA, but omitted Japan – this meant that immigration from Japan to the USA was to cease. The Japanese had warned the Americans prior to passing the act that this would have a serious negative impact on relations, but the USA passed the policy anyway. The importance of these events was that they gave the Japanese military good propaganda – proof of discrimination against Japan.

As Japan's liberal government stumbled and failed at the beginning of the 1930s with the 'success' of the Kwantung Army in Manchuria, and as the war of expansion spread in China, the Americans responded by increasing their moral condemnation of Japan and increasing their supply of aid to China. As we have already seen, relations between the USA and Japan deteriorated further with the escalation of the Sino-Japanese War in 1937.

President Franklin D. Roosevelt won the US election in November 1932 and launched a wide-ranging recovery programme, the **New Deal**, in March 1933. Therefore, the focus of the government was on the domestic situation and the acute economic crises. The US Congress passed a series of Neutrality Acts in the 1930s, which bound the US government to non-intervention in conflicts. Neutrality Acts were passed in 1935, 1936, 1937, and 1939. The isolationist mood that had followed World War One continued. However, in October 1937 President Roosevelt called for an international 'quarantine of the aggressor nations' in a speech in Chicago. The sentiment of the speech was a challenge to those in Congress that continued to promote neutrality and non-intervention with regard to events in both Europe and Asia.

US neutrality has been criticized as it prevented the Americans from helping Britain and France to deal with Nazi aggression and meant there was no US military response

US President Franklin D. Roosevelt.

to Japanese aggression in Asia up to 1941. In January 1941, President Roosevelt gave a speech in which he made it clear to Americans that a war might be coming, and clarified broader objectives should a conflict occur.

> *We look forward to a world founded upon our four essential human freedoms. The first is freedom of speech and expression – everywhere in the world. The second is freedom of every person to worship God in his own way – everywhere in the world. The third is freedom from want … everywhere in the world. The fourth is freedom from fear … anywhere in the world.*
>
> **From Roosevelt's message to Congress, 6 January 1941.**

The four values outlined in the speech were clearly opposed to those of Fascist and militaristic regimes. Hitler's invasion of the USSR in June 1941 resulted in Britain and the USA sending aid to the Soviets. For if the USSR fell to Germany, the Germans could then focus again on Western expansion. In August 1941, the Atlantic Charter was published as a result of a meeting between Churchill and Roosevelt, and it set down their joint vision for the post-war world. The Atlantic Charter included the commitment to uphold the four freedoms, ban aggression, disarm aggressor states, give self-determination to liberated states, create the **United Nations** (UN), and secure the freedom of the seas.

Roosevelt believed that these aims could only be achieved through war, but was concerned that the American public would not support a conflict. Churchill told the British cabinet that Roosevelt would look for an 'incident' to justify waging war. It seemed, at the time, that this would most likely occur in the Atlantic.

In September 1941, the Americans indeed claimed that one of their Atlantic ships, the *Greer*, carrying civilians and mail, was attacked. The *Greer* had actually been chasing a German U-boat. Roosevelt now ordered the sinking of U-boats on sight, and sent convoys to protect merchant ships. By November, although the USA claimed it was acting only 'defensively', it was in a state of undeclared war with Germany in the Atlantic.

It could be argued that Japan was a small state that suffered from over-population and a shortage of key raw materials. Thus, in order to safeguard its national power, Japan took control of Manchuria for its rich natural resources, then expanded into China in 1937, and had taken control of the coast and half of the Chinese population by 1941. Yet Japan could not make the coalition forces of nationalist and Communist Chinese surrender. The USA was supplying the Chinese to secure its own trading interests. In 1940, as we have seen, Japan had created the Greater East Asia Co-Prosperity Sphere. The new organization directly challenged American interests in the region. Japan again sought security from attack when it signed the Tripartite Pact with Germany and Italy in April 1940, and the Non-Aggression Pact with the USSR in April 1941. The USA had pursued a policy of 'biased neutrality', and this was stepped up a gear on 11 March 1941 when the Lend-Lease Bill was agreed by Congress. This provided $7 billion of arms and supplies to be used to support countries whose defence was perceived as vital for the security of the USA.

German successes over the European imperial powers meant Japan could potentially move into British, French, and Dutch colonies, and also the American protectorate of the Philippines. In July 1941, Japan gave further demonstration of its territorial ambitions by taking over Indochina. Roosevelt was focused on policy in Europe; policy towards Japan was the responsibility of Secretary of State Cordell Hull. In 1941, Hull had two choices: to increase support to China (probably through more direct military involvement) or to impose economic sanctions on Japan.

The USA imposed sanctions, but they did not achieve their objective. As it had failed to get an agreement on its terms, the USA then forced Japan into a desperate corner – threatening their oil supplies when they had only two years' supply in reserve. Without oil, Japan would be forced into retreat. These sanctions undermined the more moderate government in Japan, leaving it vulnerable to the demands of the military. Tojo became war minister and Japan took a calculated risk by bombing Pearl Harbor, intending to take out the USA's naval power before the nation could gear up for war.

The Americans did know that an attack on US interests was imminent in December 1941, as they had intercepted Japanese codes. They did not know, however, where the attack would come (they assumed it would be in the Philippines). Right-wing American historians have suggested that Roosevelt knew about the specific plan to attack Pearl Harbor, but withheld the information because this attack would finally force the USA into the war.

Activity 8

Source analysis

There were miscalculations and misperceptions on both sides. Just as Tokyo believed rightly that the United States would deal with the German threat first but wrongly that it would condone Japanese expansionism, the Americans misjudged the extent of the Japanese commitment to an empire that would end its economic insecurity and confirm its leadership in East Asia. During 1941, assuming that Japan would not go to war against a power it could not defeat, Washington tightened the 'economic noose' around Japan's neck and sent out diplomatic and economic warnings. Divisions in Washington turned a flexible sanctions policy into a virtual freeze on bilateral trade and a de facto oil embargo. Already concerned that Japan would be cut off from the raw material imports needed to make war, Tokyo was faced with this grim reality. It was to solve the strategic dilemma that General Hideki Tojo abandoned the traditional naval strategy against the United States and opted for an attack on Pearl Harbor, hoping that an enfeebled and disheartened Washington would negotiate and turn its attention to Germany. Americans, too, were the victims of their own miscalculation and, almost to the end, thought the Japanese would back down and accept their terms.

Zara Steiner, *The Triumph of the Dark* (OUP, 2013), p.1065.

1. According to historian Zara Steiner, what were the miscalculations that caused the attack on Pearl Harbor?

War in the Pacific: historiography

Left-wing historians have called Japan's war the 'Fifteen-Year War', as they argue that conflict in the region started with the Manchurian Crisis of 1931. Responsibility is put on the 'militarist Capitalist clique' who directed Japan into war. More right-wing or nationalist Japanese historians date the war as starting in December 1941 with the attack on Pearl Harbor and the invasion of South-East Asia. The *Dai Towa Senso* (Greater East Asia War), as they call it, is a view in line with the Japanese propaganda of World War Two that argued Japan was liberating Asians from Western imperialism. Michiko Hasegawa (a philosophy professor) argued that although Japan's intentions were just, the USA forced it into a war in 1941 by embargoing oil shipments, and Japan then had to fight with countries that it would have preferred to assist in friendship.

Historians have criticized this view with several arguments: the long-term anti-Chinese feeling in Japan since the war of 1894; the generally inhumane treatment of people in all occupied territories; the expansionist views of Japan's nationalist leaders; the need

CHALLENGE YOURSELF

What was the role of Australia in the outbreak of war in the Pacific?

Some historians have suggested that Jiang Jieshi's forces in China only continued to refuse to negotiate peace terms with Japan due to US aid and the hope that the US would enter the war. Some have linked Jiang's position to that of Churchill's Britain: that is, both were unable to defeat their enemies (Japan and Germany respectively) but committed to the war, gambling on ultimately being saved by the USA joining the conflict.

Consider the extent to which you agree with these suggestions.

for Japan to secure resources; and Japan's imperialist outlook. However, Japanese revisionists argue that the West was simply racist and did not want competition within its own spheres of influence in the Pacific and Asia. American historians argue that they were less anti-Japanese but instead sympathetic to the Chinese. Their pursuit of an 'open-door policy' aimed to contain all powers from expanding, which the Japanese ignored.

As students of history, you are asked to consider different historians' perspectives on the causes, course, and effects of war. By seeking to know and understand different viewpoints, you are more able to understand the importance of intellectual balance. Discuss in pairs why it is important to have intellectual balance.

When you attempt to plan and/or write an essay in history, you should attempt to write a 'balanced' response. For example, if you were responding to the question 'Why did Japan bomb Pearl Harbor?', you would include a range of arguments and evidence.

Activity 9

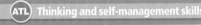

ATL Thinking and self-management skills

Source analysis

Source A

> *War sentiment in Japan had been impelled by an ultranationalist ideology that sought to preserve the traditional values of the Japanese political order, that vehemently opposed the expansion of Bolshevik influence in Asia, and that wanted to establish the Japanese Empire. Instead, war brought a social-democratic revolution at home, the rise of Communism in China, and – for the first time in Japan's history – occupation by an enemy force.*

Kenneth B. Pyle, *The Making of Modern Japan*, 2nd ed. (D.C. Heath, 1996), p.204.

Source B

> *Japanese ruling circles in the 1930s were united in their view that Japanese power and future prosperity rested on carving out a similar [to the western European powers' empires] area for themselves in Asia, reproducing in the Far East what they saw as the dominant features of Western international behaviour …*

R. Overy, *The Road to War*, 2nd ed. (Vintage, 2009), pp.405–406.

1. Read Source A. What ideological factors are identified in Source A as motives for Japanese aggression?
2. Read Source B. What motives are identified in Source B for Japanese expansionism?

Activity 10

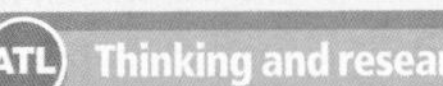

1. Look back over this chapter and copy out the chart below. Make bullet-point notes on different historians' views on the causes of the war in the Pacific. Attempt to find evidence from this chapter to support each viewpoint.

CONTEMPORARY HISTORIAN	SUPPORTING EVIDENCE

The role of the emperor in Japan's road to war

> *Once His Majesty reaches a decision to commence hostilities, we will all strive to repay our obligations to him, bring the Government and the military ever closer together, resolve that the nation united will go on to victory, make an all-out effort to achieve our war aims, and set His Majesty's mind at ease.*

From a statement by Prime Minister Tojo to Emperor Hirohito at an Imperial Conference, 1 December 1941.

At the end of World War Two, the American demand for total surrender meant that there was no guarantee of the emperor's exclusion from the Tokyo war crimes tribunal. General Douglas MacArthur, however, convinced the US government that Emperor Hirohito was needed to facilitate a stable Japan. Against the wishes of the Australian, New Zealand, Chinese, and Dutch officials, Hirohito would not stand trial as a war criminal, and he would not be held responsible for causing the war in the Pacific. In the two-year trial, 28 men were charged with war crimes and 7 were hanged. The official view was that Hirohito had basically been a prisoner of the militarists – he had had no choice but to follow their policies. The military claimed to be following the emperor's lead, but he had in fact been passive, without any real power.

However, some historians and commentators have disagreed with the view that Hirohito was passive in the events that led to the Pacific War.

> *Emperor Hirohito had stamped the orders sending troops into north China in 1937. It was later said that he did so unwillingly, yet he went on two months later to stamp orders for the dispatch of troops to central and south China as well … He became so immersed in war planning that the prime minister at the time complained of his preoccupation. Finally his own uncle assumed command of the attack on Nanjing, the Chinese capital, and moved into a hotel in Nanjing, to look on while his troops murdered over 100,000 defenseless military and civilian prisoners there. It was the first act of genocide in World War II, but when the uncle returned to Tokyo, Hirohito went out of his way to confer decorations and honors upon him ... the Sugiyama Memoranda stated that in January 1941, eleven months before the outbreak of war with the United States, Hirohito had personally ordered a secret evaluation to be made of the feasibility of a surprise attack on Pearl Harbor … Evidence taken before the Allied judges of the International Military Tribunal for the Far East, and verified by witnesses under oath and cross-examination, demonstrated conclusively that none of the 'militarists' who were supposed to have dragged Hirohito to war knew of the Pearl Harbor plan until August 1941. General Tojo, the arch 'militarist' who headed Japan's wartime Cabinet, was not told of the plan until November 1941.*

David Bergamini, *Japan's Imperial Conspiracy* (Morrow, 1971), pp.xxv–xxix.

Activity 11

Thinking and social skills

Discussion questions

In pairs, consider the following questions:

1. How far can ideology be held responsible for the cause of war between Japan and the USA in 1941?
2. Review the sections on US and Japanese responsibility for the war in the Pacific, then create a diagram of the key 'actions and reactions' of the two countries. Discuss the extent to which war in the Pacific was caused by the USA 'reacting' to the perceived aggressive action of Japan, and vice versa.

Activity 12

Thinking and communication skills

Essay planning

Plan the following essays using the war in the Pacific as your case study.

1. ***Examine the impact of economic factors in causing one 20th-century war.***
2. ***Discuss the impact of ideological factors in causing one 20th-century war.***
3. ***'Territorial factors are a key cause of conflict.' With reference to one 20th-century war, examine the validity of this claim.***

To access weblinks relevant to this chapter, go to www.pearsonhotlinks.com, search for the book title or ISBN, and click on 'chapter 7'.

Can you identify any region today where territorial factors are causing conflict?

08

Cross-regional war: World War Two – Practices

The ruins of Hiroshima after the dropping of the A-bomb, 8 August 1945.

Key concepts: Significance

As you read this chapter, consider the following essay questions:

- To what extent were economic and human resources mobilized in one 20th-century war?
- Examine the importance of air power in one 20th-century war.
- Discuss the impact of technological developments in the course and outcome of one 20th-century war.

World War Two was even more deadly than World War One. More soldiers and civilians were killed than in any war before it. The impact on civilians in particular in terms of death, destruction, and displacement also made it more of a total war than that of 1914–1918. It was also very different from previous wars in that it was a conflict of rapid movement, with major campaigns taking place not only in Central and Western Europe, but also in the Far East, North Africa, and the USSR. First, we will give a brief overview of both the war in Europe and the war in the Pacific. The war will then be analysed in terms of the nature of the fighting and the reasons why it can be considered a war of total mobilization.

The war in Europe

Blitzkrieg – the invasion of Poland (September 1939)

In the early hours of 1 September 1939, Hitler's Panzers (tanks), supported by the **Luftwaffe** (air force), smashed over the border into Poland. They rapidly cut though Poland's defences, thus making a path for the advancing infantry. This rapid and devastating method of fighting was known as ***blitzkrieg***, or 'lightning war'. Polish resistance was heroic, but ultimately futile. The USSR invaded from the east, as agreed by the Nazi–Soviet Pact, and on 29 September Poland was divided up between the two countries.

The Phoney War

After the defeat of Poland, very little happened in the next five months. Although Britain had declared war on Germany two days after the Polish invasion, it could not get troops to Poland in time to have any effect, and thus only watched as a great part of Eastern Europe fell into the hands of Hitler and Stalin. The Soviet Union invaded Finland in what became known as the 'Winter War' and took over Estonia, Latvia, and Lithuania.

Meanwhile, the French manned the **Maginot Line** and waited for the next German move. Chamberlain believed that this period of inactivity would bring Hitler to his knees and that the German leader had in fact 'missed the bus'.

The invasion of Denmark and Norway (April 1940)

Four days after Chamberlain's misguided comment, Hitler invaded Denmark and Norway. Control of Norway was important due to the need for German access to Swedish iron ore, which was vital to the armaments industry. The invasions brought about the downfall of Chamberlain in Britain, and on 10 May a coalition government was established under Winston Churchill.

The Winter War

In the Winter War, the Soviet forces were vastly superior in numbers to those of the Finnish army – 450,000 troops against only 180,000. However, the **Red Army** had recently been subjected to a political purge that had removed 50 per cent of its commanding officers. This weakness, along with the determination and high morale of the Finns, meant that Finland was able to hold out until March 1940. The fact that the Soviet losses were so large meant that this was also a humiliation for Stalin.

War in Europe		War in the Pacific	
1939			
1 Sept	Germany invades Poland		
3 Sept	Britain declares war on Germany		
1940			
9 Apr	Nazis invade Denmark and Norway		
10 May	Nazis invade France, Belgium, Luxembourg, and the Netherlands		
26 May	Evacuation of Allied troops from Dunkirk begins		
10 June	Norway surrenders to the Nazis		
	Italy declares war on Britain and France		
1 July	German U-boats attack merchant ships in the Atlantic		
10 Jul	Battle of Britain begins		
23 Jul	Soviets take Lithuania, Latvia and Estonia		
7 Sep	Blitz begins against Britain		
27 Sep	Tripartite (Axis) Pact signed by Germany, Italy and Japan		
28 Oct	Italy invades Greece		
1941		**1941**	
6 Apr	Nazis invade Greece and Yugoslavia	**26 July**	Roosevelt freezes Japanese assets in USA and suspends relations with Japan
2 June	Operation *Barbarossa* begins	**1 Aug**	USA announces an oil embargo against aggressor states
		7 Dec	Japanese bomb Pearl Harbor
		8 Dec	USA and Britain declare war on Japan
		11 Dec	Germany declares war on the USA
1942		**1942**	
13 Sept	Battle of Stalingrad begins	**4–7 June**	Battle of Midway
23 Oct–5 Nov	Battle of El Alamein	**Aug**	US Marines land in Guadalcanal
1943		**1943**	
2 Feb	Germans surrender at Stalingrad	**Jan**	Allied gains in the Pacific continue (island hopping)
16–20 Mar	Battle of Atlantic climaxes with 27 merchant ships sunk by German U-boats	**Oct**	Allies invade Philippines
13 May	German and Italian troops surrender in North Africa		
9–10 July	Allies land in Sicily		
27–28 July	Allied air raid causes a firestorm in Hamburg		
3 Sept	Allied invasion of mainland Italy		
1944		**1944**	
6 June	D-Day landings	**Jan–Feb**	US forces capture the Marshall Islands
25 Aug	Liberation of Paris		British forces make advances in Burma
2 Oct	Warsaw Uprising ends as the Polish Home Army surrenders to the Germans	**17 Apr**	Japanese begin last offensive in China
16–27 Dec	Battle of the Bulge	**15 June**	US forces invade Saipan
		July–Aug	US forces recapture the Mariana Islands
		23–26 Oct	Japanese navy suffers critical losses in the battle of Leyte Gulf
1945		**1945**	
17 Jan	Soviet troops capture Warsaw	**19 Feb**	US forces invade the island of Iwo Jima
13–14 Feb	Dresden is destroyed by a firestorm after Allied bombing raids	**3 Mar**	US and Filipino forces take Manila
16 Apr	Soviet troops begin their final attack on Berlin	**1 Apr**	US forces invade Okinawa
	Americans enter Nuremberg	**6 Aug**	First atomic bomb dropped, on Hiroshima, Japan
30 Apr	Adolf Hitler commits suicide	**8 Aug**	Soviets declare war on Japan and invade Manchuria
2 May	German troops in Italy surrender	**9 Aug**	Second atom bomb dropped, on Nagasaki
7 May	Unconditional surrender of all German troops	**14 Aug**	Japan surrenders
8 May	VE (Victory in Europe) Day	**2 Sept**	Japan formally surrenders

The invasion of Holland, Belgium, and France (May–June 1940)

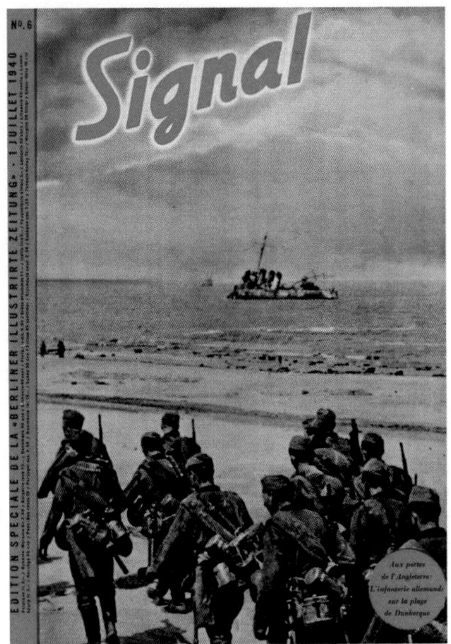

The German propaganda magazine *Signal* shows German troops on the beaches of Dunkirk, having ejected British forces from France.

Also on 10 May, Hitler launched attacks on Holland and Belgium, and then, after skirting around the end of the Maginot Line, invaded France on 12 May. The reason that the Maginot Line defences did not continue along the frontier between France and Belgium was because Marshal Pétain believed that the Ardennes forest further north would be a strong enough barrier to stop Germany attacking from that direction. However, this is exactly where the Germans broke through.

Using *blitzkrieg* tactics, Hitler's victories were swift, and within 6 days the Panzers had reached the English Channel. Only Dunkirk remained in British hands, and a third of a million troops were then rescued by the British navy and other private boats owned by fishermen. Although a great opportunity to boost British morale with talk of the 'Dunkirk spirit' (see newspaper opposite), the evacuation was in fact a serious blow for the Allies; they lost a large amount of arms and equipment and had been driven from the European mainland.

The Germans now swept southwards. Paris was captured on 14 June and the French government, now led by Pétain, requested Germany's terms for an armistice. The ceasefire agreement was signed at Compiègne on 21 June in the same railway coach that had been used for the 1918 Armistice. All of the country except south-eastern France was occupied and demilitarized, thus giving the Germans access to important submarine bases on the Atlantic coast. Unoccupied France was allowed its own government under Marshal Pétain, but in reality it had no real independence and actively collaborated with the Germans.

Hitler's Germany had achieved more in 2 months than the Kaiser's Germany had achieved in the whole of World War One. By the end of June 1940, Germany dominated Western, Central, and Northern Europe. In addition, Italy had now entered the war as Hitler's ally, and the USSR remained 'friends' with Germany in the east, under the terms of the Nazi–Soviet Pact. Franco in Spain did not actually join in the war, but remained closely associated with Germany and Italy.

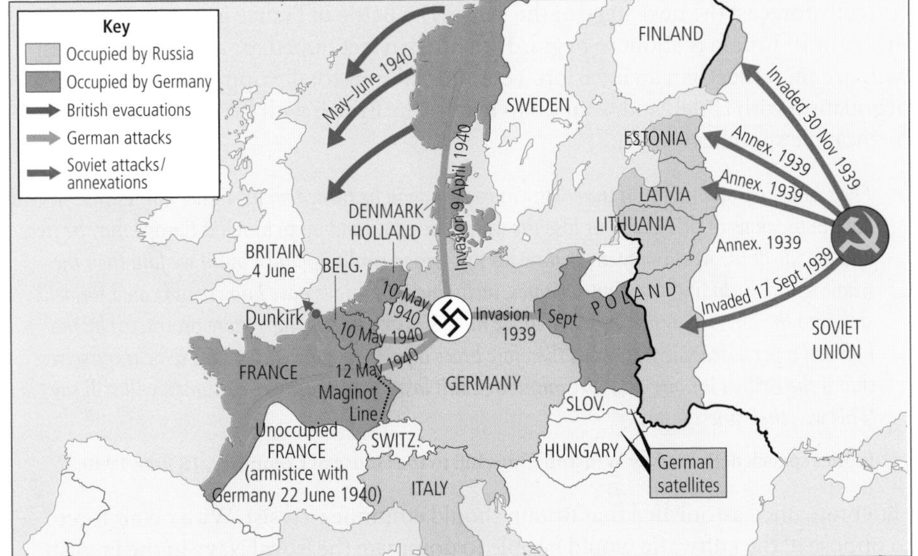

Blitzkrieg offensive, 1939–1940.

Activity 1

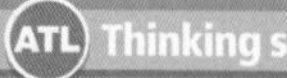

Source analysis

Source A

> *We must conclude that it [the German attack into France] was a plan well executed and incompetently opposed. But there is no doubt that the French government was weak and showed little resolve. Moral authority and executive capacity both disappeared and military defeat turned into political collapse. Essentially Hitler's military successes were based on his preparedness to take the adventurous and unexpected course. He was fortunate that military thinking lagged behind military technology. Moreover whereas the Allies were cautious and conservative, Hitler was an impatient man who was psychologically predisposed to adopt daring and mobile strategies.*

Graham Darby, *Europe at War 1939–45* (Hodder, 2003), p.18.

Source B

> *... with good battlefield aviation supporting ground forces, and an effective system of radio communication, the German military made the most of their resources against an enemy whose cast of mind was defensive and whose communication and organization at the front proved woefully deficient. The British and French concept of a war of attrition and blockade, fought partly by bombing aircraft, never materialised. The two western states lost sight in the 1930s of the most basic element of warfare – the ability to fight effectively on the field of battle itself. Both sides possessed comparable resources (the Germans had in fact fewer and poorer-quality tanks) but German military leaders emphasised high standards of training and operational preparation and technical efficiency, the very virtues that brought victory in 1866 over Austria and in 1870 over France.*

Richard Overy in Charles Townshend (ed.), *The Oxford History of Modern War* (Oxford University Press, 2005), p.140.

1. According to Darby, what factors accounted for Hitler's success in taking over France?
2. In what ways does Overy agree with Darby? What are the differences between the two sources in their analysis of the German successes?

The Battle of Britain (1940)

Britain and its empire now stood alone against Germany. On 18 June 1940, Churchill correctly forecast the next stage of the war – 'The Battle of France is over. I expect that the Battle of Britain is about to begin.' Hitler had in fact hoped for a peace agreement with Britain rather than an invasion. Yet Churchill was totally opposed to any negotiation with Hitler, and went on to inspire the British with his determination and memorable speeches:

> *The whole fury and might of the enemy must very soon be turned on us. Hitler knows that he will have to break us in this island or lose the war. If we can stand up to him, all Europe may be free, and the life of the world may move forward into broad sunlit uplands; but if we fail, then the whole world, including the United States, including all that we have known and cared for, will sink into the abyss of a new dark age made more sinister and perhaps more protracted by the lights of a perverted science. Let us therefore brace ourselves to our duties and so bear ourselves that if the British Empire and its Commonwealth last for a thousand years, men will still say 'This was their finest hour.'*

From a speech delivered by Winston Churchill to the House of Commons, 18 June 1940.

Hitler remained astonished that Britain should continue to resist. With no air force to oppose it, the Luftwaffe would be able to dominate the Royal Navy in the English

Channel, leaving Britain totally exposed to German invasion and so willing to come to the negotiating table.

Thus the Battle of Britain began in July 1940, the Luftwaffe opening their offensive with a concentrated air attack on Britain's airfields in order to gain air supremacy. The Luftwaffe then started bombing London and other major cities in what became known as the **Blitz** in an attempt to break British morale and destroy her major industries. When it became clear that Germany was unable to break the **RAF** or Britain's morale, Hitler postponed the invasion indefinitely; then in 1941 he turned his attention to his main priority – the conquest of the Soviet Union.

There are several reasons why Britain was able to survive:

- The numerical superiority of the Luftwaffe (about 1,200 bombers and 1,000 fighters to the RAF's 900 fighters) was offset by the fact that the German bombers were vulnerable once their shorter-range fighter escorts had turned for home, and they had limited range and a limited bomb load. The German Messerschmitt Bf 109 was an excellent fighter, but it also had only enough fuel to stay in the air over Britain for about 10–20 minutes. Against this, the (also excellent) British Spitfires and Hurricanes could spend much longer in the air, being over their home airfields.
- Britain had a revolutionary new warning system – radar. This minimized the impact of the RAF's numerical inferiority as it allowed the RAF to locate the incoming enemy (the radar showed up enemy aircraft when they were about 120 kilometres away) and not have to waste aircraft in patrols looking for the German planes.
- Hitler's switch to bombing the cities instead of concentrating on the RAF airfields was a fatal error. This change of target gave the RAF time to recover and to rebuild airbases. The Battle of Britain was the first time that Hitler had been stopped from achieving his aims. Britain's survival was going to be vital for keeping up the pressure on Germany, and ultimately to providing the launch pad for the allied invasion of Europe in 1944.

Exiles in Britain

After the German conquests in mainland Europe, Britain also became the base for a number of European governments-in-exile. In 1940, the governments of Poland, Norway, and the Netherlands were established in London. There were also other bodies representing Belgium, Luxembourg, and Free France. Armed forces of these countries, for example Polish fighter pilots, also took part in the defence of Britain.

RAF pilots scramble to their fighters during the Battle of Britain, 1940.

The Mediterranean and the Balkans (1940–1941)

The entry of Italy into the conflict in June 1940 spread the war to the Balkans, the Mediterranean, and North Africa. In September 1940, Mussolini sent an army from the Italian colony of Libya to Egypt. Another Italian army invaded Greece from Albania in October. Both Italian offensives failed, however. The British pushed the Italians out of Egypt, defeating them at Beda Fomm in Libya. The British then sank half the Italian fleet in harbour at Taranto and occupied Crete. The Greeks forced the Italians back and invaded Albania.

Mussolini's failures brought Hitler into both North Africa and the Balkans. General Erwin Rommel and his **Afrika Korps** soldiers were sent to Tripoli, from where the British were driven out of Libya; by June 1942 the Germans had advanced close to El Alamein in Egypt. Meanwhile, in April 1941, Hitler's troops overran Yugoslavia and Greece. Within three weeks, the Greeks had surrendered, and in May Crete was taken after a successful airborne attack. The British evacuated in May 1941.

These campaigns were significant because:

- They were severe setbacks for the Allies.
- British troops in North Africa were moved to the fighting in Greece, which weakened the British in North Africa at a time when Britain needed its strength to deal with the threat from Rommel.
- In going to assist Mussolini in Greece, Hitler's plan to attack the USSR was delayed by a crucial 6 weeks, which had an impact on the chances of the German army reaching Moscow before the harsh Russian winter set in.

Operation Barbarossa (22 June 1941)

By attacking the Soviet Union, Hitler was fulfilling his aims for *Lebensraum*, or living space, for the German people. Clearly, the natural resources of the USSR, including oil, were vast, and would be ideal for the expansion of the German race. Hitler's motives for invading the Soviet Union, however, were mainly ideological. Hitler was impatient to get on with destroying a country that was not only full of peoples he saw as inferior, such as the Slavs, but also full of Communists. During the 1930s, Hitler repeatedly expressed his belief that Communism was one of the greatest threats to German society and culture, despite acknowledging that a temporary alliance with the Soviet Union could work in Germany's interests. Hitler's military endgame, therefore, always had the Soviet Union in its sights. Even in the early stages of the war, his attention was drawn to the East and to planning for the attack, and he was clearly frustrated by Britain's refusal to make peace, which thus delayed his plans for Russia. In the end, he decided to leave Britain undefeated, believing that it would not be in a strong enough position to open a second front and that the Soviet Union would easily be defeated. He was also anxious to launch an attack on the USSR to put a stop to Stalin's own territorial gains.

Plans for the invasion, codenamed Operation Barbarossa, were drawn up at the end of 1940. The plan envisaged a three-pronged attack: in the north towards Leningrad, in the centre towards Moscow, and in the south through the agriculturally and industrially rich Ukraine.

The invasion started on 22 June 1941 and involved 121 divisions of the *Heer* (German army) backed up by massive air support in a *blitzkrieg* attack. Although the Soviets actually had greater numbers of men, tanks, and aircraft, the Germans were able to take advantage of the element of surprise. The Soviets had ignored both the warnings

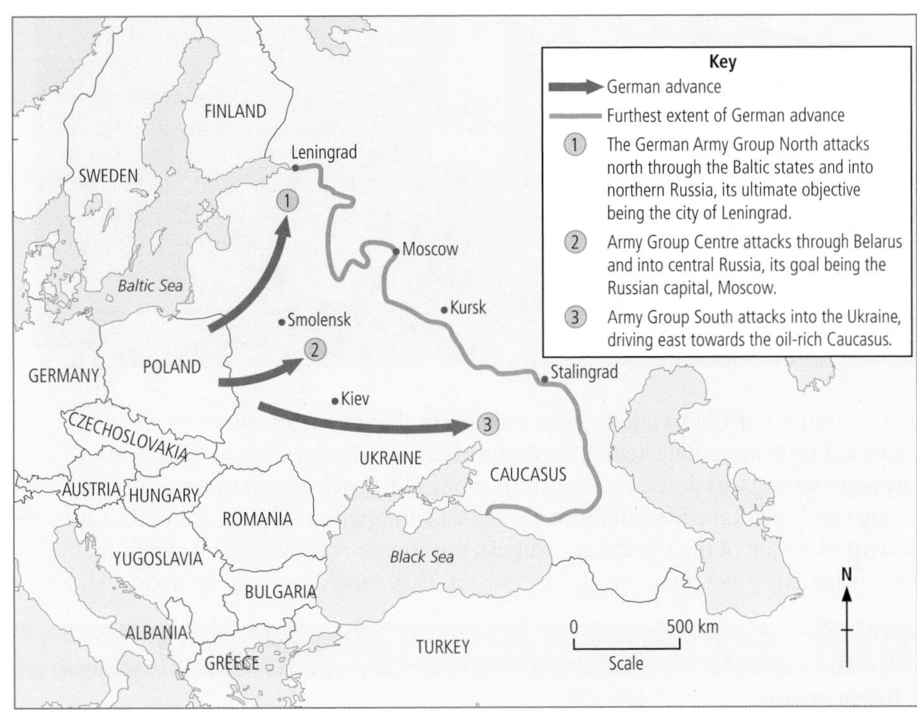

The German advance during Operation Barbarossa.

of Churchill concerning the impending invasion and also their own intelligence: Stalin presumably believed that Hitler would honour the Nazi–Soviet Pact and continue to avoid a war on two fronts. The Soviets were also still re-equipping their army and air force following the humiliating war with Finland, and the army was recovering from the impact of Stalin's purges, which had wiped out the cream of the Red Army's command.

In contrast to the Soviets' vulnerable position, the Germans attacked with the psychological advantage of knowing that their *blitzkrieg* tactics had already been successful in conquering vast areas of Western Europe. Given this situation, the Germans were able to secure dramatic successes in the first months of the war. In the north, Leningrad was surrounded and besieged. In the south, Kiev was captured, and by mid-October the German army was within 80 kilometres of Moscow. The Soviets had lost some three million men in casualties and as prisoners of war.

Yet the Germans failed to take Leningrad and Moscow. They were held back by the heavy rains of October, which turned the roads to mud, and then the severe Russian winter in which temperatures in some places fell as low as –38° Celsius. The Germans, equipped only with their summer uniforms in the expectation that they would be victorious by the winter, suffered terribly. Thousands experienced frostbite and equipment froze and failed to function. For the first time, *blitzkrieg* had failed to achieve its objectives; the great Soviet commander Marshal Georgy Zhukov launched a counter-offensive and Moscow was saved.

In June 1942 Hitler made a massive offensive towards southern Russia and the oilfields of the Caucasus. By August, the German attack had reached the city of Stalingrad and had occupied most of the city by the end of September. Yet the Russians refused to surrender, and in fact launched a counter-offensive, surrounding the Germans in a large **pincer movement**. Suffering from acute shortages of ammunition and food, and now overwhelmingly outnumbered, the Germans in Stalingrad had no choice but to surrender in early February 1943. Here was the turning point of the war on the Eastern Front.

Leningrad

The siege of Leningrad lasted from September 1941 to January 1944 and resulted in as many as 1.5 million deaths, which is more than the combined British and American casualties for the whole of the war. The inhabitants of Leningrad suffered from desperate food shortages and brought in supplies across an 'ice road' over Lake Lagoda. They were constantly bombarded by the Germans, but the city never fell.

An image of the terrible destruction at Stalingrad, 1942/1943.

In the summer of 1943, Hitler tried to launch another major attack. However, the Germans were again defeated, at the Battle of Kursk, where a German tank army 17 divisions strong was destroyed. For the rest of 1943, the German army was in retreat along nearly all of the Eastern Front. By 1944, Leningrad was liberated, and the Germans were pushed out of the Ukraine. In August, the Soviets reached Poland and Romania, and by January 1945 they were in East Prussia. They finally reached Berlin on 2 May.

Activity 2

ATL Thinking skills

Source analysis

> *Contrary to later accounts, Stalingrad was not the decisive event of the Second World War. It was far from being the largest battle on the Eastern Front. The 90,000 troops who were captured numbered only half as many as the British were to take at the end of the North African campaigns. And on the scale of military disasters it was no more significant than Timoshenko's recent disaster before Kharkhov. Yet, Stalingrad, in psychological terms, was immensely significant. It showed for the first time, that Hitler's Wehrmacht was fallible. It showed that Stalin's Red Army was not the shambolic giant with feet of clay that many experts had predicted. It sent shivers through Berlin, and gladdened the hearts of all Hitler's enemies. One cannot exaggerate its impact on the minds of Britons and Americans who at the time had no single solider fighting on European soil.*

Norman Davies, *Europe at War 1939–1945* (Macmillan, 2006), p.108.

1. According to Norman Davies, what was the significance of the Battle of Stalingrad?

Why were the Soviets able to defeat the German army?

Despite the German successes, the Soviets ended up defeating the German army. The Germans made several mistakes that contributed to their defeat:

- They were not prepared for a long campaign and they suffered from lack of supplies.
- They had inadequate equipment to face their first harsh Russian winter.
- In 1941, Hitler took over the command of the army himself, which had a disastrous impact on the conduct of the war in the Soviet Union.
- During their invasion, the Germans carried out brutal attacks against the civilian population, which made Russian resistance much stronger (see below).
- The supply lines of the German armed forces became hopelessly overstretched.
- The German army faced continual losses of aircraft and tanks that could not be replaced. Armoured divisions began the war with 328 tanks per division, whereas by the summer of 1943, they averaged only 73. The German army increasingly fell back on the use of horses, concentrating their air and tank power in only a few divisions.

In contrast to the German situation, the Soviets underwent a programme of reform and modernization. Learning from the devastating invasion of 1941, and adapting to circumstances, the Soviet army's structure was reorganized to include a much greater reliance on tanks and artillery. The air force was also reformed; now fighter-bombers and ground-attack aircraft were put together to form a concentrated air striking force, centrally coordinated using radio communications so that it could give effective support to ground troops. The installation of radios in tanks and aircraft was indeed crucial for improving overall communications. Richard Overy argues that:

> *the revolution in Soviet communications was perhaps the most important single reform … [It] gave the Soviet commanders the ability to direct large and complex operations and to hold the battlefield together.*

Richard Overy, 'The Improbable Victory', *Modern History Review*, November 1998, p.29.

Another important army reform involved Stalin withdrawing himself from military responsibility and allowing his commanders – such as Aleksandr Vasilevsky and Georgy Zhukov – much more freedom in how they conducted the war. Stalin also agreed to remove political influence over the army and restore the more traditional command structure, giving the troops back more confidence and pride.

Another key factor in the Soviet victory was the impact of patriotism. Spurred on by the atrocities committed by the Germans during their advance, which indicated what a German victory could mean, and fortified by the fact that Stalin did not abandon Moscow but remained with its civilians to resist the German attack, the Russian population united in a way not seen since the Revolution. Stalin, realizing that he could not call on the Soviets to mobilize in the name of Communism, fed this patriotism by calling on them to save 'Mother Russia'. In addition, the Russian Orthodox Church, previously persecuted by the Soviet authorities, was reinstated to provide spiritual strength.

A Soviet propaganda poster. The text reads 'Soldier, save us!', imploring the Red Army to fight hard for its citizens.

The Soviet Union lost three-quarters of its supplies of iron ore, coal, and steel, a third of its rail network, and 40 per cent of its electricity generation in the German invasion. Yet it still managed to out-produce the Germans in guns and tanks and aircraft between 1942 and 1943. This was partly due to the fact that the Soviets moved huge quantities of industrial equipment east of the Ural mountains during the German invasion – 1,360 factories in 1942 alone. In addition, the centralized nature of the Soviet state enabled the Soviet leadership to create a successful war economy. Top priority was given to producing armaments, and all factories as well as all the labour camps (gulags) were set to work for the war effort. As in the army, political supervision was decreased in the critical years to allow the planners and managers in industry to work more effectively, even to take initiative.

The Allies also contributed to Soviet success. Weapons from the UK and USA only made up 4 per cent of the amount used by the Soviets, but there were other supplies in the form of food, raw materials, and equipment that were crucial to the Soviet war effort. The Soviets also benefited from **Lend-Lease** agreements similar to those negotiated between Britain and the USA.

Activity 3

ATL Thinking and self-management skills

Review questions

1. Why were the Germans so successful with *blitzkrieg* in Europe?
2. Why did *blitzkrieg* tactics fail in the Soviet Union?
3. Summarize in bullet points or in a spider diagram the reasons for the Soviet victory over the Nazis. Which factor or combination of factors stands out as the main reason for Soviet success?

The defeat of Nazi Germany

While Stalin was fighting a very bloody war in the Soviet Union, Britain – joined by America from December 1941 – was predominantly fighting an air and sea war. Although Stalin was desperate for Britain and America to open up a second front and thus divert the Germans away from the Soviet Union, this was not possible in 1942. Roosevelt agreed that defeating Nazi Germany quickly was a priority (even though it was the Japanese who had brought America into the war), but neither the USA nor Britain yet had the resources needed to launch a major invasion of mainland Europe.

El Alamein (1942)

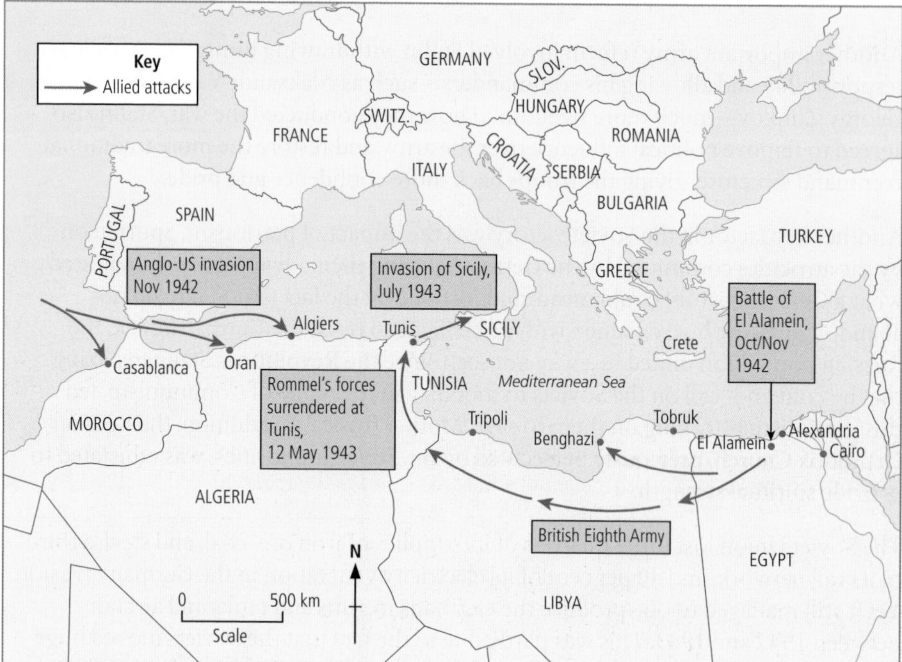

Map showing the war in the Mediterranean, 1942–1943.

Instead, Britain decided to carry on the fighting in North Africa. Rommel's forces were finally defeated in October/November 1942 at El Alamein and were forced into retreat across Libya. Early in November, Anglo-American forces landed in French North Africa in Operation Torch, and by May 1943 the whole of northern Africa had been secured.

This campaign was important for the following reasons:

- It prevented Egypt and the Suez Canal from falling to Hitler.
- It gave the Allies experience in large-scale seaborne offensives.
- It provided a launching position for the next Allied target – Italy.

The fall of Italy (1943–1945)

The southern offensive on 'fortress Europe' began on 10 July 1943, and within 6 weeks Sicily was in Allied hands. This event caused the downfall of Mussolini, who was dismissed by the Italian King. In October, Allied troops crossed to Salerno, Reggio, and Taranto on the Italian mainland and captured Naples.

Mussolini's successor, Marshal Pietro Badoglio, signed an armistice and brought Italy into the war on the Allied side. The Germans, however, were determined to hold on to Italy. German divisions were diverted to Italy and the Allies had to fight their way slowly up the peninsula. Rome was not captured until June 1944 and northern Italy did not come under Allied control until April 1945. Despite the slow nature of the campaign, the Italian war had important consequences for the Allies:

- Fascism had ended in Italy, and Germany was deprived of its most important ally.
- It tied down German divisions that were needed in Russia.
- It meant that the Allies could not be accused by Stalin of leaving all of the fighting in Europe to the Soviet forces.

The war in Italy

While the price for the Allies of the Italian invasion was high, the Italians suffered not only in terms of casualties but also in the damage caused to the cultural heritage of their country. Beautiful buildings, such as the monastery at Monte Cassino, were destroyed as the Allies fought their way up the peninsula. In addition, the domestic economic situation was desperate and the government collapsed. In April 1945, Mussolini, ousted from government, was captured by partisans, shot, and his body hung from a meat hook in a Milanese petrol station.

Operation Overlord (June 1944)

US soldiers approach the Normandy beaches during the D-Day landings, 6 June 1944.

The Allied invasion of France, codenamed Operation Overlord, began on 6 June 1944, a moment in history known as D-Day. The landings by 326,000 British, Canadian, and American troops took place from sea and air on an 80-kilometre stretch of Normandy beaches. The invasion was a result of extremely complex preparations involving a huge amount of resources. Mulberry harbours – prefabricated, temporary harbours – were built to provide anchorages for supply ships and oil pipelines were laid across the Channel. Around 4,000 ships supported the invasion and the whole assault was backed by massive airpower (12,000 aircraft in the sky on the first day of the invasion). Secrecy was also key to the success of the operation, and complex subterfuge plans were put into operation to convince the Germans (successfully) that the invasion would land at Calais rather than in Normandy.

Within a month, a million men had landed in Normandy. In the next few weeks, most of northern France was liberated, then Brussels and Antwerp were freed in the first week of September. However, German forces continued to resist and to enjoy successes. They defeated an Allied attempt to outflank the Siegfried Line at Arnhem in September 1944, and also temporarily regained ground in the Ardennes offensive (known in the West as the 'Battle of the Bulge') from December 1944–January 1945. Yet the losses in men and tanks sustained by the Germans in these battles could no longer be replaced, and the first months of 1945 saw the steady disintegration of the *Wehrmacht* (German armed forces). The Allies crossed the Rhine in March 1945. Germany was now being invaded on two fronts, and in Berlin, on 30 April, Hitler killed himself. General Dwight D. Eisenhower, the supreme Allied Commander in Europe, refused to race for Berlin to get there before the Soviets, and thus Stalin's forces were the first to arrive. On 7 May, the German government surrendered unconditionally to the combined Allied forces.

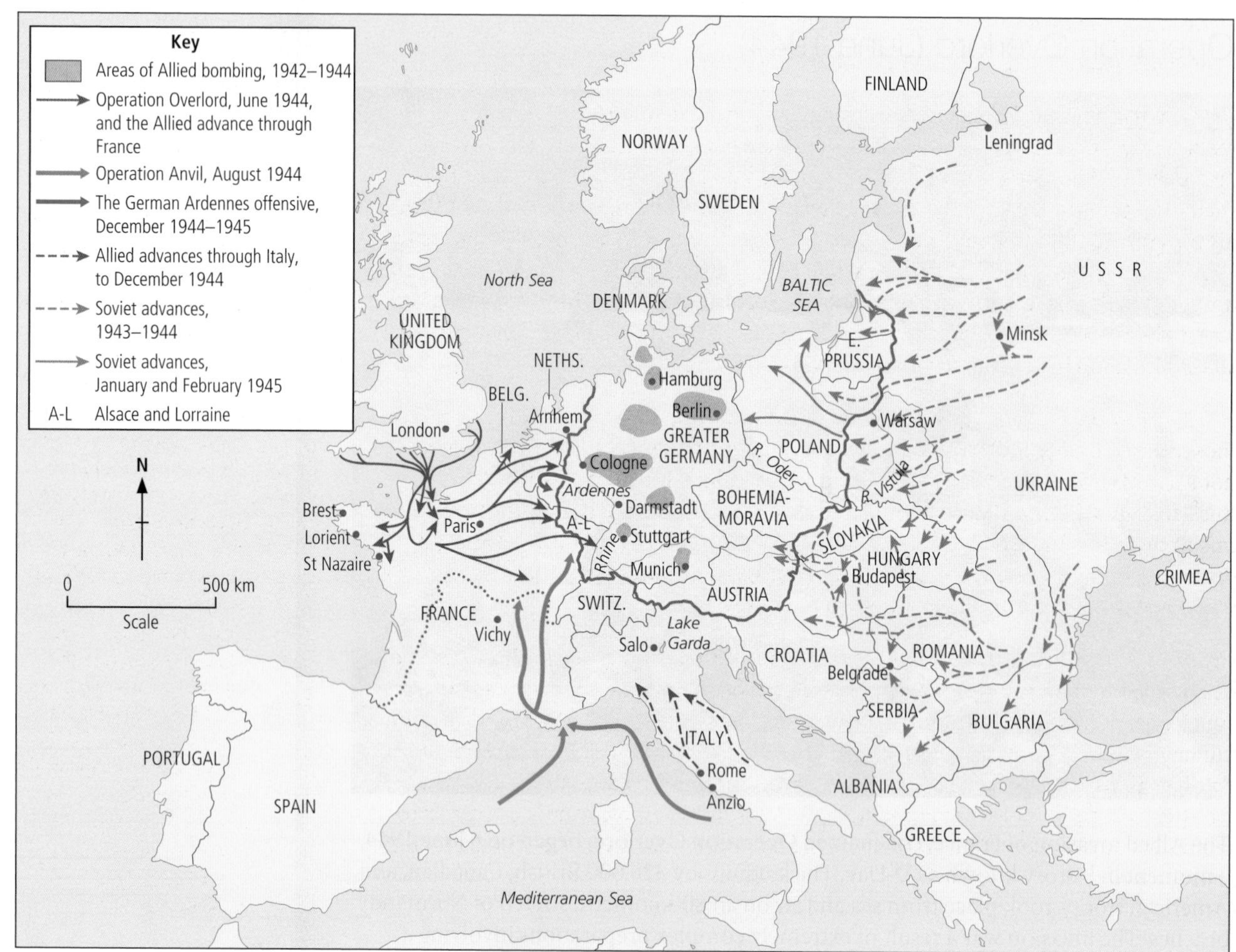

The collapse and defeat of Germany, 1944–1945.

Why did the Allies defeat Hitler?

The weakness of the Axis powers

By not committing Germany's full military capacity to the invasion of Britain in 1941, Hitler allowed Britain to survive. Britain therefore kept the war going in the West, and also in the Atlantic and Africa. The British resistance was to cause increasing problems for Germany, especially after 1942, as it had to divert resources away from the war in the East. Britain also acted as the launching pad for the bombing of Germany and Operation Overlord.

The invasion of the Soviet Union was to prove a huge mistake. It undid all the gains made by the Nazi–Soviet Pact and once again pushed Germany into a war on two fronts:

> *The effect of Operation Barbarossa was to commit Germany to war with a power which was three times her size in population, eighty times as large in area, and of much greater industrial capacity. It is hardly surprising that the major military setbacks experienced by the Wehrmacht occurred in Russia. These in turn, took the pressure off Britain and greatly assisted the latter's peripheral war effort in the Mediterranean and North Africa.*
>
> **Stephen Lee, *Aspects of European History, 1789–1980* (Routledge, 1991), p.277.**

Declaring war on the USA, which Germany did on 11 September 1941, was also a major error, and showed a serious lack of judgement on Hitler's part. He was too dismissive of America's capabilities and believed that the USA would remain in the Pacific fighting the Japanese. However, President Roosevelt made the defeat of Hitler his top priority, and US and British forces worked together to achieve this task. The USA's entry into the war allowed the Allies to invade Italy, carry out devastating bombing raids on Germany and open up the Second Front in 1944. Meanwhile, Hitler was unable to attack the USA directly, and also did not face the same unity with his allies; Mussolini in fact was a constant drain on Hitler's resources.

Hitler's personal conduct of military operations was also disastrous. This can be seen most clearly in the USSR, where he did not prepare for a winter campaign and did not allow the forces at Stalingrad to conduct an orderly retreat or breakout from the Russian trap, with the result that it had to surrender in January 1943. Another serious mistake was to concentrate on producing V-rockets when Germany could have been developing jet aircraft, which might have restored German air superiority and weakened the Allied bombing campaign of 1944–1945.

Hitler's mistakes in the conduct of the war ensured that it went on much longer than he had expected. Germany increasingly suffered from material shortages as the war continued, particularly in rubber, cotton, nickel, and, after mid-1944, oil. Although military production continued, and even increased right up until 1945, the emphasis on diversification of weapons (such as working on the V1 and V2 rockets) reduced the effectiveness of its efforts in this area. Women, for example, were not employed in munitions factories until late in the war. In addition, the German and Japanese military resented and rejected interference and direction from civilians, which prevented any useful collaboration between civilian and military experts.

The strengths of the Allies

While Hitler faced increasing economic difficulties after 1942, the resources of the Allies grew stronger. As we have seen, the USSR's economy rapidly transformed to a wartime economy and, in the factories east of the Ural mountains, Russia was producing more armaments and better-quality armaments than Germany by 1943.

V-rockets

V-rockets were unmanned long-range missiles that Hitler used against Britain in 1944 and 1945 in what became known as the 'Second Blitz'. The V1 and V2 were to be weapons of revenge – the *Vergeltungswaffen*. These were the secret weapons that Hitler boasted about, the weapons that he previously hinted would win the war for Nazi Germany. The V1s carried an 850-kilogram high-explosive warhead and travelled at 650 kilometres per hour. Between 8,000 and 9,000 V1s were launched against southern England, primarily London. Yet although they caused initial shock, their impact was limited, as V1s could be shot out of the sky by anti-aircraft fire. The V2 – the world's first **ballistic missile** – was far more dangerous. It carried a similar warhead, but travelled at such a speed that it could not be seen or heard until it exploded. These weapons spread considerable fear in London. About 1,000 V2s were fired at Britain before their launch sites were overrun by the advancing Allies. In total, they killed or wounded about 1,500 people.

The centralized state economy of the USSR proved more able than Hitler's Nazi state to produce what was needed to fight a prolonged war. Similarly, once the American economy geared up for wartime production, it also overtook the Axis powers in production of weapons. When the American war industry reached full capacity, it could turn out over 70,000 tanks and 120,000 aircraft a year.

Richard Overy points out, however, that greater economic resources and more armaments did not in themselves guarantee victory for the Allies. Key to Allied success was the fact that they 'turned their economic strength into effective fighting power' (Overy, *Why the Allies Won*, 2nd ed. [Pimlico, 2006], p.399). They learned from their mistakes of 1941 and took steps to increase the effectiveness of future combat forces. These steps involved:

- Improving the quality as well as the quantity of military forces and technology.
- Ensuring that there were excellent back-up services. In the Pacific theatre, there were 18 American support personnel for every one serviceman at the front, compared to a ratio of one to one in the Japanese forces. Stalin also paid close attention to the service of the Red Army. The chief of the Main Directorate of the Red Army Rear, General Khrulev, was responsible for the supply of the army and was treated equally to the military commanders. This was in contrast to the Axis powers, who put emphasis on operations and combat rather than on back-up organization and supplies. Men with the best organizational skills were fighting in the German army rather than helping on the civilian front with planning.
- Setting up a large civilian apparatus to support the Allied forces, which allowed them to mobilize their economic, intellectual, and organizational strengths for the purpose of waging war.

Strategic decisions made by the Allies were also vital for victory. First, the Allies made the decision to concentrate the mass of their attack on Germany; they realized that the defeat of this formidable military opponent was central to success. Thus 85 per cent of America's war effort was devoted to defeating Germany and only 15 per cent to the war with Japan. Second, the Allies poured massive amounts of money and effort into the **strategic bombing** campaign, and this had a serious effect on Germany's capacity to fight effectively at the front. Germany had to curtail its own bombing offensives and divert funds into an anti-aircraft strategy. Finally, the Allies had a tremendous will to win. Most people on the Allied side believed that this contest did not just involve the military forces, but concerned issues of life and death for whole communities and that it was a 'just' war worth fighting.

Activity 4

1. Richard Overy argues in *Why the Allies Won* that 'The war was won in 1945 not from German weaknesses but from Allied strengths.' How far do you agree with this statement?

War in the East: an overview

As we have seen, the USA was brought into the war by the Japanese attack on Pearl Harbor. The attack was brilliantly organized by Admiral Isoroku Yamamoto. There was no declaration of war. At 7.49am on 7 December, the first wave of Japanese planes, launched from nearby aircraft carriers, struck Pearl Harbor. Roosevelt, calling the attack by Japan 'unprovoked and dastardly', asked Congress to declare war on Japan, which it duly did. Britain declared war on Japan the same day. They were followed by the Latin American states of Costa Rica, the Dominican Republic, Haiti, Honduras, Nicaragua, El Salvador, Cuba, Guatemala, and Panama. On 11 December, Germany declared war on America, thus justifying those Americans who, like Roosevelt, believed that America should help Europe in the fight against Hitler. The conflict was now a world war.

Scene of the attack on Pearl Harbor, December 1941.

Meanwhile, Japan caused devastation and shock throughout the Pacific. Within hours of the Pearl Harbor attack, Japanese forces attacked Wake, Guam, the Philippines, Malaya, and Hong Kong. British naval defence depended on a new battleship, the *Prince of Wales*, and the old battlecruiser, the *Repulse*. Both were sunk by Japanese bombers on 10 December, leaving Singapore undefended. In mid-December, the Japanese also invaded Burma.

On 25 and 26 December, Hong Kong and 12,000 prisoners fell into Japanese hands. Japanese troops invaded the Dutch East Indies on 6 January 1942, and before the end of the month, British, Australian, and Indian forces had retreated from the tip of the Malay Peninsula to Singapore. This, too, was attacked and forced to surrender, along with 80,000 soldiers, in one of the worst defeats in British history.

By mid-1942, the Japanese had successfully captured the Dutch East Indies, the Philippines, and Burma. They now held a vast empire, which they labelled the Greater East Asia Co-Prosperity Sphere.

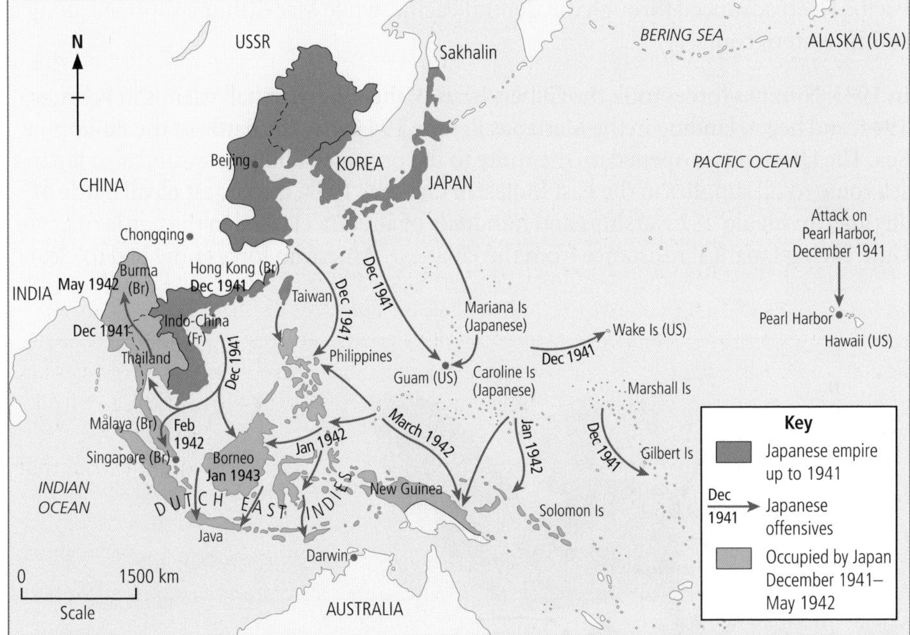

The Japanese offensive in East and South-East Asia and the Pacific, December 1941–May 1942.

The Battle of Midway (June 1942)

After these successes, however, the Japanese suffered two serious setbacks when they failed to capture Port Moresby on the south coast of New Guinea (which would have brought the north coast of Australia within reach of their bombers), or to take Midway Island in June 1942. The Japanese had hoped that an offensive against Midway Island would draw out the US Navy's vital aircraft carriers, which could then be destroyed and tip the naval balance in the Pacific in Japan's favour. However, partly due to the fact that the Americans had broken the Japanese codes and knew exactly when and where the attack was to be launched, the Americans were able to beat off the powerful Japanese naval force and to destroy three of the Japanese aircraft carriers (a fourth was sunk later in the day).

The American success at Midway proved to be a crucial turning point for the war in the Pacific:

> *Not only did the balance in the Pacific between fleet carriers now stand equal … the advantage the Japanese had lost could never be made good … Six fleet carriers would join the Japanese navy in 1942–4; America would launch fourteen, as well as nine light carrier and sixty-six escort carriers, creating a fleet against which Japan could not stand. It was now to be condemned to the defensive.*
>
> **John Keegan, *The Second World War* (Pimlico, 1997), p.229.**

Japanese retreat

Although a catastrophic defeat for Japan, the Battle of Midway did not mean that Japan had lost any territory, and America had an extremely tough time in pushing back the Japanese occupation. Beginning in January 1942 with landings in the Solomon Islands, General Douglas MacArthur (Supreme Commander of Allied Forces in the South-West Pacific Area) slowly began to recover the Pacific islands in a process nicknamed 'island hopping' or 'atoll hopping'. Superiority at sea and in the air enabled the Americans to conquer these stepping stones towards Japan.

In a two-pronged assault, Admiral Chester Nimitz (Commander-in-Chief of the US Pacific Fleet) advanced through the Central Pacific, while MacArthur continued along a south-western course.

In 1943, Nimitz's forces took the Gilbert Islands, then the Marshall Islands in February 1944, and began landing in the Marianas in June 1944 after the battle of the Philippine Sea. The US victories opened up the route to the occupied Philippines, and also Japan's sea route to oil supplies in the East Indies. In October 1944, the largest naval battle of all time, involving 282 warships and hundreds of aircraft, clashed in the battle of Leyte Gulf. Facing fanatical resistance from the Japanese, American forces now had to clear

The Allied onslaught against Japan, 1943–1945.

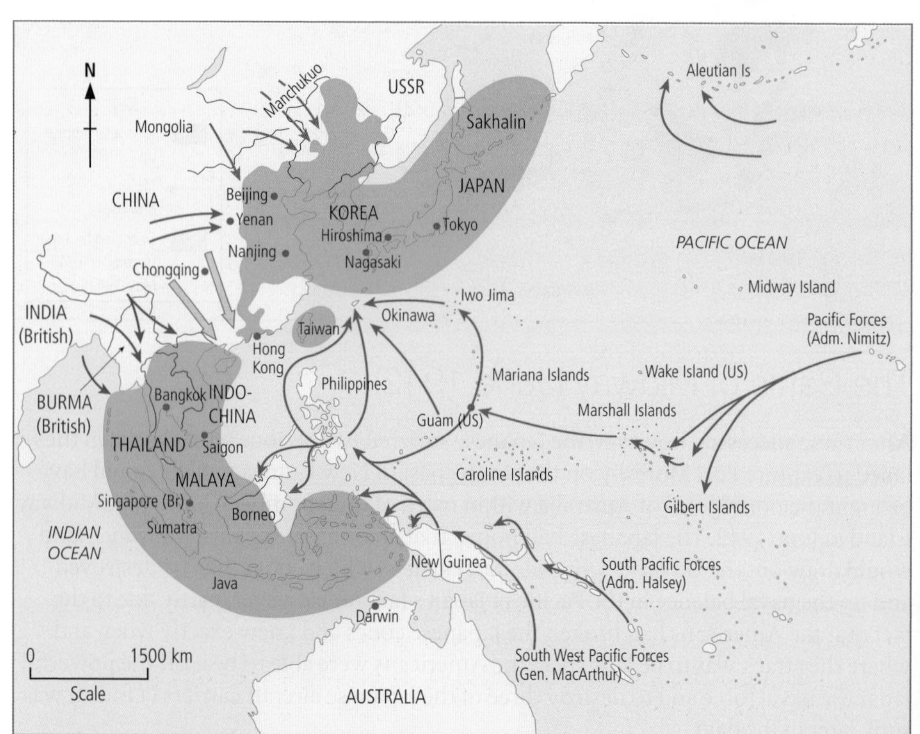

the Japanese out of the Philippines, and then the islands of Iwo Jima and Okinawa in 1945. Okinawa was the grimmest of all of these battles. The US army divisions lost 4,675 dead and missing, and the US Marine Corps 2,938. The US Navy lost a further 4,900 dead, and 763 aircraft were destroyed and 38 ships sunk. The population of Okinawa suffered terribly, with perhaps as many as 160,000 dying in the fighting. The Japanese lost 16 ships and 7,800 aircraft, 1,000 of these in *kamikaze* missions. Although the Americans took 7,400 prisoners, 110,000 other Japanese died refusing to surrender.

Meanwhile, the Allies had set up a new South-East Asia Command under Admiral Louis Mountbatten, whose objective was to clear the Japanese out of Burma and open the Burma Road to China. This objective was finally achieved in May 1945.

The atomic bomb, and the Japanese surrender

With the Germans defeated in May 1945, it was possible for the Americans to focus all of their might on the defeat of Japan. The Soviets had also promised to bring their troops to the East to help with the final assault.

Japan was clearly on the verge of defeat. Not only were the American ground forces nearly at Japan itself, through their strategy of 'island hopping', but Japan had been consistently bombed since November 1944, with devastating effects on its cities. The new Japanese prime minister, Admiral Kantaro Suzuki, tried to get the Americans to agree to a peace that would preserve the position of the Emperor. However, the Allies would not accept anything other than 'unconditional surrender'. In addition, they were concerned that if the Soviets got involved, this would ensure that Stalin received land in the East in return for his efforts; they were also concerned about the number of casualties that the US Army would suffer in a land invasion.

These were some of the factors that influenced Harry S. Truman (US president following the death of Roosevelt in April 1945) to use the new weapon possessed by the USA – the atomic bomb, or '**A-bomb**'. The American and British **Manhattan Project** had been secretly developing this weapon to use against Nazi Germany, but Germany had surrendered before it was ready.

The first A-bomb, 'Little Boy', was dropped over Hiroshima on 6 August 1945 with devastating effects, killing some 80,000 people and injuring 80,000 more. On 9 August, a second bomb was dropped on the port of Nagasaki, and another 40,000 Japanese died. After this, the Japanese government surrendered. The war was finally over.

Kamikaze

In fighting the Japanese, the Americans faced a formidable enemy. Japanese troops on the whole preferred death to surrender. Japanese warrior tradition prescribed surrender to be dishonourable, and thus many soldiers committed suicide rather than be captured. In fact, Japanese army regulations laid down that their surrender was a crime punishable by death. Another horrific aspect of the fighting for the Americans was the *kamikaze* suicide tactics used by the Japanese, in which pilots would literally fly their bomb-laden aircraft into American ships. The 1,900 suicide missions between 6 April and 22 June sank 25 ships and scored 182 hits. Ironically, *kamikaze* attacks also damaged the Japanese air force by reducing the numbers of available aircraft.

Activity 5

ATL Thinking and social skills

Discussion question

1. From what you have read, what arguments do you think Truman would have given for using the atomic bomb?

Activity 6

ATL Thinking skills

Source A

> *Based on detailed investigation of all the facts and supported by the testimony of the surviving Japanese leaders involved, it is the Survey's opinion that certainly prior to 31 December 1945 and in all probability prior to 1 November 1945, Japan would have surrendered even if the atomic bombs had not been dropped, even if Russia had not entered the war, and even if no invasion had been planned or contemplated.*
>
> **From the report of the US Strategic Bombing Survey Group, July 1946, assigned to study the effects of air attacks on Japan.**

Source B

It is my opinion that the use of this barbarous weapon at Hiroshima and Nagasaki was of no material assistance in our war against Japan. The Japanese were already defeated and were ready to surrender because of the effective sea blockade and the successful bombing of conventional weapons. It was my reaction that the scientists and others wanted to make this test because of the vast sums that had been spent on the Project. Truman knew that and so did the other people involved ... My own feeling was that in being the first to use it we had adopted the ethical standards common to barbarians in the dark ages. I was not taught to make war in that fashion.

Admiral William D. Leahy, Chief of Staff to the President of the United States, from his autobiography *I Was There* (1950).

Source C

Part of the appeal of the atomic bomb was that it allowed one plane ... to achieve what had previously been achieved by hundreds. In more than 30,000 sorties between June 1944 and August 1945, only seventy-four B-29s were lost, a casualty rate of 0.24% ... Yet seventy-four B-29s translates into nearly 900 highly trained men. Since 1940, the Allies had been applying the principle of maximum enemy casualties for minimum Allied casualties. The creation of the atomic bomb required a revolution in physics. But it did not require a revolution in the political economy of total war. Rather it was the logical culmination of the Allied way of war.

From Niall Ferguson, *The War of the World* (Penguin, 2006), p.574.

Source D

Most importantly, the bomb was part of an 'atomic diplomacy', in which the US tried to establish a post-war advantage over the Soviet Union (and, it may be argued, Britain) in Europe and Asia. In May 1945 Henry Stimson wrote that US economic power and the bomb were 'a royal straight flush and we mustn't be a fool about the way we play it'. Following this advice, Truman even delayed the Potsdam Conference with Churchill and Stalin to await the first test of the new weapon. As soon as he received news of success, the president took a tough line over issues such as Germany and downplayed the prospect of Soviet entry into the war against Japan. Truman explained, 'I have an ace in the hole and another one showing. So, unless [Stalin] has three-of-a-kind or two pairs (and I know he has nothing), we are sitting all right.' Stimson admitted, on the day after the second bomb at Nagasaki, that the US wanted to end the war, 'before the Russians could put in any substantial claim to occupy and help rule [Manchuria and Japan].'

From Scott Lucas, 'Hiroshima and History', *Modern History Review*, 1996.

1. Identify the key points being made in Sources A–D concerning the use of the atomic bomb.
2. Compare and contrast Sources A and B in their arguments against the use of the atomic bomb.
3. With reference to their origin, purpose, and content what are the value and limitations of Sources A and B for historians studying the use of the atomic bomb to end the war in the Pacific?

Activity 7

1. List the arguments for and against using the atomic bomb, as identified in the text above and in the sources. Research these arguments in more detail.
2. Now, hold a class discussion about whether the dropping of the atomic bomb was necessary to save American and Japanese lives.

Why were the Allies successful in defeating the Japanese?

The Allied victory in the Pacific and South-East Asia had several factors in common with the defeat of the Germans – the emphasis on effective back-up support for the military, and the involvement of the civilians in the military in planning and logistics, for example. As with Germany, these were areas that the Japanese had neglected. The post-war bombing survey of Japan noted the failure of the Japanese air force to provide 'adequate maintenance, logistic support, communications and control, or airfields and bases …'

Technologically, the Americans gradually overtook the Japanese in producing new fighting weapons. Although at a disadvantage at the beginning of the war, as in Europe, America learned from early mistakes and quickly pulled ahead, building up naval and air superiority, developing new planes and realizing the importance of aircraft carriers.

A critical factor behind the Allied victory lay in isolating Japan from its empire by destroying its merchant marine, navy, and naval airpower. Japan had overstretched itself in the huge amount of territory it was trying to occupy. Denied use of the empire's human resources, equipment, food supplies, and raw materials by US submarines, surface vessels, and aircraft, the nation could not possibly survive. Japan being a small island with limited industrial power, the Japanese economy simply could not match the American capacity for rapid expansion. At the end of the war, the destruction of Japan's industries and cities by systematic bombing was also an important factor in Japan's ultimate defeat. By 1945, the national infrastructure was destroyed and industry was unable to produce the weapons it needed.

How was World War Two fought?

The war on land

World War One not only had an impact on the causes of World War Two, as you have read in chapter 5, but it also had an impact on the way the war was fought. Germany had learnt from the 1918 Ludendorff offensive that in order to break through the enemy's ranks concentrated attacks by storm troopers, along with tactical air cover, were critical.

In fact, strategists in Britain, France, and Germany had all written about the need for rapid mobile attacks based on large numbers of tanks, but it was the German leadership that put these theories into practice. The result was *blitzkrieg*. Now, instead of the defensive war of World War One, there was offensive war that consisted of surprise, speed, and movement using tanks, armoured vehicles, mechanized transport, and the aeroplane. An air strike took out the opposing air force and communications centres on the ground and parachutists were dropped behind enemy lines. The swift-moving tanks and motorized infantry – supported by air power – would then split the enemy lines, and allow rapid penetration into the unprotected territories beyond, with the aim of encircling the main enemy forces and destroying them. Thus a rapid, decisive victory was achieved.

Although many historians now doubt that *blitzkrieg* was a coherent, well-thought-out strategy and believe that it was more of an improvised response, it was nevertheless well suited to Hitler's needs. He was not expecting a major war in 1939; his planning was for a widespread European war in 1943–1945, and in 1939 the German economy was not yet ready for the demands of a long war. Thus *blitzkrieg* allowed Hitler to achieve quick victories that were not too demanding in terms of casualties and resources. The speed and surprise elements of Germany's success prevented other countries from mobilizing fully for total war, and had a devastating impact on morale.

The successes and failures of *blitzkrieg*

Up until 1941, *blitzkrieg* in Europe was very successful. Although the German army was not superior in terms of actual equipment, the surprise of a *blitzkrieg* attack against an enemy that lacked the same levels of organization and morale allowed for dramatic German victories. Operation Barbarossa, however, showed the weakness of *blitzkrieg*. Despite the massive advances in the first 6 months, the German army was not sufficiently equipped to deal with such a large operation. The circumstances in which *blitzkrieg* was effective – short wars in confined areas – did not exist in the USSR. With its huge areas of land and resources, the USSR was able to withstand the initial losses, reorganize its economy and military, and fight back. By 1943, Germany had lost the key 'surprise' element of *blitzkrieg* and its enemies had learnt from their initial mistakes of 1939–1941. The Allies increasingly fought a war in the same attacking style as the Germans, with heavy use of tanks, mobile vehicles and, most importantly, air power. From 1944, the Allies had dominance of the skies on all fronts.

The war at sea

The battle for the Atlantic

For Britain, naval power was critical for maintaining the vital trade routes on which the British population depended for survival. It also allowed Britain to defend its empire and was essential to any army operation outside home waters. Thus, until 1944, Britain fought mainly a naval war. Yet even more so than in 1914–1918, sea warfare in the Atlantic was no longer about battles between large fleets and huge battleships. German naval prestige suffered a blow after the scuttling of the *Graf Spee* in 1939 (the battleship was trapped by British warships in Montevideo Harbor, Uruguay) and the sinking of the prestigious battleship *Bismarck* in the Atlantic in 1941. German capital warships were then removed from the Atlantic and as a result there were no major surface engagements in the Mediterranean and Atlantic that compared to the Battle of Jutland in World War One.

Sea warfare was now about controlling supply lines, and from 1940 to 1943 Britain and Germany fought to see who could dominate the Atlantic. Although the German U-boat fleet was small in 1939, it was developed quickly. Hitler needed the U-boats to keep Britain and the USA occupied while Germany was tied up in the Soviet Union. They were also a possible way of defeating Britain outright, and at first the German U-boats were very successful at harrying Britain's lifeline. In 1941, submarines sank 1,299 ships, and in 1942 1,662 ships, with a total tonnage of almost 8 million, were sunk. By 1943, Britain's survival was being seriously threatened by the losses of Allied shipping.

To combat the U-boats, the Allies had both to avoid them and attack them. Both strategies depended on precise knowledge of the position and movement of the U-boats. Fortunately for the Allies, mid-1943 saw the culmination of several factors that allowed them to do this, thereby eliminating the U-boat as a decisive threat.

- Britain was able to crack the Enigma codes (see the Interesting Fact box). Also, in 1943 the codes of the Royal Navy were changed, after it was discovered that the Germans had been deciphering them all along. Thus from mid-1943, the Allies had an intelligence advantage.

- By May 1943, convoys were protected by various technical innovations. Included in these was the High-Frequency Direction Finder (HF/DF, known as 'Huff-Duff'), which provided an accurate bearing towards any submarine that used its radio.
- Air power was used effectively to attack the U-boats. Long-range Liberator aircraft with short-wave radar and searchlights were able to pick out the U-boats on the surface at night. Small aircraft carrier escorts started accompanying the convoys to give protection when the Liberator aircraft were unavailable or out of range. In 1943, 149 out of the 237 German vessels sunk were victims of aircraft.

By the end of 1943, it was clear that the Allies had won the battle for the Atlantic. Richard Overy points to the importance of the British and American willingness to recognize and undertake a revolution in maritime strategy, something that the Germans were reluctant to do. After 1943, the Allies also managed to produce more ships than were being lost thanks to the dramatic increase in US shipbuilding.

Naval war in the Pacific

The revolutionary effect of aircraft in sea warfare was demonstrated even more clearly in the war with Japan. Japan used air power highly effectively at the start of the war in the attack on Pearl Harbor and also against British and Dutch ships in the Pacific. Like Germany, Japan hoped to intercept Allied shipping to prevent any reinforcements reaching the Pacific. It also hoped to destroy the rest of the US fleet, as explained. However, the Americans had huge shipbuilding capability and also had realized – even before the Europeans – that aircraft were vital to naval combat. Thus the USA already had large aircraft carriers at the outbreak of war. American ships also had radar and access to Japanese codes. These factors were crucial in their success at the Battles of Coral Sea and Midway in 1942. As explained on pages 178–179, the loss of the Japanese carrier force in the Battle of Midway put the Japanese into a position from which they could not recover, given their limited shipbuilding capacity. (In 1943 and 1944, Japanese shipyards produced seven aircraft carriers, whereas the American shipyards produced 90.)

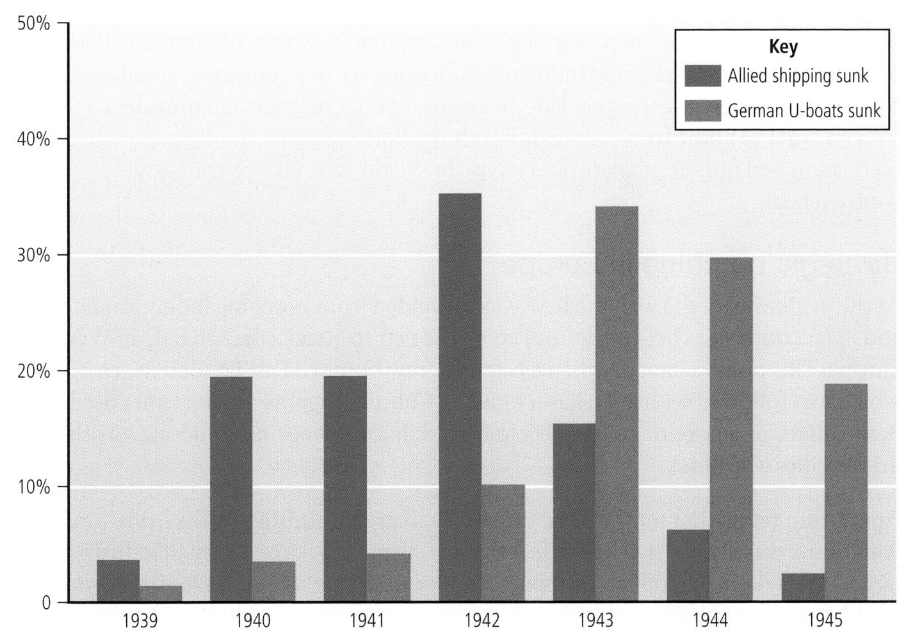

The U-boat war – annual loss of allied shipping and U-boats as a percentage of total war loss.

Enigma codes

The German military used the Enigma cipher machine during World War Two to keep their communications secret.

The Enigma machine was an electro-mechanical device that relied on a series of rotating 'wheels' or 'rotors' to scramble plain text messages into incoherent cipher text. The machine's variable elements could be set in many billions of combinations, each one generating a completely different cipher text message. The recipients of messages would know how the machine had been set up, so could type the cipher text back in; the machine would then unscramble the message. Without knowing the Enigma setting, the message would remain indecipherable.

The German authorities believed in the absolute security of the Enigma. However, with the help of Polish mathematicians who had managed to acquire a machine prior to the outbreak of World War Two, British code breakers stationed at Bletchley Park managed to crack the Enigma code.

CHALLENGE YOURSELF

Research skills 

Research further the work of intelligence at Bletchley Park. What kind of people worked there and how were they recruited? Who was Alan Turing and what was his role in cracking the Enigma code?

What was the significance of the naval war for the outcome of World War Two?

Naval warfare played a key role in both the course and the outcome of World War Two. In Europe, the German U-boat campaign, as well as bringing the British close to subsistence levels of existence, delayed the opening of a second front, preventing the build-up of the American forces in Europe until after 1943. Taking routes to avoid the U-boats also made getting supplies to the USSR and the Allied armies in Africa much more difficult than it would normally have been.

The victory of the Allies in the battle for the Atlantic was vital, therefore, in allowing Britain and the USA to prepare for D-Day. John Keegan writes that 'Had it been lost … the course, perhaps the outcome, of the Second World War would have been entirely otherwise.' The victory of the Allies on the seas also allowed them to impose crippling sea blockades on Italy and Japan, which dramatically affected the industrial strength of these countries and prevented them from sending out reinforcements to other fronts.

The war in the air

Both the war on land and the war at sea were transformed by aircraft. Both sides used aircraft as a tactical support for armies on the ground. Radio communication was used to coordinate air support, with ground-attack aircraft attacking enemy strongpoints, supply lines, troops, and vehicles. At sea, aircraft now were used to attack surface vessels and submarines, as well as to protect convoys. In supply and reconnaissance, aircraft were also applied to great effect. Supplies were now dropped by aircraft (as were soldiers in several campaigns), and aircraft were essential in supplying partisan movements behind enemy lines. Camera technology was greatly improved throughout the course of the war, making photo-reconnaissance aircraft even more effective. Aircraft were used for identifying troop movements and also targets for bombing.

Strategic bombing

While aircraft played a *supportive* role, World War Two also saw an even more radical and independent use for aircraft in strategic bombing. This type of bombing focused on destroying the military and industrial infrastructure of a country. It could also, however, be directed against civilians in an attempt to crush civilian **morale**. By focusing on the home front, strategic bombing blurred further the distinction between combatant and non-combatant, and its use in World War Two remains highly controversial.

Strategic bombing in Europe

At the beginning of the war, the RAF was forbidden from bombing indiscriminately, and in fact both sides held back from being the first to attack cities directly in Western Europe. This policy changed when a *Luftwaffe* crew bombed East London in error, which was followed with a retaliatory raid by Churchill against Berlin. Hitler used the Berlin attack as an excuse to launch a full-scale air assault against London and other British cities (the Blitz).

Apart from retaliation for the Blitz, the switch to **area bombing** by the British and Americans was also caused by the fact that precision attacks on German industrial targets in daylight led to high casualties, and localized night-time attacks were too inaccurate. In addition, strategic bombing allowed the Allies to show Stalin that they were playing their part in the war.

The key advocate of the bombing campaign in Britain was Sir Arthur 'Bomber' Harris, who was appointed commander-in-chief of Bomber Command at the beginning of 1942. Initially, bombing raids on Germany did not bring about the results that Bomber Command hoped for, and the high losses of RAF planes in 1942–1943 were making the strategy unacceptable. The effects on parts of Germany were still horrific – 40,000 dying in Hamburg in a firestorm, for instance – but they did not lead to a collapse in civilian morale and German industrial production continued to rise into 1944. However, with the introduction of the P-51B Mustang in 1944, the bombing campaign became far more devastating. This plane was fitted with auxiliary fuel tanks so that it could accompany the bombers all the way to the target; it was thus able to take on the *Luftwaffe* fighters, causing huge losses in German planes and giving the bombers easier bomb runs. In February and March 1944, the Germans lost a total of 900 fighters, a situation from which they never recovered. By June 1944, the Allies had total air superiority.

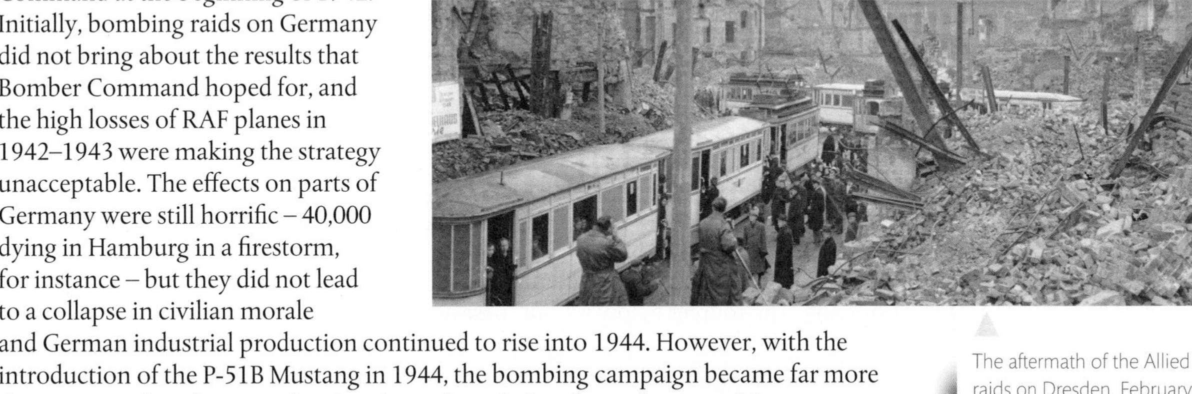

The aftermath of the Allied air raids on Dresden, February 1945.

With the *Luftwaffe* defeated, Bomber Command was able to bomb in daylight and to carry out 'precision' attacks on industrial targets such as the steel industry in the Ruhr. (The US Army Air Forces – USAAF – bombed almost exclusively in daylight. Previously the RAF largely bombed at night, while the USAAF took over in the day.) However, cities in eastern Germany such as Dresden, Leipzig, and Chemnitz were also attacked in the spring of 1945. Joint Anglo-American attacks on Dresden in February 1945 created a firestorm that killed approximately 50,000 civilians.

The Germans, who lacked a proper strategic bomber force, responded to the Allied attacks from 1944 with the V1, a pilotless flying bomb, and the V2 ballistic missile. These were targeted at London and did cause significant casualties. They could not be mass-produced, however, and were unreliable and inaccurate. They also came too late in the war to have any effect on the outcome. In fact, the rocket project did not help the German war effort, as it used up resources that would have been better spent on building more fighter planes.

Strategic bombing in the Pacific

Japan was also subjected to intense bombing. From November 1944, the USAAF, flying from the captured island bases of Saipan and Guam, began relentlessly hitting the Japanese mainland. Initially they carried out precision attacks on aircraft factories, but these gave way from March 1945 to area bombing using mainly incendiary munitions. The results were horrific for Japanese civilians living in houses made mainly of wood, bamboo, and paper. In an attack on Tokyo on 9 March 1945, B-29s flying from Iwo Jima destroyed a quarter of the city – a million homes – and killed approximately 80,000 people. In fact, in the 6 months between April and August 1945, 21st Bomber Command under the direction of General Curtis LeMay devastated most of Japan's major cities. Terrified Japanese fled to the villages; absenteeism in the factories rose to 50 per cent. A combination of sea blockade and bombing devastated the economy and left Japan on the verge of defeat. However, the ultimate expression of strategic bombing came with the use of the two atomic bombs on Hiroshima and Nagasaki, after which Japan surrendered. Thus it was air power alone that caused the final collapse of Japan; no land invasion was necessary.

The debate about strategic bombing

There have been two major criticisms made against strategic bombing: that it was morally wrong and that it was ineffective. With regard to the first point, the justifications given by the Allies were that the Germans started it (Churchill quoted Hosea 8:7 saying 'now those who sow the wind are reaping the whirlwind'), that it was the only means that Britain had of hitting back at Germany, and that it would help end the war more quickly. It was thus a strategy of necessity. Yet critics at the time, and since 1945, maintained that the devastating effects on civilian populations did not justify such use of bombing.

With regard to its effectiveness, there is again much controversy. Some historians argue that the dramatic drop in German production in 1944–1945 was due to the attacks of Bomber Command, while other historians argue that Germany's declining production figures were owed as much to the general attrition of the war as to the bombing. The sources below set out these arguments more fully.

Activity 8

ATL Thinking skills

Source analysis

Source A

There has always seemed something fundamentally implausible about the contention of bombing's critics that dropping almost 2.5 million tons of bombs on tautly stretched industrial systems and war-weary urban populations would not seriously weaken them. Germany and Japan had no special immunity. Japan's military economy was devoured in the flames; her population desperately longed for escape from bombing. German forces lost half of the weapons needed at the front, millions of workers absented themselves from work, and the economy gradually creaked almost to a halt. Bombing turned the whole of Germany, in Speer's words, into a 'gigantic front'. It was a front the Allies were determined to win; it absorbed huge resources on both sides. It was a battlefield in which only the infantry were missing. The final victory of the bombing in 1944 was, Speer concluded, 'the greatest lost battle on the German side …' For all the arguments over the morality or operational effectiveness of the bombing campaigns, the air offensive was one of the decisive elements in Allied victory.

Richard Overy, *Why the Allies Won*, 2nd ed. (Pimlico, 2006), p.163.

Source B

Harris later claimed that the bombers could have won the war on their own, had they been given the required resources. There is little evidence to suggest that area bombing (whatever we may say about its morality) contributed directly to the Allied victory. There was, for example, despite Harris' confident predictions, no general collapse in German morale. German productive capacity was reduced by about 9% in 1943 and about 17% in 1944. In mitigation, however, it is important to note three points. First, that in the dark days of 1940–41, after London and other cities had been blitzed and British forces had been expelled from Norway and France, the British felt they had to be doing something to hit back at the enemy; bombing was arguably of psychological importance. Second, that as the war dragged on, there was a need to placate Stalin, in the absence of a second ground front, to be seen to be carrying the war to the enemy, above all to deter the Soviets from signing a separate peace with Germany. Third, that area bombing operations against Germany, whatever their real effect on the ground, caused a substantial portion of German resources to be re-directed to home defence and reconstruction from other fronts; they also saved civilian lives in Britain by putting the Luftwaffe on the defensive.

From Peter Riddick, 'Strategic Bombing', in *Modern History Review*, 1994, pp.12–13.

1. Identify the key points made in Source A and explain what they reveal about the impact of strategic bombing on the outcome of the war.
2. To what extent are the views expressed about strategic bombing in Source A supported by Source B?

Activity 9

ATL Thinking and social skills

Review questions

1. What was the impact of the following on the final outcome of the war?
   a) the war at sea
   b) the war in the air
2. What technological developments in each of these areas had an impact on the nature of the fighting and the outcome?
3. In pairs, apply the same questions to World War One. Compare your answers. What are the similarities and differences in each case? (We will return to these comparisons in chapter 10 and analyse them further.)

To what extent did World War Two see the total mobilization of resources?

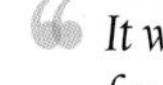

It was in the Second World War that the full force of the modern European state was mobilized for the first time, for the primary purpose of conquering and exploiting other Europeans.

Tony Judt, *Postwar* (Vintage, 2010), p.14.

Activity 10

ATL Self-management skills

1. Before reading this section, review the ways in which World War One was a total war. You may also want to copy out the spider diagram on page 70 and add to it as you read the following section.

World War One is considered to have been more of a total war and to have mobilized military, human, and economic resources to an even greater extent than World War One for the following reasons:

- Learning from World War One, governments made every effort to ensure the fullest mobilization and most efficient utilization of the human and material resources of the state.
- Because World War One had shown that the productivity of the home front was the key to victory, so World War Two saw the home front under direct attack in a way that had not occurred in the previous conflict.
- Governments used all weapons at their disposal and developed new ones during the course of the war – weapons that were capable of killing far greater numbers of civilians than ever before.
- In both the war in Europe and the war in the Far East, racial hatred led to the killing or relocation of vast numbers of civilians deemed to be untrustworthy or inferior.

The aims of the belligerents

As with World War One, the aims of the powers involved in the war were 'total'. Hitler's aims for Europe were clear; total domination and the takeover of the USSR to provide living space for the German peoples. They also involved the elimination of races considered inferior – Jews in particular – in all areas taken over by the Nazis. In combating these aims, the Allies could afford no compromise peace. They saw themselves as fighting for the freedom of Europe. The same was true in the Pacific, where the Japanese Co-Prosperity Sphere, with its aims of political, economic, and

The future impact of wartime technological innovations

World War Two saw major developments in military technology – radar, U-boat detection equipment, long-distance bombing, V1 and V2 rockets, and, of course, the atomic bomb. Of these, radar was to have a huge impact in future air and sea navigation, the V2 weapons led indirectly to rockets for space exploration and nuclear missiles, while the jet engine would revolutionize air travel. The atomic bomb, as you will read later, would affect how the Cold War was to be fought. There were other developments, stimulated by wartime needs, that would have a big impact in peacetime. The large-scale production of the new sulphonamide drugs and of penicillin (which had been discovered in 1929) saved thousands of soldiers' lives and would save thousands of civilian lives after the war.

The war also saw research into improved techniques for storing blood and plasma, and also plastic surgery for helping badly injured or burnt service personnel. Synthetic fibres such as nylon, which were used to make parachutes, would soon appear in all types of consumer products.

A 1943 US poster makes an historical link between fighting the Nazis and Japanese, and the American revolution of the late 18th century.

'Bolshevism is treading on Europe.' A German poster distributed in Belgium in 1943.

racial domination, was considered unacceptable. Although Japan called for a negotiated peace in 1945, this was rejected by the Allies, who demanded total surrender.

The racial aspect of the fighting, involving as it did whole populations, injected a greater intensity into the struggle and ensured a bitter fight to the finish. As with World War One, propaganda on both sides reinforced the need for unrestrained warfare, while also demonizing the enemy and making total victory the only goal.

The use of weaponry

As you have read, both sides used all weapons in their arsenals, and developed deadly new weapons during the course of the war in an attempt to win at all costs.

Activity 11

1. Go back over this chapter and add examples of weapons to your spider diagram to show how both sides used every means possible to achieve victory.

The impact of war on civilians

As we have seen, civilians were attacked in new ways during World War One and also suffered the effects of war in terms of rationing and deprivation. However, the large casualty figures were made up mainly of the men of the armed forces. In World War Two these proportions changed profoundly. Whereas in World War One, civilians counted for only one-twentieth of the war dead, in World War Two they counted for up to two-thirds of the deaths. This shift was because of the power of the new weaponry – the bombers, for example – and also because the new mobility of war brought the fighting to far greater numbers of people than had been the case in World War One.

Activity 12

1. Go back over this chapter. Identify examples of where civilians were either caught up in the fighting or deliberately targeted as a strategy for winning the war. Add to your spider diagram the examples and the impact on civilians.

Deportation and genocide

There was an ideological and racial aspect to World War Two that meant that certain sections of populations were deliberately targeted, with the intent that they should be deported or even eliminated entirely. In Europe, this was particularly evident on the Eastern Front following the German invasion of Poland and the Soviet Union. Hitler believed that certain races – in particular Jews, but also Slavs – were *Untermenschen* or subhuman. The space that was necessary for the Greater German Reich also meant that the existing populations in Poland and the USSR had to be destroyed or displaced. In one of the plans for German settlement drawn up by the Reich, it was estimated that:

> *the unwanted population would be closer to fifty or even fifty-seven million, assuming that 15 percent of Poles, 25 percent of Ruthanians and 35 percent of Ukrainians would need to be retained as agricultural labourers, the rest being deported to Siberia. The Russian population would wither away through the use of contraception, abortion and sterilization. The Jews would be exterminated.*
>
> **Niall Ferguson, *War of the World* (Penguin, 2006), p.442.**

Many Poles and Russians were deported to the factories and mines of the **Third Reich**, where the work there ensured almost certain death for most of them. For the Jews, special SS squads called *Einsatzgruppen* accompanied the German army as it invaded Poland and the USSR, and had the dedicated job of killing all Jews, Communist officials, and resisters they encountered. By the end of July 1941, the *Einsatzgruppen* had murdered around 63,000 men, women, and children, 90 per cent of whom were Jews. Groups other than Jews were also at risk, such as the Roma and people with mental and physical disabilities.

The method of killing such large numbers of people was, however, very time consuming and costly – mass groups of people were generally herded into remote locations and shot. The Nazis came up with a new method to deliver their 'final solution' to the 'Jewish question' – the transportation of Jews from across Europe to concentration and extermination camps where they could be eliminated either by poison gas or through overwork and starvation. The extermination camp at Auschwitz-Birkenau alone could kill 10,000 people a day.

Rape of women by the Red Army

As the Soviets pushed through to Berlin in the final year of the war, they took revenge on the German population for 3 years of brutal warfare and the atrocities that the Germans had inflicted on the Russian population. Women in the villages and towns that lay in the path of the Soviet army's advance were raped by Soviet soldiers. Clinics and doctors in Vienna reported that 87,000 women were raped in the three weeks following the Red Army's arrival in the city; and even larger numbers were raped on the Soviet march on Berlin.

The Soviet government also deported whole populations. It assumed that the minority peoples in the west were disloyal to the Soviet Union and thus the Germans on the Volga and the Tartars in the Crimea were deported. Estonians, Lithuanians, and Poles were all sent to Siberia or other parts of the USSR.

A combination of lethal factors meant that the death tolls in Eastern Europe and the USSR during the war were terribly high. At least 20 million died in the Soviet Union (some estimates put the number much higher) and more than half of these were civilian deaths. Poland suffered the greatest proportional loss of life, with 6 million deaths out of a population of 30 million. Of these, 3 million were Jews, and only 150,000 of these casualties represent deaths in military action. Overall, an estimated 1 million Roma and 6 million Jewish civilians were killed by the Nazis in their racial extermination programme.

The Japanese also had ambitions linked to racial superiority. 'The Chinese people', wrote General Sakai Ryu, the chief of staff of the Japanese forces in North China in 1937, 'are bacteria infesting world civilization.' Such attitudes were commonplace, hence the genocidal Japanese treatment of the Chinese in the Rape of Nanjing. Such brutality continued during the takeover of South-East Asia following the attack on Pearl Harbor. Figures are unclear, but some claim that up to 50,000 Chinese were massacred. Overall, 10 million Chinese died at the hands of the Japanese. Filipinos,

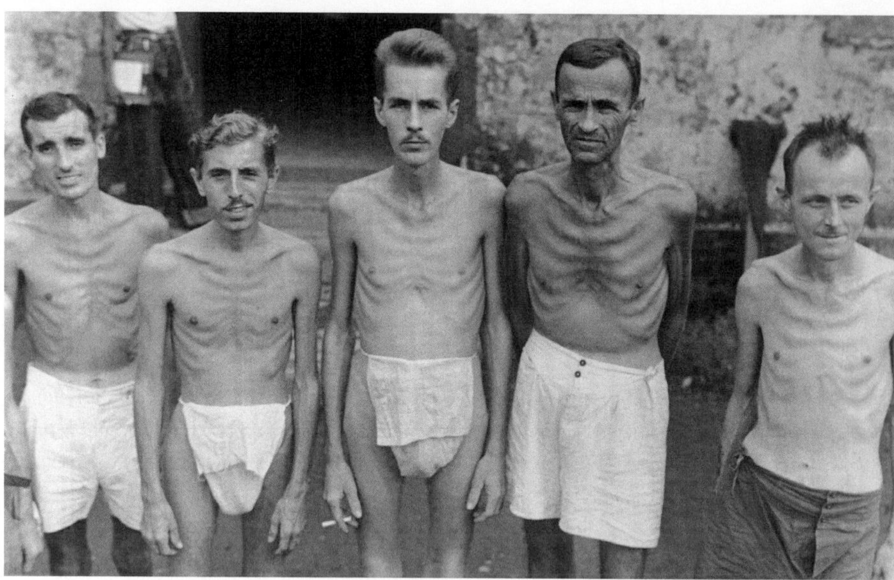

Allied prisoners of the Japanese in the Pacific War, 1941–1945.

Internment

German and Japanese civilians who found themselves living in Britain and America also suffered. It was assumed that their first loyalties would be to their country of origin. Thus Germans and Austrians in Britain were rounded up and put in internment camps. In America, more than 100,000 Japanese were relocated into camps, many losing their property or being forced to sell at very low prices. In 1988, the US Congress agreed on an apology for this policy, and gave $20,000 compensation to all surviving internees.

Indonesians, and Malays were also used as slave workers, resulting in thousands of deaths. Allied prisoners of war also suffered terribly from physical overwork, malnutrition, and abuse.

What recent examples are there in which contempt for one race of people by another has led to violence?

Activity 13

ATL Thinking skills

Source analysis

> *As the Turks had treated the Armenians, as Stalin's henchmen were treating the kulaks, Poles and other 'enemies of the people', as the Nazis were soon to start treating the Jews, Gypsies and mentally ill, so the Japanese now thought of and treated the Chinese as sub-humans. This capacity to treat other human beings as members of an inferior and indeed malignant species – as mere vermin – was one of the crucial reasons why Twentieth Century conflict was so violent. Only make this mental leap, and warfare ceases to be a formalised encounter between uniformed armies. It becomes a war of annihilation, in which everyone on the other side – men, women, children, the elderly – can legitimately be killed.*
>
> **Niall Ferguson, *War of the World* (Penguin, 2006), pp.479–480.**

1. What point is Ferguson making about war in the 20th century?

Mobilization of human resources

As with World War One, civilians were mobilized in all countries to help with the war effort. This effort was, however, on a much vaster scale than in World War One. The major combatants mobilized between a half and two-thirds of their industrial workforce, and devoted up to three-quarters of their national product to waging war. This meant that, apart from in the USA, the vital resources of the country were directed to the war effort and the populations were therefore forced to live on a restricted range of rationed food and household goods.

The number of people required to both fight and to work in the factories to produce the necessary amount of war materials was vast, and countries used different methods to get the workforce that they required.

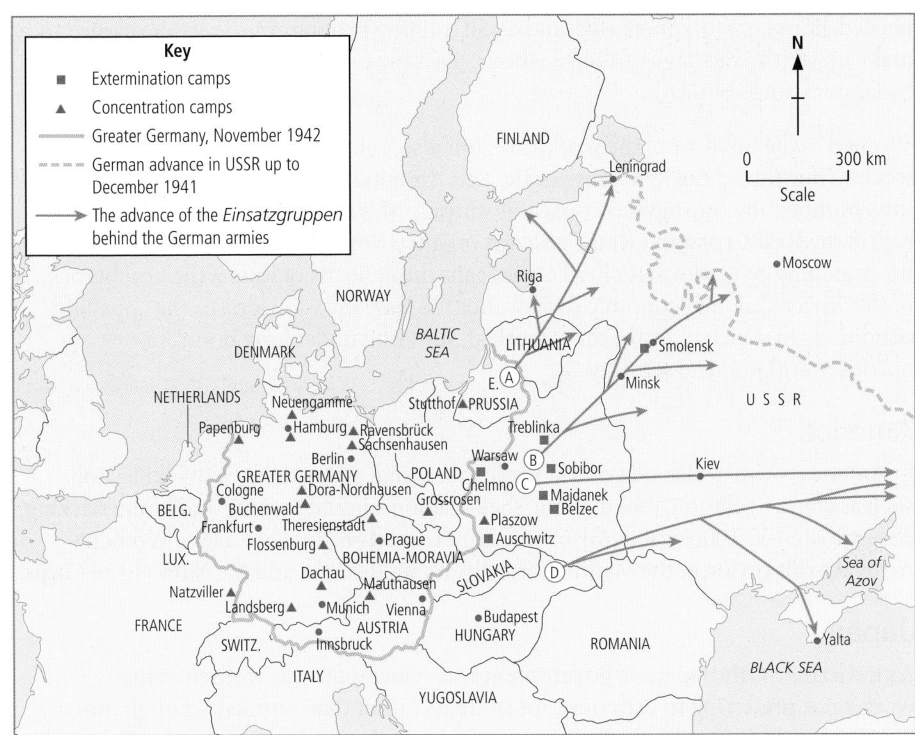

Map showing the main extermination and concentration camps in German-occupied Europe by 1942.

Britain

In Britain, military conscription was introduced from the beginning of the conflict (unlike in World War One), but it was carefully controlled to ensure that key workers were left in the important industries, such as coal mining. Industrial conscription was also introduced for women, and thus women played an even bigger role in British industry, agriculture, and administration in World War Two than in World War One.

Germany

In Germany, there was little change to the economy at the beginning of the war, as the early victories did not put much strain on the home front. When Albert Speer, the Minister of Armaments and War Production, tried to organize the deployment of human resources more effectively from 1942 onwards, he found little support. The regional and police authorities were reluctant to accept national schemes that affected their regions, and having women in the workplace went against Hitler's idea that women should focus on *Kinder, Kirche, Küche* ('Children, Church, Kitchen'). Hitler also insisted that consumer goods production remain a priority, and so workers in non-essential industries could not be transferred.

The labour force was substantially increased, however, by workers from the countries that the Germans had occupied. These workers were forcibly brought to Germany; by September 1944 there were 7,487,000 foreigners in Germany, and this constituted 21 per cent of the workforce.

Soviet Union

In the Soviet Union, the already centralized nature of the state allowed civilians to be mobilized effectively from the beginning. Coercion also played a key role. Workers were forced to move to those areas of the Soviet Union in which they were most

CHALLENGE YOURSELF

Research skills 

Research the different roles that women undertook in Britain in World War Two. How does this compare with the work that they did in World War One?

needed, hours of work increased, and crash training programmes were developed to make up for the shortage of skilled labour. Slacking or absenteeism could be punished by labour camps or death.

Women made up most of the workforce, but also volunteered to serve in the armed forces. They joined the Red Army or the Red Air Force; the latter had three regiments (two bomber and one fighter) consisting entirely of women. They also played a vital role in the **Red Cross** and **Red Crescent** organizations, and in civil defence, and fire-watching operations. Richard Overy calls the civilians of Russia the 'real heroes' of the Soviet Union's economic revival after the Nazi invasion, due to the appalling conditions in which many of them worked, suffering under long hours, poor nutrition, and political scrutiny.

A poster of 'Rosie the Riveter', a fictional female worker used by the US government in a propaganda poster campaign to encourage women to join the war effort.

America

In America, women also played a key role in war industries, doing semi-skilled jobs such as crane operation, tool making, shell loading, aircraft making and lumberjacking. An estimated 350,000 women also joined uniformed groups such as the Women's Army Auxiliary Corps, the Marine Corps Women's Reserve, and the Navy Nurse Corps.

Japan

As in Germany, the Japanese government was reluctant to use women in the workforce, preferring to use conscript students rather than women. Though more than two and a half million extra women did enter the workforce between 1940 and 1945, a much larger number did not.

CHALLENGE YOURSELF

Research a resistance group from one of the following occupied countries: Denmark, France, Belgium, Norway, or Holland. Find out how it was organized, its activities, and to what extent it had a role in the final defeat of the Germans.

Resistance movements

In all countries occupied by the Nazis, there were civilians who joined resistance groups. Also called partisans, they gathered intelligence for the Allies, used sabotage and murder against the occupiers, helped rescue shot-down Allied pilots, took Jews into safety, and fought collaborators from their own nations. Their work was vital for the Allies, but extremely dangerous, as can be seen by the contents of this poster that was put up on the walls of the French city of Nantes in 1941: 'Cowardly criminals in the pay of England and Moscow have killed, by shooting in the back, the Field Commander of Nantes on the morning of 20 October 1941. In expiation for this crime I have already ordered that fifty hostages be shot ... fifty more hostages will be shot if the guilty parties are not arrested by midnight 23 October 1941. I offer an award totaling 15 million francs to those citizens who contribute to the discovery of the guilty parties.' Resistance fighters were also involved in fighting what became, in some places, civil wars against collaborators. Such conflict became part of a wider struggle to determine the future political course after the war.

Economic mobilization and the growth of government power

Britain

As in World War One, the British government extended its powers to cope with organizing its human and economic resources. Churchill formed a **coalition government** and exercised supreme political and military power. Mines, shipping, and railways again came under state control. Rationing was introduced and, as we have seen, conscription for both men and women. Ernest Bevin, the Minister for Labour, also intervened extensively in the health and welfare of the nation, improving healthcare, setting up nurseries to look after children of working mothers, and making sure all factories employing more than 250 people had a canteen and a welfare officer. Bevin took the idea of national welfare still further by making special food rations and vitamin supplements available to young children and mothers, rationalizing the chaotic health system, and ensuring that public transport became a public service rather than a private business. This programme was to be developed further in the National Health Service and the Welfare State that was set up after World War Two.

Germany

In Germany, a single-party state already existed. Yet German planning remained confused and decentralized. In 1942 Albert Speer was put in charge of the Central Planning Board and in 1944 Joseph Goebbels, the Propaganda Minister, was appointed Commissioner for Total Mobilization of Resources for War. Yet neither appointment overcame the problems of a system that was 'poorly coordinated, uncooperative and obstructive' (Richard Overy, *Why the Allies Won*, 2nd ed. (Pimlico, 2006), p.246). Until 1943, Germany also focused on high-quality and technical sophistication rather than trying to mass produce large quantities of standard weapons. It thus failed to produce weapons on a large enough scale and, as you have read, the Soviet Union, although having a smaller industrial base, greatly out-produced the German empire throughout the war.

The Soviet Union

In the Soviet Union, the centralized all-powerful state already existed. Its survival after 1941 was due to careful planning and mass production, as well as the efforts of the Soviet people. The USSR was turned into Stalin's 'single war camp', where war production was the only priority. A single national war plan was drawn up in 1943 and the planners were given the powers for getting their objectives completed. The military share of the budget rose from 29 to 57 per cent and, unlike in Germany, Soviet planners concentrated on large numbers of weapons to be produced as simply and quickly as possible (see pages 172–173 on why the Soviets won for more information on this).

The USA

In the USA, the government also took control of industrial production. The War Production Board, which was established in January 1942, changed production priorities to the needs of the military. Thus car factories now produced tanks and planes. The War Commission recruited workers for where they were needed most and new industries were created, particularly for the production of synthetic materials. However, the USA mainly relied on American business, with its expertise in mass production and technical innovation, and it granted contracts out to the big industries to produce what was needed. Thus without changing the free-market nature of the American economy, the USA was able to expand its manufacturing capacity immensely, ending the war as the most powerful economy in the world.

Japan

Even before the attack on Pearl Harbor, the military government in Japan had strengthened its powers. In 1940, all the main political parties went into 'voluntary' dissolution, and in their place a monolithic party of national unity, the Imperial Rule Assistance Association, was set up. Trade unions were also closed down; they were replaced with the Great Japan Patriotic Industrial Association, which included employers and workers. As in Germany, however, it was difficult for the government to maintain tight control of war production due to the independent positions of the *Zaibatsu* (big companies) and the rivalries between the army and the navy.

Propaganda

Propaganda remained a key weapon of all governments in attempting to win support for the war effort. Germany and the USSR already had propaganda machines in constant action, and these played a key role in convincing their populations of the justification of their actions. Joseph Goebbels stoked the German fear of Communism in the East, and Stalin cleverly dubbed the war as the 'Great Patriotic War', in which defence of the 'motherland' rather than of the brutal communist state was to be the driving motivation of the people.

The Western democracies faced a problem in 1939 in that there was much less enthusiasm for a new war. The change in public opinion, however, came not so much from propaganda as the actions of the Axis powers. After the war scare in 1938, public opinion in Britain hardened, and generally the British were ready for war by 1939 and determined to fight, though lacking the enthusiastic response of the soldiers of 1914. In America, it was the attack on Pearl Harbor and the German declaration of war that changed attitudes.

Propaganda nevertheless remained important to the governments of both countries, and was controlled by special offices – Churchill, for example, established the Political Warfare Executive. In America, the Office of War Information was set up to help Americans understand that the purpose of the war was to defend the national belief in freedom and liberty. Propaganda and censorship were used to help maintain morale, encourage civilians to be more thrifty, get women to work, and, of course, to stress the evil nature of the enemy regime against which they were fighting.

Propaganda was also used directly in the fight against the Nazis. The radio was the most important weapon in this war. The BBC's news broadcasts came to be seen as reliable reports and were listened to in occupied countries to maintain morale and also to inform resistance movements.

British and American propaganda against the Japanese was very different from that used against the Germans. Whereas the propaganda against Germany stressed that the Nazis specifically were the evil enemy, not the whole German population, with Japan the attack was of an openly racial nature and aimed at all Japanese, not just the leaders. The attitude towards the Japanese was that they were primitive, uncivilized, and very much inferior – also that they were treacherous and barbaric.

Activity 14

Cartoon from the *Daily Mail* of 18 February 1942 (three days after the fall of British Singapore to the Japanese)

Source analysis

1. What is the message of this cartoon?
2. Look at the propaganda posters in this chapter. For each, explain the message and how this has been conveyed.

CHALLENGE YOURSELF

Thinking skills 

Research the propaganda methods of Goebbels in Nazi Germany. What different types of propaganda were used? Give examples of each type. Which were the most effective?

Activity 15

Essay planning

Turn to chapter 4, where you will find help in planning and writing comparative questions on the two world wars, and then have a go at planning the essay questions below.

1. ***Discuss the extent to which all economic and human resources were mobilized in one 20th-century war.***
2. ***To what extent was air power decisive in the outcome of one 20th-century war?***
3. ***Examine the impact of technological developments on the course and outcome of one 20th-century war.***

To access weblinks relevant to this chapter, go to www.pearsonhotlinks.com, search for the book title or ISBN, and click on 'chapter 8'.

09

Cross-regional war: World War Two – Effects

Men of the 45th Division of the US 7th Army celebrate VE Day in Nuremberg after capturing the city.

Key concepts: Consequence

As you read this chapter, consider the following essay questions:

- Discuss the international impact of one 20th-century war.
- Examine the political and economic effects of one 20th-century war.

The impact of the war in Europe

Human cost

No other war has recorded such a loss of life in so short a time. Some estimates put the number of dead at more than 50 million, with nearly 40 million of these in Europe. As you have read in the section on total war in the previous chapter, the impact on civilians in this war was huge. Perhaps as many as two-thirds of the war dead were civilians, the most extreme example of this situation being Poland, which lost a fifth of its population, almost all of the victims civilians. In fact, in Europe, only Germany and the UK suffered military losses significantly greater than civilian losses. America's casualties, meanwhile, were almost exclusively military.

Military and civilian death toll in World War Two.

	Mobilized (thousands)	Military killed (thousands)	Civilians killed (thousands)
British Empire	8,720	452	80
China	8,000	1,500	7,800
France	6,000	250	360
Germany	11,000	3,250	700
Italy	4,500	330	500
Japan	6,095	1,700	360
Poland	1,000	120	5,300
USA	14,900	407	Small number
USSR	12,500	9,500	21,500 (est.)
Total from above countries	72,715	17,509	36,600

The horror for civilians did not end with the conclusion of hostilities. More than 20 million people had been displaced during the course of the war, not just as a result of the fighting, but also due to the actions of different countries in expelling and deporting whole groups of people. Stalin and Hitler alone were responsible for the forced removals of some 30 million people.

In addition, many people were forced to move from their homes once the war was over. In German-speaking areas in Hungary, Romania, and Poland, Germans were driven from their homes and forced to move to Germany. This also happened in German lands taken at the end of the war by Russia and Poland. In all, between 1945 and 1947, approximately 16 million Germans were expelled from the countries of Central and Eastern Europe, and many died as a result of this flight to Western Europe. Thus, although the war was over, the suffering continued for many.

Economic cost

World War Two was also much more devastating economically than World War One. Unlike in World War One, the fighting in World War Two took place over nearly all of Europe. Aerial bombing was particularly destructive. Very few cities of any size were left unscathed, and the result was millions of dead and homeless people. In addition, transport and communications had been seriously disrupted, industry destroyed, and farmland ruined.

The consequence of this was that Europe was prostrate in 1945, with the 'victors' of the war (apart from the USA) emerging from the conflict almost as devastated as the losers. Food production had fallen to half pre-war production levels and 150 million people were dependent on some sort of relief food distribution during 1945–1946. Britain was bankrupted by the war, and the Soviet economy suffered badly, with much of western Russia devastated and 25 million homeless.

Political consequences

> *At the conclusion of the First World War it was borders that were invented and adjusted, while people were on the whole left in place. After 1945 what happened was rather the opposite: with one major exception boundaries stayed broadly intact and people were moved instead.*
>
> **Tony Judt, *Postwar* (Vintage, 2010), p.27.**

Compared with the peace settlement at Versailles, boundary changes after World War Two were relatively slight, with the exception of Poland, which saw its border being shifted westwards – it lost 179,000 square kilometres of land in the east and gained 104,000 square kilometres from German territories.

The new boundaries for Poland were decided at the Yalta Conference. There was no major treaty drawn up at the end of World War Two as there had been at Versailles in 1919, but the Allied leaders met twice in 1945 to make decisions about post-war Europe, first at Yalta in February, and then at Potsdam in July.

Significantly, no treaty was signed concerning the future of Germany itself. Although it was agreed at the Yalta Conference in 1945 that Germany should be temporarily divided into four occupation zones, growing hostility between the Western Allies and the Soviet Union led to a permanent division of Germany by 1949. In addition, in all the countries that the Red Army had liberated – Poland, Hungary, Bulgaria, and later Czechoslovakia – one-party regimes under Stalin's control had emerged by 1948, despite an agreement at Yalta that free elections would be allowed in all Eastern European states.

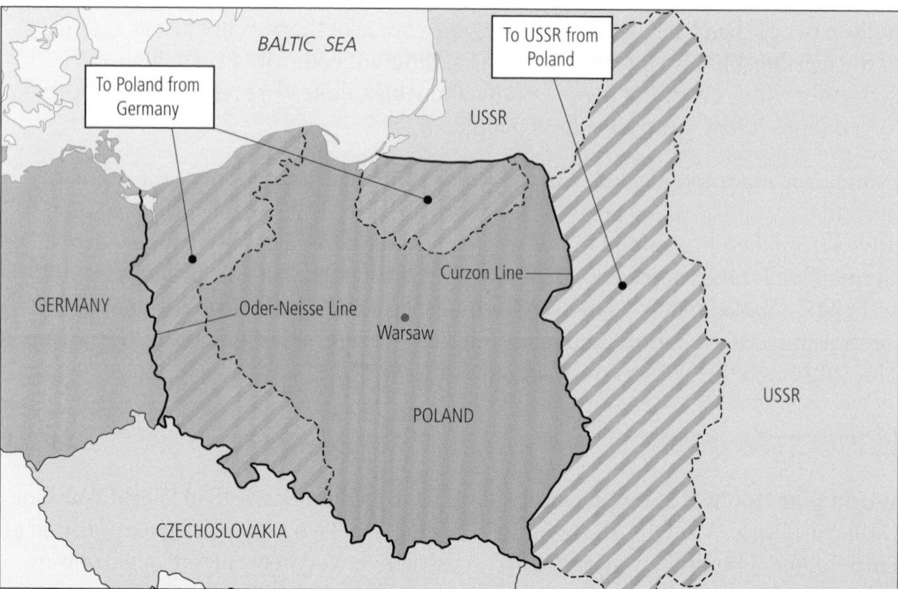

Map showing the new borders of Poland after World War Two.

Activity 1 

1. Why was no peace treaty officially drawn up with Germany at the end of World War Two?

The effects of the war on international relations

The USA and USSR emerge as superpowers

The most significant post-war development in international relations was the change in the balance of power. With some exceptions, such as Austria, the major powers before and after World War One were more or less the same. After World War Two, however, the situation changed radically. American politician Dean Acheson wrote of the post-World War Two situation: 'The whole world structure and order that we had inherited from the 19th century was gone.'

The USSR and the USA emerged from World War Two significantly more powerful than they had been before the war, while the 'old powers' of Britain and France emerged significantly weaker. Why was this?

Military reasons

- To defeat Germany, the USA had acquired the largest air force in the world, with almost 73,000 aircraft. By 1945, it also had 12 million men in the armed forces and more than 70,000 naval vessels. In addition, it possessed the atomic bomb.
- To defeat Germany, the USSR had acquired the largest land army in the world.
- France and Britain's inability to defeat Germany had changed the balance of power. They had become 'second-rank' powers. Without the USA and the USSR, there was no way that Britain could have defeated Germany on its own.
- The USSR now lacked any strong military neighbours. This made it a regional power.

Economic reasons

- The USA's economy was strengthened by the war. It was able to out-produce all the other powers put together.
- The USA was committed to more 'open' trade; its politicians and businessmen wanted to ensure liberal trade conditions and market competition prevailed. The USA was willing to play an active role in preventing the pre-war pattern of trade-blocs and tariffs from re-emerging. The USA now took the lead in international collaboration through the **International Monetary Fund** (IMF) and **General Agreement on Tariffs and Trade** (GATT).
- The USA had the economic strength to prevent a return to instability in Europe.
- The small Eastern European countries that had been created by the Treaty of Versailles were not economically viable on their own; they needed the support of a stronger neighbour, and the USSR could replace Germany in this role.

Political reasons

- For the West, the ideals of democracy and international collaboration had triumphed over Fascism. Thus liberal democracy was seen as the right path for the future.
- For the USSR, it was Communism that had triumphed over Fascism, and the Communist Party was given a new lease of life. Indeed, Communism had widespread respect in Europe because of its part in resisting the Germans. Many of the earliest resistance movements in occupied Europe had been dominated by the Communists, and immediately after the war there were strong Communist parties in several

Western European states. Also, in Asia, Communism filled the power vacuum left by the collapse of colonial empires.

- The USSR's huge losses and the role of the Red Army in defeating the Nazis gave Stalin a claim to a large role in forming the post-war world.
- The USSR had the political (as well as military) strength to prevent a return to instability in Eastern Europe. Communism could fill the political vacuum there.

Activity 2 — ATL Thinking skills

Source analysis

While the war's immeasurable costs and the destruction were not limited to Europe, it is clear in retrospect that it marked the end of the Continent's global ascendency. The demise of European dominance was a gradual process that began before 1914 and ended after 1945, yet only the bloodletting of two massive wars ensured the transfer of power away from Europe to the United States and the Soviet Union and to the near collapse of the European empires. Europe would never again be the centre of world politics, nor could it ever again claim the superior moral position that had buttressed its prestige in so many non-European regions.

Zara Steiner, *The Triumph of the Dark* (OUP, 2013), pp.1066–1067.

1. According to Steiner, what was the impact of World War Two on Europe?

The impact of the superpowers

Given the new position of the USA and the USSR in 1945, and their relative strength compared to the weakened European countries, it is not surprising that they were to become the key players in setting up the post-war settlement of Europe. After 1945, at least until 1949, Europe continued to be at the heart of international relations, but now as the battleground between the USSR and the USA, as the two superpowers came into direct conflict over how the post-war settlement should be carried out. This tension developed into what became known as the 'Cold War'. The map of Europe after 1945 was determined by this growing conflict between the USSR and the USA, with a clear divide between Eastern and Western Europe. For the USA, this situation meant an end to isolationism and the beginning of a dominant role in world affairs.

The Cold War began where it had left off in 1941, with profound distrust of Soviet motives, and an ideological divide every bit as deep as that between liberalism and Nazism. Only two years after the end of the war the American Air Policy Commission reported to Truman that the essential 'incompatibility of East and West' called for the build-up of a 'devastating' force of bombers and missiles equipped with nuclear weapons capable of operation at a range of 5,000 miles. American strategists moved effortlessly from one Manichaean world to the next.

Richard Overy, *Why the Allies Won*, 2nd ed. (Pimlico, 2006), p.404.

CHALLENGE YOURSELF

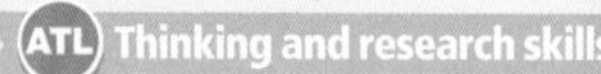

What actually is the definition of a 'superpower'? Who first used the term 'superpowers' and when? How far did the superpowers differ from the 'Great Powers' of pre-World War Two Europe?

Western Europe

One aspect of the developing Cold War was the intervention of the USA and the USSR in the economic recovery of Europe. With Western Europe's economic weakness translating into political weakness, the USA was forced to step in to provide economic aid. This took the form of the Marshall Plan in 1948; the USA was spurred into action to do this in order to prevent the weakened governments of France and Italy falling to Communism. Thanks partly to the Marshall Plan, Western countries were able to implement necessary social changes and recover economically. In fact, in the 1950s and the 1960s, Western European countries enjoyed two decades of sustained economic growth.

With the elimination of Fascism, Western Europe also saw the establishment of multi-party democracies, led for the most part by elder statesmen who had entered politics many decades before. Tony Judt explains this phenomenon:

> *The vogue between the wars had been for the new and the modern. Parliaments and democracies were seen by many – and not just Fascists and Communists – as decadent, stagnant, corrupt and in any case inadequate to the tasks of the modern state. War and occupation dispelled these illusions, for voters if not for intellectuals. In the cold light of peace, the dull compromises of constitutional democracy took on a new appeal. What most people longed for in 1945 was social progress and renewal, to be sure, combined with the reassurance of stable and familiar political forms. Where the First World War had a politically radicalising effect, its successor produced the opposite outcome; a deep longing for normality. Statesmen whose experience reached back beyond the troubled inter-war decades to the more settled and self-confident era before 1914 thus had a particular attraction … Whatever their party 'label', the elder statesmen of Europe were all, by 1945, sceptical, pragmatic practitioners of the art of the possible.*
>
> **Tony Judt, *Postwar* (Vintage, 2010), p.82.**

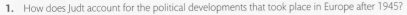

The Marshall Plan

The Marshall Plan was an American economic aid programme for Europe. It was a response to the economic devastation of Europe after the war and the fact that the USA was aware that, without economic recovery, there was a danger that Communist parties, already strong in France and Italy, would gain increasing support in Europe. The USSR refused to take part in the Plan, claiming that it was an attempt by the Americans to exercise 'dollar diplomacy' over Europe, thus establishing American economic domination. This helped to lead to the economic division of Europe as the USSR set up Comecon.

Activity 3

ATL Thinking skills

Source analysis

1. How does Judt account for the political developments that took place in Europe after 1945?
2. According to Judt, what difference was there between the impact of World War One and World War Two on political developments? Why do you think that there was this difference?

The 'social progress' that Judt mentions above took the form of new social legislation that revolutionized the role of the modern state and the expectations upon it. Every European country set up provision for a wide range of social services post-1945, though perhaps it was in Britain that the change in the role of the state was most marked. The election of 1945 swept out Churchill and the Conservative Party and returned the Labour Party, led by Clement Attlee, to office. This British government went on to establish the Welfare State, with care for the individual 'from the cradle to the grave'.

With Western and Eastern Europe divided economically, the traditional exchange between East and West was disrupted. On the other hand, the devastation of war and the Communist threat led to a greater measure of economic cooperation in Western Europe than ever before, with the formation of the European Coal and Steel Community and ultimately the **European Economic Community** (EEC) in the 1950s.

What was the impact of the war on the position of women?

As you read in the previous section, during the war, women took on jobs – from crane driving to factory work – that were normally the male domain. They also played a key role in resistance movements in occupied countries – and in the USSR women took on combat roles at the front. However, after the war there were strong pressures in all countries for women to return to the roles that they had had before the war. Although they did for the most part return to their more traditional roles, the taste of work and freedom that women had experienced played a part in contributing, in the West, to the fight for more equal rights, in terms of pay and job opportunities, that took place in the 1960s.

CHALLENGE YOURSELF

Research skills 

Continue with your research on the impact of war on women. As you did with World War One, research the position of women in different countries following World War Two. What factors, other than the impact of World War Two, caused the women's movement of the 1960s?

Eastern Europe

Between 1944 and 1948, Stalin established control over Hungary, Czechoslovakia, East Germany, Bulgaria, Romania, and Poland. This involved:

TOK

If you reflect on the 'results' of World War Two discussed here, it is clear that a historian needs to be able to understand something of each of the other Areas of Knowledge to be able to understand historical cause and effect. It is also important to realize that each of the other Areas of Knowledge has its own 'history'. Is this true of any other Areas of Knowledge?

Cominform

Cominform was founded by Stalin in 1947 in order to direct Communist party activity throughout Europe. It was the successor to Comintern (Communist International), which had been set up in 1919.

Compare and contrast the impacts of World War One and World War Two on Europe.

- the establishment of one-party rule, including installation of national leaders dependent on the USSR
- **nationalization** of private enterprise
- establishment of Soviet-style five-year plans – heavy industry was encouraged and agriculture **collectivized**.

In addition, the USSR sought to integrate its economy with those of Eastern Europe to offset the weakness of industry and agriculture in the USSR. It established the Council for Mutual Economic Assistance (Comecon). Comecon was not a massive aid programme like the Marshall Plan, but more one of economic exploitation. Each **satellite state** had to produce what the USSR needed: for example, Poland produced coal. The satellite states were not to cooperate economically with each other, however. This situation was one of exploitation for the satellite states, and economic modernization proceeded at a much slower rate. There was not, therefore, the economic regeneration that Western Europe experienced.

With no Marshall Plan, and with the priority of the USSR on heavy industry and the building of nuclear weapons, the citizens of both the Soviet Union and the satellite states suffered economic hardship in the next few decades.

This economic and political system was backed up by:

- social and ideological controls, such as Cominform, secret police
- **censorship** of all media
- suppression of religious freedom
- military presence of Soviet troops
- political purges.

Conclusions on the effect of the war in Europe

By 1949, a remarkable symmetry had emerged in Europe, with the political, economic, and military division of the continent. The Western bloc, under the domination of the USA, had a common political philosophy – democracy – and the commitment of the USA, through the '**Truman Doctrine**', to its defence. The Western states were tied to the USA and to each other economically, via Marshall Aid and the EEC, and by 1949 had a military alliance in the **North Atlantic Treaty Organization** (NATO). Similarly, the Soviet Bloc comprised Communist states, members of a joint ideological organization called the Communist Information Bureau (Cominform). They supposedly had an organization for economic cooperation in Comecon and were 'protected' by Soviet forces (the Warsaw Pact, a Communist version of NATO, was established in 1955).

Activity 4

ATL Thinking skills

Review questions

1. What was the effect of the war on the following:
   a) the international status of Britain and France
   b) the international status of the USA and USSR?
2. Why did distrust start to develop between the USA and the USSR after 1945?
3. What impact did these changes have on international relations?
4. What were the key economic effects of the war? How did the economic situation of Europe change between 1945 and 1950?
5. What political, economic, and social differences developed between Western European countries and Eastern European countries?

Activity 5

ATL Thinking skills

Read the extract below, which is taken from George Marshall's speech that he gave at Harvard University on 5 June 1947 setting out the aims of and the conditions attached to Marshall Aid.

> *Its purpose should be the revival of a working economy in the world so as to permit the emergence of political and social conditions in which free institutions can exist. Such assistance, I am convinced, must not be on a piecemeal basis as various crises develop. Any assistance that this Government may render in the future should provide a cure rather than a mere palliative. Any government that is willing to assist in the task of recovery will find full co-operation I am sure, on the part of the United States Government. Any government which maneuvers to block the recovery of other countries cannot expect help from us. Furthermore, governments, political parties, or groups which seek to perpetuate human misery in order to profit therefrom politically or otherwise will encounter the opposition of the United States.*

1. Could the response of the Americans to the economic situation in Western Europe be seen as 'altruistic'?

The impact of World War Two in Asia

The casualties of war and the extent of destruction were also huge in Asia. China had lost about 12 million people (some historians claim the toll was actually as high as 20 million), and Japan had lost more than 2 million people.

Japan

Japan was eliminated as a major power in Asia. It was occupied by the Americans under the leadership of General Douglas MacArthur, who was appointed Supreme Commander of the Allied Powers (SCAP). Unlike Germany, where the occupying forces assumed direct control due to the fact that the government had completely collapsed, SCAP was able to rule indirectly in a supervisory rule. With the emperor endorsing the process, MacArthur presided over a set of dramatic reforms. These turned Japan into a democratic state. The military and secret police forces were dissolved; anyone who had played a part in 'Japanese aggression or militarism' was purged from political office and industry; a new constitution was introduced that stated 'the Japanese people forever renounce war as a sovereign right' and declared that 'land, sea, and air forces, as well as other war potential, will never be maintained'. It also established protection for a wide range of human rights. The emperor, however, remained; MacArthur believed that he would help maintain political stability and facilitate reform.

How successful was the Treaty of San Francisco?

As we have seen, no peace treaty was signed with Germany at the end of the war. A peace treaty with Japan – the Treaty of San Francisco – was, however, finally signed in 1951. There were many problems in devising a treaty acceptable to everyone, especially with the development of the Cold War. The USSR raised many objections during the treaty meetings, seeing it as favouring Japan's relationship with America; the Soviets refused to sign it, along with Poland and Czechoslovakia. The People's Republic of China on the mainland and the Republic of China on Taiwan were not invited to the peace conference – neither were North and South Korea. India and Burma refused to participate. The Philippines, though present, neither signed nor ratified the treaty until after it became effective, while Indonesia signed but never ratified it. In total, 49 of the participating 51 nations did sign the treaty.

Under the terms of this treaty, Japan:

- renounced all claims to Taiwan, Sakhalin, and the Kuriles

- handed over the Pacific Islands of Micronesia (which had been given to Japan as a mandate after World War One) to be administered under a United Nations trusteeship
- handed over the Ryuku and Bonin Islands to the USA (though Japan still had a claim on these islands)
- accepted the judgements of the International Military Tribunal for the Far East and of other Allied war crimes courts both within and outside Japan, and agreed to carry out the sentences imposed thereby upon Japanese nationals imprisoned in Japan (see below).

The document further set guidelines for repatriation of and compensation to prisoners of war and renounced future military aggression under the guidelines set by the UN Charter. The document nullified prior treaties and set out the framework for Japan's current status of retaining a military that is purely defensive in nature. No reparations were demanded, but Japan was to help rehabilitate countries that had suffered damage because of the Japanese occupation.

As with West Germany, Japan was to become allied to the Western powers, and was to become economically strong and politically stable. It also became an important military and strategic base for the USA in its fight against Communism in Asia. On the same day that the San Francisco Treaty was signed, Japan and the USA also concluded a separate Security Treaty, in which the USA promised to defend Japan until it could look after its own defence; this meant that the USA kept military bases in Japan.

Activity 6

ATL Thinking skills

Source analysis

Source A

The treaty of peace was a treaty of reconciliation. It was nondiscriminatory, nonpunitive, and motivated by enlightened self-interest. The preamble contained a general statement of objectives and principles. Japan was to apply for UN membership (which it did, although Soviet vetoes held up Japanese entrance until 1956), and it was to maintain the new ideals of human rights and freedoms expressed in the constitution. The treaty ended the state of war and recognized the full sovereignty of the Japanese people ... Japan was to refrain from the use of force in international relations, but the treaty recognized that Japan, in keeping with the UN Charter, possessed the right of individual or collective self-defense. All occupation forces were to be withdrawn within ninety days after the treaty went into effect, but the treaty provided that some of the forces might be retained and stationed in Japan according to special agreements between one or more of the Allied power ... In its economic and political clauses, the treaty provided for nondiscrimination in relations with Japan and pledged Japan to a free economy and an unlimited right to trade.

Milton W. Meyer, *Japan: A Concise History*, 4th ed. (Rowman & Littlefield, 2012), pp.230–231.

What similarities and differences can you find between the Treaty of Versailles signed with Germany at the end of World War One and the Treaty of San Francisco signed with Japan at the end of World War Two?

Source B

Together with the San Francisco Treaty, the American–Japanese Security Treaty of 1952 was signed, leaving Japan in effect a military protectorate of the United States. That Treaty provided for the retention of American bases and allowed the United States to use the American forces stationed there in any way that would 'contribute to the maintenance of international peace and security in the Far East'. It prohibited Japan from granting military bases to any other power without American consent.

This passive and dependent role was consonant with the confused and pacifist mood of postwar Japan. But is also suited its national self-interest. Adopting an essentially nonpolitical posture allowed Japan to define its national aims in narrow economic terms and thus to concentrate the energy of its people on the tasks of improving their material livelihood.

Kenneth Pyle, *The Making of Modern Japan* (D.C. Heath, 1996), p.225.

1. According to Source A and Source B above, what were the positive aspects of the San Fransisco Treaty and the American–Japanese Security Treaty?

China

In China, fighting continued between the nationalist forces of Jiang Jieshi and the Communist forces of Mao Zedong. The conflict led to the victory of Mao in 1949 and the establishment of a Communist China. For the USA, this turn of events served to widen the fight against Communism from Europe to Asia.

French Indochina

Ho Chi Minh, a Communist who had led Vietnamese guerrillas against the Japanese, declared Vietnam to be an independent state after the Japanese had left in 1945. However, the French reoccupied their old colony of Indochina (which included Vietnam, Laos, and Cambodia). The guerrilla fighting force of the Vietminh thus fought the French, finally defeating them in battle at Dien Bien Phu in 1954. As a result, the French left Indochina.

Decolonization: the decline of European influence in Asia

The weakness of Britain and France meant that they found it increasingly difficult to hold on to their empires in Asia (and Africa). Their position of superiority and invincibility had in any case been seriously weakened by defeats inflicted on them by Japan during the course of the war. Nationalist movements, such as that led by Ho Chi Minh in Vietnam, also grew in strength during their fight against the Japanese. Condemnation of imperialism by the USA and the UN also weakened the moral arguments for having an empire.

Thus, although the Europeans tried to return, they found their old colonies unwilling to submit and, after bloody struggles, the Dutch recognized the independence of Indonesia and the French were defeated in Vietnam in 1954, and thus forced to give up Indochina. Meanwhile, Britain left India in 1947, and Burma and Ceylon in 1948. As with Europe, Asia was to become part of the Cold War as the USA and the USSR sought to increase their spheres of influence in this area.

Other effects of the war

The establishment of war tribunals

Leading Nazis appear before the International Court at the Nuremberg Trials, 1945–1946.

Tribunals were set up to try war criminals in both Europe and Asia. The Nuremberg Tribunal sat between November 1945 and October 1946. Such a trial was unique in history. Twenty-one leading Nazis were charged with war crimes and crimes against humanity. In Japan, General MacArthur carried out trials against war criminals, and 28 of Japan's leaders were tried before an international tribunal in Tokyo. Over a 6-year period, 5,700 Japanese war criminals were tried before Allied tribunals, and about 1,000 were executed.

The United Nations

World War Two, like World War One, saw the emergence of an international organization, the United Nations, which again largely came about through US initiative. The UN was intended to be more effective in peacekeeping than the League of Nations had been, but with the onset of the Cold War and the possession of the veto in the Security Council by the USA and the USSR, the UN found itself marginalized in the superpower conflicts that dominated international politics after 1945.

The arms race

With the US invention of the atomic bomb, and its use on Japan in 1945, an arms race became central to the Cold War, with the main focus on the development and acquisition of nuclear weapons. Thus the world now existed under the threat of total destruction, though the horrendous implications of using these weapons also acted as a deterrent to the USA and the USSR fighting each other directly. Although the level of tension in 1946–1950 was much greater than that after World War One, no direct war between the major powers resulted.

Activity 7

ATL Thinking and communication skills

Review questions

1. What was the impact of the Second World War on the following:
   - the popularity and expansion of Communism
   - the defeated powers – Germany and Japan

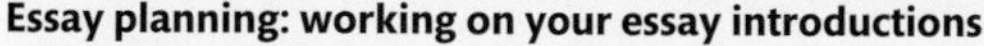

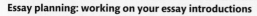

Activity 8

ATL Thinking skills

Essay planning: working on your essay introductions

After you have worked through this chapter, it should be possible now to attempt the essay set at the beginning:

Discuss the international impact of one 20th-century war.

One of the key parts of an essay is the introduction. Refer back to the essay planning guidelines at the end of chapter 2 and check what should be included in a good introduction. Then have a look at the introductions below and discuss which you think is the best one and why. Which bits of each introduction work well? How could each one be improved?

Introduction 1: World War Two dramatically changed the international situation. The European powers were now second-rate powers and America and the Soviet Union emerged as 'superpowers'. This essay will examine the reasons for this change and the impact that it would have on international relations after 1945.

Introduction 2: Following World War Two, America and the USSR emerged as superpowers and went on to dominate world affairs for the next 50 years. The reasons for this lie in the events of World War Two, which I shall explain in this essay.

Introduction 3: The world that emerged after World War Two was very different from that of 1939. The 'Great Powers' of France and Britain, who had been the key players in the 1919 settlement, were now weakened and were seen as second-rate powers. The USA and USSR had played the key roles in the defeat of Germany and now emerged as 'superpowers' in the post-war world, with military, political, and economic influence outside their own borders. Why was this, and what consequences would this have for the post-war world?

Activity 9

ATL Thinking and communication skills

Now have a go at writing an introduction for the following essay question:

Discuss the political and economic effects of one 20th-century war.

To access weblinks relevant to this chapter, go to www.pearsonhotlinks.com, search for the book title or ISBN, and click on 'chapter 9'.

Comparative study of cross-regional wars

Key concepts: Change and continuity

As you read this chapter, consider the following essay questions:

- Compare and contrast the causes of two 20th-century wars, each chosen from a different region.
- With reference to two 20th-century wars examine the role of ideology in the outbreak of wars.
- Compare and contrast the role of the war at sea in the course and outcome of two 20th-century wars.
- Discuss the role of the war on the land in determining the outcome of two 20th-century wars, each chosen from a different region.
- Compare and contrast the results of two 20th-century wars, each chosen from a different region.

You have now studied two cross-regional wars. You can use these as examples in questions that ask you to consider **two** 20th-century war case studies. Where you are asked to consider case studies from **different regions** in an essay question you will need to specify in your introduction which ones you will look at. You can use World War One in Europe and World War Two in Asia as cross-regional case studies. However, please note that you cannot use World War Two in Europe and World War Two in Asia, as these are the same case study – that is, both are from the same war.

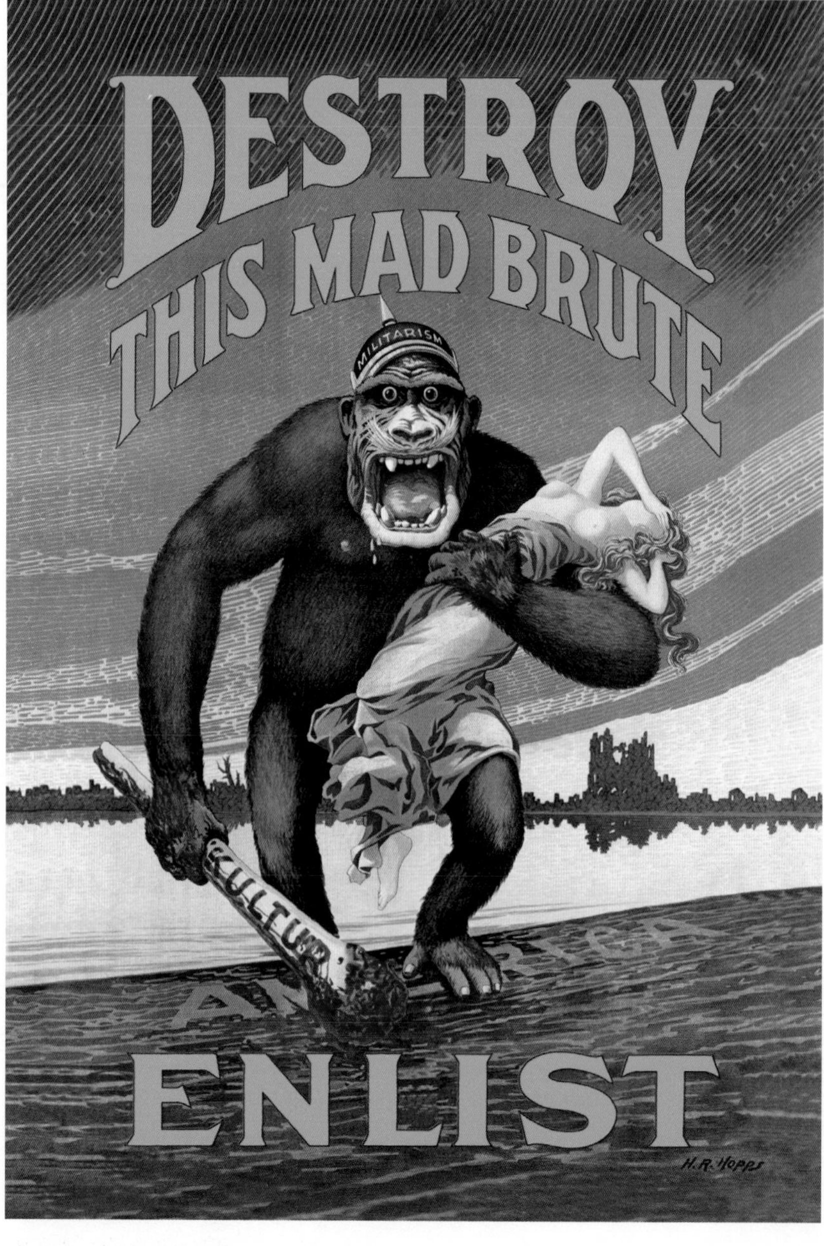

American propaganda poster by H. R. Hopps, 1917.

Compare and contrast the causes of two 20th-century wars

These are the themes that you need to consider when comparing the causes of wars:

- economic, ideological, political, territorial, and any other relevant causes
- long- and short-term causes.

Here are some areas where you might be able to make effective comparisons between the two world wars.

Comparisons between the two world wars	
World War One	**World War Two**
Ideology	
Nationalism, social Darwinism *(see source in Activity 1 for comparison of the impact of German nationalism before each war)*	Fascism, Communism, Liberal Capitalist democracy
Imperialism	
Germany's desire for colonies Conflict between Austria and Russia in the Balkans in their search for more land Britain's concerns to maintain its empire	Germany, Italy, and Japan all sought to establish and then expand their empires Britain's concern to maintain its empire
Economic factors	
War was seen as a distraction from economic problems in both Germany and Russia	Economic crises led to protectionism and contributed to the failure of collective security amongst the Western powers Economic crises, encouraged expansionism of Germany and Japan
Militarism	
The arms race from 1871 contributed to tension in Europe The naval race from 1900 caused tension between Britain and Germany	The failure of disarmament Growing militarism in Japan, Italy, and Germany
Alliances	
The Triple Alliance and the Triple Entente encouraged hostility and led to war plans that drew all powers into the crises	Shifting alliances in the 1930s led to further aggression and expansion (Axis Alliance bloc, Nazi–Soviet Pact, Sino-Soviet neutrality pact)

Here are some areas where you could make effective contrasts.

Contrasts between the two world wars	
World War One	**World War Two**
Extent of tensions	
European region was the focus of tensions and rivalries	There were cross-regional tensions between Europe, Americas, and Asia
Failure of peace settlement	
No international peace settlement existed before World War One	The failure of the Versailles settlement helped create the conditions for Hitler's rise to power
Collective action	
No international body facilitating collective security European powers were actively promoting own self-interest prior to the war; no common policies to prevent war	The League of Nations existed to keep the peace, but this failed France and Britain worked together to try to stop war via a policy of appeasement
Fear of Communism	
This was not a factor before 1914	The establishment of the USSR led to an increase in fear of Communism. It fostered the rise of Fascist states and encouraged the policy of appeasement

Contrasts between the two world wars	
World War One	**World War Two**
Economic	
Limited economic factors: for example, Germany was looking for new markets and cheap raw materials. Economic tensions in Germany and Russia contributed to governments seeking war	Important economic factors: for example, the Great Depression, affected all states and created far more wide-ranging and deep economic problems, which undermined political and social stability (see Overy source below)

The following sources highlight some of these factors.

German nationalism

Activity 1

Pressure groups started to form in the early 1890s, committed to strengthening Germany's power, as well as defending their own interests. The Agrarian League sought to protect farmers, the Pan-German League hoped to bring all Germans within a single Reich and the Navy League supported and lobbied for further naval expansion. All of these asserted an ideology of Germany's superiority and, in the case of the 20,000 strong Pan-German League, it was aggressively xenophobic and even anti-semitic. The radical nationalists looked for mass support over the long-term, targeting many of the lower classes successfully.

The German state was also nationalistic within its own frontiers towards non-German minorities – an attitude that predated the radical nationalists …

Before the First World War, German nationalism had grown in significance to the German people and become much more complex by nature. Its appeal had widened to include the lower middle class and it had progressed beyond the endemic waves of protest to a sustained tide of pressure through radical nationalist groups. No longer just an anti-foreigner attitude, it was more aggressive through the Kaiser's global ambitions of Weltpolitik, as well as having an internal focus in trying to deal with national minorities such as Poles and Danes … its insidious anti-semitism … was to re-emerge as a central feature of Nazi ideology in the 1930s.

Tim Chapman, 'The Rise of German Nationalism', *20th-Century History Review*, September 2010 (vol. 6, no. 1), p.31.

1. According to Chapman, how did nationalism show itself in Germany before World War One?
2. Identify the ways that Chapman links World Wars One and Two.

Failure of the peace after World War One

Activity 2

Such were the origins of the Second World War, or rather the war between the three Western Powers over the settlement of Versailles; a war which had been implicit since the moment when the first war ended. Men will long debate whether this renewed war could have been averted by greater firmness or by greater conciliation; and no answer will be found to these hypothetical speculations. Maybe either would have succeeded, if consistently followed; the mixture of the two, practiced by the British government, was the most likely to fail. These questions now seem infinitely remote. Though Hitler blundered in supposing that the two Western Powers would not go to war at all, his expectation that they would not go to war seriously turned out to be correct. Great Britain and France did nothing to help the Poles, and little to help themselves. The European struggle which began in 1918 when the German armistice delegates presented themselves before Foch in the railway-carriage at Rethondes, ended in 1940 when the French armistice delegates presented themselves before Hitler in the same carriage. There was a 'new order' in Europe; it was dominated by Germany.

The British people resolved to defy Hitler, though they lacked the strength to undo his work. He himself came to their aid. His success depended on the isolation of Europe from the rest of the world. He gratuitously destroyed the source of his success. In 1941 he attacked Soviet Russia and declared war on the United States, two World Powers who asked only to be left alone. In this way a real war began.

A.J.P. Taylor, *The Origins of the Second World War* (Penguin, 1963), p.336.

1. Read the source above and explain how the failure of the peace settlement at the end World War One arguably caused World War Two.

Economics and ideology

Activity 3

The world depression confirmed the pessimists of the 1920s in the argument that the capitalist system was doomed from its own nature and that some other way of organizing the economic life of the country was in the long run unavoidable … As the depression intensified during 1931 and 1932 the level of alarmism grew. Even the liberal Keynes, who insisted throughout the crisis that he remained optimistic about the long-term capacity of the system to survive, thought probably only communism could cure unemployment, though he did not like the prospect of building on what he called 'the vapours of misery and discontent.'

R. Overy, *The Morbid Age: Britain Between the Wars* (Allen Lane, 2009), p.70.

1. Read the source above. How might the economic crises of the 1930s have intensified the fear of Communism in the democratic states?

Long-term and short-term causes

Activity 4

1. Which of the causes in the tables on page 211 are long term and which are short term?
2. In pairs, create a table like the one on page 211 to compare long-term and short-term causes of the two world wars.
3. Now plan each of the questions below using World War One and World War Two as your case studies.
   - ***Compare and contrast the short-term causes of two 20th-century wars.***
   - ***Compare and contrast the causes of two 20th-century wars each chosen from a different region.***
   - ***Compare and contrast the role of ideology in causing two 20th-century wars.***
   - ***Compare and contrast the role of economic factors in causing two 20th-century wars, each chosen from a different region.***

Writing comparative essays

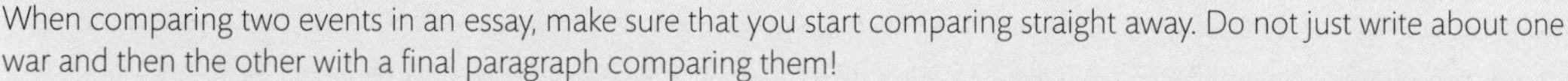

When comparing two events in an essay, make sure that you start comparing straight away. Do not just write about one war and then the other with a final paragraph comparing them!

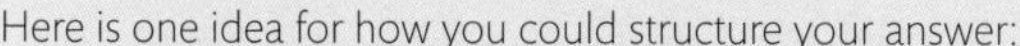

Here is one idea for how you could structure your answer:

- First point/theme: comparisons and contrasts
- Second point/theme: comparisons and contrasts
- Third point/theme: comparisons and contrasts

Or you could structure it like this:

- Deal with each thematic similarity
- Deal with each thematic difference

Practices of 20th-century war and their impact on the outcome

A soldier in a waterlogged World War One trench.

War in the air in Eastern Europe.

Theatres of War

Consider the following essay question:

> ***Compare and contrast the role of one of the following: a) war on the land, b) war at sea, c) war in the air, in the outcome of two 20th-century wars.***

1. In pairs complete this grid. The information in the coloured boxes below is to remind you of key content that could be useful evidence for each of the themes in the grid. Attempt to match this information to the correct theme.
2. Try to add more comparisons and contrasts where you can. Also add more evidence to support each theme.

Theatre of War	World War One	World War Two
Comparison Significance of war on the land on the outcome of the war		
Comparison Significance of war at sea on the outcome of the war		
Contrast Significance of war in the air on the outcome of the war		

Central Powers: failure of the Schlieffen Plan – Battle of the Marne 1914; failure of Verdun 1916; failure to capitalize on land victories in the East; Treaty of Brest-Litovsk meant an occupation force of approximately 1 million troops in East from 1917; failure of Spring Offensive 1918; defeat of Germany's allies on the land 1918.

> *The failure of [Ludendorff's] offensives did more than anything else to break the German Army's spirit [and to plunge it into an insurmountable crisis of manpower], and for all the undoubted gains in Allied fighting prowess a German defeat could otherwise have been postponed for at least another year.*
>
> **D. Stevenson, *1914–18: The History of First World War* (Penguin, 2004) p.598.**

Entente Allies: held German advance – Battle of the Marne led to the failure of the Schlieffen Plan; held Verdun 1916; successful land campaigns in 1918; impact of entry of the USA.

Battleship engagements limited and German navy fought war of blockade again using U-boats. Initially very effective; however, new technology and cheap, mass-produced US merchant boats break the blockade. Allies won war in Atlantic. British navy key to maintaining supplies and Lend-Lease materials to Europe. Navy play key role in blockading Italy after British had sunk half Italian fleet early on in war. Amphibious landings for land armies in campaign in Italy; D-Day.

Key naval battles in Pacific – Midway and Leyte Gulf – decisive for US. Amphibious landing for island-hopping. Air power in Pacific carried by navy.

The historian John Keegan argues role of Allied navies in the Atlantic and the Pacific was decisive in outcome of the war.

Air power key theatre in outcome: the Battle of Britain won in the air; air superiority in Europe by end of war allowed D-Day; Soviets out-produce Germany in aircraft on Eastern Front; air campaign and air power in Pacific – Midway; atomic bombs.

War in air crucial to war on land. *Blitzkreig*; campaigns in East; coordination via communication between air and land force – that is, tanks; air power to cover D-Day landings; air power covered island-hopping; parachuting troops behind enemy lines.

War in air crucial to war at sea. Battle for Atlantic and role of aircraft; battle in Pacific and role of aircraft carriers.

War in air crucial to home-front defeat. Bombing campaigns on Germany and Japan destroyed industrial productivity, supply lines, and morale.

Axis Powers: failure of Operation Barbarossa 1941; failure at Battle of Stalingrad 1942; Kursk 1943; Soviet forces force German retreat in East on the land; British force German retreat on the land in north Africa – Battle of El Alamein 1942; Italian campaign and removal of Mussolini; island-hopping campaigns in the Pacific; D-Day 1944 in Europe – Anglo-American force push German retreat in West.

Dreadnought Battle of Jutland 1916: German numerical victory; however, this led to withdrawal of both fleets. Britain's naval power meant able to move supplies and troops to fighting fronts and home front. German U-boat campaign attritional. Ultimately failed and led to entry of USA; British blockade of Germany ultimately more effective by end of war: 'The defeat of Germany had pivoted on control of the Atlantic' (A. Tooze, *The Deluge: The Great War and the Remaking of Global Order* [Allen Lane, 2014], p.228).

Used to support war on land: for example, reconnaissance; some bombing of front lines; support war at sea for scouting and attacks on U-boats; bombing of home front; dog-fights in the air; distribution of propaganda.

Some co-ordination of air and land towards end of war. Importance understood by end of war: for instance, Britain established an independent air force (RAF) in April 1918. Limited impact on outcome. Other theatres more significant.

Overview of themes: theatre, technology, extent of mobilization

Activity 5

ATL Social and self-management skills

1. In small groups, discuss the material in the table on the next page, adding extra details and relevant historians' views where possible.
2. Share your additional information with other groups.
3. Discuss the key areas of similarity and difference between the wars.

	World War One	World War Two	Conclusions on similarities/differences in terms of the impact on the outcome of the war
Scope and scale of fighting in the war (also casualties)			
Strategy and tactics on land	Trench warfare on Western Front War of movement on Eastern Front	War of movement War in the air and bombing	
War at sea	Blockades	Blockades	
War in the air			
Impact on civilians	Rationing	Civilian front strategic target	
Power of governments	Increased government control, e.g. Britain		

Activity 6

Before 1939, bombing wars were popularly expected to be short, sharp and decisive. The major offensives conducted by Germany, Britain and the United States were instead long drawn-out affairs, wars of attrition with high losses of men and machines, with no clear-cut end and a wide gap between ambition and outcome, a Western front of the air. The more minor operations conducted by the German Air Force in the Soviet Union or the Italian Air Force in the Mediterranean were poorly resourced and ineffective. Little of this had been predicted. The bomber offensives were regarded as unique expressions of the changing form of war, one thought to be more appropriate for an age of mass politics and scientific modernity, in which whole societies were mobilized to fight each other using cutting-edge technology to do so. 'The advent of air power,' wrote one American airman after the war, 'created total war. Prior to air power, opportunities for destruction of another nation's total strength were limited almost entirely to the destruction of the armed forces.'

R. Overy, *The Bombing War* (Allen Lane, 2013), pp.609–610.

1. What does Richard Overy highlight as misconceptions about bombing before World War Two?
2. Discuss what Overy means when he suggests that the bombing campaigns became a 'Western Front' in the air.
3. To what extent do you agree with the American airman who is quoted as saying 'The advent of air power created total war'?

Activity 7

Now plan the following essay questions:

1. ***Compare and contrast the role of technology in the course of two 20th-century wars, each chosen from a different region.***
2. ***Compare and contrast the impact of technological developments in two 20th-century wars, each chosen from a different region.***
3. ***Compare and contrast the extent of the mobilization of human and material resources in two 20th-century wars.***
4. ***Compare and contrast the significance of war in the air in two 20th-century wars, each chosen from a different region.***

Comparing the effects of World War One and World War Two

Review the impact of each war politically, ideologically, economically, and territorially. Sources A–I below will help remind you of some of the key similarities and differences in each of these areas, but you should also look back at chapter 4 on the impact of World War One and chapter 9 on the impact of World War Two.

Activity 8

Thinking and self-management skills

Copy out the grid below and summarize your information from the following sources and chapters 2 and 3 in the grid. Then have a go at planning the essay questions on page 219.

Effects of war	Similarities between World Wars One and Two	Differences between World Wars One and Two
Political		
Ideological		
Economic		
Territorial		

Similarities and differences in the *territorial* impact of the two wars

World War One

Source A

When the peacemakers gathered in Paris January 1919 to construct a peace settlement, the political map of Europe as it had existed in August 1914 had been swept away. In the course of the war, or soon after it, four empires collapsed – the Russian Empire, the Habsburg Empire, the German Second Reich and the Ottoman Empire …

At the end of the war there was a power vacuum in central and eastern Europe. Instead of three powerful, conservative empires competing against each other in the area, there were a number of small new states, trying to establish themselves politically and economically.

C. Culpin and R. Henig, *Modern Europe, 1870–1945* (Longman, 1997) p.143.

Source B

The new Europe was thus deeply divided. There was the split between victors and vanquished, which stood out most obviously in the treatment of Germany as not merely a defeated enemy but as an outcast, held responsible for the war and disarmed. There was also the linked, but by no means identical, division between the 'revisionist' countries, which wanted to change the settlement reached in 1919–21 and those which wanted to maintain it.

P. Bell, *Twentieth Century Europe* (Arnold, 2006), p.84.

World War Two

Source C

From 1870 to 1945 Europe had been at the centre of the world's events. In 1945 there was a real shift of emphasis. World power now lay with the two 'superpowers': the USA and the USSR. Both were larger, with more people, and clearly richer, than any European country could ever be.

1945 was also a dramatic turning-point in the history of the nations of western Europe. After 1945 a new dynamic appears: European unity.

C. Culpin and R. Henig, *Modern Europe, 1870–1945* (Longman, 1997) p.339.

Source D

The war changed everything. East of the Elbe, the Soviets and their local representatives inherited a sub-continent where a radical break with the past had already taken place. What was not entirely discredited was irretrievably damaged. Exiled governments form Oslo, Brussels or the Hague could return from London and hope to take up the legitimate authority they had been forced to relinquish in 1940. But the old rulers of Bucharest and Sofia, Warsaw, Budapest and even Prague had no future; their world had been swept aside by the Nazis' transformative violence.

Tony Judt, *Postwar* (Vintage, 2010), p.40.

Similarities and differences in the *political* impact of the two wars

World War One

Source E

As leader of the successful Bolshevik coup in Russia [in 1917], Lenin encouraged socialist groups to rise up against their governments and seize power. Many of the war-weary people of Europe were ready to listen. In Germany here were one million workers on strike by January 1918. In Britain, the red flag was flown over Glasgow Town Hall and there was talk of revolution in south Wales. Socialist regimes appeared briefly in Hungary and Bavaria … Fear of revolution was a powerful force in interwar politics. It gave a boost to right-wing parties and helped to bring to power Fascist regimes in Italy, Germany and elsewhere.

C. Culpin and R. Henig, *Modern Europe, 1870–1945* (Longman, 1997) p.142.

World War Two

Source F

In the immediate post-war years the sorry state of the European economy and the apparent popularity of left-wing ideologies [thus] had an uncomfortable similarity to the events of the previous decade. That these events were coupled with the expansion of Soviet influence in Eastern Europe rapidly transformed the American image of a post-war order based on co-operative security arrangements with all the victors to one that emphasized the differences between the United States and Western Europe, on the one hand, and the Soviet Union and Eastern Europe on the other. Within the European context this meant, primarily, two things: that the Truman administration viewed the recovery of Western Europe as a major precondition to international stability and American prosperity, and that the Soviet quest for security and recovery almost inevitably clashed with American goals.

Antony Best et al., *International History of the Twentieth Century and Beyond* (Routledge, 2004), p.213.

Source G

The ideological struggles for the soul of Europe which had developed after 1917 and which took violent from in the 1930s and early 1940s now assumed a new and rigid shape as a Soviet dominated, communist eastern Europe faced an American-led liberal-democratic western Europe-a division which came to seem increasingly final and immoveable as time went on.

P.M.H. Bell, *Twentieth-Century Europe* (Hodder, 2006), p.149.

Similarities and differences in the *economic* impact of the two wars

World War One

Source H

the First World War left a legacy of severe economic disruption … All over Europe industry, agriculture and transport systems had worked for four years under intense pressure, so that men machines and land were all exhausted and worn out … Europe's financial and monetary structure had suffered gravely. By contrast, some of the economic fruits and advantages of the war went to non-Europeans.

P.M.H. Bell, *Twentieth-Century Europe* (Hodder, 2006), p.85.

World War Two

Source I

The Second World War left Europe ruined and divided. The crippling of the European economy, amounting in some areas to near-destruction, meant that the continent had to struggle for life, and European predominance in the world economy already much weakened, came to an end. Western Europe came to rely on the USA, while Eastern Europe fell under the domination of the Soviet Union.

P.M.H. Bell, *Twentieth-Century Europe* (Hodder, 2006), p.145.

Now plan out these essays on the effects of war:

1. ***Discuss the impact of territorial changes as a result of two 20th-century wars.***
2. ***Compare and contrast the political results of two 20th-century wars.***
3. ***Examine the economic results of two 20th-century wars.***

Peace treaties of World War One and World War Two

Don't forget to review the impact of the post-war treaties. For World War One, this means the Treaty of Versailles, and for World War Two, the Treaty of San Francisco. See page 206 for sources on the Treaty of San Francisco and the exercise comparing these treaties.

What was the social impact of the First World War and the Second World War?

The impact of World War One and World War Two on the roles and status of women

Activity 9

Copy out the following grid and complete it, using the information in the last few chapters. Give specific examples where possible, as the situation for women varied country to country. Use the research that you have done on this topic.

	Political impact	Economic impact	Social impact	Military impact
During World War One				
Change as a result of World War One	Women get right to vote in Britain in 1918			
During World War Two				
Change as a result of World War Two				

Activity 10

1. ***With reference to two wars, examine the effects of 20th-century war on the roles and status of women.***

For the impact of World War One and World War Two on other social groups, refer back to chapters 3 and 4 for World War One and chapters 8 and 9 for World War Two.

11

Europe region: Spanish Civil War

Key concepts: Causation, consequence, and significance

Police and military searching arrested strikers in Barcelona in October 1934.

As you read this chapter, consider the following essay questions:

- Discuss the long-term and short-term causes of one 20th-century civil war.
- To what extent did foreign intervention determine the outcome of one 20th-century civil war?
- Examine the political, economic and social effects of one 20th-century civil war.

> *'A civil war is not a war but a sickness,' wrote Antoine de Saint-Exupéry. 'The enemy is within. One fights almost against oneself.' Yet Spain's tragedy in 1936 was even greater. It had become enmeshed in the international civil war, which started in earnest with the Bolshevik revolution.*
>
> **Antony Beevor, *The Battle for Spain: The Spanish Civil War 1936–1939* (Penguin, 2006), p.1.**

The Spanish Civil War broke out in 1936 after more than a century of social, economic, and political division. Half a million people died in this conflict between 1936 and 1939.

General Francisco Franco, the leader who took Nationalist forces to victory in the Spanish Civil War.

Carlism

Carlism is a political movement in Spain that looks to establish a separate line of the Bourbon family on the Spanish throne. This line is descended from Carlos V (1788–1855).

Timeline of events – 1820–1931	
1820	The Spanish army, supported by Liberals, overthrows the absolute monarchy and makes Spain a constitutional monarchy in a modernizing revolution
1821	Absolute monarchy is restored to Spain by French forces in an attempt to reinstate the old order
1833	In an attempt to prevent a female succession following the death of King Ferdinand, there is a revolt by 'Carlists'. The army intervenes to defeat the Carlists, who nevertheless remain a strong conservative force in Spanish politics
1833–1869	The army's influence in national politics increases during the 'rule of the Queens'
1869–1870	Anarchist revolts take place against the state
1870–1871	The monarchy is overthrown and the First Republic is established
1871	The army restores a constitutional monarchy
1875–1918	During this period the constitutional monarchy allows for democratic elections. The system is corrupt, however. Power remains in the hands of the wealthy oligarchs or 'caciques' Spanish Nationalism suffers when Spain is defeated in 1898 in a war with the USA
1914–1918	Spain remains neutral during World War One and experiences economic growth
1918–1923	The economy falters and 12 different governments fail to redress the crisis The regime reaches new lows in 1921, when the army, sent to crush a revolt led by Abd el-Krim in Spanish Morocco, is massacred by Moors
1923–1930	General Primo de Rivera takes control in a bloodless coup and rules for seven years, thus fatally undermining the legitimacy of the monarchy
1931	The Spanish king abdicates and the Second Republic is established

Activity 1

Study the timeline above and then read the following quotation.

> *The notion that political problems could more naturally be solved by violence than by debate was firmly entrenched in a country in which for a thousand years civil war has been if not exactly the norm then certainly no rarity.*
>
> **Paul Preston, *The Spanish Civil War: Reaction, Revolution and Revenge* (HarperPerennial, 2006), p.17.**

1. Looking at the timeline above showing events in Spain in the 19th and early 20th centuries, what evidence is there for Preston's argument?
2. Identify factors causing tension in Spain during this time (economic, military, religious, political).
3. What example of foreign intervention was there in Spain in the 19th century?

Long-term causes of the Spanish Civil War: political instability (1820–1931)

In the 19th century, Spain had struggled between periods of Conservatism and Liberalism. As you can see from the timeline above, there were several issues that caused tension and division in Spain in the century before the 1930s, fractures that were to become more acute in the decade before the civil war broke out.

Weakness of government

From 1871, Spain had been a constitutional monarchy. The king was head of state, and he appointed a prime minister who should have commanded a majority in the parliament (Cortes). Yet although the Cortes was elected by the male population, real power was held by the wealthy oligarchs, and political control shifted between their different cliques. There were two main parties, the Conservatives and the Liberals, but in fact there was no real difference between them. Elections were rigged or decided by corruption. There were no mass democratic political parties:

> *the consequence was, at a very superficial level, political stability, but beneath it tremendous social instability, because nothing ever really changed … Elections changed virtually nothing. Only a relatively small proportion of the electorate had the right to vote, and since nothing changed … the population was forced into apathy or violent opposition to the system.*
>
> **Paul Preston, *Modern History Review*, September 1991**

General Francisco Franco

General Franco was born Francisco Franco Bahamonde. He came from a military background, and had begun his career in the navy. However, as Spain's empire declined, the navy was cut down in size and Franco joined the army. He became a general after demonstrating sound leadership skills fighting in Morocco. Before the outbreak of the Spanish Civil War, Franco had been stationed on the Spanish mainland. He was active in suppressing anarchists and anti-government forces in the early 1930s – most notably in the 1934 Asturias revolt.

The role of the Spanish army

The army had a powerful political position in Spain due to its role in Spain's imperial past. It believed that it was the protector of the nation, and that this meant it had the right and duty to intervene in politics if a crisis occurred. It had intervened in this way several times: in 1820, 1871, and 1923. It did not, however, act to save the king in 1931, and this led to his exile. The army intervened again during the Second Republic and once more in 1936. It was this last intervention that was to lead to civil war.

The army was unpopular with the people. It had a reputation for brutality, it was expensive, and required heavy taxes to maintain. The army had also proved ineffective when it lost the Spanish Empire during the 19th century, and a war with America in 1898. It had also struggled to keep control of Morocco between 1906 and 1926.

The army was also in need of reform. It was too big, and had too many officers. The upper and middle classes, however, defended their interests, as they dominated the officer corps. The army was generally Conservative, but the 'Africanistas' – those who were experienced in the wars in Morocco – were the most experienced and nationalistic.

The role of the church

The Catholic Church was rich and powerful in Spain, and there had been disputes between church and state throughout the 19th century. In 1851 the Concordat made Catholicism the state religion. The state had guaranteed the role of the church in education and in elements of the economy, and the church had used its wealth to gain considerable political and social influence. It used its power to support social, political, and economic conservatism and was opposed to modernizing and liberal forces. The aristocracy was closely tied to the church; they made up the vast majority of senior clergy, and provided much of the funding for the church. This meant the church was inclined to defend the rights and status of the upper classes, which led to resentment amongst the poor. In many urban areas there were protests against the church, although it was more popular in the rural areas. Some of the educated middle class were anti-clerical and sought to limit the church's power, particularly over education.

Economic causes

The plight of the agricultural workers was a key factor in the discontent that led to the civil war. Spain was predominantly an agricultural economy, and agriculture was the chief source of employment. Unfortunately, there were fundamental problems that made it inefficient. It did not provide sufficient food, and work was only seasonal. There was the need for workers to migrate in search of work – most lived in abject poverty and the gap between rich and poor was vast. In the centre and south of Spain, land was owned in huge estates, the ***latifundia***, by the 'Grandees', who dominated the political system. In the north, peasants owned small plots of land, but often these were too small to make an adequate living.

Rioting and disorder often broke out in the countryside. The Civil Guard were deployed to ruthlessly repress any disorder. With no support from the church, some looked to groups such as the **anarchists**, who argued for the redistribution of land. Yet many of the Catholic small landholders were very conservative and resistant to socialist or anarchist ideas. The conservatism was used by the Catholic Agrarian Federation, which provided support for farmers in return for their rejection of socialist ideas; these same farmers would later support Franco and fight on his side during the war.

Industrially, there was also the need for modernization and reform. Apart from in the north, there had been little Spanish industrialization in the 19th century. Expansion was limited by endemic poverty. Workers in the towns, meanwhile, faced low wages, long hours, unregulated working conditions, poor housing, and little in the way of welfare provision. This situation led to the growth of trade unionism. But the trade unions competed with each other (for example the CNT and UGT). The unions failed to achieve anything substantial, as the employers could always find alternative labour sources from the countryside. The workers' political parties had no real political power. With no legal means of improving their situation, violent uprising appealed to many as the means to effect change.

Spain's neutrality during World War One facilitated a short period of economic boom. With the increase of exports, however, there were also shortages and inflation;

The Civil Guard

The Civil Guard was founded in 1844. Its purpose was to control the peasantry, maintain the status quo, and stamp out any anti-monarchist, revolutionary sentiment. It was particularly active in the Basque Provinces and was hated by the peasantry. It was later to play a role in supporting the Conservative landowners in resisting the reforms of the Second Republic.

UGT and CNT

The **Unión General de Trabajadores** (UGT; General Union of Workers) was the Socialist-led trade union, and the **Confederación Nacional del Trabajo** (CNT; National Confederation of Labour) was the anarchist trade union.

Colonial Spain

Spain had been a dominant European power in the 16th and 17th centuries, having colonized parts of the Americas. It had become rich in gold and silver and had continued to build a vast overseas empire. However, its power and empire had declined by the end of the 19th century. The Spanish were defeated in a war with the USA in 1898 and lost their colonial territories of the Philippines, Puerto Rico, and Cuba. Many in the army and on the right of Spanish politics wanted national regeneration.

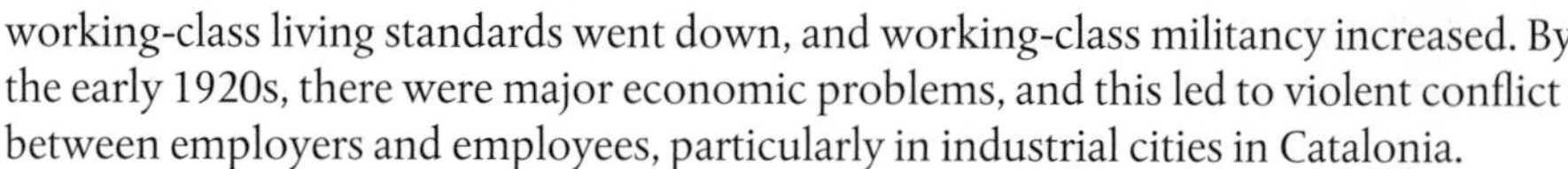

working-class living standards went down, and working-class militancy increased. By the early 1920s, there were major economic problems, and this led to violent conflict between employers and employees, particularly in industrial cities in Catalonia.

The role of the regions

A significant cause of tension was the ongoing struggle between the centralist state and Catalonia and the Basque provinces, which wanted decentralization and independence. The Catalans and the **Basques** had their own separate languages and cultures, and by the early 20th century they had their own industrialized economies and churches. Indeed, most of Spain's industries were concentrated in these regions: for example, textiles, iron, and coal industries in Catalonia, and shipbuilding in the Basque country. Protests and strikes by workers led to brutal responses from the authorities. In 1909 the army was sent in to put down riots in Barcelona, killing 200 people, and, between 1918 and 1921, 1,000 people were killed in protests in the city. Primo de Rivera – who was an experienced military official before he became prime minister in 1923, and who ruled Spain as a dictator until 1930 – took back the self-governing rights of Catalonia, and the Esquerra, a radical Catalan Nationalist party, was set up under the leadership of Luis Companys. Separatist forces supported the Republican movement that overthrew King Alfonso in 1931 (see below).

Political opposition

Prieto

Prieto, whose full name was Indalecio Prieto Tuero, was one of the leading figures of the Socialist Workers' Party (Partido Socialista Obrero Español, PSOE) in Spain. He was a prominent critic of de Rivera's government, and was appointed finance minister in Zamora's government in 1931.

There were a number of groups opposed to the political status quo in Spain, and each would play a part in the political divisions that led to violent conflict in 1936. The **Liberal** movement in Spain had achieved little in opposing Conservative forces in the 19th century, although it remained a political force and supported the revolution that ousted the king in 1931. The Partido Socialista Obrero Español (PSOE; Spanish Socialist Party) had grown in urban areas in the late 19th century, but had minimal impact, whereas the UGT was more visible in organizing strikes and protests in the urban regions. In addition, following the Bolshevik revolution, a small Communist party had emerged. The Socialists, as with the Liberals, played a significant role in the revolution of 1931, but the parties became divided over what reforms should take place. The more moderate Socialists were led by Indalecio Prieto, and the radicals were led by Largo Caballero.

The anarchists were also a major political group in Spain; as previously suggested, this was mainly due to their demand for the redistribution of land, which was popular with the peasants. The anarchists argued for revolutionary methods and boycotted all democratic processes. Their trade union was the CNT, which like the UGT was active in organizing strikes and protests. In addition, there was a more extreme anarchist faction called the **Federación Anarquista Ibérica** (FAI; Spanish Anarchist Federation), which perpetrated bombings and assassinations.

The fall of the monarchy and the establishment of the Second Republic

King Alfonso XIII (1885–1931) was not a modernizer. The impact of military defeat in Morocco and the post-World War One economic depression put pressure on the king, and after 12 unsuccessful governments during the period 1918–1923 Alfonso did not resist the army's intervention in politics when General Primo de Rivera seized power in a coup.

Primo De Rivera tried to establish an authoritarian right-wing regime to redress Spain's problems, similar to the Italian Fascist model. Although Primo de Rivera set up a military dictatorship, the king was retained and the monarchy supported the regime. The dictatorship was formerly ended in 1925, but Primo remained prime minister. He wanted to address Spain's problem of violent and militant industrial disputes and he was able to gain some tacit support from Socialists and the UGT by establishing a system of arbitration for labour disputes and some government subsidies for housing and healthcare. He also started various infrastructure programmes for railways, roads, and electrification, as well as irrigation schemes. Industrial production developed at three times the rate of output prior to 1923 and he ended the war in Morocco in 1925. Nevertheless, he ran up massive debts that put Spain into a dreadful situation when the Wall Street Crash came. He managed to alienate most of the powerful elements of society, including the landowners and the army.

> *Primo's entire revolution from above contained the seeds of its own failure. In trying to tackle the grievances of so many different groups simultaneously, he finished up satisfying none …*
>
> **Christopher J. Ross, *Spain 1812–1996* (Hodder, 2000), p.60.**

Thus De Rivera resigned in 1930, having not resolved Spain's economic problems, or brought about long-term political stability. It seemed that dictatorship as a solution to Spain's problems had failed. However, King Alfonso appointed another general to replace Primo who proved to be totally ineffectual. After promising and then delaying a general election the credibility of the monarchy was further undermined. Support for Republican movements grew and in August representatives of Republican organizations signed the Pact of San Sebastián. After municipal elections in April showed support for the San Sebastián pact's coalition of parties (Republicans, Liberals, Socialists, and Catalans), the king went into voluntary exile. This time, neither the church nor the army intervened to save him. A relatively peaceful revolution had occurred and the Second Republic was established.

Activity 2

Thinking and self-management skills

Review questions

1. Draw a mind map or spider diagram of the key issues dividing Spain by 1931.
2. Explain the events that led to the fall of King Alfonso in 1931.
3. Looking at the long-term issues in Spain and the political events of the 19th century, what problems was the Second Republic likely to face? Do you consider that war was inevitable by mid-1931?

Short-term causes of the Spanish Civil War: political polarization

Timeline of events - 1931–36		
1931	Apr	Second Spanish Republic proclaimed
1933	Nov	Spanish right wins general election
1934	Oct	Asturias uprising
1936	Feb	Popular Front government elected
	July	Army rising

Between 1931 and 1936, Spain became politically polarized. You may have already decided, in your answers to question 3 above, that civil war in Spain was likely, given the long-term structural problems and clear divisions that already existed in the 19th century and early 20th century. Nevertheless, it is important to note the following:

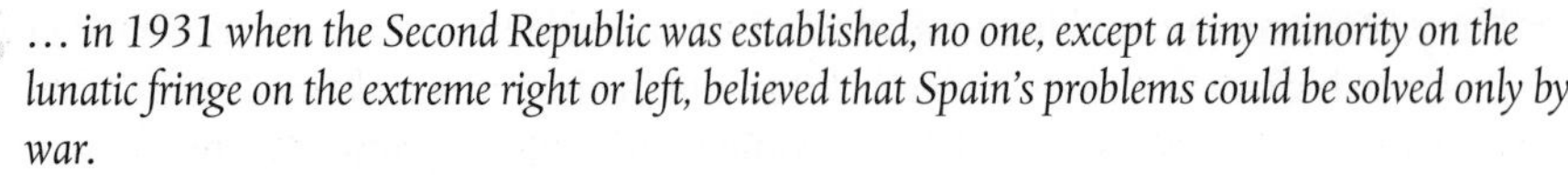

> *... in 1931 when the Second Republic was established, no one, except a tiny minority on the lunatic fringe on the extreme right or left, believed that Spain's problems could be solved only by war.*
>
> **Paul Preston, *Modern History Review*, September 1991.**

The events of the Second Republic were thus central in bringing about a situation, only 5 years later, in which large numbers of people thought war was inevitable, if not desirable.

Activity 3

A symbolic representation of the Second Republic.

1. What message about the Second Republic is suggested in this image? (Look carefully at all of the symbolism in the painting.)

The Left Republic (April 1931–November 1933)

President Manuel Azaña.

In the elections that followed King Alfonso's departure, the centre-left won, with the objective of modernizing Spain. The Cortes had 473 seats and the right won only 57. The government declared a new constitution, stating that Spain was a 'democratic republic of workers of all classes'. The constitution established that the Cortes would be elected every four years, there would be universal suffrage, a president as head of state, and freedom of worship for all religions. At first, the government was led by Prime Minister Niceto Alcalá Zamora, a wealthy liberal Catholic who wanted limited reform. Manuel Azaña, a leader of the Republican Action Party, was minister for war. When Zamora resigned after reforms of the church were passed, Azaña became prime minister, and Zamora took on the role of president. Azaña thus became the leading figure in the new regime. However, the key issues causing tension in Spain before the revolution of 1931 continued to dominate the political, economic and social atmosphere under the new left-wing government.

Azaña addressed the issue of the church's power. His speeches were anticlerical, and an attempt was made to separate the church and state, and to limit church powers.

The church was no longer in control of education, and the state payment of the clergy was to be stopped gradually over a two-year period. Divorce was legalized and civil marriages were introduced. The Associations Law 1933 prohibited priests and nuns from teaching in schools and nationalized church property. The government, which saw education as key to modernizing Spain, invested heavily in building new schools and training teachers, as the church was no longer to be responsible. Over 7,000 new schools were opened between 1931 and 1932. This was more than ten times the number built in the preceding 20 years. Although impressive, this programme was expensive.

The power of the army was also attacked; the government attempted to reduce numbers by offering early retirement on full pay, an offer taken up by 50 per cent of officers. The military academy of Saragossa was closed (Franco had been its director). Yet this policy backfired to a certain extent, as not only was it expensive for the government, but it meant that the army was radicalized; those who remained in the army were the Conservative and Nationalist core, including the Africanistas.

The desperate economic problems that existed in Spain had been exacerbated by the Great Depression: agricultural prices were tumbling, wine and olive exports fell, and land had gone out of cultivation. Peasant unemployment was rising. The effects were also being felt industrially; iron production fell by a third and steel by almost a half. Largo Caballero, Minister of Labour, initiated an extensive land redistribution programme, with compensation for landowners. In 1932, a law enabled the state to take over estates and to redistribute land to the peasants. Yet the government did not have the money for this reform, and fewer than 7,000 families had benefited from the programme by 1933. The right saw land reform as a major threat to its interests, and an attempt to copy the Soviet system.

Civil unrest and violence continued under the Left Republic, and it dealt with its perpetrators brutally. The government introduced the Assault Guard in an attempt to create a paramilitary force loyal to the Republic. There were risings by both the right (General José Sanjurjo in 1932) against the reforms, and by the left (an example was the Casas Viejas anarchist rising in 1933 – see below) against the slow pace of change. At this time, the risings were suppressed, as the majority of the army remained loyal. As for the regional issues, Catalonia was given its own parliament in 1932, as well as some powers, including law and order and dual control over education. Right-wing groups were angered by this change, as they saw it as a move towards independence for the regions and the break-up of Spain.

Each reform was perceived as an attack on one or more right-wing groups – the church, army, landowners, or industrialists. A new right-wing party, the **Confederación Española de Derechas Autónomas** (CEDA; Spanish Confederation of the Autonomous Right), was formed to defend the church and landlords. CEDA was led by José María Gil Robles, who admired the Austrian authoritarian leader Engelbert Dollfuss of the Christian Social Party, as the Spanish CEDA was not just a party of the 'right' but was based on traditional Catholic movements. Indeed, the political divisions within Spain seemed to increase under the Second Republic. The right wing opposed the reforms, sometimes with violence.

Although some historians see the failure of land reform as central to the failure of the government during this period, historian Paul Preston has argued that the right wing was in any case never going to give the regime a chance. Azaña also damaged his reputation when, in January 1933, government guards set fire to houses in the village of Casas Viejas near Cadiz in an attempt to 'smoke out' a group of anarchists. Twenty-five people were killed. This incident lost the left-wing Republic a lot of working-class support, and led even the Socialists to withdraw support from Azaña, who resigned in 1933.

Activity 4

ATL Thinking and communication skills

Review questions

1. How did the actions of the Second Republic create more tension? In what ways did they, in Paul Preston's words, 'ensure that Spain's underlying conflicts were transmitted into national politics'?
2. Look at the diagram below and explain how each of the following undermined Azaña's reforms.

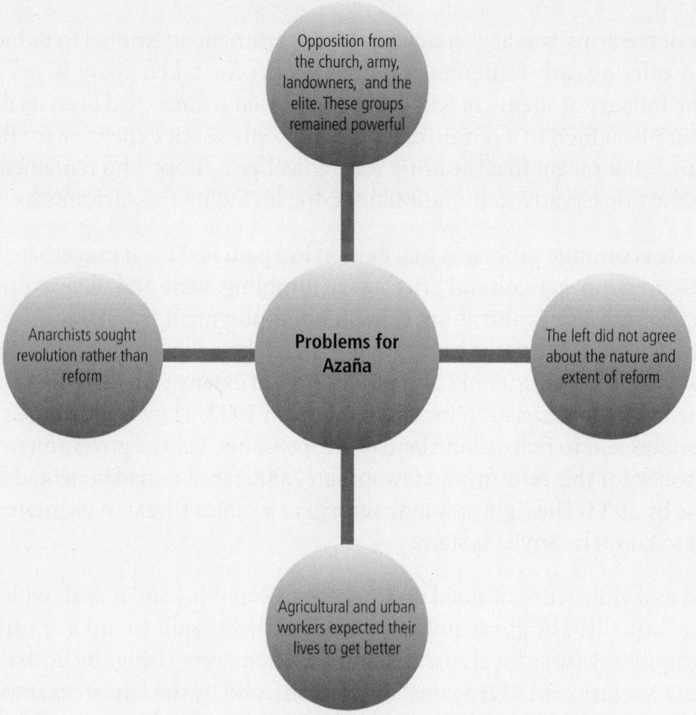

Problems for Azaña

- Opposition from the church, army, landowners, and the elite. These groups remained powerful
- Anarchists sought revolution rather than reform
- The left did not agree about the nature and extent of reform
- Agricultural and urban workers expected their lives to get better

3. In pairs, discuss how the Great Depression may have limited Azaña's reforms.

The Spanish electoral system

It is worth noting that the Spanish electoral system ensured that only a small swing in the number of votes cast had a huge effect on the parliamentary system. Indeed, the electoral system gave 80 per cent of the seats to the party or coalition that gained 50 per cent or more of the vote. Thus, although there was only a minor shift of votes from the left to the right, there was a big change in parliamentary power. The same was to happen in 1936 when the Popular Front gained control. The instability created by the electoral system was a contributory factor in the breakdown of the Second Republic.

The Right Republic (November 1933–February 1936)

In the elections of 1933, the Republic swung to the right, with the right-wing and centrist parties benefiting from the disunity of the left. Although CEDA was the largest party, the president resisted giving Gil Robles power. However, CEDA forced the government's hand in October 1934 by withdrawing support. Gil Robles was made war minister and two other CEDA party members were given cabinet posts.

The new government ruled for 2 years in what became known as the '*Biennio negro*', or 'two black years', because it embarked on systematically reversing the Left Republic's reforms. Church control was restored over education and the clergy were again to be paid by the state. Public spending was cut, particularly on education. Azaña's key economic reform – the land programme – was halted. There was an anarchist uprising in Barcelona in December 1933 and this was put down in 10 days of violence. Catalonia attempted to resist interference and declared itself independent after CEDA joined the government. Catalonia's autonomy was suspended after the Asturian miners' uprising in 1934. This rebellion was put down by troops, including Moroccan forces, after which the government censored the press and even suggested Azaña had been involved. Threats from the left of a 'general strike' increased. Historians have

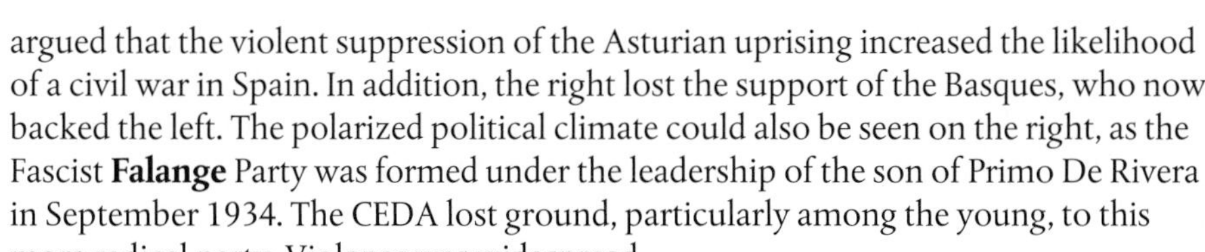

argued that the violent suppression of the Asturian uprising increased the likelihood of a civil war in Spain. In addition, the right lost the support of the Basques, who now backed the left. The polarized political climate could also be seen on the right, as the Fascist **Falange** Party was formed under the leadership of the son of Primo De Rivera in September 1934. The CEDA lost ground, particularly among the young, to this more radical party. Violence was widespread.

The political response to the Right Republic was divided. Caballero was more extreme in his speeches than the more moderate Prieto. He suggested that CEDA was the Spanish Nazi party and that the left should seek a Soviet-style solution for Spain. Thus, he articulated the parallels in Spanish politics to the broader European political landscape.

In response, Gil Robles demanded a shift to a more authoritarian approach to control the Communists in Spain. Robles' response led to more cooperation between the left's factions: Socialists, anarchists, **syndicalists**, and now Communists. Indeed, Prieto attempted to find some common ground between the left and centre groups to enable them to take on the right wing.

CHALLENGE YOURSELF

Research skills 

Research the Asturian miners' uprising of October 1934. Consider the role of the Socialists, the CNT, and the Communists, as well as the scale of the rising and its brutal suppression by the government, which lead to 4,000 casualties. In pairs, discuss the extent to which you agree that this was an *'attempted revolution'*.

The Popular Front (February–July 1936)

The right-wing coalition disintegrated as the economic and the political situation deteriorated, and in September 1935 the Prime Minister, Alejandro Lerroux, resigned after being embroiled in financial scandals. In the elections that followed in February 1936, the 'Popular Front', which was an anti-Fascist pact made up of various left-wing groups including socialists and Communists, was victorious. This idea of forming anti-fascist, or Popular Front, coalitions was supported by Stalin and pursued by the Comintern, and had been successfully implemented in France. In Spain it was not only a coalition of the left-wing groups, but also included Liberals like Azaña. The Popular Front was for many in Spain a final attempt to uphold democracy and peace, but others associated it with Stalin and the more extreme Communist supporters.

The manifesto promoted by Azaña, now returned to power initially as the prime minister and then as president, was liberal and not radical. Nevertheless, the government wanted to restore the reforms of the 1931–1933 regime, and political prisoners were released. But there was still no political consensus; Caballero's Socialists did not join the government and the right would not accept the restoration of reforms.

Falange

Falange (Phalanx) was founded by Primo de Rivera, the son of the former dictator, in 1933. By early 1936, it had 8,000 members (mainly students). They had a blue-shirted uniform. The Falange demanded a strong authoritarian leadership, but was also committed to radical social change.

The anarchists encouraged peasants to seize land, which led to an increase in violence in the countryside. They also openly recruited for their militias and organized bombings and assassinations. Open conflict between the anarchist FAI and the right wing CEDA and Falange youth movements increased. The government again faced increasing disorder. In May, the CNT called a general strike, and there were several strikes throughout June. Thousands of peasants began to occupy estates in the countryside. Gil Robles declared that a country could survive as a monarchy or a republic, but 'cannot live in anarchy'. The right wing believed that Spain was in the early throes of a left-wing revolution.

The victory of the left in the 1936 elections threw the right-wing CEDA into turmoil. Gil Robles began to use his funds to support military plans for a coup. In fact, military officers began planning for a coup as soon as the Popular Front gained power. An extreme Nationalist group of junior officers joined with senior Africanista officers, including Mola and Franco. The catalyst for the coup was the murder of a popular right-wing leader, José Calvo Sotelo, on 13 July 1936.

Azaña knew that there were plans for a coup, and attempted to prevent it by moving key military figures to remote posts. However, the conspirators had already made their plans and set a date for the coup – 18 July 1936. They had the support of the fascist Falange, the CEDA, and the monarchist 'Carlist' and '**Alfonsist**' groups. Spain was clearly polarized between two groups: those who were anti-Fascist, and those on the right who were anti-Communists.

When the details of the coup were discovered, it was initiated earlier, on 17 July, from Morocco. It spread to the mainland, and was successful in taking northern Spain and parts of Andalusia. Yet the rising failed in the main industrial areas, and the rebels did not take Madrid. Half the army had remained loyal to the Republic. Thus the coup was unsuccessful overall, and, had it remained a Spanish affair, it is quite possible that the Republicans would have won.

Activity 5 — ATL Thinking skills

1. To what extent did economic issues lead to a civil war?
2. Discuss the impact of international events on the growing divisions in Spain.

Activity 6 — ATL Communication skills

Divide the class into three groups. Organize a class debate where each group argues one of the following:

- the right wing was responsible for the Spanish Civil War
- the left wing was responsible for the Spanish Civil War
- both left and right were equally responsible for the Spanish Civil War.

Activity 7 — ATL Thinking skills

TOK

Discuss in small groups how the political and socio-economic situation of a contemporary observer influences his or her opinion of a crisis such as the Spanish Civil War.

Source analysis

Source A

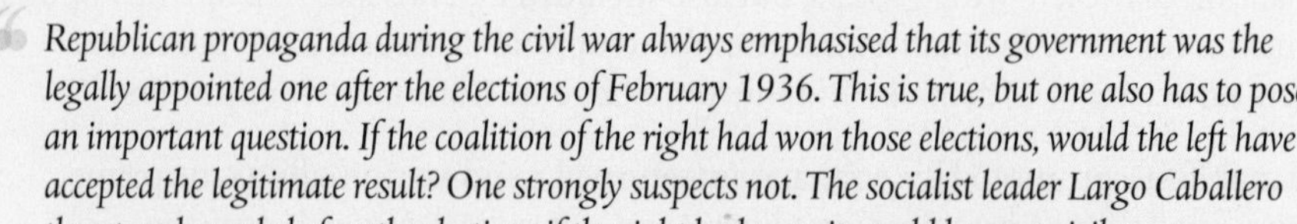

Republican propaganda during the civil war always emphasised that its government was the legally appointed one after the elections of February 1936. This is true, but one also has to pose an important question. If the coalition of the right had won those elections, would the left have accepted the legitimate result? One strongly suspects not. The socialist leader Largo Caballero threatened openly before the elections if the right had won, it would be open civil war.

The nationalists tried from the very beginning to pretend that they had risen in revolt purely to forestall a communist putsch. This was a complete fabrication to provide retrospective justification for their acts … Both sides, of course, justified their actions on the grounds that if they did not act first, their opponents would seize power and crush them.

Antony Beevor, *The Battle for Spain* (Penguin, 2006), p.xxvii.

Source B

Faced with the difficulties of modernising a backward economy and social structure in a country without strong democratic traditions, and against the background of the Depression, the Republic was facing insurmountable problems by 1936. Civil War may not have been inevitable but certainly did not come as a surprise.

Patricia Knight, *The Spanish Civil War* (Hodder & Stoughton, 1998), p.25.

Source C

The Spanish Civil War … was a class war, and a culture war. Competing visions of Spanish identity were superimposed on a bitter struggle over material resources, as the defenders of property and tradition took up arms against a Republican government committed to social reform, devolution and secularization.

Frances Lannon, *The Spanish Civil War* (Osprey, 2002), p.7.

1. What are the key causes of the civil war identified by:
   a) Antony Beevor in Source A
   b) Patricia Knight in Source B
   c) Frances Lannon in Source C?
2. Discuss the comparisons and contrasts between the views expressed in the three sources.
3. With reference to the origin, purpose, and content, assess the values and limitations of Source A for historians studying the causes of the Spanish Civil War.

Activity 8

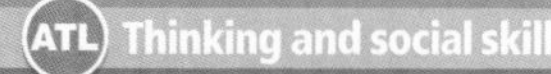

'Soft Construction with Boiled Beans (Premonition of Civil War)', 1936, by the Spanish Surrealist painter Salvador Dalí.

1. Salvador Dalí painted 'Soft Construction with Boiled Beans (Premonition of Civil War)' in 1936. In pairs, research Dalí's motives in painting this picture and what the images in the picture represent with regard to Spain in particular and war in general.

The course of the Spanish Civil War

Timeline of events – 1936–1939		
1936	**July**	Franco's forces airlifted from Morocco to southern Spain
	Aug	Britain and France begin policy of non-intervention
	4 Sept	Largo Caballero forms new Republican government
	13 Sept	San Sebastián taken by Nationalists
	Oct	Republic incorporates militias into new Popular Army
	1 Oct	Franco becomes head of Nationalist government and supreme military commander
	29 Oct	Soviet intervention begins; German and Italian planes bomb Madrid

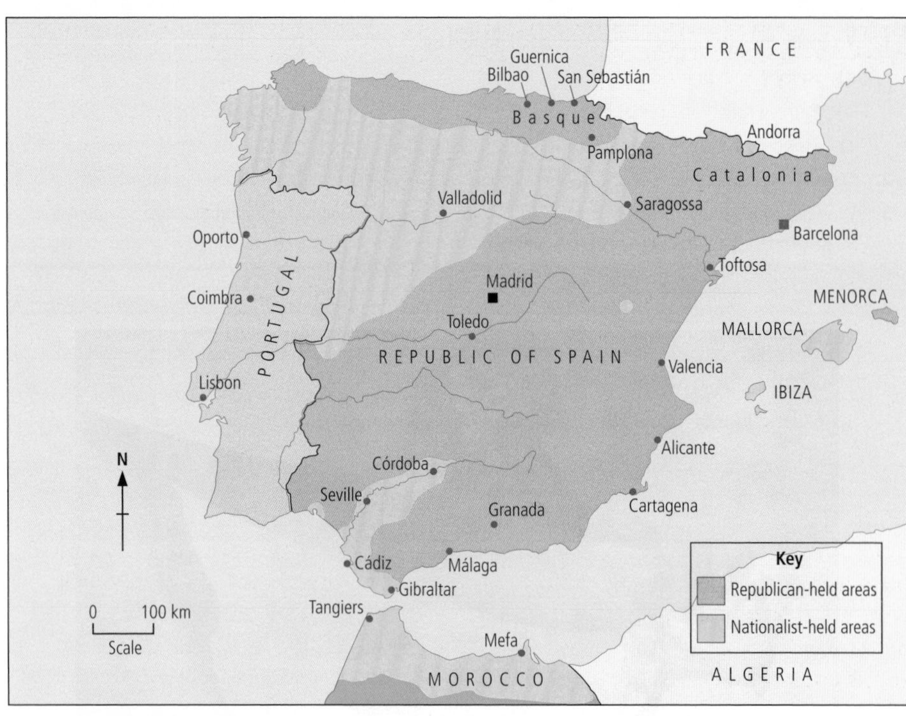

Nationalist- and Republican-held territory, July 1936.

'Death of a Loyalist', photograph by Robert Capa, 5 September 1936.

Timeline of events – 1936–1939

	6 Nov	Republican government leaves Madrid for Valencia
	23 Nov	Nationalists abandon attempt to take Madrid
1937	**Feb**	Nationalist offensive to cut the links between Madrid and Valencia fails at the Battle of Jarama Russian tanks and planes play a crucial role in the battle
	8 Feb	Fall of Málaga to the Nationalists
	Mar	Nationalist offensive to tighten the pressure on Madrid from the north fails at the Battle of Guadalajara. This was a major defeat for the Italian Army, and again Soviet equipment was vital to Republican success
	Apr	Franco unites Carlists, Fascists, and monarchists into one movement
	26 Apr	German Condor Legion bombs and destroys Guernica
	15 May	Fall of Largo Caballero
	17 May	Juan Negrin forms new government
	19 June	Fall of Bilbao to the Nationalists End of Basque independence
	July	Republican offensive to break the siege of Madrid to the west fails at Brunete
	Aug	Republican offensive to break out from Madrid to the north-east fails at Belchite
	Sept–Oct	Nationalists capture rest of northern Spain
	Dec	Newly organized Republican Popular Army captures Teruel in central Spain

Timeline of events – 1936–1939		
1938	Feb	Nationalists retake Teruel and launch the strategically crucial advance to the Mediterranean to cut Catalonia off from the rest of Republican Spain
	Apr	Nationalists reach the Mediterranean at Vinaroz Republican Spain cut in two
	July	Republican offensive on the River Ebro fails
	Nov	Nationalists drive Republicans back across River Ebro Nationalists march on Barcelona
1939	Feb	Barcelona falls to Nationalists
	28 Mar	Nationalists enter Madrid
	1 Apr	Franco announces end of war

With the assistance of Nazi Germany, General Franco airlifted 24,000 experienced troops of the Army of Africa to Spain. It was the fact that Hitler responded to Franco's pleas for help that kept Franco's efforts alive. Franco's forces landing from Morocco was coordinated with uprisings in the north of Spain. Once on the Spanish mainland, he used a policy of terror as his forces moved towards Madrid in August. Franco's success was complemented by the achievements of General Emilio Mola, who took territory in the north.

The army coup had aimed to crush the 'left revolution', but had instead politicized and radicalized many Spaniards towards the left. The supporters of the Republican regime of 1936 became known as the 'Loyalists', and those that supported the rebels called themselves 'Nationalists'. Divisions could generally be drawn by class: the workers supported the Republic, and the middle and upper classes the Nationalists. The Nationalists had the support of much of the church as well. However, alliances could also be accidental, depending on where people were when the war developed. The peasants of the north and central Spain tended to be Nationalists, while the landless

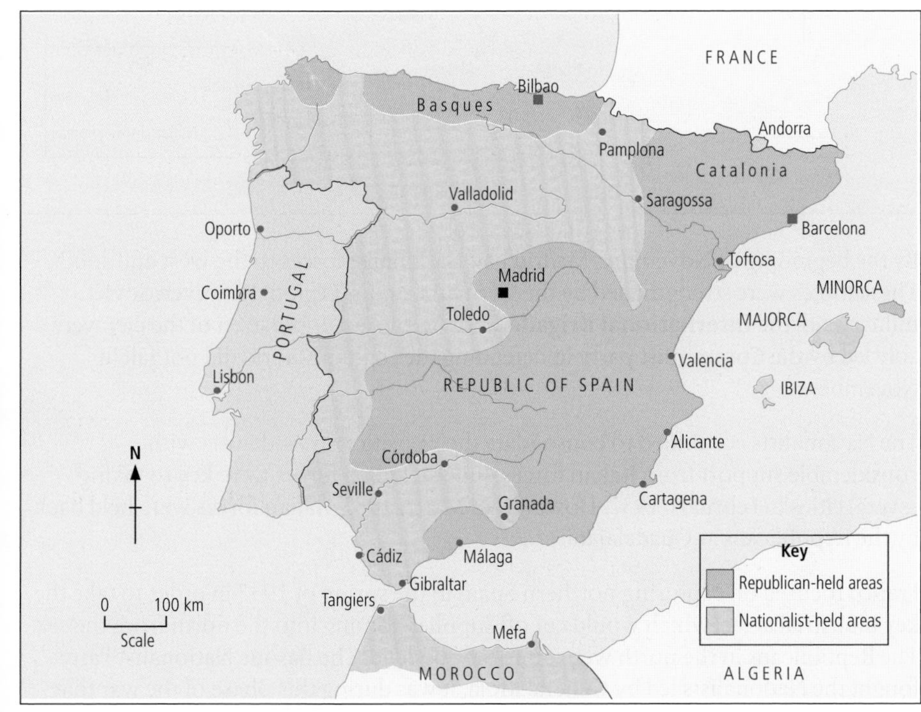

Nationalist- and Republican-held territory, October 1936.

labourers of the south followed the Republicans. The Basques and Catalans supported the Republic, as it had backed their autonomous ambitions.

Although the Nationalists made gains in the first weeks of the war, the Republic retained some advantages. It remained in control of most major cities and key industrial areas, it had Spain's gold reserves, and important elements of the military – most of the air force and navy – remained loyal. Yet, as you can see from the timeline above and the maps below, the Nationalists were able to make steady progress in pushing back the Republic.

Although the Nationalists had taken much of northern Spain in July 1936, the Republicans had defeated them in Barcelona, and in the capital, Madrid, and held most of the coastline. Franco's forces had advanced northwards from the south and had taken the city of Badajoz with great ferocity, killing over 2,000 people. However, atrocities were committed on both sides, with Republicans massacring priests, nuns, and monks. Franco's strategy was systematically to occupy territory and then purge all Republicans and their sympathizers before moving on.

Nationalist- and Republican-held territory, October 1937.

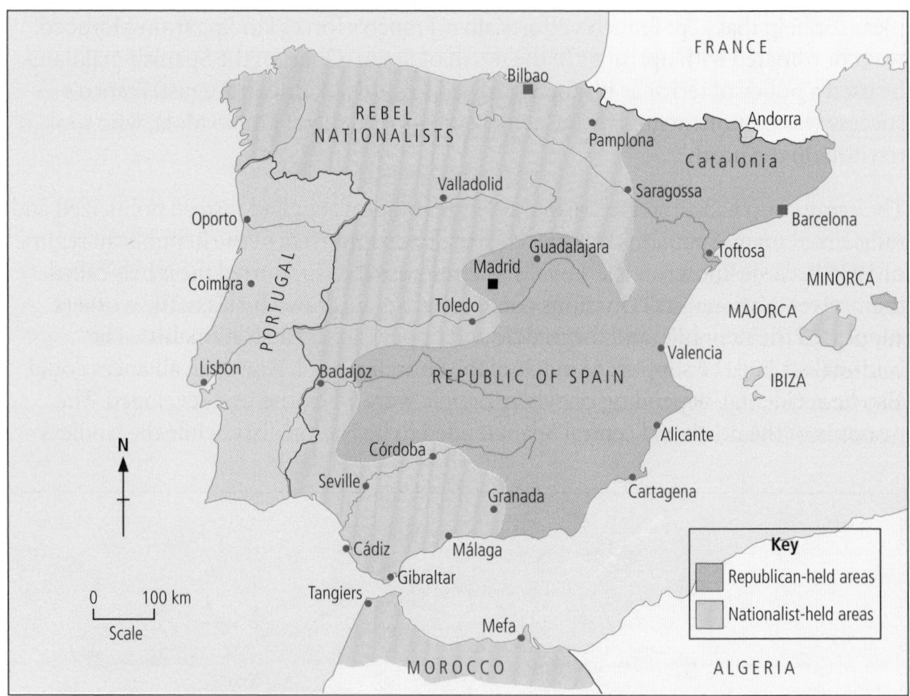

By the beginning of November, Madrid had Nationalist forces to the west and south. These forces were strengthened by the German Condor Legion. However, Soviet military aid, the **International Brigade**, and the civilian population of the city were ably led by the Communist party in defending the capital. Madrid did not fall in November.

The Nationalists continued to consolidate their position in Andalusia with considerable support from Italian forces. Indeed, Italian forces were key to taking several cities in February 1937. However, in March 1937, Italian forces were held back by the Republicans at Guadalajara.

Franco focused on capturing northern Spain in the spring of 1937 in order to take the key industrial areas, which would cut off supplies coming into the north from the sea. The Republicans in the north were politically divided. The Basque Nationalist Party fought the Nationalists led by General Mola. It was during this phase of the war that

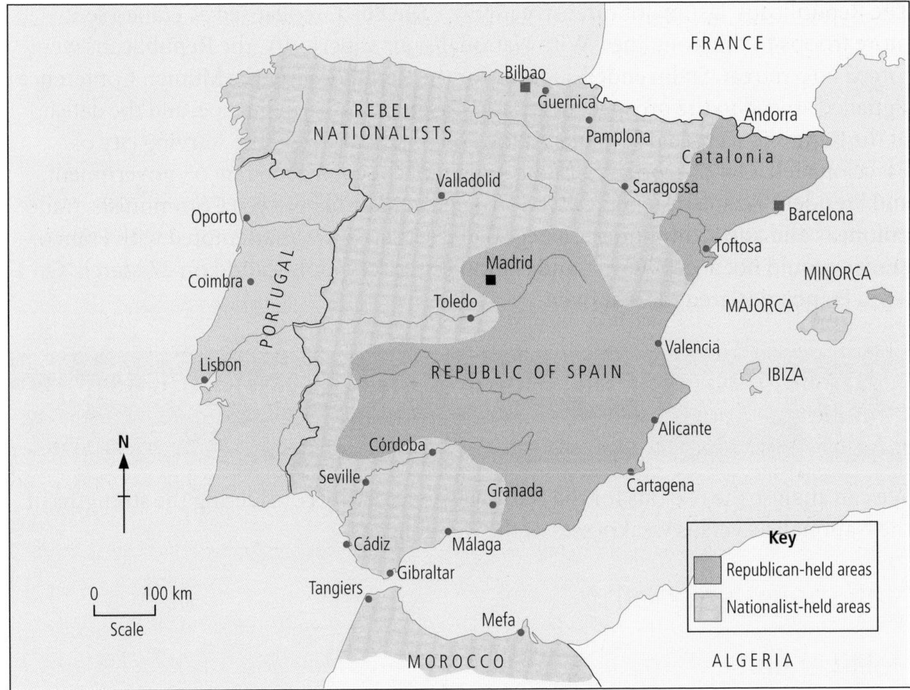

Nationalist- and Republican-held territory, May 1938.

CHALLENGE YOURSELF

Research skills (ATL)

Research the Republican offensives of Brunete, July 1937; Belchite, August 1937; and Teruel, December 1937, and examine the reasons they failed.

the bombing of Guernica was perpetrated by the Condor Legion. In June 1937 Bilbao fell after intense bombing. In October the Nationalists had captured the Asturias coalfields. Their forces had superior tanks and control of the air – the Republican air force was based centrally and the north was out of range. The loss of the northern territories was a huge blow to the Republic, as it lost valuable resources: coal, iron, and armaments industries. The Nationalist navy now could focus on attempting to blockade the Republic via the Mediterranean. By the end of April 1938, Republican Spain was divided in half (see map above).

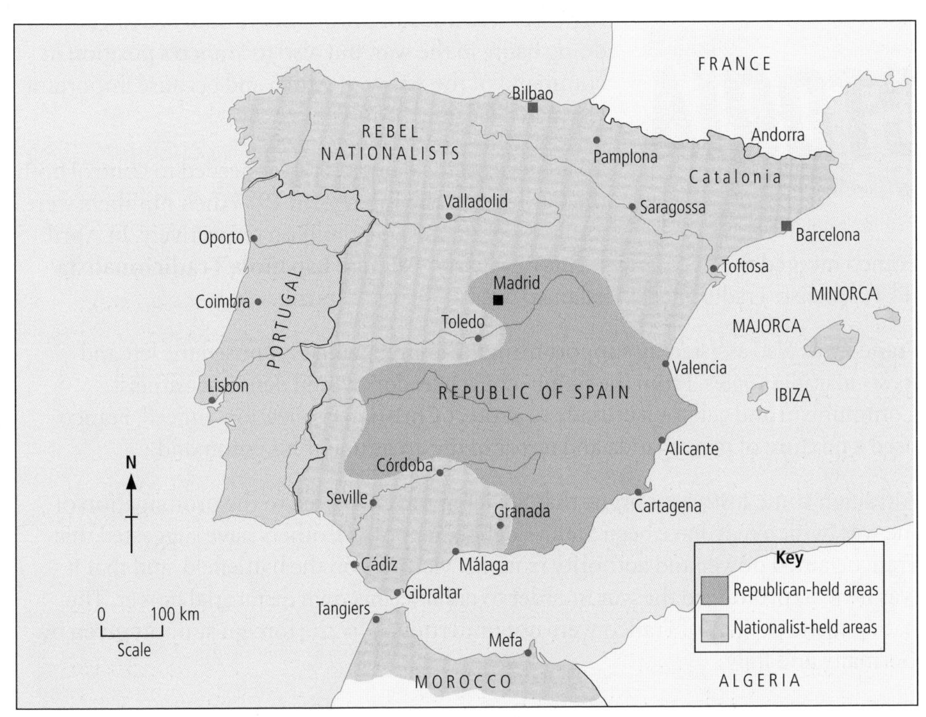

Nationalist- and Republican-held territory, February 1939.

The Republicans' last major offensive in July – the Ebro – collapsed as Franco sent more troops to the front lines. With Nationalist air superiority, the Republicans were forced into retreat. Stalin ended support for the Republic after the Munich Conference signalled an end to the prospect of an 'anti-Fascist' alliance in Europe, and the defeat of the Republic seemed inevitable. At the end of January 1939 the starving city of Barcelona fell. On 27 February, Britain and France recognized Franco's government, and President Azaña resigned. After a struggle in Madrid between Communists, trade unionists and anti-Communists, a negotiated settlement was attempted with Franco. Franco would not accept terms, and Nationalist forces took Madrid on 27 March. On 1 April Franco declared the war over.

Why did the Nationalists win the Spanish Civil War?

We can analyse the reasons for the Nationalist victory by considering the strengths of the Nationalists versus weaknesses of the Republicans.

Nationalist strengths

Political unity

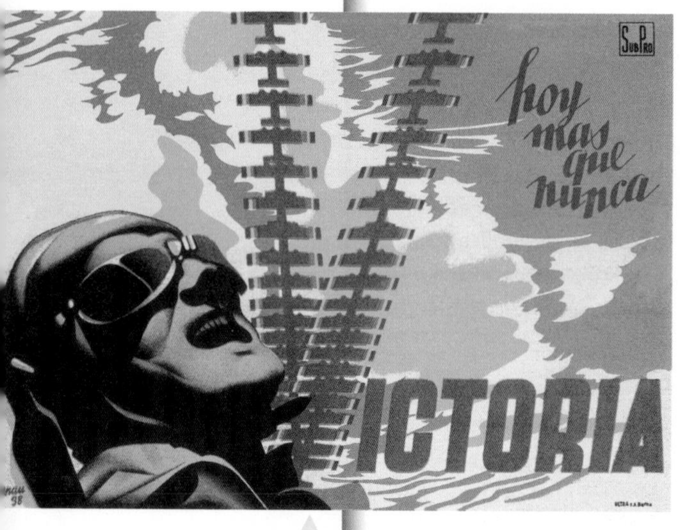

A Nationalist propaganda poster

The major strength of the Nationalists was unity. In July 1936, however, the Nationalists were almost as divided as the Republicans. Their only common aim was to overthrow the government. Initially, generals Mola, Goded, and Sanjurjo seemed more important than Franco, but after the first few weeks Franco had emerged as the leader. In September 1936, the generals decided that they needed a unified command. It was agreed that Franco would assume political and military control. He became head of government and head of state. This rise to power was due not only to other leaders dying, or doing badly in the war, but also to Franco's position in command of the Army of Africa and because important German aid came through him.

To achieve political unity, Franco needed to control both the Carlists and the Falange. In 1937 their numbers were impressive: 70,000 and 1 million respectively. In April, Franco merged the two parties. This new party, **Falange Española Tradicionalista** (FET; Spanish Traditionalist Phalanax), was under his control.

Franco was also assisted by support from the church, which opposed the left and its secular ideologies. From the pulpit, church leaders would denounce atheist Communism and call for a crusade to protect Christian civilization. Indeed, Franco used a mixture of propaganda and terror in the areas under his command.

Although some historians argue that Soviet involvement led to the prolongation of the war (which may have been Stalin's deliberate policy), others have suggested that Franco gained power and authority from his victories on the battlefield, and that it was he who prolonged the war in order to enhance his own dictatorial power. The nationalistic politics of Franco were not undermined by the foreign support given by Germany and Italy.

Military unity

Militarily, the Nationalists initially had similar problems to the Republicans – 'columns' of Carlist and Falangist militias attempted to operate alongside regular army units. In contrast, however, these militias were effectively drawn into the regular army. The Army of Africa played a significant role. It contained the best troops in the country, and it could cover for other forces while they were being trained and equipped. In open and mobile offensive operations, the Army of Africa proved itself the most effective force in the entire civil war.

The unified command was key to the Nationalists' success. Franco's leadership was accepted by the other generals and right-wing parties. The Nationalists were successful in pushing on and winning offensives, and were also able to adopt effective defensive tactics during the Republican offensive campaigns of 1937.

The Nationalists had sound communications and managed to equip their growing army throughout the civil war. They could also rely on their large number of junior officers.

Franco was an able military and political leader. He often refused to follow the more radical advice given to him by his German and Italian advisers. His concern for his troops ensured that the majority were obedient.

Economic advantage

The business community backed the Nationalists, which meant they could get credit to buy war supplies. Also, by September 1936 they were in control of the main food-producing areas. After their successes in 1937 in the north, they added the main industrial areas to their control.

The Nationalists also benefited from international trade and credit, which was not restricted. It has been estimated that the USA gave $700 million in credit during the course of the war. This meant that Franco's forces could buy all the rubber and oil they needed, often acquired from US companies.

Foreign assistance

As suggested above, some historians have argued that foreign aid was a crucial factor in the Nationalists' victory over the Republic. Hugh Thomas writes in his book *The Spanish Civil War* that the conflict 'became an international crisis whose solution was decided by external circumstances' (Eyre & Spottiswood, 1961). Indeed, the rebels benefited from more aid, which was of a better quality than that given to the Republicans, and its supply was continuous throughout the war. The Germans had airlifted Franco's army from Morocco to the mainland in the first stage of the war, at a vital moment in the conflict. The Germans also committed the Condor Legion – 10,000 troops, 800 aircraft, and 200 tanks. When the Germans sent Messerschmitt 109s in 1937, the Nationalists gained air superiority. The Italians sent 70,000–75,000 troops, 750 planes, and 150 tanks; the Portuguese sent 20,000 troops and permitted aid to pass over their long border with Spain. This assistance was significant in several ways. It allowed the Nationalists to fight in the first place, owing to the German airlift, but German planes also gave the Nationalists control of the air from 1937. Franco's command was not compromised, and, after an Italian defeat at Guadalajara, they were taken under Spanish command. The key benefit for the Nationalists, however, was not the human resources, as most of their armies were Spanish – it was the modern equipment they received.

Republican weaknesses

Spanish Civil War poster, 'They shall not pass!'

Political disunity

Caballero became head of a coalition government in September 1936. His rule was weakened by the fact that the Republicans were politically divided. Indeed, Republicans subscribed to widely different ideologies. The key divisions were between the Communists and Socialists, who believed that the 'revolution' should now be postponed until the war was won, and the anarchists, who argued that the war could only be won through revolutionary policies. The anarchists, dominant in Catalonia, Aragon, and Andalusia, encouraged 'revolution from below' in the areas they controlled, and some historians suggest that this added a crucial hurdle for the Republic, as they had to try to regain their centralized control. The Communists/Socialists had more influence in Madrid and Valencia. The regions of Catalonia, the Basque, and Asturias became virtually independent.

The war generally increased the popularity of the Communists. For example, in July 1936 the Spanish Communist Party numbered around 40,000 members, but by October 1937 it had 400,000 members. The Communist Party exploited the fact that it was the only Republican group with clear foreign support – from the USSR. However, to retain control the Communists often used 'terror' tactics, which led to some resistance even in sympathetic territories: for example, the 'May Days' in Barcelona in 1937 – see below. In addition, the Communists and Socialists wanted victory in the war to strengthen the Second Republic, whereas the anarchists wanted a new revolutionary regime.

The lack of unity between the forces of the Republic is exemplified in the 4 days of street fighting in Barcelona in May 1937 – government forces, Communists, and Socialists on one side and the anarchists and POUM on the other (this fighting became known as the 'May Days'). As a result of this turmoil, Caballero was replaced by the Socialist Juan Negrin, the Communists' choice, as leader. Negrin attacked the POUM and anarchist leaders, who were imprisoned or executed. His more authoritarian regime lasted until March 1939, when there was a military coup in Madrid.

POUM

The Partido Obrero Unificación Marxista (POUM; Workers' Party of Marxist Unification) was a small influential Catalan Marxist party that was critical of the Soviet system and was often in opposition to the Communists/Socialists, siding with the anarchists.

Military problems

The Republic lacked strong military leadership. There was no unified command, and the Communists and anarchists would not work together. Indeed, the anarchist militias and the Basques refused to be led by a central command structure. The Basques would not permit their forces to defend areas outside their own territory. In addition, loyal army officers, with potentially valuable experience, were not trusted by the Republic.

In the first vital weeks of the war, the Republic was dependent on ineffective militia units that formed haphazardly. This meant that they fought a series of local conflicts rather than one clear overall campaign. Different fronts operated separately, although to some extent this situation was due to the territory held by the Republicans. Many battlefields were not within range of their air force, and they failed to sustain offensive campaigns in 1937 at Brunete, Belchite, and Teruel. Indeed, it was not until the end of 1936 that the Republicans started to replace militias with a coherent 'Popular Army'.

Economic problems

In areas under anarchist control, industries, public utilities, and transport were taken over by workers' committees; in the countryside, collective farms were set up. However, neither of these systems could supply the needs of the Republic to fight the war. Some historians have argued that this situation was due more to the impact of the war than to a badly run government, but most believe that the collectives impaired the Republic's war effort. Production in the key area of Catalan fell by two thirds between 1936 and 1939, and the Republic was increasingly affected by food and raw material shortages. Inflation was also a problem, reaching 300 per cent during the war. At the same time, wages only increased by 15 per cent.

The international body known as the Non-Intervention Committee (NIC), established by Britain and France in 1936 for the purpose of preventing the foreign influx of support to the warring parties in Spain, also had an impact on the Republic. It banned all arms sales to the Republic, which meant the USSR was the only country willing to trade with it. Even this trade had to be paid for using the entire gold reserves of Spain. Paul Preston has argued that the Communists ultimately improved the situation by centralizing control, but this happened too late to save the Republic.

Foreign assistance

Foreign aid has been seen as a critical factor in determining the outcome of the Spanish Civil War. Some historians have suggested its role has been exaggerated; nevertheless, there is no doubt that the foreign assistance given to the Republic was far more limited than that afforded to the Nationalists. The main ally of the Republic was the USSR, and it was the Soviets who initially saved the Republic and enabled it to fight a civil war in 1936–1937. Soviet aircraft and tanks were more effective early on than their German and Italian counterparts. However, no Soviet troops were sent to fight; the USSR committed 1,000 aircraft, 750 tanks, and some advisers. In addition, this aid had to be paid for by the Republic, which sent, as we have seen, all of its gold reserves to Moscow.

The other key allies of the Republicans were the International Brigades, which were organized by the Soviet Comintern. Some 35,000 foreign volunteers went to fight in Spain. Although their role seems to have been significant in the defence of Madrid in November 1936 and in the Ebro offensive in 1938, overall, their impact was limited. In 1938, the Soviets withdrew their support and the foreign members of the International Brigades went home in October 1938 – a final blow for the Republic.

Although France sent aid initially, its support ended when it joined Britain in the policy of non-intervention, meaning that Hitler and Mussolini had no opposition in Spain from the Western democracies. This policy has been condemned by many historians.

Activity 9

1. Look back at the timelines on pages 232–233. Identify key points where foreign intervention played a significant role in the fighting.
2. In small groups, research the different countries, groups, and famous individuals that went to Spain to fight in the International Brigades (for example, the Abraham Lincoln Brigade from the USA).

Activity 10

ATL Self-management skills

Review question

1. Use this grid to summarize the key points made in the text:

	Nationalists	Republicans
Political strengths/weaknesses		
Military strengths/weaknesses		
Economic advantages/ disadvantages		
Foreign assistance		

Activity 11

ATL Communication and social skills

Group activity

1. Divide the class into two groups. One side will argue that the Nationalists' strengths won the Spanish Civil War; the other will argue that it was due to Republican weaknesses. The motion is: 'The strengths of the Nationalists won the Civil War.'

Each side must have a series of thematic and coherent arguments. To gain a point, you need to support arguments with clear evidence and examples.

Overview: foreign intervention

In general, the decision by foreign governments to get involved (or not get involved) in the Spanish Civil War was a result of both ideology and self-interest. Foreign intervention had two main effects:

- it both lengthened and intensified the war
- it meant that the Spanish issues that caused the war were overtaken and submerged by the wider ideological battles taking place in Europe.

Britain

Britain took a leading role in the Non-Intervention Committee, which was set up in August and had its first meeting in London in September 1936. Britain's fear was that the war would spread and become a general European conflict. However, three of the key members of the NIC – Germany, Italy, and the USSR – ignored it completely and became the main foreign forces in Spain. In addition, Britain's non-intervention policies were limited and tended to favour the Nationalists. It focused on preventing aid going to the Republic and allowed the Nationalists, but not the Republicans, to use Gibraltar as a communications base. In December 1936, the British signed a trading agreement with the Nationalists that permitted British companies to trade with the rebel forces. The USA also allowed American companies, such as the Texaco oil company and General Motors, to trade with the Nationalists. It would seem that Spain was sacrificed to the policy of appeasement in the same way as Czechoslovakia; Britain wanted to avoid a general war at all costs and did not want the civil war to damage its relations with Italy or Portugal.

Activity 12

Source analysis

> *... it was never more than a sham which actually worked in favour of the insurgents. A legal government was equated to a group of seditious generals. The Republic was hindered by an arms embargo from mounting an effective defence and a perfect cloak was provided for the Axis powers to continue their activities. Under British auspices, the committee would remain until the end of the war an empty talking shop. It was a perfect weapon to prevent France from making a more direct commitment, preserve consensus at home and avoid confrontation with Germany and Italy.*
>
> **Francisco J. Romero Salvadó, *Modern History Review*, February 1995.**

1. What criticisms does Salvadó make of the Non-Intervention Committee?

France

The French support for the Republic was inconsistent, and this reflected the complexity of its position towards the civil war. It was not in French interests to have a right-wing regime on its border that could join with Italy and Germany to encircle France. But French politics was also polarized, and the government feared a revolt in France should it fully commit in Spain. France was also reliant on Britain, which was more anti-Republic, for its foreign policy options. After initially supporting the Republic, France, under pressure from Britain, proposed the establishment of the Non-Intervention Committee. Although they often practised 'relaxed' non-intervention and did at times allow military aid across the border, France mainly restricted itself to humanitarian assistance. This dealt a fatal blow to the Republic, which could have benefited greatly from support from this large country on its border. The resulting reliance of the Republic on the Soviets polarized the politics of the Spanish Civil War, and associated the Republic with 'Soviet Communism'. Nevertheless, the French did not stop citizens from joining the International Brigades, which were mainly organized in France. In addition, France was the main centre for the coordination of Soviet aid.

The United States

The USA generally supported the Non-Intervention Committee and pursued its isolationist policy. The Neutrality Act, which banned arms sales to belligerents in a war, was extended to include civil wars in 1937. However, as we have seen, US companies continued to supply the Nationalists with key war supplies such as oil and cars.

The USSR

The USSR's reasons for supporting the Republic were not simply ideological. The Spanish conflict in fact presented Stalin with a dilemma. The emergence of another Fascist state would strengthen Hitler's position in Europe. On the other hand, a Republican victory could panic Britain and France into an alliance with Hitler against the threat of Communism. Such an outcome would ruin Stalin's policy of bringing

Britain and France into an alliance with the USSR to contain Hitler. Stalin was divided between these two concerns. Initially he welcomed the NIC, but seeing that Germany and Italy were able to ignore its rules, he then went on, via the Comintern, to organize the transport of international volunteers to Spain and also weapons from the USSR.

Although some historians have argued that Franco protracted the Spanish Civil War to enhance his own power, Stalin also had a motive for dragging the fighting out. The war would drain the resources of Germany, and the longer it went on the more likely it was for the war to develop into a general war. This general war would then be waged on the other side of Europe, far from the borders of the USSR.

Nevertheless, Stalin reduced Soviet support from June 1938. Not only did the Republic seem to be losing, but it now seemed that the Western democracies were set on appeasing the Fascist dictators. Stalin's aim of creating a bloc to resist Hitler ended when Czechoslovakia was abandoned by Britain and France in the Munich Agreement in September 1938.

Germany

Hitler's Germany was cautious when the appeal for help came from the rebels. He was not yet ready for a general European war. Hermann Göring was important in the decision to support the Nationalists. Both he and Hitler wanted to stop the spread of Communism, but Göring also wanted to test out his *Luftwaffe* (German airforce) in live conditions. There were economic and strategic benefits for Germany too; raw materials such as iron ore could be gained, and deploying to Spain would give Germany the potential to hamper Anglo-French maritime communications.

Hitler did not think the war would last long and only wanted to commit limited aid. Although a member of the NIC, Germany supplied the Nationalists through Portugal. As well as its support of Franco in the initial stages of the war, the Condor Legion perpetrated the now-infamous bombing of Guernica, and they played a pivotal role supporting the nationalists in taking Catalonia. The introduction of Messerschmitt 109s in 1937 gave the Nationalists superiority in the air.

German involvement was important to the outcome of the war, not only as it played crucial military roles at critical times during the fighting, but also as other governments were deterred from getting involved due to the German presence.

Italy

Italy gave the most assistance of all the foreign powers. Mussolini wanted to be involved for a number of reasons. First, involvement would be in line with his anti-Communist/Socialist/democratic outlook and his pro-Fascist stance. Second, he wished to enhance his influence as the key power in the Mediterranean, and thereby demonstrate Italy's might. Third, a Fascist victory would weaken France and prevent French left-wing influence in Spain. Another Fascist power would encircle France and put pressure on French colonies in North Africa.

As we have seen, the Italians not only sent 70,000–75,000 troops – they contributed many planes, tanks, and weapons. Italian bombers attacked Spanish cities, and their submarines were a constant threat to supplies. Italy ignored its membership of the NIC. Historians suggest that although Italy sent many troops, the significant element of its intervention was its air and naval support, particularly the blockade of Republican supplies, which helped the Nationalists to secure victory. As a wider result, the relationship between Italy and Germany was cemented in Spain.

Guernica

Pablo Picasso's *Guernica*, which has become the iconic image of the Spanish Civil War.

One of the most notorious events of the Spanish Civil War was the German bombing of the defenceless Basque town of Guernica. The Condor Legion were the perpetrators of the raid, in which 1,600 people were killed. Pablo Picasso's painting *Guernica* is not only the iconic image of the Spanish Civil War, but it has become one of the most powerful anti-war paintings in the history of art. Its powerful and terrifying image of the carnage wreaked by the bombing of civilians is recognized across the world. Indeed, its impact was considered so powerful that a copy of *Guernica* hanging in the UN was covered up when Colin Powell made the case for the Iraq War in 2003 to the world's press.

Discuss how and why a piece of art can convey such a powerful and cross-cultural message. Consider the relative role of the different ways of knowing in your discussion.

Portugal

Portugal was an important part of the foreign contribution to Franco's victory. Indeed, it was the only foreign force not compromised at any time by membership of the NIC. Not only did Portugal send 20,000 troops, but it was fundamental to supplying the rebels along the Spanish–Portuguese border, and provided a base for communications. Portugal's long-term alliance with Britain led to the British being reluctant to counter its support for the Nationalists. This was, of course, an important benefit for Franco's troops.

Activity 13

ATL Thinking skills

Source analysis

Read the sources below and answer the questions that follow.

Source A

The Nationalists maintained that Guernica had been blown up by the Basques themselves, in order to discredit the blameless Nationalists. A later version said that Republican planes dropped bombs to detonate charges of dynamite placed in the sewers. Twenty years later it was still a crime in Franco's Spain to say that Guernica had been destroyed by the Nationalists.

David Mitchell, *The Spanish Civil War* (Granada, 1982), p.92.

Source B

Our consciences were uneasy about it. After living through the raid we knew only too well that the destruction had come from the air. The Reds had hardly any planes, we knew that too. Amongst our own, we'd admit the truth: our side had bombed the town and it was a bad thing. 'But what can we do about it now?' we'd say. It was simply better to keep quiet.

From a statement by Juana Sangroniz, a Nationalist, quoted in Ronald Fraser, *Blood of Spain* (Pimlico, 1994), p.92.

Source C

In fact Guernica was a military target, being a communications centre close to the battle line. Retreating republican soldiers could only escape with any ease through Guernica because the bridge over the river was the last one before the sea. But if the aim of the Condor Legion was to destroy the bridge why did they not use their supremely accurate Stuka bombers? At least part of the aim must have been to cause maximum panic and confusion among civilians as well as soldiers. The use of incendiary bombs proves that some destruction of buildings and people other than the bridge must have been intended.

Hugh Thomas, *The Spanish Civil War*, 3rd ed. (Hamilton, 1977), p.608.

1. Compare and contrast the views expressed about the Spanish Civil War in Source A and Source B.
2. What reasons are identified in Source C for the bombing of Guernica?

Activity 14

Communication and social skills

1. As effective communicators, you should be able to express ideas and information confidently and creatively in a variety of ways – not just in your written work. Divide the class into groups. Within each group, someone should take on one of the following roles:
   - a Spanish Socialist from Barcelona
   - a Spanish Nationalist from Madrid
   - a French supporter of the Republican government
   - a German supporter of the Nationalist government
   - an Italian supporter of the Nationalist government
   - a Russian Stalinist supporter of the Republican government
   - a British non-interventionist
   - an American supporter of the Lincoln Brigade.

You must now write a speech, which should last around one minute, rallying people to join your forces fighting 'for freedom' in Spain. You must include details of why you believe your perspective to be right, and why people should fight or not intervene. Present your speech to your group, or to the whole class.

The nature of the Spanish Civil War

Although for the foreign powers the war was 'limited', for the Spanish it was a 'total' war as well as a civil war. Propaganda was used on both sides to dehumanize the enemy, even though that enemy was from the same country. Atrocities were common. Meanwhile, the targeting of civilians in bombing raids, symbolized in the attack on Guernica, offered a chilling premonition of what was to come in World War Two. There were no lines drawn between civilian and combatant.

Militarily, the Spanish Civil War seems to have been fought at a crossroads in the evolution of modern warfare. For example, in some cases, cavalry charges proved effective, as in the Nationalist attack north of Teruel in February 1938. However, the importance of new technology – particularly the dominance of airpower – in future wars became clear in Spain, shown by the crushing of the major Republican offensives of 1937 and 1938 by the combined arms of the Condor Legion. Indeed, one of the reasons that the war lasted so long was due to the fact that neither side managed consistently to gain control of the air. Control of the sea was also important, and the Italians played a significant role in maintaining supply routes for the Nationalists.

The war on land was at times similar to the attrition and stalemate battles of World War One. Defence remained easier than attack. In repeated attacks by both sides around Madrid, casualties were high, with attackers taking little ground. In other battles, the changing nature of land warfare could be seen; the tactics of *blitzkrieg* were evolving, with the application of tanks, artillery, and air bombardment to prepare an advance.

The Spanish Civil War did not develop into a guerrilla war because, as Antony Beevor writes:

> *The conditions for a universal guerrilla war simply did not exist. The best-suited regions, with the right terrain, were insufficient to have stretched nationalist forces beyond capacity.*
>
> **Antony Beevor, *The Battle for Spain* (Penguin, 2006).**

Scene from the film *Land and Freedom*, the story of a British Communist who fights for the Republicans during the Spanish Civil War.

Effects of the civil war on Spain

Human cost

The civil war had brought great human and material destruction to Spain. Around 100,000 Republicans were killed during the war, and about 70,000 Nationalists. Moreover, the killing continued after the war, as Franco launched a terror campaign to eradicate opposition. It is estimated that a further 40,000–200,000 were killed during this period, known as the 'White Terror'. Another 250,000 escaped into exile, many ending up in refugee camps in France.

Thousands of Republicans and their sympathizers were held for years in concentration camps and prisons within Spain. Often Republican children were taken from their parents to be 're-educated'. Some were placed with reliable Nationalist/Catholic families, while others were sent to orphanages where they were indoctrinated against the views and actions of their own parents. Divisions and hatred remained in Spanish society for decades.

Impact on the role of women

A female combatant during the Spanish Civil War.

CHALLENGE YOURSELF

ATL Research skills

The historian Anthony Beevor suggests that after the 1936 election victory for the Popular Front coalition a women's movement developed from the belief that the destruction of the class system would also mean the 'end of the patriarchal system' (*The Battle for Spain* (Penguin, 2006), p.107). But following the war, Franco's regime, in line with his ideology, stressed the role of women in society as homemakers and mothers. The emancipation of women that had begun under the Second Republic was ended.

Research the role played by women in the Spanish Civil War and how the war affected their role in society. Overall, the Republican women had a far more equal and active role. Nevertheless, you should not only consider the roles of key figures on the left, such as the Communist Dolores Ibarruri (La Pasionaria) and the anarchist Frederica Montseny, but also the few leading figures on the right, such as Angeles Gil Albarellos and Francisca Bohigas Gavilanes of the CEDA party. Consider the impact of women on the home front and in politics and government as well as their role on the fighting fronts.

Activity 15

ATL Thinking skills

Read the source below and answer the questions that follow.

> *The outbreak of the Spanish Civil War and the need to mobilise society for total war gave women in both zones a dramatically new participation in the functions of both government and society. As in all modern wars, the almost exclusively male preoccupation with violence created the necessity for women to take over the economic and welfare infrastructure. In the Republican zone, women not only played a crucial role in industrial production but also assumed important positions in the political, and even military establishment ... The young, politically committed women who took up arms and went to fight as militiawomen fought with great courage ... However, it was widely assumed by their male comrades that they would be best employed cooking and washing. They were also subjected to considerable sexual pressure and ... to the assumption that they were whores. Behind the lines, women ran public services in transport, welfare and health. That, together with the assumption of the role of traditional bread winner, had a dramatic effect on traditional gender relations. It was short-lived and confined to the public sphere ... As the Francoist forces captured Republican territory ... the feminist revolution of the Second Republic was reversed with extreme savagery ... In the Nationalist zone, there was no comparable emancipation of women. Republican women were punished for their brief escape from gender stereotypes by humiliations both public and private. They were dragged through the streets after having their heads shaved ... in Nationalist prisons they were beaten and tortured.*
>
> **Paul Preston, *Doves of War* (HarperCollins, 2003) p.412.**

1. In what way was there a 'feminist revolution' in the Republican zones according to Preston?
2. To what extent was this revolution limited?
3. Why was there no 'comparable emancipation of women' in the Nationalist zones?

Economic cost

Spain's economy was devastated by the war. Some 10–15 per cent of its wealth was destroyed, and per capita income was 28 per cent lower in 1939 than in 1935. Seventy per cent of Madrid's factory machinery needed to be replaced, and its communications systems, including the city's tram network, had to be rebuilt. Around a third of Spain's merchant shipping was out of action. There was high inflation due to the

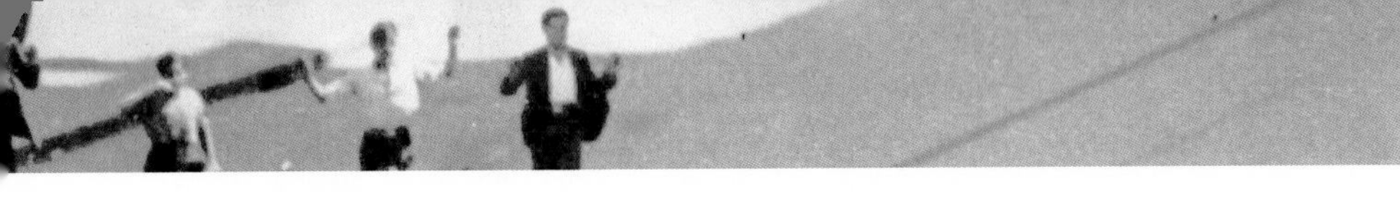

cost of fighting the war, and the method used to attempt to pay for it – printing money. Republican land reform was reversed by Franco, and Spain's agricultural economy remained inefficient and ineffective. Labourers had to tolerate periodic unemployment, and landowners were not interested in modernization. In addition, Spain had massive debts to pay. Due to the human cost of the war, there was a corresponding lack of skilled workers, and an overriding general labour shortage. Spain attempted to find foreign loans for investment, but the British demanded that debt was paid back first, and the Germans also wanted the Spanish to repay the cost of the aid sent to them before further investment was made.

The economy may have improved due to the outbreak of World War Two. Franco seems to have attempted to gain leverage over Spain's debt to Britain and France in August 1939, by offering to remain neutral and not ally Spain with Nazi Germany. He also had discussions with the Germans, presumably offering a similar exchange, in November and December. Once war broke out, Britain and France relented, and signed trade agreements with Spain (France in January 1940, and then Britain in March 1940). But the German exploitation of Spain's resources during World War Two may also have weakened the economy. The original debt remained after the war, and this gave Britain, France, and the USA influence in Franco's Spain. Spain was in isolation after World War Two and suffered famine in 1946. With industrial output at a level below that of 1918, it is possible that Spain's economy was saved by aid from the right-wing Argentine dictator, Juan Perón.

Nevertheless, in the longer term, as the Cold War took hold, Spain became less isolated, and with some reforms in the 1950s and 1960s it developed a powerful Capitalist economy. Spain industrialized and also developed a strong service industry.

Political effects

Franco emerged from the war as Spain's dictator. He remained in power until his death in 1975, ruling, as Paul Preston writes, 'as if it were a country occupied by a victorious foreign army' (*The Spanish Civil War*, HarperPerennial, 2006). Franco's regime declared that they had to save the country from Communism. As we have seen, the White Terror that ensued led to the killing of thousands of Republicans and the exodus of half a million Spaniards, which included many intellectuals – teachers, lawyers, researchers, doctors, and famous writers, poets, artists and musicians. Those that remained had to conform to Franco's authoritarian, Catholic, and conservative views.

In 1939, the Law of Political Responsibility made supporters of the Republicans (either before or during the war) liable to punishment, including confiscation of land, large fines, or even the death sentence. The law allowed for the transfer of vast amounts of land from Republicans to the state.

The key objectives of the new regime were to restore the power of the privileged class and to control the working class. Wages were cut and all industrial political activism was outlawed. The CNT and the UGT were destroyed. Employment for those Republicans who had escaped imprisonment was almost impossible. In rural areas, the inequalities and iniquities of the social and working system, described earlier in this chapter, were preserved and maintained by the Civil Guard.

All of the Republic's reforms concerning the church were repealed, and indeed the 1950s have been termed the 'era of the national church'. The historian Frances Lannon writes:

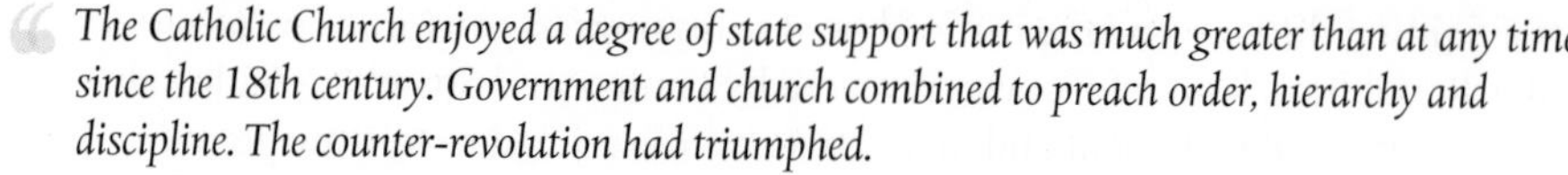

> *The Catholic Church enjoyed a degree of state support that was much greater than at any time since the 18th century. Government and church combined to preach order, hierarchy and discipline. The counter-revolution had triumphed.*
>
> **Frances Lannon, *The Spanish Civil War* (Osprey, 2002), p.88.**

The church took up the cause of the workers, and created links with their movements; Patricia Knight argues this was an attempt to infiltrate and prevent any resurgent Communist groups. The aspirations of the Basques and Catalans for autonomy were also ended. Use of Catalan, Basque, and Galician languages was forbidden and all power was centralized in Madrid. As the historian Paul Preston writes, 'behind the rhetoric of national and social unity, until the death of Franco every effort was made to maintain the division between the victors and the vanquished' (*The Spanish Civil War* (HarperPerennial, 2006), p.233).

The suppression and removal of all political opposition led to a period of political stability in Spain. Fear of state repression meant that Spain appeared more unified than it had been for decades. Nevertheless, the defeat of the Fascist powers in World War Two made Franco more vulnerable. Under pressure from the monarchists, Franco agreed to restore the king, but remained as head of state. The army also lost its pre-eminence in society after Spain's last colony, Morocco, gained its independence in 1956. Without an empire to run, and with no real external or internal threat, the old-style Spanish army became defunct.

Franco increasingly delegated control from the 1960s, and following his death in 1975 democracy was restored.

The international effects of the Spanish Civil War

USSR and Communism

The Communists had been defeated in Spain, and this undermined their international credibility. In addition, Stalin's cynical contribution to the Republican cause, and the divisions it fostered within the left wing, disillusioned many former supporters of the USSR. Thus, the Soviets lost a lot of intellectual sympathy in the West.

Although the war accentuated the hostility between the Soviets and the Germans, it also pushed Soviet foreign policy away from attempting to build an alliance with the Western powers in order to contain Germany, to one based on appeasement of Nazi Germany. It had become clear to Stalin, through their actions in the NIC, that neither Britain nor France would be a sound ally against Hitler's expansionist ambitions. Stalin began to show his interest in a possible deal with Nazi Germany as early as December 1937. His viewpoint was strengthened when Britain decided to sacrifice both Czechoslovakia and Spain in September 1938 – the Munich Agreement was the turning point. Ultimately, the new course Stalin took would lead to the Nazi–Soviet Pact in August 1939.

Hitler's Germany and Mussolini's Italy

Hitler was able to gain valuable military lessons from the war. The importance of air power was highlighted in the initial transport of Franco's forces to the mainland, as was the effectiveness of applying air cover for ground troops in *blitzkrieg*. The Germans were also able to test their bullet-resistant fuel tanks, and they discovered that their armoured vehicles needed to be able to use radio contact. The bombing of civilians also seemed, to some extent, effective. These were all important factors in the success of Hitler's campaign in Europe in 1939–1940. However, others drew the conclusion in March 1937, when the Italians were defeated at Guadalajara, that *blitzkrieg* would not work.

The war brought Germany and Italy closer together, as it further prevented a reconciliation between the members of the Stresa Front. The Rome–Berlin Axis was signed in October 1936 and the Pact of Steel in May 1939. Britain's and France's non-intervention policies and pursuit of appeasement strengthened Hitler's position. Germany also seemed to be the principal country 'defending the world from Communism'.

Hitler's position was also strengthened in Europe as the war provided a distraction from his expansion into Austria and Czechoslovakia. Relations between Franco's Spain and Germany remained good after the World War Two broke out. Although Spain was neutral, Franco allowed German planes and U-boats to refuel there, and continued to trade with Germany.

For Italy, the intervention in Spain was expensive, and, coupled with the expense of Mussolini's other war in Abyssinia, Italy was economically weakened and inclined to remain neutral when a general war began in Europe in September 1939.

Britain and France

The suffering and terror of Spanish civilians who had endured the bombing of their towns and cities made it clear that another general European war would witness horrors on a scale never seen before. This fostered public support for the policy of appeasement, as the fear that the 'bomber would always get through' was reinforced. The polarized political nature of the foreign intervention forces also led to more support for appeasement – it seemed that the warring factions would and should battle it out and exhaust one another without the democracies being dragged into the conflict. The spread of Communism, as it manifested itself in Spain, still appeared the greater threat. However, the apparent 'weakness' of Britain and France over Spain, and their wider policy of appeasement, led Hitler to change his perception of Britain. Although he had initially intended to ally with the British, by 1938 he was losing respect for Britain. Therefore, Britain's attempts to avert war by non-intervention actually encouraged Hitler to be more aggressive.

The USA

The USA remained ostensibly neutral, and although horrified by the atrocities on both sides in the Spanish Civil War, offered no tangible assistance. Indeed, the war strengthened the country's isolationist sentiment. President Roosevelt did make his 'Quarantine the Aggressors' speech in October 1937, in which he called for an international quarantine of the aggressor nations, but his words had little impact on the international situation.

The UN called for economic sanctions against Franco in 1946, and all its member states broke off diplomatic relations. In addition, Spain was excluded from the USA's massive economic recovery package for post-war Europe, Marshall Aid. The initial plan in the West was to wait for a crisis in Spain to bring about the overthrow of Franco. Yet the Americans changed their perspective on Franco's Spain as the Cold

War developed with the USSR. Franco was clearly a strong anti-Communist force and, therefore, in American eyes the 'enemy of my enemy is my friend'. This philosophy transformed into direct economic aid when the Cold War became global in 1950. In 1951, President Eisenhower agreed to the first American grant to Spain, and in return the Americans were permitted to use air bases in Spain. Spain became an ally of the USA and was permitted to join the UN.

Was the Spanish Civil War a cause of World War Two?

A number of key factors suggest that the Spanish Civil War played a significant part in the causes of World War Two:

- It emboldened Hitler by increasing his popularity at home and abroad.
- Hitler drew closer to his former enemy, Italy.
- Hitler gained practical military lessons that he would later apply to his campaigns of 1940.
- It was a distraction for Britain and France and pushed the USA further into isolation.
- It fostered a new direction for Soviet foreign policy, meaning that there could be no broad alliance in Europe to contain Hitler.
- It strengthened support for a policy of appeasement in the democracies.

Alternatively, A.J.P. Taylor, in *The Origins of the Second World War*, concludes that the Spanish Civil War was 'without significant effect' in causing World War Two.

To access weblinks relevant to this chapter, go to www.pearsonhotlinks.com, search for the book title or ISBN, and click on 'chapter 11'.

Activity 16

ATL Thinking and communication skills

Essay planning

Planning essays is an essential way to revise topics as you approach examinations. In pairs or groups, plan out the essays below. Your plan should include:

- an introduction written out in full
- the opening sentence for each paragraph setting out your 'topic'/theme of the paragraph
- bullet points setting out the evidence to go in each paragraph
- a conclusion written out in full.

Each group should present its essay plan to the rest of the class. How much overlap of content is there between the different essay plans?

Here are some hints for your planning in the first three essays.

1. *Discuss the long-term and short-term causes of one 20th-century civil war.*

You could structure this essay thematically, and consider the key issues in the long term and the short term. Your analysis should then explain why there were tensions that intensified over time. Remember to include the 'trigger' of the civil war, as this explains why the war broke out when it did.

- themes 1898–1931 – economic/social/political/military
- themes 1931–1936 – economic/social/political polarization/military (land reforms/church reforms/social unrest/reaction of right/popular front])
- trigger 1936 – the attempted coup.

2. *Examine the political, economic, and social effects of one 20th-century civil war*

You might want to include material from this chapter on the nature and impact of the war in this essay, as well as focusing on the more general results. You should structure your essay to address the political, economic, and social effects of the Spanish Civil War.

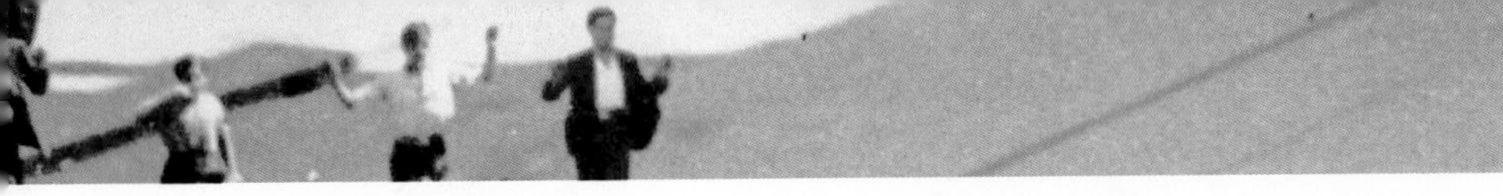

3. *Examine the role of foreign intervention in one 20th-century civil war.*

You could discuss this question in terms of how the 'nature' of the war was affected by foreign intervention:

- polarizing the complex political divisions in Spain
- increasing the brutality and casualty rate
- impacting the way the war was fought
- protracting the war.

You could then discuss this question in terms of how the 'outcome' of the war was affected by foreign intervention:

- Germany/Italy/Portugal: strengthening the military capabilities of the Nationalists
- USSR: weakening the political unity of the Republic, and then undermining its ability to wage war by withdrawing support
- NIC and neutrals benefited the Nationalists.

Now attempt to make detailed plans for the following essay questions:

- ***To what extent did political and religious divisions lead to the outbreak of one 20th-century civil war?***
- ***Discuss the role of economic issues as a cause of one 20th-century civil war.***
- ***Evaluate the impact of foreign intervention on the outcome of one 20th-century civil war.***

Here are some questions that you should consider while planning your essays:

- What are the command terms in the question? What do these suggest about how you should structure your response?
- Is there a quote that you need to refer to/explain/ come back to in your conclusion?
- Does the question require you to make a judgement?
- Where can you include historiography?

Note that IB examiners comment in their reports that the best essays are where candidates have spent 5 minutes of their time planning the essay before they actually start writing.

12 Asia and Oceania region: Chinese Civil War

Mao Zedong, leader of the Chinese Communist Party and Chairman of the People's Republic of China.

Key concepts: Consequence and significance

As you read this chapter, consider the following essay questions:

- Discuss the long-term and short-term causes of one 20th-century civil war.
- To what extent did foreign intervention determine the outcome of one 20th-century civil war?
- Examine the role of guerrilla warfare in determing the outcome of one 20th-century war.

For the first half of the 20th century, China faced political chaos. Following a revolution in 1911, which overthrew the Manchu dynasty, the new Republic failed to take hold and China continued to be exploited by foreign powers, lacking any strong central government. The Chinese Civil War was an attempt by two ideologically opposed forces – the Nationalists and the Communists – to gain central control over China. The struggle between these two forces, which officially started in 1927, was interrupted by the outbreak of the Sino-Japanese war in 1937, but started again in 1946 once the war with Japan was over. The Chinese Community Party ultimately won the war in 1949. The results of this war were to have a major effect not just on China itself, but also on the international stage.

Timeline of events - 1911–1928		
1911		Double Tenth Revolution and establishment of the Chinese Republic
1912		Dr Sun Yixian becomes Provisional President of the Republic Guomindang (GMD) formed and wins majority in parliament Sun resigns and Yuan Shikai declared Provisional President
1915		Japan's Twenty-One Demands Yuan attempts to become emperor
1916		Yuan dies/warlord era begins
1917		Sun attempts to set up republic in Guangzhou Russian Revolution
1918		Paris Peace settlement
1919		May Fourth Movement
1921		Chinese Communist Party (CCP) formed
1922		First United Front established between GMD and CCP
1925		Sun dies National government set up under leadership of GMD
1926		Jiang Jieshi becomes leader of GMD in March Northern Expedition launched in June Tension increases between Jiang and Communist Central Committee
	Jan–Mar	Communist-led strikes in central China threaten Jiang
	Apr	Shanghai massacre of Communists
	July	Communists expelled from GMD
	Dec	Guangzhou massacre
1928	**July**	Jiang has control of Beijing, declares China now united GMD now turns against the Communists

Long-term causes of the Chinese Civil War

Socio-economic factors

In 1900, China was ruled by the imperial Manchu dynasty. The vast majority of the population were peasants. Their life was hard: they worked the land, and most were extremely poor. It was the peasants who paid the taxes that in turn paid for the great Manchu imperial court. It was also the peasants who faced starvation during floods or droughts, as their subsistence farming techniques often left them with barely enough to feed their families. The population in China grew by 8 per cent in the second half of the 19th century, but the land cultivated only increased by 1 per cent. This imbalance made famines more frequent. Peasants' plots of land were reduced, although at the same time landlords increased rents; some peasants had to pay 80 per cent of their harvest. Peasants would be driven to the cities by poverty, where there was already high unemployment due to improved technology and cheap Western imports.

Map of China in 1900.

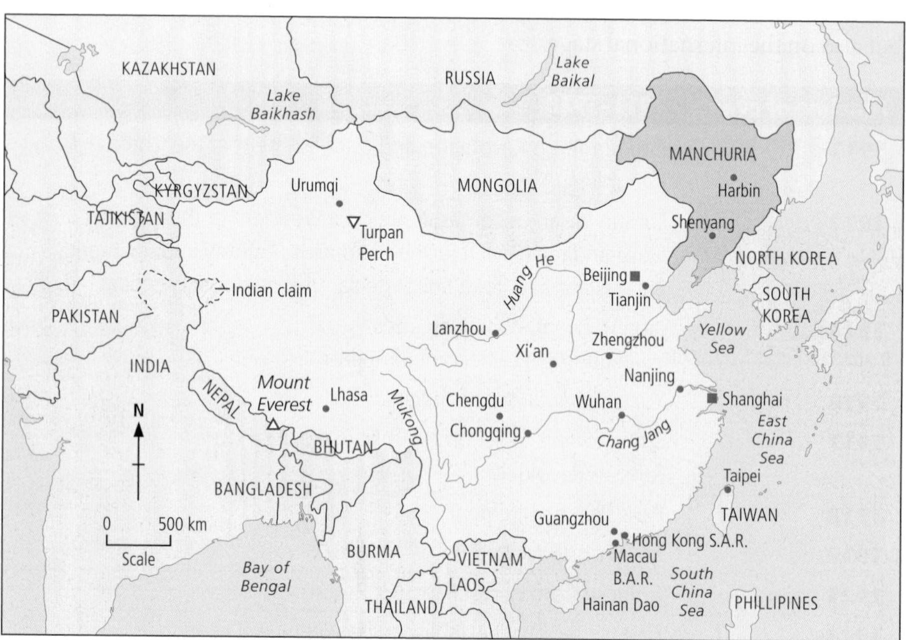

Political weakness and the influence of foreign powers

In the century that preceded the Chinese Civil War, the European imperialist powers had humiliated and exploited China and caused the destabilization of China's ruling Manchu regime. Britain had defeated China in the mid 19th century in the Opium Wars, and subsequently the great Chinese Empire was carved up into spheres of influence by the Europeans, Americans, and, at the end of the 19th century, by Japan.

China had been forced to sign unequal treaties that gave the imperialist powers extraordinary controls over Chinese trade, territory, and ultimately sovereignty. Foreigners refused to abide by Chinese laws, and they had their own extra-territorial courts. In addition, missionaries flooded into China in an attempt to spread Christianity. Inflation and corruption weakened the financial position of the Manchus. Widespread corruption among local and provincial government officials also meant that a large portion of tax revenues did not reach the central government.

In 1850, the Taiping Rebellion spread throughout southern China. The rebellion, which lasted until 1864, was part religious movement, and part political reform movement. It was only after the deaths of millions of Chinese that it was put down by regional armies. This involvement of regional armies began the move away from centralized control, which would result in the **warlord era** in the 1920s.

There had been attempts to resist Western control by sections of the educated elite in China. However, the Self-Strengthening Movement was divided as to how to modernize China, and the Manchus did not coherently support reform. China remained subjugated to the West, and faced the humiliation of defeat in war by Japan in 1895. China lost more territory to Japan when it was part of the settlement in the Russo-Japanese War (1904–1905). The extent of popular anti-Western feeling turned into widespread violent rebellion against Westerners in the Boxer Rebellion in 1899. However, without modern weaponry, the anti-foreign revolt was doomed to fail.

The Self-Strengthening Movement

The Self-Strengthening Movement was a period of reform in China lasting from around 1861 to 1895. It was essentially a response to increasing Western power and influence in China, and was an attempt to resist and redress the concessions that China had been forced to agree to – primarily with Britain. However, the movement was divided on how to 'strengthen' China, and successful reform and development generally failed.

CHALLENGE YOURSELF

Before the arrival of Europeans, China had been a great power in Asia for thousands of years. Research:

- inventions associated with the Chinese
- the political relationship that China had with its neighbouring countries
- the impact of Confucianism on Chinese society
- the Qing dynasty.

This photo of a group of Chinese Boxers illustrates their poor levels of armament compared with the contemporary European and Japanese military forces.

The overthrow of the Manchu dynasty

By the beginning of the 20th century, China was in a desperate condition, and there was a growing feeling that the ruling Manchu dynasty should be overthrown so that China could be Westernized and democracy introduced. The political weakness of the Manchu dynasty intensified with the death of the emperor and the succession of a 2-year-old boy, Pu Yi, in 1908. The former emperor's brother, Prince Chun, ruled as regent, but was not capable of conducting the essential programme of reform. Indeed, he dismissed the potential troublemaker General Jiang Jieshi and humiliated him, and he increased taxation and frustrated the business classes without any socio-economic progress being made.

Sun Yixian

Sun Yixian was the inspirational leader of the Nationalist GMD. He wanted to modernize China by adopting Western political and economic methods. His anti-Manchu government views had led to his exile to Japan. Sun put together his ideas for the future of China in the form of 'the Three Principles of the People' (see the Interesting Fact box below). However, in his view Chinese democracy would not copy that of the West. For China, the key was not the struggle for personal freedom, but for national freedom.

In October 1911, the ruling dynasty was overthrown in a revolution known as the Double Tenth. A republic was created. The revolution began when the government lost control of the military; soldiers in Wuchang revolted and rebellion spread quickly. Most provinces then declared themselves independent of Beijing. The key tensions and issues that led to this revolution would also have a significant effect on the causes of the civil war 15 years later: the impact of imperialism, anti-foreign sentiment, and the weakness of central government.

In November 1911, in an attempt to seize the political initiative, delegates from the 'independent' provinces gathered in Nanjing to declare the creation of a Chinese Republic. Dr Sun Yixian, a political exile, who had been in the USA during the revolution, was invited to be China's first president.

The imperial government attempted to use the former influential general of the Northern Army, Yuan Shikai, to suppress the rebellion, but he double-crossed them by arranging a deal with Sun Yixian. Sun agreed for Yuan Shikai to be president of the new republic in February 1912, in exchange for the end of Manchu rule in China. On 12 February 1912, Emperor Pu Yi abdicated.

The revolution, however, was incomplete. There was no real introduction of democracy, and most former imperial officials kept their positions. The impetus for the revolution was wholly Chinese, but had not been led by the middle classes. It had been the military who ignited the rising and Chinese radicals had joined in later. Michael Lynch argues that the revolution was fundamentally a revolt by the provinces against the centre:

> *The Double Tenth was a triumph of regionalism. It represented a particular phase in the long-running contest between central autocracy and local autonomy, a contest that was to shape much of China's history during the following forty years.*

Michael Lynch, *China: From Empire to People's Republic 1900–49*, 2nd ed. (Hodder, 2010), p.22.

Activity 1

ATL Thinking skills

Review question

1. How had the following weakened China in the century leading up to the civil war?
   - European imperialism
   - failure of modernization
   - regionalism.

The rule of Yuan Shikai

Yuan ruled China as a military dictator from 1912 until 1915. However, the key issues that had led to the revolution in 1911 remained unresolved. Regionalism continued under Yuan's rule and became the key obstacle to a united China. Sun's party reformed as the Guomindang (GMD) in 1912, and declared itself a parliamentary party.

The GMD and the Three Principles

The GMD had been set up by Sun Yixian in 1912. He wanted to create a unified modern and democratic China. He had returned to China after the Double Tenth Revolution in 1911, and established a government in southern China, in Canton. He also saw the need to develop a GMD army. Sun stated that he and his party had three guiding principles:

- Nationalism – to rid China of foreign influence, unite China and to regain its international respect
- Democracy – the people should be educated so that they could ultimately rule themselves democratically
- People's Livelihood – this was essentially 'land reform', the redistribution of land to the peasants, and economic development.

It is argued that Sun agreed to Yuan Shikai's rule in order to avert the possibility of China descending into civil war. The republicans were not powerful enough at this stage to take on the military. It was a lesson that both the GMD and the Chinese Communists would take on board – to win the political battle for China you needed military power.

Sun attempted to undermine Yuan's power by moving him from his power base in Beijing to the south in Nanjing to set up a new government. Yuan refused to leave. At this point the GMD was a regional power only in the southern provinces, and the republicans were not sufficiently organized to mount resistance to Yuan. A 'second revolution' failed and Sun had to flee to Japan in 1913. However, Yuan mastered his own downfall by a series of ill-conceived acts. The 1912 Republican constitution had created regional assemblies, which he abolished in an attempt to centralize power. This act further alienated the provincial powers, especially as tax revenues were centrally controlled. Yuan's final miscalculation was to proclaim himself emperor in 1916. At this point he lost the support of the military and stood down. He died three months later.

Short-term causes of the Chinese Civil War

Political weakness: regionalism – the warlords 1916–1928

A key cause of the civil war in China was the increasing lack of unity in the country by the second decade of the 20th century. Indeed, regionalism or provincialism was to play a significant role not only in causing the war, but also in its course and outcome.

With the abdication and death of Yuan, China lost the only figure that had maintained some degree of unity. China broke up into small states and provinces, each controlled by a **warlord** and his private army. These warlords ran their territories independently, organizing and taxing the people in their domains. They had their own laws and even

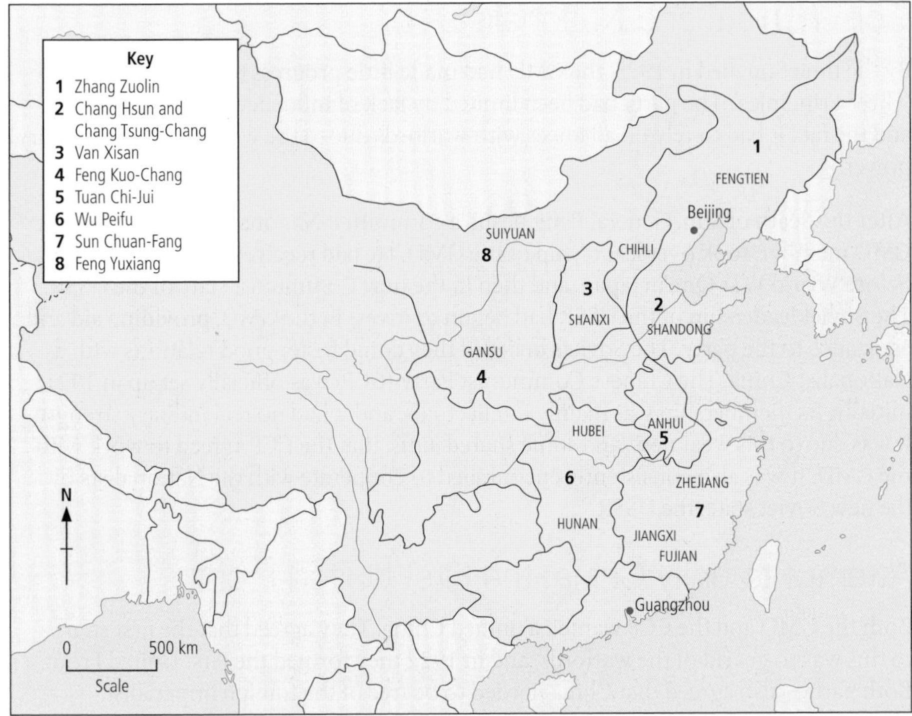

Map of China under the warlords. The marked borders are approximations only, and frequently changed.

The warlords

The warlord era can be divided into two periods: the first, pre-1920, was by default rather conservative (they wanted to preserve their own power and feudal rights); the second phase, after 1920, saw the rise of new military commanders who had not been powerful under the Republic and who were more opportunist. Although they are referred to collectively, the warlords were made up of leaders with very different aims and ambitions.

their own currencies. As warlords extended their power and wealth by expanding their territories, it was the peasants who suffered in their continuous wars. None of the warlords was willing to relinquish his armies or power to the central government.

The warlord period increased the sense of humiliation felt by many Chinese and, coupled with their desire to get rid of foreign influence, led to an increase in nationalism during the decade of warlord rule.

China had all but ceased to exist – it was in a state of internal anarchy. If the warlords remained, China would remain divided.

The May Fourth Movement

During this period, two political movements developed in response to both the warlords and foreign influence in China. The May Fourth Movement began in 1919. Students led a mass demonstration in Beijing against the warlords, traditional Chinese culture, and the Japanese. The hostility had been ignited by the Versailles settlement, in which Japan had been given Germany's former concessions in Shandong province. China, it seemed, had joined the Allies in the war only to be humiliated by them.

The significance of the May Fourth Movement was that it was dedicated to change and the rebirth of China as a proud and independent nation. Some intellectuals and students were inspired by revolutionary ideology in order to achieve these goals. The 1917 Bolshevik Revolution in Russia, led by Marxists, provided a practical example. The new Bolshevik government aimed to set up a socialist state and had also denounced the imperialists saying that all contested border claims would be dropped. Imperialism was perceived by many as the main cause of China's problems.

Other Chinese were inspired by the GMD Nationalist party, which had grown much stronger during the warlord period. Thus two groups – Communists inspired by the Bolshevik revolution in Russia, and Nationalists under the GMD – developed in China at this time. They were to come together in an alliance in 1922.

Communists and Nationalists

By the time Sun died in 1925, the GMD had made little progress towards fulfilling the 'Three Principles'. The party had been limited by lack of influence beyond the south, and the fact it had to rely on alliances with warlords due to the weakness of its military power.

Jiang Jieshi, leader of the Nationalist forces.

After the death of Sun, General Jiang Jieshi, a committed Nationalist and enthusiastic GMD member, took over leadership of the GMD. He had received military training before World War One in Japan, and then in the new Communist state of the USSR. The Soviet leadership of the USSR had begun to invest in the GMD, providing aid and assistance to the party. The Soviets believed they could foster good relations with a Nationalist China. The Chinese Communist Party (CCP) was officially set up in 1921; initially, its membership was mainly intellectuals, and it had no real military strength. It was due to this weakness, and some shared aims, that the CCP agreed to work with the GMD. It was also consistently encouraged to cooperate with the Nationalists by the new Soviet state, the USSR.

Attempt to unify China: the First United Front

Both the GMD and the CCP wanted a unified China. They agreed that the first step to this was to get rid of the warlords, and in 1922 they formed the First United Front. Both parties also agreed that China needed to be free of the foreign imperialist powers. The Third Principle of Sun Yixian, 'the People's Livelihood', was often called 'socialism', which convinced the Comintern that this was a party they could back. In addition, Jiang had studied in Moscow in 1923, and then ran the Whampoa Military Academy, which was set up and funded by the USSR to train GMD officers. Despite his Soviet links, however, Jiang was not a Communist. Indeed, he became increasingly anti-Communist, and began his leadership of the GMD by removing Communists from key positions in the party. He stopped short of breaking off the alliance with the Communists, as he knew that he must first take out his primary obstacle to a unified China – the warlords.

Jiang now determined to act on the first of the Three Principles and attempt to unify China by putting an end to the warlords' power. Together with the Communists, the GMD set out on the 'Northern Expedition' in 1926 to crush the warlords of central and northern China. This operation was a great success; by 1927, the GMD and the Communists had captured Hangzhou, Shanghai, and Nanjing. They took Beijing in 1928. Within 2 years, the United Front of the GMD and the CCP had destroyed the power of the warlords, and the GMD announced that it was the legitimate government of China and the new capital and seat of government would be Nanjing.

Activity 2

Review questions

1. Briefly explain the significance of the following on the development of China up to 1916:
   - Sun Yixian
   - Yuan Shikai
   - warlords
   - May Fourth Movement.
2. What were the key obstacles to setting up an effective central government in China in 1911?
3. What role did foreign involvement play in creating tension in China?

End of the First United Front: the GMD attacks the CCP

Despite the results of the **Northern Expedition**, China was not now unified. The **United Front** was only a friendship of convenience. What had united the CCP and the GMD – the fight against the warlords – was over, and ideology divided the two parties. The success of the Northern Expedition had been not only due to Nationalist ambitions. It was also because of the Communist promise of land to the peasants; this commitment had given them local peasant support. The Communists also had support from the industrial workers: for example, Zhou Enlai, a Communist member of the GMD, had organized the workers rising in Shanghai.

The popular support for the Communists was a key reason that Jiang decided he could no longer tolerate them in the GMD. There could be no more cooperation. Jiang was sympathetic to landlords and the middle classes, and was far more to the right than Sun had been. Areas under Communist control had seen peasants attack landlords and seize land – this could not be tolerated. It seemed to Jiang that the CCP needed to be crushed before China could truly be unified under the GMD.

Jiang now expelled all Communists from the GMD, and his attacks on them reached a peak in Shanghai in the 'White Terror' of April 1927. A powerful 'workers' army' under Zhou Enlai had proved very effective during the Northern Expedition and Jiang turned on them, using informants from the underworld of triads and gangsters – 5,000 Communists were shot. The GMD carried out similar attacks in other cities, in what became known as the 'purification movement': 'purification' meant the massacre of thousands of Communists, trade unionists, and peasant leaders. About a quarter of a million people were killed. Despite attempts to resist (Mao's Autumn Harvest Rising failed), the CCP was very nearly crushed by the end of 1927.

Ignoring the orders of the Comintern to retain the United Front, the CCP decided that its only hope of survival was for its members to flee into the mountains of Jiangsi. The GMD pursued them, determined to destroy the Communists. The civil war had begun.

Map showing the GMD's Northern Expedition, 1926–1928.

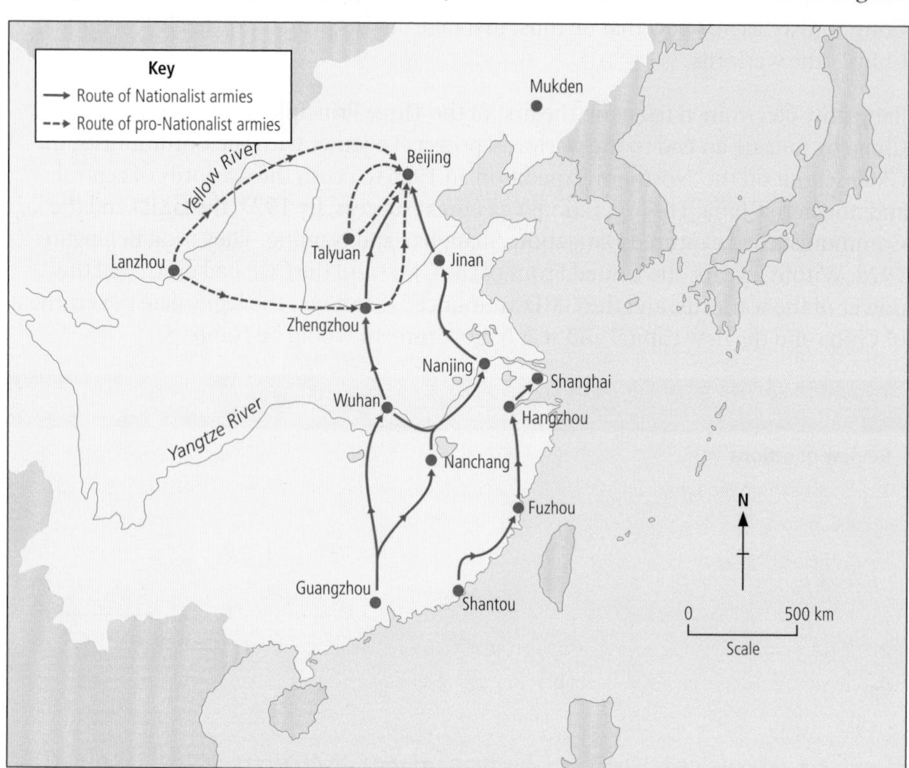

Activity 3

ATL Thinking skills

Source analysis

As his troops approached Shanghai, Chiang (Jiang) was becoming increasingly skeptical of the aims of his communist allies. Already in Ghangzhou there had been bad blood between them. Chiang believed that the Communists were preparing to have him killed. But it was the sudden success of the march north that drove the alliance apart. The CCP and the Soviets saw Chiang as a potential military dictator, a Napoleon. Chiang on his side, was becoming increasingly worried that after the liberation of China from Western influence, the CCP and the left wing of the Guomindang would put the country under Soviet control. In his diary, Chiang was increasingly critical of his Soviet advisers: 'I treat them with sincerity, but they reciprocate with deceit.' The Communists were criticizing Chiang in public and preparing to take control of Shanghai from within before his troops arrived. The clock was ticking for a confrontation.

Odd Arne Westad, *Restless Empire* (Bodley Head, 2012), pp.163–164.

1. According to Westad, why was a confrontation between the CCP and GMD likely to take place after the Northern Expedition?

Activity 4

ATL Thinking and self-management skills

Review questions

1. Why did support for Communism grow in China?
2. Why did Jiang turn against the Communists?
3. In groups, create a diagram (mind map or flow diagram) on a large sheet of paper to show the causes of the first period of civil war in China. Decide what themes you want to develop, how you are going to show long-term and short-term causes, and how you are going to show any links between the causes. Each group should then present and explain its diagram to the rest of the class.

The course of the war

Timeline of events – 1930–1950		
1930–1931		Jiang's First Encirclement campaign attacks Jiangxi Soviet, defeated by CCP
1931		Japanese attack Manchuria
		28 Bolsheviks take over Central Committee of CCP Jiang launches Second and Third Encirclement Campaigns against Jiangxi Soviet; both are defeated
1932		Japanese attack Shanghai Jiangxi Soviet declares war on Japan Fourth Encirclement Campaign begins
1933		Truce with Japan Fifth Encirclement Campaign
1934		Long March begins
1935		Survivors of Long March reach Shaanxi Soviet base
1937	Apr	Second United Front is formed
	July	Japanese invade China
	Nov	Jiang Jieshi moves government to Chongqing
	Dec	Rape of Nanjing
1940	Aug	Hundred Regiments assault on Japanese by Red Army
1944	Oct	US commander General Joseph Stilwell leaves China at Jiang Jieshi's request
1945	Aug–Oct	US Ambassador Hurley leads talks between GMD and CCP
	Sept	Japan formally surrenders in China theatre
	Oct	Agreement announced, but both sides send forces to Manchuria
	Dec	US General George C. Marshall arrives to lead negotiations
1946	Jan	Truce between CCP and GMD
	Mar	USSR begins to withdraw from Manchuria Fighting breaks out in Manchuria between GMD and CCP
1947	Jan	Marshall leaves China
	Mar	Jiang Jieshi takes Yan'an
	Oct	Mao announces land reforms
1948	Apr	US Congress passes China Aid Act – aid sent to GMD again
	Nov	Battle of Huai-Hai begins

Timeline of events - 1930–1950		
1949	**Jan**	GMD lose Battle of Huai-Hai
	Apr	CCP captures Nanjing
	May	CCP takes Shanghai
	Oct	Mao announces the establishment of the People's Republic of China in Beijing
	Dec	Jiang flees to Taiwan

Activity 5

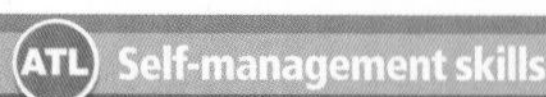

1. Look back at chapter 1 and the section on guerrilla tactics. The Chinese Civil War is a good example of guerrilla tactics working successfully against a stronger force. As you read through the rest of this chapter, note the rules for guerrilla fighting that were established by Mao, and how and why they were so successful.

Mao Zedong (Mao Tse-Tung)

Born in 1893 to a wealthy peasant family in Hunan province, in south-east China, Mao left work on the land initially to be a teacher. In 1918, he moved to Beijing and worked as a librarian at the university there. The university was a centre for many contrasting ideologies and revolutionary ideas, including Marxism. Indeed, Mao by this stage had been interested in anarchism too. Mao then moved back to Hunan and began to develop and practise his political ideas, demonstrating his skill as a trade union leader and peasant organizer. He was responsible for the shift in CCP policy from attempting to win industrial workers' support in the cities to concentrating on radicalizing the peasantry. This shift was also a realistic response to the CCP's failures to take the towns, where GMD support was strong. In 1931, Mao became the elected chairman of the Central Executive Committee of the CCP. From this time, and in this position, he began to consolidate his control over the party.

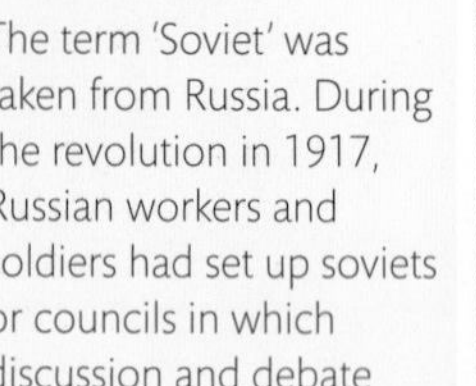

Jiangxi Soviet

The term 'Soviet' was taken from Russia. During the revolution in 1917, Russian workers and soldiers had set up soviets or councils in which discussion and debate took place.

Research Marx's theory of revolution. Explain how Mao's ideas were different from Marx's belief (and thus the Soviet model) of how revolution should take place.

The Jiangxi Soviet

The CCP were forced to retreat into Jiangxi province in order to survive the GMD onslaught. This territory become known as the 'Jiangxi Soviet'. Mao's writings suggest that the White Terror had only confirmed what he had already thought about the United Front: that this cooperation with the GMD would destroy the CCP. He also believed that the GMD and the Comintern had the wrong strategy for China, as they focused their revolution on urban areas. Mao's revolution would be based on the peasants. Essentially, this was a more realistic strategy, as the vast majority of Chinese were not urban workers but rural peasants. From a population in China of around 500 million, only 12 per cent were in urban areas, whereas 88 per cent lived in rural regions. From a total workforce of approximately 259 million, 205 million were agricultural workers and a mere 54 million were non-agricultural or industrial workers. Mao arrived at Jiangxi and organized the Jiangxi Soviet around his idea of the central revolutionary role of the peasant – 'The peasants are the sea; we are the fish. The sea is our habitat', he stated. His ideological shift away from orthodox Marxism, which placed the proletariat at the centre of the revolution, put him at odds with more orthodox members of the CCP. But his success in recruiting and organizing the peasants in the Jiangxi Soviet began to win him the argument.

Division within the CCP

Both the CCP and the GMD suffered from 'internal factionalism' during this period of the civil war. Mao's views on the revolution and how the civil war should be fought could be summarized, by 1930, in the following key points:

- The revolution will be carried out by the peasant masses, thus the peasants will be mobilized and politicized by the Red Army.
- The army's tactics will be guerrilla warfare.
- Land reform will be carried out in their areas of control.

Yet his views were not shared by the Soviet Union and the Comintern. The USSR saw the Great Depression as the beginning of the end of Capitalism, and believed that the world was on the brink of international revolution. In February 1930, Comintern official Li Lisan issued an instruction to all CCP members to attack cities in Jiangxi and Hunan. This order was known as the 'Li Lisan Line'. All the attacks failed, and the Communist army was forced into retreat. (The Comintern then blamed Li Lisan by saying he had misunderstood its orders.) The CCP in the cities was shattered, and it appeared that the party could only hold its influence in rural areas. Li Lisan was dismissed from his leadership of the CCP in January 1931.

The GMD attempts to exterminate the CCP

From 1928 to 1934, Jiang had the chance to carry out Sun's Three Principles. His government was ineffective, however, and Jiang made no progress towards democracy or land reform. His support came from landlords and the rich, and so initiatives were limited to the building of some roads and the construction of more schools. Jiang also had to face the threat of the Japanese, who took control of Manchuria in 1931.

Mao and the 28 Bolsheviks

During the military campaigns of the early 1930s Mao's position was being eroded and marginalized by the 28 Bolsheviks. The *coup de grâce* came in July 1934, when by order of the Comintern Mao was put on probation and barred from meetings. From July until the beginning of the Long March in October, when he was released, he was under house arrest.

Jiang's main goal remained the elimination of the Communists, and during this time he carried out the 'Five Encirclement Campaigns' in an attempt to destroy the Jiangxi Soviet and the CCP. The GMD strategy was to encircle the Reds and cut them off from supplies and resources. The Communists focused their strategy on survival, and based themselves in the mountains between Hunan and Jiangxi provinces. Here they built up their military force – the Red Army. Mao explained his strategy in a letter to Li Lisan in 1929: 'The enemy advances, we retreat; the enemy halts, we harass; the enemy tires, we attack; the enemy retreats, we pursue.'

Li Lisan was replaced by a group of Moscow graduates known as the '28 Bolsheviks' and the influence of the Comintern remained strong enough to remove Mao as chief commissar of the Red Army. Mao did not like these 'inexperienced men'.

The first three campaigns were launched between December 1930 and September 1931. The Red Army under Mao and Zhou Enlai faced increasingly strong GMD forces, first 100,000, then 200,000, and finally 300,000 men – and they defeated all three. Using Mao's strategy of revolutionary war, they allowed the GMD to enter their territory and begin to round up Communists, and then they attacked the fragmented units. Their knowledge of the terrain and their use of the support of the local peasants meant that they could choose the place and timing of their engagements.

Mao was not involved in the Fourth Encirclement Campaign. Zhu De was commander-in-chief of the Red Army, and he used the same tactics as before with the same results – the GMD was forced back again in March 1933.

Activity 6

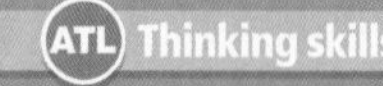

Source analysis

Source A

We split up into small, swift combat units which got in their rear and on their flanks and attacked, cutting them into segments. There's nothing secret about such tactics … [The GMD] failed because such guerrilla warfare requires not only a thorough knowledge of the terrain of the battle area but also the support of the common people.

Zhu De, Red Army leader.

Source B

The eight rules of the Red Army:

Return and roll up the straw matting on which you sleep.
Be courteous and polite to the people and help them when you can.
Return all borrowed articles. Replace all damaged articles.
Be honest in all transactions with the peasants. Pay for all articles purchased.
Replace all doors when you leave a house.
Be sanitary, and, especially, establish latrines a safe distance from people's houses.

The Eight Rules of the Red Army (1928), quoted by the American journalist Edgar Snow.

Source C

The GMD troops burned down all the houses in the surrounding area, seized all the food there and blockaded us … We were sick and half-starved. The peasants were no better off, and we would not touch what little they had. But the peasants encouraged us. They dug up from the ground the grain they had hidden from the GMD troops and gave it to us … they wanted us to win. Tactics are important, but we could not exist if the majority of our people did not support us. We are nothing but the fist of the people beating their oppressors.

Statement by CCP general Peng Dehuai, in 1936.

1. According to Source A, how was guerrilla warfare waged?
2. According to Sources B and C, why would the CCP have the support of the peasants?
3. Why was peasant support so crucial to the CCP?
4. Using these sources and your own knowledge, explain why Mao's guerrilla tactics were successful in this first phase of the Chinese Civil War. (See also chapter 1 for more discussion of guerrilla tactics.)

The Long March

Seven months later, in October, Jiang attempted his fifth and final campaign against the 'bandits'. On this occasion he had taken the advice of a German general: to adopt a gradual approach. This time a force of 800,000 men was sent in, with air cover and artillery. The Red Army could not take advantage of its previous strengths of higher mobility and local support. Outnumbered and surrounded by GMD forces, it fought and lost a final battle at Ruijin in 1934.

Military Strategy 1930–1934		
1930–1931	**1932–1933**	**1934**
Mao in charge ▼ Guerrilla warfare ▼ GMD Encirclement Campaigns 1–3 ▼ GMD campaigns 1–3 fail	Zhu De in charge of Red Army ▼ Guerrilla warfare ▼ GMD Encirclement Campaign 4 ▼ GMD campaign 4 fails	The 28 Bolsheviks in charge of Red Army ▼ 'Stand and fight' ▼ GMD Encirclement Campaign 5 (began 1933) ▼ GMD campaign 5 succeeds – German military advice. Red Army breaks out / Long March

The CCP faced annihilation. Mao decided that the only chance the CCP had was to break through the GMD's lines and set up another base. They succeeded in doing this on 19 October and then embarked on what became known as the 'Long March'. The Long March took the CCP on a seemingly impossible 9,600-kilometre trek to Shaanxi across some of the most inhospitable territory in China. It took 368 days and it led to the death of more than 90 per cent of the 90,000 Communists that broke through their encirclement at Jiangxi.

Activity 7

ATL Social and communication skills

The impact of the Long March

1. What was the Long March and why was it significant to the outcome of the Chinese Civil War?
2. In small groups, research the course and key turning points of the Long March, using the information that follows as a starting point. Your group will be writing the script of a short play or documentary based on your research. It should include the key events listed below, any extra information from your own research, areas of controversy, and an explanation of why the Long March remains important in Chinese history. You could also include historical characters and quotations from contemporaries.

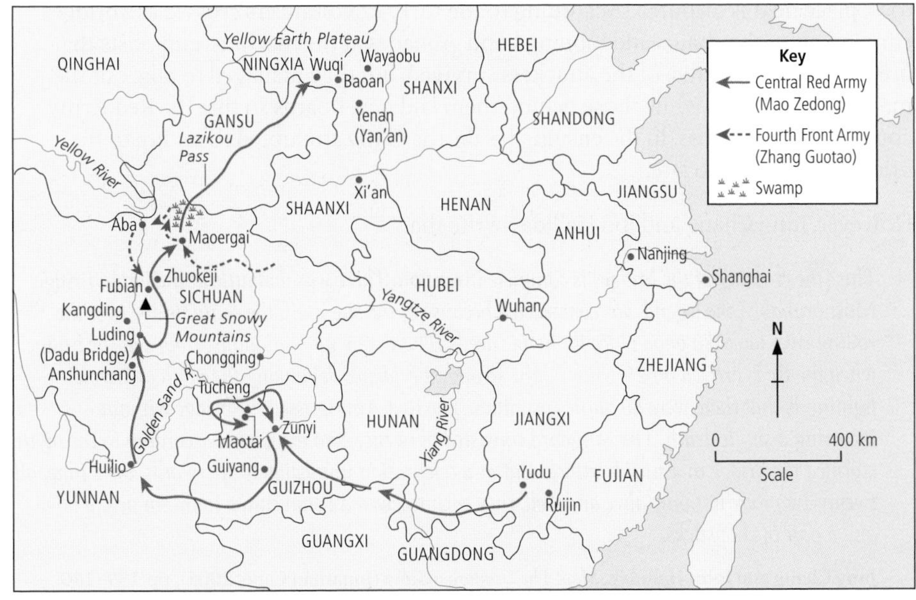

Map showing the route of the Long March.

Key events of the Long March

Crossing the Xiang River

The Xiang River was strongly defended by the GMD, and Jiang was determined not to let the CCP escape. Mao criticized the strategy the CCP used at the river, where around 50,000 died. The CCP had not used his tactics of outmanoeuvring and deceiving the GMD; they had also been loaded down with furniture and other unnecessary equipment. The 28 Bolsheviks, now in charge of the army, had simply led the CCP in a line into the river, where they were 'sitting ducks' for Jiang's forces.

The Zunyi Conference resolutions

Mao left the Zunyi Conference with a list of resolutions that summarized some of his key military ideas:

- Being weaker than the enemy, the Red Army was to concentrate its forces for selected decisive battles.
- Battles were to be avoided when victory was not certain.
- The enemy was to be lured in deep; giving up territory was not necessarily bad from a military point of view.
- The Red Army was a propagandizing team as well as a fighting force.
- Every soldier was to be told the aims and dangers of every move.

Adapted from Ross Terrill, *Mao: A Biography* (Stanford University Press, 2000), p.154

Zunyi Conference

In January 1935 the CCP, this time using guerrilla tactics, managed to capture the town of Zunyi. The 28 Bolsheviks had been discredited due to their disasters at Jiangxi and the Xiang River. At a party conference held here to determine future CCP policy, Mao established a much stronger hold over the party.

Upper Yangtze River Crossing

At Zunyi, Mao ordered that his forces 'march north to fight the Japanese', and now led the Red Army towards Sichuan to meet up with the 40,000-strong Communist army under the leadership of Zhang Guotao. Jiang pursued Mao across the far-western provinces of Yunnan and Tibet. The GMD destroyed all the boats at the Yangtze River crossing in an attempt to rout Mao's forces. Mao deceived the Nationalists that his army was constructing a bridge to cross, but sent units to a town 136 kilometres further along. Thus, while the bridge was being built, the CCP crossed the river in another place. Mao's forces got across before the GMD realized what was going on.

The Luding Bridge

Just two weeks later, with Mao forcing the pace, covering 134 kilometres in just 24 hours, the Red Army came to the Dadu River. Local people had built a bridge, using their own resources to pay for it, from 13 heavy iron chains covered by wooden planks. The river was very fast moving, but here was the only way to cross. The GMD could, and should, have blown up the bridge, but this action would have led to local outcry. Instead Jiang's forces removed the planks that covered the chains. What took place next is disputed. According to the CCP, 22 volunteers crossed the bridge, clinging on to the chains and lobbing hand grenades at the machine-gun posts that fired on them. Only five of the attackers survived, but they managed to take out the machine-gun posts, while those behind them laid new boards so that the Red Army could then rush across. In the ensuing battle, the GMD attempted to set fire to the bridge, but it was too late.

However, Jung Chang and Jon Halliday write that:

> *This [the crossing of the bridge] is complete invention. There was no battle at the Dadu Bridge. Most probably, the legend was constructed because of the site itself: the chain bridge over the roiling river looked a good place for heroic deeds. There were no Nationalist troops at the bridge when the Reds arrived on 29 May … the strongest evidence debunking the myth of 'heroic' fighting is that there were no battle casualties. The Red Amy crossed the bridge without incurring a single death. The vanguard consisted of twenty-two men, who, according to the myth stormed the bridge in a suicide attack. But at a celebration immediately afterwards, on 2 June, all twenty-two were not only alive and well, they each received a Lenin suit, a fountain pen, a bowl and a pair of chopsticks.*
>
> **Jung Chang and John Halliday, *Mao: The Unknown Story* (Jonathan Cape, 2005), pp.159–160.**

Disputes between Zhang Guotao, Zhu De, and Mao

The Long March became a much mythologized episode in Chinese Communist history. Here an idealized poster celebrates the march and its participants.

Mao had 10,000 left in his army, and this force finally met up with 45,000 men under the command of Zhang in Sichuan. The two leaders disagreed on what the Red Army's next move should be. Mao wanted to go north to the Shaanxi Soviet, where they could fight the Japanese. Zhang wanted to stay in western Sichuan, or go further west to have closer access to the USSR. They could not agree and ended up going separate ways. Zhu De decided to go with Zhang, and the two generals took the majority of forces with them. The GMD attacked them, split their forces, and Zhu fled to join Mao. Zhang's forces were virtually destroyed.

Songpan Marshes

To get to Shaanxi, Mao had to cross the unmapped and deadly Songpan Marshes, where men sank into the mud and drowned, faced attack from local tribes, and ate poisonous plants in an attempt to fend off starvation. Of the 10,000 that entered the marshes, only 7,000 made it across the 400-kilometre region.

Shaanxi

After marching 9,600 kilometres, and fighting 15 major battles and many smaller skirmishes, Mao's army arrived at the Shaanxi Soviet in October 1935. Here they set up a Communist base centred on the town of Yan'an.

Activity 8

ATL Thinking skills

Source analysis

Source A

Has there ever been in history a long march like ours? No, never. The Long March is also a manifesto. It proclaims to the world that the Red Army is an army of heroes and that the imperialists and their jackals, Jiang Jieshi and his like, are perfect nonentities. It announces the bankruptcy of the encirclement pursuit, obstruction and interception attempted by the imperialists and Jiang Jieshi. The Long March is also an agitation corps. It declares to the approximately two hundred million people of eleven provinces that only the road of the Red Army leads to their liberation. Without the Long March, how could the broad masses have known so quickly that there are such great ideas in the world as are upheld by the Red Army? The Long March is also a seeding machine. It has sown many seeds in eleven provinces, which will sprout, grow leaves, blossom into flowers, bear fruit and yield a crop in future. To sum up, the Long March ended with our victory and the enemy's defeat.

Mao reminiscing on the Long March.

Source B

When Mao finally arrived back at the Red area in north Shaanxi that was to be his base, his army was down to well below 4,000. In the last – and easiest – month of the journey, he actually lost more than half of his remaining men, between deserters, stragglers and deaths both from illness and at the hands of his own security men ... And the troops were in the worst possible shape. One officer recalled:

'We were famished and exhausted. Our clothes in particular were in shreds. We had no shoes or socks, and many people wrapped their feet with strips of blanket ... Wuqi [where they arrived] was already a very poor place but even the ... local comrades kept questioning me: how come you got into such a sorry state?'

Jung Chang and John Halliday, *Mao: The Unknown Story* (Jonathan Cape, 2005), p.172.

1. According to Mao, what was the significance of the Long March?
2. Discuss the differences between the traditional interpretation of the events at Dadu Bridge and the accounts of the Long March given by Chang and Halliday. Why might these accounts differ? You should consider the origin and purpose of each source.

Mao and revolutionary warfare

Mao's war against the GMD can be classed as a revolutionary war, as he was trying not only to defeat the GMD but also to impose a revolutionary ideology on the Chinese people.

The choice the Chinese people had was between **Maoism**, with its total restructuring of society, economy and government, and the Nationalists' policy, which basically involved maintaining the status quo. Mao believed that the peasants were central to revolutionary war, and so his priority had to be to persuade them to support the Communist cause.

Mao's revolutionary warfare consisted of several stages:

Setting up base areas

Mao planned to set up 'base areas' in which he would organize the peasants and educate them in Communist ideology. They would then, it was hoped, accept new taxes and justice systems applied by the CCP, which would be better than those they had previously endured. These base areas would be remote and thus difficult for the GMD to interfere with during this 'education process'. A constituent of the 'Eight rules of the Eighth Route Army' was to treat everyone with respect, and this very powerful idea helped to gain the support and trust of the peasants.

The organization phase

Once a base camp was set up, CCP leaders would be sent out to other villages to repeat the process. Mao called this the 'organization phase'. The aim was slowly to take over the countryside, thereby isolating the cities to allow the CCP ultimately to take political control of China.

Defending the bases

The next stage was to defend the base areas, which would not remain free from GMD attack, especially once GMD taxes were going to the CCP. Mao organized the peasants to use hit-and-run tactics, their advantage being knowledge of terrain and support of the local population. If the GMD attempted to hunt down the CCP units, they would be drawn into hostile areas, which would enable the guerrillas to attack them again and/or disappear into the local community. In this way, the 'enemy' would become demoralized and worn down. Any attempt by the GMD to wipe out the CCP presence with massive attacks and looting of villages would only increase hostility to the Nationalists and improve the position of the Communists.

The guerrilla phase

The communists could always survive by retreating, as they had in the Long March. Other bases could be set up as they retreated – these would then create more guerrilla fighters. This was the 'guerrilla phase' of the war.

Protracted war

Mao understood that his strategy would lead to a long war; indeed, the idea of a 'protracted war' was central to his thinking. However, as the numbers of guerrillas grew, and in turn the number of attacks on the enemy increased, the balance would finally tilt in favour of the guerrillas.

Seizing power

At this stage, the revolutionary war would go into the 'open or mobile phase', where guerrilla units joined together to form a conventional army. The CCP was in this last stage of guerrilla warfare when the second phase of the civil war broke out in 1946. Once in power, a period of consolidation would be needed to rid China of the remnants of the 'old regime'.

End of the first stage of the Chinese Civil War – the Second United Front, 1937

The Long March was essential for ensuring the survival of the CCP and also for making Mao the unchallenged leader. Jiang Jieshi was still determined to defeat the Communists, but he also had to deal with the threat from Japan. China had been invaded in 1931 when the Japanese took over Manchuria. Jiang initially did little about this apart from appealing to the League of Nations, as he still regarded the Communists as the more dangerous threat. He said that the Japanese 'were a disease of the skin while the Communists were a disease of the heart'.

Jiang unsuccessfully attempted to resist the Japanese attacks on Shanghai in 1932, and in May agreed to a truce. The Japanese advanced to the Great Wall in January 1933, however, and their growing control in China led to a great increase in anti-Japanese sentiment.

CHALLENGE YOURSELF

Research skills 

Research the attack on China by Japan. Why was Manchuria so appealing to Japan? What was the Mukden incident and its consequences for China, Japan, and for international relations at the time?

Mao called for another 'United Front' to fight the Japanese, and this was supported by all who had suffered under Japanese occupation, including the northern warlords Zhang Xueliang and Yan Xishan. Yet in the end it was the Comintern and not Mao that pushed the alliance between the CCP and the GMD. Stalin was worried about Japanese expansion in and from Manchuria. By 1936 he saw Jiang Jieshi as the only leader in China who could effectively fight them. The Second United Front was sealed when Jiang Jieshi was kidnapped in Xi'an by the warlord Zhang (he had been there planning his next assault on the CCP). This shocked both the Chinese and the Soviets, and although some of the kidnappers wanted to shoot Jiang, he was released on Comintern orders after 13 days.

Activity 9 — ATL Thinking skills

The kidnapping of Jiang

From all segments of society came requests for [Zhang] to release Chiang (Jiang). Most people did not believe that China could organize against Japan except under the Generalissimo's leadership. Even Stalin and the Soviets chimed in, since they believed that all alternative leaders to Chiang would be less likely to wage successful war against Japan. Zhou Enlai, Mao's second in command in the CCP, went to Xi'an to secure Jing's release. While Mao must have been fuming at seeing his archenemy get away, he knew that Stalin was keeping an eye on his every action, and that there was no other way out. He may even, in his heart of hearts, have agreed with the majority of his countrymen: With Chiang there might be little hope of ever defeating the Japanese, but without him there was not hope at all.

Odd Arne Westad, *Restless Empire* (Bodley Head, 2012), p.255.

1. According to Westad, why was Jiang released after being kidnapped?

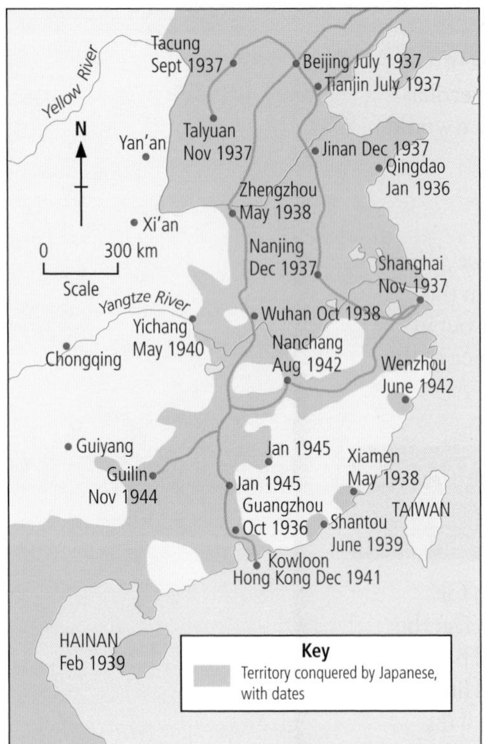

Japanese expansion in China, 1937–1944.

In April 1937 the Second United Front was formed. The civil war was suspended, and there was instead a 'National War of Resistance'. The GMD would benefit from support from the USSR, and potentially aid from the USA. The CCP benefited from the legitimacy the alliance gave them – they could no longer be dismissed as 'bandits'. The Communists also hoped that the war against Japan would exhaust the GMD.

The start of the war proper between Japan and China was triggered by an incident at the Marco Polo Bridge. There is no evidence that the clash between Japanese and Chinese troops that took place here was engineered by the Japanese. However, the fighting quickly spread, and by the end of July the Japanese had captured Beijing. In August, in the battle for Shanghai, Jiang Jieshi's forces were forced to retreat after losing around 300,000 troops. The capital, Nanjing, was relocated 1,200 kilometres to the west, to Chongqing, for the remainder of the war. Nanjing was left to face the onslaught of the Japanese. The atrocities that were then perpetrated there became known as the 'Rape of Nanjing' (see page 155).

Why was the CCP able to survive the first stage of the Chinese Civil War?

The final victory of the CCP after 1945 could never have occurred had it not been for their successes between 1928 and 1936. Why were they successful in this period?

CCP successes

- The Long March ensured CCP survival and offered a defensible base in Yan'an. It was also a propaganda victory for the CCP, who were able to use the journey to proclaim their policies to many thousands of people. They also won patriotic support for their claim to be going north to fight the Japanese.
- The march also confirmed Mao as the leader of the CCP, gave the CCP a good deal of fighting experience, and welded the survivors into a very tight, dedicated group of fanatical revolutionaries.
- Mao's offer to create a joint front with the GMD against the Japanese again won the CCP popularity, allowing them to pose as the true nationalists.

GMD errors

In contrast to the CCP, the GMD forces made several errors. Their decision to deal with the CCP before the Japanese lost them patriotic support. In addition, the poor treatment of peasants by the GMD forces further degraded their popularity. They had also failed to implement Sun's Three Principles (see page 256).

The Sino-Japanese War

The events of the war against Japan were key to explaining both the reasons for the outbreak of the second phase of the civil war and also the ultimate victory of the CCP.

The impact of the war on the GMD

The GMD withdrew its capital to Chongqing. As large areas of the GMD's support base were under Japanese occupation, Jiang Jieshi lost much-needed tax revenue. He faced the problem by printing more money, which led to high levels of inflation, and in turn impacted badly on the middle classes, who were the natural supporters of the GMD. The peasantry were also hardest hit by taxes. Other problems faced the GMD:

- Corruption was rife in the GMD army, and its troops were ill-treated and unmotivated. Conscription further alienated the peasantry.
- Although the USA sent aid to the GMD, Japanese control of the coastal ports and key land routes meant that only limited supplies could come in via the Himalayas.
- The GMD remained riddled with factions throughout the war. With rising discontent against his rule due to corruption, military failures, and inflation, Jiang Jieshi's response was increased repression, which exacerbated hostility towards the government.
- Territorially, the GMD lacked control over many of China's provinces. It really only controlled the territory around its capital in central China and areas of the south.
- The war exhausted the GMD physically and psychologically. They bore the brunt of the Japanese attacks in the early stages of the war, and throughout they continued to meet the Japanese in conventional battles, which resulted in heavy losses. Meanwhile, the CCP was fighting a guerrilla war, incurring only light losses.
- The public lost a lot of respect for the GMD in the later stages of the war, as it appeared to be waiting for the Americans to win the war.

Activity 10

Source analysis

The Communists got their chance because the Nationalists failed so completely … [The Nationalists'] notorious corruption resulted in hoarding and profiteering while millions of peasants starved … The Nationalist army was a scandal. It was largely led by incompetent generals who owed their position to cronyism … Soldiers died more from lack of food or medicine than from battlefield wounds; 10% of the army probably had tuberculosis. The army made enemies rather than friends out of the people. Peasants were conscripted into the ranks by force … often shackled to one another … it was so hated that peasants often killed Nationalist soldiers who fell into their hands ...

From June Grasso, Jay Corrin, and Michael Kort, *Modernization and Revolution in China: From the Opium Wars to the Olympics* (M.E. Sharpe, 2009), p.113.

1. Using this source, identify the key problems within the GMD army.
2. With reference to its origin, purpose, and content, assess the value and limitations of using this source to find out about the GMD's army?

The impact of the war on the CCP

Mao used the war against the Japanese to carry out his revolutionary warfare. Indeed, Mao said that 'our fixed policy should be 70 per cent expansion, 20 per cent dealing with the GMD and 10 per cent resisting the Japanese'. By March 1945, the Communists had liberated 678 out of 914 country towns and had implemented their policies in them: land reform, setting up village schools and village soviets, reducing taxes, and abolishing debt. The historian James Sheridan writes that the reason they achieved the enthusiastic backing of the peasants was 'by meeting the local, immediate needs of the peasants through reformist and radical social policies and by providing leadership for the defence of peasant communities against the Japanese. In this fashion the communists won peasant confidence and in the process began the transformation – the modernization – of rural China' (*China in Disintegration* (Free Press, 1977), p.264).

The Dixie Mission

The US Army sent an 'Observation Group', known as the Dixie Mission, to establish relations with the CCP in July 1944. The mission lasted until March 1947. Its task was to analyse the CCP politically and militarily in order to establish whether the American war effort would benefit from working with the CCP. John S. Service was responsible for analysing the CCP politically, and Colonel David D. Barrett was the military analyst.

The Dixie Mission's initial feedback was positive; it suggested that Yan'an was more effectively governed than other GMD-held territories, and was in general less corrupt. It also suggested that the CCP could be a useful military ally in China. The Dixie Mission also hosted the failed attempts by the Americans to broker an alliance between the CCP and the GMD. Their analysis of the potential of the CCP to be a sound post-war ally was not taken on board by the US government either. Indeed, those involved with the Dixie Mission were later accused of being Communist sympathizers in the 1950s, and were persecuted during the McCarthy era.

Members of the Dixie Mission in Yan'an.

The Rectification Campaign

The Rectification Campaign/Movement was initiated by the Communists to reinforce their ideology, but quickly became a campaign against intellectuals and anyone who was not in line with Maoist thinking. After approximately 10,000 people had been killed, the campaign led to Mao's position and leadership in the CCP being confirmed.

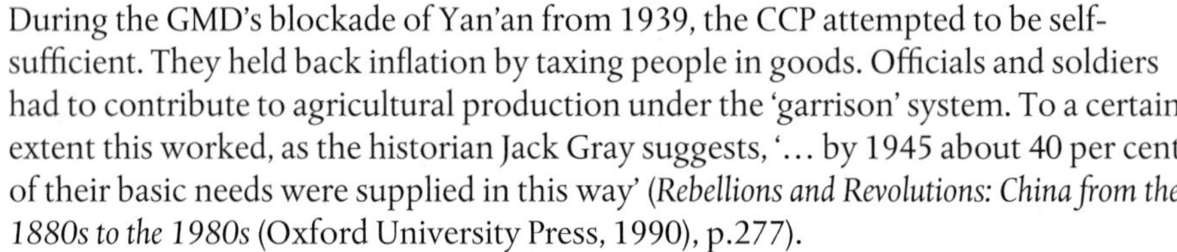

During the GMD's blockade of Yan'an from 1939, the CCP attempted to be self-sufficient. They held back inflation by taxing people in goods. Officials and soldiers had to contribute to agricultural production under the 'garrison' system. To a certain extent this worked, as the historian Jack Gray suggests, '… by 1945 about 40 per cent of their basic needs were supplied in this way' (*Rebellions and Revolutions: China from the 1880s to the 1980s* (Oxford University Press, 1990), p.277).

To establish unity within the party and to spread Maoist ideology further, a series of Rectification Campaigns were launched between 1941 and 1944. The 'correct ideas' were Mao's, and any deviation would not be tolerated. The primary ideas were the 'mass line', which meant policies were to be taken to the people and ideas taken from the people, Mao's peasant-based Communism, and the military strategy of guerrilla warfare. The Rectification Campaigns were successful in ridding the Communists of their factions, including pro-Russian groups. However, many educated Chinese who arrived at Yan'an believing that they would be helping the revolution also found themselves persecuted as class enemies and spies.

Historians do not agree on the military contribution of the CCP in the war against the Japanese. Some suggest that it was rather more limited than Mao claimed. There is little doubt, however, that there was a general perception within China and internationally that the CCP gave good leadership during the war. This perception led many Chinese to see the Communists as the true nationalists, and support the CCP rather than the GMD.

Mao used his guerrilla assaults on the Japanese as good propaganda to promote the CCP as the real nationalist force defending China. He also emphasized the support that the GMD was receiving from the USA, arguing that Jiang was nothing more than a puppet of the Western imperialists. Such sentiments fed into the long-held anti-foreign and anti-imperialist popular feelings in China.

Mao talking to the CCP in Yan'an as part of the Rectification Campaign.

Activity 11

ATL Thinking skills

Review questions

1. In what ways had the CCP been strengthened by the impact of the Sino-Japanese War?
2. In what ways had the GMD been weakened by the impact of the war?
3. 'It is absurd to speak of an historical event as "inevitable", but the Communist–Guomindang civil war almost demands that adjective. It is difficult in retrospect to see how it could have been avoided. An abyss of profound hostility and distrust, and the scars of brutal conflict, separated the two parties, to say nothing of their utterly different social philosophies' (James Sheridan, *China in Disintegration* (Free Press, 1977), p.269).

   Why was renewed civil war 'inevitable' at the end of the Sino-Japanese War, according to this historian?

Activity 12

Thinking and social skills

Discussion question

1. In pairs, discuss and make notes on the following question:

Examine the impact of foreign involvement in: a) the first phase of the Chinese Civil War, and b) the war against Japan.

You can use these notes later when planning the essays at the end of this chapter.

Second phase of the Civil War, 1946–1949

By the end of the war with Japan, the CCP was significantly strengthened, and the GMD was weakened, so much so that the Communists could move from the guerrilla warfare phase of combat to a phase of more conventional fighting. The first period of civil war (1927–1937) was an essentially Chinese war. The second period (1946–1949) would be more of an international affair. The polarization of the international political context through the development of the Cold War meant that China's civil war could not be an internal struggle alone. The war between Nationalists and Communists in China had become part of a larger Soviet–American effort to create a new post-war balance of power.

Both superpowers wanted a stable China, and a weakened Japan, and to this end they both wanted the GMD and the CCP to form a coalition government. The USSR wanted influence in Manchuria, and the USA accepted this desire to a certain extent.

Failure of the USA

The Americans worked hard to achieve a diplomatic solution between the CCP and the GMD. Yet neither side was willing to share power. General Marshall was given the responsibility of brokering a deal, and managed to get the GMD and the CCP to agree on the following terms: prepare to set up a coalition government, form a temporary state council, unite their armies in a new national army, and have free elections for local government. But as negotiations were being finalized in February 1946, both sides were moving troops into Manchuria. There would not be a diplomatic solution for China – its fate would be decided on the battlefield.

Despite the growth in strength of the CCP during the Sino-Japanese war, it is important to point out that in 1945, the GMD still had 4 million troops compared to the CCP's 1 million. The GMD also had more heavy weaponry. The events of the next three years are thus important for explaining the success of the CCP.

Initial victories for the GMD (1945–1947)

At first the GMD, with more troops and better equipment, forced the Communists to be on the defensive. Following the Japanese surrender in August 1945, the Red Army under General Lin Biao entered Manchuria to secure this important industrial region under Communist control. At the Yalta Conference in February 1945, the Allies had agreed that the USSR would invade Manchuria following Germany's surrender. The Soviets had duly invaded, and were in control when the CCP forces arrived, whereupon the Soviets gave the CCP large stockpiles of Japanese weapons. The USSR was clearly not neutral. General Albert Wedemeyer, the Allied commander of the South-East Asia Theatre, authorized Jiang to resist the Communists by using US ships and aircraft to transport 500,000 troops to Manchuria, and 50,000 American troops were sent north to occupy Beijing. The USA could no longer claim to be neutral either. Although the CCP forces were better armed than before, the GMD greatly outnumbered them. The CCP also had to fight conventionally in Manchuria, defending and holding its positions and territory. The GMD was able to force the CCP out of the cities, and in December 1945 Mao reverted to his policy of creating bases outside the cities.

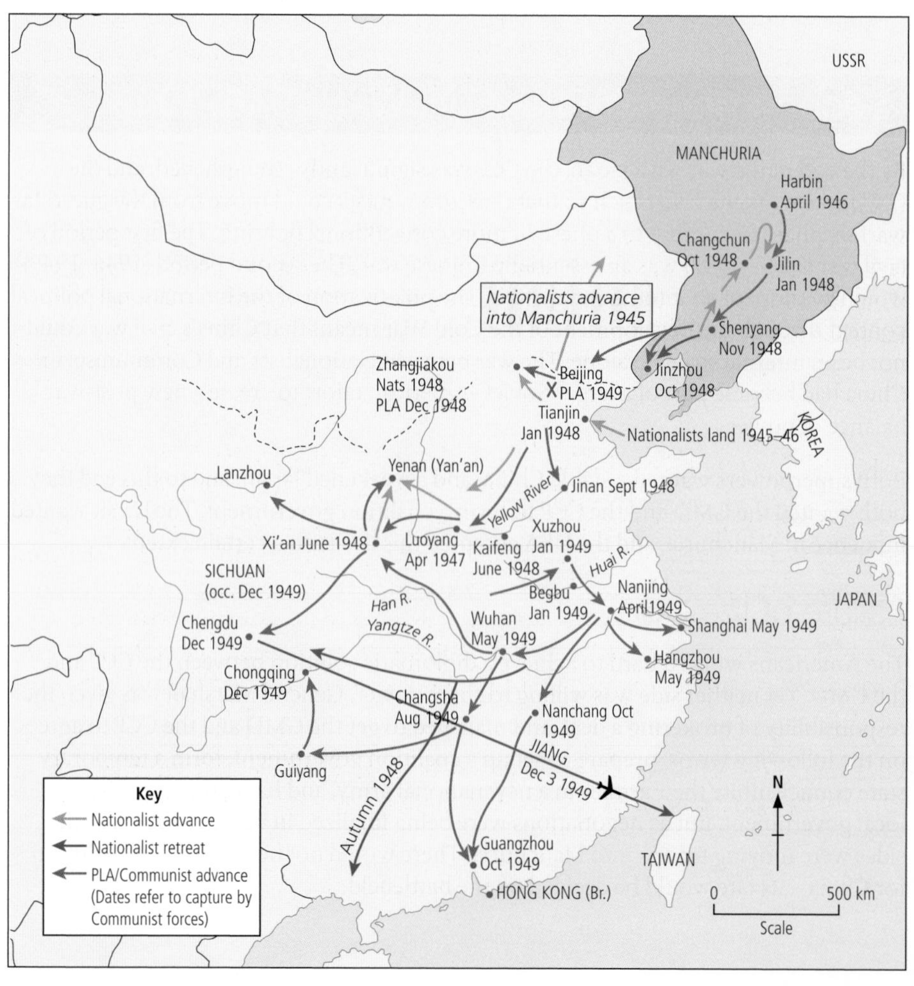

Map showing major battles and campaigns, 1946–1949.

It seemed as though Manchuria had been won by the GMD, but despite their early military achievements they continued to govern the region as they had others during the war with Japan, and this ultimately led to political defeat. Indeed, corruption was worse than it had been before, which encouraged Manchurians to support the CCP. President Truman sent General Marshall to mediate in the conflict, in an attempt to prevent a civil war and to avert US involvement in the fighting. US policy continued to be to promote a coalition government. However, the Americans were in a difficult position, as they did not support single-party states, and wanted to retain the position of mediator – even though they continued to arm Jiang Jieshi. The truce facilitated by Marshall broke down in March 1946. By May, the GMD was in control of the central area of Manchuria. The CCP demanded a ceasefire and condemned US support for Jiang Jieshi.

The CCP on the offensive (1947–1948)

At this point the US intervention, according to Jiang, played a key role in the outcome of the civil war. In June, General Marshall managed to get Jiang to agree to another truce. The ceasefire worked to the CCP's advantage, as it saved them from a final assault on their headquarters. The Communists used the time to train their forces and ready them for the war. Mao also introduced land reforms in the area. As it had done in Yan'an, land reform led to the peasants joining the Communists, as their victory would mean they could keep their land.

Fighting resumed in July, and the Red Army (now called the People's Liberation Army; PLA) reverted to guerrilla warfare. The GMD recaptured the cities of Manchuria and went on in March 1947 to take the CCP capital, Yan'an. Yet cities in Manchuria were now isolated, and Mao could use guerrilla tactics effectively; the PLA cut the GMD forces off by targeting their supply routes – the railways.

By March 1948, the remaining American advisers told Jiang Jieshi to leave Manchuria to protect his forces. At this point, the GMD and the CCP were quite evenly matched in terms of their military power and resources. Jiang refused to acknowledge that the balance had shifted unfavourably, and that the PLA now had more heavy weapons than the GMD. He fought on, but in March 1948 the CCP was in control of Manchuria. Jiang had lost 40,000 troops.

Collapse of GMD resistance

Capitalizing on its success, the PLA launched an offensive against the vital railway junction of Xuzhou. Here the Communists fought a conventional battle, relying on massed heavy artillery. The defeat of the Nationalists was a huge blow for Jiang's men, both strategically and psychologically. In the same month, January 1949, Lin Biao took the cities of Tianjin and Beijing. The whole of northern China, including Manchuria, was now under Communist control. In April the PLA launched the final series of offensives, taking Nanjing and then Shanghai in May. In October, Guangzhou was taken, and throughout November the Communists crushed the remnants of GMD resistance.

On 1 October 1949, Mao proclaimed the establishment of the People's Republic of China in Beijing, saying: 'Our nation will never again be an insulted nation. We have stood up.'

What were the reasons for the Communist success?

Strengths of the CCP

Guerrilla tactics and revolutionary warfare

The CCP used guerrilla tactics successfully in the first phase of the civil war, in the fight against the Japanese, and in Manchuria in the second phase of the civil war.

The leadership of the PLA

The PLA was led by Lin Biao, who was an excellent military commander and who was able to transform the PLA from a guerrilla fighting force into a regular army. The PLA was greatly strengthened in the final stages of the war by desertions from the Nationalist forces and through capturing enemy weapons. Owing to better conditions and political indoctrination, the PLA was a much more effective fighting force, with far higher morale than the Nationalist troops. In addition, the good behaviour of the Communist soldiers attracted much support from the peasantry.

The role of Mao

Mao's leadership was central to the Communist success. It was his leadership in the Long March and his innovative guerrilla tactics that allowed the CCP to survive and then to broaden its support base in Yan'an. He was able to take advantage of the opportunity presented by the war with Japan, and also to adapt his ideas and policies to the changing military situation. For example, although revolutionary ideas involved attacking the bourgeoisie, or middle classes, during the war against Japan, he stressed the idea that this was a *national* struggle in which all classes should cooperate.

The spread of Communist ideas

As we have seen, the Communists used the period during the war with Japan to spread Communist ideas throughout the areas they captured. The policy continued in the second phase of the civil war. Land reform continued in all rural areas captured by the Communists. As the Communists moved into the towns, they similarly spread Communist ideas. The army would take over the control of the towns, working to prevent crime, control food distribution, and establish fairer taxation systems. These activities broadened the base of support for the CCP.

The role of intelligence

The superior intelligence of the Communists in the second phase of the civil war played an important role in their victory. Jiang's Assistant Chief of Staff, Liu Fei, was a Communist spy, as was the head of the GMD's War Planning Board. This meant that the Communists knew all intended GMD moves in advance. In addition, several of the Nationalist commanders were in fact Communist agents. In Manchuria, for example, the Nationalist commander Wei Lihuang was a Communist agent, and his actions helped secure the PLA victory there. In contrast to this situation, the Nationalists were unable to infiltrate the Communists.

Activity 13

1. Give specific examples from this chapter of how guerrilla tactics were used by the Communists in their struggle.

   Add notes under the following themes:
   - Survival of the CCP from 1927
   - the Long March
   - expansion of Communist influence/control
   - the war with Japan
   - final phase of civil war 1946–1949

Jiang Jieshi's errors

Political

Jiang Jieshi continued to resist democratic changes, and his increasingly repressive regime alienated liberals and the middle classes. He failed to win mass support and his government relied on a narrow, wealthy section of businessmen and landlords for its survival. The GMD's corruption and inefficiency further alienated the middle classes and also the peasants, who bore the brunt of the unfair tax system.

Economic

Jiang Jieshi's support base was further damaged by rampant inflation, which had a devastating effect on the middle classes. Jiang only took decisive action to deal with this in 1948, when a new currency was introduced and rationing started. These reforms were too late, however, and there was economic collapse by 1949 in those areas under Nationalist control.

Military

US observers continually commented on the poor quality of many of Jiang's troops, and their low morale contributed to the high number of desertions at the end of the civil war. The behaviour of the army towards ordinary Chinese was also in sharp contrast to that of the Communist army, with its strict rules of behaviour. In terms of military leadership, Jiang also made serious mistakes – for instance, choosing to pour resources into Manchuria, far from his real bases of support. His decision to fight it out at Xuzhou was also a disaster. Furthermore, he tried to interfere too much in the actual running of the campaigns, even though he was far removed from the actual action.

What was the role of foreign support in the final outcome?

The USA

The Americans, as discussed earlier, had economic and strategic interests in China, and they had supported the GMD from the first phase of the civil war. This support should have given the GMD key advantages over the CCP, and despite the problem of getting effective aid to the GMD, the USA provided Jiang with almost $3 billion in aid and large supplies of arms throughout World War Two. At the beginning of the second stage of the civil war, the Americans transported GMD forces by sea and air to the north of China, and US troops occupied Tianjin and Beijing to hold them until the GMD were ready. In short, the USA did what it could to assist Jiang, but his regime was too ineffective to survive.

Cartoon by Leslie Gilbert Illingworth in the British *Daily Mail*, 16 September 1946. What does this show about American interests in China?

Yet some historians believe that there should have been *more* military commitment from the USA, and that this could have 'saved' China from Communism. The Americans were held responsible by Jiang for pressurizing him to agree to truces at critical times during his war on the CCP. Finally, their mere presence also gave Mao excellent anti-GMD propaganda.

The USSR

The Soviets had been rather reluctant to support the CCP, and did not in the end give them the same military and economic assistance that the GMD received from the USA. The involvement of the Comintern in the early stages of the CCP's struggle with the GMD had led to division and near annihilation in Jiang's final Encirclement Campaign. Mao waged the Rectification Campaigns to oust Soviet supporters from the CCP. The USSR had backed both United Fronts, and Stalin did not see that the CCP could win the civil war until the later stages in 1948. Some historians view the Soviet assistance in Manchuria, which also included establishing military training colleges and the training of CCP pilots, as essential to establishing the PLA as a more modern and effective force. Nevertheless, Stalin was worried that the USA would involve itself further in the Chinese Civil War, and attempted to limit Mao's successes in the later stages of the conflict. In 1949, Stalin told Mao to consolidate his gains in the north and not cross the Yangtze into southern China. Mao ignored his advice.

Activity 14

Source analysis

1. Historians, of course, often disagree on the key reasons for the CCP's victory over the GMD. Read the sources below and identify in each case what reason the historian is emphasizing as the most important for CCP victory. What similarities and differences can you identify between these interpretations?

Source A

The most important near cause for the downfall of the Nationalists was the eight-year Japanese war, which completely exhausted the government militarily, financially and spiritually. Had there been no Japanese war, the situation in China would have been very different ... [M]any of the disastrous repercussions of the war ... continued to plague the Nationalists during their struggle with the Communists. The price the Nationalists paid to win the Japanese war was also the first instalment toward its eventual downfall.

From Immanuel Hsu, *The Rise of Modern China* (Oxford University Press, 1995), p.639.

Source B

China in fact was a classical eve-of-revolution situation. The ruling elite had lost its confidence and its will to rule. In these circumstances the final victory of the Communists, although it was gained by war, was actually a political victory. In 1947 the Communist armies faced Nationalist superiority in men and materials of two-and-a-half to one. After less than a year of fighting, they had reversed the proportion, as a result of the corruption, demoralisation and frequent defection to the Nationalist armies ... The actual military events of the communist conquest of China are of little interest. The Nationalist armies, as Lenin had said of the soldiers of the tsar in 1917, voted with their feet. The war-lord allies of the Guomindang retreated into their own bailiwicks and from them made their peace with Mao Zedong.

Jack Gray, *Rebellions and Revolutions: China from the 1880s to the 1980s* (Oxford University Pres, 1990), p.286.

Source C

> *What finally undermined the Nationalist government was not war or politics but economics. The military and political success of the Communists under Mao Zedong certainly played a vital part in determining their takeover in 1949, but it is arguable that the single most powerful reason for the failure of the GMD government was inflation … By 1949 China's monetary system had collapsed, the government was discredited, and the people of Nationalist China were demoralised. Even had the Nationalists not been defeated in civil war and driven from the mainland it is difficult to see how Jiang Jieshi and the GMD could have continued to hold power in China.*
>
> **From Michael Lynch, *China: From Empire to People's Republic 1900–49*, 2nd ed. (Hodder, 2010), p.142.**

Source D

> *It is clear that a host of factors went into the Communist success … But the central factor was unquestionably the mobilization of vast numbers of Chinese, primarily peasants, into new political, social, economic, and military organizations, infused with a new purpose and a new spirit. This mobilization largely accounted for the Communist victory …*
>
> **James Sheridan, *China in Disintegration* (Free Press, 1977), p.283.**

Source E

> *The Communists won because they made fewer military mistakes than the government and because Chiang (Jiang) Jieshi – in his search for a powerful, centralized post-war state – antagonized too many interest groups in the country. As a party, the GMD was weakened by the drubbing it had got during the war against Japan. Meanwhile, the Communists became masters of telling different groups of Chinese exactly what they wanted to hear and of cloaking themselves in Chinese nationalism. Only they themselves, they insisted, were the bearers of the fate of the nation. Chiang was lampooned as a stooge of imperialism.*
>
> **Odd Arne Westad, *Restless Empire* (Bodley Head, 2012), p.291.**

Source F

> *In Yanan in 1942–43, Mao had built an efficient instrument by terrorising his power base, the members of the Communist Party. Now [by the start of 1948] he was terrorising his economic and cannon-fodder base, the peasantry, in order to bring about total, unquestioning conformity. The result was that the peasants put up little resistance to Mao's requisitioning of soldiers, labourers, food, and anything else he wanted for his goals.*
>
> *Mao regarded this process of terrorisation as indispensable for winning the war … Although people in the White areas knew quite a lot about the brutality of the land reform, not least through the hundreds of thousands who escaped, they often attributed it to passing excesses by the oppressed. In any case, they had no way of doing anything to stop Mao's advance, and having no great affection for the existing regime, often willed themselves to give Mao the benefit of the doubt.*
>
> **Jung Chang and John Halliday, *Mao: The Unknown Story* (Jonathan Cape, 2005), pp.329–331.**

TOK

How important is the study of history to our understanding of international relations today? What are the knowledge issues involved in how politicians use history? Does the study of China's relationship with the West give us a better understanding of modern foreign relations?

Activity 15

ATL Thinking skills

1. What was the impact of a) the USSR's and b) the USA's involvement in the Chinese Civil War?
2. To what extent were political/ideological factors more important to the CCP's victory than military factors?

Results of the Chinese Civil War

For China

Human cost

It has been estimated that around 3.5 million were killed in the Chinese Civil War. However, in the war against Japan (1937–45) the figures that historians have arrived at are horrific: between 15 million and 20 million people died. Of this figure around 4 million were military personnel, 10 million were civilians killed by military actions, and an additional 5 million were casualties to war-related starvation and disease. The historian Rana Mitter, in his book *Forgotten Ally: China's World War II, 1937–1945*, suggests that China's contribution to the war in the Pacific has often been overlooked in the west and had a significant impact in shaping the PRC.

Social impact

The victory of the Communists led to a social revolution in family life. A new marriage law that was passed in 1950 gave equal rights to women, forbade arranged marriages, and allowed women to hold land in their own names. Children born out of marriage were also given equal rights, and divorce was made equally available to men and women.

Likewise, centuries-old beliefs in religion were attacked. Christianity, Buddhism and Confucianism were all denounced in Communist propaganda as superstitions that could not be allowed to be part of the new China.

Economic impact

The Civil War left China economically devastated. There was widespread starvation and thousands died from hunger. Mao's new regime implemented land reform in the countryside; violence accompanied this reform as the landowners were often killed. From 1956 the CCP enforced collectivisation on the countryside and all land, tools and livestock were taken by the state from the farmers. Farmers had to hand over their grain to the state for a set price, which meant that by the mid-1950s people in the countryside were on starvation rations.

From 1952 the business community was attacked. All industry and commerce was put under the control of the All-China Federation of Industry & Commerce, and in 1956 the government took control of all private enterprises. Then in 1957, Mao launched the Great Leap Forward which was intended to bring about rapid industrialization. It was a catastrophic economic failure and led to what some historian have termed the worst man-made famine in human history.

Political impact

After the civil war, the CCP consolidated its control in China, and pursued the key ideas that it had initiated in Yan'an. The experiences of the long war were a guidebook for the new Chinese Communist regime. Society had been militarized and Mao had a god-like status. Society would be changed by short and 'total' campaigns, and all obstacles would be overcome by the power of the people. Indeed, within a year of victory Mao implemented a 'Great Terror' in which the regime eliminated all 'enemies of the Party'. Anyone could be accused of being an 'enemy' and quotas were set for those to be executed. Dikotter writes, 'School children as young as six were accused of spying for the enemy and tortured to death.' 2 million people had been killed in the terror by 1951 and a vast network of prison camps held hundreds of thousands of political prisoners. All laws were abolished and a legal system along similar lines to the Soviet Union was established. Free speech, even mild criticism of the party or regime, was silenced. One of the key legacies of the Chinese Civil War is the continued authoritarian rule by the CCP. China remains a single-party state in which individual rights and freedoms are suppressed. In 1989, when young protesters on the streets of Tiananmen Square, Beijing, were forcibly dispersed with guns and tanks, the battles of the civil war were used to justify the actions of the state.

For Asia

Mao's victory led to the globalization of the Cold War, which spread from its seedbed in Europe to Asia. Asia was now a region in which the superpowers would struggle for control and influence. The Communist victory inspired insurgencies in Indonesia, Malaya, Indochina, and Thailand. It also led to the first 'hot war' of the Cold War – the Korean conflict (1950–1953).

For the USSR

Although the CCP's victory should have been viewed as a victory for the spread of Communism and for the USSR, Stalin feared Mao as a rival for the leadership of the communist world, and he had not wanted the Cold War to spread to Asia. Jiang's GMD would have recognized disputed border territory along frontiers in Manchuria and Xinjiang as Soviet. Fundamentally, Stalin did not view Maoism as 'genuinely revolutionary' and did not agree with Mao's 'hybrid' ideology, which was a mix of traditional Chinese culture and Marxism.

Mao became convinced that Stalin planned to create a divided and weak China, which would leave the USSR dominant in Asia. He saw Stalin's policies as rooted in self-interest rather than true revolutionary doctrine. Mao later said that in 1945 Stalin refused China permission to carry out revolution and told him: 'Do not have a civil war: collaborate with Jiang Jieshi. Otherwise the Republic of China will collapse.' Mao believed that Stalin saw him as another Tito (the Communist revolutionary who became the leader of post-war Yugoslavia).

Nevertheless, once the CCP had won the civil war, Mao visited Moscow in 1950 and this visit produced the Sino-Soviet Treaty of Alliance. The USSR had become enthusiastic about the CCP's victory, and the Soviet press had poured praise and admiration on Mao and the new People's Republic of China (PRC). The US State Department referred to the alliance as 'Moscow making puppets out of the Chinese'. Soviet planners and engineers in China developed 200 construction projects in the 1950s, traditional buildings were pulled down for Soviet-style constructions, and Soviet scientific technology was prioritized in China over Chinese technology.

Sino-Soviet relations chilled again during the Korean War. When American forces, under the UN flag, came close to the Chinese border, Stalin encouraged the PRC to send troops into Korea. The Soviets gave material assistance to the 1 million Chinese troops engaged in battle, but despite this support for PRC intervention in the Korean War, Mao bitterly complained when the Soviets demanded that the Chinese pay for all weapons and materials they supplied.

Relations between the USSR and the PRC worsened dramatically after the death of Stalin. Khrushchev's attack on Stalin's cult of personality was seen by Mao as an attack on his own style of leadership, and the USSR's handling of the Cuban Missile Crisis in 1962 caused Mao to accuse Khrushchev of being a 'paper tiger'. The Sino-Soviet split worsened, culminating in border clashes in 1969.

China's relations with the USA and the West

Mao's victory led to much anxiety in the USA, and seemed at the time to shift the balance of power in the Cold War in the USSR's favour. Many in the USA initially saw the Communist victory as inevitable given the lack of support that existed for the Nationalists in China in 1949; nevertheless, as the Cold War intensified and **McCarthyism** took hold in the USA, state officials were accused of having 'lost' China. Stalin was now seen as having been the mastermind behind Mao's CCP. The USA failed to understand the different types of Communism or that there was increasing tension and hostility between Mao and Stalin. The USA also refused to recognize the PRC as a legitimate state. Instead, they backed Jiang Jieshi and the Chinese Nationalists, who had fled at the end of the civil war to the island of Taiwan, about 160 kilometres off the coast of mainland China. The Americans then ensured that Taiwan and not the PRC had China's seat at the UN.

The USA initially perceived the CCP victory as opening a new front in the Cold War – there was the Iron Curtain in Europe and now the Bamboo Curtain in Asia. Mao's victory was a key reason for the passing of a vast new military budget to fund the struggle against the spread of Communism. It also led the USA into the Korean War and confrontations over Taiwan. However, by the end of the 1960s there was a radical change by both the Americans and the Communist Chinese in their policies and strategies towards one another. During the late 1960s, China and the USA entered into a period of dialogue and rapprochement.

CHALLENGE YOURSELF

First, reflect on your understanding of the causes of war in the 20th century, and then reflect on the causes of the Chinese Civil War. Can you identify and understand the political, economic, and social causes of a war? What factors do you find more difficult to understand?

Activity 16

	GMD: Policies / Actions	CCP: Policies / Actions	Foreign intervention: Policies / Actions	Historians' comments
1927–1937				
1937–1945				
1945–1949				

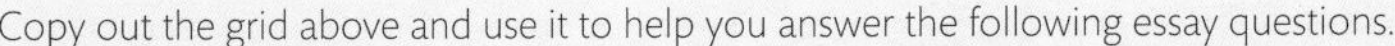

Copy out the grid above and use it to help you answer the following essay questions.

1. ***Discuss the reasons for the victory of one side in one 20th-century civil war.***

You can divide this essay into the following headings:

- strengths/successes of the CCP, 1928–1949
- weakness/failures of the GMD, 1928–1949
- the impact of the Sino-Japanese War
- the impact of foreign intervention.

2. ***Examine the role of foreign intervention in one 20th-century civil war.***

For this essay, consider

- long-term European involvement
- the impact of Japan
- the impact of the Soviets
- the impact of America.

Also try answering these questions:

3. ***Discuss the long- and short-term causes of one 20th-century civil war.***
4. ***Evaluate the impact of guerrilla tactics on the outcome of one 20th-century civil war.***

To access weblinks relevant to this chapter, go to www.pearsonhotlinks.com, search for the book title or ISBN, and click on 'chapter 12'.

Comparative study of civil wars

Key concepts: Change and continuity

As you read this chapter, consider the following essay questions:

- Compare and contrast the role of ideology as a cause of two 20th-century civil wars, each chosen from a different region.
- Compare and contrast the role of foreign intervention in the course and outcomes of two 20th-century civil wars.
- Compare and contrast the political and economic results of two 20th-century civil wars.

Republican forces in the Spanish Civil War.

Comparative study of the causes of two 20th-century civil wars

Activity 1

 Self-management and social skills

1. In pairs, make a copy of the grid below. Review the causes of the Spanish Civil War and the Chinese Civil War. Add detailed information for each case study. Draw conclusions regarding where there is evidence of comparison and where there is evidence of contrast between the case studies.

Thematic cause	Spain	China	Similarities or differences in causation?
Political/ideological • Failure of monarchy/ruling dynasty • Attempts at Republican government • Role of military in politics • Polarization of politics • Foreign influence			
Regionalism • Lack of central authority/unity • Warlords • Nationalism			

Thematic cause	Spain	China	Similarities or differences in causation?
Economic • Gap between rich and poor/ landowners and peasants/elites and urban workers • Land • Lack of economic development and modernization • Taxation • Economic crisis			
Social/religious • Lack of modernization/education • Power of church/traditional or orthodox belief			

2. When you have completed your chart/grid, identify the long-term and short-term causes from these themes for each war. Discuss the extent to which the long-term and short-term themes are similar for both case studies.

Investigate a current civil war, or a country where internal tensions may lead to a civil war. What are the causes of conflict within the state? Are there similarities with the case studies you have studied? How is the international community responding to the situation? Does this contrast with how the international community responded to the Spanish and Chinese Civil Wars?

Compare and contrast the practices of two civil wars

Activity 2

ATL Thinking and self-management skills

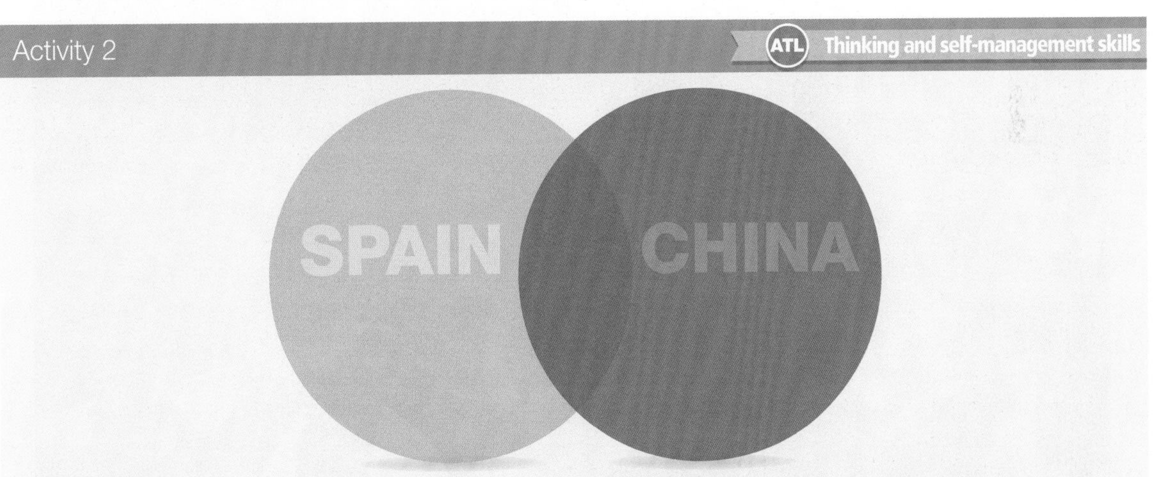

1. Sketch out a Venn diagram like the one above. Add the following to your diagram, identifying whether the factor is relevant to both wars, only to Spain, or only to China.
   - War of movement; siege warfare; trench warfare; guerrilla war
   - War on land with tanks and artillery; ground troops supported from the air; small arms; some air cover; some tanks
   - Air power; fighters and bombers; air cover for ground forces; bombing of cities; limited use of air power to support ground forces
   - Civilians targeted
   - Role of war at sea limited
   - Use of terror
   - Assistance by foreign powers.

Compare and contrast the effects of 20th-century civil wars

Chinese civilians flee fighting in final phase of the Chinese Civil War and Spanish refugees flee fighting in the Spanish Civil War.

Activity 3

ATL Thinking and communication skills

Write a short newspaper article on the effects of 20th-century war using the Spanish and Chinese Civil Wars as your case studies. You should analyse the similarities and differences between the effects of each war and include detailed own knowledge to support your arguments.

Here are some ideas to get you started:

- Destruction of industry
- Attack on middle classes
- No territorial changes
- Economic cost: loss of industry, farmland and infrastructure
- Women's rights limited and egalitarian measures reversed
- Authoritarian dictatorship
- Communist party dictatorship
- A factor in the globalization of the Cold War
- Purge and persecution of political opponents after war
- Human cost: number of casualties and deaths
- **A cause of international tension**
- Industrialization programmes
- Land reform
- Women given equal rights

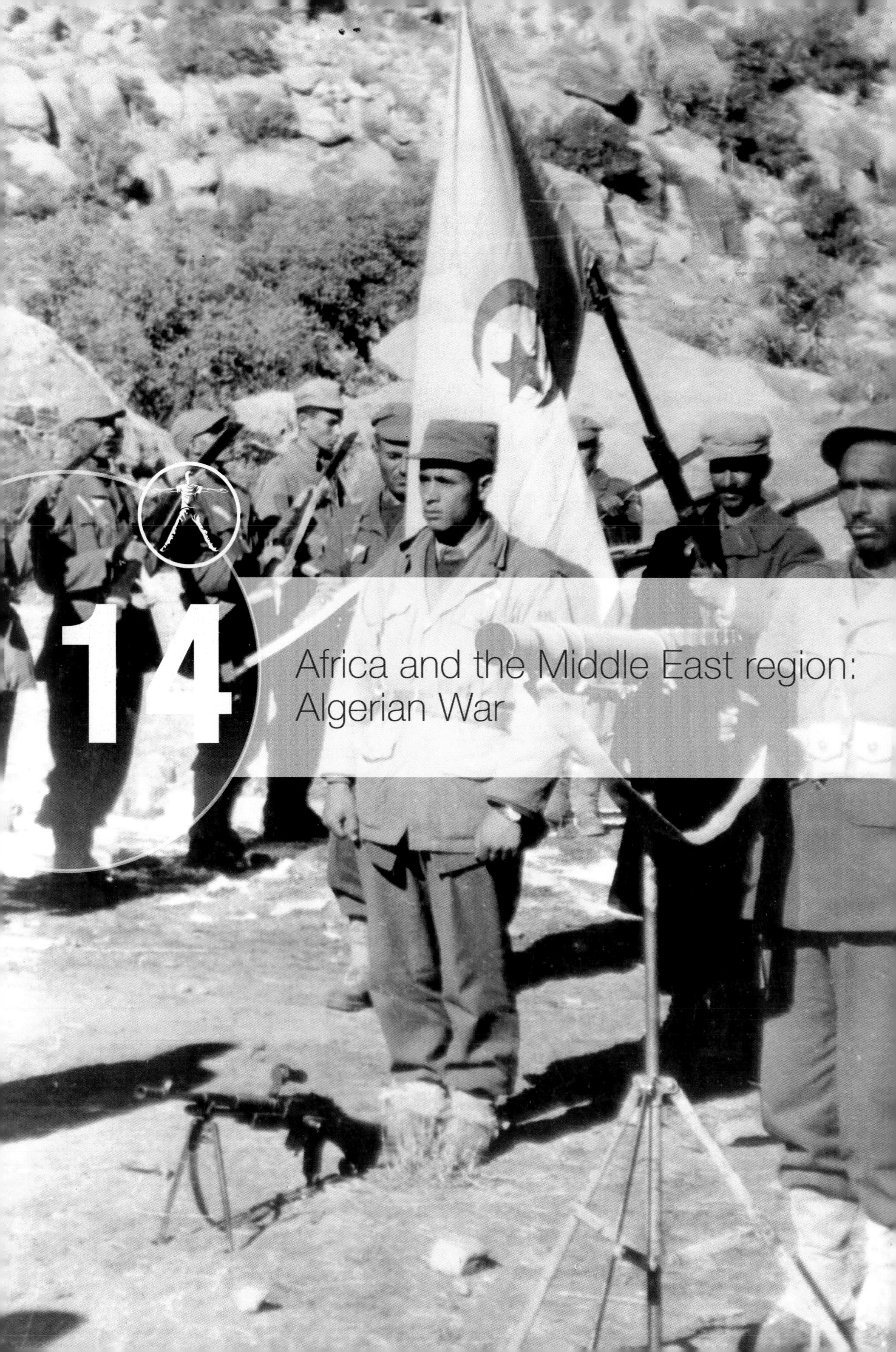

14 Africa and the Middle East region: Algerian War

Key concepts: Causation and consequence

FLN soldiers during the Algerian War, 1961.

As you read this chapter, consider the following essay questions:

- Discuss the long-term and short-term causes of one 20th-century war.
- With reference to one 20th-century war, examine the impact of guerrilla tactics in deciding the outcome.
- Examine the political, economic, and social effects of one 20th-century war.

The Algerian War of 1954–1962 was one of the most savage African struggles for independence. The war started on 1 November 1954 with an insurrection led by the Front de Libération Nationale (FLN; National Liberation Front) and it ended in 1962 when Algeria became independent. It was never a straight struggle between Algerians and the French government, however. It eventually became a four-way conflict between the Algerian nationalists, the French government, the European colonists, and, in the final stage, General Charles de Gaulle as president of the Republic of France.

The war was devastating for Algeria. During its 8 years, at least a quarter of a million Algerians died and approximately 2 million had to leave their villages. It also left France deeply scarred, and was unique in colonial wars for causing a change of government in a European country, with the destruction of France's Fourth Republic. This conflict is an example of a guerrilla war.

Charles de Gaulle.

Activity 1

ATL Thinking skills

Look back at chapter 1 and the discussion about guerrilla warfare.

1. What are the key characteristics of guerrilla warfare?
2. What factors have made guerrilla warfare the chosen style of warfare for people struggling for independence against European powers?

Charles de Gaulle

Charles de Gaulle was one of the most influential leaders of modern France. He was a brigadier general in World War Two, and, following the fall of France in 1940, he organized the Free French Forces with exiled French officers in Britain. He became prime minister in the French Provisional Government following the liberation of France in 1944, but then retired from politics in 1946. The Algerian crisis brought him out of retirement, and he was then elected President of the Fifth Republic. He finally retired in 1969.

Timeline of events - 1945-62

1945	8 May	VE Day
		Algerian revolt in Sétif followed by severe reprisals
1954	Apr	End of French rule in Indochina
	Nov	FLN created FLN insurrection and beginning of civil war
1955	Jan	Jacques Soustelle appointed as governor-general of Algeria
	Aug	FLN massacre *pieds-noirs* at Philippeville
1956	Feb	Robert Lacoste appointed as governor-general of Algeria
	Mar	Independence given to Tunisia and Morocco
	Sept	FLN explode bombs in fashionable cafes Battle for Algiers begins
	Oct	Suez Crisis
	Dec	Raoul Salan appointed as commander-in-chief in Algeria
1957	Jan	Jacques Massu's paras take over Algiers
	Nov	Battle for Algiers won by French
1958	May	Pierre Pflimlin new premier French Assembly gives de Gaulle full powers for 6 months to make a new constitution Committee of Public Safety set up under General Massu

Timeline of events – 1945–62		
	Sept	FLN announce formation of a provisional government called the GPRA based in Tunis Fehrat Abbas is prime minister
1959	Sept	De Gaulle offers Algeria self-determination
1960	Jan	*Colon* Ultras attempt coup – Barricades Week
1961	Jan	Referendum gives de Gaulle go ahead to work for Algerian self-determination Both sides agree to peace talks
	Apr	Generals' insurrection in Algiers; de Gaulle triumphs
		Organisation de l'armée secrète (OAS; Secret Army Organization) created
	May	First peace talks at Evian end in failure
1962	Feb	OAS kill 533 people
	Mar	Second Evian Conference – agreement reached and ceasefire implemented OAS continues terrorist attacks and 'scorched earth policy'
	July	Algeria becomes a sovereign state
	Sept	Ben Bella becomes president of Algeria

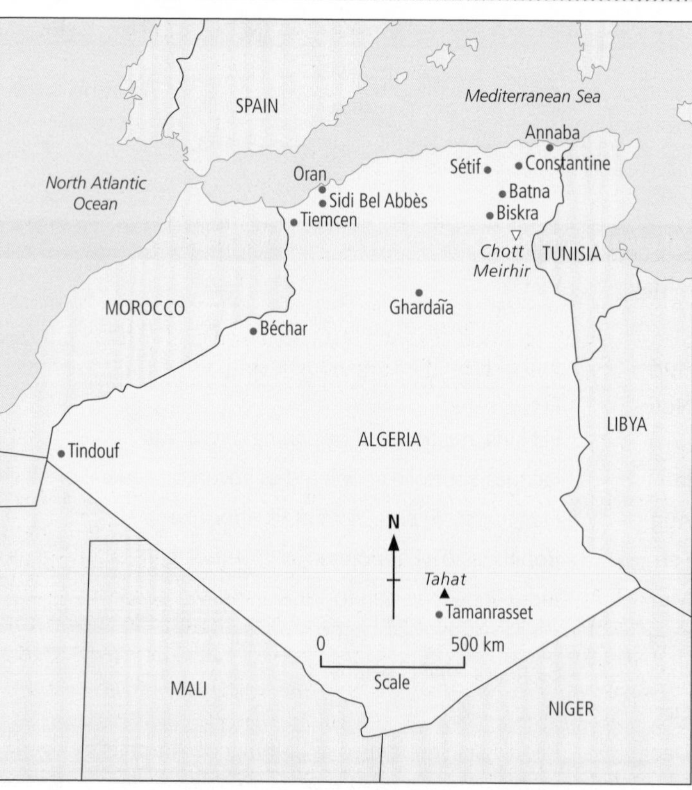

Map of Algeria.

Long-term causes of the Algerian War

Tensions in Algeria before World War Two

Algeria had been colonized by France in the 19th century. By 1841 there were already 37,374 French settlers, the ***colons***, later called the ***pieds-noirs*** (black feet) by Algerians because of the fact that they wore cheap black shoes. By 1945, there were about one million *pieds-noirs*, many of whom had been born in Algeria and who regarded it as their home. The *pieds-noirs* were an extremely diverse group both in terms of wealth and political beliefs. The extreme conservatives among this group, who resisted all change, were known as the Ultras; there were also, however, liberals (approximately 20–25 per cent) who supported reforms of some kind.

The official French policy with regard to colonies was one of 'assimilation'. This was based on the idea that French civilization was superior to all others and that the colonies would therefore benefit from being integrated into all its aspects, including its social and political institutions, French citizenship, and the French language. Thus colonies were seen as *départements* ('departments', the primary regional divisions of France itself), which, in the case of Algeria, had direct political representation in Paris. In the words of Arthur Girault, the idea of assimilation:

> *is not separation, but, on the contrary, an increasingly intimate union between the colonial and the metropolitan territory … The colonies are theoretically considered to be a simple extension of the soil of the mother country.*
>
> **Arthur Girault, *Principes de colonisation et de législation coloniale*, 1921.**

This view was particularly true of Algeria, which was dominated by the French more than any of the other French colonies, and which was seen as an integral part of France, with three *départements*.

In reality, however, French rule was racist and condescending. For the 1 million *colons* living in Algeria, maintaining the French connection was essential, as it gave them a social advantage over indigenous Algerians, who were mainly Muslim. Muslim land had been expropriated and only 2 per cent of the population owned 25 per cent of the land. *Colons* earned substantially more than the Algerian Muslims, who also suffered a high unemployment rate. This situation was not helped by the fact that the French government prevented industrialization and development of certain areas of the agricultural sector in order to prevent foreign competition with France.

Research how the idea of French assimilation compared with British methods of ruling colonies.

With regard to education, there were 1,400 primary schools for the 200,000 Europeans, and only 699 schools for the 1,250,000 Algerian Muslim children. Thus the Muslim population was in a state of near illiteracy by 1945.

The impact of World War Two on French rule in Algeria

World War Two had a decisive impact on colonial resistance movements throughout Asia and Africa. The European colonizers had been revealed as vulnerable: France had fallen to the Germans, and the British colonies of Singapore, Hong Kong, and Malaya had fallen to the Japanese. The Japanese had also helped stir up nationalism through anti-European propaganda and their promotion of local officials; their ruthless subjugation policies had also encouraged the emergence of nationalist leaders such as Ho Chi Minh in Vietnam – leaders who wanted to resist not just the Japanese but also the European rulers when they tried to return after the war.

Ferhat Abbas.

After 1945, both the USA and the USSR expressed their opposition to imperialism, and this whole concept was also undermined by the founding of the UN, with its emphasis on human rights, freedoms and self-determination. Nevertheless, the French government had no intention of fundamentally changing its colonial policy. In 1942, Ferhat Abbas, representing Algerian Muslim political activists, had drawn up his 'Manifesto of the Algerian People'. This demanded 'the condemnation and abolition of colonization' plus self-government and a constitution, allowing for immediate participation by Algerians in their own political affairs. Yet these demands were ignored, and Abbas's moderate nationalist party was dissolved in 1945.

Meanwhile, de Gaulle called a conference of colonial administrators in Brazzaville in the French Congo in 1944. The conference promised a new 'French Community' that would abolish the worst aspects of colonialism. Yet there was no suggestion of any move towards self-government. Indeed, René Pleven, a prominent French politician, asserted in his speech at the Brazzaville conference that 'there are no peoples to liberate' and that the colonial subjects 'do not want to know any other independence than the independence of France'. De Gaulle did, however, concede local assemblies.

Events outside Algeria

It is important not to look at Algeria in isolation from events that were happening elsewhere. Arab nationalism was fired by the success and the leadership of Colonel Nasser in Egypt, who had overthrown King Faroukh in 1952. In addition, the French had been defeated decisively by the **Vietminh** insurgents in Vietnam at the battle of Dien Bien Phu in 1954. Even before that, Cambodia and Laos had gained independence in 1953. Meanwhile, in two other French colonies in West Africa – Morocco and Tunisia – independence was gained in 1956.

Short-term causes of the Algerian war

The 'era of broken promises'

Frustration at this situation exploded as early as 1945. During celebrations for **VE Day** in the predominantly Muslim town of Setif, nationalist banners, which had been forbidden, appeared. When police tried to seize the banners, fighting broke out. The result was attacks on Europeans, including murder, rape, and robbery. Throughout Algeria, about 100 people were killed. French revenge was swift and bloody. Officially, 1,005 Muslims died during the savage repression. According to Algerian nationalists, 40,000 to 50,000 died. The killings had the effect of whipping up nationalist sentiment, but the French quickly restored order and therefore believed that they could carry on with colonial rule as before.

In 1946, the Fourth Republic renamed the French Empire the French Union. Based upon the principles of the Brazzaville conference, it agreed greater autonomy for the colonial people – but again there was no question of decolonization. In 1947, the Algerian Muslims did get the right to vote in Algeria, but out of the elected assembly, 60 of the deputies were to be elected by the *colons* and 60 by the Muslims, who were 90 per cent of the population. *Colons* and Muslims each sent 15 deputies and senators to Paris. In 1956, only 8 out of the 864 higher posts in the administration were held by Muslims. In addition, because many *colons* believed that the Muslims should not be able to vote at all, elections were rigged. The *colons*, who had immense influence through their deputies and pressure groups, also stopped any reforms that threatened their interests.

This period was known as the 'era of broken promises', and even moderates like Ferhat Abbas became disillusioned. He became a leader of the revolutionary FLN (National Liberation Front) along with Ben Bella. The FLN was set up in 1954 in Cairo and aimed to wage a guerrilla war against the French. Its first proclamation stated that independence was to be reached by whatever means were necessary and that 'the struggle may be long, but the outcome is certain ...'

Activity 2

ATL Thinking and research skills

1. Research and examine the impact of each of the following in the lead-up to civil war in Algeria:
- France's colonization policies
- the influence of the *colons* (*pieds-noirs*)
- World War Two
- failure of French political reform after World War Two
- events in Egypt
- events in other French colonies – Indochina, Morocco, and Tunisia.

2. Put each of the factors above under one of the following headings: economic, political, ideological, military. Which is the most significant cause of the war?

The outbreak of war

The first attack by the FLN, launched on 1 November 1954, was immediately dismissed by the French as another uprising that could easily be contained. A far more serious attack upon *colons* and French forces was launched upon the town of Philippeville in August 1955. Here, a massacre by the FLN left 123 Muslims and *pieds-noirs* dead; the French retaliatory action, according to French sources, killed 1,200 people (or 12,000, according to FLN sources).

The 50,000 French troops already in Algeria were reinforced by paratroopers and gendarmes. Jacques Soustelle was made governor-general in January 1955. Soustelle was a liberal intellectual who hoped to carry out economic and political reform. Yet he was thwarted by the *colons*, the brutality of the fighting on both sides, and the growing support for the FLN. In 1956, the French government, under pressure from the *colons*, replaced him with a less liberal governor, Robert Lacoste, who was given special powers to deal with a situation that was now spiralling out of control.

The nature of the fighting in the Algerian War

The army played a key role in the development of events in Algeria. The French defeat at Dien Bien Phu in Vietnam, they believed, was a humiliation that must not be allowed to happen again. They were thus united with the *colons* in believing that Algeria must remain under French control, although their concerns for Algeria were different from those of the *colons*:

> *The day-to-day business of administering large tracts of Algeria had become the responsibility of the army, and in the course of governing their localities had acquired a proficiency, knowledge and sympathy for the people in their care which, they judged, would not easily be supplied by anybody else.*
>
> **Peter Calvocoressi, *World Politics Since 1945*, 9th ed. (Routledge, 2009), p.513.**

When the scale of the FLN operations increased in 1955, the army started to fight the guerrillas in earnest. A key aspect to French tactics was the use of helicopters, which moved troops around and attacked over large areas from the sky. Without support from a major power, the FLN lacked anti-aircraft missiles, and the open, arid terrain made conditions easier for the French army to identify FLN forces on the ground.

Both sides targeted civilians. The FLN used terror against civilians to ensure that they did not associate with the French authorities. All Muslims were ordered to give up smoking and alcohol, or face death or mutilation. The French army purposely targeted civilians with its policy of 'collective responsibility' – that all Muslims were responsible for the guerrilla attacks. As in other guerrilla wars, a cycle of retaliation emerged whereby any FLN attack on French forces would result in the French army taking retaliatory action against civilians in an attempt to discourage support for the FLN. These actions by both sides had the effect of radicalizing both Europeans and Algerians, and also dividing the population of France.

Activity 3

Source A

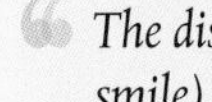

> *The disfiguring of French victims, the widespread appearance of* le grand sourire *(the broad smile), which was how the French macabrely described the Algerian practice of throat slitting, the bombing of civilian public places – these acts of terrorism aroused a comparable response.*

French soldiers began the practice of torture to obtain information and engaged in indiscriminate killing that shocked the population at home. French intellectuals vigorously protested these practices seeing that the very soul of the nation was threatened. French soldiers occasionally shivered at the thought that their behaviour was not dissimilar to that of the Nazis in occupied France. The war was thus dispiriting and disturbing, moods deepened by the lack of clearly defined military objectives, by the lack of political plan and resolve. Never recognised by the French government as a war, the struggle went on for seven years.

Raymond Betts, *France and Decolonisation* (Macmillan, 1991), p.105.

Source B

Before the crisis was over, the French army in Algeria would grow to 500 000 troops, and this within a few years of the debacle at Dien Bien Phu. Moreover, the French government was forced to send conscripts to Algeria, something it had never done in the case of Indo-China. As a result, the war affected many in France who were not enthusiastic supporters of empire, and widespread dissatisfaction with the war in North Africa developed by the late 1950s. France had freed itself from one military disaster only to become embroiled in another. As late as 1958 probably a majority of French citizens still favoured protecting the interests of the colons whatever the price. But others considered that it was a lost cause, so that French politics tended to become polarized, and France itself entered upon a particularly unstable period in its history.

T.E. Vadney, *The World Since 1945*, 3rd ed. (Penguin, 1998), p.229.

Source C

[Following the Vietnam War] … The FLN was able to pick up a blueprint of people's war ready made, although the war they fought was rather different. Lacking the Vietminh's regular military strength and its Chinese sanctuary and support, the FLN's campaign was more strongly marked by terrorism. The war began in 1954 with one of the most spectacularly deadly urban bombings yet seen, and was largely sustained by similar means. The French responded in kind, with a counter-terror … The French army had bitterly concluded that defeat in Vietnam had been due to its failure to match the ruthlessness and conviction of the Communists.

Charles Townshend (ed.), *The Oxford History of Modern War* (Oxford University Press, 2005), p.191.

1. From what you have read so far, why do you think that the FLN adopted guerrilla tactics to fight the French?
2. What kind of tactics did the FLN use?
3. What impact did these tactics have on a) the French army, and b) France (both the government and the French population)?

The ALN

The more conventional army of the FLN became known as the ALN – the Armée de Libération Nationale. It was mainly based in Tunisia. It never played a significant role in the war.

The international dimension of guerrilla tactics

The FLN was quick to realize the importance of international support and worked to develop worldwide backing for its cause. Thus, thanks to pressure from the **Arab League**, the Algerian situation was discussed at the UN and the Bandung Conference in 1955. FLN delegations were sent to Eastern and Western Europe, the USA, China, India, and Latin America. This tactic resulted in both moral support for the guerrilla fighters, with the UN putting pressure on France regarding its Algerian policy, and also material support. Weapons came to the FLN from other Arab countries, but also from Britain and America.

Activity 4

1. There have been several references to the war in Indochina/Vietnam, where the French had been defeated by the Vietminh at the Battle of Dien Bien Phu. This conflict is another excellent example of a guerrilla war.

Research:

- the reasons for this war
- the tactics used by the Vietminh
- the problems faced by the French and why they ultimately lost.

2. From what you have read so far, what similarities and differences existed between the situation in Indochina and that in Algeria?

CHALLENGE YOURSELF

Thinking skills 

Why do you think that the Algerian Civil War was not recognized as a 'war' by the French government? Can you think of conflicts today where the word 'war' is avoided by governments involved?

The Battle of Algiers

The army had the opportunity to assert its control over the direction of the war and indeed Algeria itself during the 'Battle of Algiers'. In September 1956, the FLN began an attack on the capital, one that involved brutal terrorist attacks against Europeans, Arab 'collaborators', and armed forces. Here was an attempt by the FLN to gain more international attention, and particularly shocking was the placing of bombs by Muslim women in cafes that were popular with *colon* families. Yet moving their action into the cities was a high-risk strategy for the guerrilla fighters. The French General Jacques Massu and the 10th Paratroop Division, endowed by Lacoste with the powers of civilian police, used torture and terror to destroy the FLN hideouts.

The Battle of Algiers is described in the following way by French historian Benjamin Stora:

> *It was truly 'blood and shit,' as Colonel Marcel Bigeard said, a horrendous battle, during which bombs blew dozens of European victims to pieces while paratroopers dismantled the networks by uncovering their hierarchy, discovered caches, and flushed out the FLN leaders installed in the city. Their means? Electrodes, dunking in bath tubs, beatings. Some of the torturers were sadists, to be sure. But many officers, non-commissioned officers, and soldiers would live with that nightmare for the rest of their lives. The number of attacks perpetrated fell from 112 in January to 39 in February, then to 29 in March. The FLN's command centre, run by Abbane Ramdane, was forced to leave the capital. Massu had a first victory.*

Benjamin Stora, *Algeria 1830–2000: A Short History* (Cornell University Press, 2004), p.50.

What were the results of the Battle of Algiers?

- The FLN was weakened militarily, but nevertheless continued to grow in political strength, and gained increasing support from the outside world, especially from the Communist bloc. Following the independence of Tunisia and Morocco, the FLN was able to seek sanctuary in these two countries. In 1958, the FLN announced the formation of a provisional government called the Gouvernement Provisoire de la République Algérienne (GPRA; Provisional Government of the Republic of Algeria) based in Tunis, with Ferhat Abbas as the prime minister. This development obviously complicated the situation for France. To prevent FLN attacks from these countries, the French built expensive, heavily guarded security fences along the borders. The construction programme used up vital French resources and soldiers, which then could not be used in the actual fighting in Algeria.
- The French army grew in influence in Algeria (see below), and both the army and the *colons* believed that they had been right in combating the FLN with their own tactics of force and ruthlessness.
- No solution to the situation in Algeria seemed to be in sight.

A scene from the influential film *The Battle of Algiers* (1966).

- The French faced international condemnation for their actions in Algeria and opposition to the army's methods grew within France.
- The internal crisis in Algeria precipitated a political crisis in France.

Following victory in Algiers over the FLN, the army concluded that it could not trust the existing French government to keep Algeria under French control. The *colons* were also appalled at the apparent weakness of the French government, and a new government under Pierre Pflimlin, which included no sympathizers of the *colons*, provided the trigger for a direct challenge to the young French administration. On 13 May 1958, those opposed to the French government instigated a mass demonstration in Algiers in an attempt to intimidate Pflimlin's government. Violence broke out and a Committee of Public Safety took over political power, under the control of General Massu. It was clear that the army and *colons* were united in direct and open opposition to the government in Paris.

French protesters in Algeria vent their anger against the policies of the French government.

The Battle of Algiers

The Battle of Algiers is a famous 1966 film by Gillo Pontecorvo portraying the events that took place in Algiers in 1956. It shows that atrocities were committed on both sides, and it thus caused political controversy in France, where it was banned for 5 years. Scenes of torture were in fact cut from the original American and British showings of the film. The film has seen a revival in the last few years due to the similarities between the situation faced by the French in Algeria in the 1950s and the situation faced by the Americans in Iraq following the US invasion in 2003.

What was the role of de Gaulle in the crisis?

There was confusion and panic in Paris at the situation in Algeria, and fears of a military coup in Paris itself as extremists considered launching a paratroop attack on the French capital. In this situation, the National Assembly in May voted to end the Fourth Republic and to invite de Gaulle to take power. De Gaulle was a favourite of the *colons*, who believed that he would crush the FLN and keep Algeria French. Muslims also wanted his return; de Gaulle was on good terms with the Moroccans and the Tunisians, and it was thought that he would give a generous settlement to Algeria. French politicians, meanwhile, concluded that the return of de Gaulle was the only solution to the Algerian crisis. Under a new constitution, de Gaulle was given wide powers for at least 6 months to restore order and authority. In a referendum on 28 September 1958, 79.2 per cent of those who voted supported the new constitution and the creation of the Fifth Republic.

Despite the support that de Gaulle had from the public, the army, and the *colons*, he understood that France could not be involved indefinitely in a never-ending guerrilla war in Algeria. His primary goal was to re-establish France as a world power, and in this context maintaining Algeria was costly; it impeded economic modernization and it distracted France from taking a lead in Europe. He thus concluded that negotiations and concessions to the FLN were necessary, and he also gradually realized that the terms would have to involve full independence.

De Gaulle started off by bringing Algeria back under the control of the civilian government in Paris. He allowed the army to continue to attack FLN bases. However, this was not in order to gain total control over the FLN, but rather to weaken them in order to get them to negotiate. In a major radio broadcast of 16 September 1959, de Gaulle made a speech that was a turning point in Franco-Algerian relations. In this broadcast, he announced three alternatives to the Algerian people: secession, integration, or a federal relationship in which France would provide assistance with the economy and education, and direction in matters of defence and foreign affairs. De Gaulle was thus now talking about an Algerian Algeria, and ignoring the possibility of an *Algérie française*.

Activity 5

Source A

> *'You should know that, in the last four years in Algeria, about fifteen hundred civilians of French descent have been killed, whereas more than ten thousand Muslims – men, women and children – have been massacred by the rebels, almost always by having their throats slit. In the metropolis, for the seventy-five people of French descent who lost their lives in attacks, one thousand seven hundred and seventeen Muslims fell to the killers' bullets or knives. How many lives, how many homes, how many harvests did the French army protect in Algeria! And to what slaughter would we be condemning this country if we were stupid and cowardly enough to abandon it!'*
>
> **Charles de Gaulle speaking at a press conference on October 1958, quoted in Benjamin Stora, *Algeria 1830–2000: A Short History* (Cornell University Press, 2004), p.108.**

Source B

> *Algeria is costing us – that is the least one can say – more than it is bringing in … Now our great national ambition has become our own progress, the real source of power and influence. The fact is, decolonization is in our interest and, as a result, it is our policy.'*
>
> **Charles de Gaulle speaking at a press conference on 11 April 1961, quoted in Benjamin Stora, *Algeria 1830–2000: A Short History* (Cornell University Press, 2004), p.107.**

1. What arguments does de Gaulle put forward in Source A as to why France cannot leave Algeria?
2. How do you explain the differences in the arguments put forward by de Gaulle in Source B?
3. With reference to origin, purpose, and content, assess the value and limitations of Source A to a historian studying the Algerian War.

Barricades Week and the Generals' Insurrection

De Gaulle's new policy was too extreme for the *colons* and the army. In January 1960, the *colon* Ultras rioted in Algeria, erecting barricades in what became known as 'Barricades Week'. The army took no action to stop the ensuing violence against the police and distanced themselves from the situation. Yet there was no outright rebellion; de Gaulle gave a dramatic TV address in which he made it clear that he would not give way, and in which he reminded the army that this was France's war and that 'in your mission there is no room for equivocation or interpretation'.

Barricades Week was a clear failure for the *colon* leaders. However, although the army had not directly gone against de Gaulle, the hostility of the army leaders towards his plans continued to grow. On 4 November 1960, de Gaulle made it clear that his plans were heading 'not to an Algeria governed by Metropolitan France but to an Algerian Algeria'. This declaration was followed by a referendum on his policy, in which the French voted overwhelmingly in favour of de Gaulle's position, giving him a free hand to deal with Algeria. On 15 March 1961, it was announced that peace talks between France and the FLN were to take place.

These developments were too much for the French generals. Before the peace talks could begin, the 'Generals' Insurrection', when the 1st Foreign Paratroop Regiment led by General Maurice Challe seized control of Algiers, occurred. Once again, de Gaulle used the media to end the crisis, making a radio broadcast to appeal directly to the troops.

Activity 6

'Officers, non-commissioned officers, policemen, sailors, soldiers and airmen, I am in Algiers with Generals Zeller and Jounard and in touch with General Salan so as to keep the army's oath to ensure a French Algeria, so that our dead may not have died in vain. A government of abandonment is preparing to hand over the departments of Algeria to the external organisation of the rebellion. Do you want Mers-el-Kebir and Algiers to become Soviet bases tomorrow? I know your courage, your pride, your discipline. The army shall not fail in its mission.'

Radio broadcast by General Challe on the day of the Generals' Insurrection, April 1960.

1. What does this source reveal about the aims of the French army in Algeria?

The formation of the OAS

With the failure of the conspiracy, the Ultras formed an underground army known as the Organisation de l'armée secrète (OAS; Organization of the Secret Army), which, comprised of civilians and military deserters, would use terror tactics to disrupt Algeria and France. Their actions included numerous assassination attempts on de Gaulle's life and a plan to bomb the Eiffel Tower. They also involved assassinations and bombings within Algeria, which continued with brutal ferocity during and after the peace talks. In fact, French disgust and condemnation of the OAS bombing of Paris – which resulted, amongst other casualties, in the maiming of a 4-year-old girl – meant that there was a resolve amongst the French population to end the war and restore Algeria to the Algerians.

The peace talks

Meanwhile, despite the activities of the OAS, the peace talks started at Evian. The first talks failed because of problems over whether Algeria included the Sahara. However, by the second Evian conference, de Gaulle was impatient to end a war so damaging to France's international standing, and so made far-reaching concessions. Instead of permanent guarantees for minorities, the rights of French citizens were protected for a period of 3 years, after which they could opt for Algerian citizenship. (If they decided to keep French citizenship, they would not enjoy full civil rights in Algeria.) Existing levels of French economic and technical assistance were guaranteed for the same 3-year period and French armed forces were also to withdraw after 3 years (though France could retain the lease of the Mers-el-Kebir naval base for 15 years). Most important of all, France recognized the territorial integrity of Algeria, and so gave up any hope of getting control of the Sahara and its oil (though French companies were allowed leasing rights to continue to develop oilfields).

De Gaulle said: 'We must concede these details rather than reject an agreement; for there is no comparison between the primary interest, which consists of reaching an agreement, and the secondary interest, which consists of holding a little longer certain things which, anyway, we do not reckon to hold for ever.' Algeria became a sovereign state on 1 July 1962.

Activity 7

ATL Thinking skills

French security forces round up suspected insurgents during the Algerian Civil War.

1. What is the message of this photograph?

Photos can be very useful for giving us a visual image of events. However, they are not necessarily an accurate representation of the events they are showing. When analysing a photo for its value and limitations, you need to ask key questions about it. Do we know who took the photo and for what purpose? Is there any suggestion that it was taken for propaganda purposes? Does it show the whole scene, or only part of a scene?

Activity 8

ATL Thinking and communication skills

Review activity

1. In pairs, discuss a) the role of guerrilla warfare and b) the role of other factors in determining the outcome of the Algerian War.
2. Draft an essay plan for this question and include detailed evidence from this chapter to support your points.

CHALLENGE YOURSELF

Discuss the extent to which the French public felt that the way war was being waged in Algeria was no longer in line with their principles. How far can a government act with integrity and honesty, with a strong sense of fairness, justice, and respect for the dignity of the individual, groups, and communities when fighting a war?

How far has Algeria achieved democracy and increased living standards today?

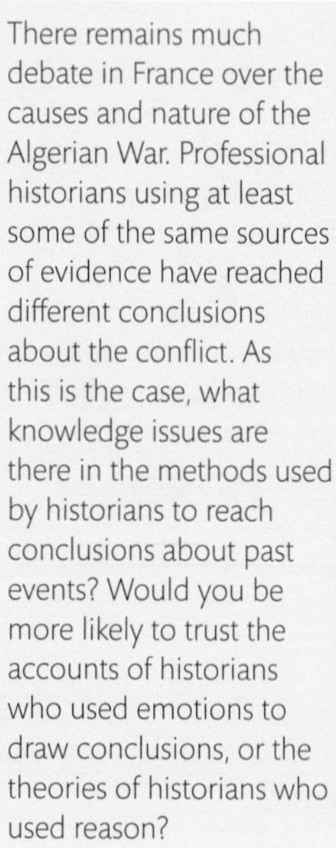

There remains much debate in France over the causes and nature of the Algerian War. Professional historians using at least some of the same sources of evidence have reached different conclusions about the conflict. As this is the case, what knowledge issues are there in the methods used by historians to reach conclusions about past events? Would you be more likely to trust the accounts of historians who used emotions to draw conclusions, or the theories of historians who used reason?

What were the results of the Algerian Civil War?

For Algeria

Human cost

The Algerian conflict was one of the most violent of the post-1945 colonial wars. More than 250,000 Algerians were killed in the war, with possibly as many as 12,000 being killed in the last attempts of the OAS to prevent a settlement. In addition, thousands suffered through being uprooted from their homes and through the massive destruction of property, as the departing *colons* destroyed buildings and facilities before they left.

Political cost

Politically, the government of the FLN did not produce stability. There was another civil war following the Evian agreement, a conflict that decided which Muslim group was to rule. It was only by the end of the summer and after another 15,000 had died that Ben Bella took control. He established a dictatorial system, purging former resistance fighters such as Ferhat Abbas, who was expelled from the FLN in 1963. In 1965, Houari Boumediène and the army overthrew Ben Bella, who was then put in prison. Boumediène ran a single-party state for 13 years, but his authoritarian socialism did not deliver the promises of higher living standards.

In 1991, the Islamic Salvation Front won the elections. However, the results were cancelled and military rule was imposed. A new civil war began as a result between the Algerian government and various Islamist rebel groups. It is estimated to have cost between 150,000 and 200,000 lives.

Economic cost

Activity 9 — ATL Thinking skills

Read the source and answer the question that follows.

Source A

After eight years of bitter civil war against the French-backed colons *Algeria won its independence in 1962, at which time almost all the* colons, *about one million in number, left the country for France. Thereafter, Algeria pursued a broadly socialist policy, first under Ahmed Ben Bella and then under Houari Boumedienne. Surprisingly, perhaps, for the rest of the 1960s Algeria enjoyed good relations with France; in fact the two countries needed each other: Algeria had oil and natural gas which France needed, France had technical expertise and could provide the aid which Algeria required for development. The withdrawal of one million* colons *meant the disappearance of most technical and other skills while the country faced unemployment levels as high as 70% of the working population. Some two million Algerians had been interned in camps during the war and a further 500,000 had become refugees in Morocco and Tunisia.*

Guy Arnold, *Africa: A Modern History* (Atlantic, 2005), p.174.

Source B

In Algeria, the conflict resulted in hundreds of thousands of dead, the displacement of millions of peasants, and the dismantling of the economy. In addition, it brought the FLN to power, a group that presented itself as the sole heir to Algerian nationalism. Benefitting from extraordinary popularity among the Algerian masses in 1962, it took root as the only party and, for nearly thirty years, negated any political or cultural pluralism.

Benjamin Stora, *Algeria 1830–2000: A Short History* (Cornell University Press, 2004), p.29.

1. According to these sources, what were:
   a) the political effects
   b) the economic effects of the war for Algeria?

For the *colons*

The European population of Algeria departed en masse; nearly 1 million returned to France (including most of the country's senior administrators). The mass exodus of the *pieds-noirs* left a vacuum in administration and business in Algeria that was exacerbated by the departure or killing of those who had cooperated with the *colons*. Ben Bella, who was elected first president of Algeria in 1963, legalized the expropriation of most foreign-owned land and hundreds of businesses that had been abandoned by the French.

For the *harkis*

The *harkis* were Algerians who had worked with the French. A report given to the UN assessed that there were 263,000 pro-French Muslims, working in all areas of administration and living in all areas of Algeria. At the end of the war, however, as the *pieds-noirs* fled to France, these people were largely forgotten. Thousands were massacred after Algerian independence, while those that did get to France (some 90,000) had great difficulties integrating into French society.

For France

In France, although there were far fewer casualties, the trauma was no less intense ... an entire generation ... found itself embarked upon a war whose stakes it did not understand. Politically, the conflict led to the fall of six prime ministers and the collapse of one Republic.

Benjamin Stora, *Algeria 1830–2000: A Short History* (Cornell University Press, 2004), p.29.

Algeria was France's last major act of decolonization. Official French casualties were put at 17,456 dead, 64,985 injured, and 1,000 missing. The war consumed 50–60 per cent of the French military budget and 10–15 per cent of the total French budget for 1954–1962. Yet with the end of its overseas conflicts and renewed focus on Europe, France then experienced a period of prosperity.

French links with Algeria continued as Boumediène concluded a series of agreements with France for the development of mining and other industries. Many Algerians, particularly the *harkis*, also migrated to France. Nevertheless, bitterness and controversy still exists between France and Algeria, with continuing debate over issues such as how the war is portrayed in French school textbooks, torture used by the French during the war, and the lack of recognition for the *harkis*.

CHALLENGE YOURSELF

Research skills

Research news articles from the past 10 years showing the continued debate over the Algerian War in France. How was the war remembered in France on the 50th anniversary of its conclusion in 2012?

Activity 10

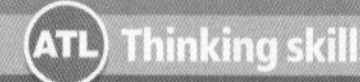

1. Explain briefly who or what the following were, and what impact they had on the course of events in the Algerian War:
   - the *colons*
   - the FLN
   - the Committee of Public Safety
   - the Generals' Insurrection
   - the OAS
   - the Battle of Dien Bien Phu
   - the Battle of Algiers
   - Barricades Week
   - Charles de Gaulle
   - the Evian conferences
2. Go back to the notes you made for the questions on page 299 about guerrilla war and add more examples of the tactics used by the FLN and on the response of the French army.
3. From what you have read so far, what problems did the French face in fighting the guerrilla tactics? Read the extract below and add to your answer.

> *A summary of this conflict illustrates the general difficulty of mounting effective counter-insurgency operations. Tough anti-insurrectionary measures, including widespread torture, which was seen as a justified response to FLN atrocities, gave the French control of the capital, in 1957. However although undefeated in battle, and making effective use of helicopter-borne units, the French were unable to end guerrilla action in what was a very costly struggle. And French moves were often counter-productive in winning the loyalty of the bulk of the population. There were also operational problems: aside from the difficulty of operating active counter-insurgency policies there was also a need to tie up large numbers of troops in protecting settlers and in trying to close the frontiers to the movement of guerrilla reinforcements, so that much of the army was not available for offensive purposes, a situation that helped the insurgents.*
>
> **Jeremy Black, *Introduction to Global Military History* (Routledge, 2005), p.43.**

Activity 11

ATL Thinking and communication skills

Use your answers to questions 2 and 3 above to help you answer the following essay question.

1. ***With reference to one 20th-century war, examine the impact of guerrilla tactics in deciding its outcome.***

Introduction: As in all introductions, you need to explain any key terms in the question. Here, you need to give a brief definition of guerrilla warfare (go back to chapter 1 to remind yourself again of the key characteristics) and explain that you are using the Algerian War as your example. You also need to put your chosen conflict into context – here, provide dates and explain that the FLN was the Algerian group carrying out the guerrilla tactics. Also set out your key argument.

Section 1: Always deal first with the issue that is given to you in the title, therefore here you need to look at the FLN's strategy of guerrilla warfare. Remember that you are not just describing the guerrilla tactics, but assessing their effectiveness. The key issue here is the impact that guerrilla warfare had on the tactics of the French army. Although guerrilla tactics were not successful in defeating the French forces or in winning the Battle of Algiers, the fact that they forced the army into retaliating with similar tactics (such as torture) alienated French public opinion against the war. It was also difficult for the French army to destroy the guerrilla forces completely or to win the support of the Algerian population, and they were forced into a costly and drawn-out struggle (see Black's comment above on this).

Section 2: Interestingly, in this war the OAS also used guerrilla warfare. How did this help the Algerian cause of independence?

Section 3: The question is asking you to make an assessment of the impact of guerrilla warfare, so, to help with this, you need to assess the contribution of any other factors to FLN success. Thus you may also want to consider here the actions of de Gaulle.

Now try these questions:

Discuss the long-term and short-term causes of one 20th-century war.

For this question you are going to structure your answer around the different thematic issues that led to conflict (such as those as identified in Activity 2 on page 292).

Examine the factors that led one side to victory in one 20th-century war.

This question is very similar to the question on guerrilla warfare, except here you can decide the order in which you deal with the different factors. The order you choose might depend on what you consider to be the most important factor – a good idea might be to deal with this factor first.

As above, points to consider include:

- the effectiveness of the FLN's guerrilla tactics
- the impact of the French army's tactics – for example, in the Battle of Algiers and the use of torture – particularly the effect that these tactics had on French public opinion
- political factors, such as the role of de Gaulle, the effect of the OAS, and how these impacted on French public opinion.

To access weblinks relevant to this chapter, go to www.pearsonhotlinks.com, search for the book title or ISBN, and click on 'chapter 14'.

Comparative study of guerrilla wars

Key concepts: Change and continuity

As you read this chapter, consider the following essay questions:

- Compare and contrast the reasons for adopting guerrilla warfare tactics and strategies in two 20th-century wars.
- Compare and contrast the role of guerrilla warfare in determining the outcome of two 20th-century wars.

An FL fighter is captured near Djebel Tarf during the Algerian War, 1958.

In examining guerrilla tactics, it is necessary to look at:

- the reasons for the choice of these tactics
- which elements of guerrilla tactics were used
- the effectiveness of these tactics and their role in determining the outcome of the conflict.

Activity 1

The basis of guerrilla war is to spread out and arouse the masses, and concentrate regular forces only when you can destroy the enemy. Fight when you know you can win. Don't fight battles you may lose.

In their operations guerrilla units have to concentrate the maximum forces, act secretly and swiftly, attack the enemy by surprise and bring battles to a quick decision. The basic principles of guerrilla warfare must be offensive and guerrilla warfare is more offensive in its character than regular warfare. The offensive, moreover, must take the form of surprise attacks.

Chairman Mao.

1. Identify and list the different elements of guerrilla warfare that are identified in this source.

The reasons for the choice of guerrilla tactics

Activity 2

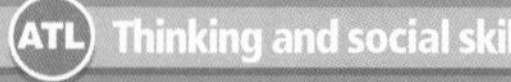

1. Work in pairs. Look at each of the following reasons as to why belligerents in a conflict might choose to use guerrilla tactics. One of you should decide which of these was relevant to the Chinese Communists; the other should decide which were relevant to the Algerian FLN. Make sure you can back up your choices with evidence. Don't forget that there are two phases to the civil war in China and you need to distinguish between the different characteristics of each phase:
   - lack of resources, arms, training, and conventional military experience compared to opponent
   - physical terrain limits conventional military operations and gives advantage to guerrilla activities
   - ideological support – revolutionary/people's war
   - practical need to win time, so that ideology can spread
   - need to shock, and generate publicity
   - opposing side's aversion to a long war
   - local traditions of resistance to authority
   - local traditions of resistance against foreign influence.

Read the following sources, which might help you to add extra information to your discussion.

Source A

Algerian geography is especially well suited to guerrilla warfare. The nation has a vast and varied terrain, from the mountain summits of over two thousand metres in the Aurès and the Djurdjura, to the High Plateaux; the landscape is remarkably different from region to region … Across the nation there are wild and undiscovered pockets very suitable for the hiding of a clandestine resistance movement … The majority of the leaders were from Kabylia and the Aurès, while most of the militants were peasants and, thus knew the territory inside-out. This put the French government at a disadvantage, as they were unfamiliar with the regions in comparison to the guerrilla militants … The geography secured the secrecy of the FLN, and enabled the militants to attack French bases and make off with weapons to power their resistance until arms could be obtained from sources abroad via the 'exterior' part of the organisation.

Sarah Hanafi, 'Guerrilla Warfare and its Role During the "Heroic Years" of the Algerian War', http://www.asfar.org.uk/guerrilla-warfare-and-its-role-during-the-heroic-years-of-the-algerian-war/

Source B

Estimated strength of Nationalist and Communist forces in China, August 1945. (Note that these statistics are just estimates and historians differ in the exact numbers that each side had. However, it is agreed that the Communists had far fewer troops.)

	Nationalists	Communists
Troops	3,700,000	320,000
Artillery pieces	6,000	600

Jonathan Spence, *The Search for Modern China* (W.W. Norton & Co., 1991), p.507.

Which elements of guerrilla warfare were used by each side?

Activity 3

1. Again, work in pairs to complete the following grid. Identify which point was relevant to each case study and how each was carried out. You should refer back to the relevant chapters to get your detailed evidence. The sources below will also help to provide extra information.

Guerrilla tactic	Algeria	China	Similarities or differences?
Mass mobilization of people behind the insurgency – winning 'hearts and minds' • land reform • disciplined behaviour of troops			
Use of terror • terror against the enemy • terror amongst own troops or amongst own civilian population			
Political campaigns • propaganda aimed at own troops • propaganda aimed at the local population			
Military tactics • ambush/surprise against regular troops and communication lines • bomb attacks in cities/against civilians			

Source A

After receiving political education, the Red Army soldiers have become class-conscious, learned the essentials of distributing land, setting political power, arming the workers and peasants etc., and they know they are fighting for themselves, for the working class and for the peasantry. Hence they can endure the hardships of the bitter struggle without complaint ... The most effective method in propaganda directed at the enemy forces is to release captured soldiers and give the wounded medical treatment. Whenever soldiers ... of the enemy forces are captured, we immediately conduct propaganda among them.

Extracts from Mao Zedong, 'The Struggle in the Chingkang Mountains', 1928.

Source B

The Three Main Rules of Discipline are as follows:
1 Obey orders in all your actions
2 Don't take a single needle or piece of thread from the masses
3 Turn in everything captured

The Eight Points for Attention are as follows:
1 Speak politely
2 Pay fairly for what you buy
3 Return everything you borrow
4 Pay for anything you damage
5 Don't hit or swear at people
6 Don't damage crops
7 Don't take liberties with women
8 Don't ill-treat captives

Instructions for the People's Liberation Army, 1947, from Mao Tse Tung, quoted in Robert Whitfield, *The Impact of Chairman Mao* (Nelson Thornes, 2008), p.26.

Source C

For month after month, life in Yenan centred on interrogations – and terrifying mass rallies, at which some young volunteers were forced to confess to being spies and to name others in front of large crowds who had been whipped into a frenzy. People who were named were then hoisted onto the platform and pressed to admit their guilt. Those who stuck to their innocence were trussed up on the spot and dragged away to prison and some to mock execution, amidst hysterical slogan screaming. The fear generated by these rallies was unbearable.

Description of life for the fighters who came to join Mao in Yenan from Jung Chang and Jon Halliday, *Mao: The Unknown Story* (Jonathan Cape, 2005), p.254.

Source D

Truly offensive action always required that the [platoon] move secretly and quickly from one point to another that was as far away as possible, since in guerrilla warfare nothing works like surprise. That meant that marches, except those in the forest, were usually done at night along ridges, in wadi beds, or at best over goat trails ... Without warning, an SAS post would be assaulted with mortar; a rural bus would be attacked and burned; or an ambush ... would patiently wait for the military convoy that informers in the neighbourhood had said was likely to pass. A hand-made mine camouflaged in the dust, would blow up a vehicle, block the convoy line, and set off machine gun fire; then came the assault. At every moment, the FLN leader's concern was to avoid the surprise of an unexpected encounter with the adversary in full strength.

Benjamin Stora, *Algeria 1830–2000* (Cornell University Press, 2001), p.63.

What was the impact of these tactics on the final outcome of the war?

Activity 4

1. In the cases of both China and Algeria, the side using guerrilla tactics achieved its ultimate goal. How important were guerrilla tactics in each case in determining this outcome?
2. In making this assessment, consider the following for each case study. Again, refer back to the relevant chapters, and use the sources in this chapter to help you.

- How effective was the attempt to win hearts and minds?
- Were there any major campaigns or battles fought by the guerrilla forces that acted as turning points in the struggle?
- How successful was political propaganda?
- What was the impact for the other side of having to fight against guerrilla tactics?

Activity 5

Consider the following essay question:

With reference to two 20th-century wars, each chosen from a different region, examine the impact of guerrilla tactics on the outcome of the conflicts.

Introduction: You need to define the key characteristics of guerrilla tactics and explain which case studies you are going to focus on.

Section 1: Consider guerrilla tactics that were effective in both countries. Remember to compare thematically, for example:

- In both China and Algeria, guerrilla military tactics achieved significant results.
- In both China and Algeria, political propaganda helped to win over the local populations.
- Both sides used terror against local populations.

Section 2: Consider contrasts between the two countries regarding effectiveness of tactics. Were there factors that were most significant in one case study and not in the other? For example, the FLN took their battle to the capital city in the Battle for Algiers, whereas the CCP remained mostly in the countryside. Did one country use terror – against its opponent or against its own fighters – more than the other?

Section 3: Weigh up the importance of guerrilla tactics against other factors. In both these cases, other factors also played a role in determining the war's outcome.

Conclusion: Here, you need to come back to the question and make a judgement as to the importance of guerrilla tactics in each case.

Now try this essay question:

Compare and contrast the role of guerrilla warfare on the course and outcome of two 20th-century wars.

Activity 6

1. Review the two case studies of guerrilla war you have studied. In pairs plan the following essay question:

   Compare and contrast the effects of two 20th-century wars, each chosen from a different region.

16

Americas region: Falklands/Malvinas War

British soldiers advancing across East Falkland Island for the final attack on Port Stanley during the Falklands War, June 1982.

Key concepts: Causation, consequence, and significance

As you read through this chapter, consider the following essay questions:

- Examine the long-term and short-term causes of one 20th-century inter-state war.
- To what extent did sea power determine the outcome of one 20th-century war?
- Discuss the political, economic and social effects of one 20th-century war.
- Discuss the role of territorial disputes in causing one 20th-century war.

Although there was no official declaration of war, Britain and Argentina went to war over the Falkland Islands/Malvinas in 1982. This conflict has been termed as one of the most 'unexpected wars' of the 20th century; 30,000 men fought over a remote group of islands with only 2,000 inhabitants. Britain and Argentina fought a war of limited mobilization in which both were restricted in their ability to deploy their human and material resources.

Timeline of events – 1828–1982		
1828	First recorded Argentine settlement in Malvinas	
1833	British take islands to prevent possible American seizure and send Argentines back to mainland	
1964	Falklands position is debated at the UN Committee on Decolonization	
1977	In November, Argentine naval manoeuvres provoke British naval response	
1979	Margaret Thatcher becomes prime minister in Britain	
1981	In December, Leopoldo Galtieri takes power in Argentina in a military coup	
1982	**19 Mar**	Argentines land at Leith Harbour, South Georgia, and raise an Argentine flag
	2 Apr	Argentine forces invade Falklands
	3 Apr	UN Security Council Resolution 502 demands cessation of hostilities and withdrawal of all Argentine forces from Falklands Britain announces Task Force to be sent to retake islands
	7 Apr	Britain declares Maritime Exclusion Zone (MEZ) of 200 nautical miles (321 kilometres) around Falklands
	19 Apr	Argentina rejects US Secretary of State Alexander Haig's peace proposal
	28 Apr	Britain establishes a Total Exclusion Zone (TEZ) around the Falkland Islands
	2 May	Submarine HMS *Conqueror* sinks battlecruiser *General Belgrano*, killing 323 Argentines
	4 May	British destroyer HMS *Sheffield* is sunk by an Exocet missile, with loss of 20 crew
	7 May	TEZ extended to within 19 kilometres of Argentine coastline UN Secretary General announces peace initiative
	20 May	UN peace initiative breaks down, ending any real hope of diplomatic resolution
	21 May	British troops land at San Carlos Bay on East Falkland
	23 May	British frigate *Antelope* hit by Argentine bombs and later sinks
	23–24 May	Air attacks lead to heavy losses for Argentines
	25 May	HMS *Coventry* and *Atlantic Conveyor* sunk, the latter by an Exocet missile

Timeline of events – 1828–1982	
28 May	Battles for Darwin and Goose Green
3 June	Bluff Cove and Fitzroy occupied by British troops Versailles Summit opens President Reagan presents five-point peace plan to British
8 June	British landing craft *Sir Galahad* and *Sir Tristram* bombed
11 June	Naval bombardment of Stanley; three islanders killed
13–14 June	Second phase of attack on Port Stanley
14 June	Brigadier-General Mario Menéndez surrenders all Argentine forces in East and West Falklands
20 June	British forces declare end to hostilities
12 July	Britain announces hostilities over the Falklands are regarded as ended Argentina makes no statement
22 July	TEZ lifted

Long-term causes of the Falklands War

The Falkland Islands as the British call them, or the Malvinas as they are known to Argentines, are a group of 780 islands in the South Atlantic. The two main islands, West and East Falklands, are approximately 500 kilometres off the east coast of Argentina, and 13,000 kilometres from Britain. A war between Argentina and Britain was 'unexpected', as they had enjoyed close relations for many years. Indeed, Britain was Argentina's largest buyer of agricultural produce. In any case, Argentina did not pose a clear threat to Britain as it was relatively isolated, and it had not been to war since the 19th century. Britain was a nuclear power (Argentina was not) and a member of the UN Security Council and NATO. Neither country had any clear economic or strategic reasons to go to war over these remote islands, whose economy was primarily based on sheep farming (there were 60,000 sheep). In addition, the Falklands were a remnant of the old British Empire, which had been in steady decline since World War Two.

Legacy of colonialism and territorial claims

The dispute over the Falklands/Malvinas began almost 150 years before the outbreak of the war itself. Britain had become an ally of Argentina in its long war of independence against Spain. After Argentina had declared itself independent in 1816, the British invested greatly in the country. Many British people went to live in Argentina, and relations between the two countries were good. However, there was one key area of tension – the Falklands. Argentina had laid claim to these islands in 1820, however, Britain occupied and controlled them from 1833, and by 1885 there was a British community of around 1,800 people on the islands. Then, in line with the broader expansion of the empire, the British gave the Falklands colonial status in 1892. The Argentines continued to claim the islands were theirs.

Following World War Two, the European empires began to collapse. Argentina pressurized the UN for the Malvinas to become an 'issue of decolonization' when it became a member state of the UN after the war. Argentina's lobbying paid off. In 1964, the Falklands position was debated at the UN Committee on Decolonization. Argentine claims were based on historical papal records from the time of Spanish and Portuguese colonial rule. The Argentines used a principle in international law whereby independent states have rights over the territories they had as a dependent state, and argued that the Malvinas, Georgias, and South Sandwich islands were part of the continental shelf of the Argentine sea. Furthermore, they claimed that British colonial claims were illegitimate. Britain based its claim on its history of effective and continuous administration of the islands since 1833, the internationally recognized principle of 'prescription' where inhabitants have a legal claim if no one else has claimed the territory, and its resolution to give the islanders self-determination as recognized in the UN Charter. Britain claimed that Argentine control would not end colonial rule, but *create* a colonial situation, as the islanders did not want to be ruled by Argentina.

In 1965, the General Assembly of the UN passed Resolution 2065, which called for negotiations between Britain and Argentina. These discussions were still ongoing in February 1982.

In 1982, there were more British people living in Argentina than in the Falklands. To most commentators in the two decades leading up to the outbreak of war, the Falklands meant nothing to the British, but they meant everything to the Argentines. Indeed, the Argentine public had been taught in school as part of the core curriculum that the islands were rightfully theirs. In contrast, at the beginning of the crisis that led to war in 1982, John Nott, the secretary for defence in Britain, had to refer to a globe to see where they were. They had no economic or strategic value at the time. There was only limited interest from the British in defending the territory, and in talks it was made clear to Argentina that the British wanted to hand them over. However, the British Foreign Office's attempts to slowly relinquish control of the islands in a process termed 'leaseback' stalled. The fundamental block to handing them over was the Falkland islanders themselves, who wanted to remain British.

Short-term causes of the Falklands War

> *Precipitated by Argentina's aggression, it was provoked by Britain's negligence.*
>
> **Hugo Young, *One of Us* (Pan Macmillan, 1994).**

Economic issues

In the early 1980s, the military regime in Argentina had serious economic problems. It had cut **public sector** spending and had tried to revive the **private sector**, but these measures had not worked and attempts to redress them made matters worse.

> *In November [1981] there had been a new run on the peso, bringing the depreciation of the local currency for the whole of 1981 to over 600% against the dollar – it set a new record even in Argentina. Financial instability had been accompanied by a deepening recession with high interest rates and a level of indebtedness threatening the survival of an increasing number of companies, particularly in manufacturing industry. During the year Gross Domestic Product had fallen by 11.4%, manufacturing by 19.2%, stirring the first symptoms of political opposition to the regime since the coup.*
>
> **Jimmy Burns, *The Land that Lost its Heroes* (Bloomsbury, 1987), pp.128–129.**

There were also economic problems in Margaret Thatcher's Britain. Unemployment had risen above three million for the first time since the global depression of the 1930s and in the final months before the outbreak of the war the worst riots of 20th-century Britain raged across cities.

Thus, it could be argued that both governments desired a foreign policy distraction from their domestic economic problems.

Leopoldo Galtieri.

CHALLENGE YOURSELF

Investigate the period known as the 'dirty wars' in Argentina. This was a period when the military dictatorships waged a campaign against suspected left-wing opponents in which approximately 10,000–30,000 people were killed. Many of these citizens were seized by the authorities and then 'disappeared'. Their families never heard from them again and did not know what had happened to them.

Political issues

General Leopoldo Galtieri had come to power in Argentina in a military coup in December 1981. In the late 1970s, the army had murdered thousands of people in what were known as the 'dirty wars', and the military had seized control in 1976. There followed a series of military **juntas**, and Galtieri's regime had continued the oppressive leadership of its predecessors. Some international observers believed Galtieri and his junta to be a Fascist-style dictatorship. He was under pressure from the military to achieve a popular success that would galvanize the regime and bring about some degree of political stability.

> *the internal situation when the military embarked upon the Malvinas landing [was] an uncontrollable deterioration of the economic crisis; contradictions in the armed forces and disintegration of its bourgeois support … and great advances in the mass movement and the struggle for democracy … Against this background, the main objective of the Junta in 'recovering' the Malvinas was to forge a new basis for consensus and to relegitimize the state …*
>
> **Alejandro Dabat and Luis Lorenzano, *Teoria y Politica* (Mexico City, 1982), translated as *Argentina: The Malvinas and the End of Military Rule* (Verso, 1984), pp.75–76.**

Margaret Thatcher became Britain's first female prime minister in the general election of 1979. She lacked authority over her own Conservative Party, and before the outbreak of the Falklands War had been one of the most unpopular prime ministers in British history. She, like Galtieri, stood to benefit politically from a foreign policy victory.

Margaret Thatcher.

In addition, she relished her reputation as the 'Iron Lady', a name given to her by the Soviets. A crisis over British territory would be an opportunity for her to live up to this image.

Before Thatcher came to power, the British Foreign Office had decided that the islanders' interests lay in handing the islands over to the Argentines. To encourage agreement from the Falkland islanders themselves, Britain limited investment and agreed that the only flights to and from the island would be dependent on Argentina.

However, the Falkland Islands Company, which was controlled by the British company Coalite, had political influence in Britain and was determined to prevent a handover. This viewpoint gained more support during the 1970s when the 'dirty war' took hold of Argentina.

Communication

It has been argued that the war was caused by a breakdown in communication between the politicians and statesmen. Indeed, the British Foreign Secretary at the time, Lord Carrington, accepted responsibility for the crisis that led to war and resigned. Carrington believed that the war could have been averted if the political regimes in Britain and Argentina had not misread the situation. The British had thought Argentina was militarily posturing to toughen its position in negotiations. They had done this on and off for over 20 years. The Argentines did not think that Britain would go to war over the Malvinas, as the regime did not understand the dynamics of the democratic political system, which was likely to encourage a forceful response from Thatcher.

Military causes

The desire to reclaim the Malvinas was strong throughout Argentina, but it was most important to the military and in particular the Argentine navy. The military-led junta that had seized power in November 1976 was determined to test Britain's commitment to the Falklands. In November 1977, they conducted provocative naval manoeuvres, but the British responded forcefully by sending a submarine and two frigates to the South Atlantic. This was sufficient to make the Argentines back down.

Significantly, British policy over the Falklands seemed confused; although talks had stalled, the British seemed to be giving signals that they would not be willing to protect the islands militarily. The results of a significant Defence Review in Britain had recommended the selling off of around a third of the Royal Navy's surface fleet. There were even rumours that the Royal Marines, one of Britain's most elite forces, was to be abolished.

Activity 1

With regard to the Falklands and its inhabitants, successive British governments had shown very little interest, and the Thatcher administration was no exception. The islands had some scientific value in so far as their minor appendage, South Georgia, provided a base for the British Antarctic Survey, but the main islands were of no strategic or economic value. The administration of the islands was unproblematic, except for the fact that they were dependent on Argentina for supplies and communication, and this served only to strengthen the Argentinian position in the dispute over sovereignty. By endorsing the leaseback proposals … the British government [indicated] it was willing to cede sovereignty [but this] was conditional on the agreement of the Islanders.

E.H.H. Green, *Thatcher* (Hodder Arnold, 2006), p.156.

1. Using the information in this chapter, to what extent was Britain giving 'misleading signals' about its position on defending the Malvinas/Falkland Islands?

Activity 2

Role play

1. Divide the class into the following two groups.
   - Group A: advisers to General Galtieri putting the case FOR war over the Falklands
   - Group B: advisers to General Galtieri arguing AGAINST war over the Falklands

Each group must review the material in this chapter and come up with a clear argument supporting their case. They may wish to divide their arguments into political/military/economic/strategic considerations.

The role of the navies

Both the British and Argentine navies could be held responsible for the immediate causes of the Falklands War. Indeed, Galtieri's coup had been supported by the commander-in-chief of the Argentine navy, Admiral Jorge Anaya, allegedly on the premise that Galtieri would back naval plans to remove Britain from the Malvinas. Admiral Anaya applied pressure on Galtieri for an invasion. In Britain, it was the key representative from the Royal Navy, Sir Henry Leach, who suggested to Margaret Thatcher that Britain was capable of retaking the Falklands. However, he was not necessarily encouraging Thatcher to go to war, and it should be borne in mind that by this point Argentina had already invaded the islands.

In Britain, John Nott's defence cuts had fallen particularly heavily on the Royal Navy. A large surface fleet seemed to have become obsolete in the context of the Cold War. Indeed, a war with the USSR would be fought for only a week, it was estimated, before nuclear weapons were used. In addition, as was later shown in the conflict, surface ships were vulnerable to air and submarine attacks. Thus, in the deep recession of the early 1980s, Nott reasoned that expenditure on the navy could be cut.

The Argentine navy had two plans to take back the Malvinas: the first was to set up an Argentine presence on South Georgia (an island approximately 1,400 kilometres from the Falklands) in a move called Project Alpha; the second was for a full-scale invasion, Operation Azul. The invasion was scheduled for some time between the end of May and mid-July, after the removal of HMS *Endurance*, as this would limit Britain's ability to offer immediate resistance. Indeed, it is argued by Duncan Anderson in *The Falklands War 1982* that the British decision to withdraw the *Endurance* was a key factor in the Argentine junta's decision to attack the Falklands in April, 1982.

HMS *Endurance*

Endurance was a Class 1 Icebreaker, and its mission was to patrol and survey the Antarctic and South Atlantic. Its role was also to maintain a physical British presence in the area and to defend British interests.

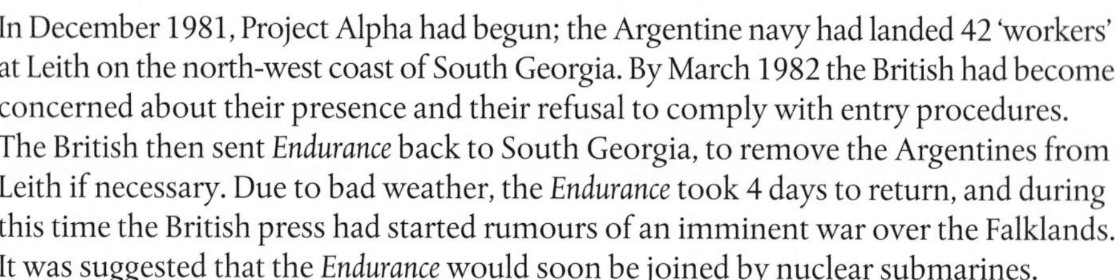

In December 1981, Project Alpha had begun; the Argentine navy had landed 42 'workers' at Leith on the north-west coast of South Georgia. By March 1982 the British had become concerned about their presence and their refusal to comply with entry procedures. The British then sent *Endurance* back to South Georgia, to remove the Argentines from Leith if necessary. Due to bad weather, the *Endurance* took 4 days to return, and during this time the British press had started rumours of an imminent war over the Falklands. It was suggested that the *Endurance* would soon be joined by nuclear submarines.

Admiral Anaya convinced the Argentine junta that reports in the British media about nuclear submarines being sent to defend the islands were correct, and that the invasion must start before the British could get forces to the region. A modified plan, Rosario, was drawn up, and on 28 March an invasion force headed for the Malvinas. This force comprised an ex-American tank landing ship, 20 US-built landing vehicles, and 900 troops, and was supported by 2 destroyers and 2 frigates. To the north of this primary invasion force was an aircraft carrier and the rest of the Argentine navy.

The invasion

On 2 April 1982, the Argentines began their attack on the capital of the Falklands/ Malvinas. Stanley became a battleground for a few hours until the defenders ran out of ammunition. Under a bombardment from the Argentines, and with Argentine troops being landed by helicopters, the local British commanders ordered their men to cease fire.

Activity 3 — ATL Thinking skills

Review questions

1. How legitimate were a) the British and b) the Argentine claims to sovereignty over the Falklands/ Malvinas?
2. What role did historical and cultural factors play in the development of the crisis in 1982?

Failure of diplomacy

War was not inevitable at this point, even though British territory had been invaded. Indeed, the British analysis of the situation was that a war that had to be waged 13,000 kilometres from home, in difficult weather conditions, against a well-equipped and locally based adversary, would be incredibly challenging. It seemed that the best response was a diplomatic one.

Margaret Thatcher, however, was worried that the press and the public would be outraged by the Argentine aggression and would not be satisfied with anything less than a military response. Although most of her advisers warned against a military campaign to retake the Falklands, the chief of defence staff was away, and in his place the First Sea Lord, Admiral Leach, persuaded Thatcher that it would be possible to win a war in the South Atlantic. In addition, he suggested that she had no other option: Britain's reputation and standing in the world were at stake.

Within hours of the Argentine landings in Stanley, the Ministry of Defence began to prepare British sailors, marines, soldiers, and air personnel for war on the other side of the Atlantic. The British armed forces assembled a massive naval Task Force, which rapidly prepared for deployment. From this point on, military timetables rather than diplomatic meetings were guiding events. The new British Foreign Secretary, Francis Pym, and the American Secretary of State, Alexander Haig, worked for a peaceful resolution.

Diplomatically, the British concentrated on isolating the Argentines and argued that they were in the wrong, as they were the 'aggressors'. The Foreign Office was able to apply years of experience to initiate a coherent international response, unlike the uncoordinated attempts by the Argentines. The British ambassador to the UN pushed through Security Council Resolution 502, which called for the immediate withdrawal of Argentine forces from the islands. On the same day, 3 April, the British got the French to agree to stop the export of Exocet anti-ship missiles, Super Etendard aircraft (which could be used for launching the Exocets), and engines for Pucara aircraft, which would impede Argentina's ability to wage war. Six days later, the EEC imposed a trade embargo.

Nevertheless, the key diplomatic effort for both Argentina and Britain was to gain the support of the USA. Galtieri's regime had gambled on some American support for Argentina, as he had a relatively close relationship with certain members of the US military. However, American support for Britain was almost inevitable due to the nature of the Cold War and the fact that Britain was a more important ally in this broader context.

Activity 4

The events of the final week before the Argentine invasion of the Falklands seem with hindsight to have possessed an awful inevitability. In Argentina the invasion machine was now in forward gear, though it is still maintained in some quarters (including American intelligence) that the final decision to go on 2 April was not made until 31 March. In London, politicians and officials appear to have been bemused and hesitant as crisis swirled towards them. Only one institution seems to have responded to the assessments of 28 March with total single-mindedness: the Royal Navy. In its case there were ulterior motives.

Max Hastings and Simon Jenkins, *The Battle for the Falklands* (Pan, 1997), p.77.

1. Max Hastings and Simon Jenkins argue that the Royal Navy was significant in the British response to the invasion. What 'ulterior' motives would the Royal Navy have for wanting or urging a military response?

The crisis intensifies

The first components of the British Task Force launched on 5 April 1982. It would take the ships 3 weeks to reach the Malvinas, therefore there was a 3-week period during which negotiations could resolve the crisis short of war. Indeed, although the crisis was intensifying, there was still hope that the mobilization and departure of the British Task Force would be a sufficient threat to Galtieri to force the Argentines to negotiate. The British carriers *Hermes* and *Invincible* set sail on 5 April, and these were followed by the departure of other ships, all of which were highly publicized in the media – the Task Force consisted of 2 aircraft carriers, 5 destroyers, 11 frigates, and 3 **nuclear submarines**. To a certain extent, this show of force had the desired effect, and there was alarm in Argentina at the scale of the British preparations for war. The Argentines responded with a build-up of forces under the command of General Mario Menéndez, who had arrived in the Malvinas to take on the role of governor.

Brinkmanship

Both sides in the crisis were engaged in a dangerous game of '**brinkmanship**' or 'bluff'. The Argentine junta continued to believe that the British military response was a bluff until the end of April 1982, and the British too thought that Galtieri had gone too far with the posturing carried out by the Argentines for 25 years. Both ultimately believed that there would be a diplomatic resolution. On 24 April, the Argentine Foreign Minister Costa Méndez arrived in the United States to review a new peace proposal drawn up by Britain's Foreign Secretary Francis Pym and the American Secretary of State Alexander Haig. Méndez rejected the plan. Peru, a supporter of Argentina, then took up the peace initiatives, but by this point the British Task Force had almost arrived in the Falklands.

The tension increased further on 28 April when Britain announced a Total Exclusion Zone (TEZ) of 200 nautical miles (370 kilometres) around the Falklands, which would come into effect as of 11.00am on 30 April. On 2 May, the British nuclear submarine HMS *Conqueror* sank the Argentine cruiser *General Belgrano* (see below for details). There could be no diplomatic solution now. Even though there had been no declaration, Britain and Argentina were now at war over the Falklands/Malvinas.

Activity 5

ATL Thinking and social skills

Read the source below and, in pairs, answer the questions that follow.

> *the Argentines' view [of the causes of the war] is perceived as a recovery of the Islands without bloodshed after 149 years of persistent claims. From the Argentine view the war was triggered by Great Britain with the British decision to sink the Argentine cruiser General Belgrano on 2nd May 1982, outside of the theatre of operations, causing the deaths of more than three hundred Argentine sailors. Until that point in the conflict, Great Britain had suffered no casualties in the Argentine recovery of the Islands.*
>
> **Major Leanoardo Arcadio Zarza, Argentine Aviator Office, School of Advanced Military Studies, Kansas, USA, in an online monograph, 2010, p.2.**

1. Evaluate the perspective of the causes of the war presented in this source.
2. Compare and contrast this view with that of the British military and government at the time of the conflict.

Map showing the route of the British Task Force to the Falklands/Malvinas, April 1982, and the British Exclusion Zone, with the position of the *General Belgrano* on her sinking on 2 May 1982.

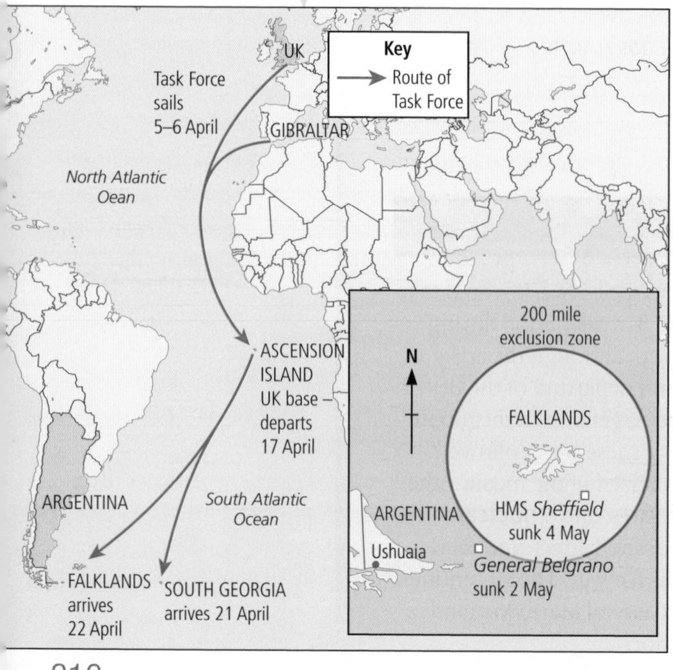

Why did the search for peace fail?

The Argentine government was not willing to negotiate for anything less than sovereignty, and the British position was similarly uncompromising. Argentina claimed the islands had been taken 'without a shot being fired' and the crowds that had gathered on the streets of Buenos Aires chanted 'Malvinas Argentina'. Argentina declared that it did not have to explain bringing about the end to the 'illegitimate British occupation of their islands'. At the UN, the Argentines defended the invasion as part of the decolonization process, saying they had 'just reclaimed their own land'.

Despite the **shuttle diplomacy** of the US Secretary of State Haig, and further attempts by the UN to secure a diplomatic resolution to the crisis, neither side would retreat from its stated aim: to restore complete British/ Argentine sovereignty to the islands. The UN could not send in a peacekeeping force until both sides had asked them to do so. Then, the British government declared a broader aim as hostilities increased – the aim of upholding the principle that 'naked aggression by anybody should not be allowed to pay'. The Argentines dismissed the British stance as an old-fashioned 'preservation of empire'. However, Argentina had broken the international rule of law with the invasion of the Falklands/Malvinas, and this fact was recognized by the UN.

Practices of the war and their impact on the outcome

> *It was a 'clean' war, in which both sides sought to avoid civilian casualties and respected the rights of prisoners.*
>
> **Commander Sandy Woodward, commander of the British Task Force.**

The Falklands War was a war of limited mobilization for a number of reasons. Britain had one of the largest navies in NATO and thus it was obviously capable of retaking the islands, but it was only willing to do so at a limited cost. The British government did not believe that the British people would support a war if there were high casualties.

At the outset, theoretically, the Argentines seemed to have many advantages over the British. They had much shorter communication and supply lines, an air force that could be operational from the mainland, and time to build their defensive positions on the Falkland Islands before the British arrived. The British appeared to have some serious military obstacles. The first of these was actually getting their fleet to the South Atlantic and preventing a single attack taking out too many troops, as the fleet was vulnerable to anti-ship missiles. In addition, coordination was difficult between different elements of the Task Force and there was friction between the navy, army, and air force.

The Argentines' war plan was to defend their position on the Falklands primarily by using their air force to cripple the Task Force before it could land troops on the islands. The British plan was first to gain control of the air and sea around the Falkland Islands and then to make an amphibious landing of ground forces. Both sides knew that the only way to ultimately win the war was to win it on the land. The British ships were in two groups. The group to the south was Commander Woodward's naval fleet, which was the advance force. This comprised two aircraft carriers and assorted warships. The objective of the first group was to gain air and sea superiority, and then the second group of ships would be able to land their troops for the land campaign.

The fighting focused on the two main islands – East and West Falkland – each only around 80 kilometres long. By the end of April 1982, the new Argentine governor and commander of the Malvinas was General Mario Benjamin Menéndez. He had 13,000 troops massed on the islands, with major concentrations on West Island, at Goose Green, and 10,000 in the hills to the west of Stanley on East Island. These hills would be Menéndez's last line of defence. Nevertheless, the Argentine plan was not to use these ground forces, but to neutralize the Task Force at sea.

> *The war for the Malvinas from the Argentine perspective consisted of two main campaigns conducted in five phases. The first campaign, the recovery, took place from 25 March until 7 April 1982. The second campaign, the defense, was fought from 7 April until 4 June 1982. Following the recovery campaign, Argentina established a Military Governor in Port Argentino, General Mario Benjamin Menendez. The Argentinean Phase III, Dominate, and Phase IV Stability, were easily achieved as there was not a single British military or civilian casualty. Phase V, enabling civil authority, took place with the transition from the British Governor to the Argentine one.*
>
> **Major Leanoardo Arcadio Zarza, Argentine Aviator Office, School of Advanced Military Studies, Kansas, USA, in an online monograph, 2010, p.32.**

War in the air

The first battle for the Falklands was in the air. The Argentine Air Force was well trained, with high-performance fighter bombers, and these could be deployed from their bases on the mainland. However, the three airfields on the islands were not long enough for jet aircraft and therefore the Argentines had to fly from their bases at home. This hampered their ability to patrol the skies and to give their ground troops close air support. It also meant that Argentine planes had a more limited fly-time over the islands.

The Sea Harrier, the main fixed-wing carrier aircraft of the British during the Falklands War.

Britain's first aim was to win air superiority, but British forces could only use the amount of aircraft they could take on their two aircraft carriers. This meant Britain had 34 planes to nearly 100 Argentine fighters. These planes also had the job of protecting the fleet, and once they had control of the air they were to cover the amphibious landings. The British air force had to accomplish all this from the very restrictive confines of the carrier decks.

The battle for control of the air began on 1 May 1982. Although the British were outnumbered, they had one key advantage – new Sea Harrier planes. This new technology had not been combat tested, but these planes could take off and land vertically and could operate from short runways. As the air battle developed, the Harriers demonstrated that they were both versatile and dependable. In addition, these jets were armed with the latest Sidewinder air-to-air heat-seeking missiles. On the first day alone, four Argentine planes were shot down by Sidewinders, and as the historians Max Hastings and Simon Jenkins assert, 'in every case in which a Sidewinder locked on, the enemy aircraft was destroyed' (Max Hastings and Simon Jenkins, *The Battle for the Falklands* [Pan, 1997]). It soon became clear that the British Harriers had the potential to destroy the Argentine air force. Using an effective combination of electronic warfare, Sea Harriers, surface-to-air missiles, and anti-aircraft artillery, the British Royal Navy destroyed more than half of Argentina's 134 combat aircraft. The Harriers were the key to Britain's war. Argentina's Mirage planes were now cut off from the islands and the British could attempt to enforce the exclusion zone in the air.

Yet the British fleet remained vulnerable, with the Argentines still able to fly from their mainland bases, and if the carriers were lost Britain would not be able to continue to fight. Indeed, the Argentines used air attacks from the mainland on the British throughout the war. Neither side gained total control in the air.

War at sea

Although the war in the air developed into a stalemate, the initial encounters at sea were to be decisive in that theatre. The way the war at sea was fought was also altered by the impact of new technology; battles would be fought using deadly missiles, including the ship-to-ship or air-launched Exocet missiles. The ability of the British to engage in the war at sea was limited by the fact that its nearest base, Ascension Island, was 5,300 kilometres from the Falklands/Malvinas. Therefore, it was vital for Britain to protect its two aircraft carriers. If they were sunk, Britain's ability to wage an air war would be destroyed. In this way, the war could be lost in a day if the carriers were taken out.

The sinking of the *Belgrano*.

On 1 May, Britain's main sea force was 160 kilometres north-east of the Falklands. To the north, Argentine warships were approaching. This group included an aircraft carrier *Cinco de Mayo*, whose onboard aircraft would soon be in range of the British fleet. To the south of the islands there was another group of Argentine ships, including a World War Two cruiser, the *General Belgrano*, and two destroyers that were believed to be armed with Exocet missiles. These Exocets had the capability of sinking a British carrier. The Argentine ships seemed to be progressing against the British in a pincer movement, moving in from both the north and the south.

The *Belgrano* and its company were being tracked by the British submarine HMS *Conqueror*. Although the cruiser was moving relatively slowly, the British were concerned that if it went into shallow water the submarine would not be able to follow. The Argentine group could then move on towards a British carrier and destroy it. However, the *Belgrano* was just outside the TEZ, so was potentially not a legitimate target. Margaret Thatcher herself was consulted and she gave the order to attack. On 2 May, the *Belgrano* was torpedoed by the *Conqueror*, which put two torpedoes into the cruiser's stern – the *Belgrano* sank in less than an hour, killing 323 of the Argentines on board; 772 men were subsequently rescued from the freezing seas.

Although there is controversy over the legality of the sinking of the *Belgrano*, there is no doubt that it had a significant strategic impact. Immediately afterwards, the entire Argentine navy turned and headed back home and remained there for the rest of the war. The Argentines feared repeated submarine attacks could destroy their fleet. Thus, the Argentine naval threat had been eliminated and Britain had won the war against Argentina's surface fleet.

Even after the sinking of the *Belgrano*, the British government still claimed that it was not officially at war. They limited their description of the conflict to 'hostilities', and argued that the British had the right to self-defence through Article 51 of the UN Charter.

Argentina now waged its war at sea against the British from the air. They had recently purchased five air-launched Exocet missiles. These missiles could seek out and destroy ships from a range of more than 50 kilometres.

On 4 May, two Argentine aircraft, each loaded with an Exocet, left the mainland and headed for the British fleet. Commander Sandy Woodward had three destroyers armed with anti-aircraft missiles defending his ships. However, the anti-aircraft missiles were unreliable against low-flying targets such as Exocets. HMS *Glasgow*'s radar picked up the approaching aircraft and sent out a warning to all other ships. The destroyer HMS *Sheffield* did not pick up the full warning, and it was simultaneously sending a message back to Britain, which blocked its radar.

HMS *Sheffield* was hit by an Exocet, and it became the first British ship to be sunk in a conflict since World War Two. Twenty men were killed and twenty-six were injured. This had a deep impact back in Britain.

As the case of the *Sheffield* demonstrated, although the British had driven the Argentine navy back home, the war at sea was far from over. Indeed, many British ships were lost supporting its land campaign as they came under attack from the air.

Activity 6

ATL Thinking and social skills

Review questions

The sinking of the *Belgrano* was a turning point. Up until then, few people had died, and most prisoners had been quickly returned via neutral countries. After the *Belgrano*, all other peace plans were doomed. Almost half of Argentina's losses in the war were killed in its sinking.

Discuss in small groups the following questions:

1. Certain Latin American and European nations supported the Argentine claim that the ship was not posing a threat to the Task Force, and Britain lost some international support. However, the attack on the *Belgrano* was popular in Britain. To what extent, in a limited war, is it more important to keep domestic opinion or international opinion on your side?
2. Review the events up to the sinking of the *Belgrano*. When was a diplomatic solution possible?
3. At what point did a war become inevitable?

War on the land

The British land campaign to retake the Falklands.

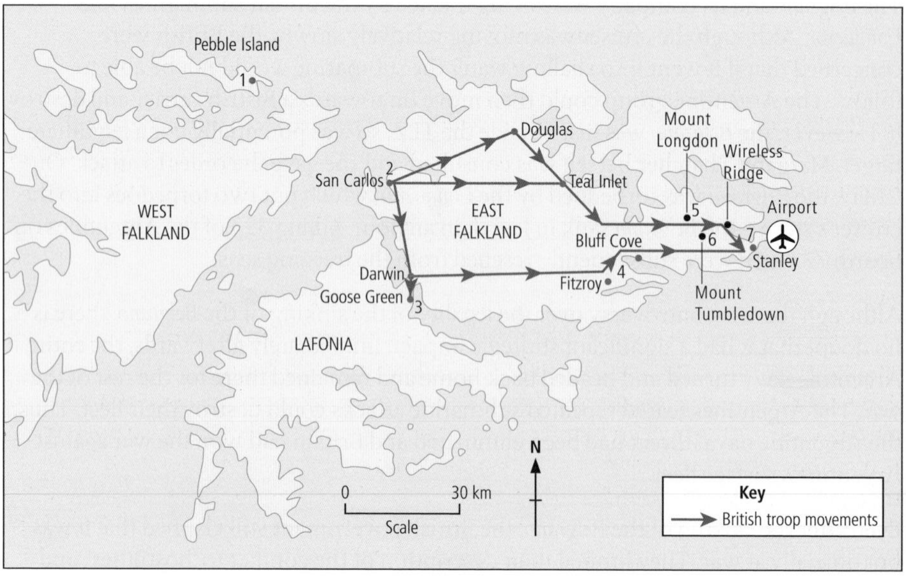

As the war in the air continued, the British had to now focus on winning on the land. The concern for the British was that the South Atlantic winter was drawing in by mid-May and flying the Sea Harriers in bad weather was almost impossible. Therefore, British commanders made the decision that they would have to risk putting in ground forces without total air superiority. This would make an amphibious landing vulnerable to

Argentine air assaults. The land war would focus on the recapture of the capital, Stanley, so the British had to land on East Island. However, the Argentines had organized sound defences in the hills surrounding Stanley, and so the British decided to land troops some distance away at San Carlos Bay in an operation codenamed Operation Sutton. The bay was not well defended and was out of range of the Argentine artillery. In addition, its surrounding hills would give protection from low-level air attack. Nevertheless, this area became known as 'bombers alley' as British forces came under relentless attack from low-flying Argentine jet planes whilst landing their troops and equipment.

On 21 May, 4,000 troops began an amphibious landing. These troops were made up of Royal Marine Commandos and paratroopers, and were led by Brigadier Julian Thompson. However, San Carlos was 80 kilometres from Stanley. To avoid having to march his men and equipment across harsh terrain in awful weather with all their kit, Thompson waited for the arrival of nine helicopters he could use as transport. The British troops dug in. The Argentines then began their air attack on the ground forces. All the supplies for Britain's land campaign were still being unloaded from ships under attack. For 5 hours, fighter bombers bombed the fleet in San Carlos Bay while the landed troops watched on helplessly. Although the hills provided some protection for the troops on shore, they hindered the British ships' radars. Five British warships were hit and one ship, HMS *Ardent*, was sinking by the end of the day. The Argentines continued their air bombardment and flew regularly at night, using Canberra bomber planes. This aerial campaign on British ground forces was sustained until the end of the war.

Although some Argentine planes were hit by anti-aircraft guns, this had little impact on the overall assault. The British ships were easy targets sitting in the bay, but they could not retreat, as it was vital for the land campaign that they unloaded their supplies. On 23 May, HMS *Antelope* was fatally hit. Eight British ships were damaged and two were sunk. Menéndez and the Argentine forces celebrated this phase of their air campaign, which was seen as a victory. The Argentine air force then prepared another campaign against the British land forces.

The next Argentine air strike seriously threatened the British land campaign. A massive supply ship, the *Atlantic Conveyor*, had begun to enter San Carlos Bay on 25 May, carrying the helicopters the ground troops needed to get across East Island to Stanley. Two Argentine aircraft released Exocets, which locked on to two frigates in the British carrier group. These ships then fired up metal foil to confuse the missiles' radar and the Exocets then locked on to a new target, the *Atlantic Conveyor*. The missiles hit the ship and destroyed all of the helicopters on board. Without these helicopters, the British land force now had to march for 4 days to cover the 80 kilometres to the capital, each man carrying up to 55 kilograms of kit.

The British split their troops into two groups. The main force of around 2,000 men marched east towards Stanley; the other force of around 500 marched south. This smaller group had been tasked to achieve a quick morale-boosting victory over the Argentines at the strategically important Goose Green. They needed to take the airstrip there, but the ground was flat and lacked any features that could be used to protect the attackers. Therefore, the plan was to attack the airfield in the dark, and then take the Argentine settlement in daylight. The British troops had to attack a well-defended Argentine position on the high ground of Darwin Hill, which was defended by minefields in front and artillery from behind.

Under the cover of darkness the attack began, but one group of men became pinned down by machine-gun fire. There were more Argentines defending the position than the British had thought. The battle raged on until dawn, when the sun rose and lit up Goose Green. The British on low ground were now exposed to Argentine fire, and could advance no further.

The British were held a mile away from the airstrip when their air support arrived. Two fighter bombers dropped cluster bombs on Argentine positions as the ground troops edged forward. Both sides were exhausted. The British then attempted to bluff a victory from the Argentines. They sent a letter threatening them with a heavy bombardment if they did not surrender. The letter also said that the Argentines would be held responsible for any civilian casualties. The threat of being blamed for civilian casualties highlights the limited nature of the war – neither side wanted civilian blood on their hands. The Argentines surrendered. Britain had won the first battle of the land campaign, and in part this had been due to deception; over 900 men surrendered to the smaller British force. The number of casualties at Goose Green was high for a limited battle in a limited war. In total, 17 British and 47 Argentine soldiers were killed, and 961 Argentines were taken prisoner. With this large Argentine force defeated the British were able to break out of the beachhead in San Carlos Bay.

Night fighting

British forces were trained to fight as effectively at night as in daylight. This capability can be highly effective against defended targets, and when fighting in open terrain. The key is to stick to the set plan, and to maintain consistent and clear communication throughout the battle. Everyone needs to know where they are, and where the enemy is. But the strategy is dangerous and difficult. Attackers have to keep moving in the dark to prevent the defenders being able to target them.

Although Goose Green was important, the key battle of the land war was the battle for the capital, Stanley. The British were now hit by a major setback. As the second group of 2,000 troops was nearing the capital, ships with reinforcements, the *Sir Galahad* and the *Sir Tristram*, were hit by Argentine bombs. The 500 men aboard should have been disembarked under the cover of darkness, but due to a series of delays and communication failures, the men had been kept on board in broad daylight. After waiting on the ships for 6 hours, the soldiers were attacked by two Argentine fighters; 49 British soldiers were killed and 115 were injured. The Argentines now had a victory in the land war, although not as significant as they suggested at the time. Menéndez believed there had been 900 British troops killed. Indeed, Menéndez thought that this would lead to a drop in British morale and would stall the advance on Stanley.

Now led by Major General Jeremy Moore, the British put 9,000 troops near the hills around Stanley. They again began their attack at night. The plan involved two phases. During the first night, troops would sweep from north to south in a three-pronged attack on Argentine positions. This movement would secure the outer ring of hills around Stanley. The largest and most important was Mount Longdon. The second night would see an assault on another ring of hills nearer Stanley; the key hill in this phase was Tumbledown. If this plan succeeded, the British would be within 3 kilometres of the capital.

The battle for Mount Longdon began on 11 June at 8.00pm and raged for 7 hours. Although the British suffered high casualties as a result of getting trapped under fire in alleyways of rock, their assault proved too forceful for the Argentines to push back. The Argentines became so desperate to repel the British that Menéndez ordered his artillery to fire down on his own positions. The British were now ready for the second phase of their plan. The 2nd Battalion of Scots Guards was tasked with one of the most difficult parts of the land campaign: the assault on Tumbledown – and they lacked experience. The Argentines had their elite 5th Marines in position, heavily armed and dug into the caves and rocks of the mountain. There were 700 Argentines, almost twice the number of British forces, and these troops also had been trained to fight at night. Initially, the British were in trouble, and their advance halted. However, 30 guardsmen then seized the initiative and climbed to higher ground so that they could fire down on Argentine positions. By the morning, the British were bombarding the remnants of the Argentine forces, and hundreds retreated towards Stanley. With the natural

Discarded Argentine kit, June 1982.

defences taken and their positions breached at Mount Tumbledown, the morale of the Argentines holding Stanley collapsed. The British surrounded Stanley, and on 14 June demanded the Argentine surrender. Menéndez agreed. Discipline in his army had broken down and the men had lost the will to fight.

Activity 7

ATL Thinking skills

War and the role of individuals

1. To what extent do you agree with the following statement?

> *It is not only the decisions and speeches of political leaders that inspire their armed forces, it is also the actions of individuals on the battlefield.*

2. Read the following case study and then discuss to what extent the actions of individuals are significant in warfare.

   Colonel 'H' Jones, leading 2nd Battalion, the Parachute Regiment, at Goose Green, decided that he would 'lead from the front'. In an act of extreme bravery, heroism or madness (depending on your interpretation), he identified an Argentine position and proceeded to attack it. (It is unclear whether Colonel H had thought he could ultimately take the Argentine position alone, or whether he was attempting to encourage his men forward with him in attack.) He charged up the hill firing his sub-machine gun, but came under heavy fire and was shot dead.

TOK

In pairs, discuss the role of individuals in history. Using this case study of the Falklands/Malvinas war, consider the role played by individuals in the causes and course of the conflict.

Activity 8

> *From Buenos Aires, Galtieri had been urging Menendez to mount a counter-offensive but Menendez knew that this was the madness of a despot and not the rational thinking of the commander-in-chief. He still had three full regiments together with some artillery, but morale was in the process of irreversible disintegration. Menendez, who felt badly let down by Galtieri, the air force and the navy, had in fact thought he was fighting a hopeless cause from the moment British troops had established their beachhead at San Carlos, but felt that he owed it to his men and his own sense of honour to put up some resistance.*
>
> **Jimmy Burns, *The Land that Lost its Heroes* (Bloomsbury, 1987), pp.394–395.**

1. According to Burns, what was the attitude of Menéndez to the development of a war on the land?

Activity 9

Thinking and social skills

1. There are mistakes, bad decisions, and miscommunications during battle, or 'the fog [confusion] of war', as it is known. In pairs, discuss whether leaders should be held responsible for mistakes made during the 'fog of war'.

The extent of mobilization: war on the home front

Due to the limited nature of the Falklands/Malvinas War, there was a correspondingly limited impact on the home front of each belligerent. There was no bombing of civilians in Argentina or an attempt to wage a sea blockade of Britain, as had been the case in the first and second *total* wars. There was no rationing or night-time air raids. Yet although Britain did not introduce conscription, the military regime in Argentina used conscripts in its army.

The war, had more of a social impact on Argentina than on Britain. For example, the Argentines had been enthusiastic consumers of Western pop and rock music, but once the war began radio stations were not permitted to play English-language music. There was also a demonstration outside the large Harrods store in Buenos Aires. The British in Argentina kept a low profile, and British schools abandoned their school uniforms so that their students could not be identified.

The Falklands War inspired patriotism in Britain such as had not been seen for decades. Here, flag-waving crowds see off the British Task Force as it heads out to the Falklands.

Nevertheless, the media was censored in both Britain and Argentina. In addition, there was the lack of effective satellite technology to get direct transmissions back to Britain, but both sides had a **jingoistic** popular press that used aggressive and often racist terminology to describe the enemy. In Britain, the BBC news presenter Jon Snow was attacked in the press and in parliament for using the term 'British' and not 'us' in his reports of the war. However, the British media managed to deliver a more accurate impression of what was going on than was the case in Argentina. Thus, although fighting a limited war, both countries ensured the press reflected the overall picture the government wanted shown to the general public.

Activity 10

1. In small groups, research the British and Argentine media coverage of the Falklands/Malvinas War, focusing particularly upon newspapers. If you include the names of prominent British papers in your searches, such as *The Sun*, *The Guardian*, *The Independent*, and *The Times* you should get a spread of political opinion. In small groups, compare and contrast the wartime headlines, looking at how the British media and the Argentine media attempted to present the conflict, and also how they used language and imagery to shape public perceptions. A significant example of jingoism was *The Sun* newspaper's inflammatory headline 'GOTCHA', relating to the sinking of the *General Belgrano*.
2. Then explore the headlines and media coverage from other countries. How consistent was the information and opinion on the war around the world?

The role of the UN

The UN acted to limit the Falklands/Malvinas War, first by attempting to find a negotiated peace, and second by preventing the escalation and spread of the conflict. The UN had passed a resolution condemning the Argentine invasion and requesting the removal of their forces. Thus, although the UN had condemned Argentina, it did not resolve to take action – it was up to Britain to act. Initially, at least, the UN resolution gave Britain the moral high ground, and Britain received support from the Security Council, on which it had a permanent seat. As the war continued, however – and particularly after the sinking of the *Belgrano* – the British strategy of keeping Argentina isolated and 'in the wrong' began to fail. Indeed, on 4 June a Security Council ceasefire resolution was supported by nine countries, including China and the USSR, with four countries abstaining. Britain was forced to use its veto, and was supported by the USA. Yet almost immediately afterwards, Jeane Kirkpatrick, the US Ambassador to the UN, announced that if it were possible she would change the American vote from a no to an abstention. It was perhaps fortunate for Britain that it had been able to stall the UN's ceasefire resolutions until the land war was well underway.

The role of the USA

Both sides recognized that the support of the USA was vital to their cause. Although the USA had developed an apparent 'special relationship' with Galtieri, he had not seen the bigger picture. Attempting to maintain its influence in Latin American was only part of US foreign policy and this involvement was not key to its overall Cold War strategy against the USSR. Galtieri's regime had gambled on the US remaining neutral. The American decision (although hesitant throughout the war) to give some support to the British was significant in its course; logistical support was given through Ascension Island in the mid-Atlantic, and without this the war would have been protracted and subject to risk by the onset of the southern winter. The British Task Force stopped en route at Ascension Island, about halfway between Britain and the Falklands, which the Americans had developed into a major military base during World War Two. This stopping point was vital for the organization of British forces. In order to wage war effectively, Britain had to set up a 13,000-kilometre supply chain using the Royal Navy and RAF. The Americans also supplied the British with 12.5 million gallons of aviation fuel. This allowed the RAF to make 2,500 flights that transported 30,000 tons of equipment and thousands of personnel. The Americans also supplied the British with missiles during the war.

In attaining American support and using its position in the Security Council at the UN, Britain's Foreign Office won the diplomatic battle of the war.

Activity 11

ATL Thinking skills

Read the sources below and answer the questions that follow.

Source A

> *The vital assumptions made unilaterally by the military junta included that Great Britain lacked strategic reach and political will to fight to recover the islands, and that the United States would remain neutral. There was no contingency branch plans or sequels developed. On April 4, 1982, the United States authorized Great Britain to use Ascension Island as an intermediate staging base. This development dramatically changed the situation for Argentina because now it put British forces only 3,000 nautical miles from the Islands.*

Argentina's lack of understanding and inaccurate appreciation of intelligence led to this critical error. The Argentine intelligence assessment stated that Argentina would be unable to hold the islands if Great Britain was supported by the United States in a recovery campaign.

Major Leanoardo Arcadio Zarza, Argentine Aviator Office, School of Advanced Military Studies, Kansas, USA, in an online monograph, 2010, p.34.

Source B

In New York at the United Nations, Spain and Panama had put forward a new resolution calling for an 'immediate ceasefire in the Islands.' When it came to a vote of the Security Council both Britain and the USA vetoed the motion. But moments after the vote had taken place, the American UN Ambassador, Jeane Kirkpatrick emerged to make a flustered statement to the press. She had voted the wrong way. Al Haig in Paris had done a last minute volte-face. He had wanted the United States to abstain, not veto the motion, presumably on the grounds that such a move would curry favour with Latin American countries. However, Kirkpatrick did not receive the instruction until after she had cast her vote, she announced to general incredulity. Not only had the United States sought to double-cross Britain, it had done so incompetently.

Richard Aldous, *Reagan and Thatcher: The Difficult Relationship* (Norton, 2012), pp.109–110.

Source C

Cartoon by Nicholas Garland, 25 April 1982, in the British *Sunday Telegraph*, 'Daddy, what will you do in the Great War?'

1. According to Source A, what was the miscalculation regarding US support for Britain that was significant in the outcome of the war?
2. With reference to the origin, purpose, and content, assess the values and limitations of Source B for historians studying the course of the Falklands/Malvinas War.
3. What is the message of Source C?

It is important that you can recognize key political figures so that you can spot them in cartoons. For example, in this cartoon you need to be able to identify the British Prime Minister, Margaret Thatcher, and the American President, Ronald Reagan. Margaret Thatcher is sitting on American President Ronald Reagan's knee while the British Foreign Secretary is playing with ships. For this particular cartoon you may also want to research the World War One poster Nicholas Garland is using as a basis.

Why did Britain win the Falklands/Malvinas war?

Britain's strong alliances served it well during the Falklands/Malvinas War and contributed to their success, as did their well-trained troops who were prepared for the difficult conditions where the fighting took place. Argentina's comparatively fewer allies put them at a disadvantage during the war. They also suffered from a poorly organized army which had inferior weaponry and flawed strategies. Read the full lists of advantages of the British and disadvantages of the Argentinians and then complete Activity 13 on page 328.

British advantages

- The British were better trained and prepared for the conditions on the Falklands. British Royal Marine Commandos, for example, were trained for cold weather and amphibious warfare, whereas the Argentines were not skilled in this kind of warfare. The British Marines, paratroopers, and other infantry were total professionals, and had good prior information about the Falkland Islands.
- The USA was a useful ally. Although President Reagan was initially hesitant, Caspar Weinberger, the US Secretary of Defense, supported the British. The key factor in US support was that it allowed Britain access to the base on Ascension Island.
- France was also an important ally. President Mitterrand wanted a strong alliance against the USSR and did not want Britain in trouble. Mitterrand blocked further sales of Exocet missiles to Argentina and hindered sales to Peru that might have gone on to Argentina. French pilots went to Scotland to assist British pilots, helping them to practise dog-fights against Mirage and Super Etendard jets. France pressured other Europeans to support anti-Argentine sanctions. In addition, France was important in influencing other countries to support Britain in the UN.
- The British were able to use their position on the Security Council of the UN in their favour, and the USSR did not veto the motion in the UN condemning Argentine actions, which was the basic justification for British action.
- The British suffered fewer casualties; there were many more Argentine losses (dead, wounded, and prisoners): a ratio of nearly 14 to 1.
- The British forces maintained high morale.
- The British benefited from luck at certain times. For example, during the final days of the land campaign, Menéndez did not realize that the British guns were down to their last rounds of ammunition, and that many of the British soldiers had not received any rations for 72 hours.

Activity 12

'In so many ways Mitterrand and the French were our greatest allies,' wrote the defence secretary, John Nott, after the war. France had earlier supplied Argentina with the mirage and Super Etendard aircraft. The Argentine navy was equipped with French-built Exocet missiles. Mitterrand now instructed the French Defence Ministry to give Britain access to Super Etendard and Mirage aircraft for training purposes. The French also supplied detailed technical information on how to tamper with the Exocet. A 'remarkable worldwide operation then ensued,' said Nott, to prevent Argentina from acquiring further Exocets. This involved the intelligence services of Britain and France working together to find Exocet missiles and render them inoperable.

Richard Aldous, *Reagan and Thatcher: The Difficult Relationship* (Norton, 2012), p.101.

1. Identify the key ways in which the French supported Britain in the Falklands/Malvinas War, as suggested in this source.
2. To what extent do you agree with the defence secretary's claim that the 'French were Britain's greatest allies' during the war?

Argentine disadvantages

- The Argentine soldiers were generally not as well trained and lacked confidence.
- The Argentines lost the sympathy of the USA. Galtieri did not respond actively to American attempts to make a peace plan, which alienated the USA.
- Argentine forces were divided. The **non-commissioned officers** (NCOs) were socially removed from the conscripts they commanded, and the conscripts themselves served in the army for only one year. Many had received little or no

Argentine forces, the Malvinas, June 1982.

training when the war began, and most had come from the tropical provinces of Argentina and were not prepared for the conditions in the Malvinas.

- Bad planning meant that the Argentines kept their best troops at home in case of an attack from Chile. They also over-reinforced their garrison in the Malvinas, which meant their troops ran low on food and supplies.

> *Contrary to some reports, a number of Argentinian officers stayed in their trenches fighting with their men during the final battles for Stanley. Their field ration was far superior to that of their men, and many, particularly the officers, had plenty to eat … [a POW] spoke of another group who, while defending Mount Longdon, had had to live only on tinned tomatoes for their last week.*
>
> **Major General Edward Fursdon, *Falklands Aftermath* (Leo Cooper, 1988), p.83.**

- Flawed strategies: the Argentines attacked warships instead of the weaker British logistical vessels. For example, if they had sunk the supply ships, the British would have struggled to wage their land campaign.
- Weaponry failings meant that many Argentine bombs did not detonate, and this reduced British losses.
- Argentine leaders made bad decisions at critical times in the fighting.
- Bad timing was a factor: the Argentines would have had a better chance of winning the war if the invasion had occurred *after* the Nott defence cuts.
- The Argentines had a lack of allies. Brazil, Peru, Ecuador, and Bolivia all supported the Argentine claims to the islands, but none endorsed the invasion, and all said they wanted to see a peaceful resolution.

Activity 13

ATL Self-management and communication skills

1. In pairs, review the bullet points above outlining the strengths of the British versus the weaknesses of the Argentinians. Makes notes on where there is an advantage or disadvantage in terms of: the war in the air; the war at sea; the war on the land; diplomacy and alliances.
2. Review the course of the war, and fill in your own copy of this grid:

	British	Argentines
Aims		
Scope and scale of fighting in the war (also casualties)		
Strategy and tactics on land		
War at sea		
War in the air		
Diplomacy and alliances		
Impact on civilians		
Nature of government		

Activity 14

Essay writing and essay planning

For following questions you can use the Falklands/Malvinas War as your case study – remember, in the examination, both questions on Topic 11 will be open and you will have to choose a relevant case study.

To prepare for the open-question examples at the end of this chapter, draft the following essay plans:

1. ***Examine the significance of a) war in the air, b) war at sea, and c) war on the land on the outcome of one war of limited mobilization.***
2. ***Discuss the role of foreign influence in the course and outcome of one 20th-century war.***
3. ***Discuss the reasons for one 20th-century conflict remaining a war of limited mobilization.***
4. ***'To win a war you need to kill the enemy's will to fight'. With reference to one 20th-century war, to what extent do you agree with this assertion?***

Activity 15

1. Briefly research relations between Argentina and Chile prior to the Malvinas War. In pairs, then research the role played by Chile in supporting the British during the conflict. It should be noted that the Chilean involvement in the war remains a source of tension between Argentina and Chile today.

Results of the Falklands War

The Falklands/Malvinas War lasted for just two and a half months. Nearly 1,000 people died: almost 700 Argentines, 252 British, and 3 Falkland islanders. The war ended without a peace treaty.

Although a brief and limited war, the conflict in the Falklands/Malvinas was significant for a number of reasons. It questioned the idea that weaker nations would not challenge stronger nations, particularly if the strong nations were nuclear powers. It was an example of how leaders in the latter half of the 20th century had not learnt from those at the beginning of the century: that is, that it was a bad idea to seek war as a distraction from domestic issues. In addition, as with other wars during the century, the Falklands/Malvinas War highlighted the dangers of miscalculating the response of other countries, governments, or leaders. Finally, for both Britain and Argentina, cultural and historical perspectives had been important in causing the war.

Results for Argentina

The political results of defeat in the war were swift in Argentina. Galtieri was removed from power within 3 days of the surrender and soon afterwards military rule was over. The authority of the army over Argentina had ended; crowds gathered in Buenos Aires shouting 'cowards' at the soldiers sent to disperse them. Under pressure from public opinion, the regime lifted bans on political parties, which finally resulted in a peaceful period of democracy. In October 1983, democratic elections brought to power Raoul Alfonsin of the Radical Party. In 1985, Galtieri and nine of his colleagues were put on trial for crimes committed during their rule, and sentenced to long terms in prison.

In terms of Argentine foreign policy, diplomacy would now be the tool used to regain the Malvinas. Some Argentine commentators, including the historian Carlos Escudé, believed 'that if Argentina had any chance at all of recovering the islands diplomatically before 1982, then after the invasion, the chances practically disappeared'. Argentina restored diplomatic relations with Britain. In September 1985, the two countries signed an agreement to promote the search for gas and oil supplies in the south-west Atlantic, which would avoid another potential issue of conflict and pave the way for future cooperation. In 1998, President Carlos Menem visited the UK on the first official visit by a leader of Argentina since the 1960s.

In the longer term, the struggle for the Malvinas continued. Argentine President Nestor Kirchner, speaking on the 25th anniversary of the end of the conflict, asserted that Britain won a 'colonial victory' in the Falklands War that was unacceptable in the eyes of the world. He went on to pledge that the islands would be returned by 'peaceful means'.

The Argentines wanted to put the war behind them and close this chapter in their history, particularly after the conviction of Galtieri's junta. However, many of those who had fought in the Malvinas could not forget the conflict. Indeed, it has been estimated that more ex-servicemen have since died from committing suicide than died in the war itself.

Results for Britain

> *I cannot agree ... that those men risked their lives in any way to have a United Nations trusteeship. They risked their lives to defend British sovereign territory, the British way of life and the rights of British people to determine their own future ... I do not intend to negotiate on the sovereignty of the islands in any way, except with those who live there. That is my fervent belief ... We went to recapture what was ours.*
>
> **Margaret Thatcher, 15 June 1982.**

Cartoon by Nicholas Garland in the British *Daily Telegraph*, 11 January 1983.

The key political impact of the Falklands War in Britain was the strengthening of the leadership of Margaret Thatcher and the control of her Conservative Party in Britain. In the 1983 general election, the Conservatives were returned to power with a hugely increased majority. Those who had not wanted war were removed, and this in turn strengthened Thatcher's position. The Conservatives were to hold power for another 15 years.

There was a wave of nationalism, and a renewed sense of patriotism ran through Britain, as could be seen in the crowds gathered at Portsmouth to greet the returning Task Force. But although public approval for the armed forces radically increased after the war, in the longer term the effects of the war on the British armed forces was marginal. British defence policy continued to focus on tanks, nuclear weapons, and war with the USSR. In addition, Britain also had to focus on its struggle at home with the IRA. Just after the Falklands victory, an IRA bomb exploded in London on 20 July 1982, killing 2 guardsmen and injuring 17 spectators. Another bomb exploded two hours later, killing 6 soldiers and injuring another 24.

The social impact of the war was a massive upsurge in national morale, and much was made in the media of the first 'crushing British victory' since 1945. The British economy also entered into a phase of recovery, leading to a period of growth and prosperity. Yet, as was the case with the Argentine veterans, many returning British troops were suffering from undiagnosed **post-traumatic stress disorder** (PTSD). Some found it difficult or impossible to forget their experiences in the South Atlantic, which resulted in a high level of alcoholism and early death among their numbers.

Nevertheless, the Falklands victory did not bring an end to the dispute with Argentina, and the British maintained a high military presence on the islands. In a message to mark the 25th anniversary of the liberation of the Falklands, the former prime minister, Baroness Thatcher, issued a rallying call to British troops in current war zones, saying that '[in] the struggle against evil ... we can all today draw hope and strength' from the Falklands victory.

Results for the USSR

The Soviet Union's analysis of the Falklands/Malvinas War was that it had seriously underestimated the military capability of Britain. This had particular implications for Soviet security in Germany, and following the war the Warsaw Pact forces that faced the British across the Iron Curtain in northern Germany were reinforced.

Results for the USA

To a certain extent, the war led to a cementing of the so-called 'special relationship' between the USA and Britain. Both Reagan and his Secretary of Defense Weinberger were given awards in Britain for their help in the conflict. However, the USA's relationship with many Latin American countries was damaged as they believed the USA had broken agreements with them when the USA gave military supplies to Britain. In addition, Britain's success in the Falklands led the USA to review its reluctance to intervene militarily in other nations and regions after its disaster in Vietnam. In 1983, US Marines were sent to the Lebanon and US forces invaded Grenada.

Results for the Falkland islanders

Three civilian women died in the war; all were killed by a British navy shell. For the Falkland islanders, their 19th-century way of life was destroyed. The population increased due to the British maintaining a high military presence on the islands – one soldier to every two civilians. Their isolation also decreased due to more regular shipping services. A new industry grew up around battlefield tourism, and television was introduced. The islands also benefited from the exclusion zone in their waters, which gave them control over profitable fishing there.

Although the war should have brought the islanders an increased sense of security, the Argentine claims to the Malvinas have not ended. Indeed, after the war the British offered to return to Argentina their war dead, but the Argentine government refused, asserting that the Malvinas were part of Argentina and the bodies must remain there. Thus for the islanders these graves are a constant reminder that the dispute continues, and that there was no concluding peace treaty to the Falklands War.

Results for the United Nations

The war also undermined the United Nations, as Peter Calvocoressi explains below:

> *The war for the Falklands was a setback for the UN as an organization and for those aspirations to world order which it embodied. For this setback the initial aggressors were overwhelmingly to blame, but the British government did not wholly escape the embarrassment of demonstrating that in a crisis a powerful state will not welcome UN diplomacy and will subordinate the rule of law and its treaty obligations under the Charter to its own assessment of national advantage and prestige. This was in 1982 no great surprise but it was not what the generation of 1945 hoped for.*

Peter Calvocoressi, *World Politics: 1945–2000* (Pearson Longman, 2001), p.159.

Activity 16

ATL Thinking and communication skills

The command terms of an essay question are important in telling you how to structure your essay, and what the focus of your key arguments should be. Below are several different possible essays for which you could use the Falklands/Malvinas War as a case study. The command terms have been underlined. In pairs, briefly discuss what each of these terms is expecting you to do in the essay and what they mean for its structure. Then draft detailed essay plans for each of the essay titles.

- ***Examine* the causes of one inter-state 20th-century war.**
- ***Discuss* the political, economic and social effects of one 20th-century war.**
- ***Discuss* why one 20th-century war remained a war of limited mobilization.**
- ***Evaluate* the contribution made by sea power and air power to the course and outcome of one 20th-century war.**
- ***To what extent* was foreign support the reason for the outcome of one 20th-century war?**
- ***Examine* the impact of economic factors in causing one 20th-century war.**
- ***Discuss* the role of 'miscommunication' as a cause of one 20th-century war.**

To access websites relevant to this chapter, go to www.pearsonhotlinks.com, search for the book title or ISBN, and click on 'chapter 16'.

17

Africa and the Middle East region: First Gulf War

A US Marine in Saudi Arabia, 1990.

Key concepts: Causation and consequence

As you read this chapter, consider the following essay questions:

- Discuss the importance of economic factors in causing one 20th-century war
- Evaluate the contribution of technology to the course and outcome of one 20th-century war
- Examine the political, social and economic effects of one inter-state 20th-century war.

On 2 August 1990, Iraqi tanks swept into Kuwait. The war that subsequently developed between a US-led coalition and Iraq was the first conflict to take place in the new international order following the end of the Cold War, and the first major conflict that the USA had undertaken since Vietnam.

The Gulf War was unique in several ways. For the first time ever, the UN had the support of both superpowers in authorizing force against a member country of the UN. Also for the first time, a coalition of over 30 countries, more than 10 of them Arab, was mobilized against another Arab state. The US President, George Bush, declared that the war was about 'a big idea ... a new world order' that would involve 'peaceful settlement of disputes, solidarity against aggression, reduced and controlled arsenals, and just treatment of all peoples'. However, this confrontation would change the whole future of the Middle East; the repercussions of the war were to lead to the US invasion of Iraq in 2003, the consequences of which are still being seen today. It would also showcase the way in which wars would be fought at the beginning of the 21st century.

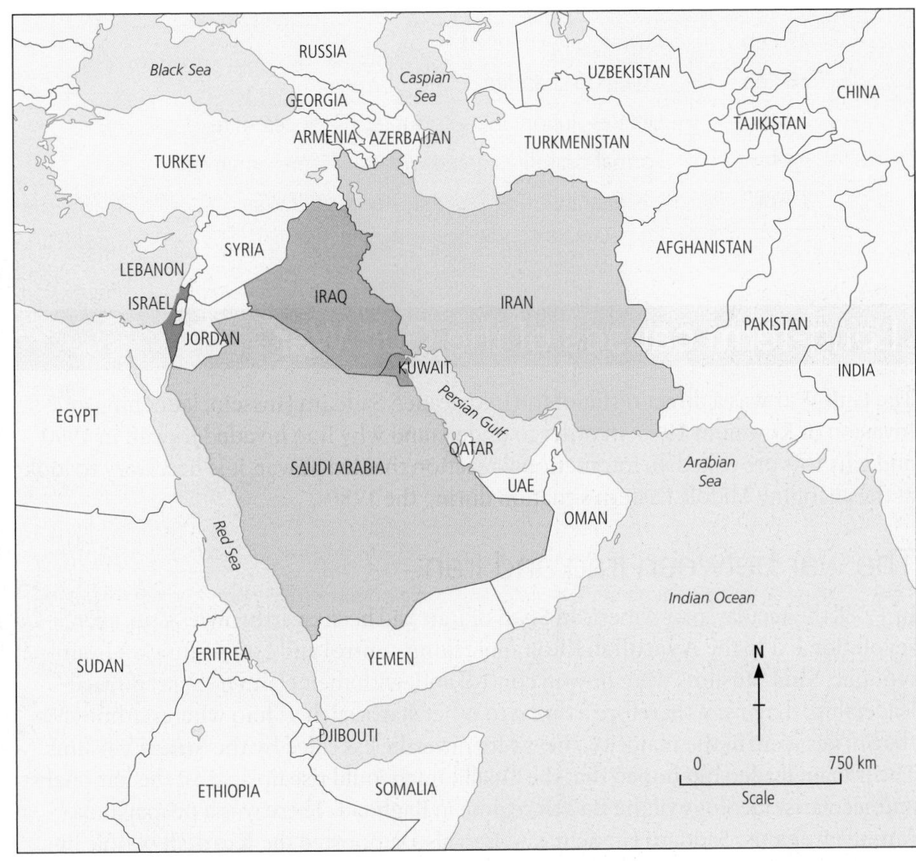

Map of the Middle East. The shaded areas indicate key regional players in the Iran–Iraq War (1980–1988) and the Gulf War (1990–1991).

Timeline of events - 1990–1991		
1990	Feb	Saddam Hussein demands money from Kuwait and United Arab Emirates (UAE)
	15 July	Saddam starts moving Republican Guard to the border with Kuwait
	25 July	Saddam meets with US Ambassador April Glaspie and reasserts lack of intention to invade Kuwait
	31 July	Iraqi and Kuwaiti delegates meet in Jeddah – no agreement
	2 Aug	Iraq invades Kuwait – UN Resolution 660 condemns Iraq's invasion
	6 Aug	UN Resolution 661 imposes trade embargo on Iraq
	7 Aug	US troops and aircraft start deploying to Saudi Arabia (Operation Desert Shield)
	29 Nov	UN Resolution 678 authorizes member states to 'use all necessary means' to make Iraq comply with previous resolutions Deadline of 15 Jan imposed
1991	15 Jan	Deadline for Iraqi withdrawal passes – Iraq does not retreat
	17 Jan	Allied air bombardment of Iraq begins
	18 Jan	Iraqi ballistic missiles hit Israel
	29 Jan–1 Feb	Battle of Al-Khafji
	24 Feb	Land campaign starts
	27 Feb	Kuwait City liberated
	28 Feb	Coalition ceasefire
	2 Mar	UN Resolution 686 sets out terms for ceasefire
	3 Mar	Formal ceasefire agreed with Iraqi representatives
	3 Apr	UN Resolution 687 formally ends Gulf War Iraq accepts conditions

Long-term causes of the Gulf War

The Gulf War was a direct result of the Iraqi leader, Saddam Hussein, launching an invasion of Kuwait in 1990. In order to understand why Iraq invaded Kuwait in 1990 and why this provoked an international reaction that led to war, it is necessary to look at the changing Middle Eastern situation during the 1980s.

The war between Iraq and Iran

In 1979, the secular, pro-American Shah of Iran had been overthrown. A popular revolution led to the **Ayatollah** Khomeini taking control and establishing an Islamic republic. **Shia** Muslims were now in control and, with their claim to Shia spiritual leadership, they were therefore a threat to other states such as Iraq where, although the Shi'ites were in the majority, they were nevertheless ruled by the **Sunni** Muslims. The Iranian leadership hoped that the Shia in Iraq would rise up against the nationalist and secularist ideology of the **Ba'ath** regime in Baghdad. There was a propaganda campaign against Saddam Hussein, and Iran also supported the **Kurdish** people in Iraq in their longstanding struggle against the Iraqi government. These provocations were the trigger for Saddam's invasion of Iran in 1980. Although Saddam Hussein

CHALLENGE YOURSELF

Research further the Sunni-Shia divide – its history, and the impact it is having today on conflicts in the Middle East. Visit www.pearsonhotlinks.com, enter the book title or ISBN, and click on weblink 17.1 to access the Council of Foreign Relations' interactive guide on this topic, which will help you with your research.

intended a short war, which would teach Iran a quick but effective lesson, it dragged on for another 8 years, ending in 1988.

Although Iraq proclaimed itself victorious in this war, the long conflict transformed Iraq from a rich and prosperous country to one that was physically damaged and crippled with debts, many of these owed to Kuwait and Saudi Arabia. In addition, Iraq faced a huge bill for repairing its war-damaged infrastructure. Western estimates put the cost of reconstruction at $230 billion. Although Iraq could rely on income from oil revenue, this was not as high as expected, due to the low prices of oil on the world market. Even if every dollar of oil revenues had been spent on reconstruction, it would still have required two decades to repair the total damage.

Saddam Hussein, leader of Iraq from 1997 to 2003.

Saddam Hussein also needed to rebuild Iraq's economy for political reasons. Inside Iraq, there had been opposition to the war. Moreover, the debts Iraq faced meant that Saddam could not follow through on promises to Iraqis of better living standards. With the end of the war, there was also huge potential for civil unrest with the planned demobilization of 1.5 million Iraqi soldiers, many of whom were Shia, and therefore a potential threat to Hussein and his regime. On the other hand, keeping such a huge standing army could also be a threat to his own security, and Saddam survived at least one **coup** attempt after the Iran–Iraq War.

Saddam Hussein's regime in Iraq in the 1970s and 1980s

Saddam Hussein was a leading member of the revolutionary Ba'ath Party, and he played a key role in the 1968 coup that brought the party to long-term power. The redistribution of land and wealth was part of the Ba'ath programme, along with a strong belief in the need to unify the Arab people. From the early 1970s, Saddam was an active member of the administration of Ahmed Hassan. During this time, he built up the security forces and put his own relatives into key positions. He also applied the socialist ideas of the Ba'ath Party by bringing all economic activity under the control of the government. This programme included nationalizing the foreign-owned oil company IBC. The increase of oil prices in the 1970s allowed the rapid economic and social development of Iraq at this time and the country began to prosper.

In 1979 Hussein became Iraqi president. He immediately ordered the deaths of dozens of government officials suspected of treason. He executed another 300 officers in 1982 for rebelling against his tactics in the war with Iran. Saddam also became notorious for using chemical weapons both in the war against Iran and in his own country against the Kurds. During a seven-month **scorched-earth** campaign in 1988, an estimated 50,000 to 100,000 Kurdish villagers were killed or disappeared, and hundreds of villages were razed.

By 1987, Saddam's army was the fourth largest in the world. He had an arsenal of **Scud missiles**, a sophisticated nuclear weapons programme underway, and deadly chemical and biological weapons in development.

The relationship between Iraq and the West

George H.W. Bush, US President from 1989 to 1993.

Although Saddam's government was clearly a violent, repressive regime, the USA had supported him in the 1980s as a counterweight to the new anti-US regime in Iran led by Ayatollah Khomeini. In 1982, the Department of State removed Iraq from its list of terrorist countries, so it could qualify for US aid and credits. Annual trade between the two countries was more than $3 billion by 1990, although most of this provided Iraq with food, weapons were also obtained through 'back door' routes. Turning a blind eye to Hussein's slaughter of thousands of Kurds with chemical weapons, other Western countries were also happy to trade with Iraq. France provided Iraq with billions of francs worth of weapons, including the technology to build a second nuclear reactor, and by 1990 Britain was Iraq's third-largest trading partner. There

The intifada

In the 1980s there was growing unrest in the **Occupied Territories** of Israel. This unrest exploded into what became known as the ***Intifada*** ('uprising') in December 1987: a rebellion by Palestinians, which included general strikes, boycotts on Israeli goods, barricades, and stone-throwing by youths against the Israeli soldiers. Saddam committed $25 million to keep the *Intifada* going. Yet ultimately the *Intifada* helped push both the Israelis and **PLO** leader Yasser Arafat (who feared he was losing control of the Palestinian situation to the more extreme **Hamas**) to the negotiating table.

was a belief in the USA and the West that Saddam Hussein could be turned away from militarism into a more moderate force in the Middle East. A National Security Directive issued by George Bush stated that 'Normal relations between the United States and Iraq would serve our longer-term interest and promote stability in both the Gulf and the Middle East'. It instructed the USA to 'propose economic and political incentives for Iraq to moderate its behaviour and increase our influence with Iraq'. Therefore, even when Saddam Hussein's behaviour became more belligerent, there was no attempt to deter him.

The decline of Soviet influence

The Middle East had, since the 1950s, been a key area in the Cold War struggle for influence between the USA and the USSR, with both superpowers supporting '**client states**'. However, in the early 1990s the policies of the new Soviet leader, Mikhail Gorbachev, were leading to a waning of influence in this area. The Soviet Union's preoccupation with its domestic problems, and the new climate of cooperation with the West, meant that it was unwilling to maintain its commitments to its client states. Thus Syria, Iraq, South Yemen, and the Palestine Liberation Organization (PLO) could no longer get economic or military, or even diplomatic, support from the Soviet Union.

This situation inevitably led to the USA stepping into the vacuum as it sought to build support for a new peace initiative between Palestinians and Israelis. This US dominance was viewed with suspicion by many Arab states, including Iraq, who saw any increased US influence as benefiting Israel only. The power vacuum was also a situation Saddam saw that he could exploit.

Activity 1

Review questions

1. What social, economic, and political problems faced Saddam Hussein by 1990?
2. What a) concerns and b) opportunities faced Saddam Hussein as a result of the Soviet Union's waning influence in the Middle East?
3. What justifications did the West give for supporting Saddam Hussein's regime?

Short-term causes of the Gulf War

Western hopes of Iraq moving to a more moderate stance evaporated in 1990 when Saddam made a series of ruthless moves. There was already a growing concern in the West over Iraq's human rights record and also over the vast amount of money that was being spent on weapons systems. In March 1990 Farzad Bazoft, a journalist working for the British newspaper *The Observer*, was executed in Iraq on trumped-up charges of spying. British intelligence also intercepted items of technology from the West that appeared to be necessary for long-range missiles and **weapons of mass destruction** (WMD). These events now put pressure on the Western countries to halt arms sales. In April, meanwhile, Saddam made a threat to use chemical weapons against Israel. He also gave more financial aid to sustain the *Intifada* and, at an Arab summit meeting in Baghdad, claimed that the enemy of the Arab camp was now 'Greater Israel'.

Meanwhile, the relationship between Iraq and Kuwait was deteriorating fast. Some disagreements between the two countries went back a long way:

- There was a long-standing argument over the frontiers between the two countries. In the 1930s, the new state of Iraq had claimed that Kuwait, formerly a British protectorate, belonged to Iraq. It also laid claim to the islands of Bubijan and Warbah at the head of the Persian Gulf.

- There was unresolved disagreement over the right to exploit the Rumaila oilfield on the Iraq–Kuwait border.
- As explained above, however, the real issue for Iraq in 1990 was its economic crisis, and in 1990 Iraq put increasing pressure on Kuwait to help it solve this crisis.
- At a summit meeting in Amman in February 1990, Saddam asked King Hussein of Jordan and President Mubarak of Egypt to inform Kuwait that Iraq not only wanted cancellation of wartime loans, but that he also needed additional funds of some $30 billion. Both requests were refused.
- Iraq also requested that Kuwait keep to **OPEC** quotas for oil output. More oil on the international market meant lower prices per barrel and thus less income for Iraq. Kuwait was the chief culprit in overproduction in a deliberate strategy to drive down the price of oil, so that more nations became dependent on OPEC oil. The long-term benefits of such a strategy were of no help to Saddam Hussein who, facing increasing political unrest at home, needed money immediately.

Iraq's invasion of Kuwait

In July 1990, the dispute with Kuwait became much more intense. Saddam Hussein started making accusations against Kuwait – that it had stolen more than $2 billion of oil from the Rumaila oilfield, which Iraq claimed as its own, and that the loans that Iraq had received during the Iran–Iraq War came from profits due to overproduction. He said that Kuwait's unwillingness to cancel Iraq's war debts constituted 'military aggression' and that Kuwait was 'stabbing Iraq in the back with a poisoned dagger'. At the same time, Saddam backed up his verbal attacks on Kuwait with a military threat; large numbers of the elite Republican Guard divisions were moved towards the border with Kuwait.

Efforts were made to resolve the crisis peacefully:

- On 27 July OPEC put up the official oil price from $18 to $21 a barrel as requested by Iraq.
- After much persuasion by the Egyptian and Jordanian leaders, an Iraqi delegation led by Izzat Ibrahim (Saddam's deputy) met Kuwaiti representatives in Saudi Arabia on 31 July. However, little progress was made, and the meeting was abandoned by Iraq, who claimed that Kuwait was acting 'against Iraq's basic interests'.

There was also a meeting between Saddam and the US ambassador to Iraq, April Glaspie. Rather than deterring Saddam from invading Iraq, it seems that Glaspie's conversation with Saddam gave the impression that the USA would take no action. She stated that 'We have no opinion on the Arab–Arab conflicts, like your border disagreement with Kuwait', although she did make it clear that differences should be solved by peaceful means. Saddam also received no warning from the USA, despite the fact that the Pentagon had detected Iraqi military divisions close to the Kuwaiti border.

Certainly, Saddam Hussein seems to have believed that the world would not act against him when, on 2 August, he launched the Iraqi invasion of Kuwait with more than 100,000 soldiers and almost 2,000 tanks. Within 12 hours of the invasion, the bulk of the resistance had been extinguished and the Kuwaiti royal family had fled to Saudi Arabia. On 28 August, Kuwait was declared to be the 19th province of Iraq.

Activity 2

ATL Thinking skills

Review questions

1. How would the invasion of Kuwait solve the problems that you identified in the review questions on page 336?
2. What reasons would Saddam Hussein have had for believing that the USA would not take any action against him?

Activity 3

ATL Thinking skills

Source A

The invasion of Kuwait promised a cure to both the economic and military legacy of the Iran–Iraq war. Kuwait's oil wealth would enable the Iraqi regime to reconstruct the state and to pay its non-Arab creditors. It would keep the army busy and far away from the capital. The claims of victory over Iran would be replaced with a real victory for Kuwait. The invasion was also seen as way to project Iraqi hegemony not just over Kuwait but also over the Gulf as a whole. This would allow Iraq to dictate oil prices and quotas to serve its own interests, as it would control 21 per cent of OPEC's total production. And, ultimately, the extension of military and economic power would enable Iraq to claim the mantle of pan-Arab leadership as the region's most powerful country, especially as it was the only country which had never even signed so much as an armistice with Israel and the only Arab state left to embrace the PLO wholeheartedly.

Antony Best et al., *International History of the Twentieth Century and Beyond* (Routledge, 2008), p.453.

Source B

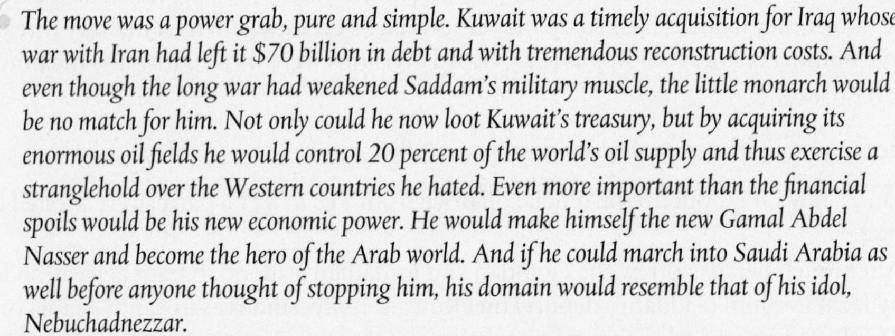

The move was a power grab, pure and simple. Kuwait was a timely acquisition for Iraq whose war with Iran had left it $70 billion in debt and with tremendous reconstruction costs. And even though the long war had weakened Saddam's military muscle, the little monarch would be no match for him. Not only could he now loot Kuwait's treasury, but by acquiring its enormous oil fields he would control 20 percent of the world's oil supply and thus exercise a stranglehold over the Western countries he hated. Even more important than the financial spoils would be his new economic power. He would make himself the new Gamal Abdel Nasser and become the hero of the Arab world. And if he could march into Saudi Arabia as well before anyone thought of stopping him, his domain would resemble that of his idol, Nebuchadnezzar.

J.G. Stoessinger, *Why Nations Go to War* (Palgrave Macmillan, 1998), p.165.

Source C

The fault here, therefore, was in not warning Saddam away from the logic of this campaign … The importance of the principle of non-aggression could have been stated far more clearly than quiet comments about the inadvisability of solving disputes through force.

L. Freedman and E. Karsh, *The Gulf Conflict, 1990–1991* (Princeton University Press, 1995), p.430.

Source D

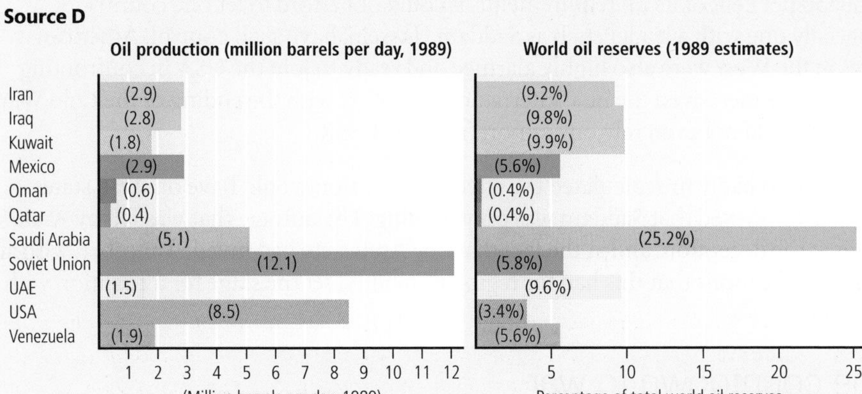

World oil production and reserves, 1989.

Source E

The invasion of Kuwait might have been averted. The 1979 Pentagon study had advised that the military needed to flex its muscles early in a crisis to deter an Iraqi invasion. But the administration never acted on that recommendation. It had not been so much a failure of intelligence as a failure to act on available information. An elementary lesson of deterrence had been lost. The Bush administration drew a line in the sand in firm, deep strokes, but not until the Iraqis had already crossed it.

The Bush's administration's commitment to its Baghdad policy was one reason. Instead of seeing Iraq's war preparations for what they were, it had embraced the most benign explanation of the Iraqi moves … the Bush's administration's desire not to cross the moderate Arabs, who also misread Iraq's intentions, also encouraged a policy of inaction. Powell's aversion to using American military to send diplomatic signals also contributed to the administration's failure to act … ironically, Powell's efforts to avoid an ill-considered use of force actually increased the prospects for American military involvement in the region.

Michael Gordon and Bernard Trainor, *The Generals' War* (Atlantic Books, 1995), p.29.

1. According to Source A, what would Saddam Hussein gain from the invasion of Kuwait?
2. Compare and contrast Sources A and B in their analysis of Saddam Hussein's motives for the invasion of Iraq.
3. What factor or factors in the above accounts explain/s why Saddam Hussein should have expected a strong international reaction to his actions?
4. In what ways does Source D support the assertions made in Source B concerning the dangers of Saddam's actions?
5. What extra reason is given in Source C for explaining Saddam's invasion of Kuwait?
6. In what ways does Source E support Source C regarding America's role in causing this crisis?

Kuwait

The **sheikdom** of Kuwait, as you can see from the map on page 333, is much smaller than its neighbours. Its small population (2 million before the invasion, of which fewer than a million were Kuwaitis), however, and its large oil resources meant that it was extremely rich. Its **GNP** was more than $26 billion in 1989. Kuwait City had become a capital city of great wealth and there were good health and education services. Yet there were also big divisions in society. The thousand or so members of the ruling al-Sabah family effectively controlled the country. In 1986 the **Emir** had disbanded the Kuwaiti parliament and in 1989 he rejected pleas to reinstate it. The bulk of Kuwaiti citizens themselves were divided into first- and second-class citizens. Half of the **emirate's** population were immigrants without citizenship or full civic rights. Nomadic **Bedouin** were denied rights because they could not prove fixed residence, as too were Palestinians and others, even if born in Kuwait.

International reaction to Iraq's invasion of Kuwait

Saddam Hussein had miscalculated the USA's reaction to the invasion. Not only was this an act of aggression by one UN country against another, but the appropriation of Kuwait's oilfields meant that Iraq would now have an unacceptable level of influence in OPEC and the pricing of oil worldwide.

There was also now the possibility of an Iraqi attack on Saudi Arabia, which would place virtually all Arab oil under Iraq's control (see Source D above) and cause economic and political instability in the region. As the USA relied on imports for about 50 per cent of its oil requirements, it could not afford to let one country, especially one with a leader such as Saddam Hussein, have such control. American allies in the West were also highly alarmed and ready to join the USA in confronting the Iraqi regime. Given the new international context with the ending of the Cold War, Saddam could not even rely on support from the USSR.

Saddam also badly miscalculated the effect the invasion would have on Arab states. Many had believed that Saddam was only bluffing. The outrage that was felt by Arab states at the deception, and at the fact that one Arab state had invaded another, with all of the implications that this had for regional stability, set the stage for a coalition with the West.

The countdown to war

The UN Security Council quickly established a comprehensive set of sanctions against Iraq. These were supported by the Soviet Union, a clear indication of the new international order that was now emerging. Meanwhile, the USA had managed to persuade King Fahd of Saudi Arabia of the need for a US force in his country in order to protect it from invasion. From 8 August, US troops started arriving in his country as part of Operation Desert Shield. Two days later, the Arab League passed a motion condemning Iraq's occupation of Kuwait and authorizing the dispatch of Arab forces to Saudi Arabia to join those of the USA.

Why was a peaceful settlement not possible?

It was hoped by many that negotiation combined with sanctions would achieve a solution to the crisis that would avoid war. Saddam did suggest on 12 August a peace plan that involved the USA leaving Saudi Arabia, Syrian troops leaving Lebanon, and Israel withdrawing from the Occupied Territories. Yet his attempt to link the wider Palestinian issue with the invasion of Kuwait was highly problematic, and was more an attempt to play for time in the hope that the coalition would become divided and weakened.

Thus, although several attempts at mediation were made, Saddam's determined intransigence on the issue of withdrawal from Kuwait made a peaceful solution increasingly unlikely. Meanwhile, international opinion was also hardened against Saddam by reports of Iraqi brutality in Kuwait and by Saddam's plans to use civilian hostages trapped in his country as human shields.

Saddam Hussein announced that citizens from any country threatening Iraq would have to stay in Iraq until the threats ended. One of the hostages, a 5-year-old British boy, Stuart Lockwood, was forced to pose with Saddam Hussein in a television broadcast, which caused much unease and consternation in the West.

Although many in Bush's administration wanted to give sanctions more time to work, ultimately Bush could not allow this to happen. There was no guarantee that they would have enough impact on Saddam himself to get him to back down, and in any case the USA did not have the time to wait and see if this would happen. It had to keep the coalition together and keep the political and military pressure on Saddam, and this situation could not be maintained indefinitely. Nevertheless, sanctions did play an important role by giving a focal point for international unity before armed conflict, and imposing economic hardship on Iraq.

Why did Saddam not respond to the military threat that faced him?

By 15 January 1991, the Allied forces had reached a figure of 555,000 men and women, and more were still arriving. Some 350,000 of these troops were American. The remainder belonged mainly to Arab and Western European forces.

The hope, other than negotiation and economic sanctions, was that Saddam would see the impossibility of taking on the might of the American war machine. Yet Saddam was overconfident, after the war with Iran, in his ability for survival. It is also possible that he believed right up to January 1991 that the Americans would not actually risk a war, and that the peace movement would grow in voice and undermine the solidarity of the coalition. He thus ended up miscalculating America's actions yet again.

The outbreak of war

On 29 November 1990, the UN Security Council had approved another resolution (its 12th of the crisis) authorizing the use, after 15 January 1991, of any necessary measures to secure the removal of Iraq from Kuwait and the restoration of its former rulers. This resolution provided the legitimate grounds for war and it was passed by 12 votes to 2 (Yemen and Cuba voting against and China abstaining). Operation Desert Shield now became Operation Desert Storm, which had the objective of militarily pushing Saddam's forces out of Kuwait. Last-minute mediation attempts all failed, and Desert Storm started on 16 January 1991.

Activity 4

Review question

1. For each of the following headings, write notes to explain the significance of each factor in contributing to the build-up of tensions and the eventual outbreak of war.

   Long-term causes of the war:
   - the Iran–Iraq War
   - decline of Soviet influence
   - Saddam's attempt to expand his influence in the region
   - Western support for Saddam.

   Short-term causes (events in 1990):
   - Iraq's economic position by 1990
   - US failure to give stronger signals concerning Saddam's actions
   - Saddam's invasion of Kuwait.
   - limited impact of sanctions
   - failure of negotiations
   - the US need to keep the coalition together
   - Saddam's miscalculations.

CHALLENGE YOURSELF

Thinking skills

Although the IBLP promotes risk-taking, this can be misinterpreted by students; a risk-taker should 'approach unfamiliar situations and uncertainty with courage and forethought, and have the independence of spirit to explore new roles, ideas, and strategies. They are brave and articulate in defending their beliefs.' Deciding to take military action to stop Saddam Hussein was a 'risk' – how far do you agree that this 'risk' was appropriate? In what other situations is taking risks appropriate? Can you also think of examples when it would not be appropriate?

Activity 5

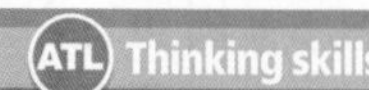

ATL Communication skills

1. Take the motion: 'This House believes that the Gulf conflict was a simple case of "blood for oil"' (see the Interesting Facts box on page 345).

Divide the class into two teams. Each team should have three speakers. The rest of the team should also help in researching and writing the speeches. Follow the standard rules for a formal debate.

Overview of the war

Activity 6

ATL Thinking skills

> *The underlying logic of the military planning was as important as the tactics. Americans would enter the enemy's territory in force and leave as soon as possible, with no entangling occupation duties or alliances with Iraqi insurgents who might take up arms against the Iraqi dictator. The stain of Vietnam would be removed by a rapid victory, and American forces would exit swiftly. Anything else was a potential snare. Even the code name of the military campaign – Desert Storm – expressed the philosophy of the war plan. Like a thunderstorm, the attacks would be furious while they lasted but limited in duration.*
>
> **Michael Gordon and Bernard Trainor, *The Generals' War* (Atlantic Books, 1995), p.ix.**

1. According to this source, what were the USA's aims in planning the military campaign against Iraq?

The Desert Storm campaign was carried out in two parts. First, there was a series of bombing attacks on Baghdad and on military targets. In more than 100,000 sorties during the course of the war, Iraq's military and industrial infrastructure was completely destroyed. Saddam responded with Scud ballistic missiles directed at Saudi and Israeli cities and by devastating Kuwait City and maltreating its citizens.

The second phase was the ground campaign against the Iraqi army itself. This began on 24 February, and within four days the Iraqis had been driven out of Kuwait. Kuwait was liberated and Saddam Hussein accepted defeat.

The nature of the fighting

The overwhelming victory achieved in the war by the US and coalition forces was due partly to state-of-the-art American weaponry. The American military had been rebuilt throughout the 1980s, and the results of their new technology were clearly seen in Desert Storm. Four developments had particular impact: **precision-guided munitions (PGMs)**, night-vision devices, space-based systems, and **stealth technology**.

The war in the air

The technological superiority of US air power was clearly shown in the opening days of the war. The first night of operations over Iraq saw the longest bombing run in history, with B-52G bombers from Louisiana making a round trip of some 15 hours. Eighty-nine per cent of the missiles dropped by these bombers hit their targets.

The total weight of bombs dropped on Iraq was just below 90,000 tons, which is the same as only 2 months' bombing in the Vietnam War. However, due to the improved accuracy of the bombs – known as 'smart' bombs – combined with the fact that the targets were more clearly defined, air power was much more effective than in the Vietnam War.

> *In stark terms, a fighter-bomber of the 1990s armed with just two smart bombs possessed such a level of accuracy that it would have taken more than 100 B-17 bombers [a World War II-era bomber] to achieve the same results.*
>
> **Alastair Finlan, *The Gulf War 1991* (Osprey, 2003), p.30.**

Yet it is also important to remember that although the Americans used 9,300 PGMs, in fact, 90 per cent of all aerial munitions used were unguided weapons.

Thermal-imaging and laser designation systems were used to guide the bombs to their target – pilots launched bombs into the 'cone' created by a laser beam locked on to the target, in order to score a direct hit. As a result of the smart bombs, the coalition forces were able to take out the Iraqi air-defence system on the first night of operations, with devastating effects on the Iraqi ability to retaliate.

The coalition air force went on to bomb command and communication facilities (second phase) and then military targets throughout Iraq and Kuwait, before focusing on Scud missile launchers, weapons research facilities, and naval forces (third phase). Night-vision devices also allowed coalition aircraft to use the cover of darkness for protection, while still being able to attack exact targets using the PGMs.

Fortunately for the coalition forces, Saddam's air force adopted a defensive position, and did not intervene. In fact, soon after the start of the war, the Iraqi air force began fleeing to Iran, possibly because Saddam wanted to keep it intact for after the war. Air supremacy was thus achieved within days of the start of the campaign.

The impact of the bombing

The technology used by the Americans in the smart bombs allowed them to destroy more targets faster, contributing to the breakdown of the Iraqi command structure and making it difficult for Saddam to coordinate his forces and mount an effective defence. The Iraqi war machine was crippled, and bridges, roads, and telecommunications equipment destroyed.

The bombing campaign also destroyed the Iraqi artillery units, and made it difficult for Iraq to operate on the battlefield. The psychological impact on the Iraqi forces of this devastating air attack must also not be underestimated.

GPS and the Gulf War

The Global Positioning System (GPS) is a satellite-based navigation system made up of a network of 24 satellites placed into orbit by the US Department of Defense (DoD). GPS satellites broadcast signals from space that are used by GPS receivers to provide three-dimensional location, (latitude, longitude, and altitude) plus the time. During the Iraq War, the DoD improved the performance of its GPS satellite navigation system to provide accuracy within 3 metres for precision guidance systems for munitions, aircraft, and ground forces, thus allowing unprecedented accuracy of fire and navigation in battle.

The land war

The technological developments mentioned above played a key role in the land war as well. The American M1A1 and the British Challenger tanks, unlike many Iraqi tanks, could move and fire at the same time. Tanks were fitted with precision munitions and sophisticated firing systems. The role of the GPS (Global Positioning System) was also essential for American forces finding their way through the desert, and the night-vision devices, such as night-vision goggles, allowed the coalition to fight around the clock.

Airpower continued to play a key role in the land campaign. During the 1980s, NATO had developed a new strategy for warfare called the **AirLand Doctrine**, which emphasized, among other things, close integration between the ground forces and a dedicated air campaign. Thus the fourth phase of air operations was part of the ground war, which started on 24 February 1991. The air attack on the Iraqi forces significantly damaged the Iraqi fortifications and minefields behind the Kuwait–Saudi border, as well as killing many Iraqi troops. When the land attack came, it quickly succeeded in driving the Iraqi army from Kuwait; it was a 100-hour rout that shattered Saddam's prediction that this would be the 'Mother of all Battles'.

The land war developed in the following stages:

- 24 February a.m.: US Marines and Saudi task forces attacked in the east into Kuwait, while in the west French and US forces launched an attack against Salman airfield.
- 24 February p.m.: US Marines and Saudi forces broke through Iraqi defences in the east and made rapid progress. VII Corps (consisting of three US armoured divisions, one US infantry division, and one British armoured division) attacked north into Iraq.
- 25–26 February: US Marines, Saudis, and Egyptians closed on Kuwait City. The escape route out of Kuwait was cut off to the Iraqis. The coalition troops that had first advanced into Iraq now moved into Kuwait.
- 27 February: Remaining Iraqi forces were surrounded, including the elite Republican Guard. President Bush announced the liberation of Kuwait.
- Hostilities cease and Iraq accepted all UN resolutions.

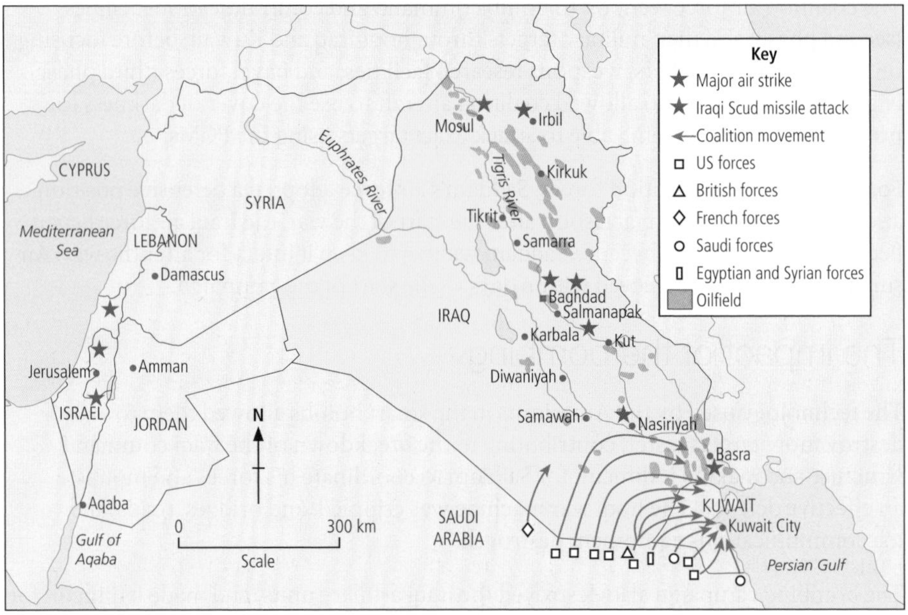

Map of coalition movement during Operation Desert Storm, 1991.

The overall commander of the coalition forces was Norman Schwarzkopf. Thanks to changes made through the AirLand Doctrine, Schwarzkopf was able to command and control his different forces with far greater authority than had ever previously been allowed, and so achieve greater coordination between the land, sea, and air units. As his forces consisted of both Western and Arab troops, he was assisted by the Saudi Commander General Khaled bin-Sultan, who controlled the forces from the Arab states. Schwarzkopf was personally very visible during the course of the war; he gave frequent press conferences, and was nicknamed 'Stormin' Norman'.

Activity 7

ATL Thinking skills

The role of technology

The general impact of technology upon the technique of modern warfare, as demonstrated in Desert Storm, was at least threefold. First, it increased the intensity of combat. Modern combat has become a round-the-clock proposition with no respite. Second, technology has made combat much more efficient. Precision munitions make it possible to do much more much faster, with fewer assets. The side benefit is less collateral damage – fewer unnecessary casualties and less unnecessary destruction. Third, the gap in capabilities between those who can exploit modern military technology and those who cannot is growing ever more significant. Precision munitions, 24-hour capability, space systems, stealth technology, and many other technologies provide the possessor with much more than marginal improvements in military capabilities. Properly used, they provide an overwhelming advantage.

D.M. Snow and D.M. Drew, *Lexington to Desert Storm: War and Politics in the American Experience* (Routledge, 1994), p.309.

1. According to this source, how have new technologies in fighting, as shown in the Gulf War, impacted on combat?

Activity 8

Research skills

1. Research the role of the following in the Gulf War:
   - the Lockheed F-117A Nighthawk stealth attack aircraft
   - AH-64 Apache helicopter
   - F-111F Aardvark interceptor aircraft
   - E-3A airborne warning and control (AWAC) aircraft
   - Patriot surface-to-air missiles
   - Scud ballistic missiles
   - Hawk surface-to-air missiles
   - Tomahawk land attack missiles (TLAM).

Public opinion on the Gulf conflict

Although many Arab governments were hostile to Saddam's actions, there was a lot of support for Saddam Hussein amongst ordinary Arabs. Part of this was due to the lack of sympathy for Kuwait. The emirate was seen as arrogant, and its treatment of foreign workers was also disliked. Iraqi propaganda during the war played on the fact that Arab soldiers were dying to save rich Kuwaiti leaders who were far from the battle zone. Similarly, in the West, a section of public opinion was sceptical about the moral reasons for the war, pointing to the fact that had Kuwait not had oil, Saddam would probably have got away with his actions. The slogan 'blood for oil' became a common cry for protesters against the war.

The sea war

The bulk of the naval forces in the Gulf War were provided by the USA, which deployed six carrier battle groups in support of operations. A real problem for the US navy was the small amount of sea space in the Gulf. Even more problematic was the threat of Iraqi mines, which were largely dealt with by the British Royal Navy (though two US ships were still holed by Iraqi mines).

The coalition navy had several roles in Operations Desert Shield and Desert Storm:

- Enforcing the UN embargo on Iraq.
- Supporting the air campaign – the US aircraft carriers carried some of the world's most advanced air defence fighters, such as the F-14 Tomcat. In addition, the new hi-tech Tomahawk land-attack missiles (TLAMs) were fired from naval vessels at targets that were considered too dangerous for the coalition aircraft.
- Persuading Iraq that the land invasion of Kuwait would come from the sea. The Iraqi navy put up very little resistance and many ships were destroyed in the act of trying to escape to Iran.

Reasons for Allied success

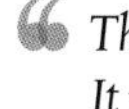

The military confrontation would take place at a time of American strength and Iraqi weakness. It would occur before the cuts in the military forces were too far along, at a time when the cold war had freed up American military resources around the world and before Iraq had a nuclear bomb.

Michael Gordon and Bernard Trainor, *The Generals' War* (Atlantic Books, 1995), p.30.

There are several reasons for the overwhelming success of the Allied coalition in the Gulf War:

The timing of the war: The US army had been modernized in the 1980s in terms of weaponry, planning, and organization, in readiness for an attack on the Soviet Union. The Cold War had only just ended, and so the US military was still at full strength. Had the conflict happened a few years later, it might well have lacked such resources.

Media coverage of the Gulf War: censorship and propaganda

With the advent of news channels such as CNN in the USA, it was now possible to watch news on the Gulf War 24 hours a day. However, civilians around the world knew far less of what was actually happening in this war than they had in the Vietnam War. Partly as a result of the political impact that unrestricted reporting had in this earlier war, the military stringently managed the media in the Gulf War: they provided the images of the bombs hitting the targets and made sure that all press teams had an escort officer who could monitor what was filmed. The media was also used by the Iraqis to their advantage, not only to illustrate the impact of US bombing on civilians, but also to show video tapes of captured US pilots forced to read prepared statements condemning the war. The Iraqi propaganda was controlled by the Information Minister Muhammed Saeed al-Sahaf, who proclaimed Iraqi victories throughout the course of the war, regardless of what was actually happening. In addition, both sides used the radio to try to win over enemy troops.

The Soviet Union at this point was also willing to work with the West, and the political unity amongst so many countries might have been difficult to achieve in following years.

The quality of military technology: As we have seen, technology was key in allowing such a rapid victory. US technological superiority – the ability to fight at night, the smart bombs, the intelligence provided by satellites, the state-of-the-art tanks and aircraft – put the coalition forces at a huge advantage.

Saddam's errors: Saddam miscalculated American will and capabilities. His military strategy was highly flawed. The failure of the Iraqi air force or ground troops to take offensive action, for instance by attacking Saudi Arabia in the early phases of *Desert Shield*, was an enormous error. The Iraqis surrendered mobility by entrenching themselves to protect Kuwait. Saddam's prediction that the entrenchments would be difficult to take, and that the Iraqis would be able to force attrition warfare on the coalition with heavy casualties, proved mistaken. He also underestimated the importance of air warfare.

Language is not only a valuable resource and tool for historians – it also can be a limitation. There is subjectivity expressed in the language of any source, and in the language used by historians themselves. During the Gulf War, the British press used the following expressions:

We have... army, navy, air force reporting guidelines press briefing	***They have...*** a war machine censorship propaganda
We... suppress neutralize dig in	***They...*** destroy kill cower
We launch... first strikes pre-emptively	***They launch...*** sneak missile attacks without provocation
Our soldiers are... boys lads cautious confident young knights of the skies loyal resolute brave	***Their soldiers are...*** troops hordes cowardly desperate bastards of Baghdad blindly obedient ruthless fanatical
Our missiles are... like Luke Skywalker zapping Darth Vader causing collateral damage	***Their missiles are...*** ageing duds killing innocent civilians
George Bush is... at peace with himself resolute statesmanlike assured	***Saddam Hussein is...*** demented defiant an evil tyrant a crackpot monster
Our planes... suffer from a high rate of attrition fail to return from missions	***Their planes...*** are shot out of the sky are zapped

Adapted from Nick Alchin, *Theory of Knowledge*, 2nd ed. (Hodder, 2006), p. 266.

Analyse the language used in this example. How might this use of language have affected British people's perception of the Gulf War? What knowledge issues might result from this language for a historian using British press reports as evidence when researching the Gulf War?

Activity 9

ATL Thinking skills

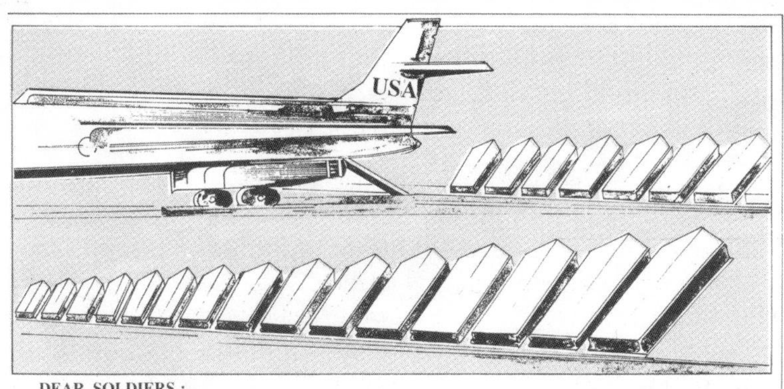
USA
DEAR SOLDIERS :
YOUR COMMANDERS HAVE SAID THAT THE WAR WILL TAKE FEW DAYS WERE THEY CORRECT ? AND CONVINCED YOU THAT LOSES WILL BE MINIMUM IN THE GROUND COMBAT, WE ASSURE THAT THEY WONT BE CORRECT

Iraqi propaganda leaflet designed for American soldiers. The caption reads: 'Your commanders have said that the war will take few days; were they correct? And convinced you that loses will be minimum in the ground combat, we assure that they won't be correct.'

1. What is the message of this propaganda leaflet, and why might Iraqis consider it to be particularly effective on American soldiers?

Throughout, Saddam was fighting not only a military battle, but a political one. He thus kept back key units so that they would be ready to fight to save his regime. His one clear strategy was that of firing Scud missiles at Israel, so that Israel would join the war and thus inflame Arab opinion, causing the collapse of the coalition. This strategy, however, failed to work.

Results of the Gulf War

Ultimately, the coalition forces stopped short of an invasion and takeover of Iraq. It can be argued that this was not in the original mandate of UN Resolution 678, and a push into Iraq would have split the coalition, particularly members from the Arab countries. Given the fact that the USA was still very conscious of the failure of Vietnam, it was also reluctant to get involved in what could have been a long, drawn-out campaign.

In military terms, the war was successful in achieving its aims as defined by the UN Security Council. Iraq had been defeated and forced to pull out of Kuwait. Kuwait's sovereignty was restored and the al-Sabah family was put back in power. However, as shown below, there was no real change in the Middle East as a result of this conflict. Saddam Hussein remained in power and the Arab states and international community remained divided as to how to deal with Iraq. The 'new world order' predicted by George Bush seemed very elusive, as new wars started in the wake of the collapse of the USSR and the disintegration of Yugoslavia.

Gulf War Syndrome

Despite initially low casualties, coalition veterans of the Gulf War have continued to die or suffer from mysterious illnesses since 1991. This has become known as Gulf War Syndrome. It is not clear what has caused this. Possible causes put forward have included the exposure to depleted uranium used in tank shells and large-calibre bullets, or a side-effect of the 'cocktail' of drugs given to soldiers to protect them from the possible dangers of biological and chemical warfare.

Casualties

For the Allies, the casualties were very low considering the huge numbers deployed. The USA lost fewer than 150 killed in action, a dramatic difference from US casualty figures in the two previous major wars involving US troops. Korea had cost the US forces more than 30,000 dead, and in Vietnam they suffered just over 58,000 dead. Britain had lost 24 killed in action and the Arab countries (not including Kuwait) suffered 37 deaths. The greatest number of soldiers killed or seriously wounded (1,500 Americans and 700 British) came from illness and accidents, including incidents of **friendly fire** or 'blue on blue'.

The Highway of Death.

One of the reasons for America's decision to end the ground war and not pursue the Iraqis back to Baghdad was an incident known as 'The Highway of Death'. This refers to a six-lane highway between Kuwait and Iraq. As Iraqis were fleeing back to Iraq along this road on the night of 26–27 February, they were bombed by American and Canadian aircraft. This resulted in the deaths of many Iraqis, and the photos of the carnage caused international concern. However, many Iraqi forces did manage to escape, along with a significant number of tanks. Jeffrey Engel writes in his book, *Into the Desert: Reflections on the Gulf War*, '... in his triumphal news conference, Schwarzkopf boasted that the gate had been shut on the Iraqi forces in the Kuwaiti theatre. In fact the barn door was never closed and a lot of horses got out' (Engel, *Into the Desert; Reflections on the Gulf War* [OUP, 2012], page 135).

The exact number of Iraqi deaths is unknown, though recent estimates suggest in the region of 20,000 (though some sources still put the figure as high as 200,000). There was much controversy over the number of civilian deaths in Iraq – reports range from 1,000 to 15,000. It is impossible to have a clear picture of civilian deaths because Iraq never released the correct figures.

In Kuwait, attacks on civilians continued after the ceasefire. This time it was due to reprisals of Kuwaiti citizens against those whom they considered were supporters of Saddam Hussein: Palestinians, Sudanese, and Yemenis in particular.

Economic effects

The cost of the damage to Kuwait, with the damage to the oilfields and loss of foreign investments, was estimated at around $30 billion. In Iraq, the effects of the 40-day bombing campaign were huge: power, water, and sanitation facilities were destroyed in Baghdad and other cities, along with roads, bridges, and telephone exchanges. One UN official who toured the country after the war described Iraq as having been 'relegated to a pre-industrial age'.

> *Iraq had suffered extensive damage in the war with the allied coalition. Within the space of six weeks, the air bombardment had destroyed more of Iraq's economic infrastructure countrywide than had the eight years of war with Iran. At the same time, Iraq still suffered the burden of debt created by that war and by additional financial burdens such as the reparations demanded for its aggression against Kuwait. Yet the continuing UN sanctions regime meant that Iraq was unable to sell its oil to earn foreign currency and was severely limited as to what it could import.*
>
> **Charles Tripp, A *History of Iraq* (Cambridge University Press, 2007), p.251.**

Environmental damage

The environmental costs of the war were also huge. They were partly due to oil spillages. On 23 January, Iraq was accused of dumping 400 million gallons of crude oil into the Persian Gulf in order to stop US Marines coming ashore. This act was the largest oil spill in history, resulting in the deaths of thousands of seabirds and marine animals. (The Iraqis denied they had acted deliberately, claiming that the coalition bombers had damaged and destroyed oil tankers.)

Retreating Iraqis also set alight 600 oil wells in Kuwait. John Stoessinger describes the effects of the destruction:

Burning oil wells in Kuwait.

> *Across the darkened landscape hundreds of orange fireballs roared like dragons, spewing poisonous vapors high into the air. From overcast skies dripped a greasy black rain polluting everything it touched. Black, choking smoke blotted out the sun. Oil-soaked workers turned in twelve-hour shifts, struggling with hand tools to control the burning flow. Some five million gallons of oil a day, worth about $100 million, were going up in flames. Oil covered thousands of acres, killing plants and animals and threatening subsurface water. Hospitals reported a dramatic increase in respiratory cases. Antipollution masks were selling briskly for thirty dollars apiece in supermarkets. Breathing, said one Kuwaiti, was 'like taking the exhaust pipe of a diesel truck in your mouth and breathing that'.*
>
> **J.G. Stoessinger, *Why Nations Go to War* (Palgrave Macmillan, 1998), pp.179–180.**

Political effects

For Iraq

It was widely believed that Saddam's humiliating defeat would trigger rebellions in Iraq by Baghdad's political and military elite, rebellions that would lead to his downfall. Indeed, there were risings, but by the Kurds in the north and Shia Muslims in the south. Saddam had enough strength and military hardware left to crush these rebellions brutally, which also caused a flood of refugees into Turkey and Iran. At first there was no international intervention, as the USA did not want to see a dismembered Iraq that would be unable to provide a counterweight to Iran. Yet eventually, international outrage at Saddam's bombings of his people caused the USA and Britain to declare no-fly zones and set up a 'safe haven' in the north for the Kurds.

In April, the UN Security Council passed Resolution 687, requiring Saddam to be completely open with all of his nuclear, chemical, and biological weapons programmes. Until he did, tough economic sanctions, including a ban on Iraqi oil exports, would remain. UN inspection teams visited Iraq in an attempt to find evidence of the weapons, although no evidence that Saddam made weapons of mass destruction (WMDs) after the war has emerged. Nevertheless, the Allies at the time remained convinced of his capacity and will to do so.

Saddam Hussein remained in complete power until the 2003 Allied invasion of Iraq. The ordinary people of Iraq suffered the most from the Allied bombing, the loss of infrastructure and also from the sanctions that were imposed after the war. As a result of the sanctions, infant mortality trebled and life expectancy fell by 15–20 years, and the general health and nutrition of the nation declined significantly.

For the USA

Desert Storm seemed to highlight a new unipolar world order, in which the USA was to play the dominant role in dealing with world problems. Ultimately, the events of this war were to lead on to the Iraq War of 2003. After the attacks on the World Trade Center and the Pentagon on 11 September 2001, the USA under George Bush Jnr moved rapidly to complete Saddam Hussein's removal from power, despite the fact that Saddam was never implicated in the events of 9/11.

CHALLENGE YOURSELF

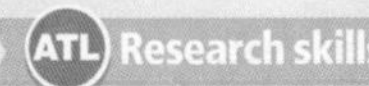

Research further into how the results of this war led to the 2003 invasion of Iraq. Look at the impact of sanctions on Iraq, the US concern that Iraq still had weapons of mass destruction, and how and why George Bush Jr linked the 9/11 attacks on the Twin Towers to Iraq.

For the Middle East region

The USA became an even stronger force in the region, which in turn provoked Muslim radicals to become increasingly hostile towards America. There was not a move to democracy in states in the Middle East, as had been hoped by the West. The National Assembly was restored in Kuwait, but with its narrow, male-only franchise. Women finally got the vote in 2005.

The Palestinian peace process was given a new boost. This impetus was not because of any earlier effort by Saddam Hussein to create 'linkage', but because Yasser Arafat's credibility had been undermined owing to his friendship with Saddam, and because the USA was now the key player and could move forward on the peace process. The result was the Oslo Accords of 1993, the first face-to-face agreement between the Israeli government and a representative of the Palestinian people.

Activity 10

Source A

Thus the coalition achieved its immediate objective of expelling Iraq from Kuwait but at a terrible cost which could only breed resentment against the West among many people in the region, while the outcome did nothing to resolve other issues troubling the Middle East – notably the Palestinian question or relations with Iran. Nonetheless, in the USA the war created a patriotic consensus on America's role as global gendarme, with what consequences only time would tell. As President Bush exclaimed, 'By God, we've kicked the Vietnam syndrome once and for all'.

T.E. Vadney, *The World Since 1945* (Penguin, 1998), p.548.

Source B

The failure to keep military objectives and political goals in harmony, however, helped ensure that the Gulf War did not lead to the hoped-for overthrow of Saddam Hussein. The American decision to end the offensive was taken in haste, in a war that was very high tempo, without an adequate consideration of how to translate the outcome of the campaign into a durable post-war settlement. This was linked to military factors, specifically the persistence of 'friction' and 'fog': a failure to distinguish victory from operational success helped ensure that the wrong decisions were taken. The civilian leadership permitted the decision to end the war to be governed by military considerations, specifically the expulsion of Iraqi forces from Kuwait: but the major goal, in fact, was political; the need to create a stable post-war situation in the Gulf, the military preconditions for such stability being ultimately a political judgement.

Jeremy Black, *Introduction to Global Military History* (Routledge, 2005), p.239.

Source C

'He who fights and runs away, lives to fight another day'. Cartoon from Nick Garland, in the British newspaper the *Daily Telegraph*, 8 March 1991.

1. According to Source A, what were the results of the war for
   a) the Middle East
   b) the USA?
2. What criticisms are made of the conduct of the war in Source B?
3. What is the message of Source C?
4. Using the sources and the information in this chapter, summarize in note form
   a) the political repercussions of this war
   b) the territorial consequences of the war
   c) the economic effects of the war.

Activity 11

ATL Thinking skills

The Gulf War as a war of limited mobilization

1. Look back at chapter 1 and the definition of limited war. How does the Gulf War meet the criteria of a limited war in terms of:
   - territory
   - weaponry
   - range of targets attacked
   - degree of mobilization?

Activity 12

ATL Thinking skills

Essay planning

Consider the following essay question:

Discuss the importance of economic factors in causing one 20th-century war.

The Gulf War is an excellent example to use for a question on economic factors, as you can consider their impact on Saddam Hussein's decision to invade Kuwait and on the USA's decision to challenge this invasion. (The 'blood for oil' debate is relevant here.)

Having discussed economic factors for both Iraq and America, you can then weigh these up against the importance of other factors. A good choice here would be to consider political factors – which caused Saddam Hussein to invade Kuwait and which led the US first to fail to prevent the invasion, and then to decide to force Saddam out of Kuwait?

Overall, do you consider economic or political factors to be more important in causing this war?

Now consider this essay question:

Examine the role of technology in determining the outcome of one 20th-century war.

Again, the Gulf War is an excellent example for a question on technology. Air warfare is particularly important for explaining the outcome of the Gulf War, so start with the impact of the US bombing. Use your research from the exercise on page 345 to help you develop your points. The application of technology in other areas was also significant, however, such as the use of satellites.

You can then weigh up the impact of technology against other factors that affected the outcome of the war, such as Saddam's strategic mistakes.

To access websites relevant to this chapter, go to www.pearsonhotlinks.com, search for the book title or ISBN, and click on 'chapter 17'.

Comparative study of limited wars

Key concepts: Change and continuity

As you read this chapter, consider the following essay questions:

- Compare and contrast the causes of two 20th-century wars.
- Compare and contrast the role of territorial disputes in causing two 20th-century wars.
- Compare and contrast the practices of two 20th-century wars of limited mobilization.
- Compare and contrast the political and economic results of two 20th-century wars, each chosen from a different region.

Burning Iraqi oilfields at the end of the 1990 war. In the foreground an American soldier stands on top of a destroyed Iraqi tank.

Causes of war

Activity 1

1. In pairs, compare and contrast the key causes of the Falklands/Malvinas War with the Gulf War. As a starting point, consider the following, and discuss which of these causal themes were similar and which were different between the case studies.
   - economic
   - ideological/political
   - territorial
   - colonialism
   - religion
   - miscalculation
2. Draft an essay plan using the Gulf War and the Falklands/Malvinas as your case studies:
   'Territorial ambitions have been a key cause of 20th-century wars.' With reference to two case studies, each chosen from a different region, assess the extent to which you agree with this statement.

Practices of war and their impact on the outcome

British soldiers in camouflage readying for battle on the Falklands/Malvinas, 1982.

Wars of limited mobilization

> *Some saw the Falklands War as associated with a bid to restore an imperial quality to Britain's role in the world. The truth is that the Falklands War did not mark a turning point in Britain's world role. It was justified on the very unimperialist principle of 'self determination' … there was no sense that the islands constituted some exciting new frontier. Most of all, the Falklands War did not change British strategy towards any of its other dependencies.*
>
> **Richard Vinen, *Thatcher's Britain* (Simon & Schuster, 2009), p.221.**

Activity 2

ATL Thinking and social skills

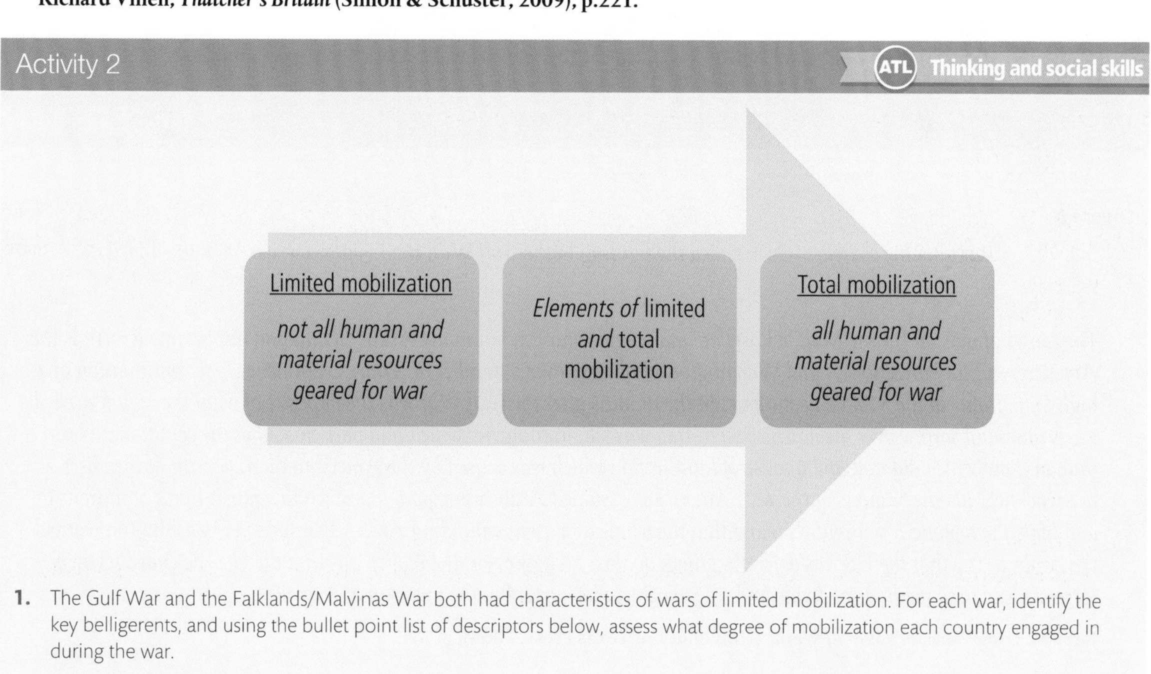

1. The Gulf War and the Falklands/Malvinas War both had characteristics of wars of limited mobilization. For each war, identify the key belligerents, and using the bullet point list of descriptors below, assess what degree of mobilization each country engaged in during the war.
   - aims and objectives
   - where the war was fought
   - use of weaponry
   - reorganization of economies for war
   - mass production of war material
   - government control and organization of military and civilians for war
   - censorship and propaganda
   - civilians a target

Now answer the following questions in pairs:

2. Which countries fought a more 'limited' war in terms of the descriptors above?
3. Which countries fought a war of more total mobilization?
4. Did the totality of the commitment of each side have an impact on the outcome of the war?
5. Why did countries fighting a more limited war of mobilization win the war?

Technological developments

Activity 3

1. Work in small groups to complete the following grid. Identify the new technology that was used in each war and assess its impact on the outcome. You should refer back to the relevant chapters to get your detailed evidence.

	Falklands/Malvinas	Gulf War	Comparison or contrast?
Role of technological developments on outcome of war			
The war at sea and technology			
The war in the air and technology			
The war on the land and technology			

Effects of war

Activity 4

Read the following source and answer the questions that follow.

Source A

In 1992, a year after the ceasefire which ended the fighting in the Gulf War, the Egyptian writer Mohamed Heikal reflected:

The causes of tension [in the Middle East] are many and complex, but many Arabs feel that an important element is the American military presence … and Washington's influence over a number of Arab governments. The continuation of a high U.S. profile in the Middle East affairs in the months after the Gulf War was the opposite of what the region needed … A profound sorrow over the destruction of Iraq was felt, in countries which had participated in the coalition no less than in those which did not, and a sense of humiliation which was caused by the American management of the crises overwhelmed all other aspects of the war. Americans assumed Arabs were glad of protection against Iraq's ambitions to dominate the region … without realising that the whole affair was wounding Arab self-respect … Washington wanted the Arabs to feel that the US was defending them against an aggressor: the reality was that the U.S. defended its own interests, and used methods of divide and rule to achieve its aims after the invasion of Kuwait.

Jerry M. Long, *Saddam's War of Words* (University of Texas Press, 2004), p.181.

1. According to Long, what were the hopes of the US regarding the impact of the Gulf War in the region?
2. According to Long, what impact did the Gulf War have on Arab states?
3. How did the US use its involvement in the war to its own advantage?

Investigate further into the results of the Falklands/Malvinas War on Argentina in the short term. Then explore the impact of the war on the Latin American region. Are there any similarities or differences with the impact of the Gulf War on the Middle East region?

Activity 5

1. Compare and contrast the following results of the Falklands/Malvinas War and the Gulf War. Copy out a diagram like the one below. Add details for each war. Shade themes that are similar in one colour and themes that contrast in another colour.

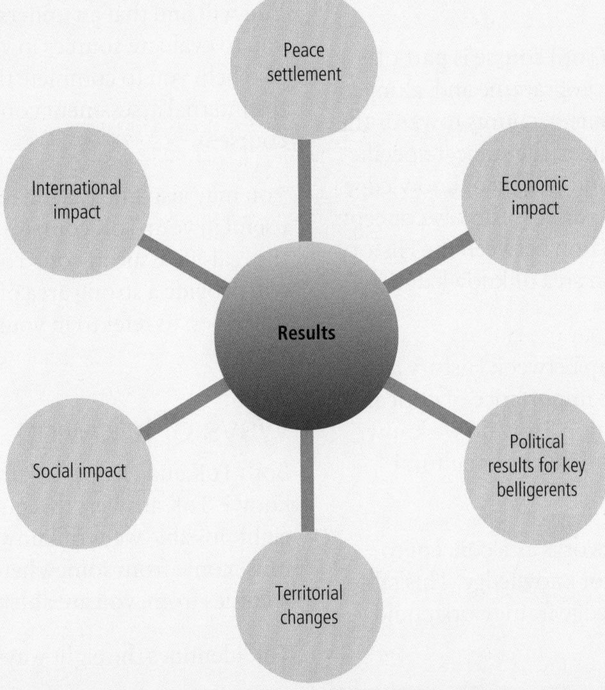

Activity 6

Draft the following essays.

- ***With reference to two case studies, each chosen from a different region, examine the role of territorial factors as a cause for war.***
- ***With reference to two case studies, each chosen from a different region, discuss the impact of limited mobilization on the outcome of wars.***
- ***Compare and contrast the effects of two 20th-century wars, each chosen from a different region.***

Theory of Knowledge

Introduction

The Theory of Knowledge (ToK) course is part of the core of the IB Diploma programme and, along with the subject-specific courses, counts towards the Diploma. History is both one of the subject-specific courses in the IB Diploma and an area of knowledge in ToK. This chapter aims to discuss the key concepts of ToK, showing the interaction between the History course and its function as an area of knowledge within ToK.

There is a substantial overlap between History and ToK, as both emphasize the importance of critical thinking. Both ask the question 'How do we know?' Both want you to understand that your cultural identity is rooted in the past.

ToK uses knowledge frameworks as a concept to differentiate between areas of knowledge. This table helps you see how a knowledge framework could apply to IB History.

Scope/ applications	• It is the study of the recorded past. • It helps us to understand that our cultural identities are rooted in the past.
Concepts/ language	• It discusses change and continuity. • It explores causation and consequences. • It recognizes the power of language in influencing thoughts and actions.
Methodology	• It has a clear, strong, and demanding methodology. • It has recognized ways of collecting evidence, questioning sources, and constructing theories. • It tests significance. • It asks 'How do we know?'
Historical development	• It recognizes that current values affect our views of the past. • It changes over time in subject matter and interpretations.
Links to personal knowledge	• It acknowledges the influence of individual historians on shared knowledge. • It allows for a range of perspectives. • It recognizes the importance of a shared history on a person's identity.

You will find that an understanding of ToK will help you to evaluate sources in your History course. It will also help you to complete the reflection section of the internal assessment component of the History course.

You may also find that an understanding of History is useful in your ToK course. It will help you to analyse the real-life issue in your ToK presentation and will provide a strong area of knowledge, with great examples, to refer to in your ToK essay.

Ways of knowing

Both ToK and History ask the question 'How do we know?' ToK answers this question by identifying eight possible ways of knowing. Your knowledge must come from somewhere and, by analysing where it comes from, you are able to assess its reliability.

ToK identifies the eight ways of knowing as:

- Language
- Perception
- Reason
- Emotion
- Memory
- Intuition
- Imagination
- Faith

You can use these concepts in ToK to assist in:

- checking the reliability of a first-hand testimony
- analysing the way emotions influence the witness and the interviewer
- determining the possible bias in the language used
- assessing the fallibility of memory
- analysing the desire to see a rational explanation for events.

You can also use them in History to assist in establishing the origin, purpose, and content of sources, in order to assess their value and limitations.

Language is one of the key ways of knowing, so here is an example exploring the use of language in the accumulation and communication of knowledge in History.

Activity 1

1. In small groups, discuss the use of language in the following source. How do historians interpret the use of language in primary sources? Is language a challenge for historians when attempting to understand the past and when primary sources are used to develop their accounts?

> *Germany cannot tolerate the deliberate degradation of the nation by the perpetuation of a discrimination which consists in withholding the rights which are granted as a matter of course to other nations ... The men who are at present the leaders of Germany have nothing in common with the traitors of November 1918. Like every decent Englishman and every decent Frenchman, we all had our duty to our Fatherland and placed our lives at its service. We are not responsible for the war but we feel responsible for what every honest man must do in the time of his country's distress and for what we have done. We have such infinite love for our people that we desire wholeheartedly an understanding with other nations ... but, as men of honour, it is impossible for us to be members of institutions under conditions which are only bearable to those devoid of a sense of honour ... Since it has been made clear to us from the declarations of certain Great Powers that they were not prepared to consider real equality of rights of Germany at present, we have decided that it is impossible, in view of the indignity of her position, for Germany to continue to force her company upon other nations.*
>
> **A speech by Hitler, broadcast on 14 October 1933.**

Activity 2

Refer back to the analysis in chapter 7 regarding the causes of World War Two in the Pacific. In pairs, read the following sources (the Steiner source is from chapter 7) about the events that led to the outbreak of the war in the Pacific in December 1941.

1. Discuss how each historian uses language to communicate their perspective on the causes of the war.
2. How does the language in each source affect your assessment of the value and limitations of each source?
3. Discuss how reason and imagination may be involved in these accounts. To what extent are reason and imagination necessary ways of knowing for historians?

> *The United States and Japan were inexorably moving toward a bloody collision in the Pacific. Several individuals and groups tried to stop the drift toward war and stimulate productive Japan–US talks ... By ... 1941, however, Japan had only two grim alternatives: reach a compromise with the US or take the gamble of going to war. The American government was in no mood to compromise and insisted that Japanese troops be withdrawn from China.*
>
> **Saburo Ienaga, *The Pacific War* [*Taiheiyo Senso*] 1931–45 (Iwanami Shoten, 1968, English translation by Random House, 1978), p.133.**

> *There were miscalculations and misperceptions on both sides. Just as Tokyo believed rightly that the United States would deal with the German threat first but wrongly that it would condone Japanese expansionism, the Americans misjudged the extent of the Japanese commitment to an empire that would end its economic insecurity and confirm its leadership in East Asia.*
>
> **Zara Steiner, *The Triumph of the Dark* (Oxford University Press, 2013), p.1065.**

Activity 3

1. In pairs, consider the ToK/language activity in chapter 17 – the Gulf War case study.

Areas of knowledge

History is one of the eight areas of knowledge identified by the ToK course. A full list of the areas of knowledge is:

- Mathematics
- Natural Sciences
- Human Sciences
- History
- The Arts
- Ethics
- Religious knowledge systems
- Indigenous knowledge systems

You can use these areas of knowledge to understand why we approach different types of knowledge in different ways. We recognize that a work of art is not the same as a chemical formula or a historical interpretation. We test them using subject-specific criteria, recognizing that a historical fact cannot be verified in the same way as a natural science fact. History uses a rigorous methodology to test its facts, but it is not the same method as used in the Natural Sciences.

Historians have their theories, their arguments, and accounts 'tested' by other historians in their field. Perhaps the way in which historians work can be considered similar to science in that their accounts are open to peer criticism, correction, and revision.

Also, history, like the Natural Sciences, uses deconstructions, and macro and micro scales. In science, there are 'general laws', but also specific experimentation, while in history you might consider broader factors. For example, when considering the causes and effects of a war a historian may focus on a specific turning-point event – such as the Munich Agreement in 1938 or the Nazi–Soviet Pact in 1939 – as a key causal factor, or the historian may consider the role of broader impersonal factors, such as ideology. Theories or ideas that are developed around broader factors may then be used to consider causal developments in another case study of war.

However, historical evidence can also be viewed as different from scientific evidence in the way it is 'found'. Scientific experimentation, 'double blind testing' and so on, are not methodologies available to the historian.

Activity 4

1. Briefly review the sources you have studied from one case study of 20th-century war in this book. With reference to specific sources, consider the following:
   - the language used by the historians
   - information included or omitted by the historians
   - details emphasized by each historian
   - analytical concepts used by each historian, and whether such concepts are liable to 'change over time'.

Find sources from different time periods: that is, sources written shortly after the war, and others that were written a long time afterwards. Consider the extent to which history can be seen as 'changing' within new theoretical frameworks.

Historians, like scientists, search for cause and effect. Some history examination essay questions will ask you to find a number of key causes and/or analyse their relative importance. As for natural and human scientists, there can be challenges for historians when establishing the difference between correlation and causation.

There are also problems in terms both of scope and depth. For example, how far back do we go when searching for the causes of a war? How much detail is relevant? This is also a problem when examining the effects of a historical episode: for example, how long after a war can events be seen as consequences of the conflict?

Activity 5

1. It is also important to consider the role of 'accident' and 'chance' in history. Can you identify any events in your war case studies where there was an element of 'chance' in the factors that caused them? How useful is the consideration of 'accidental' causation to a historian?

There is an interesting interplay between the arts and history. In one sense, the arts reflect the historical forces at play in society, but, in another sense, the arts influence history. Here follow a couple of examples exploring the complex relationship between the arts and history.

Case study 1: The First World War and the Arts

Historians often see their role as really more about highlighting and emphasizing the nature of humankind and the human condition, which is a role often associated with the arts.

Activity 6

1. In small groups, investigate poetry and art from World War One. When you have gathered a variety of examples, explore how the work of artists who fought on the front lines shaped public opinion back home. Did their work influence the actions of their governments or the way the war was fought? How has their interpretation of war affected historians? Some recent historians have challenged the view, for example, that World War One was simply 'pointless slaughter' or that the most of the soldiers were cannon fodder and 'lions led by donkeys'. However, this was the view popularized by many war poets and artists at the time, and in the French film *J'accuse*. Many historians have used these artists' interpretations as sources of evidence in their accounts.

Discuss the extent to which art influences history.

Activity 7

World War One also had an important impact on the visual arts. The Dada movement developed during the war and was specifically anti-bourgeois, anti-nationalist, and anti-imperialist – and was a reaction to what Dadaists saw as three causes of the conflict. Dadaists rejected the high value given to reason and logic, and emphasized irrationality. The movement was against beauty as the principle aim of art – they wanted their work to provoke and offend people. The mass slaughter and horror of World War One compounded Dadaist belief that there was no room for beauty in art. In societies traumatized by the war, Dada art reflected the turbulent reality of the post-war period.

1. In groups, explore the work of the Dada artists in different countries in the interwar period (between 1918 and 1935). Identify the ways in which the art reflected the post-war societies the artists lived and worked in.

Case study 2: The Spanish Civil War and the Arts

Refer to the painting by Pablo Picasso, *Guernica*, in chapter 11 on page 243. It depicts the appalling carnage and suffering inflicted by the aerial bombing of a Spanish Basque town during the Spanish Civil War. The painting had a significant impact on public opinion and compounded the fear of destructive and indiscriminate war. Its impact has lasted into the 21st century. When US officials prepared to make a statement on the war in Iraq in 2003, they realized that they were standing in front of a copy of *Guernica*. The press conference was halted whilst the painting was covered over.

Do historians paint pictures with their words, highlighting issues and events in ways that might mirror the power that artists can command with their images? If so, does the artistic method have any similarities to the methods employed by historians?

Historical development

Historical development is one of the criteria on the knowledge framework that ToK uses to differentiate between the areas of knowledge. Historical development is part of all the areas of knowledge; it recognizes that our knowledge and the way we approach that knowledge changes through time. For instance, the way we approach the Natural Sciences and what we know in this area is quite different now from 100 years ago.

You can use this concept to explore how our approach to history changes: that is, what subjects we study in History, how our views change as more information comes into the public domain, and how our current values influence our view of the past. Historians use reason to construct a logical interpretation of the past based upon the available information. Sometimes there is so much information that it is difficult to find a single thread of cause and effect in it. Sometimes there is too little information. In addition, new information becomes available as official documents are released or research is completed.

Historians are human beings with roots in their own time, place, and background. Their interpretations have an emotional and cultural context, so it is not surprising that the interpretations change over time, as society's values change.

Activity 8

Explore different historians' views of the causes of World War One. You will find that the causes of the war are as hotly contested today as they were in the 1920s. Read the source extracts in chapter 2, and answer the following questions.

1. How did the publication of classified documents decades after the war impact historians' accounts?
2. To what extent are the historians' perspectives reflecting their own culture and time?
3. What are the implications of this lack of consensus among historians, even 100 years after the outbreak of the war?
4. Does this suggest anything about the challenges historians face and the nature of historical 'truth'?

Activity 9

Read the sources below and answer the questions that follow.

Given the tenseness of the world situation in 1914 – a condition for which Germany's world policy, which had already led to three dangerous crises [those of 1905, 1908 and 1911], was in no small measure responsible – any limited or local war in Europe directly involving one great power must inevitably carry with it the imminent danger of a general war. As Germany willed and coveted the Austro-Serbian war and, in her confidence in her military superiority, deliberately faced the risk of a conflict with Russia and France, her leaders must bear a substantial share of the historical responsibility for the outbreak of general war in 1914.

Fritz Fischer, *Germany's Aims in the First World War* (W.W. Norton, 1967), p.88.

The problem with a blame-centred account is not that one might end up blaming the wrong party. It is rather that accounts structured around blame come with built-in assumptions. They tend, firstly, to presume in conflictual interactions one protagonist must ultimately be right and the other wrong ... The question is meaningless. A further drawback of prosecutorial narratives is that they narrow the field of vision by focusing on the political temperament and initiatives of one particular state rather than on multilateral processes of interaction ... You have to show that someone willed war as well as caused it ... the view expounded in this book is that such arguments are not supported by the evidence ... The crisis that brought war in 1914 was the fruit of a shared political culture. But it was also multi-polar and genuinely interactive – that is what makes it the most complex event of modern times and that is why the debate over the origins of the First World War continues ...

Christopher Clark, *The Sleepwalkers* (Allen Lane, 2012), pp.560–561.

1. With reference to the origin, purpose, and content of each source, discuss why the historians may have drawn different conclusions regarding the causes of World War One. Consider the context, culture, and era each historian is writing in and the source material available.
2. Explore some of the recent historiography on World War One. You will find historians that conclude responsibility lies with different powers and those that argue the powers were collectively responsible. Some historians agree with the historians writing immediately after World War One in the 1920s; others agree with Fischer's thesis. What does this suggest about:
   a. the impact of the availability of sources on historians accounts
   b. the impact of the context within which a historian is working
   c. the personal politics, expertise, and enthusiasms of the historian?
3. Discuss the extent to which having too many sources and too much evidence is a challenge for historians. Where sources are plentiful, does the selection of evidence become more problematic? Is bias more likely when there is a lot of evidence, or more likely when evidence is limited?

Personal and shared knowledge

ToK is interested in the links between shared knowledge and personal knowledge as it relates to history. You can use this concept to explore the role of key historians in shaping our shared knowledge, but you can also use it to investigate how our shared knowledge helps shape our own identities. One of the key concepts of IB History is that multiple interpretations are possible and one of the key concepts of ToK is that each individual should be encouraged to think critically for him or herself.

You can use the ToK concept of memory as a way into this topic. On a personal level, memory is important in creating our personalities, and on the cultural level, collective memory is important in uniting, but also in dividing, people.

Over 60 years ago the British philosopher and historian R.G. Collingwood defended the study of history, saying:

> *What is history for? … Knowing yourself means knowing, first, what it is to be a man; secondly, knowing what it is to be the kind of man you are; and thirdly, knowing what it is to be the man YOU are and nobody else is. Knowing yourself means knowing what you can do; and since nobody knows what he can do until he tries, the only clue to what man can do is what man has done. The value of history, then, is that it teaches us what man has done and thus what man is.*
>
> **R.G. Collingwood, *The Idea of History* (OUP, 2005), page 10.**

History helps us understand ourselves in the present. Our own individual 'histories' are also important in helping us understand the world we live in and our place within it. Significantly, history is used to argue and justify political positions, economic policies, the rationale for foreign policy initiatives, and relations between countries and regions. In fact, most other areas of knowledge rely to a certain extent on the use and application of history. For example, it would be difficult for a scientist to add to the body of knowledge in his or her subject in a meaningful way without knowing what had come before, and why and how something had been discovered or invented.

Activity 10

1. Investigate how your parents, grandparents, or extended family viewed the wars that you have studied, or wars that were going on around the world when they were your age. Compare and contrast their memories of these wars to those accounts you have read in this book. In what ways do they view events differently from you, or historians of the war? Do their accounts from memory highlight specific elements and omit others? What can we learn from them?

Activity 11

1. In small groups, consider how your study of the causes and effects of wars is relevant to your understanding of global events today. In what ways has your understanding of current tensions, crises, conflicts, and peace-making efforts between nations, regions, and international organizations been enhanced by studying 20th-century wars?

Activity 12

1. Can we draw lessons for the 21st-century world from our study of 20th-century wars?

Conclusion

There is a considerable overlap between History and ToK. The concepts of change, continuity, significance, causation, consequence, and perspectives are included in the IB History syllabus and they fit well into the knowledge framework in ToK.

You can use skills you develop in History to add depth and meaning to your ToK presentations and essays. You can use skills developed in ToK to help you evaluate sources and to write the reflection section of your historical investigation. You can use the methodology of History to address the real-life issues that you discuss in ToK. By collecting evidence, weighing the value and limitations of sources, and building a logical, consistent interpretation of the facts you will be able to construct sound, well-supported arguments. History is one of the key areas of knowledge in ToK.

For further information about the ToK course, consult Sue Bastian, Julian Kitching, and Ric Sims, *Pearson Baccalaureate: Theory of Knowledge*, 2nd ed. (Pearson, 2014).

FURTHER READING

Books

World War One

Albertini, Luigi, *The Origins of the War of 1914*, vol. 1, trans. by Isabella Massey (Enigma, 2005)

Beckett, Ian, *The Great War 1914–1918* (Pearson, 2001)

Bell, P.M.H., *Twentieth Century Europe* (Hodder Arnold, 2006)

Breach, R.W., *Documents and Descriptions in European History 1815–1939* (Oxford University Press, 1976)

Cawood, Ian J. and David McKinnon-Bell, *The First World War (Questions and analysis in History)* (Routledge, 2000)

Ferguson, Niall, *The Pity of War* (Penguin, 2006)

Ferguson, Niall, *The War of the World: History's Age of Hatred* (Penguin, 2006)

Fischer, Fritz, *Germany's Aims in the First World War* (Chatto & Windus, 1967)

Geiss, Imanuel (ed.), *July 1914: The Outbreak of the First World War – Selected Documents* (Batsford, 1967)

Henig, Ruth, The *Origins of the First World War* (Routledge, 1993)

Hobsbawm, Eric, *Age of Extremes: The Short Twentieth Century* (Michael Joseph, 1994)

Iriye, Akira, *The Cambridge History of American Foreign Relations, vol. 3: The Globalising of America 1913–1945* (Cambridge University Press, 1993)

Joll, James, *The Origins of the First World War* (Longman, 1992)

Keegan, John, *The First World War* (Pimlico, 1999)

Keynes, John Maynard, *The Economic Consequences of the Peace* (Skyhorse Publishing, 2007)

Laffin, John, *British Butchers and Bunglers of World War One* (Sutton Publishing, 2003)

Lee, Stephen J., *Aspects of European History 1789–1980* (Routledge, 1988)

Lowe, John and Robert Pearce, *Rivalry and Accord: International Relations 1870–1914* (Hodder & Stoughton, 2001)

Lowe, Norman, *Mastering Modern World History* (Palgrave Macmillan, 1995)

Martel, Gordon, *The Origins of the First World War* (Longman, 1987)

Strachan, Hew, *The Oxford Illustrated History of the First World War* (OUP, 2000)

Taylor, A.J.P., *How Wars Begin* (Hamish Hamilton, 1979)

Townshend, Charles (ed.), *The Oxford History of Modern War* (OUP, 2005)

Tuchman, Barbara, *The Guns of August* (Ballantine Books, 1994)

Woodward, L, *Great Britain and the War 1914–1918* (Methuen, 1967)

Wroughton, J., *Documents on World History 1: 1870–1918* (Macmillan, 1976)

The interwar years

Brogan, Hugh, *The Penguin History of the USA* (Penguin, 2001)

Culpin, Christopher and Ruth Henig, *Modern Europe 1870–1945* (Longman, 2007)

Farmer, Alan, *Introduction to Modern European History 1890–1990* (Hodder & Stoughton, 2005)

Henig, Ruth, *The Origins of the Second World War* (Routledge, 1992)

Henig, Ruth, *Versailles and After 1919–1933* (Routledge, 1995)

Lentin, A., *The Versailles Peace Settlement* (Historical Association, 1991)

Overy, Richard, *Origins of the Second World War* (Longman, 1992)

Rayner, R.M., *The Twenty Years' Truce* (Longman, 1943)

Williamson, D.G., *War and Peace: International Relations 1914–1945* (Hodder & Stoughton, 1994)

Wilson, Sandra, *The Manchurian Crisis and Japanese Society, 1931–33* (Routledge, 2003)

World War Two

Adamthwaite, A.P., *The Making of the Second World War* (Routledge, 1989)
Bergamini, David, *Japan's Imperial Conspiracy* (William Morrow, 1971)
Buchanan, Patrick, *Churchill, Hitler and the Unnecessary War: How Britain Lost its Empire and the West Lost the World* (Crown, 2008)
Calvocoressi, Peter, Guy Wint and John Pritchard, *Total War: The Causes and Course of the Second World War*, vol. 1 (Penguin, 1989)
Darby, Graham, *Europe at War 1939–45* (Hodder Murray, 2003)
Davies, Norman, *Europe at War 1939–1945* (Pan Books, 2006)
Goldston, Robert, *The Road Between the Wars, 1918–1941* (Dial Press, 1978)
Ienaga, Saburo, *The Pacific War* (Tokyo, 1968)
Iriye, Akira, *The Origins of the Second World War in Asia and in the Pacific* (Longman, 1987)
Keegan, John, *The Second World War* (Pimlico, 1997)
Lee, Stephen, *Aspects of European History 1789–1980* (Routledge, 1984)
Morris, T. and D. Murphy, *Europe 1870–1991* (Collins, 2004)
Overy, Richard, *Russia's War* (Penguin, 1997)
Overy, Richard, *Why the Allies Won* (Pimlico, 2006)
Sheehan, James, *The Monopoly of Violence: Why Europeans Hate Going to War* (Faber & Faber, 2008)
Shirer, William, *The Rise and Fall of the Third Reich* (Simon & Schuster, 1990)
Townley, Ted, *Hitler and the Road to War* (HarperCollins, 1998)

The post-war world

Best, Antony et al., *International History of the Twentieth Century* (Routledge, 2004)
Judt, Tony, *Postwar: A History of Europe Since 1945* (Heinemann, 2005)

Malvinas/Falklands War

Anderson, Duncan, *The Falkands War 1982, Essential Histories* (Osprey, 2002)
Middlebrook, Martin, *The Argentine Fight for the Falklands* (Pen & Sword Books, 2003)
Vinen, Richard, *Thatcher's Britain* (Simon & Schuster, 2009)

Gulf War

Alchin, Nick, *Theory of Knowledge* (Hodder Education, 2006)
Black, Jeremy, *Introduction to Global Military History* (Routledge, 2005)
Finlan, Alastair, *The Gulf War 1991* (Osprey, 2003)
Freedman, Lawrence and Efraim Karsh, *The Gulf Conflict, 1990–1991* (Faber & Faber, 1995)
Snow, Donald and Dennis Drew, *From Lexington to Desert Storm: War and Politics in the American Experience* (M.E. Sharpe, 1994)
Stoessinger, J.G., *Why Nations Go to War* (St Martin's Press, 1998)
Tyler, Patrick, *A World of Trouble: America in the Middle East* (Portobello Books, 2009)
Vadney, T.E., *The World Since 1945* (Penguin, 1998)

Spanish Civil War

Beevor, Antony, *The Battle for Spain: The Spanish Civil War 1936–1939* (Penguin, 2007)
Fraser, Ronald, *Blood of Spain: Oral History of the Spanish Civil War* (Pimlico, 1994)
Knight, Patricia, *The Spanish Civil War* (Hodder & Stoughton, 1998)
Lannon, Frances, *The Spanish Civil War, Essential Histories* (Osprey, 2002)

Lee, Stephen J., *Aspects of European History 1789–1980* (Routledge, 1984)
Mitchell, David, *The Spanish Civil War* (Grenada, 1971)
Preston, Paul, *The Spanish Civil War: Reaction, Revolution and Revenge* (Harper Perennial, 2006)
Thomas, Hugh, *The Spanish Civil War* (Penguin, 1977)

Chinese Civil War

Brown, C. and T. Edwards, *Revolution in China 1911–1949* (Heinemann, 1974)
Grasso, June, Jay Corrin and Michael Kort, *Modernization and Revolution in China: From the Opium Wars to the Olympics* (M.E. Sharpe, 2009)
Gray, Jack, *Rebellions and Revolutions: China from the 1880s to the 1980s* (Oxford University Press, 1990)
Hsu, Immanuel, *The Rise of Modern China* (Oxford University Press, 1995)
Lynch, Michael, *China: From Empire to People's Republic 1900–49* (Hodder & Stoughton, 1999)
Sheridan, James, *China in Disintegration* (The Free Press, 1977)
Terrill, Ross, *Mao: A Biography* (Stanford University Press, 2000)
Westad, Odd Arne, *Decisive Encounters* (Stanford, 2003)

Algerian War

Betts, Raymond, *France and Decolonisation* (Macmillan, 1991)
Black, Jeremy, *Introduction to Global Military History* (Routledge, 2005)
Calvocoressi, Peter, *World Politics 1945–2000* (Pearson, 2001)
Gildea, Robert, *France Since 1945* (Oxford University Press, 2009)
Horne, Alistair, *A Savage War of Peace: Algeria 1954–1962* (New York Review Books, 2006)
Stora, Benjamin, *Algeria 1830–2000: A Short History* (Cornell University Press, 2001)
Thorn, Gary, *End of Empires* (Hodder & Stoughton, 2001)
Vadney, T.E., *The World Since 1945* (Penguin, 1991)

Websites

To visit the following websites, go to www.pearsonhotlinks.com, enter the book title or ISBN, and click on the relevant weblink.

General websites

The following websites cover both of the world wars, plus the interwar years:

Spartacus Educational
A history site with good summaries on key individuals and events – click on Weblink 1.

The History Learning Site
Includes major sections on 20th-century history – click on Weblink 2.

The Avalon Project
Useful for primary source government documents – click on Weblink 3.

World War One and the League of Nations

First World War multimedia history
General World War One resources – click on Weblink 4.

World War I – Trenches on the web
An 'Internet History of the Great War' – click on Weblink 5.
BBC History (WWI)
The World War One section of the BBC History website – click on Weblink 6.
Eyewitness to History
Featuring numerous first-hand accounts of the war – click on Weblink 7.
World War One
General World War One information site – click on Weblink 8.
The Great War and the Shaping of the 20th Century
An extensive internet resource from PBS – click on Weblink 9.
World War One art
Excellent site for studying the art of World War One – click on Weblink 10.
The Covenant of the League of Nations
Full text of this important convenant – click on Weblink 11.

World War Two

BBC History (WWII)
The World War Two section of the BBC History website – click on Weblink 12.
worldwar-2.net
Major World War Two website – click on Weblink 13.
world-war-2.info
Includes links to features on weaponry, campaigns and personalities, plus a timeline – click on Weblink 14.
HyperWar
Major collections of World War Two primary sources – click on Weblink 15.

Spanish Civil War

Spanish Civil War 1936–39
A website featuring comprehensive links to other Spanish Civil War websites. A good starting point for your online research – click on Weblink 16.
Abraham Lincoln Brigade Archives
Website exploring the Abraham Lincoln Brigade – click on Weblink 17.
Essays on the Spanish Civil War
Collections of useful essays on this conflict – click on Weblink 18.

Gulf War

The Gulf War
A major PBS resource for studying the 1990–91 conflict – click on Weblink 19.
CBC Digital Archives
A CBC site on the Gulf War – click on Weblink 20.

Falklands War

The Falklands Conflict 1982
Major site on the Falklands War, including weapons data, chronology of events and useful links – click on Weblink 21.

Fight for the Falklands – 20 Years On
A BBC History website – click on Weblink 22.

Britain's Small Wars
An extensive website with a dedicated Falklands War section – click on Weblink 23.

Chinese Civil War

Selected works of Mao Zedong
Translations of Mao Zedong's most important works – click on Weblink 24.

Moving the Enemy: Operational Art in the Chinese PLA's Huai Hai Campaign
An online book by Dr Gary J. Bjorge, with chapters on the development of the communist forces – click on Weblink 25.

Algerian War of Independence

Pacification in Algeria, 1956–58
A downloadable report from the Rand Corporation – click on Weblink 26.

War of Independence
A history of the Algerian War of Independence – click on Weblink 27.

A-bomb: The atomic bomb, first used by the Americans in 1945 against Japan, which uses nuclear fission to release energy. It is less powerful than an H-bomb.

Afrika Korps: The German expeditionary force in Africa during World War Two.

AirLand Doctrine: Military tactics used by the US forces in the 1980s and 90s which had an emphasis on close coordination between land forces and air forces.

Alfonsist: Refers to a member of the Spanish monarchist movement that supported the restoration of King Alfonso XIII of Spain after the foundation of the Second Spanish Republic in 1931.

al-Qaeda: A militant Islamic organization, considered a terrorist group by the UN and other organizations. It was founded between 1988–89 by Osama bin Laden and others.

anarchism: The belief that government and law should be abolished.

annexation: The forcible takeover of a state's territory by another state.

***Anschluss*:** German word meaning 'connection'; used to refer to the union of Austria and Germany, which took place in 1938.

anti-Semitism: Prejudice against, hatred of, or discrimination against Jews.

appeasement: Achieving peace by giving concessions or by satisfying demands. It was the policy followed by the British government in the 1930s towards Nazi Germany.

Arab League: An organization of Arab countries in north Africa and south-west Asia, created in 1945 to promote diplomacy between its members; there are now 22 states in the Arab League.

arable land: Land used for growing crops.

arbitration: The act of settling disputes through a neutral intermediary.

area bombing: The policy of indiscriminate bombing of an enemy's cities, with the aim of destroying the enemy's means of producing military material, communications, government centres, and civilian morale.

armistice: An agreement to end fighting so that peace negotiations can begin.

arms race: Competition between states regarding numbers and/or types of weapons.

autarky: The policy of economic self-sufficiency.

authoritarian: A style of government in which there is complete obedience or subjection to authority as opposed to individual freedom.

autocracy: When power is in the hands of one person.

Axis powers: The alliance of Italy, Germany, and Japan during the Second World War.

Ayatollah: Among Shi'ites this is a title achieved by scholars who have demonstrated highly advanced knowledge of Islamic law and religion.

Ba'ath Party: Political party that ruled Iraq from 1968 and under the leadership of Saddam Hussein from 1979.

ballistic missile: A missile that is guided in the first part of its flight but falls freely as it approaches its target. It is used to deliver one or more warheads (often nuclear) to a predetermined target.

Basque: People from the Basque territories in Spain and France.

Bedouin: A group of semi-nomads who live in deserts in North Africa and the Middle East.

belligerents: The parties who are engaged in war.

Blitz: The bombing of British cities between 1940 and 1941.

***blitzkrieg*:** This term means 'lightning war' and is used to describe the German offensive tactics in the early stages of World War Two.

bloc: A group of nations that share common interests and usually act together in international affairs.

blockade: An action to prevent goods from entering or leaving a country.

Bolshevik: A member of the Bolshevik Party, which was a Russian political party that followed the ideas of Karl Marx. It seized power in October 1917.

bourgeois: Relating to the middle classes (bourgeoisie). It is usually used in a negative way in the context of Marxist writings, where the bourgeoisie are contrasted with the proletariat, or working classes.

brinkmanship: Pushing dangerous events to the brink of all-out war in order to achieve the most advantageous outcome.

capitalism: The belief that trade and industry should be controlled by private owners and for profit (as opposed to being controlled by the government).

Carlism: A Spanish right-wing political movement created in 1833. The group took its name from Don Carlos, the youngest brother of King Ferdinand VII and would-be King Carlos V.

censorship: The control of information by the government.

Civil Guard: A military force used for 'policing' duties in Spain.

civil war: When fighting takes place within one country between two or more different factions.

client states: States that are controlled or influenced by another larger and more powerful state, or which are dependent on this state for support and protection.

coalition government: A government made up of members of two or more different political parties.

Cold War: The period of international tension from the end of World War Two in 1945 to the collapse of the Soviet domination of Eastern Europe and the end of the USSR between 1989–1991.

collective security: Countries working together to maintain peace.

collectivization: The process by which private farms are confiscated by the state and collective communal farms created instead. This took place in the Soviet Union under Stalin in the 1930s.

colonial: Relating to countries that are colonies (controlled by another country), or to colonialism.

communism: A political theory that emerged in the 19th century based on the writings of Karl Marx. It claimed that all property should be owned by the community and labour should be organized for the common benefit.

***Confederación Española de Derechas Autónomas* (CEDA; Spanish Confederation of the Autonomous Right):** A right-wing political group in Spain, founded on Catholic and conservative beliefs.

***Confederación Nacional del Trabajo* (CNT; National Confederation of Labour):** The anarchist trade union of Spain.

conscientious objectors: People who refuse to fight because of religious or moral reasons.

conscription: Compulsory military service.

conservative/conservatism: This is a political philosophy that wishes to preserve and keep intact institutions, practices, and traditions. It is right wing.

constitutional monarchy: A monarchy that does not have unlimited power, but rather is restrained by written laws and has to share power with an elected parliament. Also called a 'democratic monarchy'.

***coup d'état*:** A violent or illegal seizure of power.

demilitarized zone: An area in which the deployment of military forces is not permitted.

democracy: A country governed by representatives who are elected by the people.

democratic monarchy: *See* constitutional monarchy.

deployment: To position troops in readiness for fighting.

diktat: A 'dictated' agreement in which there has been no discussion or mutual agreement.

diplomacy: Managing relations between governments of different countries by discussion and peaceful means.

disarmament: The process of decommissioning weapons.

diversionary front: A military strategy to divert the attention of opposing forces.

embargo: An order of a government prohibiting the movement of merchant ships into or out of its ports.

emir: An aristocrat or noble in Arab countries.

emirate: A political territory that is ruled by an emir.

Entente Cordiale: '*Entente*' is the French word for an 'understanding', here referring to the Anglo–French Entente of 1904.

European Economic Community (EEC): An inter-governmental organization that fostered economic integration and mutually beneficial trade arrangements between European member states.

expansionism: The policy of expansion of territory and power by a state.

Falange: A Spanish political group who wanted radical social change as well as authoritarian leadership. It was formed in 1933 and experienced rapid growth throughout the 1930s.

***Falange Española Tradicionalista* (FET; Spanish Traditionalist Phalanax):** A political group which merged the Falange and the Carlists.

fascism: Fascism is rooted in ideas that are the very opposite of liberalism. Fascists believe in limiting individual freedoms (in the interest of the state), extreme nationalism, the use of violence to achieve ends, keeping power in the hands of an elite group or leader, and an aggressive foreign policy.

***Federación Anarquista Ibérica* (FAI; Iberian Anarchist Federation):** A Spanish organization of militants, closely associated with the CNT.

feudal: Relates to a system that existed in Europe in medieval times. In theory, the king owned all or most of the land and gave it to his leading nobles in return for their loyalty and military service. The nobles in turn held land that peasants, including serfs, were allowed to farm in return for the peasants' labour and a portion of their produce. Under feudalism, people were born with a permanent position in society.

fifth column: A group of people who undermine a nation from within.

fire-control technology: The means by which artillery, missile, or tank fire is accurately guided to the target.

franchise: The right to vote.

free trade: Trade without government interference such as tariffs or customs barriers.

friendly fire: When soldiers are mistakenly injured or killed by soldiers fighting on the same side.

front: The line where two opposing forces are facing each other.

General Agreement on Tariffs and Trade (GATT): Set up in 1947, its objective was the reduction of barriers to international trade such as tariff barriers and subsidies. The functions of GATT were taken over by the World Trade Organization in 1994.

Geneva Protocol: The 1925 Geneva Protocol prohibits the use of chemical and biological weapons in war.

genocide: The deliberate extermination of a race of people.

globalization: Describes an ongoing process by which regional economies, societies, and cultures have become integrated through a globe-spanning network of communication and exchange.

GNP (Gross National Product): The market value of all goods and services produced in one year by a country.

grandees: A high ranking noble.

Great Depression: The world economic recession that took place after the Wall Street Crash in America in October 1929.

guerrilla warfare: Irregular warfare and combat in which a small group of combatants uses mobile military tactics in the form of ambushes and raids to combat a larger and less mobile formal army.

Hamas: An acronym for 'Islamic Resistance Movement', a Palestinian Islamic organization with a military section, regarded in some parts of the world as a terrorist organization.

H-bomb: A hydrogen bomb, which uses nuclear fusion to release energy. It is significantly more powerful than an A-bomb.

hegemony: The domination of one country over another.

Hindenburg Line: A German defensive position on the Western Front during the First World War.

historiography: The study of history by historians.

House of Representatives: Part of the US government that makes and passes laws. The House of Representatives and Senate make up Congress.

hyper-inflation: A rapid rise in prices that becomes out of control.

idealism: The beliefs and behaviour of someone who has ideals and who tries to base his or her behaviour on these ideals.

ideology: A set of political beliefs.

imperialism: The act of building and empire; the acquisition of colonies.

incumbents: Someone who holds an official post at a particular time.

indemnity: An amount of money or goods that is received as compensation by someone for damage or loss that they have suffered, or legal protection against future losses.

industrialization: The process by which states transfer from the use of manual labour to the use of machines.

infantry: The foot soldiers of an army.

inflation: A general increase in the price of goods and services in a country.

infrastructure: The basic equipment and structures (such as roads and bridges) that are needed for a country to function effectively.

insurgents: People who are fighting against the government or army of their own country.

International Brigade: Foreign fighters for the Republic in the Spanish Civil War.

International Monetary Fund (IMF): An international organization that oversees the global financial system.

isolationism: A policy that involves not getting involved with other countries or international problems.

jingoism: The extreme belief that your own country is always best.

junta: A military government that has taken power by force.

Kaiser: The ruler of Germany before 1918.

Kurds/Kurdish: An ethnic group in the Middle East, closely related to the Iranian people, many live in western Iran and northern Iraq.

landed aristocracy: A category of nobility in various countries over history, for which land ownership was part of their noble privilege.

***latifundia*:** Large privately owned estates of land in Spain.

League of Nations: Organization set up after World War One to ensure that international disputes were solved without recourse to war.

***Lebensraum*:** German for 'living space'. Hitler wanted to expand eastwards in order to gain living space for the German nation.

left wing: Term given to progressive parties, socialists, and communists.

Lend-Lease: US aid to Britain in World War Two. It enabled Britain to obtain war supplies for which it could not pay, under the agreement that these supplies would be returned or paid for after the war.

liberal democracy: A type of representative democracy where those in power are restricted by a constitution which safeguards the rights of citizens.

liberalism: A political ideology based on liberty and equality for all.

limited mobilization: Where a state only partially mobilizes its human and material resources for war.

limited war: War that is not total war. It is limited by the weaponry used, by its geographical location, or by its impact on the country fighting the war.

Luftwaffe: The German air force during World War Two.

Maginot Line: The French line of defence built on the border with Germany before World War Two.

mandate: In the context of 20th-century international affairs, a mandate is a territory placed under the authority or care of a European power.

Manhattan Project: Research and development project that produced the first atomic bombs during World War Two.

Maoism: Mao adapted Marxism/communism to suit the realities of China in the 1920s and 1930s. One of his changes was the argument that revolution could be achieved by the peasants, not only the urban proletariat.

Marxism: Political and economic theory of Karl Marx, which holds that human actions and institutions are economically determined and that class struggle is needed to create historical change – Capitalism will ultimately be superseded by Communism.

McCarthyism: A vehemently anti-Communist movement in the USA during the 1950s, associated with US Senator Joseph McCarthy.

***Mein Kampf*:** A book written by Hitler in 1923 setting out his political beliefs.

militarism: When there is an emphasis in a country on the importance of the military.

mobilization: When troops are made ready for war.

monarchy: A system of government where the ruler is a king or queen who reigns until their death or abdication.

morale: The feelings of enthusiasm and/or loyalty that a person or group has about a task or job.

Mujahideen: Literally 'soldiers of God', referring to the Muslim Afghan guerrilla soldiers.

nationalism: Pride for one's nation or a desire for national independence.

nationalization: When a government takes over private industry or land so that it is owned by the state.

Nazism: The ideology and beliefs of the German Nazi Party.

neo-colonial: The policy of a strong nation seeking political and/or economic control over an independent nation.

New Deal: A series of domestic programs enacted in the United States between 1933 and 1938, aimed at getting America out of the Great Depression.

non-commissioned officers (NCOs): A term used in the armed forces for leadership ranks that are junior to 'commissioned officers'. Sometimes the term is used to describe conscripted officers.

North Atlantic Treaty Organization (NATO): An association of European and North American states set up in 1949 for defence against any Soviet attack.

Northern Expedition: First United Front of the Chinese Communists and Nationalists engaged in what was called the Northern Expedition to crush the warlords and unify China in the 1920s.

Nuclear submarine: A submarine that uses nuclear power.

Occupied Territories: Refers to the territories retained by Israel after its victories in the 1967 Six-Day War. They are the West Bank, East Jerusalem, Gaza Strip, and Golan Heights.

Organization of Petroleum Exporting Countries (OPEC): An organization founded in 1960 from nations that export large quantities of oil. The organization was formed to establish policies and prices.

pacifism: The opposition to war and violence and belief in peaceful resolutions to disagreements.

Palestine Liberation Organisation (PLO): An organization founded in 1964 with the purpose of the 'liberation of Palestine' through armed struggle.

pandemic: A disease/illness that spreads over a large area, usual more than one continent.

Pan-German League: An extremist, ultra-nationalist organization in Germany which was officially founded in 1891.

parliamentary democracy: A democracy that has an elected parliament.

pincer movement: A military manoeuvre in which both flanks of an enemy force are attacked with the aim of attaining complete encirclement of the enemy.

plebiscite: A direct vote by the public on a specific issue/policy.

post-traumatic stress disorder (PTSD): The psychological and/or physical effects of experiencing extreme conditions, often associated with war; for example nightmares, depression, and panic attacks.

precision-guided munitions (PGMs): A weapon designed to hit a precise target.

private sector: The area of the nation's economy under private rather than governmental control.

proletariat: The working class, those that earn their living from manual labour. In Marxist terms the proletariat are those who must sell their labour to survive, as they own no personal capital or property.

propaganda: The particular doctrines deliberately spread by an organization or movement.

protectionism: The promotion or development of domestic industries by protecting them from foreign competition.

provisional government: The government that took over in Russia after the abdication of the Tsar in March 1917.

proxy war: A conflict between two nations where neither country directly engages the other.

public sector: The area of the nation's economy under governmental rather than private control.

puppet leader/regime: A leader or regime that is controlled by another country.

putsch: A sudden or violent takeover of a government.

rationing: The policy of giving each person a fixed allowance of provisions or food during a shortage.

Red Army/Reds (China and Russia): Communist armies.

Red Crescent/Cross: Worldwide humanitarian organization providing assistance without discrimination as to nationality, race, religious beliefs, class, or political opinions.

reparations: Money that a country which loses a war pays because of the damage, injury, deaths, etc.

republic: A state where power rests in a body of citizens that have gained power democratically.

reservist: A person who belongs to a reserve military force of a country.

revanche movement: Revenge or retaliation, often in the political context of regaining lost territory.

revisionism/revisionist: An advocate of theories that are different from established theories or doctrines.

right wing: Conservative or reactionary political views, or in opposition to extensive political reform.

Royal Air Force (RAF): The British air force.

sanctions: An action, sometimes in the form of withholding aid or trade, by one or more states towards another state, calculated to force it to comply with legal obligations.

satellite state: A political term that refers to a country that is formally independent, but under heavy influence or control by another country.

savings bonds: A bond that may be underwritten by the government.

Schlieffen Plan: Germany's war plan in World War One.

***Schutzstaffel* (SS):** Hitler's elite body guard.

scorched-earth campaign: A military campaign in which a retreating army destroys all the houses, crops, factories, etc. so that an advancing enemy cannot use them.

scud missiles: Tactical ballistic missiles developed by the Soviet Union during the Cold War.

self-determination: The right of the people of a particular place to choose the form of government they will have.

senate: The US Senate is the Upper House of the US Congress, which along with the House of Representatives forms the main legislative apparatus of the USA.

Shia (Shi'ite): A member of one of the two great religious divisions of Islam. It regards Ali, the son-in-law of Muhammad, as the legitimate successor of Muhammad, and disregards the caliphs who succeeded him.

sheikdom: A territory that is ruled by a sheikh (an Arab leader).

shuttle diplomacy: The action of an outside party in serving as an intermediary between countries in conflict.

siege warfare: The surrounding and blockading of a city or town by an army attempting to capture it.

Slavs/Slavic: An ethnic group who share some cultural and language similarities, from middle, eastern and southern Europe.

small arms: Firearms designed to be held in one or both hands while being fired.

Social Darwinism: The theory that individuals, groups, and peoples are subject to the same Darwinian laws of natural selection as plants and animals.

socialism: A system of social organization that to a greater or lesser extent attempts to give the community as a whole ownership of the means of production, capital, land, and so on.

socio-economic: The combination or interaction of social and economic factors.

stalemate: When neither side in a disagreement can make any progress.

standing army: A permanently organized military force maintained by a nation.

stealth technology: The use of advanced design and specialized materials to make an aircraft difficult or even impossible to detect by radar.

strategic bombing: A military strategy associated with total war, involving the bombing of targets that are deemed vital to an enemy's war-making capacity.

***Sturmabteilung* (SA):** Hitler's storm troopers were a political militia of the Nazi party notorious for its violence and terrorism up to 1934.

suffrage: The right to vote.

sultanate: Lands ruled by a sultan (the sovereign ruler of a nation).

Sunni: A member of one of the two great religious divisions of Islam, regarding the first caliphs as legitimate successors of Muhammad.

superpower: A nation that is sufficiently powerful to dominate international events and the policies of other nations. Used specifically to refer to the USA and the USSR after 1945.

syndicalism: A form of socialism which aimed to replace capitalism by organizing industries into confederations or syndicates.

tariff: Duties or customs imposed by a government on imports or exports.

Third Reich: The period of German history from 1933 to 1945.

totalitarian: A centralized government that tolerates no opposition to its control.

total mobilization: When a country prepares all of its fighting forces for war.

total war: A war in which a state uses all its human and material resources to fight.

Triple Alliance: The alliance of Austria-Hungary, Germany, and Italy before World War One.

Triple Entente: The alliance of Britain, France, and Russia before World War One.

Truman Doctrine: Policy of President Truman (announced in March 1947) to provide military and economic aid to Greece and Turkey and, by extension, to any country threatened by communism or any totalitarian ideology.

tsardom: Lands ruled by the tsar (sovereign ruler) of Russia.

U-boat: A German military submarine of the world wars era. The word derives from the German *Unterseeboot* (under-sea boat).

ultimatum: A final demand or set of terms, the rejection of which would have consequences.

unequal treaty: A treaty imposed on one country by another which has terms that benefit only one side in the agreement.

***Unión General de Trabajadores* (UGT; General Union of Workers):** The Socialist-led trade union in Spain.

United Front: A temporary coalition of the Chinese Communists and Chinese Nationalists. The first was to take on the warlords in the 1920s, the second was to fight Japan in the 1930s.

United Nations (UN): An international organization formed in 1945 to promote international peace, security, and cooperation.

VE Day: Victory in Europe day at the end of World War Two, celebrated on 8 May.

veto power: The power to cancel or postpone decisions or actions.

Vietminh: League for the independence of Vietnam formed in Vietnam in 1941.

Wall Street Crash: A devastating collapse of the US stock market in October 1929, which led to a global economic crisis.

war guilt clause: Clause 23 in the Treaty of Versailles in which Germany had to accept guilt for starting World War One.

warlord: A military commander who has seized power, usually in a region or specific area of a country.

warlord era: Period in China when warlords controlled different regions, between 1916 and 1928.

war of attrition: A war in which each side tries to win by wearing the other side down to the point of collapse through continuous losses.

weapons of mass destruction (WMD): Weapons that can produce devastating results in a single strike. They include nuclear, chemical, and biological weapons.

Weimar Germany/Republic: The German republic that was founded at Weimar (1919–33).

***Weltpolitik*:** Translates as 'world policy', pursued by Kaiser Wilhelm II's Germany, which aimed to build an overseas empire and a strong German navy.

Wilhelmine Germany: The period of German history 1870–1918.

Italic page numbers indicate an illustration. Bold page numbers indicate an interesting facts box.